D. S. RUSSELL

THE METHOD AND MESSAGE OF JEWISH APOCALYPTIC

D. S. RUSSELL

THE METHOD & MESSAGE OF JEWISH APOCALYPTIC

200 BC – AD 100

SCM PRESS LTD
BLOOMSBURY STREET LONDON

To my Parents
Janet and Peter Russell
and to my former Principal
Henry Wheeler Robinson

334 01007 1
First published 1964
by SCM Press Ltd
56 Bloomsbury Street London
Second impression 1971

Printed in Great Britain by
Lewis Reprints Limited,
London and Tonbridge

CONTENTS

PREFACE

TWENTY YEARS AGO, as a research student at Oxford, I was introduced to the Jewish apocalyptic literature by my honoured tutor and College Principal, H. Wheeler Robinson, whose influence can be detected in the following pages, particularly in those dealing with the 'psychology' of inspiration and of the apocalyptic consciousness. This introduction led to a deepening appreciation of what the apocalyptic writers were trying to say and a desire to understand more fully not only the times and circumstances in which they lived, but also the beliefs they held and the hopes they cherished. In 1960 I attempted an appreciation of their writings in a small volume entitled *Between the Testaments*. Its kindly reception has encouraged me to deal with the same subject at much greater length in the hope that greater justice may be done to their work.

For Jews and Christians alike this whole literature is of the utmost significance because of its claim to be 'the child of prophecy'. But for Christians it has an additional significance. Not only is it, in its teaching, a continuation of the Old Testament, it is also an anticipation of the New Testament. Christians believe that the New Testament is a continuation and fulfilment of the Old Testament, but the historical connection between the two, in respect of certain doctrines at any rate, is not always clear. The apocalyptic literature helps to bridge this gap and illustrates certain significant developments in religious belief, especially of an eschatological and messianic kind, which took place during the vital years between the two Testaments. It is not the purpose of this book to work out the theological implications of these doctrines for New Testament study. But it is hoped that the material here provided will be found useful for such a task.

It has to be remembered that the apocalyptic writers were not systematic theologians; they were not interested in exact definitions of faith, and logic was perhaps one of their lesser virtues! They were rather visionaries and poets who expressed their convictions in terms of traditional imagery, at once highly imaginary and often obscure. They were constantly inconsistent with themselves and also with the writings of other men of like mind. They tried to explain the inexplicable, to express in mere words the inexpressible mysteries of God. Inconsistency, in such circumstances, is a minor sin. Despite the hazards involved, an attempt will be made in Part III of this book to present as systematically as possible their teaching on several of the more important aspects of their faith.

Twenty years ago the Dead Sea Scrolls had not been heard of. Life then for the student of this period was much more simple—but much less exciting! A vast amount of information has suddenly become available, much of which brings into sharp focus beliefs and practices among the Jews which at best were formerly blurred and obscure. Many obscurities remain; but a clearer and more accurate view of this all-important period is now more possible than ever before. This is not a book about the Scrolls, nor do I claim to be an authority on this literature; but no study of the inter-testamental period is possible without a careful assessment of these texts. Some of them obviously belong to the class of literature known as 'apocalyptic' and so supplement the already-known apocalyptic books; others, whilst not sharing the distinctive marks of apocalyptic, nevertheless cast considerable light on the historical, cultural and religious situation within which the apocalyptic literature was produced and must be taken into account.

My indebtedness to many scholars is evident throughout the entire book, but special mention must be made of Emeritus Professor H. H. Rowley, whose friendly interest and ready help have been a constant encouragement to me. Not only has he read through the final draft and made most useful suggestions, he has also gone to considerable trouble in supplying me with books from his own library and in answering queries I have raised with him. Professor P. R. Ackroyd has likewise made a number of helpful suggestions for which I would express my deep gratitude. I must thank my colleague, the Rev. W. E. Hough, for reading through the manuscript in its completed form and for undertaking the arduous task of compiling the indexes, and also Mrs Jessie Davies for the very considerable help she has given in the preparation of the manuscript. For the understanding and patience of my colleagues and students and also of my wife and family throughout the period of the book's preparation I wish to express my grateful thanks.

Rawdon D. S. RUSSELL

ABBREVIATIONS

AJT	*American Journal of Theology*
BASOR	*Bulletin of the American Schools of Oriental Research*
BJRL	*Bulletin of the John Rylands Library*
BZAW	Beihefte zur *Zeitschrift für die Alttestamentliche Wissenschaft*
EB	*Encyclopaedia Biblica*
ERE	*Encyclopedia of Religion and Ethics*
ET	*The Expository Times*
HDB	*Hastings's Dictionary of the Bible*
HTR	*The Harvard Theological Review*
ICC	International Critical Commentary
JBL	*Journal of Biblical Literature*
JE	*Jewish Encyclopedia*
JQR	*Jewish Quarterly Review*
JTS	*Journal of Theological Studies*
LXX	Septuagint
NT	*Novum Testamentum*
NTS	*New Testament Studies*
RB	*Revue Biblique*
REJ	*Revue des Études Juives*
SJT	*Scottish Journal of Theology*
TLZ	*Theologische Literaturzeitung*
TZ	*Theologische Zeitschrift*
VT	*Vetus Testamentum*
ZAW	*Zeitschrift für die alttestamentliche Wissenschaft*

PART ONE

THE NATURE AND IDENTITY OF JEWISH APOCALYPTIC

I

THE MILIEU OF APOCALYPTIC

I. THE HISTORICAL AND CULTURAL BACKGROUND

THE RISE AND growth of the apocalyptic literature in Judaism is to be seen against the background of one of the most heroic, and at the same time one of the most tragic, periods of Israel's history. The years 200 BC–AD 100, within which the bulk of this literature was written, witness a revival of Jewish nationalism which was to have repercussions for centuries to come not only within the Jewish faith itself but also within the Christian Church. The period begins with an account of the travails accompanying the rebirth of the Jewish nation under the Maccabean leaders and the Hasmonean royal house which their descendants formed and concludes with an account of its demise at the hands of the Roman legions. The story in between tells of a constant struggle not only between the Jews and their Gentile rulers, but also between Jews and Jews; for there were divided loyalties which revealed themselves in many parties and 'sects' within the nation. The encroachments of Hellenism were regarded by the pious as a challenge to the faith and so had to be resisted even to the point of death; others, many of them in places of authority in both Church and State, welcomed its culture and readily adopted its way of life. During this period the nation was to witness the Hellenization and secularization of the High Priesthood. There was corruption in high places. Bribes were openly offered for preferment in office. Intrigue and murder were the order of the day. The affairs of State were in the hands of men who did not always reverence divine appointment to office. At last foreigners took control whose mismanagement of affairs aggravated an already critical situation and in the year AD 66 war broke out between the Jews and the Romans which was to end in the destruction of the Jewish State. The still later revolt under Bar Kochba in AD 132–5 resulted in the exclusion of the Jews from their sacred city of Jerusalem, which was re-established as a Roman city.

The religion and literature of the Jewish nation may be said to be the product of its history at every stage of its development; but this is particularly so with that expression of it in the inter-testamental period. The apocalyptic books constitute a record of these years, not in terms of historical event, but in terms of the response of faith which the nation was called upon to make. They cannot be understood apart from the religious, political and economic circumstances of the times, nor can the times themselves be understood apart from these books whose hopes and fears echo and re-echo the faith of God's chosen people. The allusions which they make to current affairs are frequently concealed beneath the guise of symbol and imagery so that more often than not it is difficult, if not impossible, to give a precise identification to this reference or that character. But they reveal quite clearly the inner side of that conflict which continued almost unceasingly throughout these three centuries; they bring to light the faith and emotions which lay behind the historical events and so make these events much more understandable than they otherwise would be.

The first, and greatest, of all the Jewish apocalyptic writings, the Book of Daniel, was occasioned by the oppression of the Seleucid ruler, Antiochus IV Epiphanes (175–163 BC), who was determined to carry through, at whatever cost, his avowed policy of Hellenization. The story of his determination to wipe out the Jewish religion altogether—his banning of the distinctive characteristics and rites of the Jewish faith and his erection of an altar to the Olympian Zeus on the altar of burnt-offerings within the Temple court in Jerusalem (I Mac. 1.54)—is too well known to require repetition here. Supporting the Maccabees in their opposition to Antiochus and his policy of Hellenization were the Hasidim (Hasideans) or 'pious ones' whose devotion to the Law and the religion of their fathers gave strong material support and full religious sanction to the revolt (I Mac. 2.42ff.). The religious outlook of these Hasidim is reflected in the Book of Daniel which, in its present form at any rate, was probably written by one of their number in the time of Antiochus Epiphanes shortly after the outbreak of the Maccabean Revolt. It is a great affirmation of faith in the overruling purpose of God which could not and would not be frustrated by the devices of evil men, however powerful and tyrannical they might be.

This same spirit is revealed, though often with less artistry and religious insight, in many other apocalyptic writings in the succeeding years. Most of these, like Daniel itself, were probably the outcome of further persecution or else were thrown up, as it were, by the political and economic pressures of the times. Those which do not bear the mark of crisis have nevertheless the same note of urgency that the time is short and the End appointed by God is near at hand. The pictures painted in these books are in sharply contrasting colours—white against black, light against darkness, good against evil, God against Satan. In particular God's chosen people are set over against the great nations of the earth which represent the powers of wickedness entrenched in the world. Just as in Daniel the great Syrian kingdom of Antiochus is condemned, so also in II Esdras and the New Testament Apocalypse, for example, the arch-enemy is mighty Rome. At other times the attack is levelled against those within the Jewish nation itself who have succumbed to the ways of the heathen. Such allusions reflect the strong party feeling which characterized Judaism throughout this entire period and contributed to the ultimate downfall of the nation.

Not only did these apocalyptic books mirror the historical situation out of which they arose, they at the same time actually helped to create it. This was inflammatory material in the hands of those who wished to appeal to the religious fanaticism which became a feature of a particular section of the Jewish people. There can be little doubt that the Zealot party, for example, found in this literature just the kind of propaganda they needed to set alight the smouldering passions of their fellow countrymen. The Jewish War of AD 66–70 was fought in the confirmed belief that the people would witness the miraculous intervention of God as declared in the apocalyptic writings. Later still, in the revolt of AD 132–5 under Bar Kochba, it was again the apocalyptic hope which inspired the Jewish people to take up arms against their overlords. Both wars resulted in tragedy for the Jewish nation, and the apocalyptic literature was finally discredited in the eyes of all but a few.

The apocalyptic literature is an example of the adage that 'man's extremity is God's opportunity'. It is essentially a literature of the oppressed who saw no hope for the nation simply in terms of politics or on the plane of human history. The battle they were fighting was on a spiritual level; it was to be understood not in terms of politics and economics, but rather in terms of 'spiritual powers in high places'. And so they were compelled to look beyond history to the dramatic and miraculous intervention of God who would set to rights the injustices done to his people Israel. The very urgency of the situation emphasized the nearness of the hour. The expression of this belief is at times fanciful and exaggerated; but book after book throbs with the passionate conviction that all that God had promised would surely come to pass. The promises made to Israel by his servants the prophets must have meaning and reality and would ultimately be fulfilled. These promises declared that God would save his people and make them great among the Gentiles. It is often said that apocalyptic is a literature of despair. But this at best is only a half-truth. With equal appropriateness it can be described as a literature of hope; God would vindicate his people once and for all and bring to its consummation his purpose and plan for all the ages.

Mention has been made of the influence of Hellenism on the Judaism of the inter-testamental period and of the different reactions to it of men and parties within the Jewish State. The word 'Hellenism' is commonly used to describe the Greek culture and civilization of the three centuries or so from the time of Alexander the Great (336–323 BC) which he and his successors in both the Greek and Roman periods sought to spread throughout the whole civilized world. It was a syncretistic system which incorporated the beliefs and legends of older religions not only of the West but also of the East. Already, before the time of Alexander, the Persian Empire had itself overcome the Babylonian Empire and had adopted many of its customs and beliefs as well as its language, Aramaic or 'Chaldee', as the language of government. When in course of time Alexander took over the Persian Empire and pressed on towards India he made a breach in the barrier separating East and West through which 'came flooding back the lore . . . and "wisdom" of the East . . . a Greek-philosophized blend of Iranian esotericism with Chaldean astrology and determinism'.[1] Such a concurrence of 'magianism', astrology and Greek paganism resulted in a highly syncretistic type of Hellenism to which the whole of Syria was particularly prone and encouraged a widespread interest in such things as occultism, magic, astrology, demonology, angelology, cosmology, anthropology and eschatology.

[1] S. B. Frost, *Old Testament Apocalyptic*, 1952, pp. 75f.

It is a debatable point among scholars in what specific ways and to what extent Persian influence made itself felt among the Jews; but it can hardly be denied that the apocalyptic teaching, for example, concerning such matters as 'the two ages', the determinism of historical events, angelology and demonology, the notion of the final judgment and eschatological ideas generally owes much to this source.[1] There is evidence, too, for the widespread influence of the old Babylonian worship of the heavenly luminaries and especially the seven planets whose movements were believed to control the lives of men and nations. This influence can be found in the astronomical sections of I Enoch, for example, and elsewhere in the apocalyptic writings where considerable interest is shown in the movements of the heavenly bodies and their influence on the affairs of men.[2] Some scholars have suggested a Babylonian origin for the stories contained in the Book of Daniel[3] where the four young men are said to be trained in 'the learning and tongue of the Chaldeans' (1.4); here, however, the word 'Chaldean' is the name given to a class of astrologers and does not signify the nation of that name mentioned elsewhere in the Old Testament.

Not only the Jews of the Dispersion, then, but also those in Palestine itself were surrounded by Hellenistic culture and civilization. Many of them, moreover, had no doubt lived for many years in direct contact with Perso-Babylonian thought and culture in Mesopotamia, where they and their fathers had been ever since the days of the Captivity. From time to time they would return to Palestine bringing back with them an appreciation of those aspects of Hellenism which were not altogether out of harmony with their own Hebrew religion. It is more than likely that many of them were attracted home during and after the period of the Maccabees as they witnessed the establishment of a strong Jewish State built around the holy Temple.

This helps to explain the rather strange fact that, although the

[1] For the influence of Iranian thought on Jewish apocalyptic see the index under 'Persia'.

[2] Of interest in this connection are the fragments of a horoscope found at Qumran which names the signs of the Zodiac spread over the days of the month and gives predictions based on thunder. J. T. Milik indicates that the *Brontologion* of this kind is well known in antiquity and points out that the specimen closest to this Qumran text is a Greek Brontologion ascribed to Zoroaster (cf. J. T. Milik, *Ten Years of Discovery in the Wilderness of Judaea*, English trans. by J. Strugnell, 1959, p. 42).

[3] Cf. J. A. Montgomery, *The Book of Daniel*, ICC, 1927, p. 22.

apocalyptic writings are on the side of 'the pious ones' in Israel and are opposed to those members of the priestly aristocracy who readily embraced the Hellenistic way of life, they nevertheless contain elements which clearly show the influence of alien thought, particularly that of Greece and Persia. The Book of Enoch, for example, shows considerable interest in the problems of astrology and cosmology and shares with, say, the Book of Jubilees and the Testaments of the XII Patriarchs a concern for demonology and angelology, whilst eschatology in one aspect or another is the prevailing preoccupation of almost every apocalyptic writer. It will be seen, however, that although syncretistic Hellenism influenced their theology deeply, their theology in its turn also influenced what they received. Despite their indebtedness to the cultural and religious world outside Judaism, they nevertheless remained true to their Jewish faith, using alien truths to unveil the fuller revelation of the only true and living God.

2. JUDAISM AND APOCALYPTIC

G. F. Moore gives the name 'normative' to that form of Judaism which attained general acceptance and authority by the end of the second century AD.[1] It finds literary expression in a corpus of tradition which can be called 'catholic' in the sense that it possesses both universal authority and in some sense finality. Just as Christianity should be judged by the line of its catholic tradition represented in the recognized teachings of the Church, so also should Judaism. It must not be judged by 'extraneous' or 'outside' books such as the apocryphal and apocalyptic literature which had neither biblical nor rabbinical authority attaching to them, but rather by its 'normative' literature, by which is meant, alongside the canonical Scriptures, the 'oral tradition' which in course of time found expression in the written records of rabbinic Judaism. Moore thus minimizes the indebtedness of Judaism to apocalyptic and argues that, since the apocalyptic books were never recognized by Judaism, it is wrong to make a primary source of them or 'to contaminate its theology with them'.[2] He would no doubt agree with R. T. Herford that 'the real strength of Judaism, the persistent vitality and unconquerable faith which enabled it to survive through all the storms which threatened to destroy it, was that which was fostered and strengthened by the

[1] Cf. *Judaism*, vol. I, 1932, p. 125. [2] *Ibid.*, p. 127.

teachers of the Rabbinical line, the Sopherim, the Pharisees, and the Rabbis'.[1] Indeed, Herford goes much further than Moore when he describes apocalyptic as a dangerous influence, the product of weak minds and unbalanced judgments, the work of men driven to the very edge of distraction and concludes that Judaism 'owed nothing of its strength and depth to Apocalyptic teaching'.[2] This judgment is contested by scholars like F. C. Porter, J. Bowman, E. Kautzsch, C. C. Torrey, J. Bloch and W. D. Davies, who have demonstrated that apocalyptic represents on the contrary a most significant development within the Judaism of the inter-testamental period. This latter judgment will, it is hoped, be amply illustrated throughout the following pages.

The name 'normative' as applied to Judaism by G. F. Moore can be misleading if only because it is a question-begging expression. There can be little doubt that what he names as 'normative literature' reflected the 'norm' for Judaism in the years which lie beyond the inter-testamental period, especially when the oral tradition came to be codified in the Mishnah some time after AD 200. But it cannot be assumed that what is now preserved therein is necessarily a reliable witness to the many-sided Judaism of the earlier centuries. Indeed, it has become increasingly clear that, however definitive and homogeneous and authoritative Judaism may have become in the later period, in earlier times there was little that was 'normative' or 'normal' about it. It cannot be taken for granted that the 'orthodox' rabbinism of the period, say, AD 70–250, is in any way a true reflection of the much more heterogeneous Judaism or indeed Pharisaism of inter-testamental times. W. D. Davies reminds us that 'it is always dangerous to impose any one mode of thought on Judaism' and that the 'Rabbinic sources represent the triumph of one stream within Judaism, the Pharisaic, and even of only one current within that one stream, that of R. Johanan b. Zakkai'.[3] If it is dangerous to do this to the Judaism which emerged after the fall of Jerusalem, it is much more dangerous to do so to the Judaism of the inter-testamental period.

Prior to AD 70 there was no recognized 'orthodoxy', nor was there any one party whose beliefs formed the norm by which Judaism

[1] *Talmud and Apocrypha*, 1933, p. 268.
[2] *Ibid.*
[3] *Torah in the Messianic Age and/or The Age to Come*, in the *JBL* Monograph Series, vol. VII, 1952, p. 53. Cf. also H. Danby, *The Mishnah*, 1933, pp. xivf.

could be judged. On the contrary there was a great variety of religious parties which were not greatly concerned about the question of orthodoxy at all. Josephus, in a well-known passage, refers to three main schools of thought in his day which he describes as 'philosophies'. These are the Pharisees, the Sadducees and the Essenes, to which he adds a fourth 'philosophy' to which he later gives the name 'Zealots'.[1] The word 'philosophies' is misleading when applied to these parties, but so also is the word 'sects' which is commonly used to describe them. There was no 'true Church' from which they had hived off or whose 'orthodoxy' they had spurned. Judaism was much more concerned with *orthopraxis* than it was with *orthodoxy*, and if the word 'sectarian' can be used at all in this connection it must refer strictly to those parties whose religious practice differed in this respect or that from the party wielding authority at that time which usually meant the Sadducees or the Pharisees or both together in an uneasy partnership.[2] It cannot be denied that the several schools of thought described by Josephus were influential in those days, but it must be remembered that numerically they were very small in relation to the total number of the population. It has been calculated that in New Testament times, for example, the Pharisees numbered about 5 per cent of the total population, and the Sadducees and Essenes together about 2 per cent.[3] Moreover, it seems likely that Josephus has exaggerated the importance of the Pharisees throughout the period he describes, and has underestimated the authority of the Zealots, who saw in themselves the spiritual successors of the Maccabees of former years.[4] It is perhaps safe to assume that the vast majority of the *'am ha'areṣ*, or 'people of the land', were virtually unaffected by the teaching of these parties and that their interest in religion was to a great extent nominal. Besides the parties described by Josephus there would no doubt be many others into which Judaism was splintered and whose names have long since disappeared. Matthew Black describes the situation within Judaism in the first century BC as 'one of a widespread and dangerously proliferating and fissiparous heteropraxis, a kind of baptizing nonconformity, with many splinter groups, extending from

[1] Cf. *Ant.* XVIII.i.1–6; *War* II.viii.2, etc.

[2] Cf. M. Black, *The Scrolls and Christian Origins*, 1961, pp. 5ff.

[3] Cf. T. W. Manson, *The Servant-Messiah*, 1956, p. 11.

[4] Cf. W. R. Farmer, *Maccabees, Zealots and Josephus*, 1956, and W. D. Davies, 'Contemporary Jewish Religion' in *Peake's Commentary on the Bible*, ed. by M. Black and H. H. Rowley, 1962, pp. 705ff.

Judaea to Samaria and beyond into the Dispersion itself'.[1] One illustration of this is provided by the Qumran Covenanters, whom most scholars have identified with the Essenes or near-Essenes, although it is just possible that they represent an influential group within Judaism whose beliefs and practices do not exactly correspond to those of the main parties familiar to us. However this group is to be identified, it is to be seen as one illustration among many of this 'nonconformist' movement whose splinter groups were to be found both in Palestine and in the Dispersion.

This fact emphasizes what has become increasingly clear in more recent years, that no rigid distinction can be drawn between the Judaism of Palestine and that of the Dispersion and that both were open to the same kinds of influence. Both found themselves confronted with Hellenistic ideas and culture which, consciously or unconsciously, shaped their religious outlook.[2] It has been argued, probably with fairly good reason, that Jewish apocalyptic (or certain expressions of it such as I Enoch) had its origin and found its inspiration in Galilee which belonged to the Dispersion.[3] The implication has sometimes been drawn that, since Galilee was wide open to Gentile and in particular Hellenistic influence, apocalyptic can rightly be regarded as a 'fringe' movement which does not represent the essential Judaism of the synagogues and schools in Jerusalem. We have seen that such an implication involves a twofold misunderstanding. Not only was there no 'essential', in the sense of 'authoritative', Judaism during this period; there was also no sharp and clear-cut distinction between the Judaism of Galilee and that of Jerusalem itself. There seems little reason to doubt that, far from being an alien or 'sectarian' element on the extreme borderline of Judaism representing a reactionary 'fringe', apocalyptic was a significant part of the accepted Jewish tradition and represented one important aspect of its life and faith.

N.B. cf. Sandmel

3. APOCALYPTIC AND THE JEWISH PARTIES

There are indications that in its origins Jewish apocalyptic was closely associated with the Hasidim, whose support was given to the

[1] *Op. cit.*, p. 8.

[2] Cf. W. D. Davies, *op. cit.*, p. 705, and also 'Apocalyptic and Pharisaism', *ET*, vol. LIX, 1948, pp. 233–7, reproduced in *Christian Origins and Judaism*, 1962, pp. 19–30.

[3] Cf. F. C. Burkitt, *Jewish and Christian Apocalypses*, 1914, pp. 28ff., and L. E. Elliott-Binns, *Galilean Christianity*, 1956, pp. 27, 38, 76.

Maccabees in their opposition to Antiochus Epiphanes. It is generally conceded that the later groups of the Essenes were descendants of these Hasidim and that the Pharisees also can trace back their spiritual ancestry to the Hasidean movement. Most are agreed that the Qumran Covenanters had their origin here also and that they emerged as a distinct party during the Hasmonean period, probably as a result of the non-Aaronite Hasmonean House taking over the high priestly office. It cannot be assumed, however, that the tradition of apocalyptic, begun in hasidic circles, was necessarily continued in or confined to any one of these known groups.

Our knowledge of the Essenes, apart from that supposed in the Dead Sea Scrolls, is very limited; but such as we have shows certain affinities with the beliefs of the apocalyptic writers.[1] According to Josephus the Essenes believed in the survival of the soul though not, it would seem, in the resurrection of the body. They had their own sacred books by whose means they were able to predict the future. From 'the books of the ancients' they learned the medicinal power of roots and the quality of stones. Their members were sworn to secrecy never to divulge the writings of the party or the names of the angels. There is no exact parallel here with the ideas contained in the apocalyptic writings; indeed, it is clear that in certain respects their beliefs do not tally. But there are interesting correspondences such as the apocalyptists' interest in prediction, their speculation concerning the future destiny of souls, their astrological lore and their interest in angelology. If it can be proved that the Qumran Covenanters were a branch of the Essenes, then the argument for Essene influence on the apocalyptic writings is strengthened. This party has been described as 'a cooled-down apocalyptic sect'[2] whose aims and ideals had much in common with those of the apocalyptic writings. There is a close connection between them, for example, in the expression of their messianic hopes, in their belief in angelology and demonology and particularly in their ideas concerning the End. They share each other's faith in the final eschatological battle, the coming judgment, the punishment of the wicked and the reward of the righteous in the life beyond. Whatever the exact relationship between them may be, they seem to have shared a common spiritual heritage. Despite these interesting similarities, however, between

[1] Cf. especially K. Kohler, 'Essenes' in *JE*, vol. V, 1903, pp. 224ff., and 'The Essenes and the Apocalyptic Literature', in *JQR*, N.S., 1920, vol. XI, pp. 145–68.

[2] R. P. C. Hanson in *A Guide to the Scrolls*, ed. by A. R. C. Leaney, 1958, p. 64.

the apocalyptists on the one hand and the Essenes and Qumran Covenanters on the other, there is not sufficient evidence to show that the apocalyptic writings necessarily had their origin here. The ideas expressed in these books, whilst shared to a large extent by the Essenes and Covenanters, probably represented the beliefs and hopes of a much greater cross-section of the Jewish people.

Another name sometimes associated with the origins of the apocalyptic literature is that of the Zealots whose messianic and eschatological ideas had no doubt also much in common with those expressed in these books. R. T. Herford, for example, in his earlier writings states quite categorically, 'The Apocalyptic literature is Zealot literature. It shows the inspiration, the ideas and religious and ethical conceptions of the Zealot Movement. . . . The Apocalyptic literature and the Zealot Movement went hand in hand, the one providing the dangerous food and the other feasting on it and calling for more.'[1] A few years later, however, the same writer retracted this judgment and confessed that he had been guilty of a too-hasty identification of the apocalyptists with a known type of contemporary Judaism.[2] The apocalyptic books would undoubtedly act as a stimulus to the Zealots, but these were revolutionaries and it is not among such men that we normally find writers of books.[3]

The exact relationship between the apocalyptists and the Pharisees has been the subject of much debate. Scholars like W. Bousset, R. H. Charles and S. Zeitlin have argued for a Pharisaic authorship, whilst others, though not necessarily confining their writing to members of any one party, have contended strongly that the apocalyptic tradition and the Pharisaic tradition are by no means opposed to each other. This position has been attacked by R. T. Herford, who maintains that, of all the types of Jews living at that time, the Pharisees were the least fitted to be the authors of such books. With the possible exception of the *Megillath Taanith* there is no instance of a book having been written by a Pharisee during these years. Their whole stress was on oral tradition and in particular on their interpretation of Torah under the forms of *halakah* and *haggadah*.[4] This is not the

[1] *The Pharisees*, 1924, p. 188; cf. also *Judaism in the New Testament Period*, 1928, p. 81.

[2] Cf. *Talmud and Apocrypha*, 1933, p. 193.

[3] Cf. *ibid.*, pp. 193f. On p. 259, however, he still maintains that II Baruch and II Esdras give expression to the feelings of the Zealots following their defeat in the Jewish War of AD 66–70.

[4] Cf. *ibid.*, pp. 191f.

method of apocalyptic and, whilst apocalyptic shows a profound reverence for the Torah, this is no justification for claiming for it a Pharisaic origin.[1] In so writing, however, Herford tends to overstate his case. In denying the Pharisaic authorship of these books he drives a wedge between apocalyptic and Pharisaism which is more imaginary than real.

It is true that reverence for the Torah was not limited to the Pharisees; nevertheless it is significant that in this respect they and the apocalyptists stood on common ground. To the apocalyptists every bit as much as to the Pharisees the written Torah was the revelation of God to his people. This can be illustrated from earlier books like I Enoch, Jubilees and the Assumption of Moses right up to II Esdras and II Baruch in the later period. The Law of God was central in their thinking and binding upon their conduct. Perhaps the most 'Pharisaic' of all the apocalyptic books is the Psalms of Solomon, written about the middle of the first century BC, when Pharisaism was a powerful factor in the State. The sentiment of these Psalms is wholly in keeping with the Pharisaic outlook and it is of no small significance for our understanding of Pharisaism, no less than for apocalyptic, that the messianic hope is here given a more central place than legalistic matters which are popularly associated with this particular party. On the other hand, in some apocalyptic writings, such as the Book of Daniel, stress is often laid on the observance of legal requirements in a thoroughly Pharisaic manner. Again, it has been claimed that the form of apocalyptic differs radically from the *halakah* form of the Pharisaic and rabbinic tradition. This is true, but it should be remembered that the Book of Jubilees, for example, not only shows knowledge of the halakic method but also gives actual illustrations of *halakot* at a stage much earlier than the rabbinic writings themselves.[2] Moreover, *halakah* was not alone in expressing the faith and teaching of Pharisaic Judaism; *haggadah* also had a significant role to play, and within the haggadic tradition we are justified in placing much of the apocalyptic lore.[3]

R. H. Charles, whilst claiming a Pharisaic origin for apocalyptic, nevertheless makes a clear-cut distinction between what he calls 'apocalyptic Pharisaism' and 'legalistic Pharisaism'. The one, he says, represents the prophetic and ethical element; the other the

[1] Cf. *The Pharisees*, 1923, p. 178. [2] See further pp. 121f.
[3] Cf. J. Bloch, *On the Apocalyptic in Judaism*, 1952, pp. 142f.

legalistic element.[1] G. F. Moore has little difficulty in pointing out the weakness of this position,[2] for, although there is a sense in which apocalyptic can truly be described as the successor of prophecy,[3] this is a very different thing from saying that it is the only or even the chief successor to the moral teaching of the great prophets. Moreover, just as 'legalistic Pharisaism' is not entirely lacking in prophetic or ethical content, so apocalyptic as we have noted is not entirely lacking in legalistic content. A somewhat different contrast has sometimes been drawn, namely, that between the ethical interest of the Pharisees and the eschatological interest of the apocalyptists. But again there is no real antithesis here at all. Deep ethical concern cannot be said to be characteristic of the apocalyptic writings, but it is certainly not absent and is often expressed, as in the Testaments of the XII Patriarchs, alongside ideas of an eschatological kind.[4] On the other hand, as we shall see presently, the writings of rabbinic Judaism which, though late, reflect the beliefs of a much earlier stage of Pharisaism, show no small interest also in eschatological speculation. These factors do not establish that the apocalyptic movement belonged in any special way to the Pharisees or that a Pharisaic authorship can be claimed for these books. The differences between them are great and cannot be denied. But they demonstrate that during the inter-testamental period there was no necessary antipathy between the two and that within the variegated Judaism of that time the 'party line' was less distinct than it came to be in later years.

We conclude that the apocalyptic writers were to be found not in any one party within Judaism but throughout many parties, known and unknown, and among men who owed allegiance to no party at all. Not all the ideas expressed in their books would be equally acceptable to all the writers of them. There were differences of emphases and even of belief; nevertheless they shared with one another a common purpose, acknowledged a common heritage and expressed a common hope in the ultimate triumph of God's kingdom in which the Jewish people would have a glorious part. The various eclectic groups which no doubt existed in Judaism during this period would find here much common ground and would be able to describe themselves, in opposition to the powers of evil around them,

[1] Cf. *Apocrypha and Pseudepigrapha of the Old Testament*, vol. II, 1913, pp. viiff.
[2] Cf. *op. cit.*, vol. III, pp. 17ff. [3] See ch. III.
[4] For the ethical content of apocalyptic see pp. 100ff.

as together the Elect, the Righteous, the Saints, the Wise, the Poor and so forth[1]—terms which frequently occur in certain of these apocalyptic writings. It is not difficult to imagine that, just as they shared their religious convictions, so they might share also their sacred books in which their hopes were expressed.

4. THE 'POPULARITY' OF APOCALYPTIC

Apocalyptic was not a 'popular' literature in the sense that it was written for the masses. It was not the product of 'ignorant and unlearned men', as has sometimes been suggested; on the contrary, it would appear to have been written for the most part by wise and learned men who were thoroughly acquainted not only with the historic Jewish faith, but also with the 'wisdom' of that time whose esoteric and magical lore owed much to non-Jewish religious traditions.[2] It is an unwarranted assumption, however, to conclude that, because it originated in a relatively restricted section of the population, it therefore represents an insignificant backwater. The evidence points rather to the fact that apocalyptic was a fairly strong current in the mainstream of Judaism in the years immediately before and after the beginning of the Christian era.

The ideas contained in these books, however, were much more widespread than the books themselves and continued to exercise a strong influence even long after the books had disappeared. They were the deposit of a varied tradition which passed through a fairly lengthy period of oral transmission and formed a link between this literature and, say, a book like that of Ezekiel in the Old Testament Canon. The popularity of such ideas at an early stage may be hinted at in Dan. 12.4 where the seer is bidden to 'shut up the words and seal the book', for 'many shall run to and fro and knowledge shall increase' (cf. also 12.9–10). Likewise at a much later stage, towards the close of the inter-testamental period, the writer of II Esdras can refer to no fewer than seventy secret books (presumably apocalyptic writings),[3] to be delivered to the wise among the people (cf. 14.13, 26, 46), which were in circulation in his day and which he mentions in the same breath as the canonical Scriptures themselves (cf.

[1] Cf. H. J. Schonfield, *Secrets of the Dead Sea Scrolls*, 1956, pp. 116f.
[2] Cf. S. Mowinckel, *He That Cometh*, English translation, 2nd ed., 1959, p. 282.
[3] See pp. 85ff., 114.

14.45–46). Reference in the Church Fathers and in later rabbinic writings confirms this widespread influence of apocalyptic and suggests that those apocalyptic books now extant are only a fraction of what must have been at one time a very considerable literature. The discovery of the library at Qumran with its profusion of apocalyptic-type literature is a further graphic indication of the significant part played by apocalyptic during this whole period.[1]

Even though the writing of these books may have been confined to relatively restricted circles within Judaism and the initial reading and study of them to certain defined strata of Jewish society, their influence would make itself felt from an early time on the life of the Jewish people as a whole. There seems little reason to doubt that during the oppressive reigns of the Herodian rulers, for example, and the troublesome years of the Roman procurators right up to the outbreak of the Jewish War in AD 66 they were a source of encouragement and strength to the nation in face of dire peril and danger. 'It may be inferred from their number and volume', writes G. F. Moore, 'that they found eager acceptance particularly in times of tribulation which inspired new ones and caused old ones to be revamped.'[2]

By far the greatest number of these apocalyptic books were written in Palestine either in the ancient Hebrew language, the tongue of the learned of that day, or in the vernacular Aramaic, the language of Jewish literature generally. In due course they found their way into the Dispersion, where they were translated into Greek and won popularity among the Jews. In Alexandria particularly they would receive great acclaim with the result that they came to enjoy there a much wider reading public than they ever had in Palestine itself. One sign of the popularity of these books is the great number of languages into which they were in due course translated—Latin, Syriac, Arabic, Armenian, Ethiopic, Coptic, Slavonic, Georgian, etc. This wide range of translation no doubt reflects the degree of popularity they came to have among the Christians,[3] but it is also an indication of the place they held within Judaism itself. Even as late as the third century AD, it would seem, apocalyptic was still held in high esteem in some parts of the Dispersion at any rate. Evidence for this comes from the Synagogue of Dura Europos (AD 245) on the Euphrates, on whose walls there appear, prominently displayed,

[1] See further pp. 40ff. below. [2] *Op. cit.*, vol. I, p. 127. [3] See pp. 33ff.

representations not only of Moses and Joshua, but also of Enoch and Ezra representing the apocalyptic tradition.[1]

The significance of Jewish apocalyptic beyond the inter-testamental period lies, strictly speaking, outside the scope of this present work, but an examination of it, however cursory, will help to put the whole subject in perspective.[2] L. Ginzberg has pointed out that in the entire rabbinic literature of the first six centuries there is not a single quotation from the extant apocalyptic literature;[3] because of this it has sometimes been too readily assumed that rabbinic Judaism would have nothing whatever to do with the teaching and ideals contained in these books. C. C. Torrey, for example, affirms that from AD 70 onwards, so great was the devotion of the Jewish leaders to the Law and the sacred Scriptures, the decision was taken to destroy as undesirable all the Semitic originals of the 'outside books', including the apocalyptic writings, and so effect 'the sudden and complete abandonment by the Jews of their popular literature'.[4] Thus, this once-popular literature was discontinued and the ideas which it perpetuated were rejected as dangerous and heretical. Such a claim is hard to substantiate, however, from the evidence of the rabbinic writings themselves. It is true that in course of time the apocalyptic books fell out of favour, but there is no evidence to support any such theory of wholesale destruction. After all, apocalyptic was ably represented within the Canon itself by the Book of Daniel and similar ideas were prominent in other canonical books. In the rabbinic writings themselves, moreover, as also in many Jewish liturgical texts, allusion is made not unsympathetically to ideas and beliefs made popular by the apocalyptic books. They express belief in such things as the heavenly bliss of the righteous, the resurrection of the dead, the heavenly banquet, the coming judgment, the fires of Gehenna, the angelic destruction of Jerusalem and the coming of the New Jerusalem, the advent of the Messiah, the travails of the messianic age, wonders and portents heralding the last days and so forth.[5] In the Talmud, moreover, there are indica-

[1] Cf. M. I. Rostovtzeff, *The Excavations at Dura-Europos*, 1936; and J. Hempel, *ZAW*, vol. LI (N.F.X), 1933, p. 289.

[2] I am particularly indebted throughout this section to J. Bloch, *On the Apocalyptic in Judaism*.

[3] Cf. *JBL*, vol. XLI, 1922, pp. 116, 131.

[4] *The Apocryphal Literature*, 4th printing, 1953, pp. 14ff. and also pp. 3f.

[5] Cf. K. Kohler, 'Eschatology' in *JE*, vol. V, 1903, pp. 209ff.; J. Bloch, *op. cit.*, pp. 92–107.

tions that not a few prominent teachers among both the Tannaim and the Amoraim, were deeply interested in the secret lore of apocalyptic tradition and occupied themselves with apocalyptic speculations.[1] It is significant that Rabbi Judah ('the Prince'), for example, who was openly opposed to such matters as angelology and esoteric mysteries and was determined to exclude these from his final recension of the Mishnah, nevertheless permitted the inclusion, for example, of a specifically apocalyptic passage recorded in *Soṭah* 9.5 in which the signs of the coming of the Messiah are described.[2] This small 'rabbinic apocalypse' is attributed to none other than Rabbi Eliezer the Great, the disciple of Rabbi Johanan ben Zakkai.[3] The name of Rabbi Akiba is also of significance in this connection. It was he who elaborated and gave order to the *halakot*; but it was this same man who awaited eagerly the coming of the Messiah and supported the revolt of Ben Kosebah, commonly known as Bar Kochba, in the abortive rising against Rome in AD 132–5. There is not sufficient evidence to prove that these early rabbis were, in fact, in possession of apocalyptic writings, but it is quite clear that they were at least familiar with the teaching of this type of literature. Nowhere do we find among them that acrimony which is to be found directed against, say, the Gospels and other Christian writings.

Despite this continued interest on the part of certain rabbis, however, it is clear that after AD 70 apocalyptic began to lose its place in the mainstream of Judaism. It is unlikely that the 'official' or 'normative' Judaism which now emerged showed any bitter hostility to these books. But it is not altogether surprising that they dropped out of use. There were certain features in them which could be deemed inimical to the 'purity' of Judaism. The theological danger of dualism, for example, about which many rabbis were deeply concerned was only one factor among many which bore the stamp of compromising foreign influence. It is easy to see, moreover, that the whole mood or sentiment of apocalyptic would be largely out of place in reformed Judaism. In the earlier days of the nation's struggle for survival, when nationalism was a power to be reckoned with, apocalyptic found a natural setting and perfect conditions for growth; the message that the kingdom of God was at hand had an urgency and relevance for all who heard it. In the world of rabbinic

[1] Cf. J. Bloch, *op. cit.*, pp. 79f. [2] Cf. H. Danby, *op. cit.*, p. 306.

[3] For further illustrations of apocalyptic passages in the Talmud, see Israel Lévi, 'Apocalypses dans le Talmud', *REJ*, vol. I, 1880, pp. 108–14.

Judaism, however, this sense of urgency had passed and the fires of nationalism had for the most part been damped down. The emphasis was now on the Law of God contained in sacred Scripture, on the 'tradition of the elders' and on the life of obedience to the revealed will of God in the light of these sacred writings. Indeed, the very fanaticism of the apocalyptists would in itself be a warning to the rabbis of the dangers inherent in such teachings. They would recall the part these books had played in actual revolts against the Roman overlords in years gone by and would no doubt be apprehensive lest their continued popularity might lead to similar tragedies in the future. Thus, they were a challenge both to rabbinic authority and to the safety of the State. Another, and perhaps decisive, factor in the decline of apocalyptic would be the rapid growth of Christianity and the adoption and adaptation by the Church of many Jewish apocalyptic writings whose messianic and eschatological teachings were eminently suitable for the purpose of Christian propaganda.[1] It has been suggested that at the time of the Hadrianic persecutions, when, for example, the study of the Torah was punishable by death, the Romans may have destroyed the apocalyptic books which they would regard as both offensive and dangerous. With the return of more peaceful times the original Hebrew and Aramaic texts would be no longer in existence. Such books as survived would owe their survival to the fact that they had already been translated into other languages, and such apocalyptic ideas as persisted within rabbinic Judaism would be the result of oral transmission.[2] This attempted solution is only a guess and cannot be proved; but it underlines the fact that, for whatever reason, the apocalyptic books were perpetuated not in the original Hebrew and Aramaic tongues but in Greek and in the many other languages of the Dispersion. By reason of the antipathy of many rabbis to them and because they were no longer available for study in their original texts, it was inevitable that they should at last fall out of use.

The relation of the apocalyptic literature to the Canon raises questions which take us far beyond the limits of our present study and can be only lightly touched upon here. Reference is made in the rabbinic writings to certain 'outside books', an expression which is taken by most scholars to mean 'books outside the Canon of Scripture'.[3] Among these were 'the books [*sic*] of Ben Sira and all books

[1] See pp. 33ff. [2] Cf. J. Bloch, *op. cit.*, pp. 37f.
[3] Cf. H. Danby, *op. cit.*, p. 387, n. 5.

which were written from then onwards' (*Tos. Yadaim* 2.13). This presumably refers to the whole group of apocryphal literature to which Ben Sira belonged, including the apocalyptic writings. The same passage refers to them as books which 'do not defile the hands' —a technical term to indicate that they are uncanonical. It is in the light of this that we are to understand another passage which, in the form in which it stands in the Mishnah, is open to misinterpretation. In the tractate *Sanhedrin* 10.1 Rabbi Akiba is represented as saying that among those who have 'no part in the world to come' is 'he who reads in outside books'. At first sight this seems to indicate that the reading of all non-canonical literature of any kind is prohibited. It is clear, however, from the interpretation given of this passage in the Gemara of both the Palestinian and the Babylonian Talmuds (cf. *j. Sanhedrin* 28a; *b. Sanhedrin* 100b) that the reference is, in fact, to the use of these books in public recitation for liturgical or instructional purposes. There is no justification for supposing that these writings were excluded from the Canon because they were disowned or proscribed by official Judaism as 'heretical'. They were left out not because of any violent hostility on the part of the rabbis, but simply because (apart from Daniel), like many other books of an apocryphal kind, they had no claim to be included. Although many of the rabbis may have been suspicious of apocalyptic for the reasons stated above, the fact that a book was apocalyptic in character did not automatically preclude its acceptance within the Canon. The tests by which any book was excluded were independent of its peculiarly apocalyptic character and applied equally strongly to many other apocryphal books which had no apocalyptic interest whatsoever.[1]

5. CHRISTIANITY AND APOCALYPTIC

We have seen that the Jewish apocalyptic books gained a considerable popularity in the Dispersion, where they were made available first in Greek and then in many other languages. In course of time the Jews there, like those in Palestine itself, came to relinquish their hold on these writings. Before this happened, however, they had already been widely acclaimed by the Christians, who adopted

[1] For an account of the criteria determining the acceptance or otherwise of any book as canonical see S. Zeitlin, 'An Historical Study of the Canonization of the Hebrew Scriptures' in *Proceedings of the American Academy for Jewish Research*, 1932, pp. 152f.; W. D. Davies, *Christian Origins and Judaism*, 1962, pp. 27f.

as their Scriptures the LXX translation of the Old Testament, which had by then incorporated certain apocryphal books, some of them of an apocalyptic kind. Those which survive no doubt represent the books which were most highly valued among the Christians. By no means all the Jewish apocalyptic writings, however, would be preserved in this way; not a few would inevitably be lost to sight; others are known only by name or by allusions to them in the Church Fathers and other early records.[1] The value of these writings would be recognized by the early Aramaic-speaking Church in Jerusalem; and as the Gentile element grew and Aramaic gave way to Greek as the language of the Christian community, their popularity would become much more widespread than before. So it is that, whereas earlier on the apocalyptic writings were preserved and treasured by the Greek-speaking Jews of Alexandria, in course of time the Christian Church appropriated them for its own use and it is within the Christian religion that they have survived. Apart from the Book of Daniel, which was early enough and popular enough to gain recognition as sacred Scripture within the Canon, the tradition of apocalyptic is, in fact, Christian and not Jewish.

The reason for the popularity of these writings among the Christians is not hard to seek. In many ways, as we have noted, they were eminently suited to the purpose of Christian propaganda and would give added authority to many of the hopes and claims expressed by the Christian Church. Their teaching concerning 'the two ages', the imminent coming of the Messiah, the messianic kingdom, the woes of the last days, the judgment of the world, the resurrection of the dead, the future lot of the wicked and the righteous—all these would have a familiar ring and would in turn influence Christian thinking deeply. Their imprint is obvious on the beliefs of the Early Church and on the New Testament writings themselves.

Some of these books were taken over just as they stood and continued to enjoy a widespread popularity over many years. Others, however, were worked over by Christian editors who made them more suitable for their purposes or interpolated them with new material expressing specifically Christian truth and sentiment. One instance of this is the Sibylline Oracles, which were freely augmented in this way. Evidence of the same kind may also be found in the Testaments of the XII Patriarchs concerning whose composition and authorship scholars are seriously divided;[2] as it stands it bears

[1] See Appendix I. [2] See pp. 55f.

the strong imprint of Christian influence and some scholars are inclined to find in it a Christian and not a Jewish document. Other books, such as II Esdras, were also augmented not so much by interpolations as by whole new sections of material of a Christian origin (cf. chs. 1–2; 15–16).

But not only did the Christian Church adopt the old apocalyptic writings in their original or revised forms, they also produced new ones of their own which, together with those of Jewish origin, continued to exercise a considerable influence. There are differences between Jewish and Christian apocalyptic, and yet they are essentially one; they represent a single type of literature with no serious break between them at all, at least where form and presentation are concerned. Indeed, so alike are they that in certain instances it is difficult, if not impossible, to distinguish between them.

By far the most significant of all the Christian apocalypses is the canonical Book of Revelation, which draws freely on Jewish traditions and in which some scholars find a Jewish nucleus in Christian guise. It is different from the Jewish apocalyptic writings especially in the place which it gives to Jesus the Messiah as the meaning and end of all human history. But familiar features of Jewish apocalyptic are evident throughout the whole book—fantastic imagery, symbolic language, angelic powers of evil, the resurrection, the judgment, the messianic kingdom, the world to come. These same features are present in many other Christian apocalypses which lie outside and beyond the New Testament Canon. Like the earlier Jewish apocalypses, many of them are known to us only by name or in fragmentary allusions. Many more have survived, among the most important of which are the Apocalypse of Peter, the Shepherd of Hermas and the Epistle of the Apostles, all of them dating from the second century AD. The first of these is of particular interest for its teaching concerning the torments of hell and the punishment of the wicked which left its deep mark on mediaeval theology. So popular did some of these writings become that they made claim for a time to canonical authority in certain sections of the Church. For the most part, however, their teaching could not bear any comparison with the Apocalypse of John or with the other accepted writings of the New Testament. In due course, like their Jewish predecessors but for different reasons, they, too, fell out of favour and with few exceptions disappeared as valued writings of the Christian Church.

II

THE APOCALYPTIC LITERATURE

1. APOCALYPTIC AND 'SECTARIAN' BOOKS

THE HELLENISTIC AND inter-testamental periods were marked by a prolific literary output,[1] the chief centre of literary interest being the city of Alexandria, from which books were despatched all over the Greek-speaking world. The Jews both in the Dispersion and in Palestine itself shared fully in this activity. More often than not the books they wrote had as their aim the condemnation of idolatry by means of ridicule and the stout defence of Judaism against the insidious influence of heathenism. Among their writings was a considerable body of literature to which the name 'pseudepigrapha' is often given on account of their form, and which are customarily classed as 'apocalypses' on account of their peculiar content. The word 'apocalypse' has the same meaning as its Latin equivalent 'revelation' and is a transliteration of the Greek word *apokalypsis* meaning 'unveiling' or 'uncovering' and signifies the disclosure of some hidden truth, particularly about God or the divine purpose. In the first place it was used to describe a vision, but in course of time it came to signify books whose contents were believed to be revealed through the medium of such visions. In this technical sense it is applied to the Book of Revelation in the New Testament and then is used to describe that whole body of literature of a similar kind prevalent among the Jews throughout the inter-testamental period. This literature is of a diverse kind, though it possesses certain fairly well-defined characteristics which mark it off from other

[1] See R. H. Pfeiffer, *History of New Testament Times with an Introduction to the Apocrypha*, 1949, pp. 60ff., 200ff.

literary productions of the same period.[1] It claims to possess secret knowledge of the future and in particular of the manner and time of the End which it is able to disclose under divine inspiration and by superhuman means.

These apocalyptic writings raise many problems of literary criticism for which no easy solution is available. Not a few of them are composite in character and contain material ranging over a period of several decades or more. Literary analysis has been made all the more difficult because of the use made of them by the early Christian Church. As we have seen, so completely did the Church adopt and adapt existing Jewish apocalyptic writings that it is often quite impossible to be certain concerning the origin of particular verses or passages or even whole books. There is no unanimity among scholars concerning the exact dates at which the several books were written, and in a few cases widely divergent views have been expressed. Not all of them, moreover, are 'apocalypses' in the thorough-going sense that others can claim that name; but they are usually included because they contain certain apocalyptic elements and obviously belong to the apocalyptic line of tradition. There is no agreed list of such books, but those generally accepted as apocalyptic or having apocalyptic elements in them are as follows, together with their approximate dates of origin.

i. The Book of Daniel (165 BC)
ii. I Enoch 1–36, 37–71, 72–82, 83–90, 91–108 (from *c.* 164 BC onwards)
iii. The Book of Jubilees (*c.* 150 BC)
iv. The Sibylline Oracles, Book III (from *c.* 150 BC onwards)
v. The Testaments of the XII Patriarchs (latter part of second century BC)[2]
vi. The Psalms of Solomon (*c.* 48 BC)
vii. The Assumption of Moses (AD 6–30)
viii. 'The Martyrdom of Isaiah'[3]
ix. The Life of Adam and Eve or The Apocalypse of Moses (shortly before AD 70)
x. The Apocalypse of Abraham 9–32 (*c.* AD 70–100)
xi. The Testament of Abraham (first century AD)

[1] See ch. IV.
[2] For evidence of a later date see pp. 55ff.
[3] It is more than doubtful that this is a Jewish apocalyptic book. See p. 59.

xii. II Enoch or The Book of the Secrets of Enoch (first century AD)[1]
xiii. The Sibylline Oracles, Book IV (*c.* AD 80)
xiv. II Esdras (= 4 Ezra) 3–14 (*c.* AD 90)
xv. II Baruch or The Apocalypse of Baruch (after AD 90)
xvi. III Baruch (second century AD)
xvii. The Sibylline Oracles, Book V (second century AD)

This list of apocalyptic writings has been considerably augmented by the so-called Dead Sea Scrolls, which have cast much light on the whole period and especially on the nature of Jewish apocalyptic itself. Many sizeable manuscripts and thousands of fragments, not a few of which are apocryphal and apocalyptic in character, have been found at Qumran and neighbouring sites. Some of these works were obviously written by members of the Qumran Community, but in the case of others the evidence concerning their origin and authorship is as yet too inconclusive for us to form a judgment. The fact that a particular manuscript was found here is no justification for assuming that it was necessarily written by a member of this party or contains a precise statement of its beliefs.

There can be no doubt, however, that writings of an apocalyptic kind had a special fascination for the members of this Community. One indication of this is the abundance of apocalyptic material, albeit in fragmentary form, to be found in their library; another is the similarity in outlook between these writings and the specifically sectarian documents produced by the party itself. From an early date, it would seem, the Qumran Covenanters were in possession of a number of the older apocalyptic books to which reference has been made above. Fragments of no fewer than seven manuscripts relating to the Book of Daniel, for example, have been found which must date from a period not much more than fifty years or so after the date of its composition. Another writing which appears among the Qumran documents is the Book of Jubilees. Not only is reference made to it in the *bona fide* writings of the party, but fragments of at least ten manuscripts of it have also been found. There is equally impressive evidence for the popularity among the Covenanters of the Book of Enoch. Portions of about ten manuscripts, written in Aramaic, have been found which correspond to four out of the five parts into which the book is divided in the Ethiopic Version which

[1] For evidence of a much later date see pp. 61f.

has come down to us. In addition to these, several fragments have been found of an Aramaic Testament of Levi and a Hebrew Testament of Naphtali.[1]

Quite apart from these already known apocalyptic works, the library of the Covenanters has produced a bewildering amount of material which has a vital bearing on our understanding of the place of apocalyptic in the inter-testamental period. These writings assume many literary forms—commentaries, psalms, books of rules, liturgies, anthologies, and the rest; but in their teaching and beliefs they have much in common with those generally known as 'the apocalyptic books', especially in their expression of messianic hopes, their beliefs concerning good and evil spirits and their conception of 'the last things'. The following is a list of Qumran works whose outlook, in greater or less degree, has a close association with the apocalyptic books listed above, even though they may not share all their characteristic marks.

i. Commentaries on Isaiah, Hosea, Micah, Nahum, Habakkuk, Zephaniah and Psalm 37
ii. The Zadokite Document (or the Damascus Document)
iii. The Manual of Discipline (or the Rule of the Community)
iv. The Rule of the Congregation
v. A Scroll of Benedictions
vi. The Testimonies Scroll (or a Messianic Anthology)
vii. Hymns (or Psalms) of Thanksgiving
viii. The War of the Sons of Light against the Sons of Darkness (or the Rule for the Final War)
ix. The Book of Mysteries
x. A Midrash on the Last Days
xi. A Description of the New Jerusalem
xii. An Angelic Liturgy
xiii. The Prayer of Nabonidus and a Pseudo-Daniel Apocalypse
xiv. A Genesis Apocryphon

Whilst these writings belong to the same religious milieu as the generally accepted apocalyptic books, there are many differences between them which give warning against a too-hasty identification of the two sets of literature or the sources from which they come. Whilst there is dependence of the Qumran texts on the known apocalyptic books, there is little if any evidence of a reverse process, nor

[1] See further p. 57.

does much of the terminology characteristic of the Covenanters appear in the other writings.

Throughout this volume, and more especially in that section dealing with the *method* of apocalyptic, particular attention will be paid to the books in the first of the two lists noted above to which the name 'pseudepigrapha' is usually given. So closely do these two belong together in their general religious outlook, however, that the evidence of the Qumran Scrolls will also be examined and used to illumine and interpret the *message* of the apocalyptic writers particularly in the expression of their messianic and eschatological hopes. A detailed analysis of these sources would take us far beyond the limits of this book. The reader will find much fuller reference in the several 'Introductions' to the apocalyptic literature and in the mass of books now available on the Dead Sea Scrolls. In the following pages only a very brief outline will be attempted so as to provide some idea at least of the literary sources to be examined in subsequent chapters.

2. THE QUMRAN TEXTS

It is quite impossible, in the light of present knowledge, to be in any way dogmatic concerning the exact dates of the various Qumran texts which have come to light. The general statement may be allowed that, in the judgment of the majority of scholars, they date in the main from the last two centuries before the Christian era and reflect the life and beliefs of a Jewish community whose settlement at Qumran can be placed, on archaeological grounds, at some point within the last third of the second century BC.

Among the very different kinds of writing found at Qumran is a distinct group of **Commentaries** on a number of biblical, and especially prophetic, books. The largest of these, and the most significant, is the commentary on the first two chapters of **Habakkuk**. Reference is made there, as also elsewhere in the commentaries, to a 'Teacher of Righteousness' who was held in very high regard by the Qumran Covenanters, and to a 'Wicked Priest' who opposed the Teacher of Righteousness and caused a disturbance on the Day of Atonement when the Teacher and his disciples were observing this festival (XI.4ff.). Concerning the Wicked Priest it is said that he defiled Jerusalem and the Temple there, that he plotted against the Poor (i.e. the Covenanters) and robbed them of their possessions (XII.2ff.). But judgment will come and he will be made to drink 'the cup of God's fury'. Those associated with him, 'the last priests of Jerusalem', who have amassed wealth and booty by plundering the peoples will in the last days be delivered into the hand of the army of 'the Kittim' who 'come from afar, from the islands of the sea' and 'trample the earth with their horses and beasts' (III.10f.). These Kittim, however, will overreach themselves and incur the vengeance of God; the time will come when he will commit into the hands of his elect the judgment of the Kittim and all the nations (V.3ff.). These Kittim have been identified by most scholars either with the earlier or later Seleucids or else with the Romans, and the Teacher of Righteousness and the Wicked Priest with many different historical figures from each of these periods. Further historical allusions are made in the commentary on **Nahum** not only to the Kittim but also to a ruler called Antiochus, a Greek king named Demetrius (on 2.12) and 'the Lion of Wrath' who 'hangs men alive, a thing never done formerly in Israel' (on 2.13). Again, different identifications have been offered for these figures which would place the events recorded in the second or first centuries BC.

These commentaries are of interest, however, not only for their historical allusions but also for their method of exegesis. More will be said about this at a later point.[1] Here we observe that the prophetic text is interpreted in terms of contemporary events. The meaning of the prophets' words had been hidden from the original writers; what they wrote had reference, not to their own day, but to 'the end of the days' in which the Covenanters were now living. The hidden meaning of these prophecies had awaited the coming of the Teacher of Righteousness by whose inspiration and insight they had now been revealed.

Of quite a different kind is the so-called **Zadokite Document** of which a considerable number of fragments have been found in three Qumran caves. This work was already known in a much more extensive text in two medieval copies which, though of different dates, obviously represent the same work. These were found in 1896–7 in the Cairo Genizah by Solomon Schechter, who published them in 1910 under the title *Fragments of a Zadokite Work*:[2] The Qumran fragments correspond to one of these manuscripts (manuscript A), which is not complete as it stands and is supplemented

[1] See pp. 180f.

[2] These documents were re-edited in 1954 by Chaim Rabin with the title *The Zadokite Documents* (2nd ed., 1958).

by the second copy (manuscript B). The title 'Zadokite Document' is derived from the name 'sons of Zadok' by which the members of the community called themselves; the title 'Damascus Document', sometimes given to it, is derived from another name by which they were called, 'the Community of the New Covenant in the land of Damascus'. Reference is again made here to the Teacher of Righteousness who had been raised up by God to lead the Covenanters after they had 'groped in the darkness for twenty years', and to their migration to 'the land of Damascus' which many scholars regard as a reference to Qumran itself. If this migration took place under the leadership of the Teacher of Righteousness, then we may possibly date this work around the year 100 BC, within forty years of the Teacher's death. The *terminus a quo* for the writing of the work is determined by a reference within it to 'the Book of the Divisions of Times into their Jubilees and Weeks' (XVI.3–4), i.e. the Book of Jubilees which, in the prologue, carries a similar title. There is, in fact, a close connection between this work and the Book of Jubilees,[1] portions of which have been found among the Scrolls; Chaim Rabin cites no fewer than fifty-eight instances where parallels in thought or expression can be detected.[2] The same writer indicates that the work consists of two different writings which he calls 'the Admonition' and 'the Laws', titles which conveniently express the contents of these writings.

The document begins with an admonition or exhortation to 'all you who have entered the Covenant' to remain faithful to God. The writer demonstrates, by reference to the history of Israel and the Community itself, the faithfulness of God, who in due course raised up for them a Teacher of Righteousness 'to guide them in the way of his heart' and to oppose 'the man of scoffing' who led the people astray. Biblical passages are used to encourage the faithful. A remnant will survive the time of evil through which they are passing and will be granted eternal life. Forty years after the 'gathering in' of the Teacher of Righteousness the wicked, including the faithless Covenanters, will be destroyed and the 'Messiah of Aaron and Israel' will appear. The coming of this Messiah is associated with 'the coming of the Teacher of Righteousness at the end of the days.' Some scholars have seen in this reference an allusion to the resurrection of the Teacher of Righteousness who is perhaps to be identi-

[1] Cf. M. Testuz, *Les Idées Religieuses du Livre des Jubilés*, 1960, pp. 179ff.
[2] Cf. *The Zadokite Documents*, 2nd ed., 1958, pp. 85f.

fied with the Messiah himself.[1] During this period of evil Belial is 'let loose upon Israel', but his rule will soon end when God will appear in judgment. The section of the work dealing with the laws of the Community refers, as we have seen, to the Book of Jubilees and also to a Book of Hagu which seems to have been highly regarded. The laws recorded here are halakic in character and are roughly grouped according to their subject-matter as in the codification of the Mishnah. The document also contains a description of certain rules relating to the organization of the Community.

The **Manual of Discipline** is a writing, presumably composed for the use of the Community's leaders, in which are set out rules and regulations dealing with matters of an ethical, ritualistic, organizational and disciplinary kind. There are indications that it may have been based on some earlier manuals of a somewhat similar nature[2] and so may not belong to the earliest days of the Community's life. Its form suggests that it may have been read aloud on the occasion, say, of the renewal of the covenant and the acceptance of novices.[3] Its chief interest, from the point of view of apocalyptic study, is in the section III.13–IV.26 which tells of the spirit of truth and the spirit of wickedness in whose ways God has appointed that men should walk. The children of righteousness are ruled by the Prince of Light and walk in the ways of light, whereas the children of wickedness are ruled by the Angel of Darkness and walk in the ways of darkness. The Angel of Darkness endeavours to overthrow the sons of light, but God and his Angel of Truth succour them. The virtues and vices of men are to be understood in relation to these two spirits. Those who walk in the way of the spirit of truth will receive joy and peace, but those who walk in the way of the spirit of wickedness will receive eternal torment and endless disgrace. This dualism is familiar elsewhere in the apocalyptic writings, as is also the theme of the triumph of the righteous and the defeat of the wicked. Another matter of considerable interest in this document is the mention of 'the Messiahs of Aaron and Israel', perhaps indicating that the members of this Community awaited the coming of two Messiahs, one priestly and one kingly.

The **Rule of the Congregation**, though attached to the Manual

[1] For a list of scholarly opinions see H. H. Rowley, *The Zadokite Fragments and the Dead Sea Scrolls*, 2nd ed., 1955, p. 53, n. 2, and p. 70.
[2] Cf. H. H. Rowley, *Jewish Apocalyptic and the Dead Sea Scrolls*, 1957, pp. 6f.
[3] Cf. A. Weiser, *Introduction to the Old Testament*, English ed., 1961, p. 460.

of Discipline, is a separate document probably of an earlier date. Its opening words make clear its eschatological interest, for 'this is the Rule for all the congregation of Israel *in the last days*'. Mention is again made of the Book of Hagu (here called Hagi) by which members of the Community are to be instructed. The purpose of such instruction is that they may serve the whole Community in judgment and counsel and that they may take part in the coming war against the nations. A place of primary importance is given to the priests in all this preparation and particularly in the description given of the Council and the meal which follows in which they are given precedence. This last reference may signify a recognized meal of the Community or it may refer to the eschatological banquet familiar in apocalyptic tradition. A kingly Messiah called 'the Messiah of Israel' takes a place at this meal subordinate to the priest in whom some scholars see the Messiah of Aaron.

The precedence of the priest is again made clear in the **Scroll of Benedictions** which was originally attached to the two previously named documents. This Scroll, as the name indicates, consists of a number of blessings to be pronounced over the faithful. It is not clear whether its use is intended for the inauguration of the messianic era or for some liturgical service in preparation for it. First comes the blessing of the whole Community, then of the High Priest, then of the priests and finally of 'the Prince of the Congregation'. The last named is presumably the kingly Messiah and some have seen in the High Priest a reference to the priestly Messiah. The interest of the Covenanters in the messianic hope is further evidenced by the **Testimonies Scroll**, which takes the form of a messianic anthology in which five Old Testament 'proof-texts' are gathered together (Deut. 5.28f.; 18.18f.; Num. 24.15–17; Deut. 33.8–11; Josh. 6.26).

The **Hymns of Thanksgiving** occupy eighteen columns and represent perhaps about twenty-five separate compositions. They breathe an atmosphere of deep piety and were probably recited or sung at one of the Community's festivals or services of worship. It is unlikely that they were written by the Teacher of Righteousness, as has been claimed, although some may have been composed by him. It is more likely that they are the work of several authors. A few hymns tell of persecution and betrayal, somewhat after the style of Jeremiah's 'Confessions', and may reflect the experience of the leader of the Community or simply of the Community itself.

As elsewhere in the Scrolls, the writers claim that God has given them a special knowledge and insight and has made them 'a discerning interpreter of wonderful mysteries'. Interest is shown in the holy angels whom God has ordained to rule over the elements and with whom the faithful will one day stand before him. Throughout cols. XIV–XVIII allusion is made, as in the Manual of Discipline, to the doctrine of two spirits in man and in the world and thanks is given for the gift of God's holy spirit. Reference is made in col. VI to 'the time of judgment' and 'battles against the ungodly' when God will overthrow wickedness and 'the sons of wickedness shall be no more'. The most significant section in this connection, however, is that contained in col. III, where the writer describes in graphic language the 'pangs' which will come upon Israel, upon mankind and upon all creation when, in the last days, God brings in his kingdom and triumphs over all his foes.[1]

The **War of the Sons of Light against the Sons of Darkness** is a remarkable document describing the final apocalyptic battle which will bring to an end this present era of wickedness and prepare the way for the era of God's favour. Whilst its interpretation is eschatological rather than historical, its description may reflect an actual historical situation; the picture it presents is idealistic, but the details of that picture are based on methods of warfare familiar at the time when the document was written. It begins (col. I) with a general description of the war between 'the Sons of Light', represented by the tribes of Levi, Judah and Benjamin, and 'the Sons of Darkness' also known as 'the army of Belial' and comprised of the armies of Edom, Moab, Philistia, the 'Kittim of Assyria' (with whom are associated the 'Kittim in Egypt') and those who have violated the covenant. Seven campaigns will be fought, each apparently of one year's duration, at the end of which the army of Belial will be destroyed. Each side will gain the advantage in three campaigns, but in the seventh the mighty hand of God will bring the victory. This same theme is continued in the final section of the document (cols. XV–XIX), which gives further details concerning the organization of the army of the Sons of Light and the tactics to be employed in battle. Here it is stated that God will effect the overthrow of the Kittim and 'the Prince of the kingdom of wickedness' by the help of his angel Michael. It has been suggested by some scholars who doubt the unity of the work that these two sections, in which the Kittim of Assyria are the chief antagonists, may have

[1] See pp. 272f.

comprised an earlier version, based on Dan. 11.40–12.3, which was later expanded by the addition of cols. II–XIV or else that cols. XV–XIX by themselves may form an appendix dependent on the rest of the document.

The description in col. I of the defeat of the Kittim in the seventh yearly campaign is followed by an account of continued fighting for another thirty-three years (except for sabbatical years) against the ancestral enemies of Israel whose names are taken from the lists contained in Genesis 10 and 25. The rest of cols. II–XIV describes in considerable detail the progress of the forty years' war, the trumpets and standards with their various inscriptions, the disposition of the army, the weapons of the soldiers, their age and number and grounds for disqualification from service, the cleanliness of the camp and the responsibility in battle of the priests and Levites who exhort God's people and seal the defeat of his enemies with a curse. The section ends with a hymn of thanksgiving celebrating the victory of the God of Israel.

The dating of this Scroll depends largely on the identity of the 'Kittim of Assyria' and the 'Kittim in Egypt'. Some see in these the Seleucids and the Ptolemies and so date it in the second century BC. Others see in them reference to the Roman army of occupation in Syria and in Egypt and claim that this identification is supported by the description given of the trumpets, the weapons and the battle formation; in this case it would date from perhaps the latter part of the first century BC. It is much clearer who 'the Sons of Light' are. They refer to the true Israel, by which is presumably meant the members of the Qumran Community. Israel, under the leadership of this priestly party, will by God's help overthrow 'the Sons of Darkness'. The priestly interest of the Scroll is evident throughout; the High Priest himself has an important role to play and the priests and Levites, though not taking part in the actual fighting, have the task of exhorting and instructing the army in time of battle.

But this is no mere military manual; it is a theological work whose aim is to prepare the faithful for the last days. There are elements in it which suggest that it is a description, brought up to date and in the guise of the writer's own day, of the battle referred to in Ezekiel 38 between Israel and the mysterious Gog of the land of Magog whom God will destroy together with his allies at the end of the age. Leading the Sons of Light is a 'mighty man' or a 'man of glory' in whom we are possibly to see a reference to the Davidic Messiah. But angels as well as men are involved in this great estachological battle which assumes cosmic and not simply earthly dimensions. By the help of God the 'Prince of Light' will overcome the 'Prince of Darkness' and cast him into the pit. God's enemies will be destroyed, but his faithful people will receive everlasting salvation in the new age which will soon dawn.

This same thought is expressed in the **Book of Mysteries**, a brief apocalyptic document, which looks forward to the time when 'knowledge will fill the world and folly will no longer be there', for 'when the children of iniquity are shut up wickedness will be banished before righteousness as darkness is banished before light'. The 'Sons of Light' are mentioned again in a **Midrash on the Last Days** which briefly interprets a number of verses brought together from various parts of Scripture. The children of Belial will devise evil plots against the Sons of Light and cause them to stumble. The kings of the nations will rage against the elect of Israel in the last days. But God will save his people by the hands of two messianic figures, 'the Branch of David' and 'the Interpreter of the Law', who will arise at the time of the End. Another work, represented by fragments in several of the Caves, is a **Description of the New Jerusalem**, written in Aramaic.[1] As the title indicates, it gives a description of the new Jerusalem and the restored Temple there in whose ritual it shows a deep interest. The measurements and furnishings of the Temple are shown in a vision to the seer, who is also acquainted with the liturgical laws which will prevail in the coming days. The work is obviously inspired by the vision of the new Temple in Ezekiel 40–48. The important place given to angels in the thought and worship of the Covenanters is indicated by an **Angelic Liturgy** which has survived in two fragments.[2] In the first of these, seven 'sovereign Princes' (*i.e.* chief angels) pronounce their blessings on the company of the faithful; in the second the theme is the throne-chariot or *merkabah* mentioned in Ezekiel 1 and 10 and which plays an important part in Jewish mysticism both of the intertestamental and the medieval periods.

Several fragments have been found of two works, written in Aramaic, which belong to the Danielic cycle of tradition.[3] The first

[1] Cf. D. Barthélemy and J. T. Milik, *Discoveries in the Judaean Desert I*, 1955, pp. 134f., and also M. Baillet in *RB*, vol. LXII, 1955, pp. 222–45.

[2] Cf. J. Strugnell, 'The Angelic Liturgy at Qumran' in *Congress Volume, Oxford, 1960, Supplements to VT*, vol. VII, pp. 318–45.

[3] Cf. J. T. Milik, ' "Prière de Nabonide" et autres écrits d'un cycle de Daniel', *RB*, 1956, pp. 411–15.

bears the title 'Words of the prayer spoken by Nabunai' and probably refers to Nabonidus, the last Babylonian king. This **Prayer of Nabonidus** has a close resemblance to the story of Nebuchadnezzar's miraculous recovery from illness as recorded in Daniel 4 and may have been the source, in oral or literary form, of Daniel's account.[1] The second work is represented by fragments of three manuscripts which apparently describe revelations given to Daniel. In this **Pseudo-Daniel Apocalypse** Daniel gives the king and his courtiers an account of world-history from the time of the Flood to the time of the End in which the author himself is living. It is probably later than the canonical Book of Daniel and may be dated around the year 100 BC.

Of somewhat less importance for our purpose is an Aramaic document, several columns of which have so far been published, which comments on the text of Genesis after the manner of a Targum. It was at first thought that the first section (col. II) of this **Genesis Apocryphon** might be a fragment of 'the Book of Lamech' of which mention is made in an early Christian list;[2] but it is now seen to be simply that portion of the commentary where Lamech is the speaker. The work is of interest because of its likeness in some respects to the Book of Jubilees. Here, too, as elsewhere in the apocalyptic literature, reference is made to Noah's miraculous birth and to Enoch as a man of superior wisdom.

3. THE LITERATURE OF THE SECOND AND FIRST CENTURIES BC

The first of the apocalyptic writings is the **Book of Daniel**, which purports to have been written in the sixth century BC towards the close of the Babylonian Captivity. The first half of the book consists of five stories concerning a Jew named Daniel who, together with his three companions, remained faithful to their religion and their God in a foreign land in face of great provocation and grievous temptation. This Daniel is presented as a wise man who is able, by God's help, to interpret dreams and forecast the course of future events. The second half of the book records four visions which came to

[1] So J. T. Milik, *Ten Years*, p. 37. A. Dupont-Sommer, however, indicates certain differences between the two accounts and judges that, in its present recension at any rate, the Qumran account is later than that of the Book of Daniel, cf. *The Essene Writings from Qumran*, English trans., 1961, p. 324.

[2] See Appendix I, p. 393.

Daniel in Babylon. These visions are not concerned with the contemporary scene in exile, but rather give a survey of subsequent history as it affects the Jewish nation from the time of Nebuchadnezzar right down to the reign of Antiochus Epiphanes in the second quarter of the second century BC.

This book has the distinction of being the only one of its kind to gain entry into the Old Testament Canon, although it is to be noted that it is set among the Writings and not among the Prophets. This fact, together with evidence of an historical and also of a linguistic kind, has led most scholars to date it, in its present form at any rate, towards the close of Antiochus's reign in or about the year 165 BC[1] and, as we have seen, to find its author or authors among the Hasidim, who gave support to the Maccabees at the time of their rising against the Seleucids.

The questions of date and authorship are closely related to the problem of the book's literary structure on which there is no consensus of scholarly opinion. Some argue strongly for a unity of authorship, even though the book as it now stands may not have been written at one time but over a period of years; others contend that in its present form it shows evidence of two or more hands.[2] In either case the sections 12.11, 12 and perhaps also 9.4–19 are to be accepted as slightly later interpolations.

The book as a whole, as we have seen, can be divided into two main sections according to the form of their contents. Chapters 1–6 record stories about Daniel and his three companions during the trying days of the Babylonian exile, whereas chapters 7–12 take the form of visions in which Daniel, by divine inspiration, is able to forecast the future. This distinction, however, is not as complete as it may appear to be. The substance of the vision recorded in chapter 7, for example, has much in common with the contents of chapter 2, and there is a certain unity about the message of the book in both these parts. A somewhat different division is possible, however, on linguistic grounds. In this case the break comes, not at the end of chapter 6 as in the previous case, but at the end of chapter 7. Apart from an introductory section which is written in Hebrew (1.1–2.4a) the bulk of the first part of the book is written in Aramaic (2.4b–

[1] For an assessment of the evidence see J. A. Montgomery, *The Book of Daniel*, ICC, 1927, pp. 57ff.

[2] The evidence is collated and presented by H. H. Rowley, 'The Unity of the Book of Daniel' in *The Servant of the Lord*, 1952, pp. 235ff.

7.28), the second part being written in Hebrew (8.1–12.13). H. H. Rowley, who advocates strongly the unity of the book and its authorship, suggests that the writer, in the stories recorded in chapters 2–6, made use of certain traditions, both oral and written, which he selected and shaped to suit his own purpose. These popular traditions concerning Daniel and his friends, written in the third person, he recorded in Aramaic, the language of the people, and circulated separately. At a somewhat later date the same writer recorded his visions in the name of Daniel so as to identify himself with the author of the stories. This transition from anonymity to pseudonymity takes place within chapter 7, which is also written in Aramaic as a sequel to the preceding stories. The visions recorded in chapters 8–12 continue the use of the first person, but are written in Hebrew, this language being more suitable for this less popular form of literature. An introduction would then be written to the whole work in Hebrew and would continue in this language up to 2.4b, where fittingly it changes over to Aramaic with the recorded speech of the Chaldeans.

Other scholars detect in the book certain differences in historical and theological outlook between the two main sections which are hard to reconcile on the basis of a single author. Many suggestions have been offered. One is that the first author may have rearranged and rewritten certain stories which he had received in a fairly fixed form concerning a traditional figure, Daniel, and his three companions who may have belonged originally to another cycle of tradition altogether; these stories he proceeded to adapt and remodel to suit the purpose he had in mind; finally he gave them their interpretation in the vision recorded in chapter 7. At a subsequent date, not far removed from the first, another author would record the visions contained in chapters 8–12 as a further interpretation of the first part of the book, at the same time writing an introduction to the whole book or translating the original Aramaic tale into the Hebrew tongue.[1]

However we are to interpret the literary structure of the book, the conviction behind the visions is the same as that behind the stories—God's purposes are greater than man's plans; he is sovereign lord over the whole history of mankind and will at last vindicate his people Israel; this vindication is drawing near, for the End

[1] Cf. E. W. Heaton, *The Book of Daniel*, 1956, pp. 47ff.

is at hand and the triumph of God's kingdom will soon appear.

The **Book of Enoch (I Enoch)**, known also as the **Ethiopic Book of Enoch**, was written originally in Aramaic, but is extant only in an Ethiopic text which itself is a translation from a Greek version.[1] Portions of the Greek text have been found representing chapters 1–32, 106 and 107. I Enoch is a composite book which, in its present form, falls into five parts. This arrangement represents a fairly common literary device among the Jews, there being a similar artificial division in the Pentateuch, the Psalms, Proverbs, the Megilloth, Ben Sira and *Pirke 'Abot.* Diverse opinions have been expressed by scholars concerning the dating of the several sections and the final editing of the whole book. R. H. Charles, for example, gives the period of its growth as 170–64 BC and reckons that it existed in its final form in the first half of the first century AD, if not a century before.[2] H. H. Rowley argues that the earliest sections are to be dated around 164 BC, *i.e.* shortly after the writing of Daniel.[3] There are a number of minor additions of later date scattered throughout the book; besides these, chapters 105 and 108 (which are absent from the Greek text) are probably to be regarded as secondary and represent later insertions.

A number of scholars have found evidence within the present text of I Enoch for a Book of Noah[4] to which reference is made in Jub. 10.13 and 21.10 and also in a Greek fragment of the Testament of Levi which R. H. Charles claims to be a source both of the Testaments of the XII Patriarchs and the Book of Jubilees.[5] He argues that this long-lost book is one of the sources of the Book of Enoch and identifies certain sections of I Enoch and Jubilees as belonging to it. These are I Enoch 6–11; 54.7–55.2; 60; 65.1–69.25; 106–107 and Jub. 7.20–39; 10.1–15.[6]

After the first five chapters which serve as an introduction and

[1] For Aramaic sections found at Qumran see above, p. 38.

[2] Cf. *The Book of Enoch*, 1912, pp. liiff., lxiv.

[3] Cf. *The Relevance of Apocalyptic*, 1945, pp. 52ff, 75ff.

[4] Support for the existence of such a book has been found in certain fragments among the Dead Sea Scrolls which may indicate a distinct 'Noachic literature' (cf. D. Barthélemy and J. T. Milik, *Discoveries in the Judaean Desert I*, 1955, pp. 84ff. and 152). An interesting feature in these fragments is the reference to Noah's miraculous birth which appears also in I Enoch 106. Similar allusion is made in the *Genesis Apocryphon* in that section of the book where Lamech is the speaker.

[5] Cf. *Testaments of the XII Patriarchs*, 1908, pp. lxix–lxx and p. 232 at v. 57.

[6] Cf. *The Book of Enoch*, 1912, pp. xlvi–xlvii, and *The Book of Jubilees*, 1902, pp. lxxi–lxxii.

may be the work of the final editor, the book may be divided up in the following way:

(*a*) The initial section (chs. 6–36) comes, it is generally agreed, from the second century BC and is among the earliest portions of the book. The probability is that it dates from the time of Antiochus Epiphanes[1] towards the end of his reign and after the writing of the Book of Daniel.[2] It tells of the fall of the angels who, through lust, brought all kinds of evil on mankind. God destroys their giant offspring in the Flood, but their spirits, as demons, are let loose in the earth. Enoch is forbidden to intercede for these angels and has to announce their doom. Judgment awaits the angels, the demons and evil men, at the close of which the Golden Age will come (6–16). Enoch, in a vision, now makes two journeys. In the first he visits the place reserved for the punishment of the angels (17–20), and in the second he views Sheol and the ends of the earth (21–36).

(*b*) The Similitudes or Parables of Enoch (chs. 37–71) are of considerable importance by reason of their references to the Son of Man. Some have seen in a number of these evidence of Christian interpolations; others consider the whole work to be post-Christian in origin. This is the only portion of the book, for example, not represented among the Dead Sea Scrolls; J. T. Milik concludes that its absence is not fortuitous and that this section was probably written in the first or second century AD by a Jew or a Jewish Christian.[3] This 'argument from silence' is not conclusive, however, and does not necessarily disprove a pre-Christian date. E. Sjöberg claims that it is pre-Christian and probably dates from the time of the first Roman procurators (*c.* 40–38 BC).[4] M. Black agrees with this finding,[5] but confesses that it is not free from suspicion of Christian influence or tampering.[6] It consists of three discourses and deals in turn with the secrets of heaven (38–44); the Son of Man, the separation of the righteous and the wicked and the punishment of

[1] Cf. J.-B. Frey, 'Apocryphes de l'Ancien Testament' in Pirot's *Supplément au Dictionnaire de la Bible*, vol. I, 1928, col. 358.

[2] Cf. H. H. Rowley, *op. cit.*, pp. 52, 75ff.

[3] Cf. *op. cit.*, p. 33.

[4] Cf. *Der Menschensohn im Äthiopischen Henochbuch*, 1946, p. 39.

[5] Cf. 'The "Son of Man" in the Old Biblical Literature', *ET*, vol. LX, 1948, p. 12.

[6] Cf. 'The Development of Judaism in the Greek and Roman Periods' in *Peake's Commentary on the Bible*, ed. by M. Black and H. H. Rowley, 1962, p. 697, sect. 608d.

the angels (45–57); the bliss of the righteous, the final judgment and the ranks and functions of the angels (58–69). The remaining chapters tell of Enoch's translation and further visions (70–71).

(*c*) The Book of the Heavenly Luminaries (72–82), which Charles dates 'before 110 BC', has no real apocalyptic reference at all, but is in the main a book dealing with the laws of the heavenly bodies and the chronological systems derivable therefrom. Particular interest is shown in the calendar and in the substitution of a solar year for a lunar year.

(*d*) The Dream Visions (83–90) are probably to be dated in the Maccabean period somewhat later than chapters 6–36. They consist of two visions vouchsafed to Enoch. In the first he witnesses the destruction of mankind in the Flood (83–84), and in the second he traces the history of Israel under the figures of oxen, sheep, shepherds and wild beasts (85–90). The destruction of Israel's enemies will be followed by the resurrection and the coming of the messianic age.

(*e*) The Apocalypse of Weeks (93.1–10; 91.12–17) is possibly to be dated also in the Maccabean period and was written under the influence of Daniel. Here history is divided into ten 'weeks', seven of which have already passed. In the seventh apostasy prevails; in the eighth the righteous prevail; in the ninth the world is written down for judgment; and in the tenth the final judgment comes and is followed by the age of bliss.

(*f*) The Book of Admonitions (91–104 with the exception of the Apocalypse of Weeks) shows no clear indication of date. Frey suggests the time of Antiochus Epiphanes,[1] but the time of Alexander Jannaeus (102–76 BC) might suit equally well or even better. It describes Enoch's admonition to his children and has a predominantly eschatological interest in which the wicked are punished and the righteous rewarded.

Several, if not all, of these sections of I Enoch had in all probability a separate circulation for a lengthy period of years before the book assumed its present form. Attempts have been made to find a common group of people behind each of them at the several stages of writing.[2] What is certain is that there was a definite 'Enoch tradition' of some antiquity which continued long after the writing of this book.

The **Book of Jubilees** is also known as 'The Little Genesis', being

[1] Cf. *op. cit.*, col. 367.

[2] Cf. C. P. van Andel, *De Structuur van de Henoch-Traditie en het Nieuwe Testament*, 1955, with English summary.

a midrashic Targum on Genesis (and part of Exodus), and sometimes as 'The Apocalypse of Moses', being in form a revelation by God to Moses on Mount Sinai. Originally written in Aramaic, it survives only in an Ethiopic version. This is a rendering of a Greek translation, only fragments of which have been preserved in Christian writings. A Latin version, based on the Greek, is available for about a quarter of the book. Jubilees is not, strictly speaking, an apocalyptic book; but it belongs to the same milieu and must be taken into serious account in dealing with that literature. Various dates have been given to it, from the fourth century BC to the first century AD; but it is generally conceded that it belongs to the second century BC, probably in the time of the Maccabees about the middle of that century.[1] Its author shows considerable interest in calendrical calculations; from its insistence on a special form of solar calendar and on fixed dates for the chief festivals, J. T. Milik suggests that it may have been written by a member of the Qumran Community.[2] There are certainly interesting correspondences between Jubilees and the Zadokite Document, for example, which make this quite a feasible proposition. It is hazardous, however, to make this identification simply on the ground of the author's calendrical ideas, for these were held by others at a date earlier than Jubilees and may well have been followed by parties within Judaism other than that of the Covenanters.[3] The book derives its name from its system of dating by which history is divided into 'jubilee' periods of 49 years each and which in turn are sub-divided into 7 weeks of years.[4] The unfolding of history will lead to the gradual revealing of the kingdom of God when men will live till they are a thousand years old.

The **Sibylline Oracles** are contained in a series of fifteen books of which three (Books IX, X, XV) are no longer available. Most of these come from Christian hands and contain material scattered throughout the first six centuries AD. Books III, IV and V are of

[1] For a discussion of the date of Jubilees see H. H. Rowley, *op. cit.*, pp. 58, 81ff., and his review of Michel Testuz, *Les Idées Religieuses du Livre des Jubilés*, 1960, in *TLZ*, 1961, Nr. 6, pp. 423ff.

[2] Cf. *op. cit.*, p. 32.

[3] For a discussion of the calendar as it relates to Jubilees and the Scrolls see especially A. Jaubert, 'Le Calendrier des Jubilés et de la Secte de Qumran: Ses origines bibliques', *VT*, vol. III, 1953, pp. 250–64; J. Morgenstern, 'The Calendar of the Book of Jubilees: its Origin and its Character', *VT*, vol. V, 1955, pp. 34–76; E. R. Leach, 'A Possible Method of Intercalation for the Calendar of the Book of Jubilees', *VT*, vol. VII, 1957, pp. 392–7.

[4] See further pp. 225f.

Jewish origin, though containing a fair amount of Christian interpolation. They were written in Greek by members of the Jewish Dispersion in imitation of earlier pagan oracles which had a great popularity in pre-Christian days. By this means the writers sought to spread knowledge of the true God among the Gentiles. The sibyl, an inspired prophetess who is here identified as Noah's daughter-in-law (III. 827),[1] unfolds the process of past history in the form of prediction. Book III is the longest and the most significant of the three Jewish Sibyls for our purpose. It comes substantially from about the middle of the second century BC (*e.g.* 97–819); other sections are later and probably date from the first century BC (*e.g.* 46–62) and the first century AD (*e.g.* 63–92). In the earliest of these sections the sibyl outlines the course of world history, extols the religion of Israel and the law of Moses and predicts the coming of the messianic age whose marks will be prosperity and peace. The same eschatological interest is shown in the two other sections, with variations on the same theme. Book IV refers to the eruption of Vesuvius in AD 79 and may be dated around AD 80. Book V makes reference to Titus (AD 79–81) and to Hadrian (AD 117–38) and is probably to be dated early in the latter's reign.

The **Testaments of the XII Patriarchs** was originally written in Hebrew and is extant in a Greek translation. There are Armenian and Slavonic versions based on this text, the former being of greater significance. A number of Aramaic fragments of the Testament of Levi which were already known[2] have more recently been supplemented by similar fragments found among the Dead Sea Scrolls.[3] These show a text longer than the Greek text of the Testament of Levi and probably reflect an earlier version. There is also extant a late Hebrew Testament of Naphtali which differs quite considerably from the Greek text.[4] A fragment of a Hebrew Testament of Naphtali has been discovered at Qumran,[5] but there is apparently no direct connection between this and the known Hebrew Testament.

[1] The numbering followed here is that given in R. H. Charles's *Apocrypha and Pseud. of the Old Testament*, vol. II, 1913, where the system of reference is to the number of lines and not to chapter and verse.

[2] Cf. R. H. Charles, *Apocrypha and Pseudepigrapha of the Old Testament*, vol. II, 1913, pp. 361–7.

[3] Cf. D. Barthélemy and J. T. Milik, *Discoveries in the Judaean Desert: Qumran Cave I*, 1955, pp. 87–91; and J. T. Milik, *RB*, vol. LXII, 1955, pp. 398–406.

[4] Cf. R. H. Charles, *ibid.*, pp. 361ff., and *Testaments of the Twelve Patriarchs*, 1908, pp. lxviff., 221ff.

[5] Cf. J. T. Milik in *RB*, vol. LXIII, 1956, p. 407, n. 1.

The problem of the origin, construction and dating of the Testaments is a very vexed question on which scholars are far from agreed. Most have followed R. H. Charles in assuming that it is essentially a Jewish work containing Christian interpolations, although there is less agreement concerning the scope of Christian influence. He gives the date of its composition as between 109 and 107 BC.[1] Since the discovery of the Dead Sea Scrolls the whole issue has had to be looked at again and many would strongly dispute Charles's 'interpolation-theory'. A. Dupont-Sommer,[2] for example, sees very little Christian influence on the Testaments and brings them into close relationship with the Qumran documents. In this he is supported by M. Philonenko,[3] who argues that the two sets of writings have, in fact, a common origin, even though they differ in certain respects, as, for example, in their expression of the messianic hope. He contends that the Testaments originated in the Testament of Levi, to which were added, at a later stage, the Testaments of Judah and Naphtali. These three Testaments then passed through the hands of a redactor belonging to the party of the Essenes who produced a shorter version. The remaining Testaments were thereafter attached to this nucleus. At a later stage a second redactor, also an Essene, expanded the text of certain of the Testaments. The final work was 'touched up' by a Christian redactor in due course, but the supposed 'Christian interpolations' can be adequately explained by reference to the second of the Essene redactors. Another critic of the 'interpolation-theory' is A. S. van der Woude,[4] who maintains that the Testaments are essentially a Jewish writing which has been rewritten and shortened in the process. Like Philonenko he finds its origin in the Testament of Levi whose existing Greek text represents a much shorter and considerably altered version of the original Aramaic or Hebrew text. Christian passages have been added but, because of the process of rewriting and abbreviation of the text, it is now impossible to separate these with any degree of certainty so as to leave behind the original Jewish work. M. de Jonge also disputes Charles's 'interpolation-theory' and at the same time disagrees with both Philonenko

[1] Cf. *op. cit.*, pp. l–liii.
[2] Cf. *The Jewish Sect of Qumran and the Essenes*, English translation by R. D. Barnett, 1954, pp. 38–57, and *The Essene Writings from Qumran*, English translation by G. Vermés, 1961, pp. 301–5, 354–7.
[3] Cf. *Les interpolations chrétiennes des Testaments des Douze Patriarches et les Manuscrits de Qumran*, 1960.
[4] Cf. *Die messianischen Vorstellungen der Gemeinde von Qumran*, 1957.

and van der Woude. He argues that the Testaments are a Christian document by a Christian author using much Jewish material in the construction of it.[1] In a later work the same writer qualifies this judgment and makes greater allowance for the part played by oral tradition, among both Jews and Christians, and sees in the Christian author or authors the last of a series of collectors or redactors of Testament material which gradually grew in size and was adapted to meet various needs.[2] He acknowledges that there may have been at least one Jewish stage in the writing of this book. A Hebrew Testament of Levi may have formed the starting-point, to be followed by a Testament of Naphtali and possibly by a Testament of Judah on the same model.[3] According to de Jonge, then, the Testaments are to be dated in the post-Christian period, since, in their final form, they are essentially a Christian work. Likewise J. T. Milik, whilst acknowledging the Essene character of the Testaments,[4] claims for them a Christian rather than a Jewish origin. A Jewish-Christian of the first or second century, adopting such Testaments as were already in existence, would complete a set of Testaments for all the twelve patriarchs using the same literary form in each case.[5]

More will be said later about the literary form of this book.[6] Here we note that it consists of the 'last word and testament' of Jacob's twelve sons to their children. Generally speaking, each testimony is in three parts—a rehearsal of significant events in the life of the patriarch, an exhortation based on what has just been said, and a foretelling of what will happen in the last days. The apocalyptic element, represented in the third part, is not very prominent, stress being laid rather on admonition of a specifically ethical kind. The book is of considerable significance, however, not only because of its ethical content but also by reason of its teaching concerning the messianic hope which is apparently associated with Levi as well as with David.

The **Psalms of Solomon**, written originally in Hebrew, survive in a Greek translation and in a Syriac version derived from the Greek. They contain several historical allusions which clearly indicate that they belong to the middle of the first century BC. In 2.30f.

[1] Cf. *The Testaments of the XII Patriarchs, a study of their text, composition and origin*, 1953.
[2] Cf. *The Testaments of the XII Patriarchs and the New Testament*, 1957, p. 550.
[3] Cf. 'The Testaments of the Twelve Patriarchs', *NT*, vol. IV, 1960, p. 188.
[4] Cf. *RB*, vol. LXII, 1955, p. 298.
[5] Cf. *Ten Years of Discovery in the Wilderness of Judaea*, 1959, pp. 34f.
[6] See pp. 120f.

reference is made to the death of Pompey which occurred in 48 BC and if, as seems probable, the collection can be ascribed to a single author a date shortly after this can safely be ascribed to these writings. There are eighteen psalms in all, two of which are of significance for their apocalyptic, or rather messianic content. Ps. of Sol. 17, after a short historical review, describes the glories of the messianic age and the Davidic Messiah in typically nationalistic terms not unlike those expressed in the Old Testament itself. Ps. of Sol. 18 continues the same theme and introduces the same Davidic king who will rule with wisdom, righteousness and strength and under whose chastening men will see the goodness of the Lord. The sympathies of the author of this collection are with the humble poor, who will not only share in the earthly messianic kingdom but will also be raised in resurrection to enjoy everlasting life (3.16).

4. THE LITERATURE OF THE FIRST CENTURY AD

The **Assumption of Moses** was written probably in Aramaic, but is extant only in a Latin version which is itself a translation of an earlier Greek version, some fragments of which are to be found scattered throughout the writings of the Church Fathers. What we have here is only part of a much larger book which, according to Charles, consisted originally of two independent works, the Testament of Moses and the Assumption of Moses, which were subsequently put together.[1] The part which now survives is of the nature of a testament and, despite its title, may contain the original Testament of Moses rather than the Assumption. There are certain indications in the text which point to a date in the first part of the first century AD. Allusion is made, for example, to the ruthlessness of Quintilius Varus, who suppressed a Jewish rising in 4 BC and other references may point to the banishment of Archelaus in AD 6. It is perhaps safe to date the book somewhere between AD 6 and AD 30.

The writer, in the name of Moses, predicts the history of Israel from the time of the entry into Canaan down to his own day. Chapters 1–5 cover the period down to the year 170 BC. There seems to be at this point a dislocation of the text caused no doubt by the misplacement of a leaf of the manuscript. Chapter 8, which tells of the persecution of Antiochus Epiphanes, should probably follow

[1] Cf. *The Assumption of Moses*, 1897, p. xlvi.

here and perhaps also chapter 9, which tells of a mysterious figure called 'Taxo' who exhorts his seven sons to die rather than deny the commands of God. Chapter 6 continues the narrative from the time of Antiochus to 4 BC, covert allusion being made to Herod the Great as the 'insolent king'. With chapter 7 the author switches over from a historical survey to a pronouncement concerning the End and the coming of the kingdom of God. This theme is continued in chapter 10, which describes the signs marking the end of the age. The rest of the book tells of Joshua's grief on hearing these things (ch. 11) and Moses' reply of encouragement to him (ch. 12). At this point (12.13) the narrative breaks off and the account of Moses' assumption, which presumably followed, is lost.

The **Martyrdom of Isaiah** is the name sometimes given to the first part of the **Ascension of Isaiah** which has been preserved in whole in Ethiopic and in part in Latin. R. H. Charles suggests that this latter book was compiled by a Christian editor from three separate writings, namely, the Martyrdom of Isaiah, which was Jewish in origin, the Testament of Hezekiah and the Vision of Isaiah, both of which were Christian in origin.[1] Parts of chapters 1–3 and 5 of the Ascension, which are generally claimed to represent the Martyrdom, give *inter alia* a prediction and account of the death of Isaiah, who is cut asunder by a wood saw. This account no doubt reflects a Jewish tradition, but there seems to be little ground in this or in any other respect for separating this section from the rest of the book or for attributing it to a Jewish source. The probability is that the Ascension of Isaiah is one book and that it is a specifically Christian apocalyptic work.[2]

The **Life of Adam and Eve**, written originally in Aramaic, can be reconstructed out of several versions, chief among which are the Latin and Greek texts. This latter is commonly given the rather unsuitable title **The Apocalypse of Moses.** It is a Jewish work containing a fair amount of Christian interpolation. Its contents indicate that it was probably written some time in the first century AD and, since the Temple is apparently still standing (cf. 29.6), we may date its composition before AD 70. It is a haggadic work concerning the lives of Adam and Eve and records incidents supplementary to

[1] Cf. *The Ascension of Isaiah*, 1900, pp. xxviff.; *Apocrypha and Pseudepigrapha of the Old Testament*, vol. II, 1913, pp. 155ff.

[2] Cf. F. C. Burkitt, *Jewish and Christian Apocalypses*, 1914, pp. 45ff., 72ff.; C. C. Torrey, *op. cit.*, pp. 133ff.

the biblical story. The apocalyptic element in the book is small but significant. The most important section in this respect is 29.4–10 in the Latin text. Here Adam, in a vision, is shown the giving of the Law, the building of the Temple, the destruction of the Temple, the Exile, the return and the rebuilding of the Temple, which will be 'exalted greater than of old'. Thereafter for a time 'iniquity will exceed righteousness'; then God will come to dwell with men on the earth. In the judgment which follows God will save and purify the righteous, but the wicked he will condemn.

The **Apocalypse of Abraham** is extant only in a Slavonic version which is apparently a translation from the Greek. It appears to be a Jewish work with a number of Christian additions and to have been worked over by a Christian editor.[1] The date of origin must be after the fall of Jerusalem in AD 70 and at any time within the next fifty years or so. The apocalyptic part of the book is confined to chapters 9–32. In a vision Abraham is given an audience with God, who recounts to him the fall of man and the subsequent idolatry of Abraham's seed which will result in the coming judgment. The present age, which lasts for twelve 'hours', is nearing its close; the End is at hand. Soon the heathen will be punished or destroyed. The trumpet will sound and God's Elect will come to gather his own people together; his enemies he will burn in the fire.

The **Testament of Abraham** is to be clearly distinguished from the previously mentioned work. The extant Greek text is found in two recensions, one much longer than the other.[2] Translations are available in Coptic, Arabic, Ethiopic, Slavonic and Rumanian. There is some doubt as to its origin and date. M. R. James judges that it is a Jewish-Christian writing which used the Apocalypse of Peter as one of its sources and that it dates from the second century AD, although in its present form it dates from the ninth or tenth century.[3] Kohler[4] and Ginzberg,[5] however, followed by Box,[6] argue with some conviction that it is a Jewish work dating from the first century AD with a number of late Christian additions. In this case

[1] Cf. G. H. Box, *The Apocalypse of Abraham*, 1919, pp. x, xxiff.

[2] G. H. Box uses the letters A and B to indicate the longer and shorter recensions, cf. *The Testament of Abraham*, 1927. In his editions of the *Apocalypse* and the *Testament* the chapter numbering alone is given.

[3] Cf. *The Testament of Abraham*, 1892, pp. 23–29.

[4] Cf. *JQR*, vol. VII, 1895, pp. 581ff.

[5] Cf. *JE*, vol. I, 1901, pp. 93ff.

[6] Cf. *The Testament of Abraham*, 1927, pp. xvff.

the Greek text may be a translation of a Semitic, possibly Hebrew, original. The book is of considerable interest, particularly on account of its eschatological teaching. Abraham, in a vision, is shown 'the world and all created things' (ch. 9); he is told that it will last for seven ages, each of a thousand years. Thereafter he is taken by Michael to the first gate of heaven, where he sees three different judgments being enacted (chs. 11ff.). No specific reference is made here to the coming of the messianic age, but this is no doubt implied in the reference to the second judgment which is to be carried out by the twelve tribes of Israel. Although this book shares the general outlook of Jewish apocalyptic, it contains features which mark it off from others in this class. In addition to those features already mentioned, there is here no sense of impending crisis, and the chief interest is in the future destiny of individual souls.

The **Book of the Secrets of Enoch (II Enoch)**, known also as the **Slavonic Book of Enoch**, was originally written in Greek, but is extant only in a Slavonic version.[1] It has been commonly assumed that it originated some time in the first century AD before the fall of Jerusalem and is the work of a Hellenistic Jew of Alexandria.[2] This assumption, however, has been strongly challenged in respect both of its Jewish origin and its early date. It is claimed that the calendrical chapters of II Enoch, for example, form an integral part of the Easter *computus* developed in the seventh century and so cannot be earlier than that date.[3] It is further claimed that the Apocalypse of Peter, far from being a derivant of II Enoch,[4] may, in fact, be its source.[5] In the following pages we shall give the benefit of the doubt to the earlier dating, bearing in mind that it is an eclectic and syncretistic book by no means free from Christian influence and may indeed be a

[1] There is another significant writing belonging to the Enoch tradition, but which lies outside the inter-testamental period. It is III Enoch, also known as the Hebrew Book of Enoch, cf. H. Odeberg, *The Hebrew Book of Enoch*, 1928. Odeberg assigns its earliest sections to the end of the first and the beginning of the second centuries AD (*ibid.*, p. 42, n. 3).

[2] Cf. W. R. Morfill and R. H. Charles, *The Book of the Secrets of Enoch*, 1896, pp. xviff, xxvff..

[3] Cf. Mrs Maunder, *The Observatory*, vol. XLI, 1918, pp. 309–16, and J. K. Fotheringham, 'The Easter Calendar and the Slavonic Enoch', *JTS*, vol. XXIII, 1921, pp. 49–56; cf. also 'The Date and Place of Writing of the Slavonic Enoch', *JTS*, vol. XX, 1919, p. 252, and K. Lake, 'The Date of the Slavonic Enoch', *HTR*, vol. XVI, 1923, pp. 397f.

[4] Cf. R. Casey, 'The Apocalypse of Paul', *JTS*, vol. XXXIV, 1933, pp. 22–23.

[5] Cf. T. Silverstein, *Visio Sancti Pauli*, in *Studies and Documents IV*, ed. by K. Lake and S. Lake, 1935, p. 93, n. 7.

Christian work representing 'a Christian continuation and counterpart of the previous Jewish Enoch'.[1]

It is doubtful whether this book belongs to the line of tradition represented by I Enoch, even though in form it is based on this latter work. After an introductory section in which Enoch announces his assumption (chs. 1–2), he experiences a vision in which he ascends through the seven heavens, where he is introduced to the wonders of each by two angelic attendants (chs. 3–21). He writes down everything that God reveals to him including his plan and method of creation, the history of the world down to Enoch's own time and on to the time of the Flood. This present age is to last for seven periods of a thousand years at the close of which the End will come (chs. 22–38). He is then given thirty days in which to teach his sons what he has seen and written down so that they may the better order their lives. The rest of the book in which these admonitions are recorded (chs. 39–66) has an ethical content which is paralleled elsewhere in the apocalyptic writings only in the Testaments of the XII Patriarchs. At last, his work ended, Enoch is translated into the highest heaven and is set down before the face of God (chs. 67–68).

The book referred to in the English Versions as **II Esdras** (Ezra) appears in the Appendix to the Vulgate as **IV Esdras** (Ezra) and is otherwise known as the **Apocalypse of Ezra**. Chapters 1–2 and 15–16 are absent from the Syriac, Ethiopic, Arabic and Armenian versions and represent later Christian additions. The Jewish apocalypse, with which alone we are concerned here, is contained in chapters 3–14 and was probably written originally in Aramaic.

It is generally agreed that the contents of these chapters come from the latter part of the first century AD; but there is divergence of opinion concerning the unity of the book. G. H. Box[2] and R. H. Charles[3] follow R. Kabisch,[4] with a few minor differences, in dissecting the book into five independent works from which a redactor, near the end of the first century AD, compiled the book as a whole. These reputed works are a Salathiel (Hebrew *Šᵉālti'el*) Apocalypse, an Ezra Apocalypse, the Eagle Vision, a Son of Man Vision and an Ezra fragment. The second and fifth of these are dated before AD 70

[1] A. Vaillant, *Le Livre des Secrets d'Hénoch*, 1952, p. ix.

[2] Cf. *The Ezra-Apocalypse*, 1912, pp. xxiff.

[3] Cf. *Eschatology*, 2nd ed., 1913, pp. 337ff, and *Apocrypha and Pseudepigrapha of the Old Testament*, vol. II, 1913, pp. 551f.

[4] Cf. *Das vierte Buch Esra auf seine Quellen untersucht*, 1889.

and the others between AD 70 and 96. More recently C. C. Torrey[1] has also argued for a composite authorship, though with much less detailed dissection. He contends that the book might more properly be called 'The Apocalypse of Shealtiel' which, in its original form and divested of later accretions, continues up to the end of chapter 13. He agrees with Box that the original seer wrote in the name of one Shealtiel (3.1) whom the compiler connected with the name of Ezra, so that the text was made to read, 'I Salathiel, who am also Ezra, was in Babylon . . .'[2] The date of this 'Shealtiel Apocalypse' he gives as AD 69 on the basis of the Eagle Vision whose prophecies, however, have been reinterpreted by later redactors in such a way as to make them now quite indecipherable. This 'rehabilitation' of the book in the name of Ezra would take place in the reign of Domitian (AD 81–96) and would coincide with the addition of an Ezra vision contained in chapter 14 in which Ezra records the Scriptures under divine inspiration; this chapter is quite different from the rest and represents an incongruous element attached to the original work.

Despite these arguments, however, the consensus of opinion is against the dissection of this book into a number of separate works of different dates.[3] In support of the literary unity of the work it has been argued that the undoubted inconsistencies to be found in it can readily be explained by reference to the author's use of different traditions which he was not disposed to harmonize with one another and indeed which he could not make to harmonize even if he were disposed so to do. The book as it stands, however, may well be the product of a single author writing near the close of the first century AD, perhaps between the years AD 90 and 100.

As it stands it records seven visions given to Ezra in Babylon. Several of them cover more or less the same ground, but it is clear that they represent different traditions and have no common basis. In the first (3.1–5.19) the seer expresses bewilderment and grief that a righteous God should allow his own people to suffer at the hands of a nation that knows him not. The sin for which Israel suffers is the result of the 'evil impulse' arising from Adam's sin. God gave them his Law, but he did not remove the 'evil impulse' from them. The angel Uriel tries to reassure him and then informs him that the end

[1] Cf. *The Apocryphal Literature*, 4th printing, 1953, pp. 116ff.

[2] For an attempted explanation of this passage see below, pp. 136f.

[3] Among those who uphold the unity of the book H. H. Rowley lists Clemen, Lagrange, Porter, Sanday, Burkitt, Violet and Gry. Cf. *op. cit.*, pp. 132ff.

of the present age is approaching and will at last come when the number of the righteous is fulfilled. In chapter 5 he is shown signs and wonders which will herald the approach of the End. This same theme is pursued in the second vision (5.20–6.34). Generation will follow generation till the End comes and God ushers in the new age and the coming judgment. In the third vision (6.35–9.25) he is told that his people will pass by narrow paths into the bliss of the other world. At the end of the age the Messiah will appear and rule for 400 years; then he and all who are with him will die. After seven days' silence come the resurrection, the judgment and the disclosure of Paradise and Gehenna. Few will be saved in those days, because each man is responsible for his lot. In the fourth vision (9.26–10.59) the seer comforts a mourning woman who represents the devastated city of Zion. Suddenly she disappears and in her place stands the magnificent new Jerusalem. In the fifth vision (11.1–12.51) the seer beholds an eagle with twelve wings and three heads whose symbolism reinterprets the fourth kingdom in Daniel 7. Under the symbolism of the eagle a review of history is given and this is followed by the appearance of the Messiah, under the symbol of a lion, who destroys the eagle and delivers the righteous. In the sixth vision (13.1–58) the Messiah appears as a man rising from the sea who flies with the clouds of heaven. With the fire of his mouth he destroys his enemies but saves his chosen people. In the seventh vision (14.1–48) the seer is told that he will be translated to be with 'the Son' until the time of the End which will soon come. Before this happens, however, he dictates under divine inspiration ninety-four books including the sacred Scriptures which had been destroyed. His task done, he ascends to heaven.

II Baruch, also known as the **Syriac Apocalypse of Baruch**, was originally written in Aramaic, but is extant only in Syriac which derives from a Greek translation of the original. There is a close literary connection between this book and II Esdras, even to the point of verbal imitation. It is generally agreed that the imitator is II Baruch. Some scholars argue that it was written soon after II Esdras; C. C. Torrey, for example, suggests that it emerged in AD 70, immediately after the 'Apocalypse of Salathiel',[1] and P. Volz gives a date around AD 90.[2] Others have argued for a date in the first decades of the second century.

[1] Cf. *op. cit.*, p. 126.

[2] Cf. *Die Eschatologie der jüdischen Gemeinde im neutestamentlichen Zeitalter*, 1934, p. 40.

R. H. Charles, following Kabisch, has attempted to dissect II Baruch into several sources of varying dates and authorship. He identifies three fragmentary apocalypses, all of them written before AD 70, and four other sections, all of them after AD 70. He suggests that the final editing took place between AD 110 and 120 and that the Greek translation is to be taken as not later than AD 130.[1] Despite Charles's argument, however, there seems to be less reason even than in the case of II Esdras to break the book up in this way. When allowance is made for the inevitable inconsistency of apocalyptic and its free use of traditional material, in literary or oral form, there seems little reason to doubt the unity of this work whose homogeneity of treatment and style indicates a single author.

The book begins with the same kind of question as is asked by the writer of II Esdras: Why do God's people suffer and their enemies prosper? God assures Baruch that the world to come is reserved for the righteous and that the destruction of Zion will hasten the coming of the future age. Twelve woes will come upon the earth at the close of which the messianic age will dawn. The Messiah will appear and the righteous dead will rise in resurrection (chs. 1–35). By means of an allegory of a cedar and a vine he is told of the destruction of the Roman Empire, which is the fourth world empire to be destroyed. The enemy is put to death by the Messiah, whose rule will stand for ever (chs. 36–46). In response to Baruch's prayer God reveals to him the nature of men's resurrection bodies and shows him the fate of the righteous and the wicked (chs. 47–52). Then, by means of the symbol of a great cloud which pours out alternately black waters and clear waters upon the earth, God makes known to him the course of world history culminating in the coming of the Messiah and his kingdom (chs. 53–76). The rest of the book deals with Baruch's admonitions to the Jews in Jerusalem and Babylon and also to the northern tribes (chs. 77–87).

III Baruch, also known as the **Greek Apocalypse of Baruch**, lies outside our period, but may be mentioned here for the sake of completeness. It was originally written in Greek some time in the second century AD and survives in a short

author was a Jewish Gnostic; R. H. Charles[1] acknowledges that 'his Judaism was tempered by a Hellenic-Oriental syncretism'.

The book is of interest for two reasons. First, it tells of the mediation of the angels who carry men's prayers and the merits of the righteous to Michael, who in turn rewards men in proportion to their good deeds. Secondly, it expresses belief in seven heavens (found elsewhere in the Testament of Levi, the Ascension of Isaiah and rabbinic literature). The seer is taken through five of these heavens (only two are mentioned in the Slavonic version) where he is shown the mysteries of God. He thereafter returns to earth and gives glory to God for all that he has seen.

5. SOME LOST PSEUDEPIGRAPHIC AND APOCALYPTIC BOOKS

The books listed above, preserved for the most part within the Christian Church,[2] represent the major and most important part of the apocalyptic literature of the period 200 BC–AD 100. There were other books, however, which flourished at this time or in subsequent years and which are known to us only by their titles or by reference to them in later writings. Such knowledge as we have comes from two main sources, from quotations in the early Church Fathers and from references preserved in a number of catalogues of canonical and apocryphal books.[3]

Reference has already been made to a lost **Apocalypse of Lamech** and a **Book of Noah,** fragments of which may be found in I Enoch and Jubilees.[4] Evidence shows that there were many others besides, mostly pseudepigraphic in character, associated with the names of Adam, Eve, Ham, Joseph, Jannes and Jambres, Moses, Eldad and Medad, Og, Solomon, Elijah, Jeremiah, Baruch, Ezekiel, Daniel, Habakkuk, Zephaniah, Zechariah, Ezra and Hezekiah.[5] The information available in many cases is so scanty that it is impossible to say which of these *apocryphal* books can, in fact, be described as *apocalyptic* or even as containing apocalyptic material. In the case

[1] *Apocrypha and Pseud. of the Old Testament*, vol. II, 1913, p. 529.

of some, however, this identity can perhaps be assumed from their reported contents or from the occurrence of the word 'apocalypse' in their title. Needless to say, it is much more difficult here than in the case of the known books to give a date to these writings and to be sure whether or not they are of Jewish or of Christian origin.

The name of **Adam**, for example, is associated with an **Apocalypse**, a **Penitence** and a **Testament** as well as with the **Life** to which reference has been made above. In the judgment of M. R. James[1] these three probably constituted one book in which were recorded a description of Adam's repentance, an admonition to his son Seth and a revelation made to him concerning the Watchers and the Flood. The name of **Seth** appears again elsewhere as a recipient of divine revelation and as the spokesman of messianic prophecies. Some of these references are unidentifiable from known sources and may suggest the existence of an independent work bearing this name. In some manuscripts of the Book of the Secrets of Enoch there is attached a fairly lengthy passage tracing the succession of the 'Enochian priesthood' through 'Methusalam' to Melchizedek, who is caught up to Paradise and so saved from the Flood. R. H. Charles considers this fragment to be the work of an early Christian heretic.[2]

Origen (*Comment. on John* 2.25; *Comment. on Gen.* 3.9) quotes from a book called the **Prayer of Joseph** which, he says, was in use among the Jews. There are hints here and there of an anti-Christian bias in it, but Origen maintains that it is a book 'not to be despised'. As the title suggests, it probably contained a lengthy prayer by Joseph; but the portions which are known to us relate rather to Jacob and belong, apparently, to a 'testament' made to his sons. Jacob here describes himself as the chief of all the angels who fought with Uriel, who is counted eighth in rank. He describes himself, moreover, as 'the first begotten of every living thing' and claims that he can read the heavenly tablets and understand the future destiny of the world. Origen (*Comment. on Matt.* 27.9) also mentions a book called the **Penitence of Jannes and Jambres** (or **Mambres**) which is probably of Jewish origin. These are the names given in Jewish legend and also in II Tim. 3.8 to the two Egyptian

manuscript tells of the penitence of Jambres's soul which his brother brought up from hell, where there was 'great burning and a pit of perdition'; but the general contents of the book are unknown. Allusion is made in the *Shepherd of Hermas* 2.3 to a book concerning **Eldad and Modad** (or **Medad**) 'who prophesied to the people in the wilderness'. These men are known to us from the reference in Num. 11.26–29, where it is said that they prophesied in the camp during the wilderness wanderings. In all probability this book gave an account of their predictions and prophecies. Hebrew legend, in the Targums and Midrashim, records that they were half brothers and that their gift of prophecy was given to them by God because they counted themselves unworthy to be numbered among the seventy elders. Among their prophecies was that concerning Magog's final attack upon Israel. It is impossible to say what part, if any, this theme played in the book bearing their names.

A number of references are made in the Fathers and in the lists of apocryphal books to the **Apocalypse** (or **Prophecy** or **Mysteries**) **of Elijah.** From an examination of the several quotations available and of two later apocalypses of the same name which may well reflect the earlier work, M. R. James concludes that the book contained 'descriptions of hell-torments, eschatological prophecy, descriptions of Antichrist and didactic matter'.[1] Origen (*Comment. on Matt.* 27.9) and others[2] state that this book is the source of Paul's words in I Cor. 2.9 ('Things which eye saw not, and ear heard not', etc.), and this may well be so. The claim of Epiphanius (*Haer.* XLII.i) is less certain that it is the source also of Eph. 5.14 ('Awake, thou that sleepest', etc.); elsewhere this verse is ascribed to an apocryphal book bearing the name of Jeremiah.[3]

At the end of the Stichometry of Nicephorus[4] six other pseudepigraphal works are mentioned—of Zephaniah, Zechariah, Baruch, Habakkuk, Ezekiel and Daniel, the last four of which are probably later additions to the original list. Clement of Alexandria (*Strom.* V.xi.77) gives a quotation from the **Apocalypse of Zephaniah** which tells how the prophet was taken up into the fifth heaven where he beheld angels called 'Lords' singing hymns to God. The **Apoca-**
lypse of Z[illegible]

indicates that this book is, in fact, a Christian writing. The book of **Baruch** may be reflected in a quotation by Cyprian (*Testimonia adv. Judaeos* III.xxix) but there is nothing to indicate that it had an apocalyptic interest. The only possible hint we have of the contents of the book ascribed to **Habakkuk** is in a Christian manuscript of the LXX which states that the stories of Bel and the Dragon come 'from the prophecy of Habakkuk the son of Jeshua, of the tribe of Levi'. The apocryphal book bearing the name of **Ezekiel** is known from several sources which indicate a Christian origin. In one place the writer gives a parable, found also in rabbinic writings and elsewhere,[1] of a lame man and a blind man who together plundered their king's garden and together were punished. From this he draws the lesson that the body will be resurrected so as to be judged together with the soul in the life beyond. The pseudepigraphal work ascribed to **Daniel** may lie behind the apocryphal 'Seventh Vision of Daniel', whose text as we now have it reflects a much later date.

[1] See below, p. 376.

PART TWO

THE METHOD OF JEWISH APOCALYPTIC

III

THE DECLINE OF PROPHECY AND THE RISE OF APOCALYPTIC

1. THE DECLINE OF PROPHECY

HEBREW PROPHECY SURVIVED the fall of Jerusalem in 587 BC and continued into the post-exilic period. The years after the Return produced men like Trito-Isaiah, Haggai, Zechariah, Obadiah, 'Malachi' and Joel as well as other unnamed prophets whose oracles are embedded in or attached to the writings of already-known prophets of the pre- or post-exilic periods. It is to be noted that just as pre-exilic prophecy was itself at times a modification and reapplication of earlier prophecy,[1] so post-exilic prophecy provided its own form of reinterpretation within the continuing prophetic tradition. This can be illustrated by reference to the scroll of Isaiah which, as it stands, is of a composite character, containing oracles of different dates attached to the original prophetic utterances. It is possible that such additions may reflect the work of an 'Isaiah-school' of prophets (cf. Isa. 8.16), who not only reapplied their master's prophecies in the altered situation of their own day, but also added to the existing corpus new oracles which were in the spirit of his declared word. Similarly, it has been suggested, the unknown prophets represented by Zech. 9–11, 12–13, 14 and 'Malachi' may have belonged to the same prophetic school as Haggai and Zechariah and so have perpetuated the same prophetic

[1] Cf. P. R. Ackroyd, 'The Vitality of the Word of God in the Old Testament. A contribution to the study of the transmission and exposition of Old Testament material', in *Annual of the Swedish Theological Institute* (ed. by H. Kosmala), vol. I, 1962.

tradition.[1] Whether we postulate the existence of such 'schools' or not, genuine prophecy continued. Even although it was 'a day of small things' (Zech. 4.10), the tradition was maintained and the word of the Lord was proclaimed (Hag. 1.13). Thus the difference between pre-exilic and post-exilic prophecy lay not so much in a new statement of prophecy as in a new application of it to changed circumstances.

The process of attaching oracles to earlier prophecies would continue until about 200 BC, when the hardening of the Prophetic Canon would make it increasingly difficult for such anonymous oracles to be incorporated in the accepted prophetic books. As the post-exilic period advanced the cryptic and apocalyptic character of some of these oracles became more pronounced and prepared the way for the full growth of an apocalyptic literature in later years.[2]

It is quite obvious, however, that alongside this sense of continuity went an increasing sense of loss that prophecy was, in fact, no longer what it used to be. Prophecy continued, but its heyday was seen to be in the past. A hint of this is given early on, in Zech. 1.4, for example, where an authoritative place is given to the 'former prophets' (*i.e.* those of pre-exilic times) by virtue of the fact that their words had been fulfilled. The same impression is given by the Chronicler who alludes to the seventy years' exile which were demonstrably a fulfilment of 'the word of the Lord by the mouth of Jeremiah' (II Chron. 36.21; cf. Dan. 9.2). And so as the Persian period gave way to the Greek, the growing sense of separation from the traditional form of Hebrew prophecy became more clearly marked, and the prophets who continued to exercise their ministry fell into disrepute.

A number of reasons can be given which help to explain this acknowledged decline in Hebrew prophecy. One is that from the time of Ezra onwards the Law Book began to exercise an ever-increasing influence on the life of the people, and 'prophetic inspiration' correspondingly began to be replaced by 'scribal inspiration'. It must not be assumed from this, however, that there was any inherent antagonism between prophecy and Torah. On the contrary, there was an essential unity between them; when, for example, in the course of time the Canon of the Pentateuch was closed, the writings of the Prophets (even though they were at that date not yet

[1] Cf. D. R. Jones, *Haggai, Zechariah and Malachi*, 1962, pp. 116, 171.
[2] Cf. especially Joel; Zech. 9–14; Isa. 24–27. See pp. 88ff.

finally defined) were also regarded as divine revelation.[1] Nevertheless the increasing authority of the Law through which God's own voice spoke to the people was undoubtedly a significant factor in encouraging the belief that prophecy belonged to the past or, at least, that prophecy was relegated to a subordinate position as a vehicle of the divine will.

A second reason for this decline in Hebrew prophecy is probably to be found in its close association with the Temple cultus. The prophetic oracle might still on occasions appeal to the conscience of the people after the manner of an Amos or a Jeremiah, but to a considerable extent it aimed at the purification of the Temple ritual. Indeed, the post-exilic prophets themselves sometimes give the impression that the era of prophecy lay in the past, whereas their own chief contribution lay in the enrichment of the formal worship of God. The exact relationship between these prophets and the Temple cultus is a vexed question, but it is clear that not a few of their oracles had their setting within the Temple worship and as part of the Temple liturgy. The association of the prophet with the cult is no doubt implied in such a passage as Ps. 74.9, which is often quoted in this connection:

We see not our signs.
There is no more any prophet;
Neither is there among us any that knoweth how long.

Here the writer laments the destruction of the Temple and bewails the neglect of (cultic?) 'signs' and the absence of a prophet. This verse is usually taken to signify the cessation or extinction of prophecy in Israel at the time of which it speaks.[2] This is a possible interpretation; but it may signify no more than that, in such a time of trouble as this, there was no prophet available to speak a word of comfort to the people.[3] Clearer testimony of the prophetic function is given by the Chronicler. Here we observe the significance of Levitic preaching in succession to the older prophetic function, and in particular the priests' responsibility for teaching the Law (cf. II Chron. 17.7ff.), which was in earlier days also associated with the prophets (cf. Isa. 1.10). In one interesting passage it is reported that the spirit of

[1] Cf. Th. C. Vriezen, *An Outline of Old Testament Theology*, English trans., 1958, pp. 69, 256.

[2] The date of this Psalm is quite uncertain. It might have been written at any time between, say, Ezra and Alexander the Great.

[3] Cf. Artur Weiser, *The Psalms*, English trans., 1962, p. 519.

the Lord came upon a Levite named Jahaziel, of the sons of Asaph, who foretold to King Jehoshaphat in true prophetic fashion the outcome of the battle with Ammon and Moab (cf. II Chron. 20.14f.). Elsewhere, however, the Chronicler hints that in his day the prophet had become a cult official whose primary responsibility was to maintain the Temple worship. He speaks, for example, of men who 'prophesy with harps, with psalteries and with cymbals' (I Chron. 25.1), thus identifying the act of prophesying with the conduct of worship. Indeed, it has been argued that the old prophetic guilds of pre-exilic times may well have become absorbed in due course in the post-exilic guilds of Temple singers.[1] Whatever degree of assimilation may or may not have taken place, it is clear that post-exilic prophecy, in certain expressions at least, differed considerably from the charismatic prophecy of pre-exilic days.

A third factor affecting the attitude to prophecy in the post-exilic period is the influence of foreign culture which for a long time had been pressing in upon the Jews and which contained elements inimical to their own religious heritage. Ever since the Captivity many of them had lived in Mesopotamia in direct contact with Perso-Babylonian thought and religion and on their return had brought back with them much of its outlook and influence. There is evidence, too, of 'a stream of Chaldean wisdom and Chaldean sages, astrologers, popular philosophers, itinerant preachers, miracle workers and charlatans which in Hellenistic times spread over the world'.[2] The oriental religions of this whole period expressed themselves often in terms of hieratic wisdom which in turn expressed itself in astrology, divination, magical rites, cultic oracles, interpretation of dreams and the study of esoteric books. No doubt this influence was felt within Judaism itself and led to the still further deterioration of the prophetic oracle. It is not surprising that prophecy in the form of oracular pronouncement or prediction which, outwardly at least, had so much in common with the heathen practice of divination should be regarded with the gravest suspicion by the religious leaders of the Jews. A significant passage in this connection is Zech. 13.2–6, where 'the prophet' is coupled with 'the idols' and 'the unclean spirit' which God will remove when he comes to purify the land. If any man appears, claiming to be a prophet, his

[1] Cf. A. R. Johnson, *The Cultic Prophet in Ancient Israel*, 1944, pp. 59f.

[2] S. Mowinckel, *Norsk Teol. Tidsskrift*, 1940, p. 236, quoted by A. Bentzen, *Introduction to the Old Testament*, English ed., vol. I, 1948, p. 172.

own father and mother will condemn him as a liar and will 'pierce him through' rather than allow him to continue to prophesy. So ashamed will a prophet be of his profession that he will disclaim any association with his class and will invent excuses for the self-inflicted wounds on his back made in times of ecstatic frenzy. It is impossible to be more precise about the dating of this particular passage than to say that it belongs to the Persian or Greek period; nor is it at all certain that it reflects the normal belief and practice of that age. But it gives some indication at least of the attitude of a section of the Jewish people to prophecy as it was then understood. Such prophets, by their unbridled feelings, dervish dances and bodily lacerations, would do much to bring the very name of prophecy into disrepute and associate it even more securely in people's minds with the idolatries of Babylon.

A contributory factor, casting further suspicion on the prophetic oracle, is perhaps to be found in the political sphere. There are indications that the exaggerated and inflammatory pronouncements of certain prophets during this period may well have been interpreted as a danger to the peace and security of the Jewish State. As in the time of Jeremiah (cf. Jer. 29.1, 8), so now, there were always irresponsible prophets whose utterances could readily lend themselves to political agitation. Such dangerous talk would of necessity be shunned by the responsible leaders of the people (cf. Neh. 6.12). Thus the prophetic oracle, in the eyes of the authorities at any rate, would be brought into further disrepute.

It is hardly surprising, in the light of these developments, that in course of time the belief came to be established within Judaism that prophetic inspiration had ceased and the voice of prophecy was dumb. It is hardly less surprising that, as men looked forward to the triumph of God's purpose in history, they should look forward also to a rebirth of prophecy which would mark the appearing of the messianic age. In I Maccabees, for example, reference is made to the fact that prophecy is a thing of the past and the belief is expressed that the time will come when God will raise up a true prophet who will interpret his Law faithfully to the people. Three passages of the book are particularly relevant in this connection. In 9.27 it is said concerning the days of Jonathan, 'And there was great tribulation in Israel, such as was not since the time that no prophet appeared unto them.' It is clear that, from the point of view of the writer, many years had passed since a prophet had last been seen in Israel. More significant still are the words of 4.46 written with reference to the purification of the Temple which had been desecrated by Antiochus Epiphanes. Judas, we are told, appointed priests to cleanse the holy place, but the problem arose as to what should be done with the altar which had been defiled by heathen sacrifices. A desision was taken and 'they pulled down the altar, and laid up the stones in the mountain of the house in a convenient place, until there should come a prophet to give answer concerning them.' The same hope of a coming prophet who would speak with an authoritative voice is expressed again in 14.41, which states that 'the Jews and the priests were well pleased that Simon should be their leader and high priest for ever, until there should arise a faithful prophet'. The hope continued to be held throughout the whole of the inter-testamental period that all the uncertainty which surrounded the interpretation of God's Law would at last be solved by a renewal of the gift of prophecy and the appearance of a great prophet in their midst who would be the precursor of the promised Messiah.[1]

This hope took two forms and came to be associated with two names. In one, the hope is expressed in the coming of a prophet like Moses as promised in Deut. 18.15: 'The Lord thy God will raise up unto thee a prophet from the midst of thee, of thy brethren, like unto me; unto him ye shall hearken.' In the other the 'faithful prophet' is looked for in the return of the prophet Elijah according to the promise of Mal. 4.5: 'Behold, I will send you Elijah the prophet before the great and terrible day of the Lord come.'[2] The first of these is identified in rabbinic literature with Elijah, who is to appear shortly before the coming of the Messiah.[3] Among the Samaritans the belief was expressed in the coming of this same prophet, called the *Taheb* or 'restorer' of all things (cf. John 4.25). Likewise in the Qumran literature the prophet foretold by Moses is referred to alongside two other messianic figures. In the *Testimonies Scroll*,[4] for example, the writer quotes certain proof texts which have

[1] With this hope in a coming prophet we may compare the reference in Ezra 2.63 where the unregistered priests have to relinquish their priestly functions until there should arise 'a priest with Urim and Thummim'.

[2] Cf. Rev. 11.3ff., where these two conceptions are combined to give the notion of the 'two witnesses'.

[3] Cf. *Menahot* 45a; *'Abot de Rabbi Nathan* 24.4.

[4] Cf. J. M. Allegro, *JBL*, vol. LXXV, 1956, pp. 174ff., and J. T. Milik, *Discoveries in the Judaean Desert I*, pp. 121ff.

for him a messianic significance. These refer to the faithful prophet in Deut. 18.18, Balaam's oracle concerning the star of Jacob in Num. 24.15ff., and Jacob's blessing on Levi in Deut. 33.8ff. The three figures alluded to in these passages are no doubt to be identified with 'a prophet and the Messiahs of Aaron and Israel' mentioned in the *Manual of Discipline* (IX.11), who are to appear at the end of the age. The relation of this prophet to the Teacher of Righteousness is not altogether clear, but it is likely that at one time the Qumran Covenanters identified the two. The function of the 'faithful prophet' as *teacher* of the people ('I will put my word in his mouth, and he shall speak unto them all that I shall command him', Deut. 18.18) finds its fulfilment in the Teacher of Righteousness who will 'rise up in the latter days' (*Zadokite Document* VI.11) and expound the Scriptures with authority given him by God. Again, in the New Testament both John the Baptist and Jesus are thought to be 'the prophet that should come', variously described as 'Elijah' or 'the prophet' or 'that prophet' (cf. Mark 9.11ff.; John 1.19ff., 45; 5.46; 6.14; 7.40; Acts 3.22f.; 7.37), and Jesus himself is said to have recognized in John the Baptist the fulfilment of the Elijah prophecy (cf. Matt. 11.14; 17.9ff.).

Further evidence for the belief that prophecy had ceased in Israel is given in the writings of the Jewish historian Josephus (*c.* AD 100), who offers more explicit information concerning the approximate date when, it was believed, God-inspired utterance had come to an end. In a passage upholding the trustworthiness of the Hebrew books over against those of the Greeks, he indicates that in his day there were twenty-two books of an inspired character among the Jews which contained 'the record of all time'.[1] Of these, five are the books of Moses; thirteen, representing the period from the death of Moses till the reign of Artaxerxes, were written by 'the prophets subsequent to Moses'. The remaining four books contain 'hymns to God and precepts for the conduct of human life'. There then follow these significant words: 'From Artaxerxes to our own time the complete history has been written, but has not been deemed worthy of equal credit with the earlier (*i.e.* the biblical) records, because of the failure of the exact succession of the prophets.'[2] That is, the true

[1] Cf. *Against Apion* I.8 (38–40). II (4) Esd. 14.44ff. refers to twenty-four 'canonical' books. Josephus may have omitted two of the disputed books or else have combined Judges with Ruth and Jeremiah with Lamentations.

[2] *Ibid.*, I.8 (41).

prophetic succession, which began with Moses, came to an end in the reign of Artaxerxes I (Longimanus) whom he identifies elsewhere with the Ahasuerus who appears in the Book of Esther.[1] This rather artificial division associated with the name of Artaxerxes is no doubt adopted so as to bring Esther within the scope of the inspired writings, for Josephus assumes that the date of the book coincides with the 'history' with which it deals. Thus Josephus gives concrete form to the prevailing belief that prophetic inspiration, which had commenced with Moses, ceased in the fifth century BC in the time of Artaxerxes, which was also the time of Ezra the scribe.

This evidence in Josephus is substantially supported by that of the rabbinic tradition. In *Pirke 'Abot* 1.1, for example, we read, 'Moses received the Law from Sinai and committed it to Joshua, and Joshua to the Elders, and the Elders to the Prophets; and the Prophets committed it to the men of the Great Synagogue.' According to later Jewish tradition 'the Great Synagogue' was 'a body of 120 elders, including many prophets, who came up from exile with Ezra; they saw that prophecy had come to an end and that restraint was lacking; therefore they made many new rules and restrictions for the better observance of the Law',[2] *i.e.* it was, traditionally at least, an authoritative body which took over the spiritual heritage of Moses and the prophets and sought to apply its teachings to the religious developments of a new age. These words of *Pirke 'Aboth* remind us again that there was no sharp antithesis in the Jewish thought of that time between the Law and the prophetic tradition, that the message of the prophets was regarded as an exposition and application of the Law of Moses, that Ezra as the reputed head of 'the Great Synagogue' embodied in the Law the aims and ideals of the prophets, and that the prophetic tradition was believed to have been replaced in the time of Ezra by the scribal tradition.

It is a frequently expressed belief in the rabbinic writings that all the prophets whom God raised up after Moses were inspired men who spoke by the holy spirit; and conversely, all inspired men after

[1] Cf. *Ant.* XI.vi.1 (184). The text reads, 'On the death of Xerxes the kingdom passed to his son Asuēros, whom the Greeks call Artaxerxes.' Asuēros is a transliteration of the Hebrew *'Ahašwerōš* (the biblical Ahasuerus) which represents the Persian *Kšayarša* which takes the form Xerxes in Greek. The LXX, however, reads 'Artaxerxes' which explains Josephus's identification of Artaxerxes with Ahasuerus as indicated above. (Cf. *Josephus*, Loeb Classical Library, vol. VI, p. 403.)

[2] H. Danby, *The Mishnah*, 1933, p. 446, n. 5.

Moses who spoke by the holy spirit were prophets. Hence, in addition to those commonly recognized as prophets, the rabbinic literature names such men as Abraham, Isaac, Jacob, David, Solomon, Zerubbabel, Joshua and Mordecai. According to one Jewish tradition there were forty-eight prophets and seven prophetesses in Israel.[1] Indeed, so closely related was prophecy to the inspiration of the spirit that when the last of the prophets died it was traditionally believed that the holy spirit ceased from Israel.[2] The last of the prophets are here identified as Haggai and Zechariah, who helped to rebuild the Second Temple, and Malachi who is regarded as their contemporary. These men thus form the link between the prophetic tradition and the scribal tradition represented in 'the Great Synagogue' and its rabbinic successors.[3] Among the prophets and as president of the assembly sat Ezra the scribe. So closely associated is he with the last of the prophets that he is on occasion identified with Malachi.[4] With Haggai, Zechariah, Malachi and Ezra prophetic inspiration ceased and prophecy itself came to an end.[5]

It has been argued that the rabbinic tradition is not always consistent in its teaching concerning the extinction of prophecy through the cessation of the work of the holy spirit, for there are certain passages which seem to indicate that the spirit was still actively at work among God's people.[6] God still appeared in the glory of the *shekinah*, for example, and spoke to them in the *bath qol*. By the aid of the holy spirit there were some among them who were able to foresee and predict the events of the future; whilst others, by their devotion and righteousness, were counted worthy to receive the gift of the holy spirit. W. D. Davies, after an examination of the evidence, concludes that 'the Rabbis . . . do not reveal any awareness that they

[1] Cf. *Megillah* 14a and *Seder ʿOlam R.*, chs. 20–21. For this whole section see G. F. Moore, *Judaism*, vol. I, pp. 237f.

[2] Cf. *Tos. Soṭah* 13.2; *Sanhedrin* 11a.

[3] Cf. *'Abot de Rabbi Nathan* 1.3: 'Haggai, Zechariah and Malachi received the tradition from the prophets; the men of the Great Synagogue received it from Haggai, Zechariah and Malachi.' Elsewhere they are themselves clearly numbered among the prophets, *e.g.* in *Megillah* 17b.

[4] Cf. *Megillah* 15a and Targum on Malachi 1.1.

[5] According to *Seder ʿOlam*, ch. 30, the prophets continued till the time of Alexander of Macedon, when their place was taken by 'the wise'. *Baba Bathra* 12a puts the cessation of prophecy at the time of the destruction of the Temple when, again, 'the wise' follow in their line of succession. See G. F. Moore, *ibid.*, vol. I, pp. 31f., and vol. III, pp. 11f.

[6] For a list of the relevant passages and an examination of the evidence they produce, see W. D. Davies, *Paul and Rabbinic Judaism*, 2nd ed., 1955, pp. 209ff.

lived in an "Age" of the Spirit', although he acknowledges that 'there may have been individuals who were conscious of the Holy Spirit as active in their lives'.[1] In a later work the same writer qualifies his statement still further, pointing out that the Qumran Covenanters, for example, were 'a community in the Spirit' who 'seem to have combined the strictest adherence to the Law with a vivid pneumatology'.[2] This evidence from the Dead Sea Scrolls indicates clearly that an awareness of the spirit may have been a more marked feature of the Judaism of the inter-testamental period than was previously recognized. There are indications, moreover, that the apocalyptic writers in particular believed that they were inspired by God in their task, even although in their writings there are relatively few references to the spirit as the direct source of their professed inspiration.[3] This consciousness of divine inspiration on their part helps us to understand more clearly their belief that they stood in the true prophetic tradition.

2. ORAL TRADITION AND APOCALYPTIC TRADITION

Reference has been made above to the belief that Moses received the Law from God on Mount Sinai and that in course of time this was committed through the prophets to 'the men of the Great Synagogue' (*Pirke 'Abot* 1.1). Part of this revelation, it was believed, was written down then or at some later time, but much of it was preserved in the form of oral tradition until, about the year AD 200, it was codified in written form. There are many passages in the Talmud and in the rabbinical literature generally which clearly assert that the oral Law, and not only the written Law, had been received by Moses at Sinai[4] and had been handed on in its complete form to successive generations.[5]

The task of interpreting the Law had been accepted as a legitimate part of legal activity even in pre-exilic days (cf. Jer. 8.8), but in the time of Ezra the scribe it received a completely new emphasis. Ezra

[1] *Ibid.*, pp. 213 and 215.

[2] 'Contemporary Jewish Religion', in *Peake's Commentary on the Bible*, ed. by M. Black and H. H. Rowley, 1962, p. 706, sect. 615a; cf. 'Paul and the Dead Sea Scrolls: Flesh and Spirit', in K. Stendahl, *The Scrolls and the New Testament*, 1958, pp. 157ff., and also in W. D. Davies, *Christian Origins and Judaism*, 1962, pp. 145ff.

[3] See ch. VI and especially pp. 164ff.

[4] Cf. *b. Berakot* 5a; *Megillah* 19b; *Exodus R.* on Ex. 34.27; *Pirke de R. Eliezer* 46.

[5] Cf. *Megillah* 14a.

is described in Scripture as 'a ready scribe in the law of Moses' (Ezra 7.6) who 'set his heart to seek the law of the Lord, and to do it' (Ezra 7.10). He 'read in the book, in the law of God, distinctly' and 'gave the sense, so that they understood the reading' (Neh. 8.8). He was followed in this by the Sopherim, who set themselves the task of interpreting the written Law of God in such a way that men could apply it to their daily lives. The revelation of God in Torah was a dynamic thing which could and should be interpreted anew in every succeeding age and applied anew to every part of human life and conduct. The work of the Sopherim was continued and developed by religious leaders who later became known as the Rabbis, whose influence was determinative of the Judaism of later generations. It is reported in *Pirke 'Abot* 1.3–12 that the tradition of the Sopherim was transmitted by Simon the Just to one, Antigonus of Socho, and that it was thereafter transmitted in pairs from Jose ben Joezer and Jose ben Johanan (*c.* 160 BC) in line of succession to Hillel and Shammai (*c.* 30 BC–AD 10). In the course of transmission their 'interpretations' or 'traditions' came to assume a sanctity and indeed a validity equal to that of the written Law itself. There were not, and could not be, two Laws, but one Law in two parts which contained the sum of divine revelation. Each part was of divine origin, of equal antiquity and of equal authority, for each had been given by God at Sinai. God's revelation of himself, of his Law and of his purpose for mankind had been given once and for all to Moses on Sinai, and having been given it was perfect and unalterable both in content and in character. Historically the development of the oral Law could be traced in part at least in definite rabbinic pronouncements and teachings. But that did not alter the fact that the whole rabbinic development of the Law had been given on Mount Sinai, for the pronouncements of even the latest rabbis represented in the tradition had been known previously by God. These men were not simply creators of this tradition, they were inheritors of it and held it in trust from God through his servant Moses. Everything in the Law, be it written or unwritten, had been foreseen by God.

But not only was Moses the fountain-head of all law-giving, he was also the fountain-head of all prophecy. To quote the words of G. F. Moore, 'The revelation to Moses was complete and final; no other prophet should ever make any innovation in the law.[1] The

[1] Deut. 4.2; 13.1 (E.V. 12.32); Lev. 27.34; *Shabbat* 104a; *Megillah* 2b; Maimonides, *Yesode ha-Torah* 9.1.

forty-eight prophets and seven prophetesses who came after him neither took away anything that was written in the Law nor added anything to it. . . . Moses is the fountain-head of prophecy in so literal a sense that it is said that he uttered all the words of the prophets besides his own.'[1] It is significant, as we have seen, that in the tradition recorded in *Pirke 'Abot* 1.1 the prophets are given an all-important place in the unbroken transmission of the Law from Moses to succeeding generations. Far from there being a cleavage between the Law and the Prophets, there is the closest possible relationship between them. This was recognized by Ezra—the 'second Moses' and 'founder of the Law'—and by his successors in the post-exilic community. Just as the great prophets had sought to expound and apply the teachings and ideals of Moses, so they in their turn, in expounding and applying the Law, believed that they were interpreting to their generation the teachings and ideals of the prophets.

In a penetrating study of the relationship of apocalyptic to Law and prophecy[2] T. W. Manson notes as significant the fact that the traditional date for the cessation of prophecy is associated with two developments, rabbinism and apocalyptic, which were to develop side by side and have a powerful influence on Judaism throughout the inter-testamental period. What is the relationship between these two? Manson suggests that they are two sides of a systematizing process and together indicate 'the Jewish attempt to answer life's fundamental problems in the light of the prophetic revelation'. On the one hand, apocalyptic is 'an attempt to rationalize and systematize the predictive side of prophecy[3] as one side of the whole providential ordering of the Universe. The other side of the systematizing process is the scribal treatment of the Law leading to the codification of the Mishnah.' The relationship is neatly put by Sabatier in a sentence which Manson quotes with approval: 'L'Apocalypse est à la prophétie ce que la Mischna est à la Thora.'

But can we define more clearly the connection between the oral tradition and the apocalyptic tradition which thus form two sides of this single process? Manson finds the common denominator, as it were, in 'the oracles of God' (*ta logia*) as set out in the Old Testament

[1] *Op. cit.*, vol. I, p. 239.
[2] 'Some reflections on Apocalyptic', in *Aux Sources de la Tradition Chrétienne* (*Mélanges offerts à M. Maurice Goguel*), 1950, pp. 139ff.
[3] See further pp. 96ff.

Scriptures. Among the several meanings of 'oracle' (*logion*) in the Greek Old Testament, two are of particular significance. One signifies a divine command; the other signifies a divine promise. These two together indicate the terms of the covenant which God has made with his people Israel (cf. Deut. 33.9). Acceptance of the covenant involves man's pledge of obedience in response to the commands of God and also the assurance of God's intervention in history, in reward and punishment, in fulfilment of his promises.

On the one hand, Israel became aware of God's commands (or demands) through two sources of influence—through the traditional rules of conduct handed down from of old, and through the living judgments of prophecy on particular concrete moral issues. From the interplay of these two influences came the codification of the divine demands in the organized Torah. The material indicating the nature of God's demands and man's obedience to them was systematically and logically arranged and at last was formed into a single all-inclusive code. On the other hand, Israel became aware of God's promises, again through two sources of influence—through a great variety of national hopes and ambitions deeply embedded in the traditions of Israel, and through the prophetic predictions of judgment and deliverance. From the interplay of these two influences came the codification of the divine purpose in the framework of the apocalypses. The material indicating the nature of God's promises was systematically and chronologically arranged and at last was formed into a single all-inclusive plan.[1]

Thus Torah and apocalyptic together shaped and determined the religious ideal of Israel during this period until, in the early Christian centuries, there came a parting of the ways when apocalyptic was abandoned by normative Juadism and became the property of the Christian Church.[2]

A most interesting commentary on the relationship between Torah and apocalyptic is given in the so-called 'Ezra-legend' recorded in II Esdras 14. It tells how one day, as Ezra was sitting under an oak tree, God called to him saying, 'I did manifestly reveal myself in the bush, and talked with Moses when my people were in bondage in Egypt; and I sent him and led my people out of Egypt, and brought him to Mount Sinai; and I held him by me for many days. I told

[1] For a treatment of the apocalyptic conception of the unity of history see pp. 217ff.

[2] See above, pp. 33ff.

him many wondrous things, shewed him the secrets of the times, declared to him the end of the seasons. Then I commanded him saying, These words shalt thou publish openly, but these keep secret' (14.3–6). These words seem to indicate—and the verses which follow substantiate the claim—that Moses received from God at Sinai not only the Torah which he was to publish openly, but also a 'secret' tradition which he was to keep hidden. The latter is presumably not the oral Law, for this was taught as openly as the written Law itself; it must refer to the apocalyptic teaching which recorded a secret tradition concerning great crises in world history and in particular the greatest crisis of all at the time of the End and which was closely associated with the name of Moses.[1] Torah and apocalyptic, then, are in this passage traced back to their origins in God's revelation to Moses at Sinai.

The writer then refers to a tradition, known also from later books,[2] that God's Law was destroyed by fire when Nebuchadnezzar captured Jerusalem in 587 BC (14.21, cf. 4.23). The reference in 14.21 ('thy Law is burnt') is specifically to the burning of the Pentateuch; but, as the context shows, the writer has in mind the rest of the Scriptures also, for as a result of this burning there is no record of 'the things which have been done by thee' (presumably the historical books) or of 'the works that shall be done' (presumably the eschatological prophecies). But the loss is greater still. The implication of the whole chapter is that not only the 'open' books of Torah, but also the 'secret' books of apocalyptic have been destroyed in the fire.

But God has raised up Ezra the scribe, the 'second Moses', to restore both the Law and the apocalyptic teaching. Just as the Lord manifested himself to Moses in a bush, so out of a bush also he speaks to Ezra (14.1–3): 'The signs which I showed thee, the dreams which thou hast seen, and the interpretations which thou hast heard—lay them up in thy heart' (14.8). The present age is fast drawing to a close and soon he will be taken up to be with the Messiah (14.9). Thereupon he prays that God will send his holy spirit that he may 'write all that has happened in the world since the beginning, even the things which were written in thy Law' (14.22). Then, like Moses on Mount Sinai, he is bidden to set aside forty days in which God's revelations will be made known to him. He is to take five chosen scribes and

[1] See further pp. 113f.

[2] This legend concerning the burning of the Law and its restoration by Ezra is recounted by a number of the Church Fathers.

dictate to them the words which God will reveal (14.24). Again, like Moses (14.6), he is told, 'Some things thou shalt publish, and some thou shalt deliver in secret to the wise' (14.26). In answer to his prayer for inspiration God bids him drink a cup 'full as it were with water, but the colour of it was like fire' (14.39). Thereupon his memory is strengthened so that he is able to remember the sacred writings which he dictates to the five scribes 'in characters which they knew not'[1] (14.42). After forty days his task is finished and the divine revelation is recorded in ninety-four books (14.44). Then comes the word of the Most High: 'The twenty-four books[2] that thou hast written publish, that the worthy and unworthy may read (therein); but the seventy last thou shalt keep, to deliver them to the wise among thy people' (14.45f.).

It has been argued by some scholars[3] that the seventy secret books refer to the oral Law which finds expression in the *halakah* and *haggadah* of the rabbinic literature. G. H. Box concedes that our author possibly understood the seventy books to *include* the halakic and haggadic literature along with the apocalyptic, but that conscious stress is laid on the latter. The language used by the writer, however, would seem to indicate that he is referring to the apocalyptic literature rather than to that of the oral legal tradition. Three times over (in 14.6, 26, 45) stress is laid on the *secret* character of certain of the books—an expression which appears frequently with reference to apocalyptic writings—which are to be delivered in due course to the wise among the people. The writer claims that these books also, like those to be published 'openly', have been restored by Ezra under the inspiration of the holy spirit. The twenty-four books which are to be published openly are those of canonical Scripture; the seventy books which are to be kept secret are those of the apocalyptic writings.

If this interpretation of II Esdras 14 is correct—that it refers to the apocalyptic tradition and not simply to the oral legal tradition—then our author is in effect claiming for the former a valued and indeed an authoritative place within Judaism. To him these writings are 'the spring of understanding, the fountain of wisdom and the stream of knowledge' (14.47). This is no small praise and no doubt faithfully records the conviction of many others in his particular

[1] This reading is found in the Syriac and Ethiopic texts. The reference here is to the square Hebrew script of which Ezra is traditionally regarded as the inventor.

[2] This reading is found in the Syriac and Arabic[1] texts.

[3] See references in G. H. Box, *The Ezra Apocalypse*, 1912, pp. 305f.

circle that this type of literature was an authentic expression of the religious hopes of Judaism and could be accorded a place alongside the oral Law itself.

Thus we see a striking similarity between these two traditions:

(*a*) Each is of divine origin, for both were received as a revelation from God.

(*b*) Each claims to be the inheritor of a long tradition within the history of Israel.

(*c*) Each is of equal antiquity, for both were made known to Moses on Sinai.

(*d*) Each is of equal authority, for both claim a place alongside the written Torah.

(*e*) Each claims the name not only of Moses, but also of Ezra the 'second Moses'. In Ezra and his five scribes—Saraia, Dabria, Selemia, Elkanah and Asiel—we may have, indeed, an attempt to match Rabbi Johanan b. Zakkai (the refounder of Judaism after AD 70) and his five famous disciples, Eliezer b. Hyrcanus, Joshua b. Hananya, Jose the Priest, Simeon b. Nathanael and Eleazar b. Arak.[1]

In the language of T. W. Manson, both are an expression of God's covenant with Israel, the one in the form of command and the other in the form of promise. They belong together and, like the written Torah itself, are also the gift of God.

3. APOCALYPTIC, EMBEDDED IN PROPHECY

It is often assumed that apocalyptic in Judaism began with the Book of Daniel in the first half of the second century BC. This, however, is at best only a half truth, for although Daniel may be the first and indeed the greatest of all the Jewish apocalyptic writings, apocalyptic itself had its origins in a much earlier period. Its roots were widespread and drew nourishment from many sources, prophetic and mythological, native and foreign, esoteric and exotic; but there can be no doubt that the tap root, as it were, went deep down into Hebrew prophecy, and in particular the writings of the post-exilic prophets whose thought and language provided the soil from which later apocalyptic works were to grow. Apocalyptic came to full flower in such books as Daniel and Enoch (though these two

[1] Cf. G. H. Box, *ibid.*, p. 314.

were of different kinds and belonged to different stocks),[1] but the seeds from which they grew had already been sown in such passages as Ezekiel 38–39, Zechariah 1–8 and 9–14, Joel 3 and Isaiah 24–27. It may be true that in certain important respects Jewish apocalyptic was not of pure Hebrew stock, but was influenced by strains from Babylon, Persia and Greece; it should be noted, however, that such influences are already to be found in post-exilic prophecy itself, from which apocalyptic sprang.

One important source of influence was undoubtedly the Book of Ezekiel, whose language, imagery and religious insights left their mark on the whole field of apocalyptic thought. Here, for example, the transcendence of God is emphasized much more than in earlier prophecies and points the way to a fuller development still in the apocalyptic writings. The prophet's stress, too, on individualism and especially on individual retribution (cf. 18.3ff.) is applied by certain apocalyptic writers to the fate of individual men in the life after death.[2] He indulges, moreover, in fantastic imagery and symbolism of diverse kinds (cf. 'the four living creatures' and the four wheels whose rims were 'full of eyes round about', etc., in ch. 1); many of his revelations come through visions and auditions (cf. his inaugural vision in 1.4–3.15); his inspiration is often ecstatic in character (cf. 3.12ff.), even to the point of catalepsy (cf. 3.25ff.). In all these respects parallels can be found in the later apocalyptic works.

In Ezekiel 38–39, which may be a slightly later addition to the writings of the prophet himself, the writer makes use of the battle motif in which the powers of evil, and in particular the Gentile nations, are destroyed (cf. 39.12ff.). Reference is made to 'Gog of the land of Magog', a mysterious figure who leads the forces of evil against God in battle. This passage is of interest for a number of reasons and illustrates several recurring features of later apocalyptic. Here, for example, allusion is made to the Dragon Myth in 38.4 where God addresses Gog in these words: 'I will turn thee about and put hooks into thy jaws, and I will bring thee forth, and all thine army.' This same theme is to be found both in post-exilic prophecy and in certain extra-canonical apocalyptic writings. Again, these chapters attempt a reinterpretation of Jeremiah's prophecy of a foe

[1] Cf. E. W. Heaton, *The Book of Daniel*, 1956, pp. 33ff., where it is rightly pointed out that there is a distinctiveness about Daniel which marks it off not only from earlier prophecy but also from later apocalyptic writings.

[2] See further ch. XIV.

from the north (cf. Jer. 1.14; 3.1–6.30), which now becomes a prophecy of the final battle which will usher in the End and establish God's kingdom.[1] This battle theme which tells of the defeat of Gog and the rout of Israel's enemies (39.12f.) becomes a familiar motif in later apocalyptic and colours deeply the picture of the final eschatological battle in which God's enemies are utterly destroyed (cf. I Enoch 90.20ff.; II Esd. 12.32; 13.37f.; Ass. of Moses 10.1ff.).

Altogether this book has about it an artificial literary style unlike that of pre-exilic prophecy and reveals, in its pictures and images, the influence of its Babylonian background. As S. B. Frost says, 'The abundant imagery of apocalyptic and its strange symbolism have, indeed, their roots in Hebrew style but have been richly fertilized by this new Babylonian type of literature which Babylonian-Ezekiel transplants into Hebrew soil.'[2]

From the time of Ezekiel onwards apocalyptic tendencies in prophecy become much more fully developed. This is seen, for example, in Zechariah 1–8, where a number of those features already noted in Ezekiel are repeated. Here, for example, considerable use is again made of visionary experience, of colourful imagery and fantastic symbolic figures which may reflect the influence of Babylonian mythology; once more the Gentiles are equated with the forces of evil and are destined to be destroyed by God in battle (cf. 6.1–8). Hope is expressed in the coming of a Golden Age (cf. ch. 8) and in the appearing of a messianic leader chosen by God (3.8, cf. also Micah 5.2ff.; Isa. 11.1ff.; Jer. 23.5ff.). Such hopes as these become increasingly common in post-exilic times and oracles expressing them come to be attached not only to post-exilic but also to pre-exilic prophecies. One other feature of Zechariah 1–8 which is of special interest for the future development of apocalyptic is the considerable increase of interest shown in angelology and the role played by Satan as 'the adversary' (3.1).[3]

Zechariah 9–14 (generally known as Deutero-Zechariah), though it has little in common with Zechariah 1–8 either in its language or in its content, takes its place in the continuing line of prophetic tradition, reapplying the message of prophecy to the conditions of its own day. There is no unanimity about its date. Some scholars place

[1] For an examination of this passage in the light of later interpretation and reinterpretation, see pp. 190ff.

[2] *Old Testament Apocalyptic*, 1952, p. 86.

[3] See further pp. 236f.

it not long after Haggai and Zechariah, but most date it much later, towards the end of the third century BC. The writers of these chapters are much occupied with matters relating to the End, the coming of a messianic deliverer and the Golden Age, the final great conflict of God's people with the forces of evil and the ultimate destruction or submission of the Gentiles. This last theme occupies the attention of prophets like Zephaniah (cf. 1.15f.) and Joel (cf. 3.9ff.). Joel in particular takes up the familiar prophetic idea of the Day of the Lord[1] and develops it in the direction of later apocalyptic thought. This great day will be a time of universal judgment on the nations of the earth when Yahweh himself will intervene in the affairs of men in a great world cataclysm.

The final judgment of the nations and the consummation of all things is again the theme of Isaiah 24–27, an addition to the Book of Isaiah dating perhaps from the third or fourth century BC. When Yahweh pronounces his judgment the earth is turned upside down (24.1) and the sun and moon are darkened (24.23). In this great cosmic catastrophe even the 'host of heaven' is to be punished (24.21), just as later on, in I Enoch 12–36, the angels receive from God their due recompense. Mention is made, too, of an eschatological banquet to which are invited 'all peoples' (25.6ff.), a feature which is to play a significant part in later apocalyptic ideas concerning the messianic age. Most startling of all the teachings of these chapters is that of 26.19 which declares that the righteous dead will be raised in resurrection to share in the final redemption of God's people. This belief is taken up and developed at great length, and with much variety of detail, by succeeding apocalyptic writers.[2]

These several Old Testament prophecies cannot be called 'apocalyptic' in the sense that the name can be applied to books like Daniel and its successors, but it can be said that they contain the 'stuff' from which apocalyptic is made—the notion of divine transcendence, the development of angelology, fantastic symbolism, cosmic imagery, the use of foreign mythology, reinterpretation of prophecy, the visionary form of inspiration, a distinctly literary form, cataclysm and judgment, the Day of the Lord, the destruction of the Gentiles, the coming of the Golden Age, the messianic deliverer and the resurrection of the dead. When at last the historical conditions for growth were right, these seeds rapidly grew into full flower in the colourful and diverse literature of Jewish apocalyptic.

[1] See further pp. 92ff. [2] See ch. XIV.

4. APOCALYPTIC, A DEVELOPMENT OF PROPHECY

The charge has sometimes been levelled against apocalyptic that it is not only imitative of prophecy but is also plagiaristic in its attempt to fulfil, by means of literary reflection, unfulfilled prophecies of the past. It is, of course, true that apocalyptic is deeply concerned about the fulfilment of prophecy[1] and that in some of these books at least a certain amount of imitation of a literary kind may be detected. But it is not *merely* imitative, and the charge of plagiarism does less than justice to the writers concerned. Indeed they give the impression that they were devout and sincere men who believed that they were following, however stumblingly, in the footsteps of the prophets. They did not punctuate their utterances with 'Thus saith the Lord', but like the prophets before them they were convinced that they had been given a message from God in dark and difficult days and were under a divine compulsion to make it known.[2]

Apocalyptic is not a substitute for prophecy—the apocalyptists would not have been so presumptuous as to make such a claim; but it is in many respects a continuation, or at least a development of it, however different it may be at times in form, feeling and content. It is 'prophecy in a new idiom'.[3] But although it may speak with a different accent and indeed in a language which is at times alien to that of prophecy, nevertheless the message it proclaims is essentially a readaptation and development of the old message within a new situation. Many of the ideas and tendencies already evident in prophecy, some of which we have noted above, are developed along new lines in the light of new needs. Similes and metaphors, especially those lending themselves to a mythological interpretation, are borrowed and reinterpreted in the light of apocalyptic expectations, whilst other elements only latent in prophecy are made to serve the same purpose.

This attempt on the part of the apocalyptists to readapt and develop the older prophetic message will be illustrated many times over in the course of the following pages. Here we observe as a case in point the use made by them of the prophetic Day of the Lord which is a common feature in the prophetic writings. The origin of

[1] See ch. VII.
[2] For the nature of apocalyptic inspiration see ch. VI.
[3] The phrase is used by B. W. Anderson, *The Living World of the Old Testament*, 1959, p. 519.

this idea is a very vexed question and does not concern us here.[1] Some have taken it to refer to God's day of battle when his enemies are to be defeated; others have seen in it 'a mythical manifestation of Yahweh in the majesty of terrible natural phenomena conquering hostile powers';[2] others have traced it back to the cult of the autumnal Feast of Tabernacles in Jerusalem in which Yahweh was enthroned as king.[3] Whatever its origins may have been, by the eighth century BC it was popularly understood by the people of Israel to signify the time when God would vindicate his people, and in particular give them victory over their enemies in the field of battle. Amos, however, saw that the logical outcome of such a belief was the doom of God's own people, for the holy God could not abide unrighteousness whether it be in the nations or in Israel itself; he thus declared that the Day of the Lord would be 'darkness and not light' (Amos 5.18), a time of judgment not only for the nations but also for Israel. Other prophets followed suit and interpreted it as a time when God would judge Israel (cf. Hosea) or Judah (cf. Isaiah, Micah) or the whole world (cf. Zephaniah). This world judgment proclaimed, for example, by Zephaniah (cf. 1.2, 3, 18; 3.8) is set forth by other prophets as well (cf. Isa. 34; Jer. 25.15ff.; Hag. 2.32). Jeremiah and Ezekiel pronounce a collective judgment on the nations and an individual judgment on the people of Israel; a glorious future for Israel is foretold and the promise is given of a great deliverer. In Joel yet another variation appears—the Day of the Lord is here presented in terms of a Great Assize in which God judges the nations of the earth; after this final world judgment the Gentiles are destroyed.

But the prophetic vision of the future is not limited to a day of final judgment. Beyond this judgment there awaits a new era, a Golden Age, when the rule of God over his people will be complete. It is an age of peace and blessedness and prosperity which will appear in 'the latter end of the days'. This phrase, found in the later prophets, expresses a future hope which is still bounded by time and history; the 'end' envisaged here is the end of an historical era and not the end of the world as the apocalyptists later came to see it.[4]

But in the post-exilic prophets we see the Day of the Lord passing over into the realm of eschatology and reaching its fullest eschatological development in the hopes expressed by the apocalyptic writers.[1] Indeed we may say that 'apocalyptic arose out of prophecy by developing and universalizing the conception of the Day of the Lord'.[2] The apocalyptists, with a mixture of spiritual insight and speculative imagination, give graphic content to this prophetic idea which the prophets themselves had left necessarily vague. They ask all kinds of questions and supply a bewildering number of answers couched often in mythological language culled from Israel's ancient past or from contemporary foreign sources. When will the great Day arrive? What will be the signs of its appearing? When will God set up his kingdom? How long will it endure? Will it be on earth or in heaven? Will the Gentiles share in it? What will be the nature of God's judgment? Will Israel also be judged? Will individual men be rewarded according to their deeds? Will the dead be raised for judgment? What is the nature of the life beyond? What of heaven and Paradise? What of hell and Gehenna? With such questions as these they build up a picture of a future hope far removed in presentation from that of Old Testament prophecy and yet vitally related to it in its essential claim that in 'the latter end of the days' will come the great Day of the Lord when God himself will be enthroned as king.

One aspect of the apocalyptic hope is of particular interest in this connection. This is the apocalyptic Day of Judgment which may be accurately described as a specialization of the prophetic Day of the Lord.[3] H. Wheeler Robinson detects in this prophetic Day four characteristics—judgment, universality, supernatural intervention and proximity. In addition he notes four features contained in it—it brings to a focus the manifestation of God's purpose in history; it is a day on which God acts and not merely speaks; it is a day on which God is shown to be victorious within this present world-order and on the stage of human history; it is a day which ushers in a new era on the earth.[4]

It is significant that all these characteristics and features are

differences, it is true, some of them no doubt the outcome of the influence of foreign thought. But the source is unmistakable and the broad outline is the same. Such differences as do appear are, for the most part at any rate, to be seen as developments of the old prophetic idea, however far removed from the prototype the final picture may appear to be.

In the prophetic Day of the Lord, for example, judgment is generally speaking to be executed on Israel as well as on the Gentiles. This holds good also of the apocalyptic Day of Judgment. But here the tendency towards individualization is much more strongly pronounced. Not only the nation, but individual men also appear for judgment before God or his Messiah. It is a judgment, moreover, not only of the living but also of the dead; the dead are raised in resurrection to receive their just rewards.[1]

Again, instead of God's judgment taking the form of a great crisis or crises in history in which the fate of the nations is determined, the Day of Judgment sometimes assumes a definitely forensic character in which, as we have seen, individuals are brought to judgment.

In the prophetic writings, moreover, the triumph of God is seen within this present world-order; but in the apocalyptic writings the emphasis comes to be laid not so much on his judgment within time and on the plane of history, as on his judgment in a setting beyond time and above history. Instead of acting through human agencies, God is seen here to act directly, intervening personally in the affairs of the world. His enemies are no longer simply human armies, but 'principalities and powers in high places'.[2]

Thus the apocalyptists took up the prophetic teaching concerning the future hope as expressed in the Day of the Lord, enlarging and enriching it out of the store of their own religious insight and experience. In this, as in so many other respects, they followed in the line of the Old Testament prophetic tradition, expounding its meaning for the days in which they themselves were then living. They were trying, in effect, to say what they believed the prophets would have said in the changed circumstances of their day. They were convinced that his chosen people still . . . that what he had promised would come to pass, and that he who had spoken of old must have a word for the present time, if only some wise and holy man could discover what it was and make it known to his countrymen.'[1]

5. APOCALYPTIC AND THE PREDICTIVE SIDE OF PROPHECY

It has sometimes been suggested that one of the chief differences between prophecy and apocalyptic is the difference between 'forth-telling' and 'foretelling', between preaching and prediction. 'Prophecy', writes R. H. Charles, 'is a declaration, a forthtelling, of the will of God—not a foretelling. Prediction is not in any sense an essential of prophecy, though it may intervene as an accident—whether it be a justifiable accident is another question.'[2] The contrast drawn here between 'prophecy' and 'prediction' and, by implication, between prophecy and apocalyptic is, however, much too sharp to stand close examination. It is inadequate for two reasons: first, because 'foretelling' played no small part in the declaration of the prophets' message, and secondly because 'forth-telling' was integral to the message of the apocalyptic writers. Nevertheless, the predictive element in prophecy had a fascination for the apocalyptists and it is to this aspect of the prophetic message that they devote so much of their interest and ingenuity.

It is true to say that the primary interest of the great prophets was in the contemporary situation and that their message was directed towards the people and nations among whom they lived. Their prophecies for the most part are to be understood against the background of the social, economic, political and religious circumstances of their own day. They were primarily preachers who addressed themselves to the iniquities and sins of the people and, in the name of the righteous God, called upon them to repent and turn from their evil ways. But the predictive element in prophecy is not simply accidental, as Charles would have us believe. It belongs to the very nature of prophecy itself. The prophets were not simply journalists who made careful note of the trend of international politics and then

1.3–2.3; 9.7, etc.). The prophet who was privileged to stand in God's secret council (cf. Jer. 23.22) could in God's name predict future events, for 'the Lord Yahweh doeth nothing without revealing his secret unto his servants the prophets' (Amos 3.7). Indeed the prophet's power to predict future events was popularly thought to be a guarantee of his worth. This was the criterion by which it was possible to distinguish a true prophet from a false: 'When a prophet speaketh in the name of Yahweh, if the thing follow not nor come to pass, that is the thing which Yahweh hath not spoken, but the prophet hath spoken it presumptuously. Thou shalt not be afraid of him' (Deut. 18.12). Sometimes the prophets' predictions took the form of a general principle, that if the people refused to repent and turn from their sins, then judgment would inevitably follow; the agent of such judgment was more often than not some foreign foe. At other times the prophets looked into the distant future for the fulfilment of their pronouncements, seeing there not only judgment but also the restoration of the nation or a remnant within the nation. In particular they looked forward to the coming of a deliverer, a 'shoot of David's line', and to the establishment of a messianic kingdom. Such 'messianic' prophecies of a coming era of peace and righteousness are to be found for the most part in post-exilic prophecies, though many have become attached to the writings of pre-exilic prophets (*e.g.* Isa. 7.14; 9.1f.; 11.1f.; 32.1f.; Micah 5.1–5; Jer. 23.5–8). Some of these predictions were no doubt fulfilled, but many more were left unfulfilled and became the object of reinterpretation on the part of other prophets and more especially on the part of the apocalyptists themselves.[1]

It is for this reason that T. W. Manson, as we have seen, can rightly describe apocalyptic as 'an attempt to rationalize and systematize the predictive side of prophecy as one side of the whole providential ordering of the Universe'.[2] There can be no doubt that the apocalyptists' interest in prophecy lay almost entirely in its predictions of the future concerning whose meaning, they believed, they had been given divine insight. In particular they were attracted by the prophecies of hope which had been a feature of pre-exilic as well as post-exilic prophecy. Predictions of judgment had indeed been fulfilled in the Captivity, but the oft-repeated hope of a glorious

[1] For a fuller account of the apocalyptic interpretation of unfulfilled prophecy, see ch. VII.

[2] *Op. cit.*, p. 142. See above, p. 84.

future had constantly been deferred—the triumph of Israel over the nations of the earth, the overthrow of all the powers of evil, the vindication of God and of those who trusted in him, the coming of a mighty deliverer of David's line, the establishment of God's kingdom which would know no end and the creation of a new heaven and a new earth where peace and righteousness would dwell. These prophecies of hope had been made in God's name; they were verily the word of God and so could not be set at naught. Their fulfilment was inevitable, for the word of God could not lie. It was obvious that they had been uttered not for the prophets' day, but for some day in the future when their true meaning and the nature and time of their fulfilment would be revealed. The apocalyptists believed that they had been raised up by God to disclose the meaning of these things and, through them, to make known the unfolding of God's plan and purpose for the world.

It is not surprising that these convictions began to be expressed at the time of the Maccabean Revolt and that they continued through the period of the Hasmonean dynasty and right down to the fall of Jerusalem and even beyond. For, as we have seen,[1] this period witnessed a revival of Jewish nationalism and a resurgence of the old hope in a new form. The prophetic expectations which had lain lifeless during the despondent years of Persian and Greek rule now sprang to life and found vivid expression in the writings of these passionately sincere men. Because of the very darkness of the hour, the light of hope seemed to shine all the more brightly. With enthusiasm the apocalyptists restated and reinterpreted and reapplied the anticipations and promises of the prophets and proclaimed that these things were on the point of being realized.

But not only did the apocalyptists take up and recast the prophetic hopes and predictions, they at the same time set about defining 'the shape of things to come'. With an abundance of symbolic imagery and mythological allusions they began to fill in the outline which they had received from the prophets. At times their vivid imaginations outstripped their spiritual insights in portraying their hopes and fears for the future, both in this life and in the life to come. But such excesses should not blind us to the real contribution which these men made to the unveiling of religious truth. It is much too facile a judgment to 'write them off' in the way that R. T. Herford does, for example, as unworthy imitators of prophecy who

[1] See pp. 16ff.

have no real contribution of their own to make to the revelation of true religion. Concerning the writers of the Book of Enoch he says, '(They) drew gorgeous pictures of the courts of heaven, spoke of the myriads of angels, the exceeding majesty of him who ruled them all, but they added nothing to the thought of God as the greatest of the prophets had left it. Certainly the prophets had had no glimpse, or no clear vision, of the future life, and certainly the writers of Enoch had much to say about it. But again, only by way of embellishing an idea already there, not by way of adding to it. . . . The writers of Enoch were not prophets, and prediction in their hands became not a creative, but a merely imitative function.'[1] However true in part this statement may be with reference to the writers of Enoch, it is not altogether fair as a judgment of the apocalyptic writers generally. Their development of predictive prophecy indicates an independence of thought and a creative power by whose means fresh insights are given into the hidden purposes of God.

So far, then, we have seen that the apocalyptist, like the prophet, 'foretold' the purpose of God in his exposition of predictive prophecy. But is there here anything to compare with the prophetic 'forth-telling' in which he declares God's message, not for some far-off distant time, but for that very day and hour? At first sight no such comparison is at all obvious; the apocalyptist's utterances are so often couched in terms of the forecasting of the End. Such a judgment, however, is only an illusion brought about by the curious device of pseudonymity which gives the reader the impression of 'prediction proper' rather than of 'history in the guise of prediction'.[2] This device should not blind us to the fact that, from the point of view of the apocalyptic writers and indeed from the point of view of the original readers, the End was not in some far off time but rather was imminent. They were vitally interested in eschatology, but to them it was an 'about-to-be-realized' eschatology. The future they foresaw was an immediate future which was about to break into the present. Their message was timely and was directed towards the contemporary situation.

In many instances the writing of these books would be occasioned by a particular situation, such as the persecution carried through by Antiochus Epiphanes in the case of the Book of Daniel, and was directed towards the needs of men within that situation. It is wrong

[1] *Op. cit.*, pp. 216f.
[2] For a consideration of the question of pseudonymity see pp. 127ff.

to think of the apocalyptists simply as prognosticators who used the unfulfilled prophecies of the Old Testament as wires to pick the lock of the distant future. No doubt in some of these books there is a degree of artificial imitation which expresses itself in something like idle curiosity, but for the most part the apocalyptists were prophetic voices who believed that the time spoken of beforehand had now come and that ancient prophecy was on the point of being realized in a manner beyond the understanding of the prophets themselves and of the rank and file of men in their own day. The device of pseudonymity would lend power to their utterances; the story of the past, with its accurate 'predictions' of historical events, would make more graphic and dramatic their message for the present and would inspire in the readers a more confident hope in the fulfilment of God's purpose in terms of the End. Here again the apocalyptists showed themselves to be true successors of the prophets, for just as the prophets had to adapt and develop the earlier message of prophecy to the new conditions of the commercial age in which they lived, so the apocalyptists had to adapt and develop the message of the great prophets to the new conditions of the age of persecution and Hellenization in which they lived. It is a travesty to regard them as a company of bizarre plagiarists imitating and perverting the pure utterances of the prophets. Despite all their strangeness and the exaggerated character of many of their ideas they were men who had a valuable and indeed unique contribution to make to the religious thought not only of the prophets but also of the whole Jewish race.

6. A MESSAGE ETHICALLY BASED

One of the greatest contributions made by the canonical prophets was their teaching concerning the ethical character of religion. God was righteous, therefore his people must be righteous; God was holy, therefore his people must be holy; God was sovereign, therefore his people must obey. They spoke and taught in the succession of Moses and within the context of the covenant at Sinai. They stood for simple faith and social obligation; they denounced social evil, perversion of justice, the oppression and enslavement of the poor, and the luxury and ostentation of the rich.

This 'social ethic' is not characteristic of apocalyptic; but it is not altogether absent. In the Testaments of the XII Patriarchs, for example, there are several references which lay stress on the demand for social righteousness. An instance of this is the Test. of Benj. 10.3: 'Do ye therefore truth and righteousness each one to his neighbour, and judgment unto confirmation, and keep the law of the Lord and his commandments' (cf. also Test. of Iss. 5.1–2; Test. of Dan 5.1–3; Test. of Asher 6.1–6). Throughout this same book moral sentiments are expressed which are at once familiar to the reader of the New Testament,[1] such as forgiving one's neighbour (Test. of Gad 6.3, 7; cf. Matt. 18.21), loving with the whole heart (Test. of Dan 5.3; cf. Matt. 22.37–39) and returning good for evil (Test. of Jos. 8.2; cf. Luke 6.27f.); or even whole phrases like those in Test. of Jos. 1.5f. (cf. Matt. 25.35f.):

> I was beset with hunger, and the Lord himself nourished me.
> I was alone, and God comforted me:
> I was sick, and the Lord visited me:
> I was in prison, and my God showed favour unto me;
> In bonds and he released me.

In almost every book men are faced with personal moral demands involving obedience to the law of God—the demands of righteousness, truth, love, forgiveness, humility, patience, meekness, care for the orphan and the widow, and many more virtues besides. Such matters as the origin of evil (cf. I Enoch 1–36; Jubilees; Test. of XII Patriarchs; II Enoch; Apoc. of Moses; Apoc. of Abraham; II Baruch and II Esdras), the suffering of the righteous and the moral government of the universe (cf. I Enoch 91–104; Pss. of Solomon; II Baruch; II Esdras; Apoc. of Abraham, etc.) are the constant concern of these men who judge history and the end of history in terms of a holy and righteous God.[2]

So concerned were they, however, with the fast-approaching End that eschatology, not ethics, was their consuming interest. But it would be wrong to imagine that these two are mutually exclusive. Behind the eschatological hopes of the apocalyptists was the deep-set conviction that the righteousness of God would at last be vindicated, that good would be rewarded and wickedness punished. However crudely presented these concepts may at times have been, they were founded on strong moral principles which were in turn founded on the moral character of God himself whose holy and righteous

[1] See pp. 55ff. above, however, for the claim made by a number of scholars that the Testaments themselves owe much to Christian influence.

[2] For a detailed examination of the ethical content of the apocalyptic writings see Maldwyn Hughes, *The Ethics of Jewish Apocryphal Literature*, n.d.

purpose for the world could not and would not be frustrated. 'Ethics', writes A. N. Wilder, 'was inextricably implied in the best apocalyptic; it was assumed. The eschatological hope was only for those who were righteous. And it was the ethical consciousness which in the first place demanded the Kingdom. From first to last we should draw our contrasts not between ethics and apocalyptic. . . . But we should draw our contrast between an ethical and a non-ethical apocalyptic.'[1]

It has often been suggested that apocalyptic is a kind of 'escape mechanism' which encourages its readers to give up all hope in this life and its values and to leave everything to supernatural intervention. It cannot be denied that this view is expressed by certain of these writers. But for the most part they were not content simply to await the great *dénouement* of history, with no concern for life's moral issues. On the contrary they recognized the moral demands of God here and now in their own lives and in the lives of their neighbours. The stories and accounts given in the Book of Daniel, for example, show quite clearly that there were many at that time who did not count the cost of martyrdom too great if only they could be counted righteous in God's sight. Their one aim was to obey God and to carry out his commandments (cf. Dan. 9.10f., 14, etc.). Even God's enemies were believed to have this self-same obligation laid upon them; and so in true prophetic fashion Daniel bids king Nebuchadnezzar, 'Break off thy sins by righteousness, and thine iniquities by showing mercy to the poor' (Dan. 4.27).[2]

Just as the apocalyptist, with his visions and dreams of the coming Golden Age, must not be too readily contrasted with the Old Testament prophet, with his emphasis on the moral demands of God, so he must not be too readily contrasted with the Pharisee with his stress on the requirements of the Law of God.[3] To each of them the Torah, and the covenant of which the Torah was a living witness, was central. In the apocalyptic writings this reverence for the Torah frequently expressed itself in a deep ethical concern every bit as sincere as the utterances of orthodox Pharisaic Judaism. 'Apocalyptic', writes W. D. Davies, 'was the outcome of a profound ethical seriousness, which was no less concerned with the observance of the

[1] *Eschatology and Ethics*, 1939, p. 32.

[2] See further H. H. Rowley, *The Relevance of Apocalyptic*, 1944, pp. 13, 162f., and R. H. Charles, *Religious Development between the Old and New Testaments*, 1914, pp. 29–32.

[3] See above, pp. 25ff.

Torah than was Pharisaism.'[1] The same writer points out that even 'the Messianic hope was relevant for ethics';[2] indeed it was commonly believed that 'the law should not only be in force in the Messianic Age, but should be better studied and better observed than ever before'.[3] R. T. Herford, who is at pains to point out the difference between the apocalyptic and the rabbinic literature both in form and content, nevertheless stresses that the link which holds the two ideas together is the fact that each attached importance to ethical ideas which, in the case of the apocalyptic writers no less than the others, were not just an afterthought but were integral to the whole apocalyptic approach.[4]

[1] *Torah in the Messianic Age and/or the Age to Come*, 1952, p. 3, n. 4.
[2] *Ibid.*, p. 48.
[3] G. F. Moore, *Judaism*, vol. I, 1932, p. 271.
[4] Cf. R. T. Herford, *op. cit.*, pp. 171, 178. For the ethical character of the last judgment see below, pp. 380ff.

IV

CHARACTERISTICS OF THE APOCALYPTIC WRITINGS

I. SOME GENERAL MARKS OF APOCALYPTIC

We have observed in the preceding chapter that apocalyptic is essentially a development of Old Testament prophecy and that the transition from the one type of literature to the other was not sudden or without previous preparation. On the contrary, distinctly apocalyptic tendencies can be traced in post-exilic prophecy from the time of Ezekiel onwards. The Book of Daniel, when it appears, does not represent an entirely new type of literature in Israel. It is born out of the past and its parentage is readily recognizable. It has the prophetic tradition as its father and faith in the ultimate triumph of God in times of peril and persecution as its mother. But though recognizable as 'the child of prophecy', apocalyptic develops traits which mark it out from its forebears. Despite its likeness to prophecy, it is nevertheless in many respects a new creation with a character and 'personality' of its own.

The character of Jewish apocalyptic throughout the inter-testamental period is complex in the extreme; there are considerable differences between one book and another, not least between the Book of Daniel and those that follow it in the apocalyptic tradition. There is, however, a homogeneity about it which justifies its classification as a distinct literary *corpus*. It is not always easy to define in what this homogeneity consists for, although it reveals certain fairly well-defined characteristics, apocalyptic is recognizable even when some of its formal characteristics are absent. It may be said to consist rather in a religious mood or temper which is different from, though related to, that of prophecy. Thus, despite the close connection between prophecy and apocalyptic, the reader is conscious of a separation between them which is perhaps greater than the difference between the pre-exilic and the post-exilic expressions of prophecy itself.

We shall consider presently certain formal characteristics which may be said to be representative of this type of literature; others of a more incidental nature may be mentioned which together build up that varied 'mood' which goes under the name of 'apocalyptic'. J. Lindblom, for example, suggests the following list: transcendentalism, mythology, cosmological survey, pessimistic historical surveys, dualism, division of time into periods, teaching of Two Ages, numerology, pseudo-ecstasy, artificial claims to inspiration, pseudonymity, and esoterism.[1] To these might be added the idea of the unity of history and the conception of cosmic history which treats of earth and heaven; the notion of primordiality with its revelations concerning creation and the fall of men and angels; the source of evil in the universe and the part played in this by angelic powers; the conflict between light and darkness, good and evil, God and Satan; the emergence of a transcendent figure called 'the Son of Man'; the development of belief in life after death with its various compartments of Hell, Gehenna, Paradise and Heaven and the increasing significance of the individual in resurrection, judgment and eternal bliss. These various 'marks' belong to apocalyptic not in the sense that they are essential to it or are to be found in every apocalyptic writing, but rather in the sense that, in whole or in part, they build up an *impression* of a distinct kind which conveys a particular *mood* of thought and belief.

E. Stauffer acknowledges the diversified character of the apocalyptic writings and the ambiguity of the word 'apocalyptic' itself when used in different contexts. He defines it in a strictly theological sense to signify 'that pre-Christian theology of history' characterized by four presuppositions. These are the principles of primordiality, conflict, eschatology and universalism. Jewish apocalyptic is vitally concerned about 'the last things', but its interest is focused on 'the beginning' as well as 'the end'. It traces back to creation and the fall the beginnings of 'salvation-history' which gives the clue to human history which in turn gives the clue to cosmic history. Apocalyptic is thus concerned not only with the history of Israel and the surrounding

[1] Cf. *Die Jesaja-Apokalypse*, 1938, pp. 101f., quoted by S. B. Frost, *op. cit.*, p. 146, n. 14, and by H. H. Rowley, *op. cit.*, p. 23, n. 2.

nations but also with history which treats of men and angels, earth and heaven, the planets and the stars. The age-long story, from the beginning to the end, has a single theme—the dramatic conflict between the kingdom of God and the kingdom of Satan; thus there emerged in apocalyptic an 'antagonistic' conception of history and the world in which demonology was incorporated into the monotheistic faith of Judaism.[1] The four principles enunciated by Stauffer might readily be increased to include another two, 'determinism' and 'supernaturalism'. The apocalyptic view of history is essentially deterministic;[2] its view of the future tends to become more and more supramundane, and its conception of the End is generally cataclysmic in character. God has set a limit to the powers of evil in the world; the era of conflict will soon be over; the triumph of God's predetermined purpose will provide the key to all life's mysteries and problems. This triumph will come, not by a gradual transformation of the universe and not by a whittling down of the power of evil, but by a supernatural and catastrophic intervention. This intervention will take the form of a great crisis, usually seen as about to happen in the writer's own day. God will break into history in a mighty act of judgment and establish his kingdom. This kingdom may be established, as in the prophets, on the present earth; but the tendency is for it to assume a supramundane character. The final triumph of God is a supernatural event in which the cosmic powers of evil are destroyed and his predetermined purpose is brought to its consummation. History is thus interpreted not simply in terms of 'the End' but also in terms of 'the above'; terrestrial history is a transcript of celestial history; the triumph of God on earth reflects his victory over 'principalities and powers in heavenly places'.[3]

These various characteristics or marks of apocalyptic give some indication of the difference in theological outlook between the apocalyptists and their prophetic predecessors. Most of these will be considered in more detail in Part Three of this book where the peculiar teaching of the apocalyptists will be examined at greater length.

In this chapter we shall examine certain features which may be said to characterize the *literature* of the apocalyptists as distinct from their *teaching*. They are these: it is esoteric in character, literary in form, symbolic in language and pseudonymous in authorship. All these factors cast light upon the method adopted by the apocalyptists

[1] Cf. *New Testament Theology*, English ed., 1955, pp. 19, 258.
[2] See further pp. 230ff. [3] See pp. 238, 244ff.

in the presentation of their message and at the same time underline still further the distinction between these writers and the Old Testament prophets.

2. ESOTERIC IN CHARACTER

The apocalyptic books claim to be revelations or disclosures of divine secrets made known to certain illustrious individuals of the past who subsequently recorded them in their secret or 'hidden' books for the instruction and encouragement of the righteous and elect among God's people. These secrets are usually made known to the seer in a dream or vision in which he is rapt to Heaven or Hades. Quite frequently this takes the form of a translation either in the spirit or in the body into Heaven where the seer is introduced to the eternal secrets of the divine purpose or even into the very presence of God himself.[1] Sometimes, too, an angelic interpreter is introduced who guides the seer in his heavenly journeyings and explains to him the meaning of things in heaven and earth.[2] The vision may consist of a review of world history right up to the time in which the writer is supposed to have lived; at other times it takes the form of prediction and relates to the future destiny of the world, the coming of God's kingdom, the judgment of the world, the punishment of the wicked and the reward of the righteous; at other times it uncovers the mysteries of the other world with its compartments for the saved and the damned, it explains the movements and functions of the heavenly bodies and reveals the secrets of the thunder, the lightning, the wind and the dew.

In three of these books—I Enoch, Jubilees and the Testaments of the XII Patriarchs—reference is made to 'heavenly tablets' on which are recorded the secrets of the ages which a few highly privileged people have from time to time been permitted to read and copy out into their own secret books. In I Enoch it is said that these 'heavenly tablets' record 'all the deeds of mankind . . . to the remotest generations' (81.2); they foretell the whole history of the world

[1] For an examination of the psychology of apocalyptic inspiration see ch. VI, where it is indicated (pp. 168f.) that this idea of translation is in some sense a development of the Old Testament idea of the heavenly Council in which the prophet shares the secret counsel of God.

[2] Compare the part played by angelic interpreters in Ezekiel and Zechariah, especially Zech. 4.

(93.2) and in particular recount the unrighteousness which will come upon the earth (106.19; 107.1). They are called 'the holy books' or 'the books of the holy ones' (103.2) by whose means the angels learn of the future (107.1) and so are able to prepare for the recompense of the righteous and the wicked (103.2f.; 106.19; 108.7). Enoch himself is bidden to 'read what is written therein, and mark every individual fact' (81.1) so that he may be able to transmit what he reads to the faithful upon earth. This same idea is to be found also in Jubilees where it is said of Jacob, for example, that at Bethel he 'saw in a vision of the night, and behold an angel descended from heaven with seven tablets in his hands, and he gave them to Jacob, and he read them and knew all that was written therein which would befall him and his sons throughout all ages' (32.21–22).[1] These same tablets predict the nature of the coming judgment (5.13) and the lot of the righteous in the messianic kingdom (23.30–32); there, too, the righteous are recorded as God's friends and the wicked as his enemies in preparation for the day of reckoning (30.21–22). For the most part, however, the 'heavenly tablets' in Jubilees form what R. H. Charles calls 'the statute book of the Theocracy'.[2] They record ritual and criminal laws[3] some of which were inscribed there and observed in heaven before being made known on earth. Only by degrees were they copied out and made known to men. Some of these teachings were openly published, but many were revealed to the patriarchs in secret books and transmitted by them to later generations (cf. 1.27; 32.21–22; 45.16). In the Testaments of the XII Patriarchs there are only three references to these 'heavenly tablets' which have more or less the same significance as in Jubilees. Not only do they predict future events (cf. Test. of Asher 7.5) which are determined beforehand by God (cf. Test. of Asher 2.10; Test. of Levi 5.4); they also record beforehand certain ritual laws which God reveals to men on the earth (cf. Test. of Asher 2.10).

The apocalyptic writers indicate that these divine revelations—disclosed in direct visions, by angelic mediation or on the 'heavenly tablets'—were written down by the ancient seers and preserved in their sacred books. Like the 'heavenly tablets' themselves these books

[1] This same incident is recorded in the Prayer of Joseph of which fragments have been preserved by Origen, Eusebius and others.

[2] *The Book of Enoch*, 1912, p. 92.

[3] Cf. 3.8–44; 4.5; 6.17–18; 15.25; 16.9, 16–29; 18.18–19; 24.33; 28.6; 30.9; 32.2ff.; 33.10; 49.1ff.; 50.6–13.

revealed not only what had been, but also what would be and related the whole purpose of God for the universe from the creation to the End-time. They had been hidden away for many generations and handed down in a long line of secret tradition, faithfully preserved until 'the last days'. These hidden books were now being revealed to the people of God! The fact that they were now at last being made known was a sure sign that the End was near. In them the faithful would find the secrets of the ages and be assured of the speedy fulfilment of God's eternal purpose for his people Israel and indeed for his whole creation.

This idea of esoteric knowledge contained in hidden books is found elsewhere, of course, in other writings of this time. Thus Josephus tells us that the Essenes had their own sacred writings and that from their study of ancient books they learned, for example, the art of medicine; the members of the sect must swear never to divulge the contents of their secret books or the names of the angels or indeed any of their secret doctrines; they made a special study of the writings of the prophets and were accurate in their predictions of the future.[1] Even more intriguing information is given in the Dead Sea Scrolls concerning the esoteric character of the Qumran sect. This is shown, for example, in their use of certain cryptic devices in the copying of their sacred books. J. T. Milik refers to the use of two different alphabets with arbitrarily chosen signs which replace the normal Hebrew characters, and of one particular manuscript where the writing runs from left to right and not, as in Hebrew, from right to left, and where Greek or Phoenician letters are occasionally inserted in place of their Hebrew equivalents.[2] These sacred books were copied and preserved in readiness for the day when God would visit his people in the last times.

The apocalyptists were convinced that the tradition in which they stood was of great antiquity and that in their secret books they were simply passing on what they themselves had received from ancient times. 'It is of these things the Most High has spoken since the days that were aforetime from the beginning' (II Esd. 9.4). There is evidence in these writings for at least two and perhaps three main lines of secret tradition concerning the crises of world history associated with the names of Enoch (with Noah), Moses (with Ezra) and possibly Daniel.

[1] Cf. *War* II.viii.6, 7, 12. [2] Cf. *op. cit.*, p. 115.

The Enoch tradition is represented by the extant Ethiopic Enoch (I Enoch), the Secrets of Enoch (II Enoch) and the Hebrew Book of Enoch (III Enoch) and is supplemented by the Book of Jubilees. In these writings, which are no doubt only part of a much larger literature, Enoch plays a central role in receiving revelations of divine secrets which he passes on to future generations. In I Enoch the patriarch recounts to his son Methuselah all the things he has seen in the 'heavenly tablets' and writes them down faithfully. Thereupon he commands his son, 'Preserve the books from thy father's hands and (see) that thou deliver them to the generations of the world' (82.1, cf. 107.3; 108.1ff.). These secret books are to be transmitted from generation to generation in various languages (104.11) for the consolation and recompense of the righteous (104.13). Sinners will alter and pervert their words and will write books of their own, enforcing heathen doctrine. But near the time of the End the secret books will be given to the generation for whom they had been preserved; they will be revealed to 'the righteous and wise and become a cause of joy and uprightness and much wisdom' (104.12, cf. Dan. 12.4, 9, 10), for they are a sign that the End is near and the kingdom of God is at hand (104.13). Somewhat the same picture is given in II Enoch where it is said that the secret books of Enoch, together with 'the writings of thy fathers, Adam, Seth, Enos, Kainan, Malaleel, and Jared, thy father' are to be distributed 'from generation to generation, and from nation to nation' (33.9–10, cf. also 47.2, 3; 48.7–9; 54.1ff.; 65.5). They are in the hands of mortal men, but God has instructed two of his angels to guard them until the time comes for them to be revealed (33.11–12). They will remain hidden and not be required until the last age (33.11); but when at last they are made known the righteous will know that the promised day is about to dawn (35.2–3).

This same tradition is noted also in the Book of Jubilees, where it is said of Enoch, 'He was the first among men that are born on earth who learnt writing and knowledge and wisdom and who wrote down the signs of heaven[1] according to the number of their months in a book' (4.17).[2]

[1] This refers to the twelve signs of the Zodiac which correspond to the twelve solar months of the year.

[2] There is evidence of this same tradition even outside the apocalyptic literature, as in Ben Sira 44.16, where Enoch is described as 'a sign of *knowledge* to all generations'.

The figure of Noah, as we have seen, features quite prominently in this complex Enoch tradition alongside the figure of Enoch himself to whom he has access and from whom he learns the divine secrets. R. H. Charles maintains that the Noah legend is older than that of Enoch and that the latter was built up on the ruins of the former.[1] Whether this is so or not, it is clear that Noah and Enoch belong to the same complex apocalyptic tradition.

The Book of Jubilees is particularly interesting in this connection. For example, the writer knows of a tradition which stretched back to Noah and through him to Enoch: 'Thus did Enoch . . . command Methuselah, his son, and Methuselah his son Lamech, and Lamech commanded me (Noah) all the things which his fathers commanded him. And I also will give you commandment, my sons, as Enoch commanded his son in the first jubilees' (7.38–39). Enoch thus passes on to Noah the fruits of his knowledge and wisdom and reveals to him those secrets which he himself has learned from God such as knowledge of the coming Flood and the need for the building of an Ark. Elsewhere we are told that he is taught the art of healing by the angels because of his resistance to the demons: 'And we explained to Noah all the medicines of their diseases, together with their seductions, how he might heal them with herbs of the earth. And Noah wrote down all things in a book as we instructed him concerning every kind of medicine' (10.12–13).[2] Before he died Noah gave these secret books to his eldest son Shem (10.14). The record does not say what Shem did with them, but he may well have passed them on to Abraham for, according to rabbinic tradition, Abraham attended the school of Shem.[3] In any case, Abraham receives what his fathers have written and passes it on to his sons. Addressing his son Isaac he says, 'Thus I have found it written in the books of my forefathers, and in the words of Enoch, and in the words of Noah' (21.10). At last the ancient writings come down to Jacob who hands them over to Levi: 'And he gave all his books and the books of his fathers to Levi his son that he might preserve them and renew them for all his children unto this day' (45.16). These words no doubt reflect the

[1] Cf. *The Book of Enoch*, 1912, pp. xlvi–xlvii.

[2] See p. 24 for the books of medicine known among the Essenes.

[3] Cf. R. H. Charles, *The Book of Jubilees*, 1902, p. 134, where it is pointed out that according to another tradition the knowledge of the calendar was passed on from Adam to Enoch, then to Noah, then to Shem and then to Abraham (cf. *Pirke de R. Eliezer* 8).

convictions of the author of Jubilees and indicate that he may have been a priest himself and a descendant of Levi.[1]

These accounts of Enoch and Noah as recipients of divine secrets recall the ancient belief that the antediluvians were men of superior wisdom. Certainly, the legends surrounding Enoch, such as we find in the apocalyptic literature, cannot be explained by reference to the Book of Genesis alone. The indications are that these legends had close affinities with mythological material of a Babylonian origin and that they were passed on as part of a living tradition into Jewish apocalyptic itself. According to Genesis 5 Enoch was seventh in line from Adam. Now, according to Berossus[2] the seventh in the list of the antediluvian Babylonian kings was Edoranchus or Euedorachus who is almost certainly the same as Enmeduranki, king of Sippar, the sacred city of the sun-god Shamash.[3] This legendary figure is presented as the founder of a hereditary guild of priestly diviners. The gods, we are told, welcomed him into their company, taught him the mysteries of heaven and earth and initiated him into the diviner's art which he then passed on to his son and to his son's sons after him. In the Genesis story not only is Enoch welcomed into the presence of God (5.22), he is also said to live for 365 years (5.23) which is a much shorter time than those of the other patriarchs mentioned in this same chapter. It is perhaps not altogether accidental that the years of Enoch's life correspond to the number of days in the solar year. It is quite likely that, on the basis of the biblical story and of Babylonian legendary material, Enoch came to be recognized in Jewish circles as the Hebrew counterpart of Enmeduranki and that such accounts of his initiation into the hidden mysteries of heaven and earth were the beginning of that developed tradition which we find in the Enochic literature. H. Ludin Jansen, in tracing the Enoch tradition back into Babylonian sources, argues that Enoch has affinities with Ea, who, together with Anu and Bel, were descendants

[1] It has been suggested that these words may allude to the work of restoration carried out by scribes and priests in the years following the conquests of Judas who 'gathered together for us all those writings that had been scattered by reason of the war that befell' (II Mac. 2.14): cf. H. J. Schonfield, *Secrets of the Dead Sea Scrolls*, 1956, pp. 9, 89.

[2] A Babylonian priest of the third century BC whose works are known in quotations from Josephus, Eusebius and George the Syncellus.

[3] For a treatment of the relation between Enoch and Enmeduranki see *Die Keilinschriften und das AT.*, by Zimmern and Winckler, 3rd ed., 1902, pp. 532ff.; J. Skinner, *Genesis*, ICC, 1910, p. 132; S. R. Driver, *The Book of Genesis*, 12th ed., 1926, pp. 78f.

of the original two deities, Apsu and Tiamat; and also with the Primal Wise Man who may be regarded as the earthly counterpart of Ea.[1] These conceptions, together with the biblical Enoch tradition, are sufficient to explain the complex Enoch figure which comes to light in the Jewish apocalyptic literature.[2] Whatever the explanation of its origin may be, it is clear that the secret tradition associated with the name of Enoch was both composite and ancient and was treasured in Jewish apocalyptic circles as part of their religious heritage.

A second line of apocalyptic tradition is connected with the name of Moses and also with the name of Ezra, the 'second Moses'. In the Assumption of Moses, for example, Moses instructs Joshua in these words: 'Receive thou this writing that thou mayest know how to preserve the books which I shall deliver unto thee: and thou shalt set them in order and anoint them with oil of cedar and put them away in earthen vessels in the place which he made from the beginning of the creation of the world' (1.16f., cf. 10.11; 11.1). The secret books which Moses gives to Joshua are to be kept preserved and hidden 'until the day of repentance in the visitation wherewith the Lord shall visit thee in the consummation of the end of the days' (1.18). Again, in the Book of Jubilees the account is given of a secret tradition made known to Moses on Sinai in which he is shown all the events of history both past and future: 'Do thou write down for thyself all these words which I declare unto thee on this mountain, the first and the last, which shall come to pass in all the divisions of the days . . . until I descend and dwell with them throughout eternity' (1.26, cf. 1.4). God then bids 'the angel of the presence' help Moses to write down those things that have happened 'from the beginning of creation till my sanctuary has been built among them from all eternity' (1.27, cf. 1.29). The reference in these verses is presumably to the secret writings contained in the Book of Jubilees itself with its apocalyptic tradition associated with the name of Moses.[3] Elsewhere reference is made to another writing which is called 'the book of the first law . . . which I have written for thee' (6.22, cf. 30.12, 21; 50.6). This is presumably the Pentateuch which

[1] See further p. 346.

[2] Cf. *Die Henochgestalt: Eine vergleichende Religionsgeschichtliche Untersuchung*, 1939; also S. B. Frost, *Old Testament Apocalyptic*, 1952, pp. 75, 165.

[3] There is evidence for the fact that at one time there existed a larger body of apocalyptic writings bearing the name of Moses than is now available. Cf. E. Schürer, *The Jewish People in the Time of Jesus Christ*, div. II, vol. III, 1890, pp. 80ff.

Moses also received from God on Mount Sinai; by implication the apocalyptic tradition as recorded in the Book of Jubilees is regarded by the author as 'the book of the second law'. That is, Moses under God is the author not only of the Pentateuch but also of the apocalyptic tradition.

If this interpretation is correct, we have here an account which corresponds to that given in II Esdras 14, where, as we have seen,[1] Ezra 'the second Moses' receives by divine revelation the twenty-four books of canonical Scripture which he has to publish openly and the seventy books representing the apocalyptic tradition which he has to keep secret. The latter are to be kept hidden away in a secret place until the time appointed when at last he will 'deliver them to the wise among thy people' (14.46, cf. 12.37–38). G. H. Box suggests that 'the number seventy doubtless has a symbolical significance, denoting what is large and comprehensive',[2] and includes not only apocalyptic writings, known and unknown, which appeared under the name of Moses, but a much wider range of apocalyptic works including II Esdras itself and this particular chapter in which these very events are recorded. It may be, however, that the choice of the number 'seventy' has a more subtle symbolical meaning than this. Several times over in the course of this chapter the word 'secret' is used with reference to these books (cf. 14.6, 26, 45). It is of interest to observe that the letters of the Hebrew word *sōd* (*swd*), meaning 'secret', have the numerical value 'seventy' (s = 60; w = 6; d = 4). It may be that this is more than coincidence and that it influenced the writer's choice of this particular number.[3] Once more the esoteric character of the apocalyptic writings is underlined.

A third possible line of apocalyptic tradition is that associated with the name of Daniel. The evidence for an ancient secret tradition of this kind is less certain than in the case of Enoch and Moses; but there is at least some indication that the Daniel of Jewish apocalyptic

[1] See pp. 28, 85ff. [2] *Op. cit.*, p. 305.

[3] Cf. Bab. Talmud *'Erubin* 65a, where use is made of the word *swd* to indicate the number 70. I owe this suggestion to P. R. Weis through H. H. Rowley in private correspondence.

It may be, of course, that the reference to the number 70 is to be traced much further back into Old Testament usage, where it is of fairly frequent occurrence and has sometimes a formulistic character, cf. the age of Kenan (Gen. 5.12) and Terah (Gen. 11.26); the number of the sons of Jacob (Gen. 46.27; Ex. 1.5), of Gideon (Judg. 8.30), of Abdon (Judg. 12.14), of Ahab (II Kings 10.1); the number of the elders of Israel (Ex. 24.1, 9; Num. 11.16ff.); the duration of Tyre's subjugation (Isa. 23.17) and of Israel's captivity (Jer. 25.11f.; Dan. 9.2; Zech. 7.5).

may reflect an ancient hero of that name known for many centuries in Hebrew, and perhaps also in Gentile, legend. The existence of such a legend is confirmed by the Book of Ezekiel, where the name, in the form *Dan'el*, appears in 14.14, 20 and 28.3. In 14.14, 20 he is associated with Noah and Job, who together are praised for their righteousness and for their powers of intercession. In 28.3 reference is made to his wisdom and to his knowledge of secret lore; 'Behold thou (the city of Tyre) art wiser than Daniel; there is no secret that they can hide from thee.' Further confirmation that there existed among the Hebrews an ancient legend concerning a hero named Dan'el has been given by the Ras Shamra tablets discovered in the north of Syria at Ugarit and dating from about the fourteenth century BC. In the legend of Aqhat[1] mention is made of one, Dan'el, a righteous man who cares for the widows and the orphans in their distress. The name is spelt here as in the Book of Ezekiel and may indicate that that prophet was familiar with Phoenician literature of this kind. There seems little doubt that the Dan'el of the Ras Shamra tablets is the same as the Dan'el of Ezekiel and that these two sources indicate the prevalence over many centuries of a legendary figure of that name.

It is not as certain, however, that this legendary figure can be identified with the Daniel of apocalyptic tradition, but the evidence is such as to make this quite probable. Of the three legendary figures mentioned by Ezekiel—Noah, Dan'el and Job—Noah is familiar to the Jewish writers of the second century BC as part of the Enoch-tradition. Job, too, is a familiar figure at this time as the reference in Ben Sira 49.8f. indicates.[2] There, in a brief allusion to the Book of Ezekiel, the writer picks out this very passage dealing with the three wise men of old and in particular mentions Job 'who maintained all the ways of righteousness' (49.9). The question is, Did the writer of the Book of Daniel (dating also from the second century BC) have in mind this passage in Ezekiel when he chose the name of Daniel as the hero of his stories? This seems likely, for the writer of this great apocalyptic work was certainly familiar with the writings of Ezekiel[3]

[1] Cf. J. B. Pritchard, *Ancient Near Eastern Texts relating to the Old Testament*, 1950, pp. 149ff.; D. Winton Thomas, *Documents from Old Testament Times*, 1958, pp. 124ff.

[2] Cf. also the midrashic Testament of Job which probably dates from the first century BC. Cf. C. C. Torrey, *The Apocalyptic Literature*, pp. 140ff., and K. Kohler, 'Testament of Job', *JE*, vol. VII, 1904, pp. 200–2.

[3] Cf. the references in 7.9; 8.9, 17; 9.12, 16; 10.4f., 6, 11. For other similarities see pp. 341f.

and in particular with the oracle contained in Ezekiel 31 (with this compare Dan. 4.10–12, 20) which is closely associated with the oracle in Ezekiel 28 where allusion is made to the man Dan'el.[1] The very fact that the ancient Dan'el was renowned for his righteousness and wisdom in revealing secrets may have had a special appeal to our writer and would provide an added reason for the adoption of his name. For here, too, Daniel and his companions are renowned both for their righteousness and their wisdom and are described as being 'skilful in all wisdom and cunning in knowledge and understanding science', being instructed in 'the learning and the tongue of the Chaldeans' (1.4).[2] If, in fact, the writer did take over the name of Dan'el from Ezekiel, he may well at the same time have taken over with it associations of a legendary character, and although such legendary material is not as obvious in the Book of Daniel as it is in, say, the Book of Enoch, the very name would carry with it certain legendary overtones and suggest the book's connection with ancient tradition.

As in the other two lines of apocalyptic tradition already mentioned so also in Daniel, the seer is bidden by God to 'shut up the words, and seal the book, even to the time of the end' (12.4, cf. 8.26; 11.35; 12.9). The prophecies and predictions contained in the book may appear strange and puzzling to the reader, but when 'the time of the end' at last arrives, then 'they that be wise shall understand' (12.10).

But the esoteric character of Daniel is illustrated even more clearly by the contents of the book which are often shrouded in mystery, and by its very choice of language. In chapter 2, for example, Daniel is summoned into Nebuchadnezzar's presence to recall the king's troublesome dream concerning the great image and to give its interpretation. He thereupon addresses Nebuchadnezzar in these words: 'The secret which the king hath demanded can neither wise men, enchanters, magicians, nor soothsayers, show unto the king; but there is a God in heaven that revealeth secrets . . . This secret is not revealed to me for any wisdom that I have more than any living, but to the intent that the interpretation may be made known to the king' (2.27–30). These verses are of singular significance for our

[1] Cf. E. W. Heaton, *The Book of Daniel*, 1956, p. 27.

[2] These same qualities of righteousness and wisdom are also associated with the name of Daniel in the History of Susanna. He appears again as a figure of wisdom in the stories of Bel and the Dragon.

understanding of the apocalyptic method, and in particular three words in them. These are 'secret' (or 'mystery'), 'interpretation' and 'wisdom'. In the Book of Daniel the word 'secret' or 'mystery' (Aramaic *raz*) occurs nine times,[1] all of them in the Aramaic section. It is a loan-word from Persian and is translated in the Greek Versions by *mystērion*. This is a key word not only in Daniel but also in the Qumran texts, where it occurs fairly frequently, together with the word *sōd*, to signify a divine mystery whose interpretation has been given to a select few. The word 'interpretation' (Hebrew *pēšer*, Aramaic *pěšar*) is also found frequently in Daniel and in the Qumran texts; in the former it occurs no fewer than thirty times, all of them once more in the Aramaic section of the book. Among the Qumran Covenanters the divine purpose is made known by the Teacher of Righteousness who is able to give the true interpretation of the mysteries communicated by God to his prophets of old. In somewhat the same way the authors of Daniel and the other apocalyptic writings believe that they, too, have been given the task of interpreting God's sacred mysteries, particularly those which appear in the form of unfulfilled prophecies within the pages of sacred Scripture.[2] But, as Daniel says, this revelation of divine secrets cannot be brought about by merely human wisdom; it requires the gift of divine wisdom for its accomplishment. It is significant that not only in the Book of Daniel but also in the only other occurrence of the word 'interpretation' in the Hebrew Scriptures (Eccles 8.1) it is closely associated with the idea of wisdom. Thus, throughout the apocalyptic books, the apocalyptist is presented not simply as a prophet declaring the coming of God's kingdom, but also as a wise man uncovering the mysteries of God's purpose.[3]

The three names associated with these three lines of secret tradition—Enoch (with Noah), Moses (with Ezra) and Daniel—do not exhaust the pseudonyms used by the apocalyptic writers, but they indicate three important lines of secret apocalyptic tradition which provided an example for others to copy. Hence there appeared from time to time writings which traced their revelations back to men like Abraham, the Patriarchs, Solomon, Isaiah, Baruch, etc. No doubt

[1] Cf. Daniel 2.18, 19, 27, 28, 29, 30, 47 (*bis*); 4.9 (4.6 in Aramaic text). It also appears in Ben Sira 8.18 ('Before a stranger do nothing secret') in a purely non-technical sense and with no eschatological reference attaching to it.

[2] See ch. VII.

[3] For further consideration of the relation between the apocalyptist and the sage see pp. 175ff.

much that is written here is imitative of what went before. Nevertheless these writers believed that what they had written had been transmitted to them from the past and could be traced back ultimately to the great hero in whose name they wrote.[1] They saw fit to shape or amend or enlarge the traditional material they had received; nevertheless they were conscious of the fact that they were not simply creators of a tradition, but also inheritors of it. What they declared in their writings they had already received as part of a rich and treasured heritage.

3. LITERARY IN FORM

Both the prophets and the apocalyptists believed that they had been given a message by God to deliver to their people. But their methods of making that message known were quite different. The prophet, for the most part, declared his message by word of mouth which might subsequently be put into writing by himself or by his disciples or by editors at a much later date. The apocalyptist, on the other hand, remained completely concealed behind his message which he wrote down for the faithful among God's people to read. God's command to the prophet was, 'Thou shalt speak unto them this word' (Jer. 13.12); his command to the apocalyptist was, 'What thou seest, write in a book' (Rev. 1.11). The prophet addressed his listeners with an authoritative 'Thus saith the Lord' (Isa. 7.7, etc.); the apocalyptist, claiming a like authority,[2] bade his readers, 'Receive this writing that thou mayest know how to preserve the books which I shall deliver unto thee' (Ass. of Moses 1.16). This stress on the literary presentation of divine truth is characteristic of the whole apocalyptic school of thought.

It is true that in the post-exilic period prophecy itself tended to become literary in form and many anonymous oracles appeared whose historical situation was completely lost to sight. But it is significant that the need was felt for these oracles, in course of time, to be attached to those of 'living' prophecy and to come under the names of known prophets of the past who had spoken in the name of the Lord. The method of apocalyptic, however, was different even from that of 'literary' prophecy of this kind, for it purported to be a message from the distant past which, as we have seen, had been preserved throughout many generations. It might have been possible

[1] For the bearing of this on the question of pseudonymity see pp. 133f.
[2] See pp. 158ff.

for the apocalyptists to convey their message by word of mouth as conveyors and interpreters of an ancient tradition which they had received from their fathers. Indeed, it is likely that there was an oral stage of apocalyptic teaching and that such teaching continued right on into the inter-testamental period. But the literary form was eminently suitable for their purpose. By the beginning of the second century BC divine revelation had come to be associated in people's minds not so much with the spoken as with the written word; the Law and the Prophets, for example, had by this time assumed their final literary shape and had acquired an authority through which God's voice could be clearly heard. It was fitting that fresh revelations should also appear in literary form. Men were suspicious of the spoken word. Might they not with greater assurance turn to the written word for new revelations of truth? This was an age which witnessed a prolific literary output not only among the Gentiles, but also among the Jews; not only among the Jews of the Dispersion, but also among the Jews of Palestine.[1] Ecclesiastes, for example, writing near the beginning of our period, could say, 'Of the making of many books there is no end' (12.12). Among the Gentiles there were many stories of secret books, some of which were said to have been found in sacred places or to have fallen from heaven. The Sibylline Oracles, for example, were of this kind and were extremely popular throughout the pagan world. This whole mental atmosphere no doubt influenced the apocalyptists in choosing the medium of 'secret' books through which to make known their message. These, moreover, were years fraught with danger for the Jews, who were severely persecuted because of their faith. To express one's hopes openly—especially if they were inflammatory, as the apocalyptists' hopes often were—would only call down the wrath of the enemy. It was much safer, and in the end more convincing, to express these things in mysterious and secret writings which only the initiated among God's people could understand.

Enough has been said to show that apocalyptic, though it is a literary production, has behind it a wealth of traditional material. This explains why Enoch, for example, appears as a composite and complicated figure corresponding neither to a historical personage nor yet to a purely literary creation; it is the deposit of several traditions going back into antiquity, some Jewish and others Gentile in

[1] Cf. E. Schürer, *op. cit.*, div. II, vol. III; R. H. Pfeiffer, *History of New Testament Times*, 1949, pp. 101ff., 197ff.

origin. But it is part of the literary technique of apocalyptic to present such traditional material in the form of a vision vouchsafed to the seer himself; and although there may well have been genuine visionary experience behind the record of this vision,[1] for the most part it belongs to this style of writing to present the apocalyptic teaching, be it traditional or original, in the form of a divine revelation.

The general pattern of apocalyptic remains the same throughout these writings, but ample room is left within them for variations of treatment. R. T. Herford makes the interesting suggestion that just as the writers of I Enoch applied the apocalyptic method to the prophetic literature and the writer of Jubilees applied it to the Torah, so it can be argued that the writer of the Testaments of the XII Patriarchs applied it to the Wisdom literature, thus bringing the three main divisions of the canonical Scriptures under the aegis of apocalyptic.[2] This presentation is perhaps too neat to be true and oversimplifies the case. But it reminds us that within the apocalyptic literature there were several emphases and indeed several types of writing. We have seen that much of it is revelatory or 'apocalyptic' in the strictest sense of the word, containing predictions and descriptions of the future or the other world as they are made known through visions, dreams and the like. The readers are exhorted to take fresh courage and to live in hope that the purpose of God, which runs from the beginning of creation to the end, will soon be fulfilled. Elsewhere it assumes an admonitory character so that a whole book, or sections of a book, take the form of a testament given by a figure of the past to his sons. This testamentary material became a recognized literary form at a fairly early stage in the inter-testamental period.[3] It is illustrated by Enoch's so-called 'Book of Admonitions for his children' contained in I Enoch 92.1–5; 91.1–11, 18–19 where the patriarch counsels his sons and grandsons and encourages them to walk in the way of righteousness. Of the same literary type are the Book of Jubilees, which contains testaments given by Isaac (cf. 31.4–22) and Jacob (cf. 45.14–16), and the Assumption of Moses in which Moses gives instructions to Joshua who will succeed him. The Testaments of the XII Patriarchs, as the name of the book implies, consists of a

[1] See pp. 164ff. [2] Cf. *op. cit.*, p. 234.

[3] Cf. J. Munck, 'Discours d'adieu dans le Nouveau Testament et dans la littérature biblique' in *Aux Sources de la Tradition Chrétienne* (*Mélanges offerts à M. Maurice Goguel*), 1950, p. 157.

number of testaments given in turn by the twelve sons of Jacob who admonish their descendants and urge them to walk before God in righteousness. This type of literature no doubt found its pattern in Scripture in such passages as the Blessing of Jacob in Genesis 49 and the Blessing of Moses in Deuteronomy 33. It would appear to have been a fairly popular literary form at this time not only among the apocalyptists but also among other groups of writers. I Mac. 2.49–70 gives a good illustration. There Mattathias the priest, near the time of his death, reminds his sons of the deeds of their forefathers from Abraham right up to Daniel; with their example before them he exhorts them to be strong and zealous for the law after which he blesses them and is 'gathered to his fathers'. More significant still is the evidence of the so-called *Zadokite Document*. This book consists of two separate documents which are usually referred to as 'The Admonition' and 'The Laws'.[1] The Admonition is a testamentary document in which the speaker, who is not identified, addresses himself to his 'children' (II.14) whom he also describes as 'ye that are in the covenant' (II.2). Reference is made to Noah, Abraham, Isaac, Jacob and their sons (III.1ff.) who are held up either as a warning or as an example to the readers. Somewhat the same literary form is found in the *Genesis Apocryphon*, which in many ways resembles the Book of Jubilees, the patriarchs themselves being the speakers.

Apocalyptic, as we have seen, differs considerably from the halakic form of writing familiar in the rabbinic literature. But this latter is not altogether lacking even in the apocalyptic books themselves, as a reading of the Book of Jubilees, for example, makes quite clear. The author of Jubilees is certainly familiar with the rabbinic method and indeed gives evidence of *halakot* at an earlier stage than the rabbinic sources themselves. Here, too, there is evidence for the influence of that form known as *haggadah*; this may be described as a development of the biblical stories rather than the biblical laws, whose development is represented by *halakah*. The apocalyptic writers were not content simply with making the patriarchs give counsel to their descendants; they were prepared even to modify and adorn the biblical narrative with haggadic comment. They embellished the old stories and glorified the patriarchs so as to make them even more edifying to their readers. A good example of this is the Book of Jubilees itself,[2] which Schürer describes simply as 'a

[1] See Chaim Rabin, *The Zadokite Documents*, 2nd ed., 1958.
[2] Here again the *Genesis Apocryphon* has much in common with Jubilees.

Haggadean commentary' on the Book of Genesis.[1] The writer deals freely with the text of Scripture and interprets its teaching in the spirit of his own age. Elsewhere, as in the Testaments of the XII Patriarchs, the text is liberally sprinkled with legendary anecdotes which have no basis in the canonical Scriptures, but which again set the patriarchs in a heroic light.

4. SYMBOLIC IN LANGUAGE

The apocalyptic literature is marked by a highly dramatic quality whose language and style match the inexpressible scenes which it tries to portray. Such scenes cannot be portrayed in the sober language of common prose; they require for their expression the imaginative language of poetry. But it is poetry quite unlike the restrained language of the Old Testament Scriptures. The apocalyptists give full rein to their imaginations in extravagant and exotic language and in imagery of a fantastic and bizarre kind. To such an extent is this true that symbolism may be said to be the language of apocalyptic. Some of this symbolism no doubt had its origin in the fertile imaginations of the apocalyptists themselves through their experience of dreams, visions and the like. But for the most part they were using stereotyped language and symbols which belonged to a fairly well-defined tradition whose roots went back into the distant past.

Some of this symbolism is taken over directly from the Old Testament, whose imagery and metaphors are adapted and used as material for graphic figurative representation. Much of it, however, has its origin in ancient mythology. This influence is traceable even in the Old Testament itself, but in apocalyptic it is much more fully developed. Over the course of the years a pattern of imagery and symbolism was evolved—indigenous and foreign, traditional and mythological—which became part of the apocalyptists' stock-in-trade. The same figures, images and ideas appear in book after book; but because of the constant adaptation and readaptation of the old figures to convey new interpretations there is no guarantee that they will have the same meaning in two successive books. More often than not the original significance of the symbol or figure is lost altogether; at other times only part of an originally complex picture is used to portray what the writer has in mind; at other times details

[1] Cf. *op. cit.*, div. II, vol. III, p. 135.

are mentioned which have no direct bearing on the matter under discussion, but are given simply because they belong to the tradition or myth which is at that moment being used.[1] Thus, though the imagery and language are for the most part stereotyped, they nevertheless lend themselves to a kaleidoscopic variation in their presentation of the divine mysteries.

An example of the influence of ancient mythology on both the canonical and the apocalyptic writings is to be found in the ancient Babylonian account of a combat between the Creator and a great sea-monster. This myth undergoes considerable modification in the Hebrew tradition, but it is still easily recognizable in several Old Testament passages where the monster is variously described as the Dragon, Leviathan, Rahab or the Serpent.[2] Both in its Babylonian and in its Hebrew form it symbolizes the chaotic deep or cosmic ocean (Hebrew *Tehōm*, Babylonian *Tiāmat*),[3] which is regarded as a place of mystery and evil. At other times it is identified with Egypt (cf. Ps. 87.4), which in several places is described under the figure of a great sea-monster (cf. Ps. 74.13ff.; Ezek. 29.3; 32.2). In Isa. 27.1 there is a significant development, for here the dragon myth is projected into the future: 'In that day the Lord . . . shall slay the dragon that is in the sea.'

This same monster reappears in several apocalyptic writings of various dates and is found also in the rabbinic tradition. In the Testament of Asher, for example, it is said that when the Most High comes to the earth to save Israel and all the Gentiles he will 'break the head of the dragon in the water' (7.3, cf. Ps. 74.13). A more detailed description is given in several other passages where mention is made of two mythical monsters called Behemoth and Leviathan (cf. I Enoch 60.7–9; II Esd. 6.49–52; II Bar. 29.4). These two great creatures, which are described at length in Job 40.15–24 and 41.1–34, are of Babylonian origin and represent the two primaeval monsters of chaos, Tiamat and Kingu of Babylonian mythology.[4] The first reference to them in the apocalyptic writings is in I Enoch 60.7–9

[1] For illustrations see pp. 126, 186.

[2] Dragon (Job 7.12; Ps. 74.13; Isa. 51.9; Ezek. 29.3; 32.2), Leviathan (Job 40.15–24; Pss. 74.14; 104.26; Isa. 27.1), Rahab (Job 9.13; 26.12; Ps. 89.10; Isa. 30.7; 51.9), Serpent (Job 26.13; Isa. 27.1; Amos 9.3).

[3] Cf. Job 7.12; 26.12; 38.8; Ps. 74.13; Isa. 51.10; Hab. 3.8; Amos 7.4. For the power of God over the deep see also Pss. 33.7f.; 93.1ff.; 107.23–32; Jonah 2.5–9, etc. In Gen. 1.2, 6ff., God the Creator saves the world from the power of chaos in the form of the primaeval ocean.

[4] Cf. H. Gunkel, *Schöpfung und Chaos in Urzeit und Endzeit*, 1895, pp. 41–69.

which reads, 'And on that day[1] were two monsters parted, a female monster named Leviathan, to dwell in the abysses of the ocean over the fountains of the waters. But the male is named Behemoth, who occupied with his breast a waste wilderness. . . . And I besought the other angel that he should show me the might of those monsters, how they were parted on one day and cast, the one into the abysses of the sea, and the other unto the dry land of the wilderness.' According to a later report it would seem that both creatures were originally sea-monsters, representing the primaeval ocean, but in course of time they were separated so that, though Leviathan retains its identity as a sea-monster, Behemoth appears as a land-monster as in the Enoch passage just quoted. This is indicated in II Esdras 6 according to which they were both brought into being on the fifth day of creation (6.47): 'Then didst thou preserve two living creatures; the name of the one thou didst call Behemoth and the name of the other thou didst call Leviathan. And thou didst separate the one from the other; for the seventh part, where the water was gathered together, was unable to hold them (both). And thou didst give Behemoth one of the parts which had been dried up on the third day . . . but unto Leviathan thou gavest the seventh part, namely the moist: and thou hast reserved them to be devoured by whom thou wilt and when' (6.49–52). Light is thrown on these last few enigmatic words by the writer of II Baruch, who gives these mythological monsters an eschatological setting and relates them to the appearing of God's Messiah: 'And it will come to pass . . . that the Messiah will then begin to be revealed. And Behemoth will be revealed from his place, and Leviathan will ascend from the sea, those two great monsters which I created on the fifth day of creation, and I kept them until that time; and then they will be for food for all that are left' (29.3–4). Here we have a conflation of two mythical allusions—the idea of an eschatological banquet (cf. Isa. 25.6) and the idea of the dragon being devoured as food (cf. Ezek. 32.4). It is the so-called 'Messianic Banquet' to which reference is made in the Qumran texts,[2] in the New Testament (cf. Luke 13.28–29; 22.30ff.; Rev. 19.9) and in rabbinic tradition.[3] At this banquet, to be cele-

[1] Presumably this refers to the day of creation; but it may have an eschatological reference, since the theme of the preceding verses is that of the coming judgment of God.

[2] See pp. 294, 320.

[3] For a list of references see J. Bloch, *op. cit.*, pp. 97ff.

brated in the messianic age, Behemoth and Leviathan will provide food for all the righteous who remain.

This same myth of the conflict between God and the monster of chaos appears in different guises in several other apocalyptic passages. It is no doubt reflected in Ezekiel's reference to 'Gog of the land of Magog' (chs. 38–39) and in the so-called 'Antichrist legend' which plays a significant part in both Jewish and Christian apocalyptic writings.[1] Sometimes the monster is identified with an historical person or persons. In the *Zadokite Document*, for example, 'the kings of the nations' are described as 'the Serpents' (VIII.10) and in the Psalms of Solomon 'the pride of the dragon' (2.29) alludes to the Roman general Pompey, no doubt under the influence of Jer. 51.34 where Nebuchadnezzar of Babylon is referred to in similar terms. In the Book of Revelation the dragon appears as Satan, the enemy of the Messiah and his saints, who will at last be bound and cast into the abyss (12.9; 20.2); other beasts, associated with this dragon, are in the end also destroyed by the Messiah who appears under the figure of 'a Lamb' (13.1ff.; 14.1ff.).

Another symbol which is to be understood against this mythological background is that of the 'heavenly tablets' to which reference has been made above. These appear in Babylonian sources as 'tablets of destiny' and play a significant part in the New Year ritual in the ceremony of fixing the destinies. Thus, when Marduk defeats the dragon Tiamat the tablets are placed in his hands, signifying that now the power and the victory belong to him. The idea of destiny is closely associated with the 'heavenly tablets' in the Jewish apocalyptic writings, but it is in the Book of Revelation that we find the closest parallel to the Babylonian myth. There 'the Lamb', because he 'hath overcome', is alone able to take the book from the hands of God and break its seven seals; this is the sign of his 'blessing and honour and glory and dominion for ever and ever' (5.1ff., cf. Ezek. 2.9).

Many other symbols throughout these writings have also a mythological origin. Sometimes their meaning, if not their origin, is fairly clear as in the case of Daniel's vision of four great beasts belonging to no recognizable species which come up out of the sea. The first is like a lion with eagles' wings (7.4); the second is like a bear, having three ribs in its mouth (7.5); the third is like a leopard with four wings (7.6); the fourth is a beast with ten horns and great

[1] See pp. 276ff.

iron teeth (7.7). By this strange symbolism the writer depicts the four great Empires of Babylonia, 'Media', Persia and Greece. At other times the significance of the symbol is lost in obscurity, as in the case of 'the sea' from which the four beasts come and 'the four winds' which blow upon it (7.2, cf. II Esd. 13.2). So also with 'the clouds of heaven' on which 'the Son of Man' appears before God (7.14, cf. II Esd. 13.3),[1] or the cloud 'ascending from a very great sea . . . full of black and white waters' symbolizing alternate periods in Israel's history (II Bar. 53.1ff.). Such symbols are part of traditional material inherited from the past whose very obscurity helps to foster an even deeper sense of secrecy and mystery.

Quite apart from those mythical creatures which appear in many forms, the apocalyptists make great use of animal figures of all kinds to symbolize men and nations. This is particularly marked in I Enoch. There the bull, for example, is used as a symbol of the patriarchs from Adam to Isaac (chs. 85–86), though in one passage it represents the Messiah and the members of his kingdom who become white bulls just like Adam (90.37–38). The righteous, such as Moses and Aaron, who come after the patriarchs, are described under the figure of sheep or lambs (89.16, 18).[2] David and Solomon are sheep until they come to the throne, when they become rams (89.45, 48). The Messiah on entering his kingdom is changed from a white bull into a lamb (90.38). Judas Maccabaeus is represented by a ram (90.14) and elsewhere by a great horn (90.9). Both the ram and the horn, common symbols of might and dominion (cf. Ezek. 34.17; 39.18, etc.), are found in other apocalyptic writings also (cf. Dan. 8.3f., etc.). The same kind of language is used also in the Testament of Joseph where the twelve tribes of Israel are symbolized by twelve harts which become twelve sheep (19.1–4) and then by twelve bulls with great horns (19.5–7) in the midst of which is a lamb, the Messiah, who treads his enemies under foot (19.8). Frequent use is made of wild beasts and birds of prey to symbolize the Gentile nations after the manner of Ezek. 39.17ff. In I Enoch 98.10ff., for example, they are described under the figures of lions, tigers, wolves, dogs, hyenas, wild boars, foxes, squirrels, swine, falcons, vultures, kites, eagles and ravens, and in Test. of Jos. 19.8 they are represented by 'beasts' and 'reptiles'. In this latter passage, however, the lion is

[1] See pp. 325, 331.

[2] The influence of Ezek. 34.3, 6, 8, is no doubt to be seen here. Cf. also Pss. 74.1; 79.13; 100.3; Jer. 23.1, where Israel is described as the sheep of God's pasture.

used to represent the tribe of Judah whilst in II Esd. 11.37 it symbolizes the Messiah; in Rev. 5.5 these two ideas are brought together and the Messiah is called 'the Lion of the tribe of Judah'. The lion of II Esd. 11.37, speaking with the voice of a man, upbraids and then destroys 'the eagle' symbolizing the mighty Roman Empire.

Just as men and nations are symbolized by animals, so good angels are symbolized by men[1] and fallen angels by stars.[2] These 'men' are sometimes said to be dressed in white garments (cf. I Enoch 87.2; 90.21; Test. of Levi 8.2, etc.); these symbolize the 'spiritual bodies' of the angels as they do elsewhere the resurrection bodies of the righteous who share in God's heavenly kingdom.[3] Again, in I Enoch 86.1ff. the fallen angels are described in terms of falling stars. Enoch, in a vision, sees a star representing Azazel the prince of the fallen angels falling from heaven to be followed by many other stars which represent all his host. These stars become bulls which sire three kinds of giants symbolized by elephants, camels and asses! At last they are brought to judgment together with the seventy angels, called 'shepherds', whom God had set to rule over his people Israel (90.20ff., cf. 89.59ff.).

One other significant form of symbolism is that of numbers. Such numbers as 3, 4, 7, 10 and 12 or multiples of them constantly recur throughout these books. Some of them, of course, already had a religious significance in the Old Testament and also in Babylonian and Persian sources, but this is considerably more marked among the apocalyptists. The number seventy, for example, is particularly common in the Jewish writings, and in the Christian apocalypses seven has pride of place as in the Book of Revelation, where it occurs no fewer than fifty-four times. Such use of numbers is quite in keeping with the apocalyptists' love of schematization and formed an integral part of their endeavours to forecast the time of the End.[4]

5. PSEUDONYMOUS IN AUTHORSHIP

Generally speaking it is true to say that Jewish apocalyptic is pseudonymous.[5] The several writers throw their prophecies into the

[1] For a similar usage in the Old Testament see Gen. 18.2ff.; Ezek. 9.2, etc.
[2] In Rev. 1.20 the stars refer to 'the angels of the seven churches'.
[3] See pp. 377ff.
[4] For a fuller treatment of this subject see pp. 195ff.
[5] In the case of Daniel, only the second part is pseudonymous, the first part being anonymous.

remote past and write in the name of some honoured figure of antiquity who, it is claimed, had received divine revelations which he recorded in a book and passed on to those who succeeded him. Many such figures appear in these writings ranging from Adam to Ezra in whose day, it was officially believed, inspiration had come to an end. More often than not the revelation consists of an account of world history culminating in the messianic kingdom or the age to come. In most cases this account is fairly clear, under its symbolical guise, right up to the age in which the apocalyptic writer himself is actually living. At that point it inevitably becomes obscure, for although the account claims to be prediction in the name of the ancient seer, prediction proper begins at the point of the author's own day. The tempo of events is then quickened, for the time is short and the End is at hand.

This method of pseudonymous writing is not peculiar to the Jewish apocalyptists, however. A similar technique was known among the Egyptians, for example, as early as the twelfth dynasty and there are indications that it was adopted also at a much later period in the years just prior to the appearance of the Jewish apocalyptic writings.[1] Of particular interest is the so-called *Demotic Chronicle*, dating from about the middle of the third century BC. Scholars are agreed that the oracles and interpretations given in this writing are no older than the Ptolemaic period, but the writer purports to be living at an earlier period in the reign of Tachos (362–1 BC). C. C. McCown suggests that the introduction, which is missing, told of the finding of ancient oracles in the time of Tachos which the finder interpreted. Certain kings of the past, to whom oracles are credited, are named; later kings, however, are not named because *ex hypothesi* they are still in the future. In this way, as in Jewish apocalyptic, past history is presented in the form of prediction whose 'fulfilment' is a source of encouragement to the readers in the Ptolemaic age.[2] A somewhat similar phenomenon is to be found also among the Greeks. This method of ascribing apocalypses to earlier writers was apparently adopted by certain philosophers who experienced visions in which they were rapt to Hades and received authoritative teachings from famous philosophers of earlier ages. The device was ridiculed by

[1] Cf. C. C. McCown, 'Hebrew and Egyptian Apocalyptic Literature', *HTR*, vol. XVIII, 1925, pp. 357–411, especially pp. 387ff.

[2] Cf. *ibid.*, pp. 390f.

other writers, but continued in vogue for some time.[1] The indications are that this was a custom quite prevalent throughout the Orient and was shared by people with different literary traditions. We need not conclude, however, that there was any necessary borrowing and in particular that the origin of Jewish apocalyptic is to be found in an imitation of Egyptian or Greek techniques. It is more likely that in Jewish apocalyptic we have an independent form of writing which represents an indigenous development and is to be explained rather in terms of the Hebrew literary tradition and the functioning of the Hebrew mind.

The phenomenon of pseudonymity is not altogether unknown in the Old Testament itself. There are differences between this and the pseudonymous authorship of the apocalyptic writings, as we shall see, but there were certain well-established precedents in the Scriptures for the apocalyptists to follow. Reference has been made above to the Blessing of Jacob, for example, in Genesis 49 as an illustration of early testamentary literature. This Blessing was written perhaps in the early monarchy and reflects the historical situation of that time.[2] The fortunes of the twelve tribes up to that point are referred back to the time of Jacob who, just before his death, discloses them in the form of predictions. Another example is that of the Book of Deuteronomy and also post-exilic legislation generally where laws are given in the name of Moses who is regarded as the author of all law-giving. In somewhat the same way many of the Psalms are credited to David, the father of psalmody; whilst such wisdom books as Proverbs (in part), Ecclesiastes and the Book of Wisdom are traced back to Solomon, who is regarded as the fountain-head of all wisdom. There is reason to believe, moreover, that some of the later prophets or their disciples may intentionally have added their writings to those of earlier prophets whose names were known and whose reputations were established. It is possible that such pseudonymous writings are to be found in passages like Isaiah 24–27 and Zechariah 9–14 which, incidentally, have an apocalyptic ring about them. Whilst there is precedent here for the adoption of pseudonymity by the apocalyptists, there are certain differences of emphasis which mark off their usage from that of the Old Testament writings. One is that, almost without exception, the apocalyptic writings are avowedly pseudonymous and

[1] For illustrations of this in the writings of the Orphic-Pythagorean schools see A. Dieterich, *Nekyia*, 1893, pp. 75, 128–33.

[2] Cf. J. Skinner, *Genesis*, ICC, 1910, pp. 507f.

make use of the device of vision, dream or trance to emphasize this particular characteristic. Again, they purposely choose certain names from antiquity and are most careful, for example by omitting to mention the names of men living after that time, to give the impression that the book is a genuine and first-hand production. We shall see that in certain cases at least the apocalyptists' adoption of pseudonymity may signify something more than a mere literary device.

Many reasons have been given for the adoption of pseudonymity by the apocalyptists. Most of them either claim or imply deception on the part of these writers. It has been suggested, for example, that it was adopted on account of the dangers of the time of writing;[1] the best way for the writer to avoid persecution was to ascribe his teaching to some individual of the past. But quite apart from the deception implied, this explanation does not indicate why pseudonymity is chosen rather than anonymity, which would have served the purpose equally well. Another reason given is what C. C. McCown calls the 'glamour of antiquity' by reason of which 'those of the Jewish age of archaism and respect for the past were compelled to adopt . . . a well-known device of their Egyptian colleagues living in a similar atmosphere of antiquarianism'.[2] But it is by no means certain that the Jews thus borrowed from the Egyptians, as we have already noted, nor does the Jewish love for 'antiquarianism' seem a justifiable reason for the adoption of this device. A more popular reason is that the apocalyptic writer would by this means be better able to gain a hearing if his writing were issued in the name of some revered figure of the past whose supposed authorship would give to it an authority it otherwise could never claim; by this means the apocalyptic books would be brought into close relationship with the books of Scripture and so secure for themselves a place in the affections of the people. This suggestion lies behind the well-known explanation of R. H. Charles, who points to the autocracy of the Law whose absolute authority made impossible the reception of fresh revelations of truth apart from that enshrined in the Law itself. The only way by which men, moved by the spirit of God, could make known their God-inspired visions was to do so by means of pseudonymous writings. 'Against the reception of such fresh faith and truth, the Law stood in

[1] Cf. J. B. Frey in Pirot's *Supplément au Dictionnaire de la Bible*, vol. I, 1928, cols. 334ff.

[2] *Op. cit.*, p. 409.

the way, unless the books containing them came under the aegis of certain great names of the past. Against the claims and authority of such names, the official representatives of the Law were in part reduced to silence.'[1] A related factor, Charles claims, was the formation of the Canon of Scripture. The Prophetic Canon was closed by the year 200 BC and so no book written after that date could hope to be included. Books continued to be admitted to the third division of the Canon, the Hagiographa, down to AD 100; but the test of their acceptance was that they should have been written as far back as the time of Ezra, when inspiration was officially declared to have ceased. In order to gain a hearing, therefore, it was necessary for the apocalyptists to issue their books in the name of some person who lived at least as early as the prophet Ezra. Daniel alone of all the later apocalyptic books gained an entrance into the Canon, though not into the Prophetic Canon, on the assumption that it was written by the ancient worthy of that name.[2]

This picture which R. H. Charles draws of the 'autocracy' of the Law whose overwhelming authority was such as to make utterly impossible the utterances of God-inspired men cannot find any substantiation in fact. This was no doubt the ideal of such men as the Sopherim whose responsibility it was to expound and apply the Law to every human interest and endeavour; but, although they possessed a pronounced moral authority among the people, it was of a limited kind and certainly could not silence the words of those who did not claim the *imprimatur* of the Law. There was, in fact, no such religious or literary censorship as Charles implies; indeed there was nothing to prevent any writer at this time issuing his book either anonymously or in his own name. Quite apart from this question of the all-sufficiency of the Law, Charles's explanation charges the apocalyptists not only with deception but also with a marked credulity in believing that such deception would be accepted by their readers at its face value.

A more practical suggestion has been offered by H. H. Rowley,[3] who explains the phenomenon of pseudonymity by reference to the genesis of the Book of Daniel. The writer, he suggests, in the first part of his book issued stories about Daniel anonymously; these were followed up in the second part with an account of his visions which

[1] *Eschatology*, 2nd ed., 1913, p. 203.
[2] Cf. *ibid.*, pp. 198ff.; *The Book of Enoch*, 1912, p. x; *Daniel*, 1929, pp. xxiiff.
[3] Cf. *op. cit.*, pp. 37ff.

he ascribed to the Daniel of his stories. The purpose was not to deceive, but simply to indicate his identity with the writer of the first part of the book. Thus, to begin with, pseudonymity was not consciously intended, but became part of the technique of apocalyptic as it was gradually copied by succeeding writers. On this reckoning pseudonymity is an artificial device and is to be explained in terms of an accepted literary convention.

But even if it be conceded that pseudonymity was commonly regarded as a recognized literary convention, it cannot be dismissed as a *mere* literary device to be judged according to the standards of modern literary etiquette. The impression given is that for the most part they are to be accepted by their readers as genuine revelations and that the writers themselves are firmly of the same conviction! That is, they are intended to be received as *bona fide* disclosures made to the ancient seer whose written records of them had been kept hidden for many generations. Indeed, it would appear that their authority is ultimately dependent upon the authority of the supposed writer and upon the venerable age of the writings which bear his name. If, then, we cannot explain pseudonymity in terms of deception, must we explain it in terms of delusion? By modern standards and judgments this might be so. But such a conclusion is quite unwarranted when we judge this practice in the light of certain factors in Hebrew 'psychology' which the apocalyptists shared with their Old Testament predecessors and for which there is no exact parallel in modern thought. These are the idea of corporate personality, the peculiar time-consciousness of the Hebrews and the significance of the proper name in Hebrew thought. It will be argued in the following pages that, although for most if not all of these writers the adoption of pseudonymity meant the following out of a literary convention, there nevertheless lay behind this a genuine sense of tradition and, in the case of some at least, an equally genuine experience of inspiration[1] both of which are to be explained in terms of their peculiar Hebrew background.

H. Wheeler Robinson has shown that the idea of corporate personality is not only familiar in Hebrew law, as when an entire family is punished or destroyed for the sin of one of its members; it also runs through the entire life and religion of Israel and does much to explain the character of Hebrew legislation generally, the Wisdom literature and the Psalms in which an individual may speak for the

[1] For a fuller discussion of the nature of apocalyptic inspiration see ch. VI.

group or the group for an individual.[1] The group comprehends all the individuals belonging to it in a 'corporate unity'; but so close is the relationship within it that 'there is a fluidity of transition from the one to the many and from the many to the one',[2] and for some purposes there is even 'an identity of the individual and the group to which he belongs'.[3] This unity, however, to which the several members belong and in which their individual lives are merged is not confined to those living at any particular time, but is extended to include past and future members as well. Thus the whole group—past, present and future—is able to 'function as a single individual through any of these members conceived as representative of it'.[4]

Now, the apocalyptists did not belong to a corporate group like that of a priestly caste or a prophetic guild,[5] but they were conscious of standing near the end of a long line of distinctive apocalyptic tradition stretching far back into the past and having its origin and inspiration in such illustrious men as Enoch, Moses, Ezra and Daniel. So conscious were they of their place within this tradition, and so indebted were they for what they themselves had received from the past, that they could rightly regard themselves not as original writers at all, but simply as inheritors and interpreters of what, under divine inspiration, they had already received.[6] But this tradition which they themselves received and represented in their

[1] Cf. 'The Hebrew Conception of Corporate Personality' in *Werden und Wesen des Alten Testaments* (BZAW, vol. LXVI), 1936, pp. 49ff.; *Inspiration and Revelation in the Old Testament*, 1946, pp. 70f., 264f.

[2] *Ibid.*, p. 264.

[3] *Ibid.*, p. 70.

[4] H. Wheeler Robinson, 'The Hebrew Conception of Corporate Personality', *op. cit.*, p. 49.

[5] The idea of corporate personality, however, was familiar to them, as is evident from a number of references in these writings. The solidarity of the nation, for example, is indicated in such a book as the Assumption of Moses, which tells how the tribes suffer vicariously for one another's sins (3.5), and receive the promise (3.9) and are glorified together (10.8). Examples of the idea of corporate personality are found throughout the apocalyptic books: The 'son of man' in Dan. 7.13 is identified with 'the people of the saints of the Most High' in 7.27. Noah can be said to be rewarded in his seed who will be for ever (I Enoch 65.12). In the Psalms of Solomon the author writes in his own name (8.1, 3, 4–7), but at other times he identifies himself with 'the saints of God' (8.28), or 'the true Israel' (1.3; 5.1ff.; 17.1ff.) or with them 'that fear the Lord in their innocency' (4.26). Jerusalem is described as a mother (II Bar. 3.1), Zion as a woman (II Esd. 10.40ff.), and Rome as a pampered virgin (Sib. Or. III. 356–7).

[6] There is a certain analogy here with the structure of the prophetic books where tradition is also an important factor in explaining later reinterpretations. See above pp. 73f.

writings could itself be traced to its source in the ancient seer whose name it bore. Thus in writing as representative of the tradition the apocalyptist was at the same time writing as representative of the seer himself. Just as all (in the apocalyptic tradition) could speak for one (the ancient seer in whose name they wrote), so one (the individual apocalyptic writer) could speak for all. In this way the apocalyptists, in their writings, were trying to express what they believed the person in whose name they wrote would have spoken had he been living in their own day. As spokesmen of the tradition, they were, in fact, spokesmen of the seer himself and could justifiably assume his name. Just as the rabbis could trace back the oral tradition of succeeding generations to Moses the fountain-head of all lawgiving, so the apocalyptists, with an equal absence of deception or delusion, could trace back *their* tradition also to Moses or to some other great figure of the past. This sense of kinship which the apocalyptists shared with the one in whose name they wrote would be accentuated all the more if, as will be argued in a later chapter,[1] their accounts reflect actual visionary experiences which they believed they received under divine inspiration. Thus S. Mowinckel, for example, can describe Enoch as ' "patron saint" of contemporary sages and apocalyptic preachers' and adds, 'just as Noah once visited him "at the end of the earth" and received mysteries revealed by him, so also the sages of the present age through prayer and fasting and study of the old books, and perhaps also by means of ecstatic exercises are able to get revelations from him to complete and give authentic interpretations of the ancient traditions'.[2] In this way pseudonymity is to be explained in terms both of tradition and of inspiration which in turn are to be understood in terms of that peculiar Hebrew psychology to which the apocalyptists had fallen heir.

This attempted explanation of pseudonymity receives greater credence when we consider it in the light of yet another factor closely related to that of the 'corporate personality' idea, namely, the time-consciousness of the Hebrews and their alleged sense of 'contemporaneity'.[3] In our own consciousness today the sense of contemporaneity can be felt strongly when in memory, for example, we live over again some vivid experience of the past or when we are

[1] See ch. VI.

[2] *Norsk Teologisk Tidsskrift*, 1940, p. 212, quoted by A. Bentzen, *Introduction to the Old Testament*, vol. I, 1948, pp. 259f.

[3] For a fuller discussion of this subject see pp. 205ff.

confronted by two similar events, one in the past and one in the present, whose 'psychical contents' give the impression that the two events or times are, in fact, identical. 'A situation or event from a time long past,' writes Thorleif Boman, 'which is prodigiously similar to our own, strikes us as modern, indeed present. . . . Strict contemporaneity is, therefore, the same as psychological identity since two psychological contents coalesce into one.'[1] Boman argues, from a consideration of the Hebrew verbal system which (he claims) expresses itself in terms of complete and incomplete action and not in terms of past, present and future time, that this particular way of thinking came easily to the Semites and especially to the Hebrews.[2] James Barr, on the other hand, denies that there is any evidence in the Hebrew verbal system for this idea of contemporaneity.[3] However cogent his arguments may be in this particular respect, there are nevertheless indications in the biblical writings that the Hebrews readily thought of history in terms of a unitary process which implied a weak sense of time-sequence and encouraged in them a strong sense of contemporaneity. In a number of passages, for example, the biblical writers describe the return of the exiles from Babylon in terms of the Exodus from Egypt; the two events are so alike in their 'psychological contents' that they can readily be equated in the writers' minds. Another example may be found in the celebration of the Passover, where the events of the Exodus, it would seem, were not only related but also, as it were, re-enacted in such a way that past and present experiences were regarded as one.[4] For somewhat the same reason the writer of the Book of Daniel could identify the events of his own day with those of the Babylonian Exile because the character of Antiochus Epiphanes's reign corresponded so closely to that of Nebuchadnezzar.[5]

The significance of such an understanding of the nature of time and time-sequence for the problem of pseudonymity becomes apparent when we realize that the apocalyptists shared with their Hebrew forebears not only the idea of 'corporate personality' but also this sense of 'contemporaneity' with which such an idea was

[1] *Hebrew Thought compared with Greek*, English ed., 1960, pp. 148–9.

[2] Cf. *ibid.*, p. 148.

[3] Cf. *The Semantics of Biblical Language*, 1961, pp. 78ff.; *Biblical Words for Time*, 1962, pp. 96, 130f.

[4] Cf. L. Köhler, *Hebrew Man*, English ed., 1956, pp. 139f. The whole context of worship is, of course, particularly relevant for this sense of contemporaneity.

[5] Cf. E. W. Heaton, *The Book of Daniel*, 1956, p. 63.

closely associated. The apocalyptic writers, like the ancient seer in whose name they wrote, stood within the apocalyptic tradition, shared the same visionary experiences and received the same divine revelations. The sameness of their respective experiences would make it possible for them to associate, to the point of coincidence, their own circumstances with those of their worthy predecessor and to see in them, as it were, a spiritual reproduction of his own. By thus telescoping the past into the present they would be able to see the two events as one. An explanation of this kind casts light on a number of passages in the apocalyptic writings, two of which may be mentioned here.[1] The first of these is the difficult passage in II Esd. 3.1–2 which reads as follows: 'In the thirtieth year after the downfall of the City I Salathiel, who am also Ezra, was in Babylon, and as I lay upon my bed I was disquieted . . . and my mind was preoccupied with my thoughts; because I saw Sion's desolation, on the one hand (matched) with the abundant wealth of Babylon's inhabitants on the other.'[2] This Ezra, in whose name the author writes, was in Babylon 'in the thirtieth year after the downfall of the City', i.e. in the year 557 BC, which was thirty years after the fall of Jerusalem in 587 BC. But these words have in all probability a twofold reference and signify the fall of Jerusalem not only in 587 BC but also in AD 70, the 'thirtieth year after' being AD 100, in which this revelation was made to the writer of this portion of the book. These two events, having the same 'psychological contents', would be easily equated in the writer's mind; and correspondingly he would be able to see in himself and in his vision at that time a 'spiritual reproduction' of Ezra and the vision which he himself had received and so could use his name without any sense either of deception or of delusion. The second reference

[1] For further illustrations see pp. 210ff.

[2] This passage raises the question of the identity of Ezra, which in turn raises the question of the unity of the book. M. R. James offers the following suggestion: 'The author of II Esdras has consciously invented an earlier Ezra, one who never returned to Jerusalem, and was taken up to heaven when his work was finished: impossible, therefore, to be identified with the historical Ezra. But to this creature of his imagination he has transferred one act which was, rather vaguely, attributed to the historical Ezra, namely, the restoration of the Scriptures, which he has transfigured into a miracle' (*JTS*, vol. XVIII, 1917, p. 168). The same writer goes on to produce evidence to show that Ezra can be identified with Salathiel and that the equation of the two names is probably based upon I Chron. 3.17. This particular problem of the authorship of II Esdras does not primarily concern us here, but the transference of the restoration of the Scriptures from the 'historical Ezra' to the 'earlier Ezra' referred to by M. R. James may perhaps find an explanation along the lines indicated in this present chapter.

is in II Esd. 14.1ff. where the author identifies himself with Ezra, and Ezra is in turn identified with Moses who stands in the same apocalyptic tradition. God, we are told, spoke to *Moses* out of a bush (14.3, cf. Ex. 3.2) and thereafter brought him to Sinai, where he remained with him 'for many days' (14.4; in Ex. 24.18, etc., this is specified as 'forty days'); on the Mount he 'told him many wondrous things, showed him the secrets of the times, declared to him the end of the seasons' (14.5). In the same chapter, however, it is also stated that God spoke to *Ezra* out of a bush (14.2, 7ff.), who then went aside for forty days (14.23, 36, 42, 44), during which time he received from God by divine inspiration not only the books of the Law, but also the books of the secret tradition (14.43ff.). The same 'psychological situation' is present in each case, so that Moses himself is seen to be identified with Ezra, who in turn is identified with the author of the book.

A third factor which helps us to understand the adoption of pseudonymity by these writers is the use of the proper name in Hebrew thought. Just as a man's personality can be expressed in terms of his family or tribe or offspring, so also it can be expressed in such things as his spoken or written word, his property or his name.[1] The name is no mere appellation; it is, so to speak, an 'extension' of the man's personality and indicates his essential being, his life, his very self.[2] Thus to honour a man's name or the name of God is to honour the one who bears it; to blot out one's name is to annihilate the man himself and all that he represents. So closely associated are the ideas of 'character' and 'name' that a change in character or circumstance often involves a change in name.[3] But a man's name is not confined simply to himself; it can be shared with others or inherited by them. It is the possession not only of the individual but also of the family or the group to which he belongs. G. Buchanan Gray observes that, especially in the post-exilic period, it was customary for a child to be called by the name of his father or grandfather.[4] This is not to be explained in terms of mere social

[1] Cf. A. R. Johnson, *The Vitality of the Individual in the Thought of Ancient Israel*, 1949, p. 89.

[2] For a treatment of the whole subject see J. Pedersen, *Israel I–II*, English ed., 1926, pp. 254–9.

[3] Cf. Abram (Gen. 17.1–9); Jacob (Gen. 32.28); Joseph (Gen. 41.45); Eliakim (II Kings 23.34); Mattaniah (II Kings 24.17); Israel (Isa. 62.2; 65.15); Simon (Matt. 16.18) and Saul (Acts 13.9).

[4] Cf. *Studies in Hebrew Proper Names*, 1896, pp. 2ff.

custom. Its significance lies in the fact that after a man's death 'the name is taken over by the son; it means that he does not die. His soul, with all its substance, great achievements, wealth, blessing, honour, everything which fills the name, lives on in the son.'[1] This practice is not confined, however, to one's own family relations; inheritance of the name is possible even in the case of strangers. Thus, from the Greek period onwards, it is customary for Jewish children to be called by the name of some famous person who is not necessarily a kinsman. By receiving this name the child receives also the contents of it and is able to share in some measure at least the life and benefits of the one who bore it.

It may be that this factor has a relevance also for our understanding of the problem of pseudonymity. We have seen reason to believe that the apocalyptic writer shared a sense of kinship with the ancient seer in whose name he wrote and indeed wrote as his representative within the apocalyptic tradition. May it not be that, by thus appropriating his name the writer thought of himself as in some way an 'extension' of his personality along the lines indicated above? If such were the case his sense of 'identification' with the man of the past would be much more complete than would otherwise be the case, for by assuming his name he would thereby be sharing in his very character and life.

But is there any evidence for this in these writings? No demonstrable proof can be given; but there are indications in several apocalyptic books that the choice of a pseudonym was not altogether arbitrary, but was in keeping with the outlook of the actual writer. Or to put it another way, there is fairly frequently a connection between the pseudonym chosen and the actual problems occupying the writer's mind. As F. C. Burkitt observes, 'The names were not chosen out of mere caprice; they indicated to a certain extent what subjects would be treated and the point of view of the writer.'[2] The author of Jubilees, for example, was deeply concerned about the supremacy of the Law and the glorification of the priesthood. It is fitting that such a man, with such interests, should write in the name of Moses who was known in Scripture both as a great law-giver and as a priest (cf. Ex. 24.6; 33.7ff.; Ps. 99.6, etc.) who had himself determined the origin of the Levitical priesthood (cf. Ex. 32.26ff.; Judg. 18.30, etc.). The same identity of interest is found also in the case of I Enoch. There the outlook of the several writers is largely

[1] J. Pedersen, *op. cit.*, p. 254. [2] *Jewish and Christian Apocalypses*, 1913, p. 18.

cosmopolitan; they are concerned not simply with the Jewish nation, but with all mankind. The visions they record tell of God's dealings with the whole human race and with the entire universe in which sun, moon and stars shine down on Jews and Gentiles alike. Once more the pseudonym chosen is a very fitting one, for Enoch may be regarded as the supreme cosmopolitan of antiquity. 'Enoch', writes F. C. Burkitt, 'was the great-great-grandfather of Shem, but he was the great-great-grandfather of Ham and Japhet, too. What was Enoch's nationality? He might appropriately reply, *Homo sum*, and accordingly no spot on the wide earth is alien from him.'[1] Very different is the narrow, nationalistic outlook of, say, the writer of II Esdras, to whom God was the God of Israel rather than of all mankind. His burning interest is in the salvation of his own people; the Gentiles, by rejecting the law of God, will be utterly destroyed or else consigned to the eternal torments of hell-fire (cf. 7.36–38; 13.38, etc.). No more fitting name could be found in Scripture to represent this outlook than that of the prophet Ezra whose ardent racial and nationalistic policy had as its aim the purification of the Jewish people and their segregation from their Gentile neighbours.

Such an explanation of pseudonymity, based on an understanding of apocalyptic 'psychology', exonerates these writers from the charge either of deception or of delusion and indicates that behind the acceptance of this particular literary convention there may well have lain a genuine sense of tradition and inspiration in and through which they saw themselves and their literature to be in the true Old Testament succession.

[1] *Ibid.*, p. 19.

V

THE APOCALYPTIC CONSCIOUSNESS

IT HAS BEEN argued in an earlier chapter that apocalyptic is not merely imitative of prophecy but is a true continuation or development of it. The same point can be further illustrated by reference to 'the apocalyptic consciousness' or the ideas held by these writers concerning human personality.[1]

An examination of the psychological terminology[2] of the prophetic writings shows clearly that 'in Israelite thought man is conceived, not so much in dual fashion as "body" and "soul", but synthetically as a unit of vital power or (in current terminology) a psychophysical organism. That is to say, the various members and secretions of the body . . . can all be thought of as revealing psychical properties.'[3] Man is regarded here as a unity of personality, not a dichotomy of body and soul or a trichotomy of body, soul and spirit. The body is not, as in popular Greek thought, the mortal shell of the immortal soul. It is so essential an aspect of personality that man can rightly be described as 'an animated body, and not an incarnated soul'.[4] This body has psychical as well as physical properties and functions which it exercises through its several members. H. Wheeler Robinson

[1] For a list of psychological terms in the apocalyptic literature see Appendix II.

[2] It is important in a study of this kind not to read back into this early period modern psychological ideas or to imagine that the experiences of the prophets or apocalyptists are necessarily explicable in terms of modern psychological language. A good working definition of 'psychology' as it is used in these pages is that given by H. Wheeler Robinson: 'Ancient "psychology" does not mean an ordered and scientific account of consciousness; it means rather that branch of anthropology which interprets the ideas held about human personality, and in this respect must throw a wide net' ('Hebrew Psychology', in *The People and the Book*, ed. by A. S. Peake, 1925, p. 353).

[3] A. R. Johnson, *op. cit.*, p. 88. [4] H. Wheeler Robinson, *op. cit.*, p. 362.

has argued that we are to find in the functioning of the various organs and members of the body 'a diffusion of consciousness'[1] in which the different parts of the body show psychical and ethical properties and can act, as it were, independently of the rest of the body. A. R. Johnson, however, has demonstrated that such an interpretation is based on too literal a reading of the text and that the phenomenon is best explained in terms of synecdoche; any one part of the body, in its exercise of psychical and ethical functions, is to be thought of as acting on the part of the whole.[2]

An examination of the relevant terminology of the apocalyptic writers shows quite clearly that their 'psychology', though influenced in part by foreign ideas, is nevertheless fundamentally Hebrew in character and represents a continuation, and in some respects an interesting and significant development, of the prophetic consciousness. A study of the psychological terminology in the apocalyptic writings is made more difficult than a similar study either in the Hebrew Old Testament or in the Greek New Testament by reason of the fact that in most cases the writings that have come down to us are in translation. This has a double disadvantage: first, a word in the original language may be rendered by two or more words in translation; and secondly, the translator may not have given to the word its original shade of meaning. For these reasons it is impossible to reach concordancial accuracy in collecting and classifying the words in question. Despite these difficulties, however, it is possible to arrive at a fairly accurate account. In this present chapter we shall examine, by means of examples, those words used by the apocalyptic writers which cast light on the ideas held by them concerning human personality.

1. PHYSIOLOGY IN ITS RELATION TO PSYCHOLOGY

(i) *The central organs.* In the apocalyptic writings mention is made of seven central organs of the body which have psychological significance. These are, in the order of their frequency of occurrence: heart (256), bowels (13), liver (8), 'reins' or kidneys (4), gall (2), spleen (1) and womb (1).

By far the most important word in this connection is the word 'heart', which occurs no fewer than 256 times. Apart from three occurrences of a non-psychological character (II Esd. 4.7; 13.3, 51

[1] *Ibid.*, pp. 362ff. [2] Cf. *op. cit.*, p. 83, n. 2.

where it is used figuratively to signify 'midst'), these fall into three main categories, the frequency of appearance in each category corresponding very closely to those in the Old Testament itself. Out of a total of 253, the word is used to denote the full range of personality or character in 99 cases, the more emotional side of human consciousness in 60 cases, the intellectual function in 69 cases and the volitional function in 25 cases.

Examples of the first category could be given from practically every one of the books under consideration. The author of the Testaments of the XII Patriarchs, for example, describes uprightness (Test. of Iss. 3.1), integrity (Test. of Iss. 3.8), purity (Test. of Napht. 3.1; Test. of Jos. 4.6; Test. of Benj. 8.2), humility (Test. of Reub. 6.10; Test. of Jos. 10.2), haughtiness (Test. of Jud. 13.2), etc., as qualities or attitudes of the heart. Numerous examples are given in the Book of Jubilees of the heart as the seat of error or of sin (cf. 37.12). This same idea is developed in II Esdras, where much use is made of the phrase 'the evil heart' (cf. 3.21).

Closely connected with this use of 'heart', and brought under this same head for the sake of convenience, is a somewhat similar use of a more specialized nature. In two cases, both in the Testaments of the XII Patriarchs, it occurs with the sense of 'conscience'. Test. of Gad 5.3, for example, reads, 'For he that is just and humble is ashamed to do what is unjust, being reproved not of another, but of his own heart, because the Lord looketh on his inclination' (cf. also Test. of Jud. 20.5). In Test. of Reub. 4.3 the word *syneidēsis* ('conscience') is used, but even this is to be regarded in all probability as a specialization from the Old Testament usage of 'heart' and not as a word with a Greek connotation.

Less characteristic, though still covering a considerable range, is the use of 'heart' to describe the seat of emotional experiences. It is described as the seat of desire (Test. of Reub. 3.6; Apoc. of Abr. 23 and 30), of love (Test. of Gad 6.3; Jub. 19.31), of mercy and forgiveness (Test. of Zeb. 5.4), of reverence and fear (Test. of Jos. 10.5); it can be merry (Test. of Napht. 9.2), or rejoice (Jub. 19.21), or bless (Jub. 22.24); it can hate (Test. of Gad 2.1) or show guile (Test. of Iss. 7.4) or grieve (Jub. 13.18); it can be disturbed (Test. of Dan 4.7) or troubled (I Enoch 95.1) or pained (Sib. Or. IV. 18–19) or afflicted (I Enoch 99.16) or afraid (Pss. of Sol. 8.6) or in distress (II Enoch 1.3) or in a stupor (II Bar. 70.2) or bloodthirsty (Sib. Or. V. 171).

More typical are the intellectual or volitional uses which, when taken together, greatly outnumber the emotional. The intellectual use is illustrated over and over again in such a phrase as 'the thoughts of men's hearts' (Jub. 12.20, etc.). In addition to the word 'heart' (Greek *kardia*) to express the intellect, we find many occurrences (32 in the Testaments alone) of the word 'mind' (Greek *nous*). But, as in the case of the word *syneidēsis* referred to above, *nous* is in all probability to be regarded as a specialization from the Old Testament usage of 'heart' and does not have here the same content which it has in Greek psychology.[1] If these occurrences of *nous*, many of which must be actual translations of an original Hebrew *lēb*, were to be added to the occurrences of *kardia*, the total number of instances of 'heart' to describe the intellectual side of consciousness would be greatly increased.

The volitional use is less common, but is nevertheless quite frequent. The writer of the Book of Jubilees, for example, uses the phrase 'to set the heart upon' with the sense of 'to decide' (cf. 25.6). It is the instrument of purpose (I Enoch 91.4) or of moral action (Jub. 1.15), and can show stubbornness when it so chooses (I Enoch 98.11).

The word 'bowels' is also used with psychological significance to express emotions of various kinds. It occurs 13 times in all, 9 of which appear in the Testaments of the XII Patriarchs; 8 of these latter have a psychical usage as have the four remaining instances in the other books. The bowels are referred to as the seat of feelings generally (Test. of Zeb. 2.1; Test. of Benj. 3.7), of compassion (Test. of Sim. 2.4; Test. of Zeb. 27.3; 28.2), of yearning (Test. of Zeb. 7.4), of trouble (Test. of Zeb. 2.4), of pain (Pss. of Sol. 2.5), and of sorrow (Test. of Jos. 15.3; Test. of Abr. 3, 5 *bis*).

The liver appears 8 times in this literature, all in the Testaments of the XII Patriarchs, and all with a psychological content. It is the seat of wrath (Test. of Napht. 2.8), of fighting (Test. of Reub. 3.3), of pain (Test. of Sim. 4.1), of distress (Test. of Zeb. 2.4; Test. of Sim. 2.4) and of suffering (Test. of Gad 5.9, 11 *bis*).

The 'reins' or kidneys appear 4 times, in each case with psychological content. They are described as the seat of distress (I Enoch

[1] It is interesting to note that *nous* and *syneidēsis* are the only Greek psychological terms which Paul uses, and that both of these, as we have seen, are specializations of *kardia* in the Hebrew sense of *lēb*. So that even for these Greek terms he is not necessarily dependent on Greek thought or Greek psychology.

60.3), of trouble (I Enoch 68.3), of prudence (Test. of Napht. 2.3) and of meditation (II Bar. 48.39). They are referred to 10 times in the Old Testament as a general emotional centre; there is no parallel there, however, to the usages in the apocalyptic writings of the 'reins' as the seat of prudence or meditation.

The gall occurs twice, once as the seat of bitterness (Test. of Napht. 2.8) and once as the seat of fighting (Test. of Reub. 3.3). The spleen occurs only once, its function being 'for laughter' (Test. of Napht. 2.8). The womb is described once as the source of blessing (Jub. 25.19).

(ii) *The peripheral organs and other parts of the body.* The phenomenon, so common in the Old Testament, of the various parts of the body representing the whole body and possessing psychical functions, is equally common in the apocalyptic writings. In Jub. 25.19, for example, we read, 'The womb of her that bare thee blesses thee thus, and my breasts bless thee, and my mouth and my tongue praise thee greatly.' Not only does the mouth praise, it may be full of blessing (I Enoch 39.7) or be an instrument of blessing (Jub. 25.4; 31.15); it can be taken possession of by God as an instrument of prophecy (Jub. 31.12) or by the devil as his instrument (Apoc. of Mos. 16.5; 17.4); it may be impure (I Enoch 5.4) or filthy (Sib. Or. III. 500) or vain (Sib. Or. V. 280) or ill starred (Sib. Or. V. 392); it can destroy (Pss. of Sol. 17.27, 39) or be bitter (Ass. of Mos. 11.4) or in need of restraint (Sib. Or. V. 439). Similar predicates are used with almost equal frequency of the lips (cf. Pss. of Sol. 13.4; 15.5; 16.10; Life of Adam and Eve 6.1; Sib. Or. V. 259, 280) and of the tongue (cf. Jub. 25.19; Pss. of Sol. 12.1–3; 13.5; 16.10; II Enoch 46.2; 52.13, 14; 60.1; Sib. Or. V. 271).

We are not surprised to read that the eye possesses the properties of lust or envy or enmity (Pss. of Sol. 4.4, 11, 15) and that it exercises an evil influence on men (Test. of Benj. 4.2). Again, the hands of men may be unholy or holy (Sib. Or. V. 399, 401). The belly may be pained because of great grief (Pss. of Sol. 2.15); the breasts have the power to bless (Jub. 25.19); the knees may be 'loosed' because of great emotion and the loins broken (Pss. of Sol. 8.5); the joints tremble because of great sorrow (Test. of Zeb. 2.5); a man's bones may be dismayed or be shaken through fear (Pss. of Sol. 8.6); his 'members' cause praises to ascend to God (II Bar. 54.7) and there his secret thoughts are stored (II Bar. 86.3).

The word translated 'flesh' is used frequently as a general term for 'mankind' (cf. I Enoch 14.21, etc.) and sometimes includes the animal creation as well (Jub. 3.29); elsewhere it refers to human nature in its capacity of weakness over against the things of the spirit (I Enoch 15.4, etc.); in a third group of references it is said to reveal ethical qualities (cf. Pss. of Sol. 4.7, which speaks of the 'corruption of his flesh'; cf. Test. of Jud. 19.4; Jub. 5.2). The indications here are that, although the flesh is weak and can be corrupted, it is not the source of sin, though it may become the seat of sin.

This examination of the terminology for the various organs and members of the body makes clear that the difference in this respect between the apocalyptists on the one hand and the Old Testament writers on the other hand is negligible. To both groups the several physical members exhibit psychical properties and each member in turn, in demonstrating these properties, is thought of as acting on behalf of the whole body.

2. THE SIGNIFICANCE OF THE USE OF THE WORD 'SOUL' (Hebrew *nepeš*; Greek *psyche*; Latin *animus*)

The uses of the word 'soul' fall into four main divisions. Out of a total of 232 occurrences it appears 11 times with reference to the principle of life; in 119 instances it denotes human consciousness in some form or another; in 46 instances it has a personal usage denoting animate objects as distinct from inanimate; and in 52 instances the reference is to the dead in a disembodied state; the remaining two occurrences stand in isolation having reference to a pre-existent life.

(i) *Life principle*. The frequent use of 'soul' in the Old Testament to denote the 'life principle' points back to what was possibly the primary meaning of the word, *viz*. 'breath'.[1] The soul as 'breath' is the animating principle of man's life. The same idea is contained in the apocalyptic writings, but this particular meaning of the word is far less frequent, appearing only 11 times out of a total of 232. In 4 of these the reference is to physical life, without any specific reference to what we should call its psychical side, as in Pss. of Sol. 17.19: 'They were wandering in desert places that their lives might be preserved from harm.' The other 7 examples indicate the life-force in

[1] But see L. Dürr, *ZAW*, vol. XLIII (N.F. II), 1925, pp. 262ff., who claims that 'throat' or 'neck' may be primary. If this is so it is a further reminder of the close relationship between physical properties and psychical functions, cf. A. R. Johnson, *op. cit.*, p. 9.

man and its various manifestations. The surviving influence of the primitive quasi-material conception of 'soul' as 'breath' is illustrated in such a passage as Pss. of Sol. 16.2: 'Within a little my soul had been poured out unto death', and in II Enoch 10.6 where reference is made to 'soulless (i.e. lifeless) gods'. In primitive thought the soul was associated not only with the breath, but also with the blood. An example of this in the apocalyptic writings is in Jub. 21.18: 'And do not eat any blood, for it is the soul', where 'blood' and 'soul' signify the principle of life in the animal creation (cf. also Jub. 7.32 and compare this with Gen. 9.4).

(ii) *Human consciousness*. A far more characteristic use of 'soul', however, is that which denotes human consciousness in its many-sidedness. Out of 119 occurrences 46 signify the full range of human consciousness; 11 more come under the heading of 'character'; 44 have a specifically emotional content; 10 refer to the seat of moral action expressing the volitional side of man's nature; 8 have an intellectual reference.

An example of the first use is in Apoc. of Moses 29.10: 'Happy shall the man be who hath ruled his soul, when the judgment shall come to pass.' Closely connected with this and hardly to be distinguished from it is its use to denote character, as when Noah enjoins his sons 'to guard their souls from fornication and uncleanness and all iniquity' (Jub. 7.20). These two groups of meanings, taken together, denote the inner life of man or man's essential being in its widest reference.

But the most characteristic use of the word is that which indicates a specifically emotional content. For example, the soul can be troubled (Test. of Zeb. 8.6) or embittered (II Esd. 9.41); it can express desire (II Bar. 35.5) or suffer agonies (II Esd. 5.34); it can hate (Test. of Gad 6.2, etc.) or love (Jub. 19.27, etc.); it can pine (Test. of Iss. 4.5) or exult (Pss. of Sol. 17.1). This predominance of the emotional element is typical also of the Old Testament, where the use of 'soul' to denote the seat of physical appetite is the only one for which an exact parallel cannot be found in the apocalyptic writings.

Sometimes 'soul' is used in conjunction with 'heart' to denote the instrument of moral action, as when it is said, 'Jacob saw that he was evilly disposed towards him with his heart and with all his soul as to slay him' (Jub. 37.24). Closely connected with this is its use to denote the strictly volitional side of man's nature. The soul purposes, resolves, decides. It is with 'set purpose of soul', for example, that a man repents of his sin (Test. of Reub. 1.9), and it is to the soul that there belongs the right of choice between the good and the bad inclinations (Test. of Asher 1.6): 'O God, our works are in our choice, yea, in the power of our own soul; to do either righteousness or iniquity in the works of our hands' (Pss. of Sol. 9.7).

Moreover, the soul like the heart exercises intellectual powers: 'O my soul, drink thy fill of understanding, and, O my heart, feed on wisdom' (II Esd. 8.4). It can take counsel or much thought (II Bar. 19.4; 21.3) and can recover the spirit of understanding (II Esd. 5.22).

(iii) *Personal usage*. Elsewhere the word 'soul' denotes that which is animate as distinct from that which is inanimate. In two cases it denotes any living creature whether it be man or the lower animal creation (Jub. 49.4; II Enoch 30.4); but more often (19 times) it signifies man alone and can be rendered by the word 'person'. In many more instances (25 times) it refers to one's 'self' or, with a pronominal suffix, it has the force of a reflexive or personal pronoun. Each of these uses can be paralleled by examples from the Old Testament.

(iv) *In disembodied state*. There is one use of the word, however, which is not found at all in the Old Testament. This distinguishes the soul from the body and conceives of it as existing separately, or as capable of so doing, in a disembodied state after death (52 times). Such a conception is a radical departure from the outlook of the Old Testament which believes that at death all that is left is a lifeless body on the one hand and a 'shade', not a 'soul', on the other. This matter will be examined at greater length in a later chapter,[1] where it will be shown that, though the apocalyptists believe in the separate survival of the soul after death, they cannot ultimately express the surviving personality in terms of soul only, but must add thereto the conception of a bodily resurrection.[2]

(v) *In pre-existent state*. Reference is made in one passage to the pre-existence of the soul in these words: 'Sit and write all the souls of mankind, however many of them are born, and the places prepared for them to eternity; for all souls are prepared to eternity, before the formation of the world' (II Enoch 24.4, 5). This, of course, is not a Hebrew belief at all, but is a Platonic doctrine which found its way into Jewish thought and into certain Jewish writings of this period (*e.g.* the Book of Wisdom and IV Maccabees). The writer of II

[1] See ch. XIV. [2] See p. 375.

Enoch was probably a Jew who lived in Alexandria and represents the orthodox Hellenistic Judaism of that place. In Palestinian Judaism the Hebrew tradition was generally followed.[1]

3. THE SIGNIFICANCE OF THE USE OF THE WORD 'SPIRIT' (Hebrew *rūaḥ*; Greek *pneuma*; Latin *spiritus*)[2]

In the Old Testament the word *rūaḥ* sometimes signifies 'wind'. In the Greek translations of the apocalyptic writings the usual word for 'wind' is *anemos*, although the word *pneuma* is sometimes found (*e.g.* Sib. Or. III. 102). In the Latin text of II Esdras it is rendered by *ventus* (*e.g.* 4.5) or *flatus* (*e.g.* 5.37), but never by *spiritus*. This particular use has no psychological significance and so does not concern us here.

The word 'spirit' appears in the apocalyptic literature 383 times with a psychological connotation. This number is considerably greater than the number of occurrences of 'soul' and is due largely to an extension of its use in more than one direction. It refers to the spirit of God (39 times), to the spirit of man (111 times) and to spirits as supernatural beings, either angelic or demonic (233 times).

(i) *Spirit of God*. Out of the 39 instances where 'spirit' is used with reference to God, in only 9 is it regarded as a purely inspirational agency, a number which is much smaller than the corresponding use of *rūaḥ* in the Old Testament. In most of the other occurrences in this literature it expresses the nature of God and his capacity to act in a particular way, especially in producing ethical results in man's behaviour. Its operation results, for example, in a man's acquiring such qualities as goodness (Test. of Sim. 4.4), or freedom from defilement (Test. of Benj. 8.2), or wisdom and discretion (Jub. 40.5). This operation of the spirit is hardly to be distinguished at times from the spirit of man himself or from those supernatural beings which have an individual existence apart from God.[3]

(ii) *Spirit of man*. More important, and much more frequent, is the use of 'spirit' with reference to man himself. As in the case of 'soul' it describes the life principle in man or in beast, or the life force which

[1] In the Ass. of Moses, which is probably a product of Palestinian Judaism, we do find the belief expressed, however, in the pre-existence of Moses, cf. 1.14.

[2] For an examination of the use of 'spirit' and 'flesh' in the Dead Sea Scrolls see W. D. Davies, *Christian Origins and Judaism*, 1962, pp. 163ff., and also in K. Stendahl, *op. cit.*, pp. 171ff.

[3] See pp. 237ff.

may depart from him under strain of fear or excitement (13 times). Again, like 'soul', it denotes the seat of the emotions (26 times), or expresses intelligence (3 times). In an important number of instances it is used to denote that aspect of man's nature which is most readily influenced by God and which is capable of taking upon itself ethical qualities of a definite nature. It can be described as holy (cf. Jub. 1.21, 23) just as in the case of the spirit of God; it can also become defiled (cf. Hebrew Test. of Napht. 10.9). Both 'soul' and 'spirit', then, are used to describe a normal element in human consciousness[1] and yet they are distinct, not only in their origin, but in the fact that 'spirit' describes human nature in its higher affinities and in its Godward aspect.[2] In a number of cases it is almost impossible to distinguish between this conception of spirit and the activity of the spirit of God himself. Even in those instances where it designates man's own consciousness there is seldom lacking the sense that the word at the same time expresses an external influence upon man, either in the form of the spirit of God or in the shape of supernatural beings.[3]

In a fairly large number of passages 'spirit' is used in a way quite foreign to the Old Testament. Like 'soul' it describes the form of man's survival after death and indicates the persistence of personality, in some form at any rate, in the life beyond.[4] This is clearly illustrated in such a passage as Apoc. of Moses 32.4 which reads: 'Rise up, Eve, for behold Adam thy husband hath gone out of his body. Rise up and behold his spirit borne aloft to his Maker.' Here

[1] There is only one instance of 'spirit' with a personal usage such as is common with 'soul'. It is in Ass. of Moses 11.16, where Moses is referred to as 'the sacred spirit'.

[2] Cf. Rom. 8.16: 'The Spirit himself bears witness with our spirit that we are God's children.' We note that sometimes Paul uses *pneuma* with reference to the higher nature of the Christian man, but at other times he uses it to denote a normal element in human nature. Cf. H. W. Robinson, 'Hebrew Psychology in relation to Pauline Anthropology', in *Mansfield College Essays*, ed. by A. M. Fairbairn, 1909, pp. 265ff.

[3] *E.g.* God may be said to send forth the 'spirit of understanding' into man, or man may be described as possessing the 'spirit of understanding' as expressive of his own nature; or again, man may be said to possess the 'spirit of anger' as a factor in his nature, but the 'spirit of anger' may be thought of in the shape of a supernatural being entering into man (cf. a *somewhat* similar conception in Hos. 4.12 and 5.4, where we read of 'the spirit of whoredoms' which is something quite positive). These uses of the word in the apocalyptic literature may be said to be a development of such an Old Testament usage as that in Isa. 11.2 which says, 'And the spirit of the Lord shall rest upon him, the spirit of wisdom and understanding, the spirit of counsel and might, the spirit of knowledge and of the fear of the Lord.'

[4] See pp. 357ff.

the spirit survives death and is so much a personality that it may readily be described as 'Adam thy husband'. Even when separated from the body it retains a conscious life of its own.

In some books the word 'soul' alone is found with this meaning (*e.g.* Sim. of Enoch; Pss. of Sol.; II Enoch; Test. of Abr.; II Baruch), and in others the word 'spirit' alone (*e.g.* the Noachic Fragments; I Enoch 108; Ass. of Moses; III Baruch); in others both 'soul' and 'spirit' are found side by side (*e.g.* several sections of I Enoch; II Esdras). This use of 'soul' and 'spirit' is found even in the oldest passages of our literature (cf. I Enoch 22.3 for 'soul', and I Enoch 22.5–7 for 'spirit'). There is a peculiar phrase in I Enoch 22.3 which speaks of 'the spirits of the souls of the dead'.

In several passages the departed spirit exists in close relation to a resurrection body conceived of either as being like the earthly body or as being of a more distinctly 'spiritual' nature.[1] The spirit of man in a disembodied state may also be thought of as departing from him in translation; but even here the idea of a bodily form is often present in the mind of the writer (cf. I Enoch 71.11).

(iii) *Supernatural beings.* One other application of the word 'spirit' falls now to be considered, for which the word 'soul' is never used as a synonym. In a large number of references (227 in all) it denotes those supernatural beings which are neither God nor man, nor yet the departed spirits of men (perhaps the nearest approach to this in the Old Testament is the 'lying spirit' in I Kings 22.21–23). These references fall into three main groups: they denote angelic beings, demons and spiritual beings not corporeally conditioned which do not clearly come within the first or second groups.

The first two groups are too common to require any illustration. In the third group the reference is more general; angels and demons are not specifically referred to, although such meanings may well be implied. In I Enoch 39.12, for example, it is said of God that 'He filled the earth with spirits', and in no fewer than 104 instances in I Enoch he is referred to as 'the Lord of spirits'. In 18 other instances the reference is to the various spirits of nature: hoar frost, hail, snow, mist, dew, rain, etc. In practically all the remaining instances these spirits influence man for good or for evil. We read, for example, of the spirit of truth (Test. of Jud. 20.1, 5) and the spirit of understanding (Test. of Jud. 20.2) which the writer regards as actual beings influencing men for good. It is this use of 'spirit' which is hardly to be

[1] For the significance of this see pp. 359, 377ff.

distinguished from that of the spirit of God acting upon man or that of the spirit of man himself. The references to these spirits influencing men for evil are much more frequent. The Test. of Reub. 2.1–2 and 3.3ff., for example, describes 'the seven spirits of deceit'. These are the spirit of fornication seated in the nature and in the senses, the spirit of insatiableness in the belly, the spirit of fighting in the liver and the gall, the spirit of obsequiousness and chicanery, the spirit of pride, the spirit of lying and the spirit of injustice.[1] This use of 'spirit' shows how influential was the belief in demonology among the apocalyptic writers, and in particular in the Testaments of the XII Patriarchs.[2]

Moreover, just as the word 'spirit' may signify a certain capacity in God and man, so it may signify such a capacity in angelic beings also. In I Enoch 61.11, for example, the writer enumerates seven virtues of the praising angels which are 'the spirit of faith . . . of wisdom . . . of patience . . . of mercy . . . of judgment . . . of peace . . . of goodness'.

4. INFLUENCE OF GREEK THOUGHT ON IDEAS RELATING TO THE CREATION AND NATURE OF MAN

There is a certain amount of evidence in these writings to show that the apocalyptists were influenced by Greek thought in their conception of human personality; but it is clear that that influence was very slight indeed compared with that of the Hebrew tradition in which they followed. The prevailing belief concerning the creation of man, for example, is that of the Genesis tradition which describes how God created Adam out of the dust of the earth and then breathed into him the breath of life (II Esd. 3.4–5; cf. Life of Adam and Eve 27.2; Apoc. of Moses 40.6; II Bar. 48.46; II Esd. 7.116; Apoc. of Abr. 20, etc.). Man is an animated body, a body made of the dust into which God breathes 'the breath of life' so that man becomes 'a living soul'.

(i) *The primal elements.* Elsewhere, however, there appear ideas and beliefs quite foreign to the typically Hebrew outlook, although

[1] In the Test. of Reub. 2.3–3.2 and 3.7, which R. H. Charles describes as an interpolation, the conception is specifically Greek in character. There we find twelve instances of the Stoic use of 'spirit' to denote the appetites or senses which, as R. H. Charles says, 'discharged themselves into the various parts of the body in the form of immaterial currents or *pneumata*'. Cf. *Apocr. and Pseud. of the Old Testament*, vol. II, 1913, p. 297.

[2] See further pp. 238f., 257.

the actual references are few. The writer of II Esdras, for example, is acquainted with the oriental doctrine that man's organism is composed of the four primal elements of earth, water, air and fire to which Philo also refers as the components of man.[1] In 8.8 we read, 'And when thou quickenest the body which thou fashionest in the womb, and endowest it with members, thy creature is preserved in fire and water . . .'; and in 4.9–10, 'But now I have only asked thee of the fire, the wind and the day that is past—things without which thou canst not be . . . the things which have intermingled with thy growth'. In these two passages three of the four primal elements are referred to—fire, water and air. The fourth element, earth, is indicated in the description of man as 'earth-born' which occurs four times in II Esdras alone (4.6; 7.46, 65; 8.35). In 5.49ff.; 10.9, etc., the earth, moreover, is referred to as a mother who bears children, the reference being to mankind.

(ii) *Man's nature*. Non-Hebrew influence is again evident in some verses in II Enoch which describe man's creation and his several natures thus: 'On the sixth day I commanded my wisdom to create man from seven consistencies: one, his flesh from the earth; two, his blood from the dew; three, his eyes from the sun; four, his bones from stone; five, his intelligence from the swiftness of the angels and from cloud; six, his veins and his hair from the grass of the earth; seven, his soul from my breath and from the wind. And I gave him seven natures: to the flesh hearing, the eyes for sight, to the soul smell, the reins for touch, the blood for taste, the bones for endurance, to the intelligence sweetness' (30.8–9). In this passage we have clear evidence of the influence of Stoic speculation and the views of human nature which came to be associated with the name of Philo.

By way of contrast we note the Hebrew influence in such a passage as Test. of Napht. 2.8: 'For God made all things good in their order, the five senses in the head, and he joined on the neck to the head, adding to it the hair also for comeliness and glory, then the heart for understanding, the belly for excrement, and the stomach for grinding, the windpipe for taking in the breath, the liver for wrath, the gall for bitterness, the spleen for laughter, the reins for prudence, the muscles of the loins for power, the lungs for drawing in, the loins for strength, and so forth.' But even this account is a compromise, and is not wholly dependent on Hebrew ideas. The reference to the five senses in the head is again an expression of Stoic thought which held

[1] Cf. *On the Creation of the World*, 51.

that man's soul was made up of eight distinct parts—the five senses, the powers of reproduction and speech, and reason which has control over the other seven.

(iii) *Dualism of human nature*. Generally speaking Hebrew psychology is distinguished from Greek psychology by reason of the fact that in the former human personality is regarded as a unity, whilst in the latter it is thought of in terms of a dualism of body and soul. According to the Orphic sects, for example, the soul's sojourn in the body is a punishment for sin; the body is the prison house of the soul. So also in the teaching of Pythagoreanism, the soul has no organic relation with the body and longs to return to that realm of pure spiritual being from which it originally came. This dualism is evident also in the writings of Plato who teaches the immortality and pre-existence of the soul. The body, which is a created thing, is inferior to the soul and a hindrance to it. At death 'the soul will be parted from the body and exist in herself alone' (*Phaedo* 66B).

There are very few references in the apocalyptic literature indicating the influence of such ideas as these. We have seen that in only one passage, II Enoch 24.4–5, is reference made to the pre-existence of the soul, although the doctrine is found in certain other extra-canonical books (cf. Wisd. 8.19; IV Mac. 13.13, 21; 18.23). A certain disparagement of the body in hinted at in I Enoch 108.7 which seems to regard asceticism as meritorious: 'For some of them are written and inscribed above in the heaven . . . the spirits of the humble, and of those who have afflicted their bodies, and been recompensed by God.' In II Esd. 7.88 the body is described as 'this corruptible vessel' from which the soul escapes at death (7.96); being mortal and corruptible it does not belong to man's essential being. Nevertheless, even though such an idea of the departed soul, existing apart from the body, reflects the influence of Greek thought, the typically Hebrew emphasis on the body as an essential aspect of personality still asserts itself, for the typical mode of survival in the after life is not just the immortality of the soul but the resurrection in which soul and body are reunited to share the glories of the world to come.

5. INFLUENCE OF HEBREW THOUGHT ON THE CONCEPTION OF THE UNITY OF PERSONALITY

A study of the psychological terminology used by the apocalyptic writers shows quite clearly that the ideas they held concerning human personality were essentially those of the Old Testament itself. The influence of Greek ideas is detectable in a few books, as is to be expected, but for the most part the tradition followed is thoroughly Hebrew.

It has been found convenient, in the above study of the various psychological terms, to treat separately the body and its members (with the heart as the most important organ), the soul and the spirit. These several terms, however, must not be taken to represent three separate 'parts' of man's being; rather they indicate three 'aspects' of his personality and signify three different lines of approach to an understanding of human consciousness. Although they may be considered separately for convenience' sake, their meaning is to be understood only in relationship. The resulting idea of personality is not a trichotomy of body, soul and spirit or a dichotomy of body and soul-spirit, but an essential unity.

One apparent exception to this is the belief expressed in the apocalyptic writings of the survival of the soul or the spirit apart from the body after death. The difficulty, however, is more apparent than real, for although the soul-spirit leaves the body at death and enters into an existence possessing a real degree of conscious life, it is generally believed that a body of some kind is necessary for the full attainment of personality.[1]

(i) *Relation of soul and spirit.* In a considerable number of cases, as we have seen, the words 'soul' and 'spirit' are regarded by the apocalyptists as synonymous terms. Both are used to denote the life principle in man, or to indicate the full range of human consciousness, or to describe the state of man's survival after death. They are not simply separate, identifiable 'parts' of personality which can be set over against each other.

E. de W. Burton, referring to the Greek writers, says, 'From Xenophanes down to N.T. times *psyche*, soul, is an individual and functional term whose definition was not in that of which it was composed but in its functions; it is the seat of life, feeling, thought. *Pneuma*, on the other hand, is a term of substance, defined not by its functions, which are very variable, but by its qualities. . . .'[2] He goes on to point out that in the Old Testament, although this substantial sense still applied to 'spirit', there was an increasing tendency to give to it an individualized sense, especially in the post-exilic literature. This

[1] For a fuller treatment of this subject see pp. 374f.

[2] *Galatians*, ICC, 1921, p. 486.

change of meaning, or rather emphasis, becomes far more obvious when we come to the apocalyptic literature, for there the substantial use is far less frequent than in the Old Testament books and the individualized use is correspondingly increased. This is a significant point for it shows a development in the apocalyptic writings toward the use of the word by Paul where the substantial sense of *pneuma* has practically disappeared; he does not use *pneuma* at all to denote 'wind', for example, and only once does he use it to denote 'breath'.[1] In this respect, therefore, the terms 'soul' and 'spirit' have been drawn more closely together in the apocalyptic writings.[2] The difference between them is not primarily one of kind but rather of aspect or approach, the spirit being expressive of that side of man's nature which may be more readily influenced by the spirit of God. We may say that 'soul' and 'spirit' together express the inner life of man in its lower and higher aspects respectively. Sometimes the word 'heart' is used as a synonym for 'soul' or 'spirit' to signify the inner life of man. But again the difference between them is one of approach and not of kind, the 'soul' stressing the emotional side of consciousness and the 'heart' stressing the intellectual or volitional.

(ii) *Relation of the body to soul and spirit.* The body and its members,

[1] In II Thess. 2.8 with reference to Isa. 11.4.

[2] Although there is a definite individualization of the spirit of God in the Jewish apocalypses there is never an actual personalization. This further development appears for the first time in Christian writings because of the influence on the writers' minds of the identification of the spirit with the person of Jesus Christ. The Holy Spirit appears as a person in the New Testament Apocalypse, for example (cf. 2.7, 11, 17, 29; 3.6, 13, 22; 14.13; 22.17). So also in the Ascension of Isaiah. In 8.18 of that book mention is made of the Trinity in these words, 'And there they all named the primal Father and his Beloved, the Christ, and the Holy Spirit all with one voice.' That the writer regarded the Holy Spirit as a person is clear also from the fact that he can refer to it as 'the Angel of the Spirit' (9.39, 40; 10.4; 11.4. 4.21 is an editorial note), or as 'the Angel of the Holy Spirit' (7.23; 9.36; 11.33); he elsewhere identifies 'the Angel of the Spirit' with Gabriel (11.4).

The paucity of references in the apocalyptic writings to the spirit of God reminds us of yet another advance made by the Christian writers in this respect. This neglect of the spirit of God was fully met by the New Testament anthropology, particularly in the Pauline interpretation of Christian experience. Some words of H. Wheeler Robinson are worth quoting here: 'The chief lacuna in the religious experience generated by Judaism . . . is the absence of any adequate development of the Old Testament idea of the Spirit of God . . . the consciousness of the immediate inspiration and presence of God, which the doctrine of the Spirit implies, had passed into more or less hopeful expectancy of some return of the heroic age. Christian hope saw that expectation realized in Christ; its experience was of the present possession of the outpoured Spirit, given through the Lord the Spirit' (*The Christian Doctrine of Man*, 1934, pp. 74f.).

as we have seen, reveal psychical as well as physiological properties and are an essential aspect of the unity of personality. If a distinction be drawn between the body and the soul-spirit it is that whereas the latter denotes the inner life of man in its lower and higher aspects, the former denotes man's outer life. The terms indicate different lines of approach to the understanding of human personality which, though many-sided, nevertheless forms a unity.

The unity of body and soul, for example, is illustrated in such a passage as II Enoch 60.2: 'He who works the killing of a man's soul kills his own soul and kills his own body, and there is no cure for him for all time.' In several passages the body is closely associated with the soul in expressing excitement or emotion. The writer of II Esd. 5.14, for example, describes the effect of a dream-vision in this way: 'Then I awoke, and my body trembled greatly; my soul also was wearied even unto fainting.' Or again, in the Test. of Dan the writer shows the psychological effect of anger first of all on the body, for it blindeth a man's eyes (2.4), and secondly on his mind, for 'it darkeneth his mind' (2.4), and thirdly on the soul, for 'it troubleth even the soul itself' (3.1). The passage continues: 'And the body of the angry man it maketh its own, and over his soul it getteth the mastery, and it bestoweth upon the body power that it may work all iniquity. And when the body does all these things, the soul justifieth what is done, since it seeth not aright' (3.2–3). That is, body and soul belong together as two aspects of the same personality.

A similar relation exists between the body and the spirit. In Test. of Sim. 5.1, for example, it is said of Joseph that he was 'comely in appearance, and goodly to look upon, because no wickedness dwelt in him; for some of the trouble of the spirit the face manifesteth'. Another passage, of greater psychological significance, is Test. of Napht. 2.2, 4 which reads, 'For as the potter knoweth the vessel, how much it is to contain, and bringeth clay accordingly, so also doth the Lord make the body after the likeness of the spirit, and according to the capacity of the body doth he implant the spirit. . . . And as the potter knoweth the use of each vessel, what it is meet for, so also doth the Lord know the body, how far it will persist in goodness, and when it beginneth in evil.' The writer here likens the body to a vessel in which the spirit is to be implanted, but his simile breaks down when he adds that the body is made 'after the likeness of the spirit' and is capable of doing good and evil just as the spirit itself which is in man. Here we see the Hebrew influence triumphing over the Greek tendency to regard the body as the temporary dwelling place of the spirit or soul.

This idea of the unity of personality in which body, soul and spirit represent three ways of looking at human personality, not three parts or sections within it, is essentially a continuation of the thought of the Old Testament and an anticipation of that of the New Testament and particularly of the Apostle Paul.[1]

[1] That Paul's conception of the body, for example, is Hebrew rather than Greek is obvious from such a verse as I Cor. 6.18: 'Flee fornication. Every sin that a man doeth is without the body; but he that committeth fornication sinneth against his own body.' To Paul's mind this sexual union was more than a union of bodies in our sense of the word; it was, in fact, a union of personalities. It is because fornication is an unworthy surrender of personality that Paul immediately condemns it as sinful; it is a sin against man's essential being. This idea of the body as fundamental to personality and as itself the essential personality, is, as we have seen, common among both the Old Testament and the apocalyptic writers.

VI

APOCALYPTIC INSPIRATION

THE APOCALYPTISTS BELIEVED they had been given a message from God and were under a divine compulsion to make it known. They were not interested, however, in supplying data to substantiate any particular theory of inspiration. Theirs was a very practical problem; they had been given a message and had to explain as best they could how they became aware of it. In particular they ascribed this message to some ancient hero such as Enoch or Moses or Abraham who is said to have received revelations from God under conditions of divine inspiration. To what extent, if any, the reported experience of the ancient seer reflects the actual experience of the apocalyptic writers it is not at all easy to ascertain.

This is a highly imaginative literature in which the inventive faculties of the writers are given free scope. In course of time a conventional literary pattern begins to emerge which, though it reveals certain interesting variations, finds expression in certain stereotyped forms of revelation such as dreams, visions, trances, heavenly journeys, angelic messages and the rest. The reader is conscious of a certain artificiality about the literature as a whole whose descriptions of visionary experiences, for example, give the impression of pseudo-ecstasy and assumed inspiration.

At the same time we have to face the fact that this is how the apocalyptic writer thought inspiration could come, and so there is at least an *a priori* argument for the possibility of his sharing such an experience. He ascribes to the one in whose name he writes such experiences as he would expect to have in a message to himself, and some of these may well have been genuine experiences in which he believed himself to be divinely inspired. After all, we must account for the fact that the apocalyptist did put his message in the form in which we find it. His frequent use of dreams, for example, suggests that a good deal of his own message came through dreams; and if the apocalyptist took his dreams seriously it would suggest that other psychical experiences were taken by him seriously also. It is, of course, a matter for inference, but it is a matter for strong inference. An examination of the various media of revelation mentioned in these writings adds considerable weight to this inference and suggests that, alongside what may be described as cases of conventional inspiration of a literary kind, there are others which have the appearance of genuine inspiration in which the writer believed that he had been privileged to share the experience credited to the one in whose name he wrote. To distinguish between the two is no easy matter, but such an examination indicates that there is probably more evidence of genuine inspiration in the apocalyptic writers than might at first be imagined.

In the Old Testament there is presented a continuous line of revelation in prophets, priests, wise men and apocalyptists who wrote or spoke, directly or indirectly, under divine inspiration. The form which their experience of inspiration took was different in each case, but each expression of it is to be understood aright only in relation to the others. In this present chapter we shall compare the inspiration of the apocalyptist and that of the prophet, with whom, as we have seen, he had much in common, and refer to an added note a comparison with the priest and the wise man. In particular we shall note certain psychological presuppositions which the apocalyptist and the prophet shared with each other in their understanding of divine inspiration.

I. INSPIRATION AS 'POSSESSION'

The apocalyptist was at one with the prophet in his belief that man's personality was accessible to supernatural influence. In pre-exilic times frequent reference is made to the *rūaḥ* (spirit) of God as a wind-like force falling upon a man and bringing about certain abnormalities in his character or behaviour.[1] It was this same *rūaḥ* from God which caused the ecstatic prophets to prophesy.[2] In the

[1] Cf. the strength of Samson in Judg. 14.6 or the madness of Saul in I Sam. 16.14, etc.

[2] Cf. I Sam. 10.6, etc.

writings of the classical prophets, however, relatively little use is made of *rūaḥ* to describe the phenomenon of inspiration. The idea of the invasive spirit of God is still to be found in their writings together with certain abnormal and 'psychopathic' elements, but there is a definite development away from the more primitive type, the chief exception being Ezekiel who may be described as a 'throw-back' in this particular respect.

Similarly in the apocalyptic writings relatively little mention is made of the spirit of God as a strictly inspirational agency;[1] but the belief is strongly expressed in the accessibility of man's nature to invasive forces sent forth from God as a means of inspiration. This idea of 'possession', common to Old Testament writers and apocalyptists, was not confined to them, but was shared by many people in the ancient world as is evidenced by the great collection of the Sibylline Oracles, for example. Those which come within our purview here are imitations of pagan oracles which are perhaps themselves imitations of the actual oracles of women 'possessed' by the god.[2] We have to make allowance for the fact that the descriptions of this type of inspiration had in all probability become, to a fairly large degree, a stereotyped convention in this kind of literature; but in the apocalyptic literature there are suggestions that the description given is more than the record of a literary convention and in fact reflects a personal experience on the part of the writer himself.

The writer of Book III of the Sibylline Oracles, for example, can speak of the message of God fluttering in his breast (162), or stirring within his breast (489–91); it is the Mighty God who is the inspirer (306); the Sibyl is 'impelled by frenzy to proclaim his word' (809–11), and beseeches him to ease her from her spell (395–6). More will be said about this ecstatic state later on, but here we note that this writer at least is familiar with it.

Human personality is accessible, however, not only to the spirit of God, but to demonic forces as well. No exact parallel to this can be found in the Old Testament, for demonology was unable to survive in the atmosphere of Yahwism.[3] In the apocalyptists, how-

[1] This use of the word *rūaḥ* is limited to the following passages: I Enoch 68.2; 70.2; 91.1; 'Mart. of Isa.', 1.7; 5.14; Test. of Abr. 4; II Bar. 6.3; 7.2; II Esd. 14.22.

[2] Cf. E. Bevan, *Sibyls and Seers*, 1928, p. 136.

[3] The reference to the 'lying spirit' in I Kings 22.21ff. probably forms a real link between the popular demonology and the general idea of the accessibility of human personality to the invasive spirit of Yahweh.

ever, demonology comes into its own, and evil spirits or demons are sent forth to invade the lives of men.[1]

2. MEDIA OF REVELATION

Another similarity between apocalyptists and prophets is to be found in the fact that, for each, the media of revelation were psychical rather than physical.[2] Such psychical phenomena as dreams, visions, trances and auditions were quite common at a lower stage of Hebrew prophecy. It is uncertain to what extent the classical prophets shared such experiences; but it seems likely that at least the beginning of their ministry was marked in this way and that such visions recurred at intervals throughout their lives. J. Skinner suggests that these 'were actually experienced by them in a condition of comparative ecstasy, in which self-consciousness was not lost, although its control of the visionary process was suspended'.[3] It would not be true to say, however, that every revelation came by some abnormal means. 'Visions and auditions, mysterious inward promptings to speech and action, are still part of the prophet's experience; but the field of revelation is no longer confined to them alone. The meaning of the vision passes into the prophet's thinking, and becomes the nucleus of a comprehensive view of God and the world, from which spring ever fresh intuitions of truth and calls to duty.'[4] The content of the message following the words 'Thus saith the Lord' might very well come from a psychologically normal experience, and not necessarily from an abnormal or ecstatic state.

When we turn to the apocalyptic writings we find that the abnormal experiences of dreams, visions, trances and auditions are far more often referred to than in the writings of the classical prophets. But as in the prophetic books so here, it is often quite impossible to say when the portrayed visionary experience is anything more than the expression of a common literary device. As R. H. Charles says, 'Just as at times the prophet came to use the word "thus saith the Lord", even when there was no actual psychical experience in which he heard a voice, but when he wished to set forth the will of God which he had reached by other means, so the term "vision" came to have a like conventional use both in prophecy and apocalyptic.'[5] It

[1] Cf. Test. of Dan 1.7; Test. of Zeb. 2.1; 3.2, etc. See further ch. IX.
[2] For examples of physical media of revelation see pp. 174f.
[3] *Prophecy and Religion*, 1940, p. 11. [4] *Ibid.*, p. 220.
[5] *Eschatology*, 2nd ed., 1913, p. 176.

must not be assumed, however, that the adoption of a conventional form of utterance and the experience of genuine inspiration are mutually exclusive. There is no guarantee, either in the prophetic or in the apocalyptic writings, that the inspired message will be passed on in its original form. The prophets, for example, in presenting their inspired message made free use of the conventional form of Hebrew poetry with its devices of parallelism and rhythmical versification; but this did not in any way affect the ultimate inspiration by which they wrote or spoke. Similarly, in the case of the apocalyptists, the fact that they made use of a common literary convention does not necessarily imply that they were devoid of inspiration. Inspiration can lay hold of the conventional and express itself through the commonest literary device. Examination of the apocalyptic writings shows that much of the literary convention there followed may well have psychological experience behind it.

3. DREAMS, VISIONS AND AUDITIONS

Writing on the subject of dreams and visions among the Semites, A. Guillaume remarks, 'When a pious, deeply religious member of such a race turns his whole attention to God, he sees more than we see, he hears what we do not hear, and his apprehension of God is, as he himself claims, immediate and intuitive.'[1] The 'psychology' lying behind such an experience is different in many ways from that of Western civilization, and if the 'abnormal' experiences of the prophets or the apocalyptists are to be understood aright they must be viewed within this setting and against the background of Semitic beliefs.

In particular, the attempted distinction between 'subjective' and 'objective', as applied to visionary experiences, would not exist for these writers. Just as in the realms of nature and history they were not careful to make any clear-cut distinction between primary and secondary causes, so in the psychological realm they believed that these abnormal phenomena had their cause in God, and as such had an objective reality. Just as, in the Old Testament prophets, the word of Yahweh, when sent forth, entered upon a history of its own as something detached from the one who spoke it, so in the apocalyptists the dream or vision or voice, having been despatched by God,

[1] *Prophecy and Divination*, 1938, p. 228.

presented itself to the mind or eye or ear of the person concerned as something of objective validity.

The apocalyptist does not say of a dream that it arose out of his own imagination or thoughts, but that it was given him or sent him by God. It was in a dream that the word of the Lord came to Abram (Jub. 14.1), that Jacob was bidden by God to return to his father's house (Jub. 29.3), that Isaac was notified concerning his death (Test. of Abr. 5), that Rebecca saw the day of her departure (Jub. 35.6), that Eve saw the blood of her son on the day of his death (Apoc. of Moses 2.2).

The vision, too, had for the apocalyptist an objective reality as when Enoch says, 'And behold . . . visions fell upon me' (I Enoch 13.4). He does not imagine that these visions rose out of his own conscious or sub-conscious experience (to use modern expressions), but that they were sent forth by God as independent media of revelation. In II Bar. 55.3 we read that the angel Ramiel presides over true visions, as though they were in existence quite apart from man's experience, stored up in the heavenly places.[1] Sometimes the vision is mediated through angels (cf. I Enoch 1.2, etc.), and at least once the way for its coming is said to be prepared by 'the holy spirit' (Test. of Abr. 4).

In two passages the phraseology used appears to signify what we should call a 'subjective' origin for the visionary experience. In I Enoch 37.4 Enoch remarks that the vision of wisdom which has been given to him has been received 'according to my insight'. What is meant here, however, is simply that there had to be on the part of Enoch a certain power of receptivity capable of appropriating and appreciating the vision once it had been imparted. Again, in Dan. 10.7 we read, 'And I Daniel alone saw the vision: for the men that were with me saw not the vision.' The writer adds, however, that as a result 'a great quaking fell upon them, so that they fled to hide themselves' (10.7), thus emphasizing the 'objective' character of the vision he had seen.[2]

Less common, but equally significant in this connection, is the

[1] Mention is made here of *true* visions, but nowhere in the apocalyptic writings does the problem arise regarding the difference between the true and the false such as we find, for example, in the book of Jeremiah, although, as we have seen, it was felt possible for the devil and his evil spirits to inspire a man just as it was felt possible for God to do so.

[2] Cf. Acts 22, where Paul hears a voice which is not heard by his retinue, though they are afraid when they see the great light from heaven.

phenomenon of audition. The idea of a voice from heaven was known to the Greeks,[1] but in practically every occurrence in the apocalyptic writings the reference is to the *bath qol* of rabbinic tradition[2] which is regarded as the echo of God's voice, if not exactly that voice itself. Audition corresponds in the sphere of hearing to the vision in the sphere of seeing; the sound of the voice does not arise out of a man's own consciousness, but is sent forth by God. Such objectivity is illustrated by an interesting reference in II Esd. 5.37 where Uriel says to Ezra, 'Show me the image of a voice', concerning which G. H. Box makes the following comment: 'The ancients believed that sound like other existences possessed form which was visible to celestial (but not to coarse human) sight. This applies also to the Deity. Such forms were only invisible on lower planes of existence.'[3]

4. EVIDENCE OF GENUINE PSYCHICAL EXPERIENCE

In many cases in these writings a clear distinction is drawn between dreams which come in sleep and visions which appear in a state of consciousness and wakefulness. But in many other cases visions are received in sleep when we should naturally expect the mention of dreams, the two experiences being apparently equated. Likewise it is sometimes difficult to distinguish the vision from the trance, for the vision sometimes appears to a person whilst he is in a trance-like state when his powers of thought and observation are in abeyance.

There are several examples of dreams giving antecedent knowledge in which, for example, Isaac (Test. of Abr. 5) and Rebecca (Jub. 35.6) saw or were reminded of the day of their death, and in which Eve saw the blood of her son (Apoc. of Moses 2.2). As with the dream so also with the vision. Enoch, for example, is shown a vision 'not for this generation, but for a remote one which is to come' (I Enoch 1.2), and Jacob is said to be able to read in visions his own future and that of his descendants on the heavenly tablets (Jub. 32.16–26). Concerning Enoch the writer of Jubilees says, 'And what was and what will be he saw in a vision of his sleep, as it will happen to the children of men throughout their generations until

[1] Cf. the *daimonion* of Socrates.
[2] *E.g.*, Test. of Abr. 10; Apoc. of Abr. 9, 10; II Bar. 13.1; 22.1; II Esd. 14.38.
[3] *The Ezra-Apocalypse*, 1912, p. 57.

the day of judgment' (4.9). The apocalyptist, in such examples as these and by his own forecasting of future events, even though from the point of view of a by-gone day, expresses his belief in such dreams and visions, if not his actual experience of them.

There are certain other references which suggest that the reported dream or vision may well have had genuine inspirational experience behind it. Sometimes, for example, the vision is said to come before sleep (Dan. 10.9) or during sleep (II Bar. 53.1, etc.) or after sleep (II Enoch 1.6). Sometimes it comes during the night (II Esd. 6.30); at other times it appears by day. This constant reference to visions coming during the night or in some state of sleep may suggest that we have here actual experiences and not merely expressions of literary convention, for night time is recognized to be conducive to inspiration, and in particular that somnolent state between sleeping and waking.[1]

The same impression is made by the account of the *effects* accompanying or following the visionary experience. Ezra, for example, tells how 'My heart was troubled within me. . . . For my spirit was greatly inflamed and my soul was in distress' (II Esd. 6.36–37). The coming of the vision puts him into a trance-like state as when he lies on the ground as one dead, his understanding being confused (10.30, cf. Dan. 8.17–18; 10.9f., 15). His heart is troubled at its coming (9.28) and it leaves him in a state of bewilderment and terror (10.27). So overwhelming is the experience that he is quite unable to express it or describe it adequately (10.32, 55, 56, cf. II Cor. 12.4). Sometimes, too, these emotional disturbances are accompanied by physical disturbances as in the case of Daniel, who found that his visions not only disturbed his spirit (Dan. 7.15) and alarmed his thoughts (7.28), but made him physically sick as well (8.27); pangs might come upon him (10.16), or he might become dumb (10.15), or even lose consciousness altogether (8.18; 10.9). Sometimes the recipient is insensible to all physical suffering, as in the 'Martyrdom of Isaiah', 5.7, where the prophet is so absorbed in a vision of the Lord that, though his eyes are open, he does not see those who are sawing his body. All these experiences are so true psychologically that it is

[1] Mozart tells us, for example, that it was at night time, when he could not sleep, that his ideas flowed far better than at other times; it was during this half-asleep, half-awake state that Wagner received the opening of the 'Rheingold'; it was during actual sleep that Tartini received the inspiration which made possible his 'Trillo del Diavolo' (cf. R. E. M. Harding in *An Anatomy of Inspiration*, 1940, pp. 10–12).

difficult to see in them nothing more than the expression of literary convention; their very nature argues strongly that they reflect the actual experiences of the apocalyptic writers themselves.

This same conclusion seems to be borne out by an example in the Testaments of the XII Patriarchs of what we today should describe as television. In the Test. of Benj. 10.1 we read, 'Now when Joseph was in Egypt, I longed to see his figure and the form of his countenance; and through the prayers of Jacob my father I saw him, while awake in the day time, even his entire figure exactly as he was.'[1] The writer is at pains to tell us that it was not a dream, for the figure appeared in the day time during a period of waking consciousness. This passage recalls that other in Num. 24.4, 16, which describes Balaam as a man 'which seeth the vision of the Almighty, falling down and having his eyes open'. It is just possible that the description in the Test. of Benj. is an attempted imitation of this Old Testament passage, and so is a fragment of prophecy; but it is more likely, because of the unusual character of the incident, that the apocalyptic writer is projecting some of his own psychical experience into his hero just as may have been done in the other examples quoted above.

5. TRANSLATION

A phenomenon unknown to the prophets of the Old Testament but common enough in Greek literature, is that of the soul or spirit of a man leaving the body and travelling through the spirit-world. Such a belief was not possible for the Hebrew prophets who could not think of the soul apart from the body as a separate conscious entity. The apocalyptists, however, *could* think of the soul apart from the body and possessing a real conscious life of its own, especially after death.[2] It is not surprising, especially in view of the prevalence of the idea in Greek thought, to find passages in the apocalyptic writings describing the translation of the spirit and its visit to the spirit-world. We read concerning Enoch, for example, 'And it came to pass after this that my spirit was translated and it ascended into the heavens, and I saw the holy ones of God' (I Enoch 71.1). Greater detail is given in I Enoch 14.8 where translation is associated

[1] Dr Charles's suggestion is quite unnecessary that this verse be emended and transferred to the beginning of 2.1; cf. *Testaments of the Twelve Patriarchs*, 1908, p. 212.

[2] See p. 147 and also ch. XIV.

with vision: 'Behold, in the vision, clouds invited me and a mist summoned me, and the course of the stars and the lightnings sped and hastened me, and the winds in the vision caused me to fly and lifted me upward and bore me into heaven.'[1] So common is this phenomenon in stories concerning legendary figures that in most of the occurrences in the apocalyptic literature we probably have nothing more than the following out of a stereotyped literary convention. At the same time, the fact that the apocalyptist could make use of such an idea shows that he gave credence to such a theory of inspiration.

But even here the influence of Hebrew psychology for which the body is essential to personality still remains strong; for in several places the translation which is described is that of the body and not that of the soul or the spirit apart from the body.[2] This is made clear in the Test. of Abraham, for example, where we read, 'I beseech thee, Lord, if I must needs leave my body, I would fain be caught up in the body, that I may see the creatures which the Lord my God has created in heaven and upon earth' (7B). God then commands Michael, saying, 'Depart, and take up Abraham in the body, and show him all. . . . So Michael went out, and caught up Abraham in the body upon a cloud' (8B). Elsewhere it is said of Abraham that he was taken up on the right wing of a pigeon and grew so weak that his spirit departed from him (Apoc. of Abr. 15; 16), and of Enoch that the angels took him up on their wings and bare him away (II Enoch 3.1), so that his soul departed from him for fear and

[1] Other illustrations of translation are: of Enoch (I Enoch 39.3f.; 71.1, 5; II Enoch 3.1; 36.1, 2, etc.), of Abraham (Test. of Abr. 7B; 8B; 9; 10; Apoc. of Abr. 12; 15; 16; 30), of Baruch (II Bar. 6.4; III Bar. 1.3, 4) and of Adam (Life of Adam and Eve 25.3).

Evidence of a similar nature is provided by the Christian apocalyptic literature. The Ascension of Isaiah, for example, tells how the soul of the prophet was taken up on high but would return to his body later (7.5, cf. 8.11, 27). It is probable that the words 'Come up hither' spoken to John on the Isle of Patmos refer also to a translation of the spirit (cf. Rev. 11.12; 17.3; 21.10). In this connection F. C. Burkitt writes, 'It is surely impossible to read the first chapter of the canonical Apocalypse of John and not feel that . . . something like it was really experienced by the Seer' (*op. cit.*, p. 41).

[2] The departure of men in the body to the realm of the dead is, of course, represented in mythological stories of Greek literature (cf. E. Bevan, *op. cit.*, p. 46), and the apocalyptists were no doubt influenced from this source in this respect. But their whole background of Hebrew psychology, which gave such an important place to the body, would be a very important factor in preparing them to accept such a view.

trembling (21.4).[1] Bodily transportations of rather a different kind are alluded to in two other passages. One is II Bar. 6.3: 'And lo, suddenly a strong spirit raised me, and bore me aloft over the wall of Jerusalem.' The other is Dan. 8.2: 'And I saw in the vision; now it was so, that when I saw, I was in Shushan the palace.' This latter reference is reminiscent of Ezekiel's transportation by the spirit to Tel-abib.[2]

In Greek literature, as we have already noted, there are many legendary stories of a man's soul, separated from the body, travelling through Heaven and Hades either after death or in a state of trance. The influence of this idea on apocalyptic thought can be readily acknowledged; but it may be that another influence, of Hebrew origin, should also be taken into account, *viz.* the idea of the Council of Yahweh. In such passages as I Kings 22.19ff., Job 1.6ff. and Isa. 6.6ff. God is described as presiding over a heavenly Council whose members are there to carry out his will. He is 'a God very terrible in the council of the holy ones' (Ps. 89.7) who 'judgeth among the gods' (Ps. 82.1) and who in the beginning spoke in the name of these heavenly beings and said, 'Let *us* make man in our own image' (Gen. 1.26). This Council is attended, however, not only by gods and angels but also by men; for it is the privilege of the truly inspired prophet to stand in its midst and hear the word of Yahweh (cf. Jer. 23.18ff.). In this connection the Old Testament emphasis is on visionary experience rather than on transportation or translation such as we have found in the apocalyptic references, but the picture is very much the same and suggests that in these apocalyptic descriptions we may well have a continuation and extension of the Old Testament idea.

The 'holy ones' or angels appear in both traditions, but in the apocalyptic writings their functions undergo certain developments. In Daniel they are described as satraps sent forth by God to govern the different countries. In I Enoch we read of the seventy shepherds or angels sent to shepherd Israel after the Captivity (89.59); Michael is described as Israel's guardian angel (90.14), whilst others are set over 'Paradise and the serpents and the Cherubim' (20.7), or mankind and chaos (20.5), and so on. Even here, however, the

[1] Cf. also I Enoch 39.3, 4; II Enoch 36.1, 2; 38.1; II Bar. 6.4; II Esd. 14.9. We are reminded of the words of Paul in II Cor. 12.2–4, where he describes how he was caught up to the third heaven, 'whether in the body, I know not; or whether out of the body, I know not'.

[2] Ezek. 3.12–15. The verb used here for 'lifting up' is the same word used for bodily translation in I Kings 18.12 and II Kings 2.16.

influence of the Old Testament is evident and the idea of the heavenly Council remains fundamentally the same.[1]

Thus, in this phenomenon of translation, illustrating one aspect of apocalyptic inspiration, it is quite possible that we are to find once again evidence of Hebrew, and in particular of prophetic, thought.[2]

6. PREPARATIONS FOR PSYCHICAL EXPERIENCE

Throughout these writings reference is frequently made to certain devices whereby it was thought possible to encourage or induce a state of inspiration. Such things as fasting, a special diet or drink, a special place or time are regarded as aids to or preparations for psychical experience. These references may very well reflect the actual practice of the various apocalyptic writers themselves.

We have already observed that in a number of cases the apocalyptic visions, for example, are said to have been received during the night. Elsewhere a special place is mentioned, like the oak tree of Mamre where Michael appeared to Abraham (Test. of Abr. 2), or Baruch saw a vision (II Bar. 6.1) or met the angel Ramiel (55.1) or wrote under the inspiration of God (77.18–19). These are probably no more than survivals of a much earlier belief, scattered throughout the Old Testament, which regarded certain trees as sacred and as places of revelation.

More significant is the practice of fasting as a preparation for psychical experience and the reception of divine revelation. Daniel, for example, sought God not only with prayers and supplications, but also with fasting and sackcloth and ashes (Dan. 9.3). Before each of his first three visions Ezra is bidden to fast for seven days.[3] He tells us that in preparation for his third vision he 'fasted seven days in

[1] The evidence of Deut. 32.8–9 (LXX), which tells how the nations are placed under the authority of angelic powers, is especially apt at this point. See below, pp. 248f.

[2] This idea of a heavenly council, as R. H. Charles reminds us, 'was developed in later Judaism to an extravagant and even blasphemous degree, in accordance with which God was represented as doing nothing without consulting this council (*Sanh.* 38b, where this statement is made). . . . When God wished to make Hezekiah the Messiah his council successfully resisted him (*Sanh.* 94a), and when he purposed to admit the descendants of Nebuchadnezzar into the Jewish Community, the angels of service would not suffer it' (*Commentary on Daniel*, 1929, p. 93).

[3] This is explicit in the case of the second vision (cf. 5.20) and the third (cf. 6.31, 35) and is implicit in the case of the first (cf. 6.35, where mention is made of fasts for *three* weeks).

like manner that I might fulfil the three weeks that had been commanded me' (II Esd. 6.35). This reference to Ezra's three weeks' fast finds an interesting parallel in Dan. 10.2, 3: 'In these days I, Daniel, was mourning three whole weeks. I ate no pleasant bread, neither came flesh nor wine in my mouth, neither did I anoint myself at all, till three whole weeks were fulfilled.' It is noteworthy that this lengthy fast was followed by perhaps the most important vision of all, just as in II Esdras the most important follows the completion of the three weeks. Again, in II Bar. 5.7 we read of a fast 'until the evening', followed by four other fasts of seven days each (9.2; 12.5; 21.1; 47.2). According to the final editor's scheme a fast is followed by a prayer which in turn is followed by a divine revelation. Similarly a fast of forty days is prescribed for Abraham before he offers his sacrifice; he is to 'abstain from every form of food that proceedeth out of the fire, and from the drinking of wine, and from anointing thyself with oil, forty days . . .' (Apoc. of Abr. 9). We see, then, that just as in the approach of a vision the person to whom it was given was affected by it in body as well as in mind and spirit, so in the preparation for a vision or any other psychical experience the mind or spirit are not the only factors involved, for the body has a vital part to play.

Of interest, too, are several references to special diets or foods prescribed as a preparation for psychical experience. The young men in the Book of Daniel, for example, are given 'pulse to eat and water to drink' (1.12) as a means of spiritual, and not only physical, well-being. The prophets mentioned in the 'Martyrdom of Isaiah' 'eat nothing save wild herbs' (2.11) so that they may the better receive God's revelation. Perhaps the clearest passage in this connection is II Esd. 9.23–25: 'If thou wilt separate thyself yet seven more days—thou shalt not, however, fast in them, but shalt go into a field of flowers, where no house has been built, and eat only of the fruit of the field; and thou shalt taste no flesh and drink no wine, but (eat) only the fruit—and pray unto the Most High continually, then I will come and talk with thee.'[1] In view of the fact that the following vision is to concern the heavenly Jerusalem, this special diet may be explained along one of two lines or along both. It may be, for example, that this partaking of the fruit (or herbs) of the field is a way of anticipating the heavenly food or manna,[2] and that Ezra,

[1] See also II Esd. 12.49–51.

[2] Cf. II Bar. 29.5, 8; Life of Adam and Eve 3.1; 4.1, 2; Apoc. of Moses 6.1; 29.3, 5, 6; III Bar. 6.11.

by taking this heavenly food, is preparing himself for the heavenly Jerusalem and consequently for his vision of it. Or, it may be explained along the line of prophetic symbolism as it appears, for example, in the Old Testament. There an act was performed by the prophet which not only symbolized the future event prophesied, but set it in motion or hastened its coming to pass. Ezra, by partaking of the food of the age of innocence, was thereby creating, albeit in vision, this heavenly Jerusalem wherein innocence and goodness dwell.[1]

In this same book reference is made in an important passage to a special drink by whose means a state of inspiration is induced. In answer to Ezra's prayer for inspiration a voice calls him, saying, 'Ezra, open thy mouth, and drink what I give thee to drink. Then I opened my mouth, and lo! there was reached unto me a full cup, which was full as it were with water, but the colour of it was like fire. And I took it, and drank; and when I had drunk, my heart poured forth understanding, wisdom grew in my breast, and my spirit retained its memory: and my mouth was opened and was no more shut. And the Most High gave understanding unto the five men, and they wrote what was dictated in order, in characters which they knew not' (14.38–42). The cup which Ezra drinks is the cup of inspiration filled with the holy spirit.

As a result of drinking it Ezra is able to repeat aloud the contents of the twenty-four books of sacred Scripture and the seventy apocalyptic writings.[2] His inspiration is infectious and is caught by the five men who write at his dictation, for they write 'in characters which they knew not' (14.42).[3] It is clear that Ezra's experience here is different from the experiences of the earlier ecstatic prophets of the Old Testament in which memory and consciousness were usually lost, for Ezra's faculties appear to have been strengthened rather than weakened and in particular his mind is clarified so that he can

[1] 'The food most appropriate in the circumstances would be that of the primaeval age, and the age of man's innocence. According to one well-known view, flesh-eating came in only after the flood, and marked a retrograde step in human development' (G. H. Box, *op. cit.*, p. 209).

[2] See pp. 85ff., 114.

[3] We are reminded of the account given in Philo of the translation of the LXX: 'They, like men inspired, prophesied, not one saying one thing and another another, but every one of them employed the self-same nouns and verbs, as if some unseen prompter had suggested all their language to them' (*Life of Moses* 2.7; quoted by Box, *op. cit.*, p. 318).

remember more perfectly the sacred writings.[1] This, then, would appear to be a case of inspiration on a higher level in which the human consciousness is not dulled but rather quickened.

The explanation of this passage seems to be that it is an attempt to rationalize previous ideas of inspiration which represented the prophet[2] as open to incursions of the invasive spirit of God and in which spirit is thought of (as in pre-exilic times) in a very material way in the form of water and with the colour of fire (14.39).[3]

This rationalization was no doubt made possible by the influence of Greek thought. There is no reference to this practice among the classical prophets of the Old Testament;[4] but from early times the Greeks were familiar with the practice of drinking wine so as to bring about a state of mind, like that of the ecstatic, in which visions were received. The magic in the wine was regarded as divine, and its presence in the body denoted the presence there of Dionysos himself.[5] The priestess of Delphi, we know, had to drink the *lalōn hudōr*—the water which causes to talk—from the sacred spring beside the temple.[6] G. H. Box suggests that this reference to the cup as a medium of inspiration has, in all probability, Essene affinities, for 'the idea of divine power being sacramentally mediated was familiar to the members of this sect'.[7]

An examination of the evidence provided by these writings points to the conclusion that there is much more here than the following out of a stereotyped literary convention or the presentation of a mere literary device. There are indications that, in not a few cases, the claim to psychical experience on the part of the ancient seer may well indicate similar experience on the part of the apocalyptic writer himself who thereby believes that he is writing under divine inspiration.

A balanced judgment may be that in apocalyptic inspiration we have a link between the original inspiration of the prophets and the

[1] Cf. 14.40: 'My spirit retained its memory', and II Bar. 21.3: 'My soul took much thought.'

[2] Cf. the possible title of this Apocalypse, *Ezras ho Prophētēs*.

[3] It is interesting to observe the close connection in the New Testament between these two elements of water and fire on the one hand and the gift of the Holy Spirit on the other. It was at the Baptism, for example, that the Spirit descended on Jesus, and it was by baptism that the Holy Spirit came upon believers; at Pentecost, when the Spirit came upon the Church, it was like cloven tongues of fire.

[4] The reference in Jer. 25.15, 16, where the cup of the wine of God's fury drives the nations mad, is something different.

[5] Cf. E. Bevan, *op. cit.*, p. 156. [6] Cf. *ibid.*, p. 157. [7] *Op. cit.*, p. 319.

more modern inspiration of a literary kind. Again and again the apocalyptist showed that he believed himself to be writing under the direct influence of the spirit of God in a manner akin to that of the prophets, and even when he accepted the conventional literary framework, as he often did, he still believed himself to be divinely inspired.

Additional Note

A. THE APOCALYPTIST AND THE PRIEST

In the foregoing pages an attempt has been made to discover the relationship, if any, between the inspiration of the apocalyptists and that of the Old Testament prophets. The relationship between apocalyptist and priest in this connection is not nearly as close, but there are certain connections which are worthy of note.

1. *Both trace their tradition back to Moses.* In the Old Testament the priest is presented as a member of a hereditary group, inheriting a priestly tradition which can be traced back, in theory at least, to Moses himself. The local shrine was the natural depository of traditions which would provide the priest with precedents in his important task of giving decisions in response to the enquiries of the people. We recall how Haggai, for example, brought to the priests a question concerning the holiness of certain foodstuffs which had been touched by a garment in which holy flesh had been carried (Hag. 2.12ff.), and observe that the priests answer him on precedent. These precedents on which the priests acted included not only the *d^ebarim* or decisions on matters of ritual, but also the *mišpatim* or judgments which came from the elders; both were brought under the aegis of the priest. These precedents went back in theory to oracles which the priest attributed to a revelation through Moses. Moreover, what was in pre-exilic days an oral tradition became increasingly in post-exilic days a literary tradition; oracles, obviously applying to a later age, were attributed to Moses under some such literary formula as, 'And God spake unto Moses, saying . . .'.

The apocalyptist differs from the priest in that he does not belong to a hereditary class; nevertheless, as we have already seen, he claims to stand in a definite tradition which traces back pronouncements to the mouth of Moses in much the same way as the priestly traditions do. Moreover, this apocalyptic tradition, like the priestly, no doubt sprang from oral beginnings, but as it has come down to us it is a literary production into which oral elements may have been incorporated. In this respect, then, there is a close parallel with the post-exilic priestly writings whose conception of inspiration may be regarded as a link between that of the prophets and that of the apocalyptists.

2. *Both give examples of physical media of revelation.* It has been noted that the priest gave decisions based on precedents and that these precedents could be traced back to an oracle. We further observe that such an oracle was frequently believed to have been received ultimately by some physical means. We must go back to some such physical device as the Urim and Thummim if we are to find the nucleus of later collections of decisions and judgments. Priestly divination was originally by sacred lot, the word *tōrah* itself signifying a casting of the sacred lot. This practice stood right over against that of the prophetic revelation which was purely psychical.[1]

In the apocalyptic writings there are only three possible references to divination by physical means. The first is in Jub. 8.11 which describes how Noah 'divided the earth into the lots which his sons were to take in possession, and they reached forth their hands, and took the writing out of the bosom of Noah, their father'. We have here something corresponding to the priestly use of the Urim and Thummim of the Old Testament. If, as has been surmised, the author of this writing was a priest,[2] he would quite naturally think of the method of the sacred lot when writing concerning the dividing up of the land. The second reference is in the Apoc. of Abr. 9. There Abraham is commanded by God to take a heifer, a she-goat and a ram, each of three years old, together with a turtledove and a pigeon. Then follow these words: 'And in the sacrifice I will lay before thee the ages (to come), and make known to thee what is reserved, and thou shalt see great things which thou hast not seen hitherto.' The reference here is, of course, to Abraham's sacrifice described in Gen. 15.9ff. The apocalyptic writer apparently expresses the belief that Abraham is able to see the events of the future in the severed pieces of the animals and birds. This belief, common among primitive

[1] A good example of priestly divination by physical means over against the oracle of the prophet by psychical means is given in I Sam. 28.6: 'The Lord answered him not, neither by dreams, nor by Urim, nor by prophets.'

[2] Cf. the exaltation of Levi over Judah in 31–32 and the reference in 45.16 to the secret traditions being in the hands of Levi's descendants.

people, that divine signs can be seen in the parts of animals and especially in the liver, is made more explicit in the third reference, II Bar. 4.4, where God says concerning the heavenly Jerusalem, 'I showed it to my servant Abraham by night among the portions of the victims.'

The fact that we have only these three references in the apocalyptic writings to revelation by physical means, but an innumerable number to revelation by psychical means, shows that the prophetic emphasis had largely ousted the other and that in this respect at least the priestly idea had practically no influence on the apocalyptists' conception of inspiration or revelation.

B. THE APOCALYPTIST AND THE SAGE

In Jer. 18.18 and Ezek. 7.26[1] mention is made of the sages alongside the prophets and the priests as recipients of divine revelation. The nature of their inspiration is different from that of both prophet and priest; nevertheless it is a genuine experience in which reference to the 'spirit of wisdom' parallels in many ways reference to the spirit of God or the hand of God in the prophetic writings.[2]

1. *Both explain inspiration ultimately in terms of possession.* H. Wheeler Robinson points out that in the Book of Job Eliphaz claims to receive a revelation by means of a supernatural voice (4.2ff.) and that in one significant passage in Proverbs something approaching an identification between the divine revelation and man's moral consciousness is made.[3] In 20.27 we read,

Yahweh's lamp is man's breath,
Searching all the chambers of the belly.

But the identification is not quite complete, for wisdom and understanding are not the result of man's genius, but of God's inspiration, as is pointed out, for example, by Elihu in the Book of Job:

There is a spirit in man,
And the breath of the Almighty giveth them understanding.
It is not the great that are wise,
Nor the aged that understand judgment (32.8–9).

[1] In the Ezekiel passage the 'wise man' of Jeremiah is replaced by the word 'elders', but no doubt the two are to be regarded as equivalent here (cf. Deut. 32.7; Job 12.12; 32.7; Lam. 2.9f.).

[2] For a fuller treatment of the inspiration of the sage than is here possible see H. Wheeler Robinson, *Inspiration and Revelation in the Old Testament*, 1946, pp. 246ff.

[3] Cf. *ibid.*, p. 247.

Wisdom is indwelling, but is not immanent; it is not a permanent element in man, for it has been sent into him by God.

In the apocalyptic writings also we find evidence of much the same idea of inspiration. In one passage, in fact, there is a very close parallel not only in thought but also in actual phraseology to the passage in Prov. 20.27 quoted above. There God says to Ezra, in answer to his prayer for inspiration that he might be enabled to restore the sacred Scriptures, 'I will light the lamp of understanding in thy heart, which shall not be extinguished until what thou art about to write shall be completed' (II Esd. 14.25). We recall that he caused the Scriptures to be written not when he was in a trance, but when he was fully conscious and in complete possession of his faculties. The divine revelation is not to be identified with Ezra's moral consciousness for he is under the influence of the inspired cup containing the holy spirit, but at the same time the two are brought into very close relation with each other.

The idea of 'possession', as we have seen, is often present in the apocalyptists' conception of inspiration. Men may be said to possess the spirit of understanding (Test. of Levi 2.3), of sanctification (Test. of Levi 18.7), of blessing (Test. of Jud. 24.2), or of grace (Test. of Jud. 24.3); but these, in their context, are more than mere temperaments reflecting man's moral consciousness—they are influences or powers sent into him by God. Sometimes these influences or powers are personalized, especially in the case of malignant spirits. Thus we read of the spirit of fornication, of insatiableness, of fighting, of obsequiousness and chicanery, of pride, of lying, of injustice (Test. of Reub. 3.3ff.), of jealousy (Test. of Jud. 13.3), of deceit (Test. of Jud. 14.8), of anger (Test. of Dan 1.8), of wickedness (Test. of Dan 5.5), of envy (Test. of Sim. 4.7) and so on.

The apocalyptic idea of inspiration, therefore, has this in common with that of the sages, that not only divine revelation but also man's conduct and everything bound up with human ethics is to be explained not merely by reference to man's moral consciousness, but ultimately to some influence or power outside of himself, acting upon him. They are at one in explaining the phenomenon of inspiration by the idea of 'possession'.

2. *Both rely to some extent at least on tradition.* One other point of resemblance between the inspiration of the apocalyptists and that of the sages is suggested by a reference in Ben Sira 39.6 concerning the student of the Scriptures:

If it seem good to God Most High,
He shall be filled with the spirit of understanding,
He himself poureth forth wise sayings in double measure.

H. Wheeler Robinson suggests that this 'double measure' may refer to that received by tradition and to his own.[1] If this be so it would indicate a parallel in the case of the apocalyptists who wrote both what they had received from the apocalyptic tradition in which they shared[2] and what they had themselves received as immediate revelations from God.

3. *Both reveal inspiration of a literary kind.* It has been noted above[3] that, although apocalyptic probably passed through an oral stage which continued into the inter-testamental period, the literary form was undoubtedly most suitable for its purpose and was truly characteristic of it. Wisdom, too, passed through an oral stage which continued into the inter-testamental period, as the evidence of Ben Sira clearly shows; but by this time the 'words of the wise' had assumed a variety of literary forms as is shown by the canonical and extra-canonical wisdom books. Although both apocalyptist and wisdom writer were recipients of immediate and personal revelation, their inspiration cannot be rightly understood apart from its relation to the literary quality of their writings. A comparison of the sages with the apocalyptists thus substantiates the conclusion at which we have already arrived that the latter stood somewhere between the original inspiration of the prophets and the more modern inspiration of a literary kind.

[1] *Ibid.*, p. 247. [2] See pp. 85ff. and compare II Esd. 14; Jub. 1.26.
[3] See p. 119.

VII

APOCALYPTIC AND THE INTERPRETATION OF PROPHECY

I. THE BACKGROUND OF BIBLICAL EXEGESIS

BETWEEN THE TIME of Ezra the scribe and the fall of Jerusalem in AD 70 the Torah came increasingly to hold a most important place in the life of the Jewish nation. The Temple continued to be a bulwark of the faith, but by the time of the Maccabees there had taken place a subtle transfer of influence from the Temple to the Torah. Indeed, throughout the Seleucid and Roman periods the Torah was recognized as the rallying-point of revolt against the incursions of Hellenistic influence. In its defence the Jews were ready not only to suffer but to die. When at last the Temple fell Judaism was able to survive because by that time its life had come to be well and truly built on the sacred Scriptures. The Jews had become 'the people of the Book'.[1]

During the whole of this period there was an equally significant development directly associated with the people's reverence for the Torah. Alongside the written Book there had been growing a mass of interpretation whose purpose was to elucidate the text of Scripture and to apply its truths to men's everyday lives. Not only were the Jews 'the people of the Book', they were at the same time 'the people of biblical exegesis'. During these years there was great activity on the part of many different parties within Judaism to reveal the hidden truths of Scripture, not only in the Pentateuch but in the Prophets as well. The Scriptures could hold such a place in the affection of the people because it was believed that they embodied the divine revelation once for all given to Moses, and carried with

[1] See the writer's *Between the Testaments*, 1960, pp. 41ff.

them divine authority. 'The Scriptures', writes G. F. Moore, 'are throughout a *revelation of religion*, in the widest meaning of that word. They are all *Torah*, not by an extension *a potiori* of the name of the Pentateuch to all the Scriptures, but because in them all . . . God has revealed what he has chosen to make known of his character and his ways, and what he requires of men in their relations to him and to their fellows.'[1]

Being a revelation of religion the Scriptures could not contradict themselves; it was the responsibility of the exegete, therefore, to defend the self-authentication of the Scriptures and to show that any differences which might appear were more apparent than real. The difficulties of such a task are hinted at in a story concerning Hananiah ben Hezekiah, a prominent member of the school of Shammai in the years before the fall of Jerusalem. There had apparently been much controversy over the Book of Ezekiel which appeared to contain teachings contradicting those of the Pentateuch, and many for this reason were in favour of rejecting it. But Hananiah, by 'burning the midnight oil' (the story says he had no less than 300 jars of it!), sat night after night in his room on the roof of his house until at last he was able to offer an exegesis which harmonized every detail and removed every apparent contradiction between the two parts of Scripture.[2]

Despite the assurance of this story, however, many difficulties of scriptural exegesis remained. Indeed, the hope is expressed in several writings that in the messianic age the obscurities and incomprehensibilities to be found in the Torah would be fully explained and clearly understood and all difficulties would be completely removed.[3] In that great day God himself would give a new interpretation of Scripture[4] and so disclose for all his people the secrets of his will.

Furthermore, being a revelation of religion the Scriptures embody revelation not only in their totality but even in their every part. Hence to the exegete every word and every phrase is of the utmost importance and has its part to play in the divine disclosure. There thus arose a form of exegesis very different from that of the modern exegete with his ideas of historical development and literary criticism. Such treatment of the text would be completely foreign to the

[1] *Op. cit.*, vol. I, p. 248. [2] Cf. Moore, *ibid.*, pp. 246f.

[3] Cf. W. D. Davies, *Torah in the Messianic Age and/or the Age to Come*, 1952, pp. 66f.

[4] Cf. *ibid.*, p. 73.

Jews of this time. 'This conception of Scripture', writes G. F. Moore, 'leads to an atomistic exegesis, which interprets sentences, clauses, phrases, and even single words, independently of the context or the historical occasion, as divine oracles; combines them with other similarly detached utterances; and makes large use of analogy of expression, often by purely verbal association.'[1] This approach to scriptural exegesis meant that the interpretation of Scripture was often forced and fanciful. A good example of this is to be found in the rabbinic treatment of the Hebrew text of Gen. 2.7 to prove the existence in man of the two 'inclinations'. There the expression for 'and he formed' is *wayyeṣer* which has a double *yodh* or 'y'. Now the word for 'inclination' in Hebrew is *yeṣer*, and since there is a double *yodh* in *wayyeṣer* this is an indication that there must be two *yeṣers*, the one being evil and the other good!

Many exegetical traditions grew up associated with the names of all the main parties in Judaism—Pharisees, Sadducees, Zealots and Essenes. In due course an attempt was made in rabbinic circles to bring order out of chaos and to establish certain rules for the proper ordering of scriptural exegesis. Rabbi Hillel (*c.* 30 BC) gave expression to the principles of interpretation current in his circle in the form of seven well-defined rules. About a century later these were expanded to thirteen by Rabbi Ishmael, and much later still, in the second century AD, to thirty-two by Rabbi Eliezer ben Joses. Alongside the 'philological exegesis' with its examination of grammatical and syntactical niceties and the dialectical exegesis of Hillel and the rest, we find recourse being taken to allegorical interpretation sometimes like, but more often quite unlike, that of Hellenistic exegesis. Whatever the method employed, there was always a profound veneration for the Scripture and a sincere desire to penetrate to its inner meaning.[2]

The description of the Jews of this period as 'the people of biblical exegesis' has found remarkable confirmation in the literature of the Qumran community. The evidence of the writings of this sect shows that the study and interpretation of the Scriptures, both the Law and the Prophets, was an imperative duty of every member. The leader of the community, the Teacher of Righteousness, was believed to be specially gifted by God for the task of exposition. He is described

[1] *Op. cit.*, p. 248.

[2] For an examination of the question of Jewish exegesis, see J. Bonsirven, *Exégèse Rabbinique et Exégèse Paulinienne*, 1938. For references to the various 'rules' of exegesis, see Moore, *op. cit.*, vol. III, p. 73.

as 'the priest into whose heart God puts wisdom to explain all the words of his servants the prophets' (*Hab. Comm.* II.7–8). He is able, by the help of God, to reveal the hidden meaning of the prophets' words which were unknown even to the prophets themselves; for these words did not refer to their own day at all, but to 'the end of the days' in which the members of the sect were then living. 'The last period extends over and above all that the prophets said; for the mysteries of God are such as to amaze' (VII.7–8). God had told Habakkuk to 'write out all that would come to pass in the last generation; but he did not grant him to know the time when these things would come to pass' (VII.1–2). The meaning of these things would be revealed by the Teacher of Righteousness 'to whom God made known all the mysteries of the words (spoken by) his servants the prophets' (VII.4–5).

Throughout these writings interpretations are given which have something in common with the methods of philological and allegorical exegesis described above which were to become characteristic of rabbinic Judaism. But for the most part the Qumran sect followed an independent line of interpretation. In their exegesis they make the following assumptions: (*a*) The text of Scripture does not, and never did, refer to the prophets' own day, but to this day in which its meaning for the first time is being clearly revealed. Thus, the exegesis given in the Commentaries and elsewhere is an interpretation, not a *re*-interpretation of prophecy. This is the true and only meaning of Scripture. (*b*) The words of the prophets relate to 'the last times'. The fact that their secret (*raz*) message has now been given its interpretation (*pešer*) by the Teacher of Righteousness, is an indication that 'the time is at hand' and that its coming is clearly associated with the Teacher himself.[1]

2. UNFULFILLED PROPHECY

The apocalyptic writers were essentially students of prophecy who believed that they had been raised up by God to make known its meaning to their people. As we have seen[2] they were particularly concerned with the predictive element in prophecy and, within that, with the problem of unfulfilled prophecy. That there were such

[1] For a treatment of this whole subject see F. F. Bruce, *Biblical Exegesis in the Qumran Texts*, in *Exegetica*, 1959 (1st British ed., 1960).

[2] Pp. 96ff.

prophecies in the Scriptures no one could deny. The prophets had said many things difficult to understand in the light of subsequent events. They had made many promises, on the authority of God's revelation, which had never been fulfilled. They had spoken of a Golden Age to be ushered in by 'the Day of Yahweh' when his people would be vindicated and the powers of evil would be utterly destroyed; the day would come when the nations would flock to Jerusalem, the metropolis of the earth; God would raise up a mighty deliverer whose kingdom would last for ever; there would even be a new heaven and a new earth in which righteousness and peace would reign eternally. These prophecies had been uttered in God's name and his word could not be broken. But the fact remained that these things had not come to pass. The hope which the prophets had set forth had continually been deferred, and with each deferment had come increasing disillusionment.

This problem had been felt by many right through the Persian and Greek periods when the Jews were utterly in subjection to foreign powers and their hope for the future was at its lowest ebb. Ample evidence of this can be found in the prophetic writings themselves in the form in which they have come down to us. Critical scholarship has clearly shown that, in the case of many of these books, the words and activities of the prophets have been worked over by later editors and interpolators in an attempt to re-cast or re-interpret certain prophecies so as to revive the old hopes in a new form and to adapt them to new circumstances in the life of the nation.

This process is clearly marked in several of the Old Testament prophecies, but in none, perhaps, more than in the Book of Isaiah, which may fairly be described as an anthology of prophecies gathered round the utterances of Isaiah of Jerusalem as their central core. S. B. Frost identifies four types of 'glossing' in this particular book. The first type corresponds to the 'historical' expectation of the prophets, without any distinctively eschatological overtone; the second is eschatological in emphasis, but in the pre-exilic style with its promise of the coming Golden Age and 'happiness ever after'; the third emphasizes the eschatological note and interprets the End in terms of cosmic phenomena; the fourth consists, not of short glosses or interpolations in the nature of comments on existing oracles, but of complete literary works which Frost describes as 'fabricated apocalypses'.[1] This process, illustrated here by reference to Isaiah,

[1] *Op. cit.*, pp. 112ff.

can be traced, though to a lesser extent, in other prophetic writings also; here again the additions to the original oracles range from textual glossing to literary compositions, from simple comments to complete reinterpretation. For the most part these 'extra-prophecies' are anonymous, but in some cases (*e.g.* Isa. 24–27; Zech. 9–11; 12–14; Isa. 40–55) the additions may have been intentional; if this is so, then we have in such instances occurrences of pseudonymous prophecy.

Writing of the prophetic books J. Hempel says, 'Their object is to be a witness to a future age that it may recognize the truth of God and his prophet at the moment when the catastrophe breaks in, and that belief in Yahweh may thereby be held fast. Prophetic literature was intended to be read in the future, in the last age, and not in its own age. This distinguishes it from the detached oracle, uttered in an actual situation. . . . To an increasing extent the literature has preserved the oracles only, and forgotten the concrete situation.'[1] This applied particularly to those 'extra-prophetic' passages which, as we have seen, tended to stress the eschatological character of the divine promises.

3. THE METHOD OF APOCALYPTIC INTERPRETATION

A landmark in the history of 'interpretative prophecy' is reached in the period of the Maccabees and the subsequent struggle of the Hasmonean House. During this time hopes which for centuries had lain dormant now sprang to new life. As a result of the persecutions which the people were having to undergo the conviction was born that God himself would intervene and establish his kingdom, thus bringing to their fulfilment the age-long promises through his servants the prophets. What God had foretold would come to pass, if not in the present age, then in a new age which was about to dawn. The ancient prophecies were to be read in terms of 'the End' and were to be interpreted and reinterpreted so as to fit into the great final drama in which the triumph of God and of God's people would be made known over all the nations round about. Prophetic promises became apocalyptic assurances. In answer to the prophets' cry, 'How long, O Lord, how long?' the apocalyptists gave the year, the day and the hour! In the course of their writings they claimed to

[1] 'The Literature of Israel', in *Record and Revelation*, ed. by H. Wheeler Robinson, 1938, pp. 65f.

give an answer to all those outstanding problems which unfulfilled prophecy had for long raised in the minds of the people. This 'fulfilment of prophecy' is to be found not only in isolated passages in which certain words and phrases of the prophets are taken up and recast with reference to the future, but in the whole range of apocalyptic teaching. Its entire message—the Golden Age, the Day of Judgment, the overthrow of evil, the transcendent Messiah, the Two Ages, rewards and punishments, even the doctrine of the resurrection and the life to come—is an attempt to bring to the point of fulfilment the prophetic message and so to vindicate the purposes of Almighty God whose word could not be broken.

The method of interpretation adopted by the different apocalyptic writers follows the same general pattern in the various writings:

(i) It is clear from what has been said that the apocalyptists' interpretations of prophecy were, for the most part, the result of literary reflection. They scrutinized the writings of the prophets for clues concerning the future destiny both of Israel and of the Gentiles and in particular for unfulfilled predictions which were capable of ingenious exegesis. We have noted that such reinterpretations and adaptations were to be found already within the writings of the prophets; but the apocalyptists went to far greater lengths than any before them. Not only did they interpret prophecy (cf. Jer. 25.11 and Dan. 9.2ff.), they were prepared to reinterpret previous interpretations already given in earlier apocalyptic books (cf. Dan. 7 and II Esd. 12.11–14). Even within a previous apocalyptic book, whose calculations had not been proved correct, they were prepared to make adaptations and changes and further suggestions (*e.g.* in Dan. 12.11–12). At a later stage Christian apocalyptists adopted somewhat the same practice and adapted former Jewish apocalyptic writings for their own purposes not only by interpreting them in the light of Christ but also by interpolating phrases and even whole passages of a distinctly Christian character.

(ii) An important factor reinforcing the claim of apocalyptic to be a fulfilment of prophecy is the device of pseudonymity. Past history is here presented in the form of unfulfilled prophecies which are seen to have their fulfilment in later events subsequent to the time of the supposed writer. There then follows a further account of unfulfilled prophecies relating to the actual writer's own day or to 'the time of the End' whose fulfilment is promised in the very near future. The fact that the earlier prophecies are seen to have been fulfilled gives strength to the expectation that the later ones will be speedily fulfilled also.

J. Hempel points out that 'through this scheme of prophecy, both fulfilled and still to be fulfilled, even the universalistic cosmological eschatology (*i.e.* of apocalyptic) maintains a close connection with the actual and contemporary prophesying of the ancient prophets, however much the two may differ in their literary character'.[1] He asserts that this conception is of significance not only for the history of literature, but also for the idea of revelation itself. No longer is God's deed bound up with his word as it is in ancient spoken prophecy; the content of revelation breaks free from what happens here and now and, as timeless event, has reference to the consummation of all things. But though revelation is set free from a particular time, it is still bound up with the people of Israel and in this we are to find the link between apocalyptic and the living prophecy of the Old Testament.

(iii) Again, it is to be noted that the apocalyptic writers applied themselves to the task of reinterpreting the promises of the prophets in the sure belief that their true meaning was to be found within the context of the End Time. Such prophecies had a secret or hidden meaning whose interpretation was intentionally concealed by God till the last days. These last days were now at hand and God had at last revealed the secrets of his eternal purpose to his saints, who were bidden to record them in their books that the wise among the people might read and understand. Their task was to examine ancient prophecy and, under the inspiration of God, reveal what had been hidden from many generations. The time was at hand; the things foretold by the prophets were about to take place. This conception of prophecy and its method of interpretation has much in common with the outlook of the Qumran Covenanters. Both accepted unfulfilled prophecy as a mystery or secret (*raz*) whose interpretation (*pešer*) they had been called by God to make known.

(iv) In their interpretation of Old Testament prophecy, moreover, the apocalyptists quite regularly drew upon non-biblical tradition, making free use of cosmic mythology with its profuse symbolism and of foreign ideas generally, culled more often than not from Babylonian and Persian sources. This practice, of course, is to be found already even within the Old Testament Scriptures, but in the apocalyptic literature it is put to much greater use. But in thus borrowing foreign

[1] *Ibid.*, p. 67.

ideas to interpret prophecy, the apocalyptic writers seldom failed to give new significance both to the ideas borrowed and to prophecy itself. 'The Jews', writes F. C. Porter, 'knew how to borrow what they liked and use it as they liked. They knew how to appropriate foreign mythological figures without the mythology, and even dualistic conceptions without the dualism, and could build a Babylonian story of creation into their system, and the Persian idea of a ruling evil spirit, without giving up their monotheism.'[1] This is true of the Jews in general and of the apocalyptists in particular.

Sometimes only part of the apocalyptic tradition in question is relevant to the interpretation of a particular prophecy, and yet the whole of it may be recorded, as in the case of Daniel's vision in chapter 7 of that book where reference is made to 'the four winds' and to 'the sea' out of which the beasts come. These details, we know from other sources, have significance in themselves in the tradition on which the writer is drawing,[2] but in this particular passage and for the purpose which the author of Daniel has in mind, they play no part at all in the task of interpretation.

Again, an apocalyptic writer may borrow imagery or symbolism from traditional sources or from earlier prophecies which have already been made use of, and in so doing he may completely change the meaning of what he borrows. An illustration of this is the use of the four differently-coloured horses in Revelation 6 which have been suggested to the writer by the four chariot-horses in Zechariah 6. The symbols are more or less the same, but their significance in each case is quite different.

Or he may borrow a symbol from tradition, detach it from its original context and imbue it with a completely new meaning. An example of this is the symbol of the eye; in Egyptian tradition, for instance, the ubiquitous eye of Horus symbolizes the fertilizing power of the sun, but in apocalyptic usage it becomes a potent symbol of God's omnipresence as in the eyes on the rims of Ezekiel's heavenly chariot (Ezek. 1.18) or in the four living creatures of the Book of Revelation (Rev. 4.6, cf. also Zech. 3.9; 4.10).

(v) We have seen, then, that the apocalyptists, in their work of interpretation, sometimes use the traditional to explain the actual, in the form of unfulfilled prophecy. But on occasions the reverse process is followed and the actual is used to explain the traditional.

[1] *The Messages of the Apocalyptical Writers*, 1905, p. 59.
[2] Cf. S. Mowinckel, *He That Cometh*, English trans., 1959, pp. 351ff.

An example of this is the three and a half years referred to in Dan. 7.25. In its context this refers to the duration of the persecution which the Jews were to suffer under Antiochus Epiphanes. But in course of time, in Christian apocalyptic, the *actual* period is taken to represent the *traditional* period of tribulation which would prevail before the Second Advent of Christ and the duration of the reign of Antichrist (Rev. 11.2f., cf. also 12.14; 13.5), so that 'the figure of Antichrist is very largely the figure of Antiochus "writ large" and thrown upon the screen of the future'.[1]

(vi) More will be said later about the part played by chronology and numerology in the apocalyptic writings,[2] particularly with reference to their attempts to forecast the 'time of the End'. Here we observe that, in their attempts to fulfil unfulfilled prophecy, they make fairly frequent use of what we might call allegorical arithmetic in which much play is made with figures and cycles and number patterns. Such calculations as these led inevitably to frustration and disappointment on the part of the people when it was found that the appointed time had come and gone and the End was not yet. This led to reinterpretations of the original prophecies, with fresh calculations, in which the time limit was still further postponed. In later years such forecasters were referred to by the rabbis, disparagingly, as 'calculators of the (messianic) end'. 'He who announces the messianic time based on calculations', says Rabbi Jose, 'forfeits his own share in the future' (*Derek Ereṣ Rabba* 11). This same sentiment is expressed in *Sanhedrin* 97b in these words: 'Cursed be they who calculate "the End", because they argue that since "the End" has arrived and the Messiah has not come, he will never come.' Nevertheless, calculations of this kind had a great fascination for many, and such speculations were rife from the Maccabean period onwards.

4. INFLUENCE OF PROPHETIC LANGUAGE AND THOUGHT

Throughout the apocalyptic literature the thought and imagery of the Old Testament prophets is frequently taken up and fitted into a new pattern of ideas, more often than not of an eschatological character. Sometimes the borrowing is unconscious and at other times it is done of set purpose after reflection on the old prophetic writings.

[1] H. T. Andrews, 'Apocalyptic Literature', in *Peake's Commentary*, 1919, p. 433.
[2] See pp. 195ff.

An illustration of this is in Dan. 12.2–4 whose roots can perhaps be traced back to three different Old Testament prophecies representing three different sources of influence. In 12.2 we read: 'Many of them that sleep in the dust of the earth shall awake, some to everlasting life, and some to shame and everlasting contempt' (RV margin: 'abhorrence'). Prophecies concerning the restoration of the nation under the figure of a resurrection from the dead had already been made familiar by Hosea, who speaks of the time when God will 'ransom them from the power of the grave' (13.14), and by Ezekiel in his famous vision of the valley of dry bones (37). But more significant still for our purpose are the words of Isa. 66.24: 'And they shall go forth, and look upon the carcasses of the men that have transgressed against me: for their worm shall not die, neither shall their fire be quenched; and they shall be an abhorring unto all flesh.' In this passage the writer pictures the destruction of unfaithful Israelites outside the city of Jerusalem in the presence of the righteous. It is highly probable that the writer of Daniel had this passage in mind when he used the phrase 'some to shame and everlasting abhorrence'. This is indicated not only by the general content of the verse but also by the use in both passages of the word *dera'ōn*, meaning 'abhorrence', which is to be found in the Old Testament only in these two verses. The influence of Isa. 66.24 is no doubt to be detected also in I Enoch 27; in both passages the apostate Jews are tortured by fire in the sight of the righteous, in the one case outside Jerusalem and in the other case in Gehenna. The words which immediately follow those quoted above, in Dan. 12.3, may also be traced back to earlier prophecy. There it is said, 'And they that be wise shall shine as the lights of the firmament; and they that turn many to righteousness as the stars for ever and ever.' Reference here to 'the wise' echoes the words of Isa. 52.13 concerning the wisdom of the Servant, whilst the phrase 'they that turn many to righteousness' is paralleled in the words of Isa. 53.11: 'Through his knowledge shall my servant make many righteous' (RV margin). It is more than likely that the author of Daniel had in mind the figure of the Suffering Servant in writing this verse and that his very phraseology is influenced by what he read there. Again, in Dan. 12.4 Daniel is bidden to seal the prophecies of his book till 'the time of the End' when there will be many eager to read and understand its message: 'Many shall run to and fro and knowledge shall be increased.' These words read like a conscious adaptation of Amos 8.12: 'They shall run to and fro to seek the word of the Lord, and shall not find it.'[1] Thus Amos's words of judgment are transformed into words of hope and are applied to the time of the End.

Another interesting passage is Dan. 4.10–18 which describes Nebuchadnezzar's dream of a great tree, reaching to heaven, which gives shelter to the birds and beasts and provides food for all mankind. The tree, symbolizing the king, is to be cut down, and only the stump is to be spared. The source of this story is no doubt Ezek. 31.1–9 where, in an oracle against Egypt, the Pharaoh is likened to a mighty cedar whose downfall will be a warning to all who lift themselves up in pride against God. The sequel to this story, in 31.10–14, gives its application and tells how the felling of the tree has repercussions even in Sheol itself (cf. 17.1–10, 22–24). This is reminiscent of the taunt song in Isa. 14.4–20 which tells how the Babylonian king sought to 'exalt his throne above the stars of God' so as to become as the Most High. God's judgment is given in these words: 'Thou shalt be brought down to Sheol, to the uttermost parts of the pit' (cf. also Ezek. 28.1–10, 11–19). E. W. Heaton suggests that behind this complex passage lies a mythological theme connected with the garden of Eden (cf. Ezek. 31.8f.) and that it may reflect an old legend concerning the 'first man' who sought to become as God.[2]

The same writer emphasizes the connection of the author of Daniel with the wisdom of the scribal schools and indicates that his method of writing, especially in chapters 1–6, is that of the Hebrew *mašal*. This word, meaning 'popular proverb' in its earliest use, comes to signify the 'parable' or 'allegorical story' which is used frequently in rabbinic literature, for example, to expound Scripture. Here the writer of Daniel uses stories or legends or traditions of the past to teach the lessons of wisdom to the people of his own day.[3] In chapter 2 he shows a particular interest in the story of Joseph as recorded in Genesis 41; it is clear from a comparison of the form of the two stories and from an examination of parallels in thought and even in language that Daniel's account is modelled on the earlier narrative and on its device of dream-interpretation.

Again in Dan. 11.30 the writer says concerning Antiochus, 'Ships of Kittim shall come against him.' This reference is no doubt inspired by Num. 24.24, where Balaam prophesies that 'ships shall

[1] The Jewish commentator Rashi quotes this passage with reference to Dan. 12.4, cf. Montgomery, *Daniel*, ICC, *ad loc.*

[2] Cf. *The Book of Daniel*, 1956, pp. 148f. [3] Cf. *ibid.*, pp. 44ff.

come from the coasts of Kittim'. This name, which originally referred to a town in Cyprus, came to signify the Mediterranean coastlands. Here, in Daniel, it is interpreted to signify a fleet which halted the advance of Antiochus in his campaign against Egypt. It is of interest to note that the Qumran covenanters interpret 'the Chaldeans, that bitter and hasty nation' mentioned in Hab. 1.6, by the term 'Kittim': 'Its interpretation concerns the Kittim, who are swift and mighty in war' (*Hab. Comm.* II.12–14). Here again the expression probably refers to the Romans, though some scholars argue that the reference is rather to the Seleucids.

5. CONSCIOUS ADAPTATION OF PROPHECY

The illustrations given above indicate that the writer of the Book of Daniel at any rate was familiar with the writings of the prophets and of other Scriptures and that he quite freely used verses or even whole passages to convey his message. For the most part the use which he makes of Scripture in these references hardly amounts to interpretation or reinterpretation. They are simply illustrations of the influence of the Old Testament writings upon his thinking and expression. There are certain other instances, however, where a conscious attempt is made to reinterpret former prophecies and in particular to adjust and adapt words and phrases to make them fit into a new set of circumstances prevailing in the author's own day. This practice can be illustrated from a number of apocalyptic books, but, as in the instances noted above, it is seen most clearly and most frequently in the Book of Daniel.

One of the most significant examples of such reinterpretation of prophecy, which had a considerable influence on subsequent apocalyptic thought, is based on the passage Ezekiel 38–39. There we are told that Israel is to be invaded by certain nations from the north whose names are given as Rosh, Meshach and Tubal (38.2; 39.1). Already in the Old Testament and in tradition beyond the Old Testament the north was regarded as a place of menace and mystery.[1] This hostile army is individualized and given the name 'Gog of the land of Magog' (38.2). Many attempts have been made to explain these names, but none is altogether satisfactory. The

[1] Cf. the Ras Shamra tablets, where the north is the mythological home of the gods.

second name, 'Magog', may, in fact, owe its origin to a glossator whose contribution to the passage was yet to have important repercussions in future reinterpretations of this prophecy.

Not only is Ezekiel 38–39 a source of later reinterpretation, it is itself a reinterpretation of earlier Old Testament prophecies. This is clearly acknowledged in 38.17, where it is said concerning Gog, 'Art thou he of whom I spake in old times by my servants the prophets, which prophesied in those days for many years that I would bring thee against them?' The allusion here is no doubt to such passages as Jer. 1.14; 3.1–6.30 and Zeph. 1.7, 14ff.; 3.8, where reference is made to a mysterious foe from the north who would be the instrument of divine wrath. Herodotus identifies these with the Scythians (I.103, 107; IV.1). As Ezekiel reads these prophecies he realizes that they have not been fulfilled, and so he recasts them in a new form with a new emphasis. He fits them into the framework of an eschatological vision in which he describes the final battle of history which would mark the breaking in of the rule of God. This idea of an onslaught made by the Gentiles on Palestine was to become a fairly common motif in later apocalyptic and is to be found in the Old Testament itself. In Zech. 14.2ff., for example, the nations gather together to sack Jerusalem; but God comes to their aid and delivers them. A reference to the same menace may be found in Joel 2.20, where allusion is made to 'the northerner' whom God will drive 'into a land barren and desolate'. This semi-historical, semi-mythological reference is a reminder that Ezekiel himself, in individualizing the northern nations as 'Gog', may well have been expressing a well-established tradition concerning an evil monster who leads the powers of evil.

This interpretation of earlier prophecies which we find in Ezekiel 38–39 is further reinterpreted in later Jewish apocalyptic writings and deeply influences the conception of Antichrist[1] and 'the Man of Sin'[2] as they appear in Christian writings. Although the expression 'Antichrist' first appears in Christian writings the idea is to be found in earlier Jewish apocalyptic works. M. R. James, basing his findings on Bousset's studies on the subject, states that in his opinion 'there was among the Jews a fully developed legend of Antichrist—perhaps oral but more probably written—which was accepted and amplified by Christians'.[3] No doubt the influence of Persian thought is to be

[1] Cf. I John 2.18, 22; 4.3; II John 7. [2] Cf. II Thess. 2.3.
[3] 'Man of Sin', in *HDB*, vol. III, 1900, p. 227.

traced in such a conception, but the seed of the idea was ready to hand in Ezekiel's prophecy of Gog and Magog.

In the LXX of Ezek. 38.2 Magog becomes the name of the people who inhabit the land rather than the name of the land itself, and this is possibly the interpretation of the text of 39.6.[1] A similar topographical allusion is made in Sib. Or. III.319f. where 'the land of Gog and Magog' is set 'in the midst of the rivers of Ethiopia'; in this passage these names may refer to the Nubians who returned from Egypt with Antiochus when he despoiled the Temple (cf. also III.512ff., 632ff.).[2]

Elsewhere they more clearly represent the heathen nations who will make their final assault against God's people as a prelude to the coming of the messianic kingdom. This assault takes different forms and the heathen nations are variously described. The language of Dan. 11.40ff., for example, is reminiscent of Ezekiel's picture of Gog's attack on Israel (Ezek. 38.1f.) and of Isaiah's picture of the Assyrian invasion of his own day (Isa. 8.7f.; 10.5ff.; 31.8f.). There we have a description of an invader from the north who will 'overthrow and pass through' with chariots and horsemen and many ships and will meet his end somewhere between the Mediterranean and Mount Zion (11.45). The passage as a whole, from verse 21 onwards, describes the career of Antiochus IV, but towards the end details of his death are given which do not correspond to the facts known about Antiochus. The writer is apparently modifying his account so as to fulfil the old prophecy that God's great enemy will 'fall upon the mountains of Israel' (Ezek. 39.4, cf. Zech. 14.2; Joel 3.2, 12f.; Isa. 14.25).

This is certainly how the writer of the *War of the Sons of Light*, etc., interpreted this particular passage in the Book of Daniel. In his description of the final battle between 'the sons of light' and 'the sons of darkness' he is patently adapting to his own purpose the language of Dan. 11.40ff., and his treatise has not unfittingly been called a midrash on this section of the Book of Daniel.[3] The 'sons of darkness' are identified as 'the Kittim of Assyria', the reference being apparently to the Roman armies stationed in Syria. Of interest in

[1] Cf. also Jub. 9.8. Magog is mentioned as a son of Japheth in Jub. 7.19 and the land of Gog is mentioned in Jub. 8.25.

[2] Cf. R. H. Charles, *Apocrypha and Pseudepigrapha of the Old Testament*, vol. II, 1913, p. 384.

[3] F. F. Bruce, *op. cit.*, p. 63.

this connection is the fragmentary commentary on Isa. 10.28–11.4 which interprets Isaiah's account of an Assyrian invasion in terms of the Kittim. In the great eschatological battle before the coming of the kingdom the Kittim will be slain. The 'scion of David' will hold sway over the heathen nations 'at the end of days'; among those to be vanquished by him is Magog, who is singled out in this document for special mention (*Commentary on Isa.* 11.1–4).[1]

In I Enoch 56.5ff. further reference is made to this eschatological battle; here the angels stir up God's enemies and in the end utterly destroy them. The old biblical account, however, is reinterpreted still further, for the enemy is here identified with contemporary enemies of Israel; in place of Gog and Magog the writer substitutes the names of the Parthians and the Medes. Somewhat the same picture is given later in II Esd. 13.5, 33f., where 'an innumerable company of men' are 'gathered together from the four winds of heaven' to do battle against the Messiah who destroys them by supernatural means. Again, in II Bar. 70.7–10 the Messiah summons the nations to appear before him; some are spared and others destroyed. Later still, in Rev. 20.7–9, the process of individualization is taken further. Here Gog and Magog stand side by side, like two 'demon kings', as the allies of Satan himself; they come to do battle against God, but fire comes down from heaven and devours them.

Another example of reinterpretation of prophecy within the apocalyptic literature concerns the 'four great beasts' rising out of the sea whose appearance to Daniel in a vision is recorded in Daniel 7. The background to this vision does not concern us here, although it is itself a good illustration of how the roots of apocalyptic imagery can often be traced back to ancient mythology, whether indirectly through earlier prophecies or directly through contact with foreign ideas. The first beast is like a lion with eagles' wings (7.4); the second is like a bear, with three ribs in its mouth (7.5); the third is like a leopard with four wings (7.6); the fourth is a beast with ten horns and great iron teeth (7.7). By this means the author identifies the four great Empires of Babylonia, 'Media', Persia and Greece. Later on in the same chapter he describes how sentence of death is pronounced on the fourth beast: 'The beast was slain and his body destroyed, and he was given to be burned with fire' (7.11), and this is followed by the advent of the messianic kingdom 'which shall not be destroyed' (7.14).

[1] Cf. T. H. Gaster, *The Scriptures of the Dead Sea Sect*, 1957, p. 346.

This great hope, however, was not realized; yet another prophecy remained unfulfilled. Its fulfilment must be sought by a reinterpretation of its symbolism. This is exactly what is done by the writer of II Esdras many years later who re-adapts Daniel's prophecy of the fourth beast to suit the situation of his own time. In a vision he sees an eagle, having twelve wings and three heads, rising out of the sea (11.1ff.) which is attacked and destroyed by a lion (11.36ff.). The writer makes clear his reinterpretation in these words: 'This is the interpretation of the vision which thou hast seen. The eagle which thou sawest come up from the sea is the fourth kingdom which appeared in vision to thy brother Daniel. But it was not interpreted unto him as I now interpret it unto thee' (12.10–12). The fourth beast of Daniel, representing Greece, is now taken, under the figure of the eagle, to represent Rome,[1] the three heads no doubt signifying Vespasian, Titus and Domitian. The lion, representing the Messiah, will arise in the time of the third head, and destroy the eagle; he will rebuke and destroy the unrighteous, but will deliver his own people with mercy and make them joyful until the End shall come (12.34). Here, then, is a clear case of reinterpretation in which a former apocalyptic prophecy is re-adapted to suit the writer's own circumstances when he expected the End to come.

The writer of Daniel, in his description of the fourth beast, remarks that it had ten horns (7.7) representing ten kings (7.24). In the midst of the ten horns there grew up another little horn (7.8) which would 'wear out the saints of the Most High'; these would be given into his hand 'until a time, times and half a time' (7.25). The reference here is to Antiochus Epiphanes; the enigmatic allusion which follows might be translated 'until a year, (two) years and half a year', and so indicates a period of three and a half years. No doubt this is to be taken as a 'round number', being half of the traditional number seven,[2] and refers to the period during Antiochus's reign when the Jewish Temple was desecrated and given over to heathen worship (25th December, 167 BC–25th December, 164 BC, cf. II Mac. 10.5). At the close of this period Antiochus's power would be overthrown and the End would come when the kingdom would be given to 'the saints of the Most High' (7.27).

A slightly different account is given in 8.14, where it is said that the tribulation will have to be endured for 'two thousand and three

[1] In *ʿAbodah Zarah* 1b, a similar interpretation is given of Dan. 7.23.
[2] Cf. E. W. Heaton, *op. cit.*, p. 189.

hundred mornings (and) evenings', *i.e.* for the period during which 2,300 morning and evening sacrifices will be offered, *viz.* for 1,150 days, or three years and two months. It may be that this number indicates an attempt to define more closely the round number 'three and a half' previously given, but its exact significance remains a mystery. Whatever its meaning may be, the writer comes back to his original reference and in 12.7 indicates that the End will come after 'a time, times and an half'. A later writer, however, recognizing perhaps that the End had not come with the 1,150 days and wishing to particularize the prophecy of three and a half years, states that the length of time during which the Temple would lie desecrated is to be 1,290 days (12.11), *i.e.* three and a half years.[1] A still later hand extends the prophecy even further and makes the time of waiting 1,335 days (12.12), an enigmatic figure whose significance is quite unknown. This is a clear case of prediction being reviewed and recast by later hands in the light of the apparent failure of earlier attempts to indicate the time of the End. As we have already noted,[2] the tradition of three and a half years' tribulation before 'the End' was known to the writer of the Book of Revelation. For forty-two months (Rev. 11.2; 13.5) or 1,260 days (11.3) the holy city would be trodden under foot (11.2). At the end of this time Antichrist would be overthrown and Christ would reign. The number 'three and a half' would no doubt in course of time become stereotyped within Christian as well as Jewish apocalyptic tradition and it is probably for this reason that the drought of three years in the time of Elijah (I Kings 18.1) becomes three years and six months in Luke 4.25 and James 5.17.

6. ALLEGORICAL ARITHMETIC

From the time of Daniel onwards many attempts were made, in the apocalyptic literature and elsewhere, not only to interpret or reinterpret prophecy, but also to calculate the lengths of different epochs of history and in particular the time of the End. In this exercise of allegorical arithmetic the numbers 7, 70 and 490 frequently appear as does the number $3\frac{1}{2}$ which we have already examined. To these writers numbers have meaning, and meaning can be expressed in terms of numbers.

[1] In months of 30 days each this is $36 + 6 + 1$ (intercalary) $= 1,290$ days.
[2] See p. 187.

(i) This process is perhaps most clearly seen in the case of Daniel concerning whom Josephus remarks that he 'did not only prophesy of future events, as did the other prophets, but he also determined the time of their accomplishment' (*Ant.* X.xi.7). He is alluding here to Dan. 9.2 which reads, 'I Daniel understood by the books (*i.e.* the Scriptures) the number of the years, whereof the word of the Lord came to Jeremiah the prophet, for the accomplishing of the desolations of Jerusalem, even seventy years.' The reference is to Jer. 25.11–12 and 29.10 where the prophecy is given that after seventy years' captivity[1] the king of Babylon will be punished and his land made desolate (25.12), and God will cause his people to return to their own land (29.10). Daniel, reflecting on this promise, is deeply troubled because he knows that it has not been realized except in a very partial manner. But the promises of God through his servants the prophets cannot fail. There must therefore be some hidden meaning in these words. As he is thus meditating and questioning, the angel Gabriel appears to him and explains the secret of the 'seventy years' (Dan. 9.21ff.). These 'seventy years' are to be interpreted as 'seventy weeks of years' or seventy heptads of years, *i.e.* 490 years.

It may be that this reinterpretation of Jeremiah's prophecy was suggested as a result of the writer's comparing the Jeremiah passage with two other portions of Scripture. In II Chron. 36.21 it is said that the people were carried into captivity in Babylon 'to fulfil the word of the Lord by the mouth of Jeremiah, until the land had enjoyed her sabbaths; for as long as she lay desolate she kept sabbaths, to fulfil three score and ten years'. A somewhat similar statement is made in Lev. 26.34f., 'Then shall the land enjoy her sabbaths', etc.; in this same chapter God says concerning his people, 'I will chastise you seven times more for your sins' (26.18). It cannot be proved, but it is quite possible, that these passages taken together gave the writer of Daniel the idea that each year of Jeremiah's prophecy should be interpreted as a *sabbatic* year, *i.e.* that each year represented a period of seven years. If this is so, it is an illustration of the use of Scripture to reinterpret Scripture in the light of unfulfilled prophecy.

The angel Gabriel interprets the meaning of Jeremiah's seventy years in terms of historical events since the fall of Jerusalem and in

[1] In the Ep. Jer. of v. 3 (= Bar. 6.3) this is given as 7 generations.

terms of the fast-approaching End. The seventy heptads are divided up into three periods, their lengths being determined by certain significant events.

The first period is to last for seven 'weeks' (*i.e.* forty-nine years): 'From the going forth of the commandment to restore and to build Jerusalem unto the anointed one, the prince, shall be seven weeks' (9.25). The *terminus a quo* indicated here is probably to be taken as the year 587 BC, when Jerusalem fell to the Babylonians. At that time the promise was given that God would bring back the captives and rebuild the ruined city (cf. Jer. 30.18; 31.38–40). Forty-nine years after this event, in 537 BC, Cyrus issued an edict permitting the rebuilding of the Jerusalem Temple (II Chron. 36.22; Ezra 1.1) and as a consequence the rehabilitation of the Zadokite line of priests. The allusion to 'the anointed one, the prince' would then be a reference to Jeshua the High Priest who returned to Jerusalem in that same year.

The second period is to last for sixty-two 'weeks' (*i.e.* 434 years): 'After three score and two weeks shall the anointed one be cut off, and shall have nothing; and the people of the prince that shall come shall destroy the city and sanctuary' (9.26). The most likely interpretation of this verse is that it refers to the High Priest Onias III who was assassinated in 171 BC (cf. II Mac. 4.33–36). The removal of Onias from office marked the end of the Zadokite line of high priests and so, like the accession of Jeshua in earlier days, was a highly significant date. One apparent difficulty is that the period between 537 BC and 171 BC adds up to 366 years which is about sixty-eight years short of the 434 years indicated in the 'threescore and two weeks'. Schürer indicates that at this time there were no adequate means of determining the correct chronology and that Daniel is obviously following some current view on the matter.[1] He points out that Josephus later on, in several passages,[2] also miscalculates certain dates to the extent of forty or fifty years. Like the author of Daniel, Josephus is probably, in certain references at least, following other sources or traditions.[3] F. F. Bruce is probably correct in stressing that this period of sixty-two 'weeks' is a schematic

[1] Cf. *op. cit.*, div. II, vol. III, pp. 53f.

[2] *E.g. Wars* VI.iv.8; *Ant.* XIII.xi.1; XX.x.1.

[3] Schürer (*op. cit.*, p. 54) gives another illustration of miscalculation of dates. He refers to the Jewish Hellenist Demetrius, who, like Daniel, reckoned about 70 years too many in his treatment of approximately the same period, cf. Clement of Alex., *Strom.* I.xxi.141.

number and that the accuracy or inaccuracy of the calculations is of little importance.[1]

The third period is to last for one 'week' (*i.e.* seven years): 'He (*i.e.* the oppressor) shall make a firm covenant with many for one week; and for the half of the week he shall cause the sacrifice and the oblation to cease . . .' (9.27f.). This presumably refers to Antiochus, who would enlist the support of apostate Jews (cf. I Mac. 1.10–15) for seven years (171–164 BC). For the second half of the 'week' (*i.e.* commencing 167 BC) he would desecrate the Temple and cause the sacrifices to cease. At the end of this time will come the 'consummation' when 'wrath shall be poured out upon the desolator' (9.27). The writer is here probably walking 'by faith not by sight' in thus foretelling the End in three and a half years' time after Antiochus's act of desecration. As things turned out, the Temple was cleansed and rededicated in exactly three years, on 25th December 164 BC. But the End was not yet. The interpretation which Daniel gives of Jeremiah's seventy years was seen to require reinterpretation itself. Several attempts were made in subsequent years by apocalyptic writers and others to interpret Daniel's prophecy either in whole or in part, particular attention being given to the fulfilment of his final heptad in which succeeding generations believed they were then living.[2]

(ii) An attempted reinterpretation of Daniel's prophecy is given in Test. of Levi 16–17 the text of which is none too easy to understand. In these two chapters, and also in chapter 14, the writer scathingly criticizes the behaviour of the priesthood and describes

[1] Cf. *op. cit.*, p. 61. I am indebted to Dr Bruce for several of the points made in this section.

He indicates that in Eusebius, *Demonstratio Evangelica* VIII.ii.58, allusion is made to an early Christian interpretation of this passage (probably to be traced to Hippolytus), which takes 'an anointed one, a prince' to refer to the line of Jewish High Priests from Jeshua to Alexander Jannaeus in 103 BC. He suggests that in its original form this interpretation was Jewish and not Christian and that the 'anointed one' had reference to the Zadokite priesthood from Jeshua to Onias III; the period was then extended to include the high priesthood of Alexander Jannaeus so as to make a reinterpretation of the prophecy applicable to the Roman period; cf. also p. 81.

[2] Josephus (*Ant.* XX.x.1 (237): 'The city continued 7 years without a High Priest') seems to identify the final heptad with the 7 years' vacancy in the high priesthood between the time of Alcimus and the time of Jonathan (160–153 BC). Elsewhere (*War* VI.v.4(312f.)), however, the text seems to indicate that 'the prince who is to come' (Dan. 9.26) and oppress the people at the beginning of the final heptad is Vespasian (AD 69–79).

in detail the apostasy of the priests and the profanation of their holy office. Reference to the seventy weeks of Dan. 9.24 is made in 16.1: 'And now I have learnt that for seventy weeks ye shall go astray, and profane the priesthood, and pollute the sacrifices' (cf. 17.1). No indication is given of the *terminus a quo* of this prophecy and such historical allusions as seem to be made are very difficult to identify. R. H. Charles claims that these chapters are by a later hand than that of the author of the bulk of the book. He argues for the years 70–50 BC as the most likely date of their composition.[1] Whatever the exact meaning of the passage is, it is probably an attempt to expound Daniel's earlier prophecy to include the period of the Hasmonean House. The position is made even more complicated by the reference in 17.2–9 to a period of seven jubilees in connection with the seventy weeks already alluded to (cf. 17.1). Once more there is no indication given as to when this period of jubilees is thought to begin. These verses were probably originally independent of the passage in which they are now embedded. There is here, then, a conflation of two attempts at prophetic interpretation. In one the seventy 'weeks' of Daniel are interpreted, as in that book, as seventy heptads or 490 years; in the other, it may be, the final heptad of Daniel's vision is interpreted as seven jubilees, *i.e.* 450 years (taking a jubilee as fifty years as in Ass. of Moses 1.2; 10.12).[2]

(iii) It is of interest to observe that these two numbers play a part also in the hopes of the Qumran community as illustrated in the *Zadokite Document*. The relevant text reads, 'And in the epoch of wrath, 390 years after he had given them into the hand of Nebuchadnezzar, king of Babylon, he visited them. . . . But they were like the blind and like them that grope their ways for twenty years. And God considered their works, for with a perfect heart did they seek him; and he raised for them a Teacher of Righteousness to lead them in the way of his heart and to make known to the last generations that which he would do to the last generation, the congregation of the faithless' (I.5–12). This states that, after 390 years' captivity,[3]

[1] Cf. *Testaments of the Twelve Patriarchs*, 1908, pp. 53ff.

[2] In Ass. of Moses 3.14 the duration of the Captivity is given as 77 years. This may indicate a combination of two ideas, the 70 years of Daniel and the 7 years of the final 'week'. But, more likely, it signifies simply an indefinite number as in Gen. 4.24 and Matt. 18.22.

[3] Cf. Ezek. 4.4f., which tells how the prophet Ezekiel is to lie on his left side for 390 days representing 390 years of captivity. This is the reading of the Masoretic text. The LXX, no doubt correctly, reads 190 years.

God restored his people; twenty years later he raised up a Teacher of Righteousness. Later on in the same work it is stated that forty years after the death of the Teacher of Righteousness 'the men of war' will be consumed in the great final battle (XX.14–15). The sum of these numbers is 450 years. If we add forty years, representing the duration of the Teacher's ministry, we have the figure 490 which may well represent the seventy heptads of Daniel's prophecy.[1]

(iv) The number 70 plays a significant part also in the Book of Enoch. In chapters 1–36 it is stated that from the time of the Flood to the time of final judgment will be 'seventy generations' (10.12), but in chapters 83–90 the writer works out the scheme of world history in a much more detailed way. In the second of two visions recorded here he gives an outline of Israel's history under the figure of oxen, sheep, wild beasts and shepherds (chs. 85–90). Attention is focused on the period from the Captivity onwards when Israel has been made to suffer greatly under the rule of the Gentiles. The sheep, representing Israel, are torn in pieces by wild beasts, representing the Gentiles. God apparently remains unmoved at this spectacle and calls seventy 'shepherds' to whom he gives the responsibility, one after another, of 'pasturing' the sheep. He tells them how many of the sheep they may allow to be destroyed; but they exceed their orders and slay more than was required of them. Careful note is taken of their misdeeds with which they will be confronted on the Day of Judgment when they will be punished for their sins.

This account of the seventy 'shepherds' is a reinterpretation of the seventy years of Jeremiah. It divides up Israel's history, from the time of the Captivity, into four periods ruled over by twelve, twenty-three, twenty-three and twelve 'shepherds' respectively. There is no chronological exactness in these figures. The duration of each 'shepherd's' rule is called 'an hour' (89.72); but these 'hours' are of unequal and indeterminate duration, and so it is idle to calculate the significance of these numbers in terms of years. At the same time the context makes quite clear the limits of the several periods. The first period of twelve 'hours' extends from the Captivity to the return of the captives in the time of Cyrus (89.68–71). The second period of twenty-three 'hours' extends from Cyrus to Alexander the Great (89.72–77), the Greeks or Macedonians being represented by eagles (90.2). The third period, also of twenty-three 'hours', extends from

[1] This suggestion is made by F. F. Bruce, *op. cit.*, p. 60.

Alexander the Great to Antiochus Epiphanes (90.1–5). The fourth period, again of twelve 'hours', extends from Antiochus Epiphanes down to the time of the End and the last judgment (90.6–19). Just before the last period begins, lambs are born to the white sheep which are no longer blind as all the others before them had been (90.6); these are the *Hasidim* who were in existence before the Maccabean Revolt and who played such an important role in that uprising. Horned lambs then appear representing the warlike Maccabees. Among these is a sheep from which sprouts a great horn (90.9), representing no doubt Judas Maccabaeus who led the revolt of his fellow Jews against Antiochus. Eagles, vultures, ravens and kites, representing the Gentiles, swoop upon the sheep, but have no power over the great horn (90.12ff.). A great sword is then given to the sheep, with which they scatter and slay the birds and beasts (90.19). The angel Michael, who is introduced as 'that man' in verses 14 and 17, now appears and states that the last twelve 'shepherds' had destroyed much more than their predecessors had done. Thereupon God smites the earth which swallows up the birds and beasts. Then follows the judgment scene (90.20–27) in which the 'stars', or fallen angels, are judged and found guilty and are 'cast into an abyss, full of fire and burning' (90.24). Likewise the seventy 'shepherds' are found guilty and are cast into the fiery abyss (90.25). God then builds a new Temple for the sheep, the birds and beasts that remain are converted, the dispersed sheep are gathered together, the slain sheep are raised to life again to share in the messianic kingdom (90.28–36). There is then born a white bull, representing the Messiah (90.37). The birds and beasts make petition to him and are themselves changed into white bulls. Thus they return to the state of the first man Adam, who is described as a white bull (85.3), before the occasion of the Fall.

The hope here expressed is a familiar one, that soon, very soon, the End will come and the messianic kingdom will be ushered in. The number '70' comes, no doubt, from Jer. 25.12 and 29.10, and the symbolism of the shepherds is derived, as in Deutero-Zechariah, from Ezekiel 34. R. H. Charles has argued strongly[1] that the 'shepherds' mentioned here represent angels and further suggests that 'there may be some distant connection between the seventy angels here and the seventy guardian angels of the Gentile nations'.[2]

[1] Cf. *The Book of Enoch*, 1912, pp. 199ff. [2] *Ibid.*, p. 200.

The idea of a heavenly Council of angelic beings presided over by Yahweh is, of course, already familiar in the Old Testament.[1] But there are also suggestions in the Old Testament, the LXX, the Targums and the rabbinic literature as well as in apocalyptic sources that God set guardian angels over the nations of the earth to direct their affairs.[2] These guardian angels form a heavenly counterpart of the Gentile rulers into whose power God has given his people from time to time because of their wickedness. It is in the light of this prevalent belief that we are to understand the interpretation of the seventy 'shepherds' in the Book of Enoch. God's people Israel is handed over into the power of the nations to live under the dominion of their guardian angels. But the time of their domination will soon come to an end. Because they have abused their trust, they will be brought under the awful judgment of God, but the faithful in Israel will be established as God's own people.

[1] Cf. I Kings 22.19ff.; Job 1.6ff.; Isa. 6.6ff.; Ps. 89.7; Jer. 23.18ff. See above, pp. 168f.

[2] For an examination of this evidence see pp. 244ff.

PART THREE

THE MESSAGE OF JEWISH APOCALYPTIC

VIII

HUMAN HISTORY AND DIVINE CONTROL

FOR APOCALYPTISTS AND Old Testament prophets alike history is the sphere of divine revelation whose meaning is to be understood in terms of 'the mighty acts of God'. The apocalyptists differ from the prophets in their interpretation of the end of history and in looking beyond history for the fulfilment of these 'mighty acts' in an age in many respects different from that in which men now live.[1] But basically they express the same beliefs and share the same tradition, finding the ultimate meaning of history in the working out of the divine purpose.

In this chapter we shall examine the apocalyptic conception of history in relation to the prophetic, noting similarities and differences between the two outlooks. We begin with an examination of the nature of time and of eternity which, in a sense, form the warp and woof of history, on which the divine pattern can be clearly traced.

I. THE NATURE OF TIME AND ETERNITY

It has been customary in recent discussions on 'time in the Old Testament' to distinguish between 'chronological time' (time in terms of sequence or measurement) and 'realistic (or psychological) time' (time in terms of content or event) and to stress that the latter is characteristic of the Hebrew way of thinking.[2] This characterization

[1] See pp. 219ff.

[2] Cf. O. Cullmann, *Christ and Time*, English trans., 1951; J. Marsh, *The Fulness of Time*, 1952, and article 'Time' in *A Theological Word Book of the Bible*, ed. by A. Richardson, 1950, pp. 258–67; H. W. Robinson, *Inspiration and Revelation in the Old Testament*, 1946, pp. 106–22; J. A. T. Robinson, *In the End, God . . .*, 1950; Th. Boman, *Hebrew Thought compared with Greek*, English trans., 1960.

of time by content rather than by measurement, it is contended, implies an evaluation with which we have nothing to correspond today, in the Western world at any rate. Among the Hebrews there was nothing, for example, corresponding to our idea of clock-time.[1] They thought of time not as an abstract idea, but rather in terms of the quality of the event or occurrence which it marked. 'Time is charged with substance or, rather, it is identical with its substance; time is the development of the very events. . . . The colourless idea of "hour" meaning time in a purely quantitative way, is far from the old Israelite conception.'[2] The passing of time is essentially a succession of real content; not its measurement, but rather its substance, its quality, its character was what mattered for the Hebrews. They were not absorbed, as we are today, in a historic consciousness. Nor did they think of time in terms of past, present and future. They were not interested in historical events simply as 'time divisions'. Time for them was a process coloured by event or filled with content.

This whole approach has more recently been vigorously attacked by James Barr,[3] who points out that in fact chronology plays a very significant part in the Old Testament and that it is an unwarranted assumption to set over against this a 'qualitative' conception of time as characteristically Hebrew. He doubts whether, in fact, it is possible, on the evidence available, to postulate a purely biblical view of time at all which differs radically from our own.[4] In this he agrees with W. Eichrodt, who holds that 'the important thing for the Bible lies not in the idea of time itself but elsewhere, in the use made of the historical sequence for the presentation of an encounter with God'.[5]

We are not concerned here with the rightness or wrongness of these different points of view except in so far as they cast light upon our understanding of time among the apocalyptic writers. In the case of their writings the field of investigation is more limited than in the case of the Old Testament books; nor, as we should expect, is there the same consistency of outlook. Nevertheless it is clear that, on the whole, they are in this respect inheritors of the Old Testament

[1] The only reference to 'clock-time' in the Old Testament is in Isa. 38.8 and II Kings 20.9–11, which describe the 'steps' of Ahaz which acted as a gnomon or sun-dial.

[2] J. Pedersen, *Israel I–II*, 1926, pp. 487, 489.

[3] Cf. *The Semantics of Biblical Language*, 1961; *Biblical Words for Time*, 1962.

[4] *Biblical Words for Time*, p. 153.

[5] *Ibid.*, p. 144; cf. W. Eichrodt, 'Heilserfahrung und Zeitverständnis im Alten Testament', *TZ*, vol. XII, 1956, pp. 103–25.

tradition. But, as in so many other connections, they adapt what they adopt and develop what they receive along lines of their own special interest.

One example of this is to be found in their use of chronology. Both Eichrodt[1] and Barr[2] are surely right in stressing that chronology occupies a not-unimportant place in the thought of the biblical writers.[3] There is plentiful evidence in the Old Testament for a carefully enunciated chronological system, particularly in the writings of the Priestly school, whereby the dates of such great events as the Flood, the Exodus from Egypt and the building of Solomon's Temple could be worked out. Sometimes this was done in relation to the creation of the world, but at other times it was done in relation to its end. The genealogies of the patriarchs, for example, recorded in Genesis provide material for a chronology which, it would appear, is intended to fit into a particular theory concerning the time of 'the End'. The chronological system which forms the basis of the Priestly work seems to imply that the world will last 4,000 years from the time of creation, i.e. four periods, each of a thousand years.[4] It is calculated, on the basis of the Masoretic text, that the Exodus from Egypt took place in the year 2666 after creation.[5] This is almost exactly two-thirds of 4,000. If the Exodus thus took place at the end of two-thirds of the world's history, the remaining one third would end about the time of the Maccabees and the writing of the Book of Daniel.[6] If these dates are not arbitrary, but are given by design, then we may with some justification trace back such arithmetical speculations connected with the End to the writers of the Priestly school.

That other speculations of a somewhat similar kind were in vogue both before and during the inter-testamental period is further evidenced by the chronological variations to be found in the Samaritan Version of the Pentateuch, the LXX, Josephus and, say, the Book of Jubilees. The apocalyptists, as we have seen, were fascinated by chronologies and delighted in speculations of an arithmetical kind.[7]

[1] Cf. *ibid.*, pp. 113ff. [2] Cf. *op. cit.*, pp. 26ff.

[3] See R. H. Pfeiffer, *History of New Testament Times*, 1949, pp. 200ff., and the list of books mentioned there.

[4] Cf. E. Jacob, *Theology of the Old Testament*, English trans., 1958, p. 318, n. 1.

[5] Cf. Ex. 12.40 together with Gen. 11.10–32; 21.5; 25.26; 47.9, 28.

[6] Cf. E. Jacob, *ibid.*, p. 318, n. 1, and L. Köhler, *Hebrew Man*, English trans., 1956, p. 41, n. 1.

[7] See pp. 195ff. for 'allegorical arithmetic' and also pp. 224ff. for the apocalyptists' systematic arrangement of history.

The writer of II Baruch could say, 'With the Most High account is not taken of much time nor of a few years' (17.1), for 'hours are as a time, and days as generations' (48.13). But the writer of II Enoch is in this respect more representative of the apocalyptic outlook when he says, 'And the Lord saw all man's works, and created all his creatures, and divided time, and from time he fixed the years, and from the years he appointed months, and from the months he appointed days, and of the days he appointed seven. And in these he appointed the hours, measured them out exactly, that man might reflect on time and count years, months and hours, their alternation, beginning, and end, and that he might count his own life, from the beginning until death, and reflect on his sin, and write his work bad and good' (65.3–4, cf. 40.4; 43.1; 48.4). Divisions of time, their duration and their measurement are all of the utmost significance in tracing out the divine purpose and its fulfilment in the time of the End. Even among the apocalyptists themselves there were speculations of different kinds in this same respect. W. Bousset, for example, has shown from a comparison of II Esd. 9.38ff., 10.45f., Josephus *Ant.* VIII.iii.1 (61f.), X.viii.5 (147f.), and the Ass. of Moses 1.2, 10.12 that one method of calculation among the Jews of this period dated the Exodus in the year 2501.[1] The Book of Jubilees, moreover, apparently basing its calculations on the chronology of the Samaritan Version of the Pentateuch, assumes the year 1307 for the Flood and on this date builds up 50 jubilees of 49 years each from creation to the conquest of Palestine. On this calculation the year of the Exodus is given as 2410. These dates, like that of 2666 provided by the Masoretic text of the Pentateuch, would no doubt be used as fixed points from which to make further predictions concerning the time of the End.[2]

This interest of the apocalyptists in the measurement of time can be seen also in their descriptions of the heavenly bodies as dividers of time and in the complicated calendrical calculations with which such considerations were closely connected. In I Enoch 72–82, for example, the writer describes the movement of the sun through its twelve 'portals', the different phases of the moon and the movement of the stars, and sets forth the laws of the heavenly bodies from which there can be no deviation 'till the new creation is accomplished'

[1] Cf. 'Das Chronologische System der biblischen Geschichtsbücher', *ZAW*, vol. XX, 1900, pp. 136ff.

[2] Cf. J. Skinner, *Genesis*, ICC, 1910, pp. 134ff., 233ff.

(72.1). Their measurement of time can always be relied upon for 'the sun and stars bring in all the years exactly, so that they do not advance or delay their position by a single day unto eternity' (74.12). Such measurements and divisions of time are of the greatest importance for the fixing of the calendar and so for the determination of the ordained festivals. By this means the writers of Jubilees and I Enoch 72–82, for example, advocate a solar year of 364 days, made up of twelve months of thirty days each plus four intercalary days.[1] This unrealistic and impracticable system of measurement was no doubt adopted because it found support in the biblical tradition in the Priestly account of the Flood.[2]

Chronology, then, played an important part in the thinking of the apocalyptic writers, even more so than in the case of the Old Testament writers themselves. But this fact does not of itself invalidate the claim that to these men, as to the biblical writers, time was of significance in terms of content and quality and character. This is suggested in such a verse as II Enoch 43.12 which says, 'As one year is more honourable than another, so is one man more honourable than another', *i.e.* the year can be called 'honourable' because 'honour' marks the character or content of that year, just as in the Old Testament a day can be called 'good' or 'evil' for the same reason (cf. Jer. 20.14; Job 3.3), its identity being determined by the event which took place within it. Thorleif Boman uses the expression 'psychological (or psychic) time' to express this concept over against what he calls 'chronological time' and claims that the former is characteristic of the Semitic mind and is distinguishable from the European way of thinking.[3] This cannot mean, however, that the writers with whom we are dealing had no interest in chronology, as the above paragraphs make plain, nor can it mean that there is nothing at all corresponding to it in the Western mind. What it does mean is that these men were disposed to think of time concretely in terms of its content and purpose perhaps much more readily than we are today.

[1] Cf. Jub. 6.29–38. So also II Enoch 48.1; the ordinary year of 365¼ days, however, is accepted in II Enoch 14.1. The Qumran Covenanters probably used the same calendar as that presented in Jubilees; according to this reckoning the religious festivals each year would fall on the same day of the week.

[2] Cf. R. H. Charles, *The Book of Jubilees*, 1902, pp. 56f. E. R. Leach, however, argues that it was, in fact, a practical calendar and not just a religious fiction; cf. *VT*, vol. VII, 1957, pp. 392–7.

[3] Cf. *op. cit.*, pp. 137ff.

The relevance of this idea of time-consciousness for an understanding of the phenomenon of pseudonymity has been discussed above where it has been argued that the apocalyptists' sense of 'contemporaneity' made it possible for them to associate, to the point of coincidence, their own circumstances with those of the men in whose names they wrote.[1] This same factor casts light also on certain other matters in the apocalyptic writings which are otherwise difficult to explain. One is the occurrence, in some of these books, of the transfer of one man's functions to another. An illustration of this is given in II Baruch where the language used of Baruch himself is at times reminiscent of that used concerning Moses or Enoch. In 76.2–3, for example, God says to Baruch, 'Thou shalt surely depart from this earth, nevertheless not unto death but thou shalt be preserved unto the consummation of the times. Go up therefore to the top of that mountain, and there will pass before thee all the regions of that land.' These words remind us of the tradition concerning Moses that he did not, in fact, die, but was taken up from Mount Nebo to be with God. This association with Moses is made clearer still in the verses which immediately follow. There Baruch is bidden by God to go and instruct the people for forty days before being taken up (76.4–5); this, like the forty days given to Ezra in which to restore the Scriptures (II Esd. 14.23), may well reflect the forty days spent by Moses on Mount Sinai (Deut. 9.9, 18). Elsewhere in the same book allusion is made to Baruch in terms which would more appropriately fit Enoch. In 13.3 it is said, 'Thou shalt therefore be assuredly preserved to the consummation of the times, that thou mayest be for a testimony.' This is strongly reminiscent of Enoch, who was not only 'preserved' by his translation to heaven, but was also 'set as a *sign* . . . that he should *testify* against all the children of men, and that he should recount all the deeds of the generations until the day of condemnation' (Jub. 4.24, cf. 10.17; II Enoch 40.13; 53.2; 64.5). In 59.5–11 the writer once more refers to 'the consummation of the ages' in terms familiar to the reader of the Book of Enoch where the revelations recorded are ascribed to Enoch himself; here, however, they are ascribed not to Enoch but to Moses. A further occurrence of the same feature is in II Esd. 14.50, where another transference of function takes place, this time from Enoch to Ezra, for there Ezra is described as 'the scribe of the knowledge of

[1] See pp. 134ff.

the Most High for ever and ever', a title which is elsewhere used of Enoch.[1]

It may be that the transference of attributes from Enoch to others was due to the increasing popularity of the Enoch literature among the Christians of the first century and a corresponding hostility to this figure on the part of the Jews,[2] or to the fact that the apocalypses which followed Enoch were simply imitations of the original tradition.[3] These explanations may answer the question *why*, but they do not explain *how* such a transference was deemed possible. It is not enough to dismiss such a feature as an altogether arbitrary act on the part of the later apocalyptic writers. A more adequate explanation may be found in terms of the 'psychological identity' of the people concerned, who together stood within the apocalyptic tradition and together shared the divine secrets.

This explanation of time in terms of 'contemporaneity' may help to elucidate certain other passages where, for example, the unities of space and time are neglected in rather a strange way. One illustration of this is in II Bar. 10.2 where God speaks to Baruch, 'Tell Jeremiah to go and support the captivity of the people unto Babylon' (cf. also 33.2); the following verses tell how Jeremiah departed as the Lord had commanded him and went there with the people. This, of course, does not agree with the biblical account, which states how Johanan the son of Kareah took Jeremiah and Baruch with him, not into Babylon, but into Egypt (Jer. 43.4–7). R. H. Charles argues for a faulty record at this point and comments that 'we have here a violation of the true historical tradition'.[4] It is hardly likely that the reference to Babylon instead of Egypt should have arisen by reason of an inadequate knowledge of the historical facts, nor is there any justifiable reason for questioning the text. May it not be that, by associating in his mind two different times each having the same 'psychological content', the apocalyptist is able to identify Jeremiah's departure to Egypt, virtually as a captive, with the people's departure to Babylon, and thus to speak of Jeremiah as being one with the people in their Babylonian captivity?[5]

[1] Cf. I Enoch 12.3f.; 15.1. In II Enoch 22.11 it is used of the archangel Vretil.

[2] Cf. R. H. Charles, *The Apocalypse of Baruch*, 1896, p. 22.

[3] Cf. S. B. Frost, *Old Testament Apocalyptic*, 1952, p. 167.

[4] *Apocrypha and Pseudepigrapha of the Old Testament*, vol. II, 1913, p. 485, and *The Apocalypse of Baruch*, 1896, pp. 13f.

[5] R. H. Charles quotes one other example where, he says, 'the unities of time are sacrificed to suit the dramatic purposes of the writers'. This is in II Bar. 1.1,

Another illustration is provided by I Enoch 39.3ff., where the picture of the righteous and the angels surrounding the Elect One points to a time *after* the history of the world has come to an end and the judgment is passed; but the fact that the angels still intercede for men points to a time *before* the end of the world and the final judgment. This 'confusion of thought', as we might be inclined to call it, becomes understandable if we see it in the light of the apocalyptists' weak sense of time-sequence which need not interpret time rigidly in terms of 'before' and 'after'.

It is not surprising that biblical writers and apocalyptists alike, being concerned with the character of temporal events and not simply with the bare measurement of time, should find difficulty in expressing such a supra-temporal idea as that of eternity and that their attempts to do so should meet with an arithmetical breakdown. Thus the Psalmist can say of God, 'A thousand years in thy sight are but as yesterday when it is past' (Ps. 90.4). The apocalyptist, too, can say, 'One thousand years are as one day in the testimony of the heavens' (Jub. 4.30, cf. II Peter 3.8; *Ep. of Barn.* 15) or concerning the new age soon to be ushered in, 'One hour of the age, the same is a hundred years' (Apoc. of Abr. 28); eternity can be reckoned as seventy generations (I Enoch 10.5, 12) or as five hundred years (I Enoch 10.10) or as 'many weeks without number for ever' (I Enoch 91.17). In these references, then, there is a unity between time and eternity. Eternity is not other than time; it is the totality of time, sharing with it the same character which pervades and constitutes both.

This is substantially the conclusion which Oscar Cullmann reaches in his consideration of the biblical view of the relationship between time and eternity.[1] James Barr, however, argues over against

where we are told that the word of the Lord came to Baruch, in the twenty-fifth year of Jeconiah, predicting the captivity of the people of Jerusalem. Jeconiah, says Charles, began to reign in 599 BC, when he was 18 years of age (II Kings 24.8), and after three months he was carried into captivity where he was still called king. His twenty-fifth year would therefore be 592 BC, *i.e.* two years before the approach of Nebuchadnezzar. This would mean that there were two full years between the prediction and the actual fulfilment of it. But in 6.1 we are told that only one day elapsed between the prediction and its fulfilment, for 'on the morrow' the city was taken (see *The Apocalypse of Baruch*, 1896, pp. 1, 2). This difficulty is resolved, however, and Charles's comment quoted above is unnecessary, if, as is more likely, Jeconiah began to reign in 597 BC and not in 599 BC (cf. Oesterley and Robinson, *A History of Israel*, vol. I, 1934, p. 459).

[1] Cf. *op. cit.*, pp. 61ff.

Cullmann that, since Genesis 1 and other biblical sources suggest that time began with creation, it may not be entirely non-biblical to think of time also as having an end.[1] This is certainly the belief of some at least of the apocalyptic writers who state, over against those already mentioned, that with the coming of eternity time vanishes. In II Enoch, for example, eternity is described as 'a time of not counting, endless, with neither years, nor months, nor weeks, nor days, nor hours' (33.1–2, cf. 33.11); it is the eighth eternal 'day' which follows the six days representing the six thousand years of the world's history and the one day of rest representing the one thousand years which come after (33.2). Following the final judgment, 'when all creation visible and invisible, as the Lord created it, shall end . . . then all time shall perish, and the years, and thenceforward there will be neither months nor days nor hours, they will be stuck together and will not be counted' (65.6–7). In the after-life there will be no measurement of time, 'for the first will receive the last, those whom they were expecting, and the last those of whom they used to hear that they had passed away' (II Bar. 51.13, cf. II Esd. 5.42; Matt. 19.30); time will be hidden from them, and will no longer age them (II Bar. 51.8–9).

Of significance in this respect is the doctrine of the two ages, familiar in the rabbinic writings as well as in apocalyptic, in which 'this age' is set over against 'the age to come'.[2] The world-age will end and the eternal-age will begin. 'The Most High has not made one age, but two' (II Esd. 7.50); the day will come when 'the age which is not yet awake shall be roused, and that which is corruptible shall perish' (II Esd. 7.31). The age to come is not simply the completion of this present age; it is altogether different from it. The beginning of the one marks the end of the other when time itself will end and eternity begin.

2. TIME AND THE RECURRENCE OF EVENTS

S. H. Hooke, in his attempts to determine a myth and ritual pattern in Jewish and Christian apocalypses, refers to the view, common in the ancient world, of time as a vast circle in which history is understood in terms of a recurring cyclic process. He claims

[1] Cf. *op. cit.*, pp. 75f., 145f.
[2] For a fuller treatment of this subject see pp. 266ff.

that 'in the apocalyptic books themselves we find abundant evidence of the dream of one great final revolution of the wheel of the divine purpose, setting all things right. . . . Here the preoccupation with time in its aspect of recurrence finds expression in calculations of mystic periods, days, weeks, half-weeks, weeks of years and an appearance of strange minuteness and accuracy.'[1]

The Cyclic Theory of the Ages assumed different forms in the ancient world, in some at least of which the belief was expressed that the whole world followed an ever-recurring cycle of change.[2] Of particular significance in this respect was the Great Year of the Babylonians, based on the movement of the heavenly bodies, particularly the planets, and forming the centre of complicated astrological study. In the course of some thousands of years these bodies, in their rotation, came round full circle at which point, it was believed, an old age was completed and a new age begun. This new age had reference not only to the revolution of the heavenly bodies, but also to the recurrence of terrestrial history. In its Babylonian form this idea was associated with the sacred number 12,960,000 ($= 60^4 = 3{,}600^2$), the numerical expression of the law of the universe, which was believed to govern not only the life of the universe but also the life of man. When applied to time it represented 12,960,000 days or 36,000 years (taking 360 days as one year) representing the Babylonian cycle, in one form of the theory at any rate. There is, in fact, no unanimity about the duration of such cycles, 432,000 being another figure sometimes given. It is to be observed that this figure, like the others, is also a multiple of 60, the Babylonian system of numbering being sexagesimal.

The number 36,000 represents the duration of what came to be called the great 'Platonic Year'. In this presentation of the theory there is an alternation of two ages which repeat themselves as long as the universe lasts. In the first the universe, as it were, moves forward; in the second it moves backward to the place from which it began. The revolution forward leads to the Golden Age. In this rotation the processes of life are in many respects the opposite of those which men experience now. During this age, for example, men are born old, but gradually grow younger as time moves round. The

[1] 'Myth and Ritual Pattern in Jewish and Christian Apocalypses', in *The Labyrinth*, 1935, p. 221, and also in *The Siege Perilous*, 1956, p. 132.

[2] Cf. 'Ages of the World' in *ERE*, vol. I, 1908, pp. 183ff., especially 'Greek and Roman' by K. F. Smith, 'Jewish' by E. N. Adler, 'Zoroastrian' by N. Söderblom.

earth gives birth to them and sustains them with food. It is a time of happiness and plenty, with no strife, no pain, no toil. The 'turn of the age', when the universe begins to change direction, is indicated by great cosmic disturbances, prominent among which are devastations caused by fire and flood. Men no longer grow young, but grow old and die. With another full turn of the circle, the universe again reverses direction and moves on once more toward the Golden Age. Those who had died in the previous cycle and were buried in the earth now rise up. They are born old and gradually grow young and eventually disappear.[1]

According to Berossus, the Babylonian astrologer and missionary, the universe passes through a number of Great Years each with a summer and a winter. 'Their summer took place when all the planets were in conjunction at the same point of Cancer, and brought with it a great conflagration. On the other hand, their winter came when all the planets were joined in Capricorn, and its result was a universal flood. Each of these cosmic cycles . . . was an exact reproduction of those that had preceded it. In fact, when the stars resumed exactly the same position, they were forced to act in identically the same manner as before.'[2]

This cyclic view of time and history was known to the writers of the Old Testament (cf. II Sam. 11.1; I Kings 20.22; Isa. 29.1; Job 1.5) and was given at least tacit acceptance by Ecclesiastes: 'That which hath been is that which shall be; and that which hath been done is that which shall be done; and there is no new thing under the sun. Is there a thing whereof men say, See, this is new? it hath been already, in the ages which were before us' (1.9–10). But any such theory of time, which involved belief in ever-recurring cycles of change, was ultimately incompatible with the Hebrew belief in God as Creator and with the prophets' stress on the *eschaton* as the completion of world-history. Their emphasis was on the unique acts of God in history leading to the salvation of his people; these acts pointed forward to a climax in history in which his rule would be established over all.[3]

This old idea of the *magnus annus*, as the Romans called it, became particularly prominent from the time of Alexander's conquests

[1] Cf. *ibid.*, pp. 197f.

[2] F. Cumont, *The Oriental Religions in Roman Paganism*, 1911, p. 176, quoted by T. F. Glasson, *Greek Influence in Jewish Eschatology*, 1961, p. 78.

[3] For a fuller treatment of this subject, see pp. 263ff.

onwards. At that time the dividing wall between East and West was broken down and this resulted in a mingling of cultures in which the Jews of Palestine and the Dispersion shared. There are indications in the apocalyptic literature that these writers, not surprisingly, were familiar with the cyclic view of time and were influenced by it. In several of their books we find reminiscences of the old Babylonian or the more recent Greek accounts. In the Book of Enoch, for example, the part played by the planets, the stars, and the other heavenly bodies reminds us strongly of the relation which these bodies have to the measurement of time in the Babylonian system. Again, in Jub. 23.25 we have a reminder of the old belief that men are born old in the forward revolution of the universe: 'All the heads of the children will be white with grey hair, And a child of three weeks will appear old like a man of one hundred years',[1] a strange phenomenon which is to be one of the signs foreshadowing the appearance of the kingdom (cf. Sib. Or. II. 155). In at least one apocalyptic book several references are made to the earth bringing forth children in somewhat the same way as in the Greek form of the cyclic myth (cf. II Esd. 5.49ff.; 10.9, etc.). Again, the idea of the destruction of the world by fire, which is a feature of certain apocalyptic writings, was found not only among the Persians but also among the Stoics, for whom this was a prominent feature in their cyclic theory of time. Alongside this went the other recurring catastrophe associated with the *magnus annus*, destruction by flood. These two catastrophes, as we have seen, were features in the Chaldean account of the Great Year. No doubt allusion to this is to be found in such a passage as the Life of Adam and Eve 49.3: 'On account of your transgression, our Lord will bring upon your race the anger of his judgment, first by water, the second time by fire; by these two will the Lord judge the whole human race' (cf. Sib. Or. III. 761).

Indications of the cyclic view of history have sometimes been found in the familiar idea that the End of Time will resemble the Beginning of Time.[2] This is a constantly recurring theme of Jewish and Christian apocalypses and, of course, has its roots in Old Testament prophecy. There will be a new heaven and a new earth; Paradise will return and everything will be perfect as it was at the first. The presentation of this belief may well have been influenced by this particular view of history during the inter-testamental period,

[1] Cf. Hesiod, *Works and Days*, 180–1. [2] See further p. 182.

but it is by no means certain that the cyclic theory necessarily lies behind it.[1]

Despite their familiarity with the cyclic view of time, however, it cannot be said that this idea was characteristic of the apocalyptic writers as a whole. S. H. Hooke's contention that in these books there is 'abundant evidence' for this particular theory must be seriously qualified, especially if what he has in mind is a belief in the recurrence of historical events. The apocalyptic theory of the Two Ages, for example, reveals a way of thinking which is very different from the popular conception of recurrent world-ages of a cyclic kind and is indeed a denial of it. Their stress, too, on eschatology and the place they give to the *eschaton* in their interpretation of history is in itself a refutation of the cyclic view of the universe in general and of history in particular. These hopes differed in a number of respects from those of the prophets, but like them the apocalyptists looked forward to the climatic triumph of God over evil in terms of the End and not in terms of a universal cycle of events in which history repeats itself in a series of endless revolutions.

3. THE UNITY OF HISTORY

We moderns readily assume history to be a unity. All civilized peoples, we believe, are joined together on the basis of certain common characteristics of life and habit which they share with one another, *i.e.* we assume a unity of history because we assume a unity of human nature.[2] But this conception of the unity of history did not originate with the moderns. It was in fact passed on to us by the early Christian Church which taught that all men were 'one in Christ Jesus' and that the whole of history was unified through God's purpose in him.[3] Here, however, the unifying principle was not the idea of the unity of human nature, but rather the belief in the overruling purpose of God. But this idea did not originate even with the

[1] See T. F. Glasson's chapter on 'The End and the New Beginning' in *op. cit.*, pp. 74ff., and his reference to N. A. Dahl's essay on 'Christ, Creation and the Church' in *Background of the N.T. and its Eschatology*, edited by Davies and Daube, 1956, pp. 422ff.

[2] Compare, for example, Marx's economic unity which finds the clue to the solution of this problem in the class struggle.

[3] 'It was Christianity which taught men to say with the poet Francis Thompson, "I view all mundane happenings with the Fall for one terminus and the Millennium for the other".' (H. Wheeler Robinson, *The History of Israel*, 1938, p. 233).

Christian Church. Christians themselves received it from the Jewish apocalyptic writers who interpreted the whole of history—past, present and future—in terms of God's unifying purpose.

R. H. Charles maintains that this idea of the unity of history originated with the apocalyptists, who were true pioneers in this respect. 'It was thus apocalyptic', he says, 'and not prophecy that was the first to grasp the great idea that all history, human, cosmological and spiritual is a unity—a unity that follows inevitably as a corollary to the unity of God as enforced by the O.T. prophets. Thus whereas prophecy deals with the present destinies of individuals and nations, and their future destinies as arising organically out of the present and on the present earth without reference to the life of the individual after death, apocalyptic dealt with the past, the present, and the future as linked together and forming one whole, and thereby sought to justify the ways of God to man.'[1] Elsewhere the same writer says, 'The O.T. prophet dealt with the destinies of this nation or of that, but took no comprehensive view of the history of the world as a whole. . . . Hence Daniel was the first to teach the unity of all human history, and that every phase of this history was a further stage in the development of God's purposes.'[2]

Such a claim, however, does less than justice to the Old Testament prophets and enhances the reputation of the apocalyptists in a way they hardly deserve. It is more accurate to regard the apocalyptists as middle-men rather than as pioneers in this regard. What they did was to carry still further the sense of divine purpose, which was already to be found in the prophets, as the unifying principle of all human history. As we shall see, they greatly widened the scope of the idea and developed it in ways hitherto unknown; but in this as in other respects they were acting as interpreters of prophecy, leaving their own peculiar mark on what they transmitted.

The unity of history, as R. H. Charles himself indicates, is a corollary of the unity of God. The monotheistic faith and belief in his all-embracing purpose belong together. The one grows out of the other and is an inevitable development of it. Monotheism became explicit, perhaps for the first time, with Deutero-Isaiah; but for some considerable time before this it was at least implicit in the teaching of earlier prophets. Amos, for example, does not expressly state that Yahweh is the only God, but for all practical purposes he takes this

[1] *Commentary on Daniel*, 1929, p. xxv; cf. *Eschatology*, 2nd ed., 1913, p. 183.
[2] *Commentary on Daniel*, 1929, pp. cxiv–cxv.

for granted. The gods of the surrounding nations—Hadad, Dagon, Melek, Melkart, Chemosh—are to be completely ignored. Yahweh is not only the creator of the physical universe and the controller of all natural phenomena, he is the controller of peoples and their history as well. His interest and control are not confined to Israel. Damascus, Gaza, Edom, Tyre, Moab and Ammon must all come before him for judgment and receive punishment at his hand (Amos 1.3–2.3). Assyria is a mighty nation, but she is a mere tool in the hand of God. Yahweh will use her to carry out his purpose just as it pleases him, and when that task is done she will be destroyed (Isa. 10.5–19). Indeed, it was the rise of Assyria that forced the prophets to enlarge their ideas of God, for he must now be regarded as equal to the task of controlling and governing that great world empire. Even the great migrations of the past are now seen by the prophets to be the work of Yahweh; not only did he bring up Israel out of Egypt, it was he also who brought up the Philistines from Caphtor and the Syrians from Kir (Amos 9.7). God's control is over all, and none can escape from him even though he dig into the depths of Sheol itself (Amos 9.2). The prophet's glance sweeps indiscriminately over the past, present and future, uniting all history into a single plan, conceived and controlled by God; for Yahweh is controller also of the destinies of men and nations.

Such considerations as these point to the fact that in the prophets, rather than in the apocalyptists, we are to find the pioneers and originators of this idea of the unity of history. It may be true, as R. H. Charles says, that 'whereas prophecy incidentally dealt with the past and devoted itself to the present and the future as rising organically out of the past, apocalyptic, though its interests lie chiefly in the future as containing the solution of the problems of the past and present, took within its purview things past, present and to come.'[1] This must not be taken to mean, however, that the prophets did not thereby grasp the idea of the unity of history. It is fairer to say that, though the prophets grasped the idea, it was left to the apocalyptists to complete the logic of it and to work it out in terms of their own historical situation and in terms of their convinced belief concerning the fast-approaching End.

'The knowledge of history', writes H. Wheeler Robinson, 'is not the mere accumulation of facts. We must relate these data to one another, and trace their connections.'[2] The apocalyptists, in a much

[1] *Eschatology*, 2nd ed., 1913, p. 183. [2] *Redemption and Revelation*, 1943, p. 167.

more thorough and systematic way than the prophets, set about relating these data to one another, and traced the connection between them in terms of the divine purpose and the divine initiative in history. They saw and interpreted the events of history *sub specie aeternitatis* and observed in the apparent confusion of history an order and a goal.

It has often been said that the apocalyptists took a pessimistic view of history and that, in their writings, they endeavoured to 'contract out of history' by looking beyond it and above it for the fulfilment of their hopes and dreams. But this point of view presents only one side of the picture. It is true that, by and large, they believed that things were going from bad to worse, that the present world-order was 'past redemption', that an end would have to be made of history which had become corrupt through its capitulation to the powers of evil. And yet they were not forlorn men, wringing their hands in despair. They were men of faith who could see within history, through history and beyond history the working out of God's triumphant purpose, not only for themselves as a nation, but also for men from every nation who were prepared to follow the way of righteousness. In face of the tyrannies of their Greek and Roman oppressors they believed in the ultimate victory of God and the establishment of the kingdom of God. In a world where evil was in the ascendancy and persecution was the lot of the righteous, they believed in their destiny as the People of God and in the triumph of his almighty purpose over men and demons. They believed that 'man's extremity is God's opportunity'. This extremity, the End, was near. The promises made to their fathers were about to be fulfilled. The great *denouement* of history was close at hand. In it God would take the initiative as he had done from the very beginning of time.

The hopes and fears of the apocalyptic writers are to be judged, then, against the background of the events and circumstances of the days in which they wrote. Their writings, like boiling lava from a volcano, were thrown up out of explosive historical circumstances over which they themselves had no control. They cannot be rightly understood apart from the situations and the times in which they were written. These were critical times for the Jewish people. The years between the Maccabean Revolt and the fall of Jerusalem in AD 70 are marked by a series of crises which are reflected in one apocalyptic book after another. On the surface the struggle appeared to be between Jews on the one hand and Greeks and Romans on the other, between Judaism and Hellenism; but, in fact, it was between the powers of darkness and the powers of light, between the kingdom of Satan and the kingdom of God.[1]

Because they believed they stood so close to the End the apocalyptists were able to take in the whole of history at a glance and recite its meaning in terms of the divine purpose. Within this purpose the people of Israel had a high destiny which they dared not evade. F. C. Burkitt draws attention to this by pointing out that during the two and a half centuries before the fall of Jerusalem the whole world was confronted in a new way by the fact of the Jewish nation. In pre-exilic times the Hebrews had not differed greatly in respect of thought or custom from the surrounding nations. After the return from Captivity, the Jews were a distinctive people, but they were a Church rather than a nation, and played no significant political role. But from the time of Antiochus Epiphanes the Jewish nation became, as never before, 'a kingdom of this world, an alternative to civilization as then understood, actually before the eyes of men'.[2] By no stretch of the imagination could it be compared in material resources or in military power with the great empires of the Seleucids or the Ptolemies; none the less it believed it had an imperial part to play in the history of civilization. F. C. Burkitt illustrates this point by comparing the prophecies in Jeremiah and Ezekiel, which were directed against the nations, with those in Daniel: 'In Jeremiah and Ezekiel we have announcements of Divine vengeance upon the enemies of Israel, but it is all piecemeal and detached. In Daniel, on the other hand, there is a philosophy of universal history.'[3] In support of this he quotes some words of Edwyn Bevan: 'The great Gentile kingdoms, like the Greek supremacy of the Seleucids and Ptolemies which seemed so overwhelming and terrible, are shown as phases in a world process whose end is the Kingdom of God.'[4] The apocalyptic visionaries looked at history and saw it whole. They looked at contemporary history and recognized that their own nation had a vital part to play in it. They refused to measure their destiny in terms of wealth and armies, but rather in terms of the purpose of Almighty God. Daniel, in his visions in chapters 2, 7 and 8, sees the fall of Babylonia, Media, Persia and Greece. There is nothing parochial about his outlook. He is a patriot, but he is a cosmopolitan as well.

[1] See ch. X.
[2] *Jewish and Christian Apocalypses*, 1914, p. 4.
[3] *Ibid.*, pp. 6–7.
[4] *Jerusalem under the High Priests*, 1920, p. 86.

God is the God of the whole earth; Judaism is the embodiment of religion for all mankind; Israel is the instrument for the establishment of his world-wide rule. From where they stood the apocalyptists could see the past, the present and the future in one continuous perspective. They were not so much conscious of its continuity, however, as they were of its wholeness.

This point, together with several others mentioned above, is brought out in the account of Nebuchadnezzar's dream given in Daniel 2. There the writer describes four great world-empires in terms of a statue whose 'head was of fine gold, his breast and his arms of silver, his belly and his thighs of brass, his legs of iron, his feet part of iron and part of clay' (2.32–33). Here we may see evidence for belief in a gradual deterioration which illustrates the apocalyptist's 'pessimism' and his despair of the present age. The Babylonian Empire is of gold (2.38), the Median Empire of silver (2.39), the Persian Empire of brass (2.39), and the Greek Empire of iron and clay (2.40ff.). The author is not particularly concerned, however, about the continuity of these empires and their relation to one another. 'The unfolding of history is of little importance; . . . the four empires which come one after another are all present at the end of the last empire.'[1] This is reminiscent of the poor sense of time-sequence on the part of the earlier Hebrew writers and of their habit of measuring time and history by their content rather than by their place within an historic sequence. The climax of the vision is reached in the description of a stone 'cut out without hands' which smashed the statue in pieces and then became a great mountain which filled the whole earth (2.34f.). This stone is the kingdom of God which takes the place of the kingdoms of this world. Elsewhere it is made clear that this kingdom will be given into the hands of Israel who will share in God's great triumph over the nations of the earth (cf. 7.13, 18, 27). This small kingdom of Israel is set over against the mighty kingdoms of the earth and in direct opposition to them. It is not inferior to them; on the contrary, they will perish, but to Israel will be given 'the kingdom and the dominion, and the greatness of the kingdoms under the whole heaven' (7.27). By reason of their own historical situation and the part they were called to play in the affairs of the nations, the apocalyptists were able to adopt a much more cosmopolitan outlook and to see history as a unity in a manner quite impossible for the prophets who had gone before them.

[1] E. Jacob, *Theology of the Old Testament*, English trans., 1958, p. 196.

These writers, then, were not so much students of history as they were interpreters of history. They believed that the happenings of history have a meaning and that that meaning is to be understood in terms of the goal toward which history is moving. They believed, too, as we shall see, that human life and destiny have meaning and that that meaning is to be found in belief in the resurrection of the dead, *i.e.* even the fate of individuals is influenced by their sense of history and their interpretation of it as purposeful and meaningful. But God's purpose was not confined to the lives and destinies of men and nations. The whole universe was his concern. The history of the physical universe as well as the history of the human race was involved in his eternal purpose. God had been working from the very beginning and was working still. All the events of history were directed toward a single goal—the establishment of the kingdom of God—in which the divine purpose would be vindicated once and for all.

We have already seen, however, that in the minds of some of these writers there is a discontinuity between time and eternity, between history and beyond-history, between this age and the age to come. H. Wheeler Robinson reminds us that, if we are to meet all the difficulties involved in the problem of the relation of time to eternity, we must try to resolve three dualities into what he calls 'transparent unities'. 'The dualities are that (*a*) history must vindicate God, and yet is inadequate within itself to do so, (*b*) the values of history which . . . require a temporal order for their actualization, also require an eternal order for their interpretation and justification, (*c*) the temporal must be so taken up into the eternal, that its process, as well as its product, has meaning and value for God.'[1] The apocalyptic writers cannot be said to have succeeded in resolving these dualities into unities, although they are at least one in seeing the need for an eternal order. The characteristic note struck by most of them, as we have seen, is not the sameness of this present age and the new age, but the difference between them. A dualism is maintained between the present age of ungodliness and the future age of righteousness (cf. Apoc. of Abraham 29; 31; 32). The universe cannot ultimately be reduced to a harmonious whole, for 'the Most High has made not one age but two' (II Esd. 7.50). This teaching, as we shall see more clearly later on,[2] is fundamental to our under-

[1] *Op. cit.*, p. xlii. [2] See pp. 266ff.

standing of apocalyptic thought. And yet, however different they may be from each other, the temporal and the eternal are joined together by ties that cannot be broken. This link is the purpose of God which reaches through history into eternity and will find its vindication in the salvation of God's own people. The apocalyptists see this vindication to be one of the righteous nation and the righteous individual who take part in the messianic kingdom. In the apocalyptic writings, then, there is after all a unity wider than that of mere world history; it is a unity in which the temporal is taken up into the eternal by means of those moral and spiritual qualities which make up the purpose of God—a purpose which, whilst finding its actualization in history, must seek its justification beyond history.

4. HISTORY SYSTEMATICALLY ARRANGED

We have observed that the apocalyptists shared with the canonical prophets a belief in the unity of history. But so far there have been few indications that they made much advance on the contribution made by their predecessors. That advance came when the apocalyptists began to work out history systematically in vast periods and also deterministically. Writing of Nebuchadnezzar's empire as described in the Book of Daniel, S. B. Frost comments, 'That a kingdom should be weighed in a balance and found wanting is the very stuff of prophecy; that it should be divided is a pronouncement of divine judgment in the very nature of an Isaiah; but that it should be *numbered* is the thought of an apocalyptist alone. The whole school is impregnated with the conception of periods predetermined by divine decree.'[1] We shall consider presently the question of the determination of history. Here we observe the apocalyptists' love of systematization and schematization. The history of the world is divided up into great epochs characterized either by 'millennia' of varying lengths or by the rise and fall of great empires. This succession of world-empires provides a complete scheme of world-history which God has ordained beforehand and which together form a whole, a unity. There is no unanimity in these books about the number or duration of the various eras or empires, although certain fairly well-defined traditions are followed by most of the writers. The various schemes are worked out with mathematical precision. The resulting

[1] *Op. cit.*, p. 186.

impression is one of artificiality. At the same time this method of writing helps to bring out the apocalyptists' love of symbolism, for the schematization of history has symbolic significance, and makes more graphic the reality of the approaching End.

We have already observed that the writer of the Book of Daniel divides up history, from the time of the Captivity onwards, into seventy weeks of years or seventy heptads of years on the basis of Jeremiah's prophecy.[1] These seventy weeks of years are themselves divided into three periods of seven 'weeks', sixty-two 'weeks' and one 'week' after which will come the End. Again, in the Test. of Levi 16–17 the scheme of seventy weeks of years is adopted but, it would seem, the first heptad is interpreted as seven jubilees. In I Enoch 1–36 the period from the Flood to the final judgment is given as seventy 'generations' (10.12). In I Enoch 83–90 Israel's history, from the Captivity onwards, is ruled over by seventy 'shepherds' whose reigns are of unequal length. These seventy reigns are in turn divided into four periods or ages ruled over by twelve, twenty-three, twenty-three and twelve 'shepherds' respectively.[2] This division of history into four ages appears also in the Book of Daniel in terms of the four metals (ch. 2) and the four great beasts (7.3) and no doubt reflects the classical idea of the division of the world into the Gold, Silver, Bronze and Iron Ages.

Further allusion is made to the division of history into vast periods in II Esd. 14.5 which tells how God spoke to Ezra concerning Moses, saying, 'I told him many wondrous things, showed him the secrets of the times, declared to him the ends of the seasons.' As G. H. Box points out, this refers to 'the secret tradition regarding the crises of the world's history (measured by certain periods of time) which was associated with the name of Moses.'[3] Two books are of particular interest in this connection—Jubilees and the Assumption of Moses. In the former God discloses to Moses at Sinai the history of the world both past and future (Jub. 1.4, 26); in the latter, Moses reveals to Joshua the things which are to come (Ass. of Moses 1.6ff.).

The Book of Jubilees, as its name indicates, adopts a system of dating based upon the Old Testament idea of the jubilee. Here, however, each jubilee is reckoned as forty-nine years and not as fifty years as in the Pentateuch.[4] The choice of this number is in

[1] See pp. 196f. [2] See pp. 200f. [3] *The Ezra-Apocalypse*, 1912, p. 308.
[4] R. Jehuda also assumes jubilee periods of 49 years in *Nedarim* 61a.

itself significant as indicating the author's love of symmetry ($49 = 7 \times 7$; 7 is a sacred number). He calculates the period from the creation to the Exodus in terms of forty-nine 'jubilees', each of which lasts for seven 'weeks of years', *i.e.* forty-nine years. Hence the total duration is $49 \times 49 = 2{,}401$ years. In 50.4 it is stated that forty-nine more years elapsed before the entry into Canaan. This brings the figure to 2,450 years representing the period from creation to entry into the Promised Land. Michel Testuz argues that the book gives indication of a division of time greater than those of 'weeks of years' or of jubilees.[1] He sees evidence for the division of world-history into three eras or ages which he describes successively as the Age of the Testimony, the Age of the Law and the New Age. The first of these lasts for forty-nine 'jubilees' and is completed with the flight of the Israelites out of Egypt; the second, whose duration is not specified, begins with the revelation of the Law to Moses on Sinai; the third ushers in the kingdom 'when the heavens and the earth shall be renewed' (1.29) and God himself will descend and dwell with his people throughout eternity (1.26).[2]

In the Assumption of Moses reference is again made to jubilees as a measurement of world-history. Here, however, each is taken to represent a period of fifty years, as in the Pentateuch. The duration of world-history is given as eighty-five jubilees. The evidence is in 1.2 which states that 2,500 years had elapsed before the death of Moses, and in 10.12 where Moses says to Joshua, 'From my death until his (*i.e.* God's) advent there will be 250 times.' A 'time' here represents a year-week, so that from Moses' death until the advent of God in judgment will be 250×7 years, *i.e.* 1,750 years. Thus the duration of world-history is given as $2{,}500 + 1{,}750$ years, *i.e.* 4,250 years or 85 jubilees.[3]

This schematization of history is developed even more in that section of I Enoch known as the Apocalypse of Weeks (93.1–10;

[1] *Les Idées Religieuses du Livre des Jubilés*, 1960, pp. 138f., 172ff.

[2] 'At that time (*i.e.* the first century), the belief was widespread among the Jews that world history consisted of three epochs: first, the period of chaos—*tohu bohu*; then the period of the Torah beginning with the revelation on Mount Sinai; and finally, the hoped-for period of the Messiah' (L. Baeck, *The Pharisees*, English trans., 1947, pp. 72f., quoted by W. D. Davies, *Torah in the Messianic Age and/or the Age to Come*, 1952, p. 79). This judgment is based chiefly on the words of *Sanhedrin* 97b and *ʿAbodah Zarah* 9b, which read, 'The world is to exist 6,000 years: the first 2,000 years are to be void; the next 2,000 years are the period of the Torah; and the following 2,000 years are the period of the Messiah.'

[3] See R. H. Charles, *The Assumption of Moses*, 1897, p. 44.

91.12–17). There the history of the world is divided into ten 'weeks' of unequal lengths, each of which is marked by some great event. From the point of view of the writer seven 'weeks' are in the past, and three are still to come. These three represent the messianic age at the close of which the final judgment takes place.[1]

The number 7 appears in several other apocalyptic writings in this same connection. In the Testament of Abraham, for example, Death shows Abraham 'seven fiery serpents' heads' (ch. 17), which symbolize the seven ages into which the world is divided (ch. 19), each of which presumably lasts for 1,000 years. This same belief in seven ages is expressed also in II Enoch 33.1–2 whose calculations are obviously based on the idea of a world-week of seven millennia corresponding to the seven days of creation. Just as the six days of creation were followed by one day of rest, so the 6,000 years of world-history will be followed by a rest of 1,000 years.[2] At the close of this era of rest the eighth 'eternal day' will begin.

In several other passages history is divided into twelve parts. The Test. of Abraham 7B, for example, agrees with chapters 17 and 19 in putting the world's duration at 7,000 years, but here this period is divided into 'twelve hours of the day'. Similarly in the Apocalypse of Abraham the present age lasts for twelve 'hours' (ch. 20), but in this case each 'hour' represents a period of 100 years (ch. 28). These twelve 'hours' or 1,200 years are probably to be regarded as extending from the founding of Jerusalem by David (cf. II Esd. 10.46) to the destruction of the last Temple by Titus.[3] A twelve-fold division of history, representing the period before the coming of the messianic kingdom, is given in Baruch's vision of the cloud with black and white waters; these waters, which symbolize the periods of world-history (II Bar. 56.3), are poured out upon the earth twelve times (53.6).[4] Again, in the Latin text of II Esd. 14.11, we read that 'the world-age is divided into twelve parts; nine parts of it are passed already, and the half of the tenth part; and there remain of it two parts, besides

[1] World history is divided into 10 generations according to Sib. Or. IV. 47–85. In I Enoch 18.16 and 21.6 it is stated that the punishment of the fallen angels will last for 10,000 years. For traditions concerning the duration of the messianic kingdom and the final judgment, see ch. XI.

[2] Cf. Ps. 90.4: 'A thousand years in thy sight are but as yesterday'; also Jub. 4.30.

[3] Josephus says that this period extended over 1,179 years (*War* VI.x.1 (439)).

[4] In II Bar. 27.1ff. it is the period of 'woes' preceding the messianic kingdom which is divided into 12 parts.

the half of the tenth part'; in the Ethiopic text it is divided into ten parts and not twelve, half of the tenth part remaining.[1]

There is, then, a considerable variety of tradition here, but in each case world-history is systematized and schematized in a way unlike anything to be found in the Old Testament prophets. These divisions of time, whatever their number or duration may be, form a unity of history through which the divine purpose can be traced. This present age is brought to a close either by the establishment of the messianic kingdom or by the coming of the final judgment.

The question arises, where did the apocalyptists learn to think in this way? How are we to explain this idea of the division of history into vast periods in a way so unlike that of the Old Testament prophets? The answer is to be found in their environment, and in particular in the influence of Hellenistic and more especially of Persian beliefs. The source of the account in Daniel 2, for example, in which the four ages of the world are represented by four metals—gold, silver, bronze and iron—is to be found in Greek thought both at this time and at a much earlier period.[2] This division of world-history into four ages is not confined, however, to the Greeks. It is to be found also among the Persians and is characteristic of the teaching of Zoroastrianism. The dating of the literary sources of Zoroastrianism is a notoriously difficult problem. But, though most of this literature comes from the post-Christian and indeed post-Mohammedan eras, it 'undoubtedly contains material of far greater antiquity'.[3] There it is stated that the world is to last for 12,000 years and that this period is divided into four eras of 3,000 years each. During the first 3,000 years the great god Ahura-Mazda (Ormazd) produces spiritually those creatures which will enable him to gain the victory over evil; these creatures remain during this period spiritual 'intangible bodies' (*Bundahishn* 1.8); everything remains invisible.[4] During the second 3,000 years 'everything proceeds by the will of Ahura-Mazda' (*Bundahishn* 1.19); the evil spirit, Angra-

[1] Cf. the half-week in Daniel 9.27 = the last $3\frac{1}{2}$ years of tribulation.

[2] Cf. T. F. Glasson, *op. cit.*, pp. 2–3. Glasson refers to J. Duchesne-Guillemin, who 'points out that the metal-myth was well known in Greece; there is no indication that the Book of Daniel derived it from Iran, where it only appears very late'; cf. *Ormazd et Ahriman*, 1953, p. 78, and contrast S. B. Frost, *op. cit.*, p. 187.

[3] N. Söderblom, 'Ages of the World (Zoroastrian)', in *ERE*, vol. I, 1908, pp. 205–10.

[4] Cf. II Enoch 24.4: 'For before all things were visible, I alone used to go about in the invisible things.'

Mainyu (Ahriman) tries to oppose Ahura-Mazda, but remains in a state of confusion of thought throughout the whole period; during this time Ahura-Mazda creates the material world and, in its final stages, man himself; the *fravashis*, or spirits, of men had already existed, but now they assume bodily form. During the third 3,000 years there is 'an intermingling of the wills of Ahura-Mazda and Ahriman' (*Bundahishn* 1.19); the evil spirit rushes into creation, gains the ascendancy and exercises power over men; with the commencement of this period the history of mankind begins, *i.e.* it is to continue for 6,000 years through the second and third trimillennia; Zarathushtra (Greek *Zoroaster*), it is said, was born thirty years before the close of the second trimillennium, *i.e.* at the centre point of human history. During the fourth 3,000 years Ahura-Mazda gains the victory through a deliverer, Saoshyant, who is Zarathushtra himself or one of his descendants and who appears at the close of each of these remaining 3,000 years; at last 'the evil spirit is disabled, and the adversary is kept away from the creatures' (*Bundahishn* 1.20); Angra-Mainyu is then thrown into the abyss and the end of the world arrives; the dead are raised and judgment follows; all men are purified by fire and a new age begins.

This brief sketch of Zoroastrian teaching is of obvious significance in the light of the beliefs of the apocalyptic writers indicated above. The Iranian writers divided up history into great world epochs and worked it out in elaborate schemes and systems of measurement much in the same way as the apocalyptic writers did. It is surely more than coincidence that the number 12, which plays such an important part in Zoroastrianism, should appear so frequently in the apocalyptic divisions of history. We have already noted, moreover, that in certain apocalyptic (and Talmudic) writings the duration of the world is calculated on the basis of the six days of creation, each day representing 1,000 years. This, too, may well reflect the Zoroastrian reference to the life of mankind as covering the last two trimillennia of world-history. However much the details of the two schemes may vary, this much seems plain, that the Jewish apocalyptists were deeply influenced by the Iranian conception of world-epochs and used it to develop, systematize and universalize the idea of the unity of history which they had already received from their prophetic predecessors in the Old Testament tradition. The extent of this influence will become even clearer when we come to consider more fully the apocalyptic conception of 'the last things'.

5. HISTORY DETERMINED BEFOREHAND

The apocalyptists believed not only that history had been systematically arranged, but also that this arrangement had been ordained by God from the very beginning, *i.e.* those vast eras of time into which history was divided had been predetermined by the will of God and must follow the pattern which had already been set for them. Their number and their duration were both fixed beforehand. There was therefore an inevitability about history; through travail and persecution it would move unerringly to its predetermined goal—the defeat of evil and the establishment of God's kingdom in the time of the End. The past was fixed; the future was fixed also. To the apocalyptists there was 'an absolutely fixed future, in which they saw not the inevitable results of present conduct, but the violent reversal of present conditions'.[1] 'Determinism thus became a leading characteristic of Jewish apocalyptic; and accordingly its conception of history, as distinguished from that of prophecy, was often mechanical rather than organic.'[2]

This is particularly clear in such books as I Enoch and Jubilees, for example, where the belief is expressed that human life and historical events are regulated and even determined by the movements of the heavenly bodies. In Jubilees it is said of Enoch that 'he wrote down the signs of heaven according to the number of their months in a book . . . and what was and what will be he saw in a vision of his sleep, as it will happen to the children of men throughout their generations until the day of judgment' (4.17, 19). The twelve 'signs of heaven' in this passage correspond to the twelve signs of the Zodiac, and the whole passage has reference to I Enoch 72–82 and 83–90 where the same thought is expressed at greater length. These heavenly bodies, which determine the destinies of men, are themselves controlled by angels in whose hands lies the fate of men and nations.[3]

[1] F. C. Porter, *The Messages of the Apocalyptical Writers*, 1905, pp. 66f.

[2] R. H. Charles, *Eschatology*, 2nd ed., 1913, p. 206.

[3] J. T. Milik indicates several references in the Dead Sea Scrolls where the same belief is to be found, *e.g. Hymns of Thanksgiving* I.23–25, 27–29; VII.28ff.; IX.16f.; X.1ff.; XII.10f. He refers to a work from Cave I which 'teaches the physical characteristics of people born under a given sign of the Zodiac, and the exact proportion of their share in the world of the Spirits of Light, and in that of the Spirits of Darkness' (*Ten Years of Discovery in the Wilderness of Judaea*, English trans., 1959, p. 119).

We hear a great deal in these writings about the heavenly tablets on which God has recorded the fixed order of historical events. From this there can be no deviation at all. What God has set down must come to pass, or, as Daniel puts it, 'that which is determined shall be done' (11.36). On the heavenly tablets are recorded 'all the deeds of mankind, and of all the children of flesh that shall be upon the earth to the remotest generations' (Jub. 1.29). All things created have been foreseen by God; the destinies of Israel and of the Gentile nations have been determined beforehand by him (Ass. of Moses 12.4f.). He alone knows the goal of the generations (II Bar. 48.3, etc.). The whole course of history is predetermined, and the Day of Judgment will come when the fixed number of the elect has been reached (II Esd. 4.35f.; 11.44; 14.5).

Weight is given to this conviction, that all history has been determined from the beginning, by the device of pseudonymity. The apocalyptic writers believed that God had given to them a secret knowledge of times past and times to come. By placing themselves in the past, as it were, and by writing from the standpoint of the hero of the past, they were able to see the intervening years of history up to their own time in terms of the future. That which actually has been is now that which shall be; that which has been accomplished is that which will be accomplished. History is related in terms of foretelling; accomplished fact is related in terms of predetermined purpose. The pattern of the past is the pattern of the future. The whole is determined and will lead up to the End. It is because the future is determined, as the past has been, that the apocalyptists can claim to have foreknowledge and secret knowledge of that which is yet to be.

Men could not alter what had been predetermined by the divine will. But they could try to discover at what point they themselves stood in the scheme of history unfolded for them by divine revelation. By identifying fixed points in the scheme with fixed events in history they could discover where they themselves stood and how near they were to the End. Such calculations became an important part of the apocalyptists' task; they invariably showed that the apocalyptists themselves were living in the last days very near to the final crisis of history. This belief was, in a number of cases, strengthened by reason of the fact that the times in which they lived were times of great travail and distress. This predeterminism of history, making possible the calculation of times and seasons, emphasizes still further the apocalyptists' strong sense of the unity of history, made one by the overruling purpose of Almighty God.

A consideration of the determinism of history leads into another closely related subject, that of the relationship between human freedom and divine control. The apocalyptists, as we have seen, interpreted the events of history in terms of the divine purpose which ran through it from beginning to end. But, more often than not, men are God's agents in the carrying out of his purpose. In their estimate of history, therefore, the apocalyptists take into account the activity of men as well as the purpose of God. Thus, alongside their conception of history deterministically ordained, or rather together with it, we find the problem of human freedom and its relation to the pre-ordaining will of God.

Writing of the Old Testament prophets H. H. Rowley says, 'The divine activity in history does not override human freedom. It but uses it to serve the divine will. The event of history can be looked at merely from the human side, and read in terms of moral purpose and the exercise of physical and material forces; or it can be viewed in terms of the divine purpose it serves.'[1] So it is also with the apocalyptic writers. The clash of human freedom and divine control had not as yet become a conscious problem, so that these two apparently contradictory points of view could be expressed side by side without any intellectual difficulty. For the most part, the point of view of the apocalyptic writers is that of 'normative' Judaism as expressed in Rabbi Akiba's celebrated statement: 'All is foreseen, but freedom of choice is given' (*Pirke 'Abot* 3.16). The writer of the Book of Jubilees, for example, can say that each man's path is set out for him and that the heavenly tablets already contain the record of his judgment, but he at the same time counsels each man to take heed that he walks not in the way of transgression lest judgment be written down against him (5.13; 41.24ff.). Again, the writer of the Pss. of Solomon 14.5 avows that God 'knoweth the chambers of the hearts before they had their being'; but the same writer can state that the course of a man's life, whether it be good or evil, is a matter for that man's choice: 'O God, our works are in our choice, yea, in the power of our own soul: to do either righteousness or iniquity in the works of our hands' (9.7).[2] In II Enoch it is stated that each man's work has

[1] *The Relevance of Apocalyptic*, 1944, p. 144.

[2] This is the probable reading of this difficult verse; cf. Ryle and James, *The Psalms of the Pharisees*, 1891, pp. 95f.

been written out before his creation (53.2); but elsewhere in the same book it is clearly stated that God bestowed on man at the creation the gift of free-will so that he might be able to distinguish the way of light from the way of darkness, the knowledge of good from the knowledge of evil (30.15). Each man continues to enjoy free-will, says another writer, for we 'are still in the spirit and the power of our liberty' (II Bar. 85.7); each possesses a faculty whereby moral judgments are made possible, for 'each of the inhabitants of the earth knew when he was committing iniquity' (48.40). God's will is free to do as he thinks fit; so also is the will of man (Apoc. of Abr. 26).

But not only is man's life predetermined, his after-life is predetermined also. For, long before the final judgment comes God divides the spirits of the children of light from the spirits of the children of darkness (I Enoch 41.8). Man's portion is laid in the balance before God and nothing that he can do can alter what God has prescribed for him (Pss. of Sol. 5.6). Even before a man is born there has been 'a place prepared for the repose of that soul, and a measure fixed how much it is intended that a man be tried in this world' (II Enoch 49.2). In the 'Mirror of the World' Abraham sees the whole world divided into two, God's people on the right side and the heathen on the left (Apoc. of Abr. 21). Everything was 'already planned beforehand' (Apoc. of Abr. 22). The wicked or the heathen are Azazel's 'portion' who have been assigned to him from the beginning (Apoc. of Abr. 22). The future state of both righteous and wicked has been predestined by God, 'for corruption will take those that belong to it, and life those that belong to it' (II Bar. 42.7).

But, as in the case of man's life, so in the case of his after-life, much will depend on the choice he himself has made. 'Of those who were born from him (*i.e.* Adam)', says one writer, 'each one of them has prepared for his own soul torment to come, and again each one of them has chosen for himself glories to come' (II Bar. 54.15). The same writer concludes, 'Adam is therefore not the cause, save only of his own soul, but each one of us has been the Adam of his own soul' (II Bar. 54.19). Reference is made in several books to the weighing of the actions of men in the after-life so that their destinies can be decided upon. Enoch, for example, sees the deeds of the righteous being weighed in a righteous balance (I Enoch 41.1, 5; 43.2; 61.8, cf. III Bar. 11.9; 12.4, 5; 15.2, 3). In addition to the test of weighing, the writer of the Test. of Abraham describes the trial of men's works by fire (ch. 13). The works of the righteous are preserved in treasuries awaiting the final judgment (II Bar. 14.12, etc.). These works which decide the destinies of men are themselves decided by the decisions which men make whether of good or evil. Men must choose for themselves, but God shows his readiness to help his creatures. Men must pray that God will strengthen them to do his will (Jub. 21.25; 22.10), for with his strength they will at all times be able to choose the right.

Man's actions, then, may help to determine the events of history in its temporal and eternal aspects; but the whole time-process is both determined and unified by the working out of God's eternal purpose.

IX

ANGELS AND DEMONS

I. THE WORLD OF SPIRITS

IT IS OFTEN said that, in its highest reaches of religious thought, the Old Testament expresses belief in God in terms of 'ethical monotheism'. But it must be remembered that monotheism, for the Old Testament prophets, had a connotation very different in many respects from that which it has in modern thought. It is false to assume that the Old Testament writers, however exalted their conception of the Godhead might be, conceived of God as alone in isolated majesty over against men, the creatures of his will. There is ample evidence to show that this conception of monotheism was held in conjunction with a belief in a spiritual world peopled with supernatural and superhuman beings who, in some ways, shared the nature, though not the being, of God.

In the Pentateuch, the Prophets and the Writings frequent reference is made to many kinds of ministering 'angels', messengers or servants of God who form his divine retinue and wait upon him, ready to do his bidding. The origin of these angelic beings does not concern us here, but the development of the idea is probably to be traced back to the belief in many gods who were thought to hold sway over the various nations and countries of the earth. The growth of angelology is, on this view, an indication of the demoting of the gods of the heathen and the increasing transcendence of the God of Israel. This process would be greatly facilitated by the influence of Persian thought and by its teaching concerning the world of spirits,[1] but the material for such a doctrine was ready to hand in the beliefs already expressed in the Old Testament itself.

[1] See pp. 257ff.

Reference has already been made to the idea in the Old Testament of a heavenly Council in which Yahweh presides over the company of his 'messengers' or 'sons of God'[1] and which may be attended not only by God's ministering angels but also by his 'servants the prophets' (cf. Jer. 23.18ff.). This Old Testament picture is basic to the more developed notions of angelology to be found in later Judaism, even though there are to be found there developments which have no precedent in the biblical writings. There is evidence in Deut. 32.8 (LXX) for the belief that God divided the nations of the earth among the 'sons of God' and gave them authority to rule over them;[2] elsewhere in the same book it is stated that Yahweh's own people 'went and served other gods, and worshipped them, gods whom they knew not, and whom he had not given (lit. divided) unto them' (29.26). That is, it was Yahweh who allotted these gods to the nations as their objects of worship whilst confining the worship of himself to Israel alone. In an earlier chapter the same language is used concerning the worship of the heavenly bodies which the heathen regarded as gods; the people of Israel are warned to take heed 'lest thou lift up thine eyes unto heaven, and when thou seest the sun and the moon and the stars, even all the host of heaven, thou be drawn away and worship them, and serve them, which the Lord thy God hath divided unto all the peoples under the whole heaven' (4.19). These allusions build up a picture of Yahweh surrounded by his ministering angels to whom he delegates authority over the nations of the earth and whom the nations accept as objects of worship. Yahweh sits in his glorious majesty, 'a God very terrible in the council of the holy ones, and to be feared above all them that are round about him' (Ps. 89.7).

These 'angelic councillors' or 'messengers' are there to do the will of God, whether it be to bring blessing as in the case of Abraham (Gen. 18.1ff.) or to bring destruction as in the case of the Egyptians (Ex. 12.23). Even in the case of the 'destroying angels' there is no inherent evil; it is at the express command of God that they are to carry out their task. In the well-known passage in Job 1, 'the Satan' is one of 'the sons of God', *i.e.* he belongs to the company of angelic beings who form his Heavenly Council and wait upon him to do his will. This figure has, at this particular stage, few if any of the sinister characteristics which later came to be associated with his name. He is

[1] See pp. 168f.; cf. I Kings 22.19ff.; Job 1.6ff.; Isa. 6.6ff.; Pss. 82.1; 89.7.
[2] See further pp. 248f.

referred to by name three times in the Old Testament, all of them occurring in post-exilic writings—in Job 1; Zech. 3.1–9, and I Chron. 21.1. In the first two passages the word 'Satan' is used with the definite article and means 'the tester' or 'the adversary'; it is not yet a proper name but is simply descriptive of his function as a minister of Yahweh. In the first of these passages he shows himself anxious to put Job to the test; in the second he is more than anxious and is rebuked by God for falsely accusing Joshua the High Priest. In the third reference 'Satan' is used as a proper name; the development of his character in the direction of evil is now more marked than hitherto; he tempts David to flout God by numbering the people against his will. In the parallel passage in II Sam. 24.1 it is God himself who incites David to this act, but the writer of I Chron. 21.1 feels compelled to transfer the responsibility from him to his angelic servant. This last reference indicates a tendency which was to become more clearly marked during the inter-testamental period. But as yet it had made but little progress. Satan is still regarded as a messenger of God and as a member of his heavenly retinue who acts in the name of God and at his divine command.

In the inter-testamental period, particularly as illustrated by the apocalyptic writings, there is a remarkable development in Jewish thought concerning the world of spirits and angelic beings generally. Certain factors may help to explain why this development came about. One is the growing transcendence of God, to which reference has already been made. This tendency had been in evidence from the beginning of the post-exilic period, and as time passed it became more and more pronounced. The belief in angels—already familiar and well established in the Hebrew tradition—formed a vital bridge between God and his universe which otherwise would have been difficult to construct. But there was a second factor of equal significance. Ever since the days of the Captivity the problem of suffering had been a great mystery to the Jewish people, especially as it applied to their own nation and to the righteous men within their nation. Attempts had been made to explain it, but none was wholly satisfactory. The problem of suffering, moreover, was only one aspect of the much bigger problem of moral evil which formed the subject matter of not a few writings of this period. There gradually grew up, no doubt under the influence of foreign thought, the notion that the angels to whom God had given authority over the nations and over the physical universe itself, had outstripped their rightful authority and had taken the power into their own hands. No longer were they simply God's envoys to whom he gave the charge of punishing those who denied his rule; they themselves became part of the rebellious family and took upon themselves the right to reign. They refused any longer to take their orders from God, but were either rulers in their own right or were prepared to take their orders from someone other than God who, like themselves, had rebelled against the Almighty. Thus the problem of human suffering was seen to be but part of the greater problem of cosmic evil. Every part of the created universe was affected by it, and human life had to be lived out under its shadow. The same force of evil could be seen in microcosm in human history and in macrocosm in cosmic history. Human life and the life of the universe were in the grip of malignant powers who had wrested the authority from the hands of God. Thus those 'tendencies toward evil' which appear in the biblical references to 'the Satan' reach their full extent in the apocalyptic writings where Satan and his legions are presented as arch-enemies of God, bent on controlling and so ultimately destroying not only the human race but even the cosmos itself.

But not all the angels rebelled against the authority of God. Myriads upon myriads remained faithful to him. 'The kingdom of God' faced 'the kingdom of Satan', their angelic armies drawn up in battle array. Thus the world of spirits is divided into two. On the one side are the angels who remain true to God, who execute his will and direct men in the way they ought to go; on the other side are the fallen angels and demons who obey the chief of the demons and commit all kinds of wickedness upon the earth. This present world is now in the hands of these 'principalities and powers'; men's lives are in the power of Satan and his angels. God bides his time. The End will come, the kingdom of Satan will be routed and the kingdom of God established not only in human life but throughout the whole universe.

Corresponding to these two spiritual forces in the universe the writer of the Testaments of the XII Patriarchs indicates that 'two spirits wait upon man—the spirit of truth and the spirit of deceit (or error)' (Test. of Jud. 20.1).[1] In this same writing the spirit of

[1] With this verse we may compare a passage in the *Manual of Discipline* (III.13–IV.1) which deals with 'the two spirits'. There it is said that God assigned to man two spirits—the spirit of truth and the spirit of wickedness which war against each other within the heart of man (III.18). The righteous walk in the way of 'the

deceit is associated with Beliar (or Belial) who is set in opposition to 'the Lord' (Test. of Jud. 25.3, etc.), and (in its present form at any rate) the seven evil spirits are set over against the seven good spirits (Test. of Reub. 2.1ff.). W. F. Albright describes this teaching as a 'modified dualism' which deeply influenced Christianity but which was in course of time rejected by normative Judaism.[1] But S. B. Frost rightly points out that 'when we speak of the "modified dualism" of the apocalyptists we must give full value to the adjective'.[2] The word 'dualism' with respect to apocalyptic belief must be as carefully defined as the word 'monotheism' with respect to the teaching of the Old Testament. What we find expressed in the Testaments of the XII Patriarchs, for example, is an 'ethical dualism'[3] which basically has much in common with the 'ethical monotheism' of the canonical prophets. As E. Stauffer points out, 'This way of thinking[4] has nothing at all to do with a metaphysical or ontological dualism.'[5] It is with this in mind that the same writer remarks, 'Apocalyptic does not think dualistically. But in wrestling with the problem of theodicy it has reached a point where it cannot but adopt a demonology; and in this way the Old Testament monotheistic theology of history has been built, by the introduction of

---

prince of light'; the wicked walk in the way of 'the angel of darkness' (III.21ff.). On the one side are 'the spirits of light' whom God loves, and on the other side 'the spirits of darkness' whose ways he hates (III.25ff.). In the verses which follow (IV.2–14) the writer gives a catalogue of virtues and vices in terms of 'the two spirits'. This expression of 'ethical dualism' has much in common with the Johannine writings in the New Testament with their description of the contrast between light and darkness (I John 2.11) and between 'the spirit of truth' and 'the spirit of error' (I John 4.6), etc.; cf. M. Black, *The Scrolls and Christian Origins*, 1961, p. 134.

The passage in the *Manual of Discipline* referred to above is almost reproduced in the *Didache* I.1ff. and in the *Ep. of Barnabas* 18–20 (cf. J. T. Milik, *op. cit.*, p. 118). J. T. Milik comments thus: 'Although dualist, the Essenes' doctrine of the world and the human soul does not go beyond the limits of biblical monotheism; it is God who will bring about the final victory of Good over Evil. Although a Persian influence can be detected, orthodoxy remains safe' (*ibid.*).

R. C. Zaehner judges that the extraordinary likeness between the teaching of the *Manual of Discipline* concerning 'the two spirits' and Zoroastrian teaching concerning the nature and origin of evil seems to indicate direct borrowing on the Jewish side, cf. *The Dawn and Twilight of Zoroastrianism*, 1961, pp. 51ff.

[1] Cf. *From the Stone Age to Christianity*, 2nd ed., 1957, p. 362.

[2] *Op. cit.*, p. 241. [3] The phrase is used by Matthew Black, *op. cit.*, p. 134.

[4] He is referring in particular to the words of the Test. of Asher 5.1: 'There are two in all things, one against the other'; but what he says might equally well apply to the other aspects of the Testaments' teaching noted above.

[5] *N.T. Theology*, English trans., 1955, p. 65.

ancient Persian ideas, into a dynamic monotheism, an understanding of the world and its history that can be called "antagonistic".'[1]

Only with such qualifications as these can we speak of 'the dualism of apocalyptic thought' in this connection. It is a dualism which does not and cannot contradict their monotheism. There were obvious dangers involved in such an 'antagonistic' faith, and no doubt this was one of the factors that ultimately made the apocalyptic writers unpopular with the rabbis.[2] But these writers took pains to safeguard their monotheistic belief in a number of different ways. In Jub. 2.2, for example, it is stated that 'on the first day (God) created the heavens which are above the earth and the waters and all the spirits which serve before him'. These spirits or angels were created by God and owe their very existence to him.[3] 'The angelic mythology of Judaism', writes G. F. Moore, 'is a naïve way of imagining the mediation of God's word and will in the universe by personal agents . . . they do not consciously infringe upon the belief in his omnipresence or omniscience.'[4] No matter what their own intentions might be, the angels were agents of the divine will. It was God who gave them power to administer the universe and even to lead the nations astray. Even the demons are subordinated to God and cannot act without his permission. It is by the permissive will of God that the Prince of Darkness himself continues his way until now. There will come a day of reckoning when God's authority will be acknowledged by all.

2. THE GROWTH OF ANGELOLOGY

When we enter the inter-testamental period we find that belief in angels has grown to proportions unknown in the Old Testament writings. Details of their numbers, their names, their functions, their natures are given which, though in many cases having their beginnings in the canonical Scriptures, far outstrip anything to be found there. Among the apocryphal books by far the greatest interest in angelology is taken by the apocalyptic writings.[5] But so hetero-

[1] *Ibid.*, p. 258, n. 3. [2] Cf. W. F. Albright, *op. cit.*, p. 362.

[3] The rabbis argued in a similar way that God had no partner in creation. They, however, state that the creation of the angels was on the third or the fifth days. See Moore, *op. cit.*, vol. I, p. 381, n. 3.

[4] *Ibid.*, pp. 404f.

[5] This interest is evident also in the Dead Sea Scrolls. For a convenient list of the names and functions of the angels in these writings, see T. H. Gaster, *The Scriptures of the Dead Sea Sect*, 1957, pp. 316f. See also reference to the Angelic Liturgy, p. 47 above.

geneous is the information given that it is impossible to systematize the belief into the form of a doctrine.

As early as the time of Daniel and I Enoch there had grown up in Judaism a prolific angelic tradition whose broad outlines are familiar to us right through the whole of the inter-testamental period. The writer of Daniel tells us that 'a thousand thousands' ministered to the Ancient of Days, and 'ten thousand times ten thousand stood before him' (7.10, cf. Rev. 5.11). The same picture is presented in I Enoch where God is said to come 'with ten thousand of his holy ones' (1.10, cf. Jude 14). There is nothing very unusual about this, for even in the Old Testament itself the same kind of picture is presented (*e.g.* Job 25.3).

In the apocalyptic literature, however, the angels are now arranged into a well-drilled hierarchy, with officers and ranks like those of a great army. In Jub. 2.2, for example, we read, 'He created . . . the angels of the presence and the angels of sanctification, and the angels of the spirit of fire and the angels of the spirit of the winds, and the angels of the spirit of the clouds, and of darkness, and of snow and of hail and of hoar frost, and the angels of the voices and of the thunder and of the lightning, and the angels of the spirits of cold and of heat, and of winter and of spring and of autumn and of summer, and of all the spirits of his creatures which are in the heavens and on the earth.' Here, it would seem, we have three distinct categories or 'orders' of angels. First, 'the angels of the presence'; second, 'the angels of sanctification'; and third, the angels who are set over the natural phenomena. The first two form together a superior class of beings and are called 'these two great classes' (Jub. 2.18); their functions are clearly distinguished from the third inferior class.[1]

Sometimes those belonging to the superior class are referred to as 'ministering angels' who wait upon God and hold themselves ready to run his errands. Such angels 'minister before the Lord continually' (Jub. 30.18). In the Similitudes of Enoch they are described as 'Seraphim, Cherubim, and *'ōpannim*: and these are they who sleep not and guard the throne of his glory' (I Enoch 71.7, cf. 61.10). The Seraphim and Cherubim are familiar to us from the Old Testament; the *'ōpannim*, meaning 'wheels', are simply personifications of the chariot-wheels in Ezekiel's vision (Ezek. 1.21) which are now regarded as angels. A fourth category is mentioned in this Enoch passage; these are the 'watchers' or 'wakeful ones' who are first

[1] Cf. M. Testuz, *op. cit.*, pp. 75ff.

mentioned in the Book of Daniel (4.10, 14, 20) and to whom frequent reference is made throughout I Enoch.

Closely related to this function of 'ministering' is that of intercession for men. This belief is to be found, of course, even in the Old Testament itself (cf. Zech. 1.12; Job 5.1; 33.23); but in the apocalyptic books it finds much greater prominence, particularly in the Book of Enoch. In I Enoch 15.2, for example, God says to the Watchers, 'You should intercede for men, and not men for you', as if this duty of intercession was something naturally expected of them (cf. 12.6; 14.7). Elsewhere intercessory prayer is the prerogative of the archangels Michael (I Enoch 40.9; 89.76) and Gabriel (40.6) and indeed of all the ministering angels (39.5; 47.2; 104.1; cf. Rev. 8.3, 4). Sometimes the angels have the responsibility of mediating between men and God and of conveying men's petitions to him, as in I Enoch 99.3: 'In those days make ready, ye righteous, to raise your prayers as a memorial, and place them as a testimony before the angels, that they may place the sin of the sinners for a memorial before the Most High' (cf. also 9.2–11). Again, in the Test. of Levi 3.5 the angels of the presence are described as those 'who minister and make propitiation to the Lord for all the sins of ignorance of the righteous'; and in the Test. of Dan 6.2 the interceding angel, Michael, is described as 'a mediator between God and man'.[1]

It is the responsibility of the angels, moreover, to guide men in the right way of life,[2] to watch over their lives and to report to God what they see of good or evil. In Jub. 4.6, for example, the angels say, 'We announce when we come before the Lord our God all the sin which is committed in heaven and on earth, and in light and in darkness, and everywhere.'

Yet another function of the superior class of angels is to reveal to men God's secrets concerning earth and heaven. It is an angel who reveals to Enoch, for example, 'what is first and last in the heaven in the height, and beneath the earth in the depth, and at the ends of the heaven, and on the foundation of the heaven' (I Enoch 60.11). These secrets are recorded in 'the books of the holy ones'; from them the angels can learn of the future and so prepare for the recompense of the righteous and the wicked (cf. I Enoch 103.2; 106.19; 108.7). Enoch was able to draft a calendar of days and months and years

[1] Cf. Paul's use of the phrase in I Tim. 2.5.

[2] For the relation of the angels to 'les deux voies morales', see M. Testuz, *op. cit.*, pp. 93ff.

(Jub. 4.18) because he was 'with the angels of God these six jubilees of years, and they showed him everything which is on earth and in the heavens, the rule of the sun, and he wrote down everything' (Jub. 4.21). Men and women commit evil on the earth because the Watchers made known to them God's holy mysteries (I Enoch 16.2f.). Likewise Azazel 'taught all unrighteousness on earth and revealed the eternal secrets which were preserved in heaven, which men were striving to learn' (I Enoch 9.6).

One significant development during this period is that, for the first time in Jewish history, the angels are given personal names which are associated with specific duties or responsibilities assigned to them by God. An early occurrence of such names is in the Book of Daniel. There reference is made to Michael as 'one of the chief princes' (10.13), as 'your prince' (10.21) and as 'the great prince' (12.1) who will champion Israel against 'the prince of the kingdom of Persia' (10.13) and 'the prince of Greece' (10.21). Another angelic figure mentioned here is Gabriel (8.16; 9.21) who appears frequently elsewhere in company with Michael. In a number of passages in I Enoch the names of four principal angels or archangels are given together. These are Michael, Raphael, Gabriel and Uriel (9.1f.) or Phanuel (40.6ff., cf. 54.6ff.; 71.8ff.). They are described as 'four presences' who stand 'on the four sides of the Lord of Spirits' (40.2). Elsewhere, however, seven archangels are mentioned whose names include the four already referred to. These are Uriel, Raphael, Raguel, Michael, Saraqael, Gabriel and Remiel (I Enoch 20.1–8, cf. 81.5; 87.1ff.; 90.22; Rev. 8.2). Reference is made to them also in the Test. of Levi 8.1f., where they are described as 'seven men in white raiment'. The various functions performed by these seven archangels are set out in I Enoch 20.2ff. There it is said that Uriel is 'over the world and over Tartarus', Raphael is 'over the spirits of men', Raguel 'takes vengeance on the world of the luminaries', Michael is 'set over the best part of mankind and over chaos', Saraqael is 'set over the spirits who sin in the spirit', Gabriel is 'over Paradise and the serpents and the Cherubim', and Remiel is 'set over those who rise'. These two separate traditions of four and seven archangels are brought together in Rev. 4.5, 6, which speaks of 'the seven spirits of God and . . . four living creatures full of eyes before and behind'.

Those angels so far mentioned belong to the number of the principal or superior angels, the *élite*, as it were, of the heavenly hierarchy.

But, as has already been indicated, there were many other angels whose responsibilities were more humble and less exacting. In Jub. 2.2, quoted above, a long list of such spirits is given in which it is stated that each of the natural elements and each of the seasons has its own angel who is responsible to God for its proper functioning. This same thought is expressed also in I Enoch 60.11–24, where the writer mentions, among others, spirits of thunder, lightning, sea, hoar-frost, hail, snow, frost, mist, dew and rain (cf. also II Enoch 5.1f.; 6.1f.). In I Enoch 75.3 it is stated that Uriel has been 'set for ever over all the luminaries of heaven . . . that they should rule on the face of the heaven and be seen on the earth, and be leaders for the day and the night, *i.e.* the sun, moon, and stars, and all the ministering creatures which make their revolution in all the chariots of the heaven'. In II Enoch 4.1–2, however, it is said that the heavenly bodies are controlled by 200 angels who are described as 'the elders and the rulers of the orders of the stars'. To the popular imagination the multitude of the stars did not simply represent the angelic hosts (cf. I Enoch 80.6; II Esd. 6.3); they were regarded as actual living creatures. Thus in I Enoch 85–90, for example, the story of the fallen angels[1] is told in terms of stars which fall from heaven (*e.g.* 86.1ff.).[2] These stars are in the end judged by the seven archangels and cast into the abyss (I Enoch 88.1ff.).

In several of these writings the idea is developed of angel custodians not only of the elements and the heavenly bodies, but also of individual men, particularly the righteous whom God regards as 'the apple of an eye' (I Enoch 100.5). Perhaps the earliest reference to this belief is in Jub. 35.17 where it is said that 'the guardian of Jacob is great and powerful and honoured, and praised more than the guardian of Esau'.[3] Much more significant than this, however, is the notion that not only individuals but also nations have their guardian angels. To this important idea we now turn.

3. GUARDIAN ANGELS OF THE NATIONS

One important aspect of the development of angelology during this period is the belief in guardian angels set over the nations of the

[1] See pp. 249ff.

[2] In Rev. 1.20 the same language is used to describe 'the angels of the seven churches'.

[3] Cf. also Test. of Jud. 3.10; Test. of Dan 5.4; Test. of Jos. 6.7, etc. See also Matt. 18.10 and Acts 12.15.

earth. These guardian angels, it would appear, form a heavenly counterpart of the Gentile rulers into whose power God has, from time to time, given his people because of their wickedness. Wars and the like which take place among the nations upon earth have their parallel in wars in heaven fought out between the several guardian angels and their retinues. According to some writers, at any rate, the two orders are related to each other in such a way that the events in heaven are believed actually to determine the events on earth. When a particular guardian angel gains the ascendancy over his fellows, the nation over which he has been appointed also gains the ascendancy over the other nations of the earth; similarly when he is defeated in the heavenly warfare his charge on earth is defeated also. These angelic powers are given free course by God, but only for a season and only by his permissive will. They are under the sovereign will of God and are ultimately answerable to him for the use or misuse of their power and authority; so it is also with the earthly rulers and the Gentile nations. Just as these rulers and nations will be judged, so their guardian angels will be judged also. Indeed the judgments upon earth are involved in the judgments in heaven. Before a nation can be judged and punished, its angel ruler must first be dealt with.[1] The key to terrestrial history is to be found in celestial event. History thus assumes a supramundane character; its meaning is to be found not only at the end of history, but also above history in the realm of spiritual being.

This general idea of guardian angels appointed to rule over the nations of the earth assumed several different forms and made up the background to both Jewish and Gentile thought during the inter-testamental period. It is reflected in a number of biblical and extra-biblical passages. The most significant of these, among the apocalyptic writings, are to be found in Dan. 10.13, 20, 21; 12.1; Jub. 15.31–32; I Enoch 89.59ff.; 90.20ff.[2] In Dan. 10.13ff. it is said that an angel, possibly Gabriel, appears to Daniel in a vision and tells how he has been prevented from coming earlier because of the opposition of 'the prince of the kingdom of Persia' (10.13). This 'prince' (cf. Jub. 5.15) is the guardian angel of Persia, as becomes clear from the subsequent account. Gabriel is assisted, however, by the arch-

[1] Cf. Clinton D. Morrison, *The Powers that Be*, 1960, p. 20.

[2] Cf. also Test. of Levi 5.6; Test. of Dan 6.1f.; Ass. of Moses 10.1; II Bar. 67.2f.; Apoc. of Moses 32.3; III Bar. 6.1. See E. Langton, *The Ministries of Angelic Powers*, n.d., pp. 94f.

angel Michael who is described as 'one of the chief princes'. This Michael is the guardian angel of God's own people, Israel. The angel of the vision informs Daniel that he is about to return 'to fight with the prince of Persia'; as soon as this conflict is over he will join battle with 'the prince of Greece' (10.20). Only Michael stood beside him in his conflict; but their victory is assured for 'it is inscribed in the writing of truth' (10.21). The future destinies of these 'princes', like those of the nations they champion, are predetermined by God. Victory is assured, for 'at that time shall Michael stand up, the great prince who standeth for the children of thy people' (12.1). He will lead his people through trial and tribulation to the final triumph over all their foes.

The second apocalyptic passage of significance in this connection is Jub. 15.31f. There we read, 'There are many nations and many peoples, and all are his, and over all hath he placed spirits in authority to lead them astray from him. But over Israel he did not appoint any angel or spirit, for he alone is their ruler, and he will preserve them and require them at the hand of all his powers in order that he may preserve them and bless them.' One difference between this and the Danielic passage is that here the Gentiles only are under the dominion of angels. Israel is reserved for God alone and no mention is made of Michael within this context. The same idea is reflected in Ben Sira 17.17 which reads, 'For every nation he appointed a ruler, and Israel is the Lord's portion.' In Jubilees it is stated that the purpose of his appointing angels over the nations is 'to lead them astray from him'.[1] Elsewhere this function is ascribed to the demons (cf. 10.3, 8; 19.28). The suggestion of R. H. Charles is no doubt correct when he says, 'We may assume that the statement in our text is made on the same principle as many in the Scriptures (cf. Isa. 6.9; Matt. 13.14; Mark 4.12, etc.), in which the ultimate result of an action or a series of actions is declared to have been the immediate object of them.'[2]

The third reference to these guardian angels is in the Dream Visions of I Enoch. In 89.59ff. we are told that God gives his people, here symbolized by sheep, into the hands of seventy 'shepherds' who are to exercise discipline over them. God numbers his sheep and tells the shepherds how many may be destroyed and how many are to be

[1] In rabbinic writings generally the purpose is that they should lead the nations in the right path.

[2] *The Book of Jubilees*, 1902, p. 112.

spared. But he indicates that the shepherds will go beyond their permitted limit and will slay more sheep than God commanded. A record is to be taken of how many they destroy by God's permission and how many by their own caprice. The shepherds do as God said they would. They slay more than they were bidden. They deliver them to the power of lions and tigers and wild boars who destroy them. In 90.22ff. an account is given of the judgment of the seventy shepherds; they are found guilty and are cast into the fiery abyss.

R. H. Charles brings forward strong arguments to prove that the 'shepherds' represent angels and concludes that 'there may be some distant connection between the seventy angels here and the seventy guardian angels of the Gentile nations'.[1] For many generations God himself had been the Shepherd of Israel. But Israel had sinned against God and forfeited his care and protection. This conviction, together with the growing awareness of God's transcendence, would prepare the way for the belief that he had committed them to the care of 'under-shepherds' in the form of the guardian angels of the nations. In this way it was possible to explain the calamities which had befallen Israel ever since the fall of Jerusalem and the captivity of their people. They had suffered by the permissive will of God. But the angels, into whose hands God had committed them, had overstepped their rightful authority; the people had 'received of the Lord's hand double' for all their sins (Isa. 40.2). The angels would receive their due punishment as recorded in I Enoch 90.22f. This passage recalls Isa. 24.21ff. where it is stated that 'in that day the Lord will punish the hosts of the high ones on high, and the kings of the earth upon the earth'. This order of judgment—first the angels and then the earthly rulers—is the same as that in I Enoch and reflects the general belief that, before God judges any nation or ruler, he first judges the guardian angel whose charge they are.

Mention may be made here of a Hebrew Testament of Naphtali which, in its present form, is probably to be dated in mediaeval times.[2] M. de Jonge argues that, though it is late and secondary, it may go back to a much older text. He claims that both the Hebrew and the Greek Testaments go back to an original Testament of Naphtali and that in some places at any rate the Hebrew text may

[1] *The Book of Enoch*, 1912, p. 200.
[2] See R. H. Charles, *Tests. of the XII Patriarchs*, 1908, App. I.

be closer to the original.[1] There it is said that in the time of Phaleg 'the Lord came down from his highest heavens, and brought down with him seventy ministering angels, Michael at their head. He commanded them to teach the seventy families which sprang from the loins of Noah seventy languages. . . . But the holy language, the Hebrew language, remained only in the house of Shem and Eber, and in the house of Abraham our father, who is one of their descendants' (8.4–6).

Behind all these passages lies Deut. 32.8–9. This passage describes the division of the nations of mankind and the choosing of Israel to be God's own people. The Hebrew text reads thus: 'When the Most High gave to the nations their inheritance, when he separated the children of men, he set the bounds of the peoples according to the number of the children of Israel (*b^e^ne Yisra'el*). For the Lord's portion is his people; Jacob is the lot of his inheritance.' Instead of 'according to the number of the children of Israel' the LXX reads 'according to the number of the angels of God' which may reflect the reading 'the sons of God' (*b^e^ne 'el* or *b^e^ne 'elohīm*) in the original Hebrew text, *i.e.* all the nations of the earth are given over into the control of angelic powers, but Israel is reserved for Yahweh alone. G. F. Moore and others argue that the reading of the Hebrew text gives an entirely acceptable sense. 'The number of the children of Israel' is given as seventy in Scripture (Ex. 1.5), and this is the number of the nations which are said to have sprung from Noah's three sons (Gen. 10).[2] It may well be, however, that the LXX reports the original text and this claim has been recently strengthened by the discovery at Qumran of a Hebrew text with the reading 'according to the number of the sons of God'.[3]

The Palestinian Targum on Deut. 32.8 shows a knowledge of both readings and combines both traditions in one. There it is said that the Most High divided mankind 'among the seventy angels, the princes of the nations' at the time of the dispersion at the Tower of Babel; at the same time 'he established the boundaries of the peoples corresponding to the number of the persons of Israel who went down into Egypt'.[4]

[1] Cf. *The Testaments of the XII Patriarchs*, 1953, pp. 52–60, and his article with the same title in *Novum Testamentum*, vol. IV, 1960, pp. 196ff.

[2] Cf. G. F. Moore, *op. cit.*, vol. I, p. 227. In Jewish tradition there are said to be seventy languages spoken by men, cf. *Sanhedrin* 17a end, *Tos. Soṭah* 8.6.

[3] Cf. M. Burrows, *The Dead Sea Scrolls*, 1956, p. 319.

[4] Cf. Moore, *op. cit.*, vol. I, p. 227; vol. III, p. 62.

The evidence given above, though some of it is late in its present form, indicates that the idea of guardian angels appointed over the nations may well have sprung from the account in Deut. 32.8f. and that, in particular, the seventy shepherds of I Enoch 89 and 90 and the seventy guardian angels of the Gentile nations have a common lineage. If this Deuteronomic passage is the seed-bed of this idea, the conditions of the Greek period were especially favourable for its growth to full flower, for during this same period the belief was prevalent among the Greeks and others that God ruled the world by means of intermediary agencies who are sometimes described as the 'shepherds' of the nations.[1]

4. FALLEN ANGELS AND THE ORIGIN OF EVIL

Great concern is expressed in a number of the apocalyptic writings concerning the problem, and in particular the origin, of evil in the world. Several different explanations are given. Sometimes these are given separately; at other times the solution is of a composite character.

One popular explanation is based on the account given in Gen. 6.1–4, which tells how 'the sons of God came in to the daughters of men'. Christian tradition, from the earliest days, identified these *b^ene 'elohīm* or 'sons of God' with the descendants of Seth whose offspring represented a superior race. But the scriptural reference is undoubtedly to heavenly beings or angels who lusted after the daughters of men.[2] This ancient myth is taken up by the writer of I Enoch 6–36, for example, and is repeated, with variations and embellishments, in a number of other apocalyptic writings. I Enoch 6 tells how two hundred angels, elsewhere called 'watchers',[3] bound themselves to one another and to their leader Semjaza by an oath to take wives from among the children of men and to beget children. The names of nineteen of their leaders, 'chiefs of tens', are here given (6.7); the name of the twentieth is Azazel (cf. 10.4) whose leadership is apparently on a par with that of Semjaza. The motive given for their descent from heaven is that they lusted after the comely

[1] See further pp. 260f.

[2] Cf. I Enoch 86.1ff.; 106.13; Jub. 4.15; 5.1ff.; Test. of Reub. 5.6f.; Test. of Napht. 3.5; II Enoch 7.1ff.; 18.1ff.; II Bar. 56.10ff.; see also Jude 6; II Peter 2.4.

[3] Dan. 4.13, 17, 23; I Enoch 10.7, 15; 15.2; 16.1f.; 19.1–3; Jub. 4.15; II Enoch 18.1–5, etc.

daughters of men (6.1–2). Elsewhere, in Jub. 4.15, it is stated that they were sent down from heaven by God himself to instruct men 'that they should do judgment and righteousness on the earth'. This tradition is reflected in I Enoch itself where it is said that the fallen angels taught men much knowledge and many crafts (cf. 7.1; 8.1ff.). Whatever the motive may have been, the result of this unlawful association was that the whole earth became corrupted; bloodshed and lawlessness were spread abroad (9.1). To the seduction of the daughters of men by these fallen angels is due the depravity of the whole human race. The cries of men rise up to heaven; Azazel and Semjaza are bound and imprisoned until the final judgment when they will be 'led off to the abyss of fire and to the torment and prison in which they shall be confined for ever' (10.13, cf. II Peter 2.4; Rev. 20.2f.). Michael is commanded to 'destroy all the spirits of the reprobate and the children of the Watchers, because they have wronged mankind' (10.15).

This reference to 'the children of the Watchers' picks up the account in 7.2ff. which tells how the fallen angels and the women whom they coveted produced 'great giants whose height was three thousand ells' who committed all kinds of sins against God's creatures and began to slay one another. These giants are called evil spirits, or it is said that, when they died, evil spirits proceeded from their bodies: 'The giants who are produced from the spirits and flesh shall be called evil spirits upon the earth, and on the earth shall be their dwelling. Evil spirits have proceeded from their bodies. . . . And the spirits of the giants afflict, oppress, destroy, attack, do battle, and work destruction on the earth, and cause trouble: they take no food, but nevertheless hunger and thirst, and cause offences. And these spirits shall rise up against the children of men and against the women, because they have proceeded from them' (15.8, 9, 11). These evil spirits or demons, according to this writer, are not destroyed by the Flood, but continue their work of inciting to sin right up to the final judgment (16.1).[1] To their solicitations is due the corruption of mankind.

Substantially the same story is told in the Book of Jubilees (cf. especially chs. 5 and 10). Noah prays that God will destroy from off the earth these malignant spirits, the offspring of the Watchers: 'As for these spirits who are living, imprison them and hold them fast in

[1] Cf. 10.6; 16.1; 19.1. The same belief is expressed also in Jub. 10.5–11 and is alluded to in Matt. 8.29: 'Art thou come hither to torment us before the time?'

the place of condemnation, and let them not bring destruction on the sons of thy servant, my God; for these are malignant, and created in order to destroy' (10.5). In answer to his prayer God gave orders for all the evil spirits to be bound, but at the request of their leader, Mastema, he bound only nine-tenths of them and allowed one-tenth to roam the earth 'that they might be subject before Satan on the earth' (10.11). These evil spirits make men suffer from all kinds of diseases; they corrupt them and lead them astray. Noah, however, was instructed in all kinds of medicine. 'Thus the evil spirits were precluded from hurting the sons of Noah' (10.13). It was they who encouraged men to wage war against one another and to enslave their brothers (11.2ff.); they influenced them to make molten images and incited them to worship idols (11.4). They led them on 'to do all manner of wrong and sin, and all manner of transgressions, to corrupt and destroy, and to shed blood upon the earth' (11.5). Once again, as in the Book of Enoch, the writer of Jubilees makes clear that evil does not come from God, but rather from evil spirits who continue their work, but only with the permission of the Almighty.

Further allusions to these angelic marriages and the origin of demons are made in I Enoch 86.1ff., where the fallen angels are represented by stars. Enoch sees a single star, representing Azazel, falling from heaven, which is followed by many other stars representing all his host. On reaching the earth these stars become bulls which 'began to cover the cows of the oxen'. The offspring of this union were 'elephants, camels and asses' representing three kinds of giants. These wrought such havoc on the earth that men 'began to tremble and quake before them and to flee from them' (86.6). In 90.20ff. an account is given of the judgment of these stars together with the seventy 'shepherds' who had abused their trust.

In the Testament of Reuben women are warned not to adorn their heads or their faces, because it was for this reason that the Watchers lusted after them and begat giants in the earth (5.6). Again, in the Testament of Naphtali, it is said that it was on account of the Watchers who 'changed the order of their nature' that God 'made the earth without inhabitant and fruitless' through the Flood (3.5). There is no reference in the Testaments to the origin of demons or evil spirits, but frequent mention is made of them as the cause of all kinds of evil on the earth.[1]

[1] For a detailed list of occurrences see pp. 404f.

Here, then, is one explanation of the origin of evil, prominent in the earlier apocalyptic writings, which had a great influence on Jewish thought at this time—that sin, in its many forms, can be traced back to the rebellion or the fall of angels and more especially to their demon progeny whose evil brood fill the air and hover continually over the earth, the home of their mothers.

This, however, is not the only explanation of the origin of evil to be found in the apocalyptic writings. In a number of cases an historical explanation is sought in the Paradise story as recorded in Genesis 3. Already we see this appearing side by side with the 'Watcher theory' in the Book of Jubilees (*e.g.* 3.17–35) and in the Testaments of the XII Patriarchs (*e.g.* Test. of Levi 18.10, 11); it is found also in II Enoch (*e.g.* 30.15f.; 54.15f.), the Apocalypse of Abraham (*e.g.* 23; 24), II Baruch (*e.g.* 23.4; 48.42, 43; 56.5, 6), II Esdras (*e.g.* 7.11, 12), the Apocalypse of Moses (*e.g.* 11.2; 19.3), and III Baruch (*e.g.* 4.16).

In those books which put forward the Adam story as an explanation of the origin of human sin, the principle of human freedom is nevertheless commonly accepted. Sin may be traced back to Adam's 'fall' (Apoc. of Abr. 23), but man is himself responsible for his own sin (Apoc. of Abr. 26). Indeed, men are said to suffer in so far as they are themselves participators in the sin which Adam their father committed (III Bar. 4.16). Adam is referred to as the primary source of sin (cf. II Bar. 18.2); but each man is answerable for his own transgressions and can determine his own destiny. This is clearly stated in II Bar. 54.15, 19: 'For though Adam first sinned and brought untimely death upon all, yet of those who were born from him each one of them has prepared for his own soul torment to come, and again each one of them has chosen for himself glories to come. . . . Adam is therefore not the cause, save only of his own soul, but each one of us has been the Adam of his own soul.' Here Adam's sin is the cause only of physical death (cf. also 17.3; 23.4; 54.5); it is given as the cause of spiritual death in only one passage in II Baruch, *viz.* 48.42 (cf. also II Esd. 3.21, 22; 4.30; 7.118–21), but once again it 'is not due to the incapacity of man for righteousness after the fall, but to his following of his own choice in the steps of Adam'.[1]

This idea of a 'fall', then, explained in terms of the 'Watcher'

[1] R. H. Charles, *Apocrypha and Pseud. of the Old Testament*, vol. II, 1913, p. 507.

theory or the 'Adam' story, expressed the popular theology of the Judaism of this period. Another theory, however, representative of the technical theology of the rabbis, played a significant part. This is the theory of the *yeṣer ha-raʿ* or 'evil inclination'. In Gen. 6.5 the evil *yeṣer* is described as something in man for which he himself is responsible; but in Gen. 8.21 it is implied that it is given by God as an inherited infirmity. This apparent contradiction runs right through the rabbinic treatment of the subject. 'It is never doubted that God made the evil *yeṣer*, yet man is responsible for controlling and subduing it.'[1] The rabbis did not believe in a continuous transmission of the evil inclination, however; its possession by a man is not to be explained along hereditary lines; each person receives it directly from God at his birth or at conception. This fact sets it right over against the Adamic theory of the 'fall'.

This idea of the evil inclination plays a significant part in a number of the apocalyptic writings. In the Testaments of the XII Patriarchs, for example, it is stated that there is a good as well as an evil inclination in man: 'If the soul take pleasure in the good inclination all its actions are in righteousness. . . . But if it incline to the evil inclination all its actions are in wickedness' (Test. of Asher 1.6, 8).[2] More important for our purpose is the evidence of II Esdras which at least implies that there is in Adam a good as well as an evil *yeṣer*. A key passage in this connection is 3.21–22: 'For the first Adam, clothing himself with the evil heart, transgressed and was overcome; and likewise also all who were born of him. Thus the infirmity became inveterate; the Law indeed was in the heart of the people, but (in conjunction) with the evil germ;[3] so what was good departed, and the evil remained.'[4] The *yeṣer ha-raʿ* is described by this writer as 'the evil seed' (4.30) which, being sown in the heart of Adam,

[1] F. C. Porter, 'The Yecer Ha-raʿ', in the *Yale Bicentenary Volume of Biblical and Semitic Studies*, 1901, p. 108.

[2] Other references to the *yeser* in man in the Tests. of the XII Patriarchs are as follows. God knows the good inclination (Test. of Napht. 2.5); he tries it (Test. of Jos. 2.6); he rewards according to it (Test. of Jud. 13.8); it is not in the power of the spirit of Beliar (Test. of Benj. 6.1ff.); it does not admit of any evil desire (Test. of Reub. 4.9); it receives no glory from men (Test. of Benj. 6.4); it is blinded by fornication (Test. of Jud. 18.3); it is made angry by envy (Test. of Sim. 4.8); men must destroy the evil inclination by their good works (Test. of Asher 3.2), for it is such that it blinds the mind (Test. of Jud. 11.1).

[3] Cf. Rom. 7.7f., 20f.

[4] This statement that the Law which is planted in man's nature is unable to gain the mastery over the evil *yeṣer* contradicts the teaching of rabbinic theology. Cf. *Suk.* 52b, 'The Law wears away the *yeṣer ha-raʿ* as water wears away stone.'

results in the 'evil heart'.[1] It is this 'evil heart' which estranges men from God (7.48), for it is transmitted from Adam to his descendants. This is stated quite clearly in 7.118f.: 'O thou Adam, what hast thou done! For though it was thou that sinned, the fall was not thine alone, but ours also who are thy descendants. For how does it profit us that the eternal age is promised to us, whereas we have done the works that bring death?' Here Adam is responsible for the perdition of the whole human race, but neither here nor anywhere else in the book is it clearly stated what the connection is between Adam's sin and the sin of his descendants.

It is not surprising that the doctrine of free-will and the sense of individual responsibility are very weak indeed in II Esdras. The thought is there, as in 8.56–60, which affirms that man wilfully defiled the name of God, and, having received liberty, 'despised the Most High, scorned his Law, and forsook his ways'. But it is significant that, for the most part, such free-will as man has he uses for doing what is wrong. Evil is ingrained in the human race; man's infirmity is inveterate (3.22).

5. SATAN AND HIS DEMONS

We have observed that, according to a widespread tradition, evil is to be traced to its origin in the fall of the angels called Watchers and in the birth of their giant offspring and their demon progeny. There is another ancient tradition, however, which states that evil agencies existed even before the fall of these angels. In the Similitudes of Enoch (I Enoch 37–71), for example, an account is given of a number of 'Satans', ruled over by a chief 'Satan' (53.3; 54.6). They are apparently to be distinguished from the Watchers for, unlike them, they have ready access into heaven and are able to come before the Lord of Spirits (40.7). The function of these evil spirits—for such they are—is threefold: to accuse men who dwell upon the earth (40.7), to tempt men to do evil (69.6) and to act as angels of punishment (53.3; 56.1; 62.11; 63.1). In 69.4–12 a list of five Satans is given, together with an account of their misdeeds. Of particular interest are the first two Satans. These, we are told, 'led astray all the sons of God, and brought them down to the earth, and led them astray through the daughters of men' (69.4f.). Elsewhere in the same

[1] Expressed in the Latin text by the phrases *cor malignum* or *cogitamentum malum*.

book it is said that God regards the Watchers as culpable because of 'their unrighteousness in being subject to Satan' (54.6). These same Satans who led them astray will themselves in the end torture them for their misdeeds. Enoch sees them casting 'the kings and the mighty' into 'a deep valley with burning fire'; there, too, he sees them preparing 'their instruments, iron chains of immeasurable weight . . . for the hosts of Azazel (*i.e.* the Watchers), so that they may take them and cast them into the abyss of complete condemnation' (54.3, 5).

The same tradition of rebellion in heaven before the fall of the angels is referred to again in II Enoch. There Enoch is brought to the second heaven where he sees angels 'awaiting the eternal judgment' (7.1). He asks who they are and is told, 'These are they who apostasized from the Lord, who obeyed not the commandments of God, and took counsel of their own will and transgressed together with their prince' (7.3). The name of their prince is given in a later chapter as 'Satanail' (18.3);[1] he is said there to rule over the 'Grigori' who are confined in the fifth heaven. More evidence concerning the character and works of Satanail is given in other parts of the book. He is described as an archangel who 'entertained an impossible idea' that he should set up his throne higher than the clouds of heaven and be equal in rank with God himself (29.4). God, however, throws him down from the heights together with his angels and he is left 'flying in the air continually above the abyss' (29.5). Part of Satanail's plan was to entice the Watchers in the fifth heaven to revolt with him. Some of those who responded were cast down with him and imprisoned in the second heaven, as we have seen (7.3; 18.4); others went down to the earth and seduced the daughters of men (18.4) and were thereafter imprisoned beneath the earth (18.6, 7).

When Adam was created, Satanail was envious of him and planned to make another world so as 'to rule it and have lordship over it' because 'things were subservient to Adam on earth' (31.3). He is called here 'the devil' and 'the evil spirit of the lowest places' (31.4). On leaving heaven he who was formerly known as Satanail became known as Satan (31.4). Not only had he designs against Adam, he also 'entered and deceived Eve' and caused her to sin (31.6).

The same story is told, with variations, in the Life of Adam and

[1] In Test. of Dan 5.6 he is referred to as 'your prince Satan'.

Eve 12–17. There Satan is called 'the devil' (12.1) and 'this Adversary' (17.1). He tells Adam that it was on his account that he had been expelled from heaven. When God made Adam in his own image, Michael commanded the angels to worship him. The devil refused to do so since Adam was younger than himself. It was Adam who ought to worship the devil! The angels who were under the devil followed his example and refused to worship also. Michael warned them that God would be wroth, but the devil threatened that if God were wroth with him, he would set his throne above the stars of heaven and be like the Highest (15.3). Accordingly God banished him and his angels from their glory and hurled them to the earth. There the devil deceived Eve and caused Adam to be banished from the Garden of Eden (16.4). Details of his deception of Eve are given in the Apoc. of Moses 15ff. There the devil entices the serpent to co-operate with him and allow him to speak through his mouth. He appears in the Garden 'in the form of an angel[1] and sang hymns like the angels' (17.1). Then, speaking through the mouth of the serpent he entices Eve and causes her to sin (17.4). This association of Satan with the serpent is to be found in other Jewish writings of the period and appears also in the New Testament Apocalypse (cf. 12.9; 20.2).[2]

We have seen that different names are given to the prince of the demons in the various apocalyptic writings. He is called the devil or Satanail or Satan. Alongside him (in the earlier apocalyptic literature) and merging with him (in the later apocalyptic literature) are several other 'princes' or 'chiefs' of angels or demons. The names of Semjaza and Azazel are mentioned in the Book of Enoch, including the earliest chapters, as being responsible for the bloodshed and lawlessness which prevailed on the earth following the descent of the angels (9.6f.). Semjaza is bound by Michael for seventy generations to await the final judgment when he and his associates will be thrown into the fiery abyss (10.1ff.). Azazel, because he 'hath taught all unrighteousness on earth and revealed the eternal secrets which were preserved in heaven' (9.6), is bound by Raphael and cast into the desert to await the day of judgment when he will be cast into the fire (10.4–8). It was he, according to one source (I Enoch 83–90),

[1] Cf. II Cor. 11.14.

[2] No doubt the serpents referred to in Luke 10.19 are to be associated with, or even identified with, demons: 'Behold I have given you authority to tread upon serpents and scorpions, and over all the power of the enemy.'

who, as a star, fell first from heaven, to be followed by the other fallen angels who defiled themselves with the daughters of men (86.1ff.; 88.1f.).

According to the Book of Jubilees the evil spirits are ruled by one, Mastema (10.8, etc.),[1] whose aim it is, throughout the whole course of history, to lead men astray from the way of God. He sends forth his spirits 'to do all manner of wrong and sin, and all manner of transgression, to corrupt and destroy, and to shed blood upon the earth' (11.5). In these passages Mastema is hardly to be distinguished from Satan. Each rules over a class of fallen angels whose members bear the name and the character of their leader (cf. 49.2).

In the Testaments of the XII Patriarchs the demons are ruled over by a chief called Beliar who is called 'the prince of deceit' (Test. of Sim. 2.7) and is identified with the devil (Test. of Napht. 8.4). If the soul inclines to the evil inclination, then it is ruled by Beliar (Test. of Asher 1.8). But the time will come when God will 'redeem all the captivity of the sons of men from Beliar' (Test. of Zeb. 9.8). In the end Beliar will be bound (Test. of Levi 18.12) and will be cast into the fire for ever (Test. of Jud. 25.3).

Here, then, we have the picture of a great angelic host and an innumerable company of evil spirits and demons of every kind marshalled under the leadership of a demon prince. They have taken control not only of man's nature but also of the world in which man lives. They are arrayed like a great army just as, on God's side, the hosts of heaven are drawn up under the control of the Lord of Hosts.

6. THE INFLUENCE OF FOREIGN THOUGHT

The conception of angelology and demonology which we find in the apocalyptic writings is much more developed and varied than it is in the Old Testament writings. So great is the change that it is extremely hard to believe that what we find in the apocalyptic books is simply the natural growth of ancient Jewish traditions, however intermingled these may have been in earlier days with foreign ideas from Babylonia and elsewhere. It is most significant that this change is to be detected in the centuries following the conquest of Alexander the Great and especially in the two centuries or so before Christ.

[1] In the Dead Sea Scrolls the word *msṭmh*, meaning 'enmity', appears several times as a common noun. Some scholars translate it as a proper noun in *Zadokite Document* XVI. 5. Cf. C. Rabin, *The Zadokite Documents*, 1958, p. 75.

This, as we have seen, was a period in which the Jews were strongly influenced by Hellenism whose culture embraced religions and philosophies not only of the western Mediterranean peoples, but also of countries and nations much further to the east. Among these was the religion of Persia whose influence on Palestine had been felt previously in exilic and post-exilic times and again following the conquests of Alexander.[1] Scholars have differed in their estimates of the extent to which Persian thought has influenced apocalyptic ideas, but most are agreed that that influence existed and that, in particular, the development of angelology and demonology is to be understood against the background of Persian teaching on this subject.

As has been pointed out above, Persian dualism is in many respects different from that form of it which we find in the apocalyptic writings. Nevertheless, in the common apocalyptic picture of angels and demons opposing each other under rival princes, we have something strongly reminiscent of the religious outlook of the Zoroastrian faith. The picture of ranks of demons set out in descending order to be found frequently in the Persian system is common also among the apocalyptists, as, for example, in the Book of Enoch. Corresponding to this is the picture of ranks of angels graded according to the authority they have been given or have won over their fellows.

Reference has already been made to the seven archangels who appear with personal names in the apocalyptic writings. A hint as to the origin of these names is given in the *Bereshit Rabbah* on Gen. 18.1, where it is recorded that 'the names of the angels, such as Michael, Raphael and Gabriel, they (the Israelites) brought from Babylon'. This statement no doubt reflects a genuine tradition that the practice of giving personal names to angels came into Palestine from Babylon; but it does not necessarily mean that this practice originated with the Babylonians. Indeed, it is more likely that the origin is to be found in Zoroastrianism which, in post-exilic times and even before, had permeated the Babylonian religion. It has been further suggested that the number 'seven' is also of Persian origin in this connection and that the seven archangels of apocalyptic lore emerged under the influence of the archangels of the Persian hierarchy called Amesha Spentas. There are at least two objections to this theory that the Amesha Spentas are the prototype of the arch-

[1] Cf. R. C. Zaehner, *The Dawn and Twilight of Zoroastrianism*, 1961, pp. 20–22, 51–52, 57–58.

angels. One is that the names in the respective lists do not in any way tally with each other. The second is that the Amesha Spentas were in fact only six and not seven in the Zoroastrian system;[1] at a much later date they are recognized as seven, but this is probably due to the reverse influence of Jewish thought on Persian. In all probability the number seven which occurs in the apocalyptic accounts is due to Babylonian influence and originated in the worship of the seven 'planets' (strictly the sun, the moon and five planets) which were regarded as deities who controlled the lives of men and nations.[2] The idea that the stars and other heavenly bodies represent and are angelic beings and objects of worship is to be found in both the Babylonian and the Persian systems.

A correspondence between the Persian and the Jewish systems of belief is to be found in the fact that in each of them certain angels are appointed to rule over the natural phenomena and are themselves regarded as personifications or manifestations of the powers of nature. There is some reason to believe that the Amesha Spentas themselves were of this kind and that they, too, represent personifications of the elemental powers. Moreover, as in the apocalyptic writings so also in the Persian, the angels are set over the seasons. In the latter the different parts of the calendar are introduced by different angels who are given authority over each month which bore the name of the angel under whose rule it was placed.[3]

Reference is made on occasions in the apocalyptic writings, as we have seen, to the existence of guardian angels not only of the elements but also of human beings.[4] A correspondence has been found between this notion and that of the *fravashis* in the Zoroastrian system which tells of 'the swiftness and might, the beauty, the helpfulness, the friendship of the powerful, pre-eminent guardian angels of the true believers' (*Yasht* 13.1). The *fravashis* have been described as 'the pre-existent external souls of all good men and women . . . on whom the very maintenance of the cosmos depends',[5] or 'the

[1] For a description of the six Amesha Spentas see R. C. Zaehner, *ibid.*, pp. 63ff.

[2] The immediate source of the seven archangels of apocalyptic lore is no doubt to be found in Ezek. 9.2–11, which tells how 'six men (*i.e.* angels) came from the way of the upper gate . . . and one man in the midst of them, clothed with linen, with a writer's ink-horn by his side'. This last reference clearly reflects the figure of the god Nabu who records in the book of fate.

[3] Cf. M. Testuz, *op. cit.*, p. 79, n. 1, and also J. Duchesne-Guillemin, *Zoroastre, étude critique avec une traduction commentée des Gatha*, 1948.

[4] See p. 244. [5] R. C. Zaehner, *op. cit.*, pp. 76, 146.

imperishable, purely spiritual, prototype of deities, but also of men who are true believers',[1] or as 'the spiritual counterpart of a man'.[2] This notion is much more widespread than in Persian literature,[3] but it may have found its way into Judaism from this quarter.

J. H. Moulton and others believe that this picture of the *fravashis* may lie behind the idea expressed in the apocalyptic writings of 'princes' and 'angels' appointed to rule over communities of people and also behind the idea of the guardian angels of the nations. Moulton indicates that, in Persian thought, the idea of the *fravashi* was not confined to the individual but was associated with the house, the family, the clan, the district.[4] This view is challenged by T. F. Glasson who sees in the Greek idea of superhuman guardians and shepherds allotted to the nations a more likely source than the Persian to account for this Jewish emphasis: 'Those who look to Persia have to argue that, while there was originally a counterpart to each individual, the Jews developed this idea and extended its application from individuals to nations. If, however, we look to Greece, no such surmises are required; the same thought already exists and is even expressed in similar terminology.'[5]

The same writer points again to Greek ideas, rather than Persian, as the immediate source of the account given in the apocalyptic writings of angel marriages and the origin of demons. He indicates four aspects of this story which find correspondence in the two literatures. These are the mating of gods and women; demons as the product of this union; demons as the surviving spirits of supermen of a past era; and God's anger at the unnatural mating of the divine and the human.[6] He further indicates that there are close parallels between the Greek stories of the Titans and the accounts of the fallen angels in the apocalyptic writings. Both instruct men in the arts of civilization; both are bound in chains beneath the earth and are subsequently cast into the fire.[7]

When we turn to a consideration of demonology the influence of Persian thought is more obvious. At the head of the 'hosts of darkness' stands Angra-Mainyu (Ahriman), the 'Enemy-Spirit', the prince of the demons who himself created the demons and from the bodies of

[1] W. O. E. Oesterley, *The Jews and Judaism during the Greek Period*, 1941, p. 273, n. 1.

[2] J. H. Moulton, *Early Zoroastrianism*, 1913, p. 245.

[3] Cf. *ibid.*, p. 324.

[4] Cf. *ibid.*, pp. 274, 325.

[5] *Greek Influence in Jewish Eschatology*, 1961, pp. 72ff.

[6] Cf. *ibid.*, pp. 57ff.

[7] Cf. *ibid.*, pp. 62ff.

whose followers, when they died, demons were born. Immediately beneath him in rank are six arch-demons. These form Angra-Mainyu's inner council and are responsible for carrying out their leader's diabolical plans. Outstanding among them is the demon Aeshma, whose name appears in that of Asmodaeus (*Aeshma daeva*) in the Book of Tobit. Alongside these are over fifty other demons who personify the evil forces in the world and in particular the evil moral qualities in man such as arrogance, false speech, greed, sloth, lust, etc. On a lower level still are 'the wicked' made up of innumerable demonic figures who are the instigators of all kinds of evil in the universe.[1] The similarity between this ordered array of demonic powers and the picture presented in the apocalyptic writings can hardly be accidental.

The relationship between the idea of Satan and that of Angra-Mainyu is a very complicated one. One obvious difference between them is that, whereas Satan is believed to be a rebellious angel, created by God and dwelling in heaven, Angra-Mainyu is an independent spiritual power of evil owing nothing to the creative power of Ahura-Mazda but rather sharing with him in the work of creation. In the apocalyptic writings, however, the Satan of Jewish tradition gradually takes upon himself the characteristics of Beliar who is described as the chief of the demons. This figure of Beliar or Satan-Beliar has much more in common with the Persian Angra-Mainyu. Beliar, for example, is not depicted as an angel, but is a spirit of evil utterly opposed to 'the Lord of Spirits'. Both these demon princes stand at the head of their respective demon hosts and both exercise the same functions of accusing, seducing and destroying.[2]

Reference has been made above to the association of Satan with the serpent in the story of Adam's fall in the Garden of Eden (*e.g.* Apoc. of Moses 17.4) and to its reappearance in the New Testament (*e.g.* Rev. 12.9; 20.2). In somewhat the same way Angra-Mainyu is also closely associated with the serpent in the Persian account. A late source, containing much earlier material, tells how this evil spirit sprang from the earth in the shape of a serpent and so infested the earth with its poisonous spawn that no place was left even for a needle (*Bundahishn* 3). Elsewhere reference is made to 'the Serpent Dahaka' (*Azhi Dahaka*) who appears in human form but from whose

[1] Cf. A. V. Williams-Jackson, 'Demons and Spirits (Persian)', in *ERE*, vol. IV, 1911, pp. 619f.

[2] Cf. E. Langton, *Essentials of Demonology*, 1949, pp. 68ff.

shoulders there grow two snakes planted there by a kiss from Angra-Mainyu.[1] Demons are here associated with many kinds of animals and reptiles; the most terrible are the serpents, among whom *Dahaka* holds the highest place.

The illustrations given above indicate that the Jewish apocalyptic writers were influenced, then, not only by their Hellenistic environment, but also by the cultures of Babylonia and Persia. But it is easy to overstate the case for such external pressures and to overlook the fact that much of this thought, especially as it relates to angelology, is indigenous or is at least part of a tradition which can be traced a great deal further back than the time of the apocalyptic writings themselves and earlier than the conquests of Alexander. There is reason to believe that Jews and Samaritans alike may have shared a common tradition relating to angelology, demonology and eschatology which ante-dated perhaps the reforms of Ezra and which came to light in the apocalyptic writings of the centuries immediately preceding and following the birth of Christ.[2] It is certain that there were borrowings in this realm from external sources, but, as so often happens, these borrowings would be largely unrecognized as such by the borrowers and would be naturally accepted as part of the traditional faith of their fathers.

[1] Cf. A. V. Williams-Jackson, *op. cit.*, p. 620.
[2] Cf. M. Gaster, 'Parsiism in Judaism', *ERE*, vol. IX, 1917, pp. 639f.

X

THE TIME OF THE END

I. 'THE HOUR IS AT HAND'

WE HAVE ALREADY seen that the apocalyptic writers endeavoured, by interpretation and reinterpretation of earlier prophecies and predictions, to forecast the time of the End.[1] This, however, should not blind us to the fact that, to the majority of these writers and in particular to the writer of the Book of Daniel, the fact of the End and its imminence were of much greater importance than their ability to predict the day or hour of its arrival. They were convinced that God would make an end of evil and usher in his kingdom and that they themselves were soon to witness its appearing. The End might come at any moment and they were to see its coming with their own eyes. There was an air of eager, even desperate, expectancy that soon, very soon, God's rule would suddenly and devastatingly break in and God himself, either in person or through his Messiah, would right all wrongs and reward the patience and longsuffering of the righteous.

This sense of eager expectancy was, of course, part of the popular messianic hope of the day. It is clearly seen in the New Testament in the ministry of John the Baptist, in the message of Jesus and in the witness of the Early Church,[2] and is amply illustrated in the writings of the Qumran Covenanters.[3]

Throughout the inter-testamental period, it seems certain, there were several popular traditions concerning the coming of the End which would lend weight to the belief that the people were at that time living in the last days. The apocalyptists, writes H. J. Schonfield, 'were conscious that they were playing a leading part in the last Act

[1] See pp. 96ff. [2] Cf. II Tim. 3; II Peter 3; I John 2.18. [3] See pp. 272f.

of a stupendous Cosmic Drama begun in the dawn of time; and this Act was regarded as having opened around the commencement of the second century BC in the Great Apostasy which gave rise to Chasidism. . . . And so began the age of apocalypse, or revelation. An age which believed that upon itself had fallen the ends of all the ages, that it was to witness the consummation, the catastrophic curtain to the drama of humanity.'[1] The writer of the Book of Daniel lived in this age and shared this belief. 'Go thou thy way till the end be,' he is told, 'for thou shalt rest, and shalt stand in thy lot, at the end of the days' (12.13). It is obvious that this book was written during and for the time of the End (cf. 8.17, 19). 'The hour is at hand.' This is its abiding message—not its calculations and predictions and prognostications. All these are secondary to the conviction that the time is short and the End will speedily come. Other writers followed the way that Daniel pioneered, taking up his calculations and reinterpreting them in the light of the circumstances of their own day. But behind their repeated prognostications the message of Daniel remained the same—the time is short, the End is at hand. Even with the passing of the years and the non-appearance of the End, their faith did not falter. The day had long been delayed, but this delay could not last much longer. The consummation would speedily come. 'For the youth of the world is past, and the strength of the creation is already exhausted, and the advent of the times is very short, yea, they have passed by; and the pitcher is near to the cistern, and the ship to the port, and the course of the journey to the city, and life to consummation' (II Bar. 85.10).

It is against this background of hope-deferred that we are to understand the eager expectation of the apocalyptic writers who lived in the assurance that God's reign of righteousness would soon begin.

2. THE NEW ESCHATOLOGY

The controversial question of the origin of eschatology in Hebrew thought lies outside the boundaries of this study and does not really affect our understanding of the many and varied eschatological beliefs which form the extremely tangled web of apocalyptic during the inter-testamental period. It is perfectly true, as R. H. Charles points out,[2] that 'prophetic eschatology' and 'apocalyptic eschato-

[1] *Secrets of the Dead Sea Scrolls*, 1956, pp. 112f.
[2] Cf. *Eschatology*, 2nd ed., 1913, pp. 177ff.

logy' must be carefully distinguished from each other because each has its own peculiar conception of 'the last things'. But such a reminder as this requires at least two qualifications. One is that, despite the obvious differences between them, there is an underlying unity; the broad lines of prophetic teaching can be traced right on into the apocalyptic writings and remain an essential part of their teaching despite the many changes and developments which took place in the process. The second qualification is that the word 'eschatology', when applied to the prophetic utterances, has a different connotation in certain fundamental respects from that which it has in the apocalyptic tradition. S. Mowinckel, for example, argues strongly that in Israel there was no pre-prophetic or indeed prophetic eschatology in the strictest and indeed the only true sense of that word.[1] The future hope often expressed in the prophets is not to be interpreted in terms of 'the last things', for 'the last things' in the sense of 'the end of the world' do not constitute part of their teaching at all.

What we find expressed in the prophetic writings is a future hope of a coming kingdom bound up, more often than not, with the restoration of David's line. This was essentially a picture of an earthly kingdom, political in character, nationalistic in outlook and military in expression. Although here and there it envisaged the hope of a universal salvation for the nations, for the most part it was a hope for Israel alone in a kingdom of this world. God's people would be delivered from the power of their enemies who would fall before the awful judgment of God. God himself would reign as king with or without the help of his 'Messiah'. At this stage, however, the terms 'kingdom' and 'Messiah' did not have the nuances which later came to be associated with them and which, in Christian thought at any rate, became inextricably associated with the old prophetic ideas. In the writings of Deutero-Isaiah, however, the future hope became increasingly supra-terrestrial and transcendent. The hope of restoration was here viewed in terms of the miraculous intervention of God in such a way that the present world order would be completely transformed. He describes, in language associated with and no doubt derived from the cult, the victory of Yahweh over the powers of the universe and his enthronement as king. Others follow Deutero-Isaiah in this emphasis and look forward not only to a renewed creation where none will hurt or destroy, but also to a new heaven

[1] Cf. *He that Cometh*, English trans., 2nd ed., 1959, pp. 126ff.

and a new earth. Despite the flights of poetic imagination in which these hopes are expressed, the scene of God's kingdom is still this present world order, however, with Jerusalem as its centre and the surviving people of Israel as its citizens.

But already the way was being prepared for a remarkable development in the expression of Israel's future hope. Its roots can be traced back into the teaching of Old Testament prophecy, but its subsequent growth may owe something to the influence of Persian ideas.[1] This new conception of the last things is not consistently presented throughout the apocalyptic writings but a certain pattern of beliefs appears unlike that of the prophets in a number of very significant respects. The phrase 'the latter end of the days' was fairly familiar in the Old Testament Scriptures and especially in the writings of the prophets where it referred to the far-distant future or more specifically to the coming of the messianic age,[2] but in the apocalyptic writings it took on a new meaning and gained an entirely new significance. It now signified not simply the end of Israel's enemies, but the termination of history, the end of the world itself. Because of this the future hope of the apocalyptists can truly be called 'eschatology', a doctrine of 'the last things'.

'Eschatology', writes Mowinckel, 'is a doctrine or a complex of ideas about "the last things", which is more or less organically coherent and developed. Every eschatology includes in some form or other a dualistic conception of the course of history, and implies that the present state of things and the present world order will suddenly come to an end and be superseded by another of an essentially different kind.'[3] This dualistic view of the world, which is characteristic of apocalyptic eschatology, finds expression in a doctrine of two ages which states that 'the Most High has not made one age but two' (II Esd. 7.50). Over against 'this age' (Hebrew *ha ʿolam haz-zeh*; Greek *ho aiōn houtos*), with its sin and corruption, is set 'the age to come' (Hebrew *ha ʿolam hab-ba'*; Greek *ho aiōn mellōn*) in which evil will be routed and wrongs will be set right. It is to be observed that these

[1] R. C. Zaehner argues that 'a Judaeo-Christian dependence on Zoroastrianism in its purely eschatological thinking is . . . not at all convincing. . . . We have no evidence as to what eschatological ideas the Zoroastrians had in the last four centuries before Christ', *op. cit.*, p. 57. For the influence of Zoroastrianism on the Jewish conception of life after death, however, see below, pp. 385ff.

[2] Cf. Gen. 49.1; Num. 24.14; Deut. 4.30; 31.29; Isa. 2.2; Jer. 23.20; 30.24; 48.47; 49.39; Ezek. 38.16; Hos. 3.5; Micah 4.1; Dan. 2.28; 10.14.

[3] *Op. cit.*, p. 125.

two phrases have overtones of a cosmic character which they could never have had within, say, the context of Old Testament prophecy. This present age is in the control of evil powers and has itself become contaminated with evil and wickedness of every kind. But these evil powers are no longer the great empires and kings of which the prophets had spoken; they are 'principalities and powers in high places', demonic beings under the control of their leader Satan, Beliar, Mastema, the Devil.[1] The whole presupposition of apocalyptic eschatology is that of a 'pessimistic-dualistic view of the Satanic corruption of the total world-complex'.[2] God had entrusted the government of the world to the care of his angelic rulers, but they had rebelled against him and had stolen it from his control. The world was no longer God's kingdom; it lay in the hands of evil cosmic forces which were bent on the destruction of mankind and of the world itself.

Because it is in the hands of Satan and his angels, this present age is 'full of sorrow and impotence' (II Esd. 4.27); it is corruptible (II Esd. 4.11) and a 'world of sickness' (II Enoch 66.6) so that men's hearts fail them when they think of it (II Esd. 4.2). How great a contrast this is with the age to come! 'The ways of this world become narrow and sorrowful and painful and full of perils coupled with great toils. But the ways of the future world are broad and safe, and yield the fruit of immortality' (II Esd. 7.12–13). This present age, with all its evil and corruption, will, however, soon pass away for 'the age which is not yet awake shall be roused, and that which is corruptible shall perish' (II Esd. 7.31, cf. II Bar. 44.9, 12). Wicked men and all the powers of evil will be punished for 'the Lord shall visit them in the consummation in the end of the days' (Ass. of Moses 1.18, cf. II Bar. 27.15; 29.8). Vengeance will be taken at the end of the age not only on wicked men (II Bar. 54.21, cf. II Esd. 7.47; 8.1f.), but also on those evil spirits which have corrupted the earth (I Enoch 10.13ff., etc.).

'The present age', we are told, 'is not the End. . . . But the Day of Judgment shall be the end of this age and the beginning of the eternal age that is to come; wherein corruption is passed away, weakness is abolished, infidelity is cut off; while righteousness is grown, and faithfulness is sprung up' (II Esd. 7.112–14). This new age will

[1] See above, pp. 254ff.

[2] R. Bultmann, *Theology of the New Testament*, English trans., vol. I, 1955, pp. 4–5.

come when the number of God's elect is fulfilled (II Esd. 4.36). There will come a time when 'the age which is about to pass away shall be sealed: then the books shall be opened' (II Esd. 6.20). This present age is 'fast coming to its end' (II Esd. 4.26); already by far the greater part of it is past and only a short time remains (II Esd. 4.44–50; 14.11). The End will not be long delayed, for 'creation is already grown old, and is already past the strength of youth' (II Esd. 5.55).

The present evil age, symbolized by Esau, will be at once followed by the glorious age of Jacob (II Esd. 6.9). The present age will pass away (II Bar. 48.50), but the new age will never pass away (II Bar. 44.11). Into it will be gathered the righteous who have died in their righteousness, for 'the earth shall restore them that sleep in her' (II Esd. 7.32, etc.).[1] This eternal age will be quite unlike the one that has gone before: 'Then the times shall perish, and there shall be no year, nor month, nor day, and there shall be no hours nor shall they be reckoned. There shall be one eternity, and all the just who shall escape the great judgment of the Lord shall be gathered together in eternal life and for ever and ever the just shall be gathered together and they shall be eternal. Moreover, there shall be no labour, nor sickness, nor sorrow, nor anxiety, nor need, nor night, nor darkness, but a great light. . . . And incorruptible paradise shall be their protection, and their eternal habitation. For all corruptible things shall vanish, and there shall be eternal life' (II Enoch 65.7–10).

This whole picture is very different from that presented by the Old Testament prophetic hope. No longer, for example, is the future hope simply nationalistic in the sense that it is circumscribed by the boundaries of any one nation or people; it is universalistic in the sense that God's salvation extends to the righteous and his judgments fall upon the wicked. No longer is the nation as such the only object of God's redemption (although, as we shall see, the thought of the nation remains a powerful factor in this respect); there emerges a future hope for the individual who will share in the coming kingdom by means of resurrection. No longer are God's enemies confined to men of flesh and blood; they are the demonic powers of darkness who have entrenched themselves in God's vast universe and in the heart of man. No longer are God's battles fought with sword and spear; they now assume cosmic proportions and involve the whole

[1] For the significance of the resurrection belief in this connection see pp. 366ff.

universe. Thus apocalyptic eschatology becomes more and more transcendent, with stress from first to last on the supernatural and the supra-mundane. Deliverance will come, not from men, but from God himself who will bring in his kingdom and usher in the age to come.[1] This will mark the fulfilment and triumph of God's eternal purpose which has been from the beginning and will continue to the very end.

Here, then, is an eschatology which represents a new interpretation of human history and human destiny, or at least an interpretation which clearly reveals new emphases and insights, an eschatology which is at once 'dualistic, cosmic, universalistic, transcendental and individualistic'.[2]

The foregoing description of the 'new eschatology' to be found in the apocalyptic books may be summed up and tabulated in the following way:[3]

(*a*) The 'future hope' of Old Testament prophecy becomes strictly 'eschatology' when it finds expression in a dualistic view of the world.

(*b*) This dualistic view of the world finds expression in a doctrine of two ages and involves a transcendental view of the coming kingdom.

(*c*) This new order generally takes the form of a new beginning, free from that corruption which had all along affected creation.

(*d*) The transformation which is thus wrought is not evolutionary but cataclysmic.[4]

(*e*) It is brought about not by human or historical (*i.e.* political and military) forces, but by supernatural powers.

(*f*) It takes the form of a cosmic drama in which divine and demonic forces are at work.

(*g*) It is related to the thought of the individual's destiny after death and includes the ideas of resurrection and judgment.

(*h*) Its completion is the work of God and marks the fulfilment of his plan for the world.

[1] For the relation of the messianic kingdom to the age to come see pp. 291ff.

[2] S. Mowinckel, *op. cit.*, p. 271.

[3] Following Mowinckel, *ibid.*, pp. 125f., 270ff.

[4] An exception to this is the Book of Jubilees, whose author apparently believes that the messianic age has already set in. Its growth would be gradual; men would grow in spiritual stature and nature would become gradually transformed, cf. 1.29; 4.26; 23.26–28, and also Isa. 65.17ff.; 66.22.

It is clear from what has been said above that the this-worldly, national and political hopes of the prophets are very different in character from the other-worldly, universal and transcendent hopes of the apocalyptists. Nevertheless it would be a mistake to imagine that these two complexes of ideas, expressed separately in this way, lend themselves to an easy division and fall naturally into two well-defined and opposite categories. There is, in fact, a considerable measure of overlapping which defies analysis and refuses to be categorized.

It is a mistake, for example, to imagine that the prophetic hope and the apocalyptic eschatology represent two successive phases of religious belief, the national and political expectation being succeeded in course of time by the universal and transcendental, for even in the apocalyptic writings themselves the familiar Old Testament pattern of the coming kingdom is still to be found.[1] Nor do they represent two definite lines of development within the same books or two statements of belief which can be systematically arranged over against each other. For the most part they are fused together into a complex whole which defies characterization. At times, indeed, fusion becomes confusion as, for example, in the Similitudes of Enoch (I Enoch 37–71) where the earthly and the heavenly are strangely combined in one. At yet other times, as in II Esdras and II Baruch, the two conceptions are separated from each other in such a way as to make necessary the compromise of a temporary kingdom established on the earth whose place will ultimately be taken by an eternal kingdom not of this world.[2] It is misleading, moreover, to regard the national and political idea of the kingdom as native to Old Testament thought and so to the true Hebrew tradition and to dismiss the universalistic and transcendental idea as a borrowing from Zoroastrianism and so completely foreign to Hebrew thought. Even if it be conceded that apocalyptic eschatology was partly influenced by Zoroastrian eschatology,[3] but it is a mistake to oversimplify the position by a too careful categorizing of the eschatological material. Rudolf Otto rightly points out that 'the new motives which are active in the eschatology of late Jewish apocalyptic are far from being absolutely and radically alien to ancient Israelite religious feeling, for in that case we should have had to do with a syncretism in the sense of mechanical addition, and the eschatology of late Judaism

[1] Cf. Pss. of Sol. 17.21–51; Sib. Or. III. 652–9. See further pp. 286ff.

[2] For the idea of the millennium see pp. 291ff. [3] See p. 266.

would then be simply and solely an alien phenomenon, which is not the case. Rather they work upon germinal ideas found even in ancient Israel.'[1] Even in the case of borrowings from Zoroastrianism, such is the genius of Hebrew thought and the strength of the Yahweh religion, that much of what was taken over was completely transformed and made to fit into the familiar pattern of Old Testament faith in the God of power and righteousness. In taking over such ideas from foreign sources the apocalyptists were nevertheless aware of their place within the prophetic tradition. They read and interpreted the ancient prophecies in the light of the new 'wisdom' which had been given to them with its interest in astrology, angelology, cosmology and the rest, and in terms of the new eschatological expectations of their day. Thus, Zoroastrian ideas of an eschatological kind were not superimposed on earlier Hebrew beliefs, but were incorporated into their interpretation and understanding of ancient Scripture as part of its fulfilment in the working out of the purpose of God.

The popular Old Testament view of the future hope with its military leader and earthly kingdom continued, then, to hold a secure place in the religious aspirations of the mass of the people during the inter-testamental period. But from the time of Daniel right through to the end of the first century AD there can be sensed a tension between this and the 'new eschatology' with its dualistic outlook and transcendental interpretation of God's purpose which was never really resolved within Judaism. This tension, as will be seen in a later chapter, is particularly evident in the relationship between the Messiah and the Son of Man.

3. SIGNS OF THE END

The hope is expressed throughout these writings not only that the End will come soon, but also that God in his mercy will shorten the predetermined time of waiting: 'For the Most High will assuredly hasten his times, and he will assuredly bring on his hours' (II Bar. 83.1, cf. 20.1; 54.1; Mark 13.20; *Ep. of Barnabas* 4.3). The time will speedily come when there will be a 'showdown' between the kingdom of God and the kingdom of Satan. This dramatic conflict between the *civitas dei* and the *civitas diaboli*, which has been going on from the very beginning of the world and which has swept up into its toils

[1] *The Kingdom of God and the Son of Man*, 1943, p. 39.

men and beasts and all created things, will reach its grand finale. The powers of evil will make their last desperate attempt to overthrow the powers of good. They will launch their attack upon God's people and upon God's whole universe. Sin and wickedness will do their worst and bring desolation and woe in their train before God's kingdom is established and the End at last will come.

This picture of judgments and woes, coupled with the expression of hope in the final triumph of God, recalls the familiar Old Testament picture of the Day of Yahweh when God would be acknowledged as king.[1] Sometimes the coming of this great Day is the result of the direct intervention of God himself; at other times he acts through his chosen Messiah who establishes his kingdom upon the earth. Sometimes 'the kingdom of God' is identified with 'the kingdom of the Messiah'; at other times the two are distinguished and the earthly kingdom of the Messiah is followed by the transcendent, heavenly kingdom of God.[2] 'The Day of the Messiah', like 'the Day of Yahweh', is ushered in by portents and signs of a supernatural order which herald the triumph of God over all his foes.

The name given in later Jewish and Christian writings to this period of distress before God's final triumph is 'travail pains of the Messiah'. The idea goes back to Hos. 13.13 (cf. also Isa. 26.16–19; Micah 4.9–10; Hag. 2.6) and finds its way, through such passages as Zech. 14.13 and Dan. 12.1, into the main stream of apocalyptic thought. Within the New Testament it appears in the so-called 'Little Apocalypse' of Mark 13 where the listed 'woes' are called 'the beginnings of the birth pangs' (13.8, cf. Matt. 24.8). The same idea is set forth at greater length in Rev. 12.1–6, where the writer describes the birth of the Messiah or the messianic community from the womb of the true Israel which is likened to a woman who 'crieth out, travailing in birth, and in pain to be delivered' (12.2).

This last passage finds a remarkable correspondence and precedent in the *Hymns of Thanksgiving* among the Dead Sea Scrolls where reference is made to the birth of children to a woman in great travail, in these words:

> I am in distress
> like a woman in travail with her firstborn,
> when her pangs come,
> and grievous pain on her birth-stool,
> causing torture in the crucible (*i.e.* womb) of the pregnant one;

[1] See pp. 92ff. [2] See pp. 291ff.

for sons have come to the waves of death,
and she who conceived a man suffers in her pains;
for in the waves of death she gives birth to a man-child;
with pains of Sheol he bursts forth
from the crucible of the pregnant one,
a wonderful counsellor with his power (III.7–10).[1]

This has generally been taken as a description of the birth of the Messiah—a Wonderful Counsellor (cf. Isa. 9.6)—who would emerge at the time of the End from the midst of the true Israel, represented no doubt by the Qumran Community, to establish God's kingdom. It seems more likely, however, that the picture represents the emergence, not of the Messiah, but of God's redeemed people through great toil and suffering. This is suggested not only by the use of the plural 'sons' to describe the woman's offspring, but also by the apocalyptic language used throughout the entire hymn[2]—the seas roar, the foundations rock, the abysses boil, Sheol and Abaddon open wide, the doors of the Pit are closed upon the devisers of wickedness. In the following hymn (III.19–36) the theme is continued—the 'torrents of Belial' rain down consuming fire which destroys the foundations of the earth; the flinty rocks become torrents of pitch; they burst into Abaddon; earth's foundations shake and tremble; the war of 'the heavenly mighty ones' scourges the earth; destruction is determined and these things will not end before the appointed time.

As far back as the time of the Book of Daniel the apocalyptic tradition had clearly declared: 'There shall be a time of trouble, such as never was since there was a nation even to that same time' (Dan. 12.1). Subsequent writers reiterated this prophecy[3] (*e.g.* Ass. of

[1] Translation by Millar Burrows, *The Dead Sea Scrolls*, 1956, p. 403.

[2] Cf. M. Black, *The Scrolls and Christian Origins*, 1961, pp. 149f.

[3] This, of course, is also characteristic of later rabbinic theology and of extra-canonical Christian apocalypses. In the Mishnah, for example, we read these words: 'With the footprints of the Messiah presumption shall increase and dearth, reach its height; the vine shall yield its fruit but the wine shall be costly; and the empire shall fall into heresy and there shall be none to utter reproof. The council-chamber shall be given to fornication. Galilee shall be laid waste and Gablan shall be made desolate . . .' (*Soṭah* 9.15, translation by H. Danby, *The Mishnah*, 1933, p. 306).

An illustration of the same thing from the Christian point of view is given in the *Didache* 16.3ff.: 'For in the last days *the false prophets* and corrupters shall be multiplied, and the sheep shall be turned into wolves, and love shall be turned into hate. For as lawlessness increaseth, *they shall hate one another and shall persecute and betray. And then* the world-deceiver *shall appear* as a son of God; *and shall work*

Moses 8.1) and indicated certain signs which would mark the near approach of the End.[1] An early account of these is given in Jub. 23.13ff.:

> For calamity follows on calamity, and wound on wound, and tribulation on tribulation, and evil tidings on evil tidings, and illness on illness, and all evil judgments such as these, one with another, illness and overthrow, and snow and frost and ice, and fever, and chills, and torpor, and famine, and death, and sword, and captivity, and all kinds of calamities and pains. And all these will come on an evil generation, which transgresses on the earth: their works are uncleanness and fornication, and pollution and abominations. . . . For all have done evil, and every mouth speaks iniquity and all their works are an uncleanness and an abomination, and all their ways are pollution, uncleanness and destruction. Behold the earth will be destroyed on account of all their works, and there will be no seed of the vine, and no oil; for their works are altogether faithless, and they will all perish together, beasts and cattle and birds, and all the fish of the sea, on account of the children of men. And they will strive one with another, the young with the old, and the old with the young, the poor with the rich, and the lowly with the great, and the beggar with the prince, on account of the law and the covenant; for they have forgotten commandment, and covenant, and feasts, and months, and Sabbaths, and jubilees, and all judgments. And they will stand (with bows and) swords and war to turn them back into the way; but they will not return until much blood has been shed on the earth, one by another.

In subsequent writings this list of 'woes' is repeated and supplemented with many frightening details. One evident sign which appears in practically every account is that of fearful *war*[2] in which nation will rise up against nation: 'And it will come to pass in those days that all the inhabitants of the earth will be moved one against another . . . and passion will seize him who is peaceful, and many will be roused in anger to injure many, and they will rouse up armies in order to shed blood, and in the end they will perish together with them' (II Bar. 48.32, 37). There will be 'tumult of nations, confusion

---

signs and wonders, and the earth shall be delivered into his hands; and he shall do unholy things, which have never been since the world began' (trans. by J. B. Lightfoot, *The Apostolic Fathers*, 1912, p. 235).

[1] The chief passages relating to these 'signs' are as follows: Dan. 12.1; I Enoch 80.2–7; 99.4, 5, 8; 100.1ff.; Jub. 23.13–25; Sib. Or. III. 538f.; 633ff.; 796ff.; V. 512ff.; Ass. of Moses 8.1; 10.5; Apoc. of Abraham 29f.; II Bar. 25–27; 32.1; 48.32ff.; 70.2ff.; II Esd. 5.1–12, 50–55; 6.21–24.

[2] Cf. in particular the theme of the *War of the Sons of Light against the Sons of Darkness*.

of leaders, disquietude of princes' (II Esd. 9.3, cf. Matt. 24.7ff.). Men will hate one another and provoke one another to fight; foolish men will assume control and lead their fellows into confusion so that many will fall by the sword (II Bar. 70.3ff., cf. 27.4). Even friends will attack one another suddenly as if they were enemies and the whole earth will be stricken with fear (II Esd. 6.24, cf. 5.9; Jub. 23.16; II Bar. 70.6). There will be an utter *lack of human sympathy* so that people will abandon their babes and their children without any qualms of conscience (I Enoch 99.5, cf. Micah 7.6), and men will kill their own brothers and slay their own sons and grandsons from sunrise till sunset (I Enoch 100.1–2).

Alongside these signs there will be *earthquakes* (cf. II Bar. 27.7; 70.8; II Esd. 9.3), *famines* (cf. II Bar. 27.6; 70.8; II Esd. 6.22) and *destruction by fire* (cf. II Bar. 27.10; 70.8; II Esd. 5.8): 'And it will come to pass that whosoever gets safe out of the war will die in the earthquake, and whosoever gets safe out of the earthquake will be burned by the fire, and whosoever gets safe out of the fire will be destroyed by famine' (II Bar. 70.8). *Mysterious powers* will take control of nature: 'Suddenly shall the sown places appear unsown, and the full storehouses shall suddenly be found empty' (II Esd. 6.22). The fruits of the earth will cease to grow at their appropriate time (I Enoch 80.3); there will be no wine or oil (Jub. 23.18). Rain will be withheld (I Enoch 80.2) and God will make the heavens like brass and the earth below like iron so that men will neither sow nor plough (Sib. Or. III. 539ff.).

Fearful and mysterious portents will appear for which there is no rational explanation. Blood trickles forth from wood, stones speak with a voice, the birds take sudden flight, salt appears in fresh water, mysterious voices speak forth in the night,[1] fire bursts forth from the earth, wild beasts desert their haunts and women give birth to monsters (II Esd. 5.5–9); pregnant women bring forth premature infants at three or four months, and these live and dance (II Esd. 6.21, cf. Matt. 24.19).

There will also be *portents in the heavens* reminding men that the End is near. References to the sun, moon and stars in a state of confusion are common enough in the Old Testament (cf. Isa. 13.10; Ezek. 32.7; Joel 2.31; 3.15, etc.). Here the same idea is taken up and developed by the apocalyptists along lines of their own: 'The horns

[1] Cf. the account given by Josephus of strange portents and of the mysterious voice heard in the Temple, *War* VI.v.3 (289, 296ff.).

of the sun will be broken and he will be turned into darkness; and the moon will not give her light, and be turned wholly into blood. And the circle of the stars will be disturbed' (Ass. of Moses 10.5, cf. Rev. 6.12–13; 8.12). The sun and the moon will alter their courses so that they do not appear at their proper times (I Enoch 80.4–5, cf. Sib. Or. III. 801–3); indeed, the sun will shine by night and the moon by day (II Esd. 5.4). The same utter confusion is evident also among the stars which change their courses (II Esd. 5.5); they alter their orbits and fail to appear at the seasons prescribed for them (I Enoch 80.6, cf. Rev. 6.13). Swords appear in the night sky and in the morning; footmen and horsemen make their way as to battle through the misty clouds (Sib. Or. III. 806f., cf. II Macc. 5.2–3).

4. ANTICHRIST

Closely associated with these 'signs of the End' is the figure of 'Antichrist', who, it was believed, would appear in the last days to do battle with God himself. Though the actual term first appears in Christian writings, the idea is very much earlier and probably reflects a well-established and fully developed legend familiar to the writers of the apocalyptic books.[1] The roots of this idea can be traced back into the Old Testament itself, especially to Ezek. 38–39 where Gog of the land of Magog is presented as the leader of those forces of evil which set themselves up in opposition to God. Indeed, they can be traced further back still into those mythological notions of a conflict between God and the monster of chaos, traces of which are to be found within the Old Testament itself.[2]

Another important factor in this connection is the influence of Persian eschatology with its account of warfare between Ahura Mazda and Angra Mainyu. This is seen in a number of apocalyptic writings where Beliar, for example, is pictured as a prince of the demons who sets himself up in opposition to God himself. Elsewhere a description is given of a great eschatological battle in which God defeats and slays the devil in the last days (*e.g.* Ass. of Moses 10.1ff.).

Antichrist, as we shall see, sometimes assumes the identity of a human figure, but the mythological background of the idea keeps shining through. What is here presented is, in fact, an individualizing and historicizing of the mythical monster of chaos or the satanic prince of wickedness who will in the end be destroyed by the hand

[1] See above, pp. 191f. [2] Cf. H. Gunkel, *Schöpfung und Chaos*, 1895.

of God. 'Whether regarded as a mere man or as the incarnation of this demonic spirit, we have the figure of a powerful king or ruler, subduing men beneath his evil sway, filled with the sense of his own importance, setting himself up to be equal with God, claiming divine honours, and trampling on the saints.'[1] The identity of Antichrist might change from generation to generation, but his nature remained the same and was recognizable in those who, like Antiochus or the Emperor Nero, dared oppose the will of God.

The earliest reference to this idea of Antichrist in the apocalyptic writings is in the Book of Daniel, where he is identified with Antiochus Epiphanes. It is not at all surprising that this terrible oppressor and persecutor of the Jews should be seen as the embodiment of the spirit of evil who would in the end be destroyed by God. He is here described as a king coming from the mysterious north supported by chariots, horsemen and many ships who will overthrow country after country and enter into 'the glorious land' (11.40–41). He is pictured as 'a little horn' who will pluck up three other 'horns', *i.e.* kings, by the roots (7.8). He speaks boastfully (7.8) and even speaks words against the Most High (7.25; 11.36). He wears out the saints of the Most High and sets himself to 'change the times and the law'. For three and a half years he is allowed to reign, but in the end judgment will come and his dominion will be taken away (7.25–26); he will be slain, with none to help him (11.45).

This role of Antichrist was in course of time transferred to other rulers who replaced Antiochus as the object of the Jews' hatred and fear. In the Ass. of Moses 8.1ff. a description is given of one who is called 'The King of the kings of the earth and one that ruleth with great power'. The context indicates that this is yet another allusion to Antiochus or, perhaps, to a figure which combines the features of Antiochus and Herod the Great.[2] Again, in the Pss. of Solomon 2.29 the Roman general Pompey is described as a 'dragon' and the writer beseeches God 'to turn the pride of the dragon into dishonour'.[3] Such a picture recalls the figure of the mythological dragon of chaos which, according to ancient tradition, God will utterly destroy.

The figure of Pompey may again be indicated in II Bar. 40.1f.

[1] H. H. Rowley, *The Relevance of Apocalyptic*, 1945, p. 146. For a discussion of the origin of the idea of Antichrist see *ibid.*, pp. 30ff.

[2] So W. Bousset, 'Antichrist', in *ERE*, vol. I, 1908, p. 579a.

[3] This representation is no doubt under the influence of Jer. 51.34, where Nebuchadnezzar of Babylon is described in similar terms.

which tells how 'the last leader of that time will be left alive, when the multitude of his hosts will be put to the sword and be bound, and they will take him up to Mount Zion, and my Messiah will convict him of all his impieties, and will gather and set before him all the work of his hosts. And afterwards he will put him to death.' The identity of the figure, however, is not clear; but it apparently is to be recognized as a human and not as a supernatural being. Another possible reference to Antichrist is perhaps to be found in II Esd. 5.6, which states that 'one whom the dwellers upon earth do not look for shall wield sovereignty'. Again, the reference is presumably to a human ruler who tyrannizes over the people of God. But no clue is given concerning his identity.

There are several other instances, however, where Antichrist does not appear as a human figure at all, but is the embodiment of none other than Beliar himself, the personification of wickedness and the leader of the hosts of iniquity. In the Testaments of the XII Patriarchs, for example, frequent reference is made to Beliar as the arch-enemy of God. In the last days, we are told, many will 'forsake the commandments of the Lord' and 'will cleave unto Beliar' (Test. of Iss. 6.1), but God's Messiah will wage war against him and rescue those whom he has taken (Test. of Dan 5.10). In the end he will be routed and 'cast into the fire for ever' (Test. of Jud. 25.3). Here we see more clearly than in any of the references so far given the influence of Persian dualism and in particular the influence of the demonic figure of Angra Mainyu to whom Beliar, in so many respects, corresponds.

The figure of Beliar appears again in Sib. Or. III. 63ff. There it is said that he will perform many signs and raise the dead, but these things will be of no effect; he will deceive many, but God will bring forth 'fiery energy' from the earth and burn up both Beliar himself and all who put their trust in him. It is here stated that Beliar will come 'from the stock of Sebaste', *i.e.* Samaria. For this reason, and on the strength of the description of him given in this passage, it has been suggested that the reference here is to Simon Magus who is depicted as Beliar or Antichrist. The reference, however, may be to the Emperors; if so, Beliar here represents the return of the Emperor Nero.[1] In either case this would be yet another instance of Antichrist assuming human form.

[1] So H. C. O. Lanchester (*Apocrypha and Pseud. of the Old Testament*, vol. II, 1913, p. 380), following R. H. Charles (*Ascension of Isaiah*, 1900, p. lxviii). He

In this same passage it is stated that, on the death of Beliar, 'the world shall be under the dominion of a woman's hands obeying her every behest' (III. 75ff.). But God will intervene and bring her rule to an end. The whole firmament will collapse upon the earth and the sea; land and sea will be burned by 'a ceaseless cataract of raging fire' and the whole of creation will be cast into 'one molten mass and clean dissolve'. Bousset sees in this figure a reference to the mythical Sea Monster which was originally regarded as feminine.[1] Others have suggested that the woman is to be identified with Cleopatra, who here assumes demoniacal properties.[2] Lanchester gives as his opinion that the identification of the woman with Rome is the most probable explanation.[3] The reference in Revelation 17 to 'the great harlot' is reminiscent of this account and may well belong to the same line of tradition.

One other interesting passage remains to be considered in this connection. In the Testaments of the XII Patriarchs it is stated that the tribe of Dan opposes the Lord by provoking Levi and fighting against Judah (Test. of Dan 5.4). In 5.6–7 the writer goes further and asserts that the prince of the tribe of Dan is Satan and that 'all the spirits of wickedness and pride' will conspire, through Dan, 'to attend constantly on the sons of Levi, to cause them to sin before the Lord'. R. H. Charles, who dates the latter verses in the middle of the first century BC, underlines the importance of this passage and maintains that it is 'the most ancient authority we at present possess for the view which connected the tribe of Dan with the Antichrist'.[4] He points out that even in the Old Testament itself Dan is associated with idolatry (cf. Judg. 18.30; I Kings 12.29), and in the rabbinic literature the account of his history is painted in dark colours. Irenaeus (*Haer.* V.xxx.2), moreover, interprets this particular verse with reference to Antichrist and comments that, because of this

---

regards lines 62–92 as a later passage dating from the latter part of the first century BC (*op. cit.*, p. 371).

In the Ascension of Isaiah 4.2–5.1a, which is Christian in origin, Antichrist is an incarnation of Beliar and is identified with the Emperor Nero. He will hold sway for three years, seven months and twenty-seven days which corresponds, in the Julian calendar, to the 1,335 days mentioned in Dan. 12.12 (cf. H. H. Rowley, *op. cit.*, pp. 135–6).

[1] Cf. *The Antichrist Legend*, English trans. by A. H. Keane, 1896, pp. 99f.
[2] Cf. Schürer, *op. cit.*, div. II, vol. III, p. 284. [3] Cf. *op. cit.*, p. 371.
[4] *Testaments of the XII Patriarchs*, 1908, p. 128.

association, Dan's name is omitted from 'the number of them which were sealed' in Rev. 7.5–8. H. H. Rowley, on the other hand, finds no reference whatever to Antichrist in the Test. of Dan 5.6–7, nor can he find any association between the two figures in the Book of Revelation where Antichrist is quite evidently of different identity altogether.[1] Even if this be so, however, the passage is of considerable significance as part of the case history of the development of the Antichrist legend within both Judaism and Christianity.

5. CREATION AND RE-CREATION

The apocalyptic writers teach that God's creation has been usurped by Satan and his legions and lies under the power of wickedness. The redemption which God will bring about will involve not only man himself and not only the nation of Israel, but also the whole created universe. The usurped creation will be restored; the corrupted universe will be cleansed; the created world will be re-created. Thus, throughout these writings, there is a close relationship between God's act in creation and his act in redemption. This act of redemption is an act of re-creation to be realized either in the messianic kingdom or the age to come. 'Even the irrational creation, heaven and earth, and therefore the whole universe in the strict sense, is transformed, the old destroyed and a new and glorious one made in its stead.'[2]

This idea is, of course, to be found in the Old Testament itself (*e.g.* Isa. 65.17; 66.22); but in the apocalyptic writings it finds renewed expression.[3] A gradual transformation of the world is envisaged in the Book of Jubilees (1.29); elsewhere it is generally sudden and catastrophic (I Enoch 91.16f., etc.). Such a belief was not, of course, confined to Jewish writers, but was a feature of much of the oriental thought of that time. In the popular neo-Pythagoreanism of the inter-testamental period, for example, the idea of a periodic renewal of the world was a familiar one and was held in conjunction with the belief that the universe had to pass through ever-recurring cycles of change.[4]

[1] Cf. *op. cit.*, p. 64. [2] Schürer, *op. cit.*, div. II, vol. II, p. 130.

[3] Cf. Jub. 1.29; I Enoch 45.4; 72.1; 91.16f.; II Bar. 32.6; 57.2; II Enoch 65.7, cf. also *The Manual of Discipline* IV.25; *Hymns of Thanksgiving* XI.13–14; XIII.11–13; Matt. 19.28; II Peter 3.13; Rev. 21.2.

[4] See above, pp. 213ff.

The influence of foreign thought is again to be found in the fairly frequently expressed belief that the created universe would in the end be destroyed by fire. We have already observed that, according to oriental thought, those cycles of change through which the universe was to pass would be accompanied by great cosmic disturbances, chief among which would be devastations caused by flood and fire.[1] These catastrophes are a feature of Babylonian teaching, and in Iranian eschatology the element of fire plays a very important part indeed. There it is believed that men will pass through the judgment of fire after which will appear the new age with its new heaven and new earth. But such teaching was not confined to Zoroastrianism; it formed part of the common belief of the times and was a prominent feature, for example, of Stoicism. But, once again, this idea of judgment by fire was not uncommon in the Old Testament,[2] although the total destruction of creation by this means is not found there as it appears in the apocalyptic writings.

Destruction first by water and then by fire is mentioned in the Life of Adam and Eve 49.3: 'On account of your transgression, our Lord will bring upon your race the anger of his judgment, first by water, the second time by fire; by these two, will the Lord judge the whole human race' (cf. also II Peter 3.10ff.). Destruction of the world by water is mentioned a number of times in these writings;[3] but much more frequent mention is made of the coming judgment by fire, particularly in the Sibylline Oracles.[4] There it is said that, at the time of the judgment 'a cataract of fire' will pour out of heaven (III. 54); all mankind will be destroyed by 'fire upon the earth' (III. 542, cf. II Bar. 27.10; 70.8); 'fire and cataclysm of rain' together with 'brimstone from heaven' will execute God's terrible judgment (III. 690f.). In Dan. 7.9–10 it is said of the 'Ancient of Days' that 'his throne was fiery flames' and that 'a fiery stream issued and came forth from before him'. God's wrath, as a flame of fire, goes forth against sinners (Pss. of Sol. 15.6f.); and the souls of the wicked are tortured in the fires of Hades (Apoc. of Abr. 31, etc.).

But God's judgment upon sinners and upon the world is not his

[1] See above, p. 215.

[2] *E.g.* Isa. 66.15f.; Jer. 4.4; Ezek. 21.31; Amos 5.6; Zeph. 1.18, etc.

[3] Cf. Jub. 5.11–12; I Enoch 10.2; 83.3–4; Sib. Or. III. 690f.

[4] Cf. Dan. 7.9f.; I Enoch 17.1, 4f.; Pss. of Sol. 15.6f.; Sib. Or. III. 54, 542, 690f.; IV. 176; II Bar. 27.10; 70.8; II Esd. 5.8; cf. also *The Manual of Discipline* II.8; *Hymns of Thanksgiving* III.29ff.; *War of the Sons of Light, etc.* XIV.17; and I Cor. 3.15; II Thess. 1.7f.; II Peter 3.6ff.; Rev. 19.20; 20.10, 14f.; 21.8.

final word. The re-creation of the universe which follows is expressed in many different ways throughout these writings. One significant principle in this respect is that the End should in some way correspond to the Beginning. What the Creator willed and planned at the time of his creation of the world will reach its fulfilment in the last days when he will redeem his universe, rectifying and restoring what has gone wrong and bringing to perfection what has already been created. This notion had already found expression in certain Old Testament passages (*e.g.* Isa. 11.6–8; Ezek. 34.25–27) and was a feature of current oriental thought. It is an accepted tenet in much rabbinic literature and is found in both Jewish and Christian apocalyptic. In the *Epistle of Barnabas* 6.13, for example, it is stated on divine authority, 'I will make the last things as the first.' Within the Jewish apocalyptic writings the same thought is expressed by the writer of II Esdras, who states that, just as 'in the beginning of the terrestrial world' God created the universe, 'so also the End' will come through him alone (6.1–6). There will be a correspondence between the two, for after the judgment 'then shall the world be turned into the primaeval silence seven days' (7.30, cf. II Bar. 3.7).

The exact relation between the Beginning and the End is complex in the extreme and affords no simple analysis. But N. A. Dahl, on the basis of an analysis of Christian and Jewish sources, has suggested a differentiation of the main types of correlation under seven heads.[1] These are the *analogy* of the old creation in describing the new, the one being parallel to or a type of the other (cf. Isa. 65.17; 66.22; Jub. 1.29; I Enoch 91.16; II Esd. 7.30ff.; II Peter 3.12f.; Rev. 21.1, 5); the *restitution* of the perfect order of the original creation (cf. Test. of Levi 18.10f.; Jub. 23.26ff.; I Enoch 90.37f.; Rom. 3.24; 5.2; 8.19ff.; Col. 1.15–20; Rev. 20.13; 21.4); the *transformation* of the old creation (cf. Isa. 26.1ff.; 60.19f.; Dan. 12.3; I Enoch 45.4f.; II Bar. 51, etc.; Rev. 21.13); the *identity* of the new with the old (cf. I Enoch 24–25, etc.; Rev. 2.7; 21.1, 14, 17, 19); the *reservation* of certain aspects or certain elements of the first creation (cf. II Esd. 6.49f.; II Bar. 29.4); the *perfection* of the old creation in the new which is itself included in the initial act of creation; and finally, the *pre-existence or predestination* of certain things which have remained from the beginning in the mind of God and will appear at the end (cf. II Esd. 4.36f.; 7.70; Rev. 17.8; 21.2, etc.).

[1] Cf. 'Christ, Creation and the Church', in *Background of the N.T. and its Eschatology*, ed. by Davies and Daube, 1956, pp. 422ff.

Throughout the apocalyptic writings frequent use is made of the idea of Paradise[1] to express this correspondence between the Beginning and the End. Sometimes the Paradise which is to appear at the end of the age is earthly in character (cf. Test. of Levi 18.10f., etc.) and is believed to be among the original works of creation (cf. Jub. 2.7; II Enoch 30.1; II Esd. 3.6; 6.2f.).[2] At other times, particularly in later apocalyptic books, it is transcendental and heavenly in character and is identified as the abode of the souls of the righteous (cf. I Enoch 61.12; 70.3f.; II Enoch 8.1ff.; II Bar. 4.3; 51.11; II Esd. 6.26; 7.28, 36ff.; 13.52; 14.9, 49). More often than not this transcendental Paradise partakes of the nature of both the earthly and the heavenly or else stands over against the earthly Paradise as its heavenly counterpart, yet remains in the closest possible relationship with it.[3] In II Enoch Paradise is situated in the third heaven (42.3) and seems to be identified with the earthly Paradise in the Garden of Eden. To this heavenly Paradise the souls of the righteous go after the final judgment (cf. II Enoch 42.5; II Esd. 8.53; Rev. 2.7). It is a place of bliss (II Esd. 7.36–38, 123) and is set in opposition to Gehenna, the place of torment for the souls of sinners (II Esd. 7.36). Apart from II Enoch, where the purely spiritual character of Paradise is most in evidence, even in those writings where its transcendental nature is emphasized 'the transcendent and superterrestrial never becomes the merely spatial, abstract, invisible, intangible, and empty'.[4]

Closely associated with this idea of the return of Paradise at the end of the age is that of the heavenly Jerusalem which, like Paradise itself, has been prepared beforehand by God at the beginning of his creation (cf. II Bar. 4.2–6). Here again there is a mingling of the earthly and the heavenly, the latter being more prominent in those writings which appeared in the years following the fall of Jerusalem in AD 70.

In certain of the earlier books the old Jerusalem, it is believed, will be purified as a preparation for the coming of the messianic kingdom (cf. I Enoch 10.16–19; 25.1; Pss. of Sol. 17.25, 33) or as

[1] The term 'Paradise' is of Persian origin and signifies a garden or orchard. The Greek equivalent is used in the LXX to translate 'the garden' of Eden. It occurs three times in the New Testament (Luke 23.43; II Cor. 12.4; Rev. 2.7).

[2] Observe that in Zoroastrian teaching Ahura Mazda creates the spiritual world before the earthly world.

[3] See further pp. 378f.

[4] S. Mowinckel, *op. cit.*, p. 275.

the centre of the temporary messianic kingdom (cf. II Bar. 29; 39–40; 72–74; II Esd. 7.27–30; 12.32–34; 13.32–50); elsewhere it is said that it will be replaced by the new Jerusalem (cf. I Enoch 90.28f.; Test. of Dan 5.12f.) which comes down from God out of heaven and is a counterpart of the earthly Jerusalem (cf. II Bar. 4.3; 32.2–4; II Esd. 7.26; 8.52–53; 10.44–59; 13.36 and also Gal. 4.26; Heb. 12.22; Rev. 3.12; 21.2, 10). Glimpses of the heavenly Jerusalem have been given beforehand to Abraham and Moses (II Bar. 4.4–5), and the apocalyptic seer himself sometimes claims to have seen what is yet to be revealed (cf. II Esd. 10.26f.; Rev. 21.2ff.). But its final revelation is reserved by God until after the final judgment when that which has been kept hidden in heaven will at last be made known.

Behind this picture of re-creation and redemption, then, is the strong conviction that God's purpose, which embraces the life of the whole created universe, will at last reach its glorious fulfilment. The powers of wickedness will be routed and creation itself will share in the salvation of God.

XI

THE MESSIANIC KINGDOM

I. THE IDEA OF THE KINGDOM

THE EXPRESSION 'THE kingdom of God' or 'the kingdom of heaven', so common in the New Testament, is not to be found anywhere in the Old Testament or in the apocalyptic writings. Nevertheless, the *idea* of the kingdom, in which the sovereignty of God is yet to be revealed, is basic to the teaching of both bodies of literature. Moreover, although much is said about the coming of a messianic kingdom in which the fortunes of Israel, or a remnant within Israel, would be restored and the surrounding nations judged, the figure of the Messiah is frequently absent, *i.e.* the Messiah and the messianic concept are not always or necessarily found together.[1] In the apocalyptic writings, as indeed in the Old Testament itself, the coming of the kingdom marks the great climax of history. The apocalyptists are interested, not so much in the process of history, as in the goal of history which, to them, is the kingdom. Or rather, they are interested in the course of history in the measure in which it leads to its completion and fulfilment in the kingdom. The Gentile kingdoms, like the Greek supremacy of the Seleucids and Ptolemies which seemed so overwhelming and terrible, are shown as 'phases in a world process whose end is the kingdom of God'.[2] There is an inevitability about the course of history because there is absolute certainty about the establishment of the kingdom of God. This conviction is based on their faith in God who 'ruleth in the kingdom of men and giveth it to whomsoever he will' (Dan. 4.17). It gives both meaning and purpose to life as they know it, with all its oppression

[1] See further p. 309.

[2] E. Bevan, *Jerusalem under the High Priests*, 1920, p. 86.

and suffering, and offers a solution to the mystery of God's dealings with his people Israel.

2. THE KINGDOM ON THIS EARTH

It has been pointed out above[1] that the dualistic view of the world, characteristic of much of the apocalyptic literature, finds expression in a doctrine of two ages in which 'this age' is set over against 'the age to come'. 'The age to come', however, is understood in different ways in different writings. In the earlier stages of this literature the idea prevailed that the messianic kingdom or Golden Age would come upon earth as the final act of history. This would be preceded by a judgment in which God and/or his Messiah would rout evildoers and punish the enemies of his people. In some cases the dead, or a portion of them, would be raised to life in resurrection to share in this kingdom which would be eternal. At this stage of writing men were not concerned to look at anything which might lie beyond the kingdom itself. It was an end in itself. This was the climax of history in which the blessings of God, both material and spiritual, would be their portion. It was the religious and political fulfilment of their national history. The picture of this coming kingdom might be idealized; nevertheless, it belonged essentially to this world. Because the kingdom was eternal or of unmeasured or immeasurable duration, it was in effect at this stage synonymous with 'the age to come', although this latter phrase is to be found only in the later writings.[2]

An example of this is given in the **Book of Daniel**. There it is said that 'the God of heaven shall set up a kingdom, which shall never be destroyed, nor shall the sovereignty thereof be left to another people; but it shall break in pieces and consume all these kingdoms, and it shall stand for ever' (2.44). Its sudden appearing is likened to a stone 'cut out without hands' (2.34) hurtling down a mountainside to smash in pieces a great image representing the mighty kingdoms of the earth (2.31ff.). It is a kingdom for whose coming God himself is responsible and in which his sovereignty will be acknowledged by 'all the peoples, nations and languages' (7.14); all the peoples of the earth will serve him (7.27). It is to be given to 'the saints of the Most High' who will bear rule in it with the full authority of God (7.13, 18, 27); it is an earthly kingdom in which the surviving members

[1] See pp. 266ff.
[2] Cf. G. H. Dalman, *The Words of Jesus*, English trans., 1902, p. 151.

of the nation will share together with some of the more illustrious dead who will be raised by resurrection to take part in it (12.2). This kingdom, unlike any that have gone before, will be an everlasting kingdom in which evil of every kind will be destroyed (7.18, 27).

In **I Enoch 6–36** the coming of the messianic kingdom is preceded by 'the day of the great judgment' in which not only wicked men (22.10–11; 27.2) but also Azazel, demons and fallen angels will be punished or destroyed (10.6; 16.1; 19.1). Reference is made in 22.13 to a resurrection and it is at least implied that, as in Daniel, righteous men will be raised to take part in the kingdom together with those who are still alive. The description of the blessings of the kingdom shows quite clearly that it is to be a Golden Age here upon the earth. The righteous 'shall live till they beget thousands of children, and all the days of their youth and their old age they shall complete in peace' (10.17, cf. 25.6). The earth will be cleansed of all defilement and sin and from all oppression by their enemies (10.20ff., cf. 25.6). All the Gentiles will become righteous and worship God (10.21). The soil will produce abundant crops so that 'each measure (of seed) shall bear a thousand, and each measure of olives shall yield ten presses of oil' (10.19). Jerusalem, with its holy Temple, will be the centre of the kingdom (25.5). There God will plant the tree of life that the righteous may eat thereof and be glad (25.4ff.). But the blessings of the kingdom are not devoid of ethical content, for in it 'truth and peace shall be associated together . . . throughout all the generations of men' (11.2).

The writer of **I Enoch 83–90** is less sensuous in his conception of the kingdom than the author of 6–36, but the ground-plan to be found here is essentially the same as that to be found there and in the Book of Daniel. God, we are told, smites the Gentiles in their final assault against Israel (90.18). Thereafter he sets up his throne on the earth and judges all those, angels and men, who have done evil (90.20–27). The city of Jerusalem, as in the previous section, is to be the centre of the new kingdom. But here it is not simply a purified city; it is an entirely new city set up by God to replace the old and on its original site (90.28f.).[1] The surviving Gentiles become subservient to Israel (90.30). Those who have been dispersed are

[1] For the idea of a new Jerusalem brought by God from heaven see further II Bar. 32.2; II Esd. 7.26; 13.16; Rev. 21.2, 10. This hope is based on certain Old Testament prophecies such as Ezek. 40–48; Isa. 54.11, 12; 60.1ff.; Hag. 2.7ff.; Zech. 2.6–13.

gathered together and those who have been slain are raised in resurrection to take their place in the kingdom (90.33). The Messiah then appears, into whose likeness the righteous are transformed (90.37f.), and to whom all the Gentiles make petition.

In the **Testaments of the XII Patriarchs** the Messiah has a significant part to play in the coming of the kingdom. He makes war against the enemies of Israel and against Beliar whose captives he sets free (Test. of Dan 5.10–11); he then binds Beliar (Test. of Levi 18.12) and casts him into the fire (Test. of Jud. 25.3). There is a resurrection of certain Old Testament heroes and of the twelve patriarchs and then of all men, some to glory and some to shame (Test. of Benj. 10.6–8). Thereafter comes the judgment in which both Israel and the Gentiles receive their due recompense (Test. of Benj. 10.9ff.). The kingdom is set up with its centre in 'the new Jerusalem' as in I Enoch 90 above, and is to the glory of God for ever; this city will no longer suffer desolation nor will Israel be led captive, because God himself will be in the midst of it (Test. of Dan 5.13). The idea of the kingdom, then, is still an earthly one and of eternal duration in whose glories even the Gentiles are permitted to share.

In the **Sibylline Oracles III** it is said that God will send his king, or Messiah, who will lift the curse of war from all mankind (652–6). The people of God will be laden with wealth and will arouse the envy of the Gentiles. These will attack the land and encircle Jerusalem in an attempt to ravage the Temple there (657–72). But God will send his judgment upon them; there will be terrible portents in the heavens, and the earth itself will shake (672–88). Wars will be added to natural catastrophes, and men and beasts will be utterly destroyed (689–701). But God's own people will live in peace around the Temple; God himself will encircle them and free them from all war (702–9). The Gentiles will be so impressed by what they see that, repenting, they will go in procession to the Temple there to ponder his holy law (710–31). The blessings of the kingdom here described consist of abundance of corn, wine and oil and every good thing that the mind of man can imagine; these things will be possible because it will be a time of peace throughout all the earth (741–59). The kingdom which God will establish will be 'for all ages'; into it and to the Temple there men will bring their gifts from many lands (767–74). Here, then, is a picture quite in keeping with Old Testament expectation—an earthly kingdom which will know eternally the blessings of the Lord God and in whose benefits the whole wide world will share. Unlike some other apocalyptic writings of the second century BC this book makes no reference to a resurrection or to the participation of the dead in the glories of the kingdom.

In the **Psalms of Solomon 17** the coming of the kingdom is described in terms of a powerful, militant king who will come and shatter unrighteous rulers, free Jerusalem from their tyranny and thrust out sinners (17.24–27). This mighty ruler, a descendant of David's line (17.23), will gather his people together and rule over them in righteousness (17.28–30). He will divide the land among them and make the heathen nations serve under his yoke (17.30–32). He will purge Jerusalem and make it holy so that nations will come from the ends of the earth bringing exiled Jews with them to see God's glory (17.33–34). In **Ps. of Sol. 18** the same kind of picture is presented and the mighty ruler is identified with God's anointed, *i.e.* the Messiah (18.6). R. H. Charles states that 'the messianic kingdom in the Psalms is apparently of temporary duration, for there is no hint of the righteous dead rising to share in it'.[1] This judgment, however, is rather difficult to substantiate. Although the resurrection is not mentioned in Pss. 17 and 18, there are several references to it in Pss. 1–16, where it is stated that the righteous are raised to 'eternal life'[2] (cf. 3.16; 9.9; 13.3; 14.2, 7). What we have here, then, is the familiar picture of an earthly kingdom, eternal in duration, ruled over by God's Messiah under whom the Gentiles will be made to serve.

A rather different, and much more complicated, picture is presented by the writer of the **Similitudes of Enoch** (**I Enoch 37–71**). At the end of the age the supernatural and pre-existent Son of Man[3] comes to take his place 'on the throne of glory' where he sits as judge (cf. 45.3; 48.2f.; 49.4; 61.8ff.). The dead are raised in resurrection and appear before the Son of Man for judgment together with the angels and the kings of the earth (cf. 51.1ff.; 54.1ff.; 61.5, 8). Sinners and the godless are driven off the earth (cf. 38.3; 41.2; 45.6; 53.1ff.; 54.1ff.), whereupon God transforms the heaven and the earth and makes them both a place of blessing (45.4–5). The kingdom thus established is universal in its scope, for 'all who dwell on the earth and sea and islands shall bring to him gifts and presents and tokens of homage' (53.1, cf. 46.4–6; 52.3f.; 62.5ff.). Like the

[1] *Eschatology*, 2nd ed., 1913, p. 270.

[2] For the significance of this phrase see pp. 369f. [3] See pp. 342, 351.

kingdom of the Son of Man in Daniel, it is everlasting—'the Elect One standeth before the Lord of Spirits, and his glory is for ever and ever, and his might unto all generations' (49.2). The actual setting of the kingdom—in a transformed heaven and earth (45.4–5)—is none too clear. The context of this passage indicates that the throne of the Son of Man is to be set up on the earth where his elect dwell 'that he may be potent and mighty on the earth' (52.4, cf. 45.4). On the other hand the elect are to dwell with the Elect One[1] (cf. 61.4) whose dwelling-place is with the Lord of Spirits in prison (cf. 49.2). This dual character of the kingdom and the obscurity which surrounds it, writes S. Mowinckel, 'is inherent in the nature of the subject, in the superterrestrial logic of the kingdom . . . the writer is dealing with realities of faith which do not belong to the empirical world'. The picture presented here is that of 'the eschatological *communio sanctorum*, the society of the holy, the new, distinctive, eschatological people of God, consisting of both the elect in heaven and the elect on earth'.[2]

3. THE KINGDOM IN HEAVEN

We have seen that, even in the case of those writings where the kingdom is established on this present earth, there is a tendency on the part of some writers to idealize the conception and to view its centre, not as the old Jerusalem, but as a new Jerusalem which is either a purification of the old (*e.g.* I Enoch 6–36) or a replacement of it (*e.g.* I Enoch 83–90). We have seen, too, that in the Similitudes of Enoch this teaching has gone a bit further and the kingdom is now seen to be established not only on a transformed earth but also (and this is something new) in a transformed heaven.

In the **Assumption of Moses**, however, this tendency goes a bit further still. In chapter 10 the writer states that God's kingdom 'will appear throughout all his creation' (10.1). No Messiah is mentioned here, but when God himself goes forth from his throne in heaven the whole earth trembles (10.3–4). Signs and wonders appear in earth and heaven (10.4–6). God punishes the Gentiles and destroys their idols (10.7). His angel takes vengeance on all his enemies (10.2). Satan himself is destroyed and sorrow departs (10.1). The days of Israel's mourning will be ended; she will be exalted 'to the heaven of the stars' and will rejoice to see the sufferings of her foes in Gehenna

[1] This is the probable reading of the text. [2] *Op. cit.*, p. 406.

(10.9–10). There is no resurrection mentioned in this presentation and no earthly kingdom. The whole conception is supramundane and the kingdom is viewed as a kingdom of heaven.

4. A TEMPORARY KINGDOM FOLLOWED BY 'THE AGE TO COME'

In this tendency we can see the influence of the 'new eschatology' with its emphasis on the transcendent and other-worldly and its belief in the doctrine of the two ages. Its effect can be even more clearly seen in certain other writings, moreover, which visualize neither an eternal earthly kingdom nor an immediate heavenly kingdom, but rather a temporary kingdom on earth to be followed by a timeless eternity in heaven. Here, for the first time, a distinction is made between the messianic kingdom and the age to come. The messianic kingdom, which belongs to this present age and marks its glorious climax, comes to an end and gives way to the age to come. No longer do the judgment and the resurrection come at the beginning of the messianic kingdom; they come at its close and inaugurate the final age which is heavenly and eternal and in which all earthly wrongs are set right by the retributive justice of God. Thus in the majority of the later apocalyptic writings especially, the sequence is 'this age' followed by 'the messianic kingdom' followed by 'the age to come'.

This pattern is characteristic of certain later writings, as has been noted, but there is evidence for it also in two much earlier books, I Enoch 91–104 and the Book of Jubilees. **I Enoch 91–104** includes the so-called Apocalypse of Weeks (93.1–10, 91.12–17) which may have been incorporated into the larger work by the author himself or by the editor of the whole book.[1] In the Apocalypse of Weeks world history is divided into ten 'weeks', the first seven of which are now past. These seven weeks are times of iniquity which reach their climax in the seventh week, described as a period of apostasy (93.1–10). At the beginning of the eighth week the messianic kingdom appears and is described as a time of righteousness in which sinners will be delivered into the hands of the righteous (91.12). This kingdom continues from the eighth week till the tenth week. During this time houses are built for the righteous and a Temple for God's

[1] See R. H. Charles, *The Book of Enoch*, 1912, p. 224.

glory (91.12–13). True religion is revealed to all men, sin is banished from the earth, and the world is prepared for judgment (91.14). This great judgment comes at the end of the tenth week. Vengeance will be taken on the angels; there will be the creation of a new heaven in which men will live in goodness and righteousness for all eternity (91.15–17). No resurrection of the body is mentioned here. The transitory kingdom, established on a sinful earth, cannot be the goal of the righteous dead, but only heaven itself.[1] The other chapters within which the Apocalypse of Weeks is set make no reference to a kingdom on earth but to a time of reward or of punishment in the age to come. The righteous will shine 'as the lights of heaven' (104.2) to which their spirits ascend (103.4); the wicked will go down to Sheol and 'be wretched in their great tribulation' (103.6–7).

The evidence of the **Book of Jubilees** is much less clear, but here again we may detect the idea of a temporary kingdom. The author seems to believe that he is living at the very beginning of the messianic kingdom in which God will come to dwell in Zion in a new sanctuary throughout all eternity (1.17, 26, 29). The coming of the kingdom is in no way dramatic or cataclysmic; on the contrary it is gradual. Heaven and earth will be renewed gradually as men themselves grow in spiritual perception (cf. 1.29; 4.26; 23.26–28 and also Isa. 65.17; 66.22). Men will begin to study the laws of God in those days and return to the path of righteousness (23.26); their lives will be prolonged and will reach the age of a thousand years, the span originally planned for them by God (23.27, cf. 4.30); they will live lives of joy and peace, for there will be no Satan or any other evil destroyer to hurt them (23.29). All this evidence seems to suggest the idea of an eternal kingdom on earth (cf. especially 1.17, 18, 26, 29) and is supported by the words of 23.11 which suggest that the judgment comes before the establishment of the kingdom. There is no resurrection referred to and so there is no share for the righteous dead in the earthly kingdom. 'Their bones will rest in the earth and their spirits will have much joy' (23.31) in a blissful eternity. R. H. Charles acknowledges the evidence for an eternal earthly kingdom and a judgment preceding its foundation. Nevertheless, he contends that, by its very nature, its gradual and progressive transformation cannot allow for a judgment at any point in its development. He

[1] The idea of the creation of a new heaven was a familiar one in the Old Testament (cf. Isa. 65.17; 66.22; Ps. 102.26). Belief in the dissolution of the heavens is to be found in Persian thought also.

concludes that the final judgment must come at its close when punishment will be meted out (4.19) to sinful men (4.24), to the fallen angels (5.10) and to Mastema and his evil progeny (10.8).[1]

In **II Enoch** very little is said on the subject of the messianic kingdom, but the information given there is of considerable significance in the light of later developments, especially within Christian circles. God gives Enoch an account of the creation of the world from the beginning right down to the time of Adam's sin (24.1–32.1). In six days God created the heavens and the earth, and the seventh day God blessed because in it he rested from all his labours (32.2, cf. Gen. 2.3). The story of creation gives the key to the duration of the world, for a thousand years in God's sight are but as one day (cf. Ps. 90.4). The world will last 7,000 years (33.1) at the close of which will come 'a time when there is no computation and no end' (33.2). The implication here is that the history of the world will run for 6,000 years and then there will be a 'rest' of 1,000 years when God will establish his kingdom. Here, then, we have the beginnings of a belief in a millennium, in the literal sense of a kingdom which is to last 1,000 years. This idea is to play a significant part in Christian expectation in later years.[2] There is no Messiah mentioned here and no information is given about the nature of the messianic kingdom. But there will be a time of judgment, for just as God came the first time to bless, so he will come a second time to punish (cf. 32.1; 48.1). The righteous will be raised in 'spiritual bodies'[3] to dwell in Paradise, a curious combination of the earthly and the heavenly, 'between corruptibility and incorruptibility' (8.6) wherein 'all corruptible things shall pass away' (65.10).

The nature and identity of the temporary kingdom is more clearly marked in **II Baruch,** although there is a certain lack of consistency in its teaching in this regard.[4] Here again the writer seems to envisage a temporary kingdom on this earth to be followed by an eternity in heaven. In 39.3ff. he describes the rise and fall of four great empires familiar to the reader from the account in Daniel 7. At the time of the

[1] Cf. *The Book of Enoch*, 1902, p. 150, and also M. Testuz, *op. cit.*, p. 169.

[2] Cf. Rev. 20.2–6, where it is said that the saints will reign with Christ for 1,000 years. This same number is given as indicating the duration of the kingdom in the Arabic Version of II Esd. 7.28.

[3] See further pp. 377ff.

[4] We shall assume here the unity of the book, whilst recognizing that the author may well have made use of several different sources. See above, pp. 64f., and compare H. H. Rowley, *op. cit.*, pp. 133ff.

consummation 'the principate of the Messiah will be revealed' (39.7) and the fourth world empire (presumably Rome) will be destroyed. Its leader will be brought before the Messiah for judgment after his hosts have been destroyed and he himself will be put to death (40.1–2). The principate of the Messiah will then stand for ever; his kingdom is on earth and will last as long as the earth endures (40.3). No judgment, apart from that on the nations already mentioned, is directly alluded to in this context, although a final judgment is perhaps implied in 36.11 which points forward to a time of great anguish and torment.

Another section of the book (chs. 53ff.) describes how, after a period of war and natural catastrophes (70.7–8) the Messiah will come and summon all the nations, some of whom he will spare and others destroy (72.2). Thereafter will dawn the age of joy and rest when 'anxiety and anguish and lamentation will pass from amongst men, and gladness will proceed through the whole earth' (73.2). Once again the horizon is limited to this present earth, and the judgment is that of the nations. In chapter 59, however, a judgment other than that of the Gentiles is hinted at; there the writer speaks of 'the mouth of Gehenna' and 'the likeness of future torment' (59.10–11).

Again, in chapters 27ff. the sensuous nature of the kingdom is clearly demonstrated. At the same time it is evident that, although the kingdom is to be set up on earth, it is to be on an earth idealized and transformed to a much greater extent than in the earlier books which present the idea of an eternal this-worldly kingdom. Thus when 'the Messiah will begin to be revealed' (29.3) the earth will produce its fruits on a great scale—'on one vine there will be a thousand branches, and each branch will produce a thousand clusters, and each cluster will produce a thousand grapes, and each grape will produce a cor of wine' (29.5). The winds will bring every morning 'the fragrance of aromatic fruits' and in the evenings the clouds will distil 'the dew of health'; the members of the kingdom will be fed with manna from on high[1] for they have come to 'the consummation of time' (29.7–8). At that time also the great mythical monsters, Behemoth and Leviathan, will be used as food for the righteous in the great 'messianic banquet' (29.4).[2] The messianic

[1] In Ps. 78.25 manna is described as angels' food; cf. Rev. 2.17, 'To him that overcometh will I give of the hidden manna.'

[2] Cf. also II Esd. 6.49f. and see further pp. 124f., 320.

kingdom belongs to this present age and is to last 'until the world of corruption is at an end' (40.3, cf. 21.19). Indeed, it marks the end of corruption (31.5; 44.9) and the beginning of incorruption (43.2; 74.3, cf. 85.5) and is the prelude to 'the new world which does not turn to corruption those who depart to its blessedness' (44.12). It is none too clear what part, if any, the righteous dead play in the messianic kingdom. A hint of this may be given in 30.1–2 which reads, 'When the time of the Messiah is fulfilled, he shall return in glory. Then all who have fallen asleep in him shall rise again.' Some scholars[1] take this to refer to the Messiah's coming to earth, in which case the resurrection is to a share in his earthly kingdom. Others[2] take it to refer to the Messiah's return to heaven at the close of his temporary kingdom, in which case the resurrection is to a life of heavenly bliss (cf. 51.10). In 50.2–4 the dead are raised presumably to a life on earth, for their bodies retain their old physical marks.[3] But on the day of judgment which follows the righteous enter into 'the world which does not die' (51.5). 'For in the height of the world shall they dwell, and they shall be made like unto the angels, and be made equal to the stars, and they shall be changed into every form they desire, from beauty into loveliness, and from light into the splendour of glory' (51.10). In the heavenly Paradise (51.11) they will live a life that is free from evil in a world which ages not (51.16).

The writer of **II Esdras**, like the writer of II Baruch, has also attempted to weave together various strands of apocalyptic tradition concerning the kingdom of God and 'the last things'. The result is not all of one piece or of one consistent pattern. The picture presented, however, is apparently that of a temporary earthly kingdom to be followed by an eternal state in heaven.

The time will come, we are told, when 'the city shall appear that now is not seen' (7.26).[4] The reference here is to the New Jerusalem which is elsewhere associated with Paradise and is established in heaven (cf. 8.52; 10.26f.; 13.26; II Bar. 4.2–6; Rev. 21.2). Here at

[1] *E.g.* B. Violet, *Die Apokalypsen des Esra und des Baruch*, 1924, p. 246, and H. H. Rowley, *op. cit.*, p. 99.

[2] *E.g.* R. H. Charles, *The Apocalypse of Baruch*, 1896, p. 56.

[3] For the nature of the resurrection body see further pp. 374ff.

[4] This is the likely reading of the Greek text. The Latin text, reflected in the R.V. translation, reads 'the bride shall appear . . . that now is withdrawn from the earth'. See W. O. E. Oesterley, *II Esdras*, 1933, p. 70; B. Violet, *op. cit.*, p. 73; L. Gry, *Les dires prophétiques d'Esdras*, vol. I, 1938, p. 147; H. H. Rowley, *op. cit.*, p. 95.

once we are confronted with a distinct incongruity, for the passage as a whole deals with a temporary and earthly kingdom, but this allusion is presumably to an eternal and heavenly Jerusalem. Thereafter the Messiah[1] will be revealed 'with those who are with him' (7.28)—those like Enoch and Elijah, for example, 'who have not tasted death' (6.26).[2] According to one tradition within the book (the so-called 'Eagle Vision', 10.60–12.35) the Messiah (12.32), symbolized as a lion (11.37), destroys the fourth kingdom of Daniel's vision (11.39, cf. Dan. 7.3), symbolized by a three-headed eagle (11.1ff.) which is here interpreted of the Roman Empire.[3] He judges, rebukes and destroys the enemies of God (12.33f.), but his own people 'he will deliver with mercy and . . . will make them joyful until the End come, even the Day of Judgment' (12.34). The kingdom which he sets up is on this earth and is to last for 400 years (7.28).[4] There is no resurrection to mark its inauguration; the righteous dead do not participate in it at all; it is for the surviving righteous in the land (7.28, cf. Pss. of Sol. 17.50). At the end of 400 years the Messiah and all who take part with him in the kingdom will die (7.29). For the next seven days the world is turned into primaeval silence (7.30, cf. Gen. 1.2; II Bar. 3.7–8). At the end of this time the new age will dawn, 'the age which is not yet awake shall be roused, and that which is corruptible shall perish' (7.31). 'The earth', it is said, 'will restore those that sleep in her' (7.32). There will be a general resurrection so that all men may be judged. The great judgment will last for a week of years (7.43) during which period 'the furnace of Gehenna' and 'the Paradise of delight' will be made manifest over against each other (7.36). Nothing specific is said about the setting of the final age, but the picture presented is in keeping with that of the 'new eschatology'. The temporary

[1] The text reads 'my son Jesus', which is a Christian correction. The Versions read, 'my son the Messiah' (Syriac and Arabic) or 'my Messiah' (Ethiopic and Armenian).

[2] According to apocalyptic tradition several other names appear in this list, *e.g.* Jeremiah (II Mac. 2.1ff.; 15.13; Matt. 16.14), Baruch (II Bar. 6.8; 13.1–3; 25.1; 43.2; 46.7; 48.30; 76.1–3) and Moses (*Ant.* IV.viii.48 (326); Matt. 17.3–4; Mark 9.4–5; Luke 9.30–33). See Oesterley, *op. cit.*, p. 56.

[3] The three heads no doubt represent Vespasian, Titus and Domitian. The kingdom is to come during Domitian's reign.

[4] This number is no doubt arrived at by a combination of Ps. 90.15 ('Make us glad according to the days wherein thou hast afflicted us') and Gen. 15.13 ('And they shall afflict them 400 years'), cf. *Sanh.* 99a; *i.e.* the messianic kingdom will last as long as Israel's oppression in Egypt.

earthly kingdom passes and the eternal heavenly kingdom is ushered in. The 'days of the Messiah' give place to 'the age to come'.

Throughout this whole process, from Daniel to II Esdras, we find evidence, then, of a tension between a this-worldly kingdom and an other-worldly kingdom. In the earlier period especially the former of these predominates and even when, in later years, the influence of the latter makes itself increasingly felt it does not oust from people's minds the earlier hope whose roots can be traced back into the ancient prophetic expectations. In their teaching concerning a millennial or a temporary kingdom to be followed, through resurrection and judgment, by 'the age to come' they were expressing a compromise which witnesses to the strength of that traditional faith which looked forward to the establishment of the rule of God not only over his own people in their own land, but also over all people throughout the whole earth.

5. THE SALVATION OF ISRAEL AND THE JUDGMENT OF THE GENTILES

During the inter-testamental period the eschatology of Judaism in general and of apocalyptic in particular was primarily concerned with the salvation of Israel as the people of God. Some of these writers interpreted their beliefs about the last things in terms of the fate of individual souls after death,[1] but in the main their eschatological hopes were predominantly nationalistic. These nationalistic hopes, which found constant expression from the time of the Maccabees right down to the fall of Jerusalem in AD 70, were projected, as it were, into the future. The Jewish nation, a kingdom of this world, fell heir to the kingdom of God. In a number of apocalyptic books a distinction is made between 'the righteous' and 'the wicked' on purely ethical grounds without any reference to nation or race (*e.g.* I Enoch 91–108); but for the most part the tendency is to identify 'the righteous' with Israel and 'the wicked' with the Gentiles. In the coming kingdom the Gentiles will witness the triumph and vindication of God's people. 'The kingdom and the dominion, and the greatness of the kingdoms under the whole heaven' will be given to 'the people of the saints of the Most High' (Dan. 7.27). The *whole* Jewish nation, moreover, will share in this inheritance and not

[1] See p. 367.

simply the three (or two and a half) tribes of which, it was believed, the existing nation was then composed;[1] the 'lost tribes' of the ancient northern kingdom will be restored and take their place in the final triumph of the true Israel of God.

But although the apocalyptists are more or less agreed concerning the future destiny of Israel, there is far less agreement concerning the fate of the Gentiles. This holds good of Judaism in general and indeed of much Old Testament prophecy of the post-exilic period. Between the years 170 BC and AD 70, or even later, Judaism showed itself to be a virile missionary faith, seeking to win not only renegade Jews but also Gentile sinners to faith in the true God. Jewish 'missionaries' of this time could no doubt find ample justification for their action in the writings of the Old Testament prophets. The hope was there envisaged that the day would come when the coastlands would wait for God and in his arm they would trust (Isa. 51.5); the nations would look to him and be saved, for there was none else beside him (Isa. 45.20, 22). Gentiles would beg the exiled Jews to let them return with them to Jerusalem because God was with them (Zech. 8.23). Jerusalem's gates would be open continually to receive the wealth of the nations (Isa. 60.11). The holy Temple would be called God's 'house of prayer for all peoples' (Isa. 56.7). The time would come when God's blessing would be shared not only with 'Israel, my inheritance', but also with 'Egypt, my people' and 'Assyria, the work of my hands' (Isa. 19.25).

But in other prophecies the Gentiles continued to be presented as the traditional enemies of Israel who would face the awful wrath of God (Isa. 63.1–6) and be destroyed by his fury (Isa. 34.1ff.). The Lord would have 'a controversy with the nations' and destroy them utterly (Jer. 25.29–38). The day of the Lord would be 'a day of vengeance that he may avenge him of his adversaries' (Jer. 46.10). The Gentiles are presented as the very incarnation of evil (Zech. 14.1ff.) or identified with the great universal power of evil, at once cosmic and earthly, whose doom is writ (Ezek. 38–39). Even when

[1] Cf. Test. of Benj. 9.2; II Bar. 62.5; 77.19; 78.1; II Esd. 13.40. Information varies concerning the number of the 'lost tribes'. There are ten according to the Latin Version of II Esd. 13.40; nine and a half according to II Bar. 62.5; 77.19; 78.1 and the Syriac, Arabic and Armenian Versions and certain Ethiopic MSS of II Esd. 13.40; nine according to other Ethiopic MSS of II Esd. 13.40 and also the Ascension of Isa. 3.2. The remaining tribes, who make up the existing Jewish nation, are identified as Judah, Benjamin and Levi, cf. Hebrew Test. of Napht. 3 and *War of the Sons of Light against the Sons of Darkness* I.2f.; III.14; IV.15.

they are spared and given a place in the future age of blessedness, they are forced to do so under threat of dire punishment (Zech. 14). Even though God invites 'all peoples' to share in his great banquet (Isa. 25.6–8), nevertheless 'the kings of the earth' are cast into the pit (Isa. 24.22) and the great world-powers are destroyed (Isa. 27.1ff.).

These diverse Old Testament prophecies are reflected in the apocalyptic writings of the inter-testamental period. The judgments expressed there range from a liberal universalism, in which the nations share with Israel the blessings of the kingdom, to their complete destruction and the assigning of them to hell fire. The former attitude is more characteristic of the earlier apocalyptic writings; the latter is found in certain others which no doubt reflect dark days of persecution, particularly after the fall of Jerusalem in AD 70.

A generous view of the Gentiles is taken in certain books dating from the second century BC. This was a time of danger and persecution for the Jewish nation—of danger from foreign culture, of persecution from foreign armies. In this period of bitter hostility and recrimination, these writers were supremely confident that this state of affairs would not long continue and that the day would speedily come when the Gentiles would acknowledge the glory of Israel and worship the true and only God. According to I Enoch 10.21, for example, all the Gentiles will become righteous and offer to God their adoration and worship. Indeed, the Jewish nation is seen to have a vital part to play in the conversion of the Gentiles. In the Sibylline Oracles III it is described as 'a guide to life for all mankind' (195f.), through whose mediation the nations will make their way in procession to God's Temple there to ponder his law and supplicate the Eternal King (716ff., cf. 725ff.); from every land they will bring frankincense and gifts to the house of the great God (772ff.); in the coming kingdom they will have a share in the blessings that it brings (740). This same attitude is to be found also in the Testaments of the XII Patriarchs, where it is clearly stated that the twelve tribes of Israel will at last be gathered to the glorious Temple together with 'all the Gentiles' (Test. of Benj. 9.2; 10.5, 9f.; cf. Rev. 21.24ff.; 22.2). In the priesthood of the Messiah of Levi 'the Gentiles shall be multiplied in knowledge upon the earth, and enlightened through the grace of the Lord' (Test. of Levi 18.9). The angel Michael intercedes not only for 'the nation of Israel', but also for 'all the righteous' (Test. of Levi 5.7). In one place (Test. of Napht. 8.3) it is stated that 'the righteous of the Gentiles' will be gathered together when God comes 'to save the race of Israel'; but elsewhere in the book the reference is simply to 'all the nations' for whose ultimate salvation God deeply cares. It is the duty of Israel so to live that they will win the Gentiles (Test. of Levi 14.4ff.). The law of God was given not for Israel only, but 'to lighten every man' (Test. of Levi 14.4, cf. II Esd. 7.21); thus God has willed the salvation of the Gentiles as well as the Jews. In the messianic kingdom all men everywhere will come to acknowledge him as the only true God.[1]

In certain other apocalyptic writings, however, there is a hardening of attitude towards the Gentiles and a narrowing down of that universalistic outlook which characterized some of the earlier works just considered. Here the enemies of Israel are destroyed, whilst those who have not provoked Israel, or having done so have repented, are given a servile place in the kingdom as the bondslaves of the people of God (cf. Isa. 61.5ff.). This attitude is expressed by the writer of II Baruch in these words: 'My Messiah . . . will both summon all the nations, and some of them he will spare and some of them he will slay. These things therefore will come upon the nations which are to be spared by him. Every nation which knows not Israel, and has not trodden down the seed of Jacob, shall indeed be spared. And this because some out of every nation will be subjected to thy people. But all those who have ruled over you, or have known you, shall be given up to the sword' (72.2–6). Here again it is the hostile nations that are destroyed (cf. 40.1ff.), and the neutral nations that are spared (cf. 68.5).

This same pattern appears also in three other books of a much earlier date—Daniel, I Enoch 83–90, 91–104, and the Psalms of Solomon. In Daniel the coming of the kingdom brings the destruction of the Gentiles (2.44, cf. 7.11f.); but when it is established 'all

[1] For a full note on the universalism of the writer of the Testaments of the XII Patriarchs see R. H. Charles, *Testaments of the XII Patriarchs*, 1908, pp. 210ff. He lists the following passages where the salvation of the Gentiles is foretold: Test. of Sim. 6.5; Test. of Levi 2.11; 4.4; 5.7; 8.14; 14.4; 18.9; Test. of Jud. 25.5; Test. of Dan 6.2, 7; Test. of Napht. 8.3; Test. of Asher 7.3; Test. of Benj. 9.2; 10.5. In certain other passages references to the Gentiles, it is claimed, are interpolations. These are Test. of Sim. 7.2; Test. of Jos. 19.11; Test. of Benj. 3.8; 11.2. Three other passages are said to be out of their context or else are corrupt: Test. of Jud. 24.6; Test. of Zeb. 9.8; Test. of Sim. 6.4. This last reference, it would seem, is rejected rather arbitrarily because it is in conflict with 4.4 (this is given as 6.4 in Charles's text) and all the rest of the Testaments. In this connection it is of interest to note the bitterness of the Jews to the Samaritans in Test. of Levi 7.

the peoples, nations and languages' will serve 'the saints of the Most High' (7.14). Again in the Book of Enoch a sword is given to the righteous who execute judgment on the oppressors (91.12); or God smites the earth which swallows up the hostile Gentiles like Korah and his followers of old (90.18, cf. Num. 16.31ff.). As a result the neutral nations look to the path of righteousness (91.14); they are converted and do homage to the people of God (90.30, 33, 35, cf. Isa. 14.2; 66.12, 19–21). In the Psalms of Solomon the Messiah is the instrument of God's punishment on the Gentiles. With the coming of the kingdom he 'shall destroy the godless nations with the word of his mouth' (17.17), and those that remain will be made to serve under his yoke and will come from the ends of the earth to see his glory (17.32ff.). The Gentiles, then, have a place in the future kingdom, but it is in complete subservience to Israel, the true people of God.

A further step is taken in several other apocalyptic writings where an even harsher view is expressed concerning the future destiny of the Gentiles. There they are condemned simply on the ground that they are Gentiles. The contrast between 'the righteous' and 'the wicked' is essentially the contrast between the Jewish nation and the other nations of the earth. Ethical considerations take second place to ethnic qualifications. The fate which was reserved, in certain other writings, for the sworn enemies of Israel is now meted out to all Gentiles. That fate is eternal torment or else annihilation. Either way they have no share at all in the blessings of the messianic kingdom. The writer of the Book of Jubilees, for example, expresses his bitter hatred of the Gentiles (cf. 24.28ff.) who are to be driven out of Palestine (23.30, cf. 50.5). God has put them under the authority of angels who will lead them astray and effect their destruction (15.31). Again, in the Assumption of Moses the enemies of Israel (10.10) are identified with the Gentiles (10.7) and are consigned to the flames of Gehenna (10.10).[1]

But this bitterness towards the Gentiles finds its fullest expression in two other books, the Similitudes of Enoch and II Esdras, although in both there is a lack of consistency which is, of course, characteristic of apocalyptic teaching as a whole. In I Enoch 50.2–5 it is said that the righteous will triumph over the wicked and as a result the Gentiles will repent and be saved. Those who remain unrepentant

[1] This is the reading of the emended text proposed by R. H. Charles, cf. *Assumption of Moses*, 1897, p. 43.

will be shown no mercy, but will utterly perish.[1] Elsewhere in this same book, however, little or no hope is held out to any of them. All who dwell upon the earth, at the time of the judgment, will bring to the Elect One 'gifts and presents and tokens of homage' (53.1), but these will be of no avail; they will be destroyed and be banished from the face of the earth and will perish for ever and ever (53.2). None will be saved and none will be able to escape (52.7). Punishment is meted out especially to the Gentile kings and rulers (cf. 38.4, 5; 46.4–8; 48.8–10; 53.5; 54.2; 55.4; 62.1, 3, 6, 9–11; 63.1–12) who will be removed from their thrones and be filled with shame, and 'worms shall be their bed' (46.4–6). They will be filled with anguish when they look upon the Son of Man and will fall down before him supplicating him for mercy; but their prayers will be of no avail. God will deliver them up to the angels who will execute vengeance upon them so that they become a spectacle to the righteous who will rejoice to see their fearful plight (62.1ff.).

Somewhat the same picture is presented also in II Esdras. Once again it is suggested that some of the Gentiles at least will be spared and will submit themselves to God and to his people Israel. As a sign of their submission they will bring in to God's Messiah exiled Jews as an oblation (13.13, cf. Pss. of Sol. 17.34 and also Isa. 66. 18–20). But for the most part the writer contemplates nothing less than the utter destruction of the nations. The law of God, given by God to the Jews, had also been offered to the Gentiles; in it they had been shown what they should do to live and what they should observe to avoid punishment (7.21, cf. Test. of Levi 14.4). But they rejected the law and so brought punishment upon themselves. On the Day of Judgment the nations will be raised from the dead and will be condemned to eternal torment because they have denied the Lord and have despised his commandments. The pit of torment and hell is reserved for them (7.36–38, cf. Matt. 25.31f.). The judgment, however, is not only ethnic, it is also ethical in character; first and foremost it is a world-judgment and then it is individual.[2]

Elsewhere in this same book, in the so-called Vision of the Man

[1] Charles remarks that this passage is inconsistent with the rest of the Similitudes and belongs to the same sphere of thought as chs. 83–90 and 91–104. Accordingly he would regard it as an interpolation. This need not necessarily be so. Allowance must be made for such inconsistency of thought in a writing of this kind.

[2] See further pp. 382f.; cf. G. H. Box, *II Esdras*, 1912, p. 124, and P. Volz, *Jüdische Eschatologie von Daniel bis Akiba*, 1903, p. 85.

from the Sea (13.1–58), it is said that in the last days 'an innumerable multitude' will be gathered together to make war against God's Messiah (13.5, 34). These represent the united armies of the heathen nations who, according to ancient tradition (cf. Ezek. 38–39), would attack Israel and be defeated at the inauguration of the messianic kingdom. The Messiah fights against them, not with human weapons, but by supernatural powers. 'A fiery stream' issues out of his mouth (13.10, cf. Dan. 7.10; I Enoch 62.2; Pss. of Sol. 17.27)[1] which 'burned them all up, so that suddenly nothing more was to be seen of the innumerable multitude save only dust of ashes and smell of smoke' (13.11). Having destroyed his enemies, the Messiah then gathers together 'another multitude which was peaceable' (13.12, 39, cf. Pss. of Sol. 17.28 and Isa. 11.12). These are the ten tribes which had been led away captive by the Assyrians (13.40). They now share with their brethren in the other tribes the blessings of the kingdom.[2]

The bitterness here expressed by the writer of II Esdras against the Gentiles is to be understood against the background of persecution which the Jewish nation as a whole had to suffer, first in the time of the Seleucids and then in the time of the Romans. It reflects the troubled years following the capture of Jerusalem in AD 70 and is in keeping with the trend in Judaism generally. From this time forward, and especially from the close of the first century AD, the harsher view prevailed and the universalism of the earlier years was gradually replaced by that spirit which could be satisfied only with the annihilation of all the other nations of the earth.[3]

[1] This picture is no doubt based on Isa. 11.4. [2] See above, pp. 297f.

[3] Cf. P. Volz, *op. cit.*, pp. 322–5, and F. Weber, *Jüdische Theologie*, 1897, pp. 364–9, 376.

XII

THE TRADITIONAL MESSIAH

I. THE TERM 'MESSIAH' AND ITS OLD TESTAMENT BACKGROUND

TO JEWS AND Christians alike the term 'Messiah' is a word full of strong overtones derived from a long history of religious belief. It is a 'loaded' word full of preconceived notions concerning Jewish eschatological hopes and Christian 'messianic' expectations. It is easy, but entirely misleading, to read back into the Old Testament for example those contents of meaning which the word came to have in later Judaism and in the Christian Church. In these latter references the term 'Messiah' is used as a title or even a proper name to designate an eschatological figure who is associated with 'the latter end of the days' and with the coming of the kingdom of God. As such it is a technical term and can properly be written with a capital 'M' to distinguish it from the earlier Old Testament use of the word which is without such nuances.

In the Old Testament the Hebrew word *mašiaḥ* (Greek *messias*) is strictly an adjective meaning 'anointed' which, with the definite article, signifies 'the anointed one'. Basically it indicates one who has been set apart by God for the fulfilment of some special purpose. As such the expression is used most often in connection with the kings of Israel who, on their succession to the throne, were anointed with oil. This was a sacred act in which the king was set apart as a 'holy' man by the priest to the office of kingship, an office which possessed priestly and sacral functions. As God's 'anointed' the king ruled over his people on behalf of God himself. Thus the name 'Yahweh's anointed' is given to Samuel (I Sam. 24.6, 10; 26.16; II Sam. 1.14, 16), to David (II Sam. 19.21; 23.1), to Zedekiah (Lam. 4.10), and in general to all the kings of David's line. In one most unusual instance it is given even to the Persian king, Cyrus (Isa. 45.1), who, according to the writer, was called by God and set apart for the special purpose of restoring Yahweh's people to their own land.

In the post-exilic period, when the monarchy had ceased to exist, the sacral functions which had been assumed by the kings in pre-exilic times were taken over by the priesthood. In course of time the High Priest assumed the status, if not the name, of king. It is not surprising that, on his assuming office, he also was anointed with oil (cf. Ex. 29.7; Lev. 8.12; Ps. 133.2). There are indications that this act of anointing was carried out even in the case of priests other than the High Priest (cf. Ex. 29.21; Lev. 8.30); but special mention is made of the latter as 'Yahweh's anointed' or 'the Anointed One' as the expression was previously used of the king himself. Reference to this is made, for example, in Zech. 4.14, where Zerubbabel, Jehoiachin's grandson and so a descendant of David, and Joshua the High Priest are called 'the two sons of oil'.[1]

In I Kings 19.16 the account is given of the anointing of a prophet. Elijah is there bidden to anoint three men with the express purpose of wiping out the House of Omri. These men are Hazael king of Syria, Jehu king of Israel, and Elisha the prophet. This last reference may indicate a wider use of anointing in the setting apart of prophets, although this is by no means certain. The words of Isa. 61.1, 'Yahweh has anointed me', etc., are probably to be understood in this way. The anointing of prophets is referred to again in one other rather curious passage. In Ps. 105.15 (= I Chron. 16.22) God says, 'Touch not mine anointed ones, and do my prophets no harm.' The reference here is to the patriarchs of old who, according to late biblical and post-biblical usage, are described as prophets.

It is clear, then, from what has been said above that the 'anointed one' in the Old Testament has reference to an actual historical person and in particular (especially in pre-exilic times) to the kings of Israel who reigned as the earthly representatives of Yahweh himself.

In the prophetic books, however, we find a significant development which was to have a most important bearing on the future 'messianic hope', even though in this connection the word *mašiaḥ* itself does not appear. Allusion is made there to the coming of a

[1] Another suggestion is that 'the two sons of oil' may refer to two priests, the High Priest and his deputy.

Golden Age, the future kingdom of God, in which the fortunes of Israel, or a remnant within Israel, will be restored, the surrounding nations judged and an era of justice and peace ushered in. In a number of these prophecies this future age of blessedness is ruled over by an ideal leader who, like the anointed king of Israel, also represents Yahweh. There was a strong tradition, recorded for example in God's promise to David in II Samuel 7 and fostered by the prophets of the south,[1] that the ruler of the coming kingdom would be of the House of David. He is described as 'a prince' or 'a righteous branch' or 'David' or 'a scion of David' or 'a shoot out of the stock of Jesse'. The allusion, then, is to an actual historical kingship, with particular reference to the restoration of the Davidic line. This hope persisted after the fall of Jerusalem in 587 BC. Indeed, there is good reason to believe that the majority of these references may belong to the post-exilic period; even here, despite the disappearance of the monarchy (or perhaps because of it) the thought is still that of 'a scion of David's line' who will be raised up by God to rule over the coming kingdom.

In some of these passages the writer has in mind a contemporary king. In Hag. 2.23, for example, Zerubbabel is described as the chosen of Yahweh and is envisaged as the promised ruler of the coming kingdom. Even more explicit is the reference in Zech. 3.8 and 6.12 where Zerubbabel is described as 'the Branch'; no doubt his symbolic name ('a shoot out of Babylon') would facilitate his association with the hope of a restoration of David's line. But this hope of restoration in the person of Zerubbabel came to nothing, and many years were to pass by before it again came to be associated with a contemporary figure.

There are other passages, however, where the historical setting of the future hope is less apparent and in which the ideal character of the coming kingdom and the ideal characteristics of the coming ruler are stressed.[2] This ideal ruler is of the stock of David (Isa. 11.1ff.,

[1] II Sam. 7, recording Nathan's prophecy concerning David's House that it would be 'established for ever', is no doubt post-exilic in its present form (cf. H. P. Smith, *The Books of Samuel*, ICC, 1899, pp. 297f., and R. H. Pfeiffer, *Introduction to the Old Testament*, 1941, pp. 370f.). Nathan may well have made such promises to David at his anointing; but from the literary point of view Mowinckel, for example, describes it as 'a faithful cult-historical reflection of a common cultic situation' (*op. cit.*, p. 100, n. 3).

[2] Cf. especially Isa. 9.6f.; 11.1f.; Jer. 23.5ff.; Micah 5.2ff.; Zech. 9.9. The dating of these prophecies, whether pre-exilic or post-exilic, does not concern us here.

etc.); he will be invested with superhuman power and be enabled to overcome his enemies (Isa. 9.6ff.); he will bring peace to God's people (Isa. 9.6; Zech. 9.9) whose fortunes will be changed when he comes to rule in the strength of Yahweh his God (Micah 5.4); he will rule with justice and righteousness (Isa. 9.7; 11.1ff.; Jer. 23.5f.) and will be the saviour of the poor (Zech. 9.9); God will give him the kingdom and his throne will be established for ever (II Sam. 7.13, 16).

Those passages which refer to the ideal leader of the coming kingdom are popularly known as 'messianic prophecies'. But this is a question-begging expression, for the fact is that in none of them is he ever given the name 'Messiah' nor indeed is the word *mašiaḥ* used with reference to him. Where the term *mašiaḥ* does appear in these writings it refers, not to this ideal ruler, but to some reigning king. There has been much dispute among scholars concerning the use of *mašiaḥ* in the so-called 'messianic Psalms' where it apparently refers to the ideal king of the future kingdom. But Mowinckel and others have shown good reason to believe that in these psalms we are dealing, not with a future eschatological figure, but rather with a reigning king of Israel. These are, Mowinckel would conclude, 'royal psalms' to be used at the enthronement of the king in Jerusalem on the occasion of the festival appointed for that purpose. They are written in the language of the cult and have to do with the reigning monarch who is described as the Lord's 'anointed' in keeping with regular Old Testament usage.

The word *mašiaḥ*, then, is never used in the Old Testament as a technical term for the 'Messiah', nor is it used with reference to the future ideal king. This association belongs to the literature of later Judaism and plays a significant, if limited, part in the writings of the apocalyptists. The expression 'Messiah', as used in later Judaism and in the New Testament, is derived from the Old Testament word *mašiaḥ*, descriptive of the ancient kings of Israel; but the meaning and content of the two words are very different. As we shall see, even in its technical sense the word retained much of its national and political association; but in course of time, as a result of the development of religious ideas within Judaism itself and under the influence of eschatological ideas from outside, there grew up a conception of the Messiah different in many respects from the 'messianic' expectations of the Old Testament Scriptures.

2. THE FIGURE OF THE MESSIAH IN THE APOCALYPTIC LITERATURE

The figure of the Messiah as it appears in the apocalyptic literature is to be viewed against the extremely complex background of eschatological beliefs which, as we have seen, characterized Jewish religious thought during the inter-testamental period. Partly at least through the influence of Persian ideas and in particular the dualistic view of the world in which 'this age' was set over against 'the age to come', there grew up in Judaism an eschatology markedly different from the future hope expressed in the prophetic writings. Already there had been set up a tension between this-worldly, national and political elements on the one hand, and other-worldly, universal and transcendent elements on the other hand which could not easily be resolved. It is in connection with these two 'eschatologies' that the name 'Messiah' at last appears in the apocalyptic writings as a technical term for the eschatological figure chosen by God to play a leading part in the coming kingdom. In each case a leader appears whose nature and function correspond to that future hope with which he is associated. The position is summed up by Mowinckel in these words: 'The Messianic conceptions of certain circles produced the picture of a Messiah who is predominantly this-worldly, national and political, whereas the views of other circles produced the picture of a predominantly transcendental, eternal and universal Messiah . . . these two complexes of ideas are *in part* represented by different names, "Messiah" and "Son of Man".'[1] In some writings these two conceptions are clearly distinguished; in others they are brought together; yet nowhere are they completely fused. Together they form part of that complex eschatology which is the background of the inter-testamental literature and also of the New Testament faith.

In this chapter we shall examine the idea of the Messiah as it appears in certain apocalyptic writings, in so far as it can be distinguished from that other originally distinct, yet related concept, the Son of Man. This figure, it will be seen, has much in common with the Old Testament picture of the ideal leader of the coming kingdom who will deliver his people from the power of their enemies—the Babylonians, the Persians, the Seleucids, the Romans—and rule over them as king. Despite the many eschatologizing features which come to be associated with his name, the Messiah is, in one strand of

[1] *Op. cit.*, p. 467.

messianic expectation at least, essentially a historical and political figure.

The traditional Old Testament hope, then, of the coming of a 'messianic' prince as the leader of the coming kingdom persists in this literature. But just as in the Old Testament the ideal leader is not necessarily or always associated with the Golden Age, so in the apocalyptic literature the Messiah is not indispensable to the eschatological kingdom. Indeed, in a fairly considerable number of writings of the period (apocalyptic and otherwise) in which the messianic hope is in the forefront, the figure of the Messiah is not even mentioned. One example of this is the Book of Daniel. In 9.25, 26 we read, indeed, of 'an anointed one, a prince' and of another 'anointed one (who) shall be cut off'; but in neither case is the reference to the messianic prince of popular expectation. In the former case it is the High Priest Joshua who is indicated, and in the latter it is another High Priest, Onias III, who was put to death in the days of the Maccabees. Similarly the figure of the Messiah is absent from I and II Maccabees, Tobit, the Wisdom of Solomon, Judith, Ben Sira, Jubilees, I Enoch 1–36 and 91–104, the Assumption of Moses, I Baruch and II Enoch.

It is surely an overstatement to say with S. H. Hooke that 'with one or two unimportant exceptions, the Messianic element is central' in Jewish apocalyptic.[1] On the other hand it would be wrong to regard it as no more than an accidental or incidental element in the development of apocalyptic eschatology. The whole idea is too deeply rooted in the traditional lore of Hebrew prophecy to dismiss it as lightly as this. But at best the Messiah plays a secondary role in the majority of these writings. It is quite conceivable, of course, that a writer like the author of the Book of Daniel could entertain the idea of a ruler at the head of the coming kingdom even though he makes no mention of any such figure; but the very fact that no such mention is made clearly indicates the relatively insignificant part this figure plays in his thoughts. These particular writers apparently see no need for a human Messiah, for the coming kingdom is the work of God himself. This is suggested even in certain other apocalyptic writings where the figure of the Messiah actually does appear. Sometimes, for example, he appears only *after* God himself has established the kingdom (cf. I Enoch 90), or the period of his rule is said to be for a strictly limited period (cf. II Esdras). The emphasis, then, is not so much on the

[1] *The Siege Perilous*, 1956, p. 129.

Messiah and his ushering in of the kingdom as it is on the kingdom itself as a mighty act of God.

From the political angle this, of course, is not really surprising, for the fact is that during the Persian period the hope of a future leader of David's line had fallen more and more into the background. A number of factors were responsible for this. One was the cessation of the monarchy and the rise in significance and power of the priests and the House of Zadok;[1] another was the decline of prophecy, although the influence of the older prophetic books would continue to be felt; a third was the political situation in which the Persian authorities would rightly regard the continuance of such hope in the restoration of the royal house to be a menace to the security of the State. The result was that emphasis came to be laid increasingly on the kingly rule of God himself in the coming kingdom and on the prime necessity of keeping his holy Law.

3. THE LEVITIC MESSIAH

But the time was to come when, once again, men's hearts were stirred with hopes that at long last the messianic age was about to be realized and that God would raise up one who would be the instrument of his purpose. There are indications of this during the period of the Maccabees and Hasmoneans who were descendants, not of the House of David, but of the House of Levi. In particular the hopes of the people came to be centred in Simon, brother and successor of Judas Maccabaeus. In the year 142 BC Simon was acknowledged by

[1] An interesting side-light on the increasing sacerdotal interest in religion is provided by a late addition to the Book of Jeremiah. This is 33.14–16, which repeats the Jeremianic oracle in 23.5–6 concerning 'David a righteous branch'. This shows a continuation of the Davidic hope at the date when this later oracle was written. But even more revealing is a significant variation in the text. Whereas in Jeremiah's oracle the name 'Yahweh our righteousness' is given to the ideal Davidic king (23.6), in the later oracle it is given to Judah or Jerusalem (33.16). It is further asserted that the House of David will never lack Levitical priests to sacrifice continually. There is no suggestion here, of course, of a leader other than one from the House of David, but it is interesting to observe the setting of this 'messianic' hope in 'the temple piety of later Judaism through the combination of the Messiah with the Levitical priesthood' (H. Ringgren, *The Messiah in the Old Testament*, 1956, p. 36).

We note, too, the way in which Ben Sira, at the beginning of the second century BC, gives pride of place to the priesthood. 'Aaron and his descendants are the subjects of long and glowing eulogiums (45.6–24). . . . On the other hand Sirach depreciates the kingly dynasty' (R. H. Charles, *Eschatology*, 2nd ed., 1913, p. 284).

the people as 'leader and high priest for ever, until a trustworthy prophet should arise' (I Mac. 14.41), *i.e.* he was appointed leader and High Priest with hereditary rights, the first Maccabee to be so recognized.[1] The blessedness of his reign is described in characteristically 'messianic' terms in I Mac. 14.8ff.: 'And they tilled their land in peace, and the land gave her increase, and the trees of the plain their fruit. The ancient men sat in the streets, they communed all of them together of good things, and the young men put on glorious and warlike apparel. . . . He made peace in the land, and Israel rejoiced with great joy: and they sat each man under his vine and his fig tree, and there was none to make them afraid.' But neither here nor elsewhere is Simon referred to as 'the Messiah'.

The writer of the Book of Jubilees also declares that the future power in Israel will lie, not with the House of David, but with the House of Levi. God will give to Levi and his seed 'greatness and great glory'; he will 'make them great unto all ages. And they will be princes and judges, and chiefs of all the seed of the sons of Jacob;

> They will speak the word of the Lord in righteousness,
> And they will judge all his judgments in righteousness'
> (31.13–15).

This same hope is expressed also in the Test. of Levi 8.14 which reads, 'A king shall arise in Judah (better, 'out of Judah')[2] and shall establish a new priesthood' which will be called by 'a new name'. R. H. Charles took this to refer to John Hyrcanus, representing the Hasmonean House; the 'new name' would then refer to the title 'priests of the Most High God' anciently borne by Melchizedek (Gen. 14.18) and revived by the Hasmonean High Priests when they displaced the legitimate Zadokite priesthood from office.[3] T. W. Manson, however, has argued strongly that the 'new name' refers rather to 'sons of Zadok', *i.e.* to the Zadokite priesthood founded by Solomon.[4] If this is so, then there is no reference here to Hyrcanus or the Hasmonean House, and the passage is seen to be in harmony with the possible beliefs of the Qumran Covenanters in this same

[1] Some scholars have found in Ps. 110 an acrostic on the name Simon (Simeon) and maintain that it refers to Simon Maccabaeus. Such an interpretation, however, does violence to the Psalm and in any case depends upon an incomplete acrostic. It is more likely that it refers to a pre-exilic king of Judah.

[2] Cf. T. W. Manson, *JTS*, vol. XLVIII, 1947, pp. 60f.

[3] Cf. *Testaments of the XII Patriarchs*, 1908, pp. li, 45.

[4] Cf. *op. cit.*, pp. 60f.

connection.[1] But whatever the interpretation of the passage may be, there is again no mention here of a Messiah.

Of significance for this study are several passages in the Testaments of the XII Patriarchs where reference is made to the tribes of Judah and of Levi together, Levi being accorded the more honourable place. As the text now stands allusion is made to the coming of two Messiahs who will apparently stand side by side in the coming kingdom, one from the House of Judah and one from the House of Levi. An examination of the relevant passages raises a number of very difficult problems concerning the dating of this document and also concerning its composition and authorship—whether it is in fact a Jewish book with later Jewish and Christian interpolations, or whether it is substantially Christian in the form in which we now have it.[2]

According to R. H. Charles the historical background of the book is the period of the Hasmonean House in the thirty or forty years preceding the breach of Hyrcanus with the Pharisees.[3] He finds ample evidence throughout the Testaments for belief in a Messiah of Levi.[4] In only two cases, he claims, is any reference made to a Messiah of Judah—in the Test. of Jud. 24.5–6 and the Test. of Napht. 4.5. These, however, represent first-century additions, when the hope of a Messiah from Judah reappeared after the eclipse of the Hasmonean House.[5] Charles, therefore, recognizes the hope of a Messiah from Levi as alone original to the text.

G. R. Beasley-Murray, however, claims that 'the juxtaposition of the Messiah from Judah and the Messiah from Levi is too deeply rooted in the fabric of the book for either element to be discarded.'[6] He argues that, Christian interpolations apart, the book is essentially a unity in which two Messiahs are presented, one to act as king and the other to act as priest in the coming kingdom. Such is the exalted view of the Hasmoneans held by the author that the priest is given precedence over the Davidic king. He rejects Charles's claim that

[1] See pp. 320f. M. de Jonge, however, argues that the Test. of Levi 8.12–15 reflects a Christian interpolation and that vv. 14–15 refer to the priestly and kingly office of Jesus Christ; cf. *Novum Testamentum*, vol. IV, 1960, p. 211, n. 1, and *The Testaments of the XII Patriarchs*, 1953, pp. 45–46.

[2] See pp. 55ff. [3] Cf. *op. cit.*, pp. liff., xcviif.

[4] The passages he cites are Tests. of Reub. 6.7–12; Levi 8.14; 18; Jud. 24.1–3; Dan 5.10–11; Jos. 19.5–9, cf. *ibid.*, p. xcviii.

[5] Cf. *ibid.*, p. xcvii; cf. also Lagrange, *Le Judaïsme avant Jésus-Christ*, 1931, p. 129.

[6] *JTS*, vol. XLVIII, 1947, pp. 1ff.

references to a Davidic Messiah are later Jewish interpolations, but supports his claim that a Levitic Messiah belongs to the original text. He reduces Charles's references, however, to two passages whilst admitting that 'only one passage sets this forth without any ambiguity'. This passage is Test. of Reub. 6.5–12 which reads as follows:[1]

> Therefore, (then, I say unto you), ye will be jealous (against the sons of Levi), and will seek to be exalted over them; but ye shall not be able. For God will avenge them (and ye shall die by an evil death). For to Levi God gave the sovereignty (and to Judah with him and to me also, and to Dan and Joseph, that we should be for rulers). Therefore I command you to hearken to Levi, because he shall know the law of the Lord, and shall give ordinances for judgment and shall sacrifice for all Israel until the consummation of the times, as the anointed High Priest, of whom the Lord spake. I adjure you by the God of heaven to do truth each unto his neighbour and to entertain love each for his brother. And draw ye near to Levi in humbleness of heart, that ye may receive a blessing from his mouth. For he shall bless Israel and Judah, because him hath the Lord chosen to be king over all the nation. And bow down before his seed, for on our behalf it will die in wars visible and invisible, and will be among you an eternal king.

M. de Jonge, however, gives a different interpretation to these verses. In his book on the Testaments[2] he suggests that the words in verses 11b–12 following the phrase 'for he shall bless Israel and Judah' are an additional note referring back to Judah and so have no reference to Levi as Charles and Beasley-Murray assume. Thus the whole section 6.5–12 is to be regarded as a typical Levi-Judah passage.[3] In a later treatment of the subject, however, he retracts this view, particularly in the light of evidence from the Dead Sea Scrolls[4] and accepts the view that verses 11b–12 spoke originally about Levi. But he notes certain differences between this passage and the Scrolls and judges that Christian influence can be detected here. In 6.8 also he sees evidence of a Christian redactor who claims that the Levitical

[1] The quotation is from Charles's translation. He indicates by brackets what he takes to be interpolations.

[2] *The Testaments of the XII Patriarchs, a study of their text, composition and origin*, 1953.

[3] Cf. *ibid.*, p. 89; cf. also A. S. van der Woude, *Die messianischen Vorstellungen der Gemeinde von Qumran*, 1957, pp. 195ff.

[4] Cf. *NT*, vol. IV, 1960, p. 210. He refers especially to the *War of the Sons of Light, etc.* V.1; XV.4–8; XVI.11–14; XVIII.3–6, where the tribe of Levi plays a significant role.

priesthood will be succeeded by Christ the High Priest as in Hebrews 7.11.[1]

The second passage which, according to Beasley-Murray, testifies to a belief in a Levitic Messiah is Test. of Levi 18.2–9:

Then shall the Lord raise up a new priest.
And to him all the words of the Lord shall be revealed;
And he shall execute a righteous judgment upon the earth for a multitude of days.
And his star shall arise in heaven as of a king,
Lighting up the light of knowledge as the sun the day,
And he shall be magnified in the world.
And he shall shine forth as the sun on the earth,
And shall remove all darkness from under heaven,
And there shall be peace in all the earth . . .
And the glory of the Most High shall be uttered over him,
And the spirit of understanding and sanctification shall rest upon him (in the water).
For he shall give the majesty of the Lord to his sons in truth for evermore;
And there shall none succeed him for all generations for ever.
And in his priesthood the Gentiles shall be multiplied in knowledge upon the earth,
And enlightened through the grace of the Lord:
In his priesthood shall sin come to an end,
And the lawless shall cease to do evil.

Once more Charles thinks that the writer had John Hyrcanus in mind; but there is no justification at all for this view. What we have here is an idealized picture, no doubt based on what the author had seen of the achievements of the Hasmonean House, but without specific reference to a Hasmonean Messiah or indeed to any historical figure. As H. H. Rowley says, 'The functions assigned to the Messiah of Levi go beyond the achievements of the Hasmoneans, but it is possible that the author idealized a conception which was based on what had been done by the Hasmoneans, and thought of a coming priest who would overthrow all the forces of evil.'[2] Lagrange,[3] Mowinckel[4] and others argue that the messianic references here are not concerned with any specific person who is to be acknowledged as

[1] De Jonge follows a different reading from Charles here and translates either until the consummation of the times of the (an) anointed High Priest' or 'until the consummation of the times of Christ the High Priest', *ibid.*, p. 211.

[2] *Jewish Apocalyptic and the Dead Sea Scrolls*, 1957, pp. 12–13.

[3] Cf. *op. cit.*, pp. 127ff. [4] Cf. *op. cit.*, pp. 288f.

Messiah, but rather with the founder of a dynasty. It is the dynasty (in this case the Hasmonean House) which will collectively fulfil the function of the Messiah and will reveal in its succession of priest-kings all those qualities which are elsewhere ascribed to the Davidic Messiah himself. Rowley disputes this, however, and argues that the messianic functions here described are best understood as 'inhering in a person'. They go beyond those functions which could be ascribed to the Hasmonean House, however idealized, and in many respects correspond to those of the ideal Davidic king who was conceived of as an individual in the thought of the prophets.[1]

Most scholars have followed R. H. Charles in seeing certain Christian interpolations in this eighteenth chapter of the Test. of Levi (*e.g.* the phrase 'in the water' in verse 7), whilst retaining the chapter as a whole. Its originality, however, has more recently been called in question. Matthew Black, for example, expresses doubt about its Jewish origin and concedes that perhaps the whole chapter should be regarded as entirely Christian.[2] M. de Jonge has argued this position at greater length.[3] His analysis of 18.2–9 leads him to conclude that, as it stands, this passage is dependent on the New Testament and in several respects agrees with the Christology set forth in the Epistle to the Hebrews. It may, however, contain elements which derive from the Qumran sect or a related group. There are certain correspondences between the messianic figure of this chapter and that described in certain parts of the Scrolls,[4] but the redaction of the text has been so thorough that it is very difficult to separate the pre-Christian and possibly Essene elements.

This brief survey gives some indication of how complicated and confused is the evidence concerning the messianic hope expressed in the Testaments of the XII Patriarchs. It seems likely, however, that the glories and achievements of the Hasmonean House had inspired at least some among the people with the hope of a Messiah from the tribe of Levi in whom they saw many of those traits long associated with the tribe of Judah. Even if this were so, disillusionment would soon set in as the people witnessed the increasing secularization of the High Priesthood. Inevitably the old hope of a Davidic Messiah

[1] Cf. *The Relevance of Apocalyptic*, 1945, p. 61.

[2] Cf. *ET*, vol. LX, 1948–9, pp. 321f.

[3] Cf. *The Testaments*, etc., *ad loc.*; *Novum Testamentum*, *art. cit.*; cf. also M. A. Chevallier, *L'Esprit et le Messie dans le Bas-Judaïsme et le Nouveau Testament*, 1958, pp. 125–30, and van der Woude, *op. cit.*, pp. 210–14.

[4] See pp. 319ff.

would begin once more to assert itself. For the re-emergence of this brand of the messianic hope there is ample evidence in the apocalyptic literature.

4. THE DAVIDIC MESSIAH

The Jewish literature of the times and the Gospel narratives both show clearly how popular was men's expectation of a Messiah from the House of David. Among the apocalyptic books the most significant in this connection are the Testaments of the XII Patriarchs and the Psalms of Solomon.

As already noted there is a considerable disagreement among scholars concerning the evidence presented by the present text of the Testaments. Those difficulties of a critical nature which we saw to apply in an assessment of a Levitic Messiah apply here also. Out of the many passages which link the tribes of Levi and Judah together Charles, as we have seen, singles out two which may indicate belief in a Davidic Messiah—the Test. of Jud. 24.5–6 and the Test. of Napht. 4.5. But he has no hesitation in dismissing these as interpolations or as passages which originally referred to a Messiah from Levi.[1] The evidence thus confirms his theory that only a Messiah from Levi is presented in this book.

This position is again attacked by G. R. Beasley-Murray,[2] who claims that throughout the Testaments, and especially in the Testament of Judah, there is indisputable evidence of belief in a Davidic Messiah. He singles out three passages in particular—Test. of Jud. 17.5–6; 22.2–3; 24.1–6. The last of these reads thus:

> And after these things shall a star arise to you from Jacob in peace,
> And a man shall arise (from my seed), like the sun of righteousness,
> Walking with the sons of men in meekness and righteousness;
> And no sin shall be found in him . . .
> Then shall the sceptre of my kingdom shine forth;
> And from your root shall arise a stem;
> And from it shall grow a rod of righteousness to the Gentiles,
> To judge and to save all that call upon the Lord.

Charles saw in these verses two independent messianic fragments. As they stand, verses 1–3 refer to a Messiah from Judah, but he omits the words 'from my seed' as an interpolation and takes the passage to refer to the Messiah from Levi. He further concludes that verses

[1] Cf. *op. cit.*, pp. 95, 142. [2] Cf. *op. cit.*, pp. 1ff.

5–6, referring to a Messiah from Judah, are also the work of the same interpolator.[1] Beasley-Murray, however, contends that the passage hangs well together and affords reliable evidence for a Messiah from Judah. The Testaments, therefore, give evidence for belief in two Messiahs, one from David and one from Levi, in which the priestly ruler is given precedence over the kingly. This 'double messianism', moreover, fits in well with the book as a whole which links together the *tribes* of Levi and Judah as the agents of God's salvation. At the head of each of these tribes is a deliverer, with his own distinct function to perform, through whom the kingdom will come: 'And now, my children, obey Levi and Judah, and be not lifted up against these two tribes, for from them shall arise unto you the salvation (of God). For the Lord shall raise up from Levi as it were a High Priest, and from Judah as it were a king (God and man), he shall save all (the Gentiles and) the race of Israel' (Test. of Sim. 7.1–2).

M. de Jonge, however, holds that in the original Levi-Judah passages it is unlikely that reference was made to two Messiahs.[2] He disputes the claim that two deliverers are mentioned in Test. of Sim. 7.1–2 and states that the present text predicts the coming of only one messianic figure. He further suggests that in the passage underlying these verses only the two *tribes* are mentioned and that the redactor's intention was to indicate that Jesus Christ was both High Priest and king.[3] He agrees that the Test. of Jud. 24.1–6, quoted above, can be divided into two parts and that originally the whole passage dealt with Judah and Levi. But the parallels between these verses, the Testament of Levi 18 and the Gospel narratives of Jesus' baptism in the River Jordan, indicate that this is a Christian composition, perhaps incorporating material from the Qumran (or other related) sect. It is impossible to reconstruct the original text or to cull from it any possible messianic expectations.

But the main source of this belief concerning a Davidic Messiah is the Psalms of Solomon, to be dated about the middle of the first century BC some years after Pompey had ended the rule of the Hasmonean House. The specifically messianic references are to be found in Ps. of Sol. 17.23–51 and in Ps. of Sol. 18.6–10. To the writer of these psalms the members of the priestly House were 'sinners' who 'assailed us and thrust us out. . . . They laid waste the throne of David in tumultuous arrogance' (17.5, 8). The deliverer whom God

[1] Cf. *op. cit.*, p. 95. [2] Cf. *NT*, vol. IV, 1960, p. 218. [3] Cf. *ibid.*, pp. 213–14.

will raise up will be a king of David's line. This identification is not actually made in Ps. of Sol. 18, but in Ps. of Sol. 17 the reference is quite specific. He is introduced in these words: 'Behold, O Lord, and raise up unto them their king, the Son of David' (17.23). Here, too, for the very first time in this literature the name 'Messiah' is used as the title of the coming king. Twice over he is called 'the anointed of the Lord' or 'the Lord Messiah' (17.36 and in the title of Ps. of Sol. 18); this indicates that at long last the expression 'Messiah' is being used in its technical sense with reference to the ideal king of the future and is brought into relation with the messianic concept.

It is clear from what is said of him that the Davidic Messiah, in spite of all the honours and titles that are ascribed to him, is a thoroughly human being whose kingdom will be established upon the earth with its centre in Jerusalem. But God will equip him with those qualities which he will require for the exercise of his mission. He will rule over his people in righteousness (17.28f., 35; 18.8) and wisdom (17.42; 18.8); he will chasten them that he may direct them in the way of righteousness (18.8); in their national assemblies his word will be as the word of an angel (17.49). He will allow no unrighteousness to lodge in their midst; his subjects will be all holy and sons of God (17.28ff.). He himself will be 'pure from sin'; he will rely upon his God who will 'make him mighty by means of (his) holy spirit' (17.41–42). He will put his trust not in armed might or in gold and silver, but in the Lord who is his king (17.37f., 44). The blessing of God will be with him (17.43) so that he will shepherd his flock faithfully, allowing none to stumble (17.45). It is significant that, in describing these qualities of the coming Messiah, the writer lays considerable stress on his moral and spiritual equipment and on his readiness to inspire those same qualities in the hearts of those over whom God has called him to rule.

But this is not the full picture of the Messiah as presented in these Psalms. Over against this presentation of a righteous and religious leader we have that of a military leader whose responsibility it is, under God, to crush the heathen and to set his people free from their tyranny and oppression. He will shatter unrighteous rulers and purge Jerusalem from nations that trample her underfoot (17.24); he will destroy godless nations with the word of his mouth (17.27). He will gather together a holy people who have been dispersed and will lead them in righteousness (17.28, 50); he will divide the land among their tribes and remove aliens from among them (17.30f.). The heathen nations will serve under his yoke, and will come from the ends of the earth to see his glory and the glory of the Lord bringing with them as gifts God's exiled people (17.32ff.).

Throughout the rest of the first century BC and in the first Christian century the figure of the messianic king lived on in the hearts of the people, as the New Testament makes abundantly clear. But no longer was he thought of simply as coming after God had established his kingdom; rather was he God's instrument in the establishment of it, and his foremost task was the destruction of God's enemies from the face of the earth. In the popular imagination increasing stress was laid on the national and political aspects of his work, and the future hope was viewed, particularly in times of persecution and national unrest, in terms of deliverance from the alien power of Rome (cf. Matt. 21.9). The Messiah was regarded by many as a military deliverer of the Zealot type who would rid the country of their hated enemy. And so there arose a series of 'false Messiahs' who incited the people against the common foe—Hezekiah the 'brigand' whom Herod executed, his son Judas the Galilean and his brother Menahem, the prophet Theudas in the time of the procurator Cuspius Fadus (cf. Acts 5.36), the Egyptian Jew who was put to death by the procurator Felix (cf. Acts 21.38), another Jew who led his followers out into the wilderness in the time of Festus, and Simon bar Kochba whose revolt was quelled in A.D. 135.

5. THE MESSIAH AND THE DEAD SEA SCROLLS

We have already considered the claim that, in the Testaments of the XII Patriarchs, there is evidence for belief in two Messiahs side by side—one from Levi and the other from David. The relation between the Testaments and the Scrolls is a point of much debate, but it is agreed by perhaps most scholars that this belief was shared also by the Covenanters of Qumran among whose writings, as we have previously observed, fragments have been found of an Aramaic Testament of Levi and a Hebrew Testament of Naphtali.

The clearest indication of such a belief in two Messiahs, it is claimed, is to be found in the *Manual of Discipline* which states that the members of the Community will continue to live according to the original discipline 'until there shall come a prophet and the Messiahs of Aaron and Israel' (IX.11). The plural 'Messiahs' or 'anointed ones' is clearly indicated in the text. These same three figures appear again in the *Testimonies Scroll*. In this document the writer quotes three texts from the Pentateuch which have a bearing on the future hope. The first concerns the Prophet whom God will raise up from among their brethren (Deut. 5.28f., together with 18.18f.); the second gives Balaam's prophecy about the star out of Jacob (Num. 24.15–17); the third is Moses' blessing on the tribe of Levi (Deut. 33.8–11). It has been suggested that the Prophet may have been identified with the Teacher of Righteousness, though this is not at all certain. What is more certain is that, according to Jewish tradition, the star of Balaam's oracle was believed to refer to the Davidic Messiah. It is reasonable to suppose that in this document the three figures mentioned are the Prophet, the Davidic Messiah and the Aaronic Messiah.

Moreover, in the Scrolls as in the Testaments, there are indications that the priestly Messiah is given precedence over the kingly Messiah, recalling perhaps the relative positions of priest and king in the ideal commonwealth of Ezekiel 40–48. This is shown in the *Rule of the Congregation* where the subordination of the kingly Messiah is made plain in a section dealing with an eschatological banquet. It reads thus: 'Let no one begin to eat bread or drink wine before the priest, for it is his province to bless the first mouthful of bread and wine and to stretch forth his hands first upon the bread. Thereafter the Messiah of Israel may stretch forth his hands upon the bread' (II.18–22). The expression 'the Messiah of Israel' does not occur in the Old Testament or indeed anywhere else in later Judaism; but it obviously refers to the Warrior Messiah of popular Jewish expectation.[1] It is assumed by those who find a dual messianism in the Scrolls that the priest mentioned here is 'the anointed one of Aaron', although this is not specifically mentioned in this context. Reference to the kingly Messiah appears again in company with a High Priest in a fragmentary collection of *Benedictions*; the former is called 'the prince of the Congregation' and is the Warrior Messiah; the messianic character of the priest is less certain and indeed the text leaves doubt as to the identity of the one who is to be blessed.

In the *Zadokite Document* reference is made in several places to 'the Messiah of Aaron and Israel' (XIV.19; XIX.10, cf. also XII.23), and elsewhere to the future coming of a Messiah who shall arise 'from

[1] In certain texts from Cave IV he is called 'Shoot of David', *i.e.* he is the traditional 'Messiah of Judah'; cf. J. T. Milik, *Ten Years of Discovery in the Wilderness of Judaea*, 1959, p. 127.

Aaron and from Israel' (XX.1) forty years after the 'gathering in' of the Teacher of Righteousness (XX.14–15). The singular word 'Messiah' is difficult to square with the belief that in these writings as a whole we have a doctrine of two Messiahs; and so it has been suggested that this is 'a secondary correction by a mediaeval copyist' who was familiar with the Jewish tradition of only one Messiah.[1] This explanation, however, must be ruled out, for corroboration of the singular 'Messiah' has, in fact, been found in a document from Cave IV.[2] J. T. Milik holds that in this passage the priestly Messiah has taken over the title of the kingly Messiah, although elsewhere (*e.g.* in VII.18ff.) 'the old dyarchy subsists under new names'.[3] No doubt if we could be more certain about the relative dating of the several documents, we should be in a much better position to understand the variations within the messianic hope of the Qumran Covenanters. In any case it is unwise to expect perfect consistency of eschatological expectation in any apocalyptic group, and the Qumran Community is no exception.

Belief in a priestly leader and a kingly leader would find precedent in the joint leadership of Joshua and Zerubbabel, the two 'sons of oil', in the early days of the Second Temple (cf. Zech. 3–4). Several hundred years later, at the time of the Second Jewish Revolt we find the High Priest Eleazar joining forces with the messianic figure of Simon bar Kochba in the fight against the Romans (AD 132–5).[4] The very nature of the Qumran sect itself may give a clue to an understanding of the situation. It was perhaps natural that this religious community, made up of laymen and priests, but having priests as their leaders, should envisage the deliverance of God coming through a king and a priest together. Certainly the expectation of a kingly Warrior Messiah is quite clearly established in these writings. If in fact they believed also in a Levitic Messiah, it is very unlikely that such a belief could have arisen out of admiration for the Hasmonean priestly House of Levi. They themselves were loyal sons of Zadok and would look forward to the coming of a Messiah of Zadok's line which alone, to them, represented the true High Priestly office.

[1] Cf. K. G. Kuhn, in *The Scrolls and the New Testament*, edited by K. Stendahl, 1958, p. 59.

[2] Cf. 4QDb. See J. T. Milik, *op. cit.*, p. 125. [3] *Ibid.*, p. 126.

[4] In both these illustrations, however, it is the secular leader who plays the more prominent part.

Despite the evidence noted above, however, a number of scholars dispute the claim that a doctrine of two Messiahs is taught in the Scrolls. It is pointed out, for example, that in the *Zadokite Document*, as we have seen, there is no justification for altering the singular 'Messiah' into a plural, and that there is a perfectly good explanation of the text as it stands. The phrase 'the Messiah from Aaron and from Israel' or 'the Messiah of Aaron and Israel' signifies that he will come from the Community as a whole which is made up of priests and of laymen. In any case, in this same document the Messiah of Aaron and Israel reveals functions which identify him with the Warrior Messiah for whom there is ample evidence in many parts of the Scrolls. A number of scholars recognize him in the 'man of glory' in the *War of the Sons of Light*, etc. (XII.10; XIX.3) who plays an important part in the eschatological battle at the time of the End. Mention is made here also of 'the holy one of Adonai' and of 'the king of glory'. It has been suggested that the former is the High Priest and the latter is to be identified with the 'man of glory', *i.e.* the Warrior Messiah. On the other hand, 'the holy one of Adonai' and 'the king of glory' may refer to the same person, namely, the Messiah.[1]

Again, it is not at all clear that the reference to the priest in the *Rule of the Congregation* is in any way truly messianic. The description given there of the eschatological banquet is probably based on Ezek. 44.3 which describes the celebration of the meal which is to be partaken by the Davidic Prince (*nasī'*) at the inauguration of the new Temple in Jerusalem.[2] This idea of an eschatological banquet is, of course, a familiar one in the apocalyptic tradition.[3] In such circumstances it is quite natural that the priest should preside and that the messianic prince should take a subordinate place. This precedence on the part of the High Priest does not necessarily mean that he is to be regarded as a messianic figure. One apparent obstacle to the interpretation of a single Messiah is the evidence already noted in the *Manual of Discipline* which refers to 'a prophet and the Messiahs (anointed ones) of Aaron and Israel'. The simple answer may be that the plural here is the result of a scribal error; or the reference may be simply to 'a duly anointed high priest and a duly anointed king',[4]

[1] Cf. M. Black, *op. cit.*, pp. 155f.

[2] Cf. *ibid.*, pp. 146f. It is significant that in the Scrolls the Messiah of Israel is also called by the name *nasī'*.

[3] See pp. 124f., 294.

[4] Cf. T. H. Gaster, *The Scriptures of the Dead Sea Sect*, 1957, p. 15.

without any technical sense attaching to the word 'anointed'. Matthew Black points out that the word 'Messiah' was not as yet the technical term it was soon to become in Jewish circles; but wherever he appears in later Jewish tradition 'the Anointed One *par excellence*' is the secular leader. This emphasis, he claims, is beginning to emerge in the Scrolls and it is under the influence of the 'messianic' expectations of Ezekiel for whom the Davidic prince alone has a significant role to play.[1]

M. de Jonge suggests that in the Qumran texts, as in the Testaments of the XII Patriarchs, there is a variety of messianic expectation to be found and that it is impossible to define in any way accurately the historical and literary relationship between these two bodies of literature.[2] Some scholars who have seen only one Messiah in the Scrolls have identified him with the Teacher of Righteousness whose resurrection would usher in the messianic age.[3] This is not justifiable on the evidence in the Qumran literature. It is just possible that the Teacher's disciples may have expected his resurrection after a period of forty years and on the eve of the messianic age. If so, it is possible that they thought of him in the way in which popular tradition thought of Elijah, as a forerunner of the Messiah, although there is no indication at all that he is in any way to be identified with that prophet. In any case, there is no suggestion that his followers accorded him messianic status.

[1] Cf. *op. cit.*, p. 148. [2] Cf. *op. cit.*, p. 218.
[3] Cf. A. Dupont-Sommer, *The Dead Sea Scrolls*, English trans., 1952, p. 44.

XIII

THE SON OF MAN

WE HAVE ALREADY seen that, during the inter-testamental period and even before, there had been emerging in the thought of Judaism an eschatology very different in many respects from the national and political hope which had inspired the prophets of the Old Testament. Its emphasis was on the transcendent, the supernatural, the supramundane. It was by no means unrelated to certain eschatological ideas already expressed in the Old Testament prophets, but it revealed traits which indicated the influence of foreign ideas, particularly perhaps of a Zoroastrian origin. Corresponding to this 'new eschatology', and forming one expression of it, was the belief in a mysterious figure called 'the Man' or 'the Son of Man' who appears in several apocalyptic writings. This enigmatic figure—his origin, his identity, his characteristics—has been the subject of much scholarly controversy. One reason for this has been the use of the term by Jesus to describe himself, the nature of his ministry and the future hope associated with the coming of God's kingdom in the Gospel tradition.

I. THE LITERARY SOURCES OF THE EXPRESSION 'SON OF MAN'

The first occurrence of 'the Son of Man' in the apocalyptic literature is in Dan. 7.13. This chapter describes a vision in which the seer sees four great beasts coming up out of the sea, each one different from the others. The first three bear a resemblance to known animals; the first is 'like a lion', the second 'like a bear' and the third 'like a leopard'. The fourth animal bears no comparison, so terrible and destructive is it (7.1–8). The interpretation given is that these four beasts represent four kings (7.17) or kingdoms (7.23). During the time of the fourth kingdom the 'Ancient of Days' suddenly appears in all his blazing glory; he takes his place on a fiery throne and passes judgment on all mankind. The fourth beast is destroyed, and the other three have their dominion taken away (7.9–12). At this point there appears on the scene 'one like unto a son of man' who comes 'with the clouds of heaven' to stand before the Ancient of Days, *i.e.* he is conveyed on the clouds into God's heavenly Council where he stands in the divine presence. It is a royal audience at which this 'son of man' is given 'dominion and glory and a kingdom, that all the peoples, nations and languages should serve him: his dominion is an everlasting dominion, which shall not pass away, and his kingdom which shall not be destroyed' (7.14).

This figure is likened to a 'son of man' (*i.e.* presumably a human being) just as the four other figures are likened to beasts. This in itself suggests that, like them, it is to be interpreted symbolically. In the verses which follow the writer makes clear what this interpretation is. Just as the four beasts represent four kings or kingdoms, so the 'son of man' represents 'the saints of the Most High' (7.18). These will suffer persecution from the fourth beast for a specified time (7.25); but the day of reckoning will come and its dominion will be taken away and it will be destroyed (7.26). 'And the kingdom and the dominion, and the greatness of the kingdoms under the whole heaven, shall be given to the people of the saints of the Most High: his kingdom is an everlasting kingdom, and all dominions shall serve and obey him' (7.27).

L. Dequeker has argued[1] that Dan. 7 as it stands shows clear indications of two redactors, the second of whom radically altered the original meaning of the passage. The expression 'the saints (holy ones) of the Most High', he claims, belongs to the original vision and refers to God's 'holy ones' or angels. This phrase, or rather the Hebrew equivalent of the Aramaic phrase here, appears once only in the Dead Sea Scrolls in the *Zadokite Document* (XX.8). But the word 'holy' by itself is found frequently in the Scrolls, in the Old Testament and in other non-biblical texts including the pseudepigrapha as a substantive where, with relatively few exceptions, it

[1] Cf. 'Les Saints du Très-Haut en Daniel VII', in J. Coppens and L. Dequeker, *Le Fils de l'homme et les Saints du Très-Haut en Daniel VII*, 1961, pp. 13–54.

signifies supernatural beings or angels. 'The saints of the Most High', then, refers to the angels who are to be God's agents in bringing in the heavenly kingdom. The kingdoms of the world, symbolized by the beasts, are now under the dominion of evil forces; but with the coming of the kingdom the new world will be governed not by evil forces but by the angels. The first redactor did not alter this basic idea, but simply applied the prediction of the End to his own day. The second redactor, however, writing very soon after the original author, gives an altogether different interpretation to the whole passage. He reduces the phrase 'the saints of the Most High' to 'the saints' (7.21, 22), and elsewhere, by adding a single word, changes the original conception completely. In 7.27 he now speaks of 'the *people* of the saints of the Most High' after the manner of 8.24 (cf. 'the holy people') which is a kind of *midrash* on chapter 7. Thus the conception of a universal dominion exercised by the angels is changed into a universal dominion conferred upon the pious Jews in the last days. The kingdom is still the work of God, but it is interpreted now in nationalistic terms. God will intervene in favour of the elect; Antiochus will be defeated and the Jewish people will receive the dominion for ever and ever.[1] However this figure of the 'son of man' or 'the saints of the Most High' was originally interpreted or came to be interpreted in later times, it seems likely that in its present context it signifies the triumphant people of God in the coming eschatological kingdom, *i.e.* it represents the redeemed Israel or the righteous remnant within Israel to whom God will give the victory over their enemies in the time of the End.

As it stands the 'son of man' can hardly be interpreted in terms of a Messiah, as a number of older scholars have done,[2] or indeed, except symbolically, of any individual.[3] Some scholars have argued for a compromise position between an individual and a corporate interpretation. Whilst acknowledging the collective nature of the figure, they would not exclude the thought of a leader who not only

[1] Dequeker refers to M. Kruse's contention that the 'interpolations' in Dan. 7 are to be regarded as *pᵉšarīm* ('interpretations') rather than as 'glosses' and are in keeping with the exegetical method adopted in the *Habakkuk Commentary* among the Dead Sea Scrolls, cf. *ibid.*, p. 30, n. 74. See also pp. 180f. above.

[2] For an exhaustive note on the various interpretations given by different scholars see H. H. Rowley, *Darius the Mede and the Four World Empires*, 1935, pp. 62–64.

[3] This applies also to the argument that the 'son of man' is the angel Michael, cf. *ibid.*, p. 63.

represents the kingdom but also stands as its head.[1] The tendency towards individualization is a feature of certain later apocalyptic writings[2] where it may be feasible to see such an oscillation between an individual and a corporate representation. This interpretation, however, seems less likely in the case of the 'son of man' in Daniel 7. Here, it would appear, it is a corporate figure in which the human and the humane triumph over the beastly and the bestial by the greatness and the power of God. It is a prophecy of the final triumph of God's people in God's kingdom in God's appointed time. As such it is in line with the popular hope expressed elsewhere throughout the apocalyptic writings in which the Davidic Messiah may or may not play a part.

The next apocalyptic book in which the figure of the Son of Man appears is the Similitudes of Enoch (I Enoch 37–71) which is perhaps to be dated in the Roman period or earlier still in the Maccabean age. Judgments have varied concerning the unity of this book and especially on whether or not the Son of Man references occur in Christian interpolations. It is unwise to dogmatize on this point, but the weight of evidence favours the claim that the book is in fact a literary unity,[3] and that the so-called Christian interpolations are part of the text. There is no indication here of any attempt to bring the teaching of the book concerning the Son of Man into line with that of the Gospels; indeed in chapter 71, as we shall see, the Son of Man is identified with an actual historical person who is not Jesus but none other than Enoch himself.[4] What we have here is an essentially Jewish book comprising a literary unity, at least where the Son of Man passages are concerned.

In a number of places throughout the Similitudes the expression 'Son of Man' or simply 'Man' is used (cf. 46.1–6; 48.2–7; 62.5–9, 14; 63.11; 69.26–29; 70.1; 71.17) to describe a being who is elsewhere in the same book designated 'the Elect One' (cf. 40.5; 45.3; 49.2; 51.3; 61.8; 62.9, cf. also Luke 9.35; Acts 3.14) or 'the Righteous One' (cf.

[1] See the references in H. H. Rowley, *ibid.*, p. 63, and also J. Coppens, 'Le Fils d'Homme Daniélique, etc.', in J. Coppens and L. Dequeker, *op. cit.*, pp. 55–101.

[2] See pp. 381ff.

[3] This is the opinion, for example, of Erik Sjöberg, *Der Menschensohn im Äthiopischen Henochbuch*, 1946, pp. 33f., whose only qualification is that he finds in the work four Noachic passages; cf. also J. Bowman, 'The Background of the term "Son of Man" ', *ET*, vol. LIX, 1948, p. 286, and M. Black, 'The "Son of Man" in the old biblical literature', *ET*, vol. LX, 1948, p. 12.

[4] See pp. 348f., 351f.

38.2) or 'his Anointed' (cf. 48.10). In all cases except one (62.7) the demonstrative 'this' or 'that' is used with it in the Ethiopic text. This usage is capable of at least two interpretations. It can be argued that the demonstrative is used simply to refer back to the first occurrence of the term in the very first vision and so means simply 'the man aforementioned'. On the other hand it may be that 'the demonstrative is used to indicate the translator's opinion that the term Son of Man is being used in a special sense' and that it has the effect of 'putting "the man" in inverted commas and writing man with a capital M'.[1] If this is so, then the expression does not simply signify 'a man' or 'a certain man', but a Man in a very special sense, the mention of whose name would mean something of significance to those who heard it or read it.

He is presented here as a heavenly being with no prior human existence whatsoever. His face has the appearance of a man and yet it is 'full of graciousness like one of the holy angels' (46.1). He looks human, but he is a supernatural angelic being who stands in a very special relationship to God himself. The Lord of Spirits has chosen him (cf. 46.3; 48.6) and kept him to carry out in his name a work which is yet to be revealed. God's choice of him was made 'before the creation of the world and for evermore' (48.6). 'His name was named before the Lord of Spirits' before the sun, the signs of the Zodiac and the stars were made (48.3); in the purpose of God he was concealed from the beginning (62.7) and 'his glory is for ever and ever' (49.2).

And yet, although he is supernatural and divine, nevertheless as 'the Elect One' he stands as the representative and head of 'the elect ones', that heavenly company of righteous men who will one day inherit the kingdom which God has promised to his chosen people (cf. 62.8, 14, etc.). He himself is called 'the Righteous One' (38.2f., cf. 39.6; 53.6) because he typifies the inheritors of God's heavenly kingdom. Indeed righteousness occurs prominently among those characteristics which mark him out from angels and men; he is one who possesses righteousness and in whom righteousness dwells (46.3, cf. 38.2f.; 39.5f.; 49.2; 53.6f.; 62.2f.). He is not only righteous himself, he is able to effect righteousness by bringing salvation to God's own people (cf. 38.3; 47.4, etc.) who will one day be exalted to be with him (cf. 62.8, 14). But righteousness is only one of many

[1] T. W. Manson, 'The Son of Man in Daniel, Enoch and the Gospels', *BJRL*, vol. XXXII, 1950, p. 178.

such God-given qualities which belong to the Son of Man, for

> In him dwelleth the spirit of wisdom,
> And the spirit which gives insight,
> And the spirit of understanding and of might (49.3, cf. 46.3; 49.1; 51.3; Isa. 11.2).

Of particular interest to the apocalyptists is a knowledge of the secret lore of the universe, those divine mysteries concerning the beginning of the world, its continuance and its end. These, we are told, are hidden with the Son of Man (62.6). Not only does he 'rule over all that is hidden' (62.6), he is able to reveal all their treasures (46.3) and pour forth from his mouth 'all the secrets of wisdom and counsel' (51.3). Even the 'secret ways' of the angels are not concealed and will be judged by him (61.9). But the greatest secret is the Son of Man himself who has been not only chosen but also hidden before the creation of the world (48.6) and preserved in God's presence (62.7). But one day he will be revealed; indeed he has been revealed already to the elect by the wisdom of the Lord of Spirits (48.7); they rejoice greatly 'because the name of the Son of Man had been revealed unto them' (69.26). The time is coming when 'the Righteous One shall appear before the eyes of the righteous' (38.2) in all his glory and splendour and will take his seat on the throne of God's glory. God sets him on a throne just like his own (55.4) and even sets him on his own throne allowing him to share his divine glory (51.3; 61.8). He sits on his throne as judge of heaven and earth, of men and angels, of the living and the dead. He causes sinners to be destroyed from off the face of the earth (69.27, cf. 38.2f.) so that 'all evil shall pass away before his face' (69.29); he deposes kings and puts down the mighty from their seats and breaks the teeth of sinners (46.4); they will all be terrified at the sight of him (62.5) and will be full of shame before him (63.11). Not only will those on the earth come under his judgment, the dead and the very angels in heaven must also come before him:

> And he shall judge all the works of the holy (ones) above in the heavens,
> And in the balance shall their deeds be weighed (61.8).

'Azazel and all his associates and all his hosts' will be judged by him in the name of the Lord of Spirits (55.4). None will be able to withstand or deceive him, for

> He shall judge the secret things,
> And none shall be able to utter a lying word before him;

For he is the Elect One before the Lord of Spirits according
to his good pleasure (49.4).

But the judgment of sinners is not the only function of the Son of Man. He comes also to deliver the elect and the righteous and to bring them salvation:

And the righteous and elect shall be saved on that day,
And they shall never thenceforward see the face of the sinners
and unrighteous (62.13, cf. 51.2).

The nature of this salvation is nowhere described at length except in terms of the destruction of the wicked. The blessings of his rule are related in terms reminiscent of the words of Deutero-Isaiah:

He shall be a staff to the righteous whereon to stay themselves
and not fall,
And he shall be the light of the Gentiles,
And the hope of those who are troubled in heart (48.4, cf. Isa. 42.6;
49.6; 61.1, 2).

But this salvation is not confined to those who dwell on the earth; those also who have perished and departed from this life will be able to 'stay themselves on the day of the Elect One', for they will be raised to share in the kingdom of the Son of Man (61.5).

Chapters 70 and 71 are of peculiar interest because of the relationship there described between Enoch and the Son of Man. In 70.1–2 the writer describes the translation of Enoch as recorded in Gen. 5.24, and in the following verses continues the account in the first person. The particular point of interest is in verse 1 where it is said that Enoch is 'raised aloft to that Son of Man and to the Lord of Spirits'. Stranger still are the words of 71.14 where Enoch himself is greeted with these words:

Thou art the Son of Man who art born unto righteousness,
And righteousness abides over thee,
And the righteousness of the Head of Days forsakes thee not.

R. H. Charles finds these words so difficult that he arbitrarily alters the text to read, 'This is the Son of Man', etc. We shall consider presently some attempted explanations of this strange identification.[1]

The figure of the Son of Man appears again in the post-Christian apocalyptic writings, II Esdras, II Baruch and the Sibylline Oracles V; but the part he plays here is much less prominent than in the

[1] See pp. 348f., 351f.

Similitudes of Enoch. In II Esdras he appears as 'the form of a man' (13.3) or 'the man' (13.5, 51) or 'this man' (13.3), and in the Sibylline Oracles V as the 'blessed man from the plains of heaven' (414f.). The so-called Vision of the Man from the Sea, recorded in II Esdras 13, shows clearly the transcendent character of the Son of Man. The seer in a dream sees a storm-tossed sea, and coming out of the midst of it 'as it were the form of a man' who 'flew with the clouds of heaven' (13.1–3). At his look everything trembles, and all who hear his voice are destroyed by fire (13.3–4). A great multitude of men assemble to make war against him; thereupon he carves out a great mountain and flies up upon it (13.5–7). He then destroys this great host with 'a fiery stream' which comes forth from his mouth (13.10) and calls to himself 'another multitude which was peaceable' (13.12). Later on, in the interpretation of the dream, it is said that the mountain to which he flies is Mount Zion or the heavenly Jerusalem (13.35f.), the fire is the Law (13.38) and the peaceable multitude are the ten captive tribes (13.40) who are united with the other two tribes in Palestine (13.48) to enjoy his kingdom of peace. The similarity between this 'Man' and the 'Son of Man' in the Similitudes is evident in a number of respects. What we have here is more or less the same transcendent figure 'whom the Most High is keeping many ages and through whom he will deliver his creation' (13.26). One difference is, however, that here he does not as obviously assume the role of judge in the last days. Elsewhere in the book it is shown that God himself will sit as judge at the time of the final judgment and after the resurrection of the dead (cf. 7.31–33). But as in the Similitudes so here, the Son of Man is a splendid, heavenly figure who will one day appear before the righteous in all his glory; everything that pertains to him is a divine secret, for 'just as one can neither search out nor know what is in the deep of the sea, even so can no one upon earth see my Son, but in the time of his day' (13.52). In him the mysteries of God's purpose are concealed, but when he appears what is hidden will at last be revealed.

2. SON OF MAN AS MESSIAH

The ideas of the Son of Man and the Messiah are not only different in their origins,[1] they also represent in their development two separate strands of eschatological expectation and indicate two distinct

[1] See pp. 304ff., 345ff.

emphases of 'messianic' hope. It is probable that, for the vast majority of the Jewish people, these two ideas had little or no connection with each other. Their significant association would be understood only by a relatively small group of apocalyptic writers. In some quarters, as we have seen in the previous chapter, the traditional idea of the Jewish Messiah prevailed. In other quarters, however, this traditional figure is replaced by or transformed into the figure of the transcendent Son of Man; sometimes the name 'Messiah' is retained, at other times not; sometimes no connection with the national figure is discernible, at other times certain characteristics are revealed which show the interrelation between the two modes of thought. And so in course of time 'there emerged a Messianic figure both eternal and transcendental, and also historical and human, in an eschatology both historical and also supra-historical and absolute'.[1]

In Daniel 7, as already indicated, no mention is made of the Messiah as the deliverer of his people, and certainly the Son of Man who appears there does not assume this role. The relationship between these two figures in the Similitudes of Enoch, however, is less clear. H. H. Rowley, for example, categorically asserts that 'there is no evidence that the Son of Man was identified with the Messiah until the time of Jesus'[2] and that that association was first made by Jesus himself. He supports this by pointing out that, whereas Jesus did not apply the term 'Messiah' to himself during his ministry and indeed charged his disciples to tell no man that he was, nevertheless he openly used the expression 'Son of Man' of himself. In the Similitudes of Enoch, he maintains, the Son of Man is not equated with the Messiah in the technical sense of that term. Here we have no human deliverer who can in any way be associated with the Old Testament hope, but a purely transcendent figure.[3] Others, like W. F. Albright, argue that even before the time of Jesus there was a certain amount of fusion between the two figures.[4] It is of interest to note that the writer of I Enoch attaches to the transcendent Son of Man certain characteristics which were already familiar to the tradition of the Messiah: he is righteous and wise, he is chosen by God, he receives the homage of kings, he is a light to the Gentiles and is actually called 'the Anointed One' of God (48.10; 52.4).[5]

[1] S. Mowinckel, *op. cit.*, p. 436. [2] *The Relevance of Apocalyptic*, 1945, p. 29.
[3] Cf. *ibid.*, p. 56. [4] Cf. *From the Stone Age to Christianity*, 1957, pp. 378ff.
[5] N. Messel regards these references to 'the Anointed One' as secondary, cf. *Der Menschensohn in den Bilderreden des Henoch* (BZAW, vol. XXXV), 1922, p. 31. T. W. Manson gives a collective interpretation: see below, pp. 350ff.

These references do not necessarily connect him with the Davidic earthly Messiah, and indeed the whole picture rules this out, but they may indicate that thus early the title 'Son of Man' has acquired a 'messianic' ring.

We have already seen that in II Esdras 13 the Son of Man appears as a truly transcendent figure. It is significant, however, that even here he is given the title 'my servant'[1] (13.32, 37, 52, cf. 7.28; 14.9) and reveals a number of characteristics which belong to the national hope associated with that name (cf. 13.33ff.). He is regarded as the Jewish Messiah, although the actual name is not used here to describe him nor is he to be thought of as a human figure of David's line. This identification, however, is much more pronounced in certain other sections of the book. In the so-called Eagle Vision, for example, in 10.60–12.35, the writer gives a reinterpretation of the vision recorded in Daniel 7 in which a lion appears and destroys the eagle symbolizing the Roman Empire (11.37; 12.1ff.). The lion represents the great deliverer of the coming age and is called 'the Messiah . . . who shall spring from the seed of David' (12.32),[2] *i.e.* he is the earthly Messiah. This identification is made even more explicit in 7.28–29 where he is specifically called 'my Messiah'[3] or 'my servant the Messiah'[4] who, it is said, will die at the close of the messianic kingdom (7.29). This same identification is made by the writer of II Baruch (cf. 29.3; 30.1; 39.7; 40.1; 70.9; 72.2), who declares that at the time of the consummation 'the principate of the Messiah will be revealed' (39.7). The person of the Messiah is here left rather vague, but again it is clear that an earthly, human Messiah is envisaged whose kingdom, we are told, will last as long as the earth itself endures (40.3). Thus in these writings we find the transcendent figure of the Son of Man taking upon himself traits associated with the Jewish Messiah, and the traditional figure of the Messiah assuming characteristics belonging to the Son of Man to the point of identification between the two figures.

This interrelation of the names 'Messiah' and 'Son of Man' thus

[1] The Latin text reads *filius meus*, which no doubt renders the Greek *ho pais mou*. This may mean either 'my son' or 'my servant'. The latter meaning is more likely in this context, as it is more common in the later use of the word. It thus corresponds to the Hebrew *ʿabdī* meaning 'my servant' in the original text.

[2] The word for 'Messiah' is in the Latin text, but not in those of the Syriac and other oriental versions and may be a Christian interpolation.

[3] Ethiopic, 'my Messiah'; Ar.², 'the Messiah'; Arm., 'the Messiah of God'. The Latin reading *filius meus Jesus* is an obvious Christian alteration.

[4] In Syriac and Ar.¹

indicates the tension which, as we have observed, had developed between this-worldly and other-worldly elements in apocalyptic eschatology. This tension was relieved in some writings by the introduction of an interim kingdom, a 'millennium', in which, after a preliminary judgment, the Messiah would reign upon the earth for 1,000 years (cf. II Enoch 32.2–33.2; Rev. 20.4–7). Sometimes the duration is given as 400 years (cf. II Esd. 7.28); at other times the kingdom lasts for an indefinite period (cf. II Bar. 40.3). This interim kingdom marks the close of the present aeon and is itself followed by the general judgment, the destruction of the world, the new creation, the resurrection[1] and the beginning of the new age of bliss.[2] The introduction of this idea of a millennium is in itself an indication of the compromise which the apocalyptic writers adopted between the two strands of expectation and shows how the idea of the Messiah, albeit in supramundane form, not only survived but also triumphed over the powerful influence of the concept of the Son of Man.

3. MESSIAH, SON OF MAN AND SUFFERING SERVANT

As we have seen, the Synoptic Gospels indicate that, whereas Jesus frequently used the expression 'Son of Man' with reference to himself,[3] he discouraged the use of the title 'Messiah' throughout the length of his public ministry. This suggests that, at least in those Jewish circles represented by his disciples, there was at that time no obvious association between the two terms. The Davidic Messiah was a concept clearly understood by them; the Son of Man—whatever they may have understood by it—was something altogether different. When Jesus interpreted his messiahship in terms of the Son of Man he was bringing together two concepts hitherto unequated in the thought of popular Judaism.

But not only did he interpret his messiahship in terms of the Son of Man; he interpreted it also in terms of the Suffering Servant. In reply to Peter's words 'Thou art the Messiah', he at once 'began to teach them that the Son of Man must suffer many things . . . and be killed' (Mark 8.30–31). The astonishment with which these

[1] A first resurrection at the beginning of the millennial reign of Christ is referred to in Rev. 20.4.

[2] See above, pp. 293ff.

[3] For a collective interpretation of the Son of Man even on the lips of Jesus see p. 338 and cf. T. W. Manson, *The Teaching of Jesus*, 1931, p. 227.

words were met is an indication that, in these circles at any rate, there was no thought of associating, far less equating, the ideas of the Messiah and the Suffering Servant of the Lord. It may well be that both ideas can be traced back to common roots in, say, the cultic rites of the Jerusalem Temple; but they each go their separate ways and represent distinct lines of Jewish expectation. So distinct, and indeed diverse, are they that in New Testament times the very thought of a suffering and dying Messiah was an offence to the God-fearing Jew (cf. Matt. 16.21ff.; Mark 8.31; 9.31f.; Luke 24.20f.; Acts 17.3; I Cor. 1.23; Gal. 5.11, etc.).

In post-Christian Jewish tradition, as represented by the Targums and the Talmud, reference is made to a certain Messiah ben Ephraim or Messiah ben Joseph who is to fall in battle fighting against the enemies of Israel; according to one account he is killed by one Armilus (*i.e.* Romulus = Rome). But there is no justification for identifying this figure with the Suffering Servant of Isaiah 53 or of reading it back into pre-Christian times. As H. H. Rowley says, 'There is no serious evidence of the bringing together of the concepts of the Suffering Servant and the Davidic Messiah before the Christian era, or of the formulation of the doctrine of the Messiah ben Ephraim at so early a date.'[1] What relationship if any, then, is there between the Messiah-'Son of Man' and the Suffering Servant during this period, and in particular what evidence do the apocalyptic writings provide?

The evidence of the Targum on Isa. 53 has often been alluded to in this connection. But the relevance of this passage is more apparent than real. There the Servant is identified with the Messiah, but the interpretation given to this whole chapter is radically different from the original intention of the Old Testament prophet. The Messiah here presented is the Messiah of David who will triumph over the heathen and all the enemies of God's people. The suffering he has to endure is reduced to the barest minimum and is completely devoid of that vicarious quality which we find in the biblical passage; indeed it can hardly be called suffering at all, for it consists simply in the exposure of himself to those dangers he will be obliged to face in the coming struggle with the heathen before his final victory is assured. The actual sufferings and death undergone by the Servant in the biblical passage are transferred one after another to the enemies of Israel and are accomplished by the victory of the Messiah. There is

[1] *The Servant of the Lord*, 1952, p. 85.

no mention here of an atoning death; indeed there is no reference to a suffering and dying Messiah. On the contrary, the conflict and toil which he is called upon to endure will lead only to his ultimate glorification. Thus the whole picture is recast to give prominence to the national and political figure of the Davidic Messiah.

The word 'servant' is used in II Esdras and in II Baruch to describe the Messiah from the seed of David. In II Esd. 7.29, for example, the Messiah is described by God as 'my servant' and reference is made to the fact of his death at the close of the interim kingdom which he will set up upon the earth. There is no suggestion here, however, of a 'suffering Messiah', nor has his death anything at all to do with atonement, nor is it of the nature of a vicarious offering. He is not even killed by his enemies or by disease. He simply ceases to exist. The reference to his death is almost casual, as if it were something to be fully expected in the natural course of events. In the millennial kingdom he has reached the peak of his triumph and it is quite natural that at its close he and 'all in whom there is human breath' should die. The world is then transformed into primaeval silence for 'seven days' at the close of which the new age begins (7.30–31). In the resurrection which follows, the Messiah will presumably rise with the others and continue his work as God's 'servant'. In no sense is this messianic figure associated with the Suffering Servant of the Lord.

Some scholars have seen reference to a suffering Messiah in two other writings, one of them among the Qumran Scrolls and the other among the apocalyptic writings. The first is a variant reading of Isa. 52.14 in the *St Mark's Scroll* which, it is claimed, gives evidence for a messianic interpretation of the Suffering Servant. The translation given of the Masoretic text in the Revised Version reads, 'His visage was so marred more than any man', etc. The word here rendered 'marred' is *mišḥat* from a root *š-ḥ-t* (to mar, spoil). The variant reading in the Qumran text, however, has the letter *yodh* added to the received consonantal text. It has been argued[1] that this reading represents the word *mašaḥtī*, from the root *m-š-ḥ*, meaning 'I have anointed'[2] and so has a messianic connotation. If this interpretation is correct the reference here, unlike the Targumic reference

[1] *E.g.* by D. Barthélemy in *RB*, vol. LVII, 1950, pp. 546–7, and W. H. Brownlee in *BASOR*, vol. CXXXII, 1953, pp. 10ff., and vol. CXXXV, 1954, pp. 33ff.

[2] A. Guillaume, in *JBL*, vol. LXXVI, pp. 41–42, accepts the reading *mašaḥtī*, but compares it with the Arabic *masaḥa* (to mar) and translates 'I have marred'.

mentioned above, would be to a priestly and not to a kingly Messiah. But it is doubtful whether, in fact, this suggested derivation and interpretation of the word is justifiable. The rendering given by Barthélemy for example—'I have anointed him so that his appearance surpasses that of a man'—is forced in meaning and strangely out of context. It is much more likely that the text should be pointed to read *mošḥatī*,[1] from the root *š-ḥ-t*, with the sense, '(His visage) was marred'. In this case there is no messianic reference in the word at all.

The second reference is in the Test. of Levi 18.6 which reads,

> The heavens shall be opened,
> And from the temple of glory shall come upon him sanctification,
> With the Father's voice as from Abraham to Isaac.
> And the glory of the Most High shall be uttered over him,
> And the spirit of understanding and sanctification shall
> rest upon him (in the water).

Recalling the story in Genesis 22 of God's command to Abraham to sacrifice his son Isaac, Matthew Black comments, 'There can be no doubt that the voice of the Father to his Messiah in Levi 18, a voice like Abraham's to Isaac, is the voice of parental authority calling for the obedience of a beloved Son to the point of complete readiness to offer Himself in Sacrifice.'[2] This allusion recalls the words of Isa. 53.7 and is echoed in the New Testament, particularly in the Epistle to the Hebrews. For this very reason, however, Black is inclined to think that the whole chapter is Christian in origin.

But what about the relation between the Suffering Servant and the Son of Man? Some scholars maintain that Daniel's visions may have been dependent originally on the Servant passages in Deutero-Isaiah and that the Son of Man in the one is representative of the Suffering Servant in the other.[3] There are similarities in language, for example, between the two bodies of literature. In each case

[1] This is the reading suggested by A. Rubinstein, for example, in *Biblica*, vol. XXXV, 1954, pp. 475–9, who identifies it as 'a *hophʿal* participle in the construct state with a *yodh* ending', other examples of which can be found in the Masoretic text. G. R. Driver (in private correspondence) likewise interprets it as 'a *hophʿal* participle plus *hireq compaginis*'. The meaning 'marred' is accepted by J. Reider in *BASOR*, vol. CXXXIV, 1954, pp. 27–28, and also, as we have seen, by A. Guillaume in *JBL*, vol. LXXVI, pp. 41–42.

[2] 'The Messiah in the Testament of Levi 18', *ET*, vol. LX, 1949, p. 322.

[3] Cf. M. Black, 'Servant of the Lord and Son of Man', *SJT*, vol. VI, 1953, pp. 1ff., and F. F. Bruce, 'Qumran and Early Christianity', *NTS*, vol. II, 1956, p. 176.

reference is made to 'the wise' (Isa. 52.13; Dan. 12.3) who make 'the many' righteous (Isa. 53.11; Dan. 12.3) and who suffer in obedience to the will of God (Isa. 53.3ff.; Dan. 11.33, 35). But such similarities extend beyond the mere use of words and phrases. There is a correspondence also in the ideas associated with these two figures. Daniel's Son of Man, representing God's faithful people, is called upon to endure suffering in much the same way as Deutero-Isaiah's Servant. Their enemies will make war with the saints and prevail against them (7.21), and will 'wear out the saints of the Most High' (7.25); those who are 'wise among the people . . . shall fall by the sword and by flame, by captivity and by spoil, many days' (11.33); by this means they will refine, purify and cleanse the whole nation (11.35). The idea of vicarious suffering, so prominent in Deutero-Isaiah, is perhaps not completely absent from this conception of the Son of Man.

There are indications in the Gospels that Jesus was influenced in his thinking by both Deutero-Isaiah and Daniel and that he interpreted his messianic ministry in terms of a unitive exegesis of these two books. He brought together the two ideas of Suffering Servant and Son of Man and interpreted them together in terms of his own life and death and resurrection.[1] It would seem, however, that Jesus was not the first to interpret Deutero-Isaiah and Daniel together in this way, for the Qumran Covenanters thought of their particular mission along somewhat similar lines.[2] They called themselves 'the wise' (Hebrew *maskilim*, cf. Dan. 11.33, etc.), 'the Remnant' and 'the saints of the Most High' (cf. Dan. 7.27), and believed themselves to be in the true line of succession of 'the wise' in Daniel who were to endure grievous suffering for 'many days' (Dan. 11.33). But they equally clearly saw in themselves the fulfilment of the ministry of the Servant. In quite a number of places throughout the Scrolls the language used to describe the role of the Covenanters closely resembles that of Deutero-Isaiah.[3] They call themselves 'true witnesses for justice' (cf. Isa. 43.10, 12) and 'the elect by God's will to make atonement for the land' (cf. Isa. 43.1) and describe their vicarious suffering in language which sometimes resembles that of Isaiah 53.

[1] Cf., for example, Mark 1.14f., where the 'good news' of Isa. 61.1 is combined with the 'kingdom of God' of Dan. 2.44.

[2] Cf. F. F. Bruce, *op. cit.*, pp. 176ff., and M. Black, *op. cit.*, pp. 1ff.

[3] Cf. especially *Hymns of Thanksgiving* VIII.35f.; *Manual of Discipline* VIII.5ff.; *Rule of the Congregation* I.1–3.

They seek, by study of the law, by submission and by suffering to effect atonement for the sins of the people and to turn them to righteousness in the manner of the Servant of the Lord. Their work is to be accomplished by the Community as a whole but, as F. F. Bruce remarks, 'if the whole Community had its mission prescribed in terms of the mission of the Servant, it is not difficult to understand how some smaller body, or even an individual, acting or speaking in the name of the Community, could be referred to in similar terms.'[1] This is illustrated in the *Manual of Discipline* where, at one point, the propitiatory role is played by a council of fifteen men (VIII.1ff.), and in the *Hymns of Thanksgiving* where the writer speaks in the name of the whole community after the manner of the Servant. If the variant reading in the *St. Mark's Scroll* of Isa. 52.14, quoted above, does in fact refer to a messianic figure, then it would be quite natural that he should be regarded as the representative of the whole community or the whole people.[2]

In the Similitudes of Enoch the description of the Son of Man contains certain words and phrases which recall the description of the Suffering Servant in Deutero-Isaiah, and some have seen here a synthesis of these two figures. William Manson has conveniently tabulated these words and phrases and compared them with similar references used elsewhere concerning the Davidic Messiah and the Suffering Servant.[3] Each is chosen by God, is called the Lord's Anointed, is endowed with wisdom and righteousness, is a light to the Gentiles and receives the homage of kings. The very name 'Elect One', by which the Son of Man is known, comes from Isa. 42.1, and it may well be that the title 'the Righteous One' is taken from Isa. 53.11. Matthew Black sees evidence here that Deutero-Isaiah as well as Daniel has been 'the inspiration of the Similitudes',[4] although he acknowledges that vicarious and redemptive suffering, which is the chief function of the Servant, is nowhere ascribed to the Enochian Son of Man.[5] S. Mowinckel, however, refuses to accept that the individual expressions from Deutero-Isaiah are sufficient to prove that the figure of the Son of Man in the Similitudes finds the source of its inspiration there.[6] He acknowledges that the influence of the

[1] 'Biblical Exegesis in the Qumran Texts', in *Exegetica*, 1959, p. 55 (1st British ed., 1960, p. 62).

[2] So Bruce, *ibid.*, pp. 55f. (1st British ed., 1960, pp. 62f.).

[3] Cf. *Jesus the Messiah*, 1956, pp. 173f. [4] *ET*, vol. LX, 1948, p. 15.

[5] Cf. *SJT*, vol. VI, 1953. p. 10. [6] Cf. *op. cit.*, p. 421.

Servant Songs can be detected in the Similitudes' description of the Son of Man; but he argues that the picture of the Servant which underlies this figure, like that in the Targum on Isaiah 53 described above, is not the true Servant at all. 'It is the triumphant, Jewish Messiah, who has here lent to the portrait of the Son of Man certain decorative details, which he himself borrowed unjustifiably from the Servant of the Lord.'[1] Nowhere is there any indication that the Son of Man suffers or dies after the pattern of the Servant; nowhere are the content of the Servant Songs or the vicarious mission of the Servant read into his character and work. Indeed, what strikes us is not the similarity but the stark difference between the two figures. The Servant suffers pain, humiliation and death, and by the vicarious offering of himself brings to men expiation of their sins; the only involvement of the Son of Man in the affairs of mortal men is to judge the world, to destroy God's enemies and to deliver his people from their hands. The deliverance wrought by the Son of Man is not salvation from the power of sin, but deliverance from the oppression of their enemies. He is the terrible judge of sinners, not the Saviour of men's souls.

4. THE SON OF MAN AND THE BIBLICAL TRADITION

We have seen reason to believe that the Book of Daniel may well have been influenced by Deutero-Isaiah and that, in particular, the figure of the Son of Man may be in some sense representative of the Suffering Servant. The question now arises, Are there any indications which show the dependence of the Son of Man idea on other biblical books, and are these indications such as to prove the indigenous growth of this belief within the Hebrew tradition? We shall examine several Old Testament references with which, it may be claimed, the Danielic Son of Man has some connection and try to ascertain the relation between these and the apocalyptic sources where this expression occurs.

The first occurrence of the phrase in the apocalyptic literature, as we have seen, is in Dan. 7.13 where it translates the Aramaic *bar 'enaš*, meaning 'a member of the human race' or 'an individual human being'. The Hebrew equivalent of this expression, *ben 'adam*, is found in Ps. 8.4f. which may provide a further insight into its meaning:

[1] *Ibid.*, p. 414.

What is man that thou art mindful of him?
And the son of man (*ben 'adam*), that thou visitest him?
For thou hast made him but little lower than God,
And crownest him with glory and honour.

In these verses and in those that follow, man is seen in his creaturely weakness over against God, and at the same time in his God-given dignity over against the rest of creation. This double relationship is evident again in Ezekiel's use of the phrase where it occurs no fewer than eighty-seven times with reference to the prophet himself.[1] There Ezekiel's essential humanity is stressed over against the majesty of God; and yet as God's inspired prophet he possesses a dignity which the lower creation cannot share. This conception may have influenced the writer of the Book of Daniel, for there would appear to be a correspondence between the general features of the vision recorded in Daniel 7 and the prophet's recorded experience in Ezekiel 1. In each case there appears a throne set on wheels and aflame with fire (Ezek. 1.4, 15f., 21, 26, and Dan. 7.9f.) on which sits God himself in appearance like a man (Ezek. 1.26f.) or one Ancient of Days (Dan. 7.9f.); this chariot-throne is accompanied by a great cloud (Ezek. 1.4) and the Son of Man comes with the clouds of heaven (Dan. 7.13); in each case there appear four great beasts (Ezek. 1.5ff., and Dan. 7.3ff.) which, though their appearance and functions are different, emphasize as in Ps. 8.4f. the distinction between man and the animal creation.[2]

Another significant passage which may well have influenced the Danielic idea of the Son of Man is Psalm 80, particularly verse 17, which reads:

Let thy hand be upon the man of thy right hand,
Upon the son of man whom thou madest strong for thyself.

Here again, as in Psalm 8 and Ezekiel, we find the dual reference to the 'son of man' in his human weakness and in his special relationship with God. This is emphasized even more by the contrast that is drawn between the son of man whom God strengthens and the boar and wild beasts mentioned in verse 13. Much more significant, however, is the fact that there the expression 'son of man' is used as a collective symbol to represent the Israelite nation[3] just as the boar

[1] Daniel is also addressed as *ben 'adam* in Dan. 8.17.
[2] Cf. J. Bowman, *op. cit.*, p. 285.
[3] Cf. J. Bowman, *ibid.*, p. 284, and M. Black, *op. cit.*, p. 11.

and the wild beasts are used to represent the heathen nations round about.[1] Israel in its human frailty is 'the man of thy right hand' whom God will 'make strong' and so enable to fulfil his purpose in the world.

In Daniel 7, as we have seen, the Son of Man appears as a symbolic figure representing 'the people of the saints of the Most High'. T. F. Glasson argues that this figure was taken from I Enoch 14 which he would date in pre-Maccabean times.[2] As in Daniel 7 so in I Enoch 14, God is seated on his wheeled throne surrounded by his angels; his presence is accompanied by streams of fire; his raiment is as white as snow; a man (identified in I Enoch with Enoch himself) is borne into God's presence on the clouds of heaven (cf. also II Enoch 3.1). Glasson concludes that the 'original' of Daniel's Son of Man was none other than the patriarch Enoch himself, even though the author of Daniel 7 did not identify him as such. This explains why in the Similitudes of Enoch the Son of Man appears as an individual and not as a group figure and also why in chapter 71 of that book Enoch himself can be identified with the Son of Man.[3] This argument is, of course, based on the assumption that I Enoch 14 can be dated before the Book of Daniel, a claim which is by no means certain.[4] Moreover, as we shall see,[5] both Daniel and I Enoch may have been drawing upon a common tradition which would adequately explain the similarities between the two texts. H. H. Rowley, however, finds sufficient explanation of the symbolism of Daniel 7 within the chapter itself without any recourse either to I Enoch 14 or to external sources apart from the testimony of Scripture. The Danielic Son of Man transcends the heathen nations in honour and dignity just as man himself transcends the beasts. He comes with the clouds and is from above; they come from the sea and are from below.[6]

It has been argued that the occurrence of the Son of Man in the Similitudes of Enoch can be equally well explained on the same presuppositions and that it is no more than an imaginative development of the figure which already appeared in Daniel 7. This view finds support in the fact that in I Enoch 71.7ff. (cf. also 14.18f.) the

[1] Cf. E. L. Curtis, *HDB*, vol. I, 1898, p. 556a.
[2] Cf. *The Second Advent*, 1945, pp. 14ff. [3] See further pp. 348f., 351f.
[4] Cf. H. H. Rowley, *The Relevance of Apocalyptic*, 1945, pp. 75ff.
[5] See further pp. 345ff.
[6] Cf. *Darius the Mede and the Four World Empires*, 1935, p. 62, n. 2, and also E. L. Curtis, *op. cit.*, p. 556.

description of God's throne is largely derived from Ezekiel 1 and Daniel 7[1] and that the Son of Man passages read like a *midrash* or commentary on Daniel 7. Take, for example, 46.1ff.:

And there I saw one who had a head of days,
And his head was white like wool,
And with him was another being whose countenance had the appearance of a man,
And his face was full of graciousness, like one of the holy angels.

Then follows the explanation of the 'other being'—who he is, what he is and what is his relationship with the Ancient of Days:

This is the Son of Man who hath righteousness,
With whom dwelleth righteousness,
And who revealeth all the treasures of that which is hidden,
Because the Lord of Spirits hath chosen him,
And whose lot hath the pre-eminence before the Lord of Spirits in uprightness for ever.

The connection between this passage and Daniel 7 is obvious;[2] but this in itself does not explain the differences that obviously exist between the presentations of this Son of Man in these two passages or what is the exact relationship between them.

An interesting suggestion is made by T. F. Glasson who interprets the origin of the Son of Man in the Similitudes along these lines.[3] When God appears at the end of the age, the Son of Man (whom Glasson calls here 'the Messiah') appears also and takes part both in the judgment and in the reign which follows. Glasson recognizes Dan. 7.13 as the source of the expression 'Son of Man' in the Similitudes; but he looks to the Dream Visions of I Enoch (*i.e.* chs. 83–90) for an explanation of this twofold function undertaken by the Son of Man. There it is stated that God was assisted in the work of judgment by an angel (90.20) who is probably to be identified with Michael. The writer of the Dream Visions interpreted the Son of Man of Dan. 7.13 in terms of this Michael. But also in the Dream Visions the

[1] Note that the wheels (*'ōpannīm* in Hebrew) of the chariot-throne in Ezek. 1 become angels called 'Ōpannīm in I Enoch 71.7, cf. 61.10. Similarly the 'whirling wheels' (*galgalīm* in Hebrew) of Ezek. 10 and Dan. 7 become the angelic Galgalīm in III Enoch. See above, p. 241.

[2] Note also the similarity of this passage with Isa. 11.2: 'The spirit of the Lord shall rest upon him, the spirit of wisdom and understanding, the spirit of counsel and might, the spirit of knowledge and of the fear of the Lord.'

[3] Cf. *op. cit.*, pp. 28f.

writer introduces the figure of the Messiah under the symbol of a white bull (90.37) who appears after the judgment and is born from the community. Thus in I Enoch 83–90 we have two figures alongside God—Michael who assists him in judgment and the Messiah who assists him in the reign which follows. Glasson concludes that in the Similitudes these two offices are combined in the figure of the Son of Man who appears as judge and as king in the kingdom which follows.

This is an ingenious theory; but it is only a theory and is built on rather shaky foundations. As S. B. Frost points out,[1] the occurrence of an angel in 90.20 is dependent on an emendation of the text and in any case he is nowhere specifically identified with Michael, nor is there any evidence that the writer brought such a figure into relationship with the Son of Man of Daniel 7. Most significant of all perhaps, this theory does nothing to explain the fact that the Old Testament 'Day of the Lord' now becomes the 'Day of the Elect One' (cf. 61.5) and that the judgment is now placed in the hands of the Son of Man.

A much simpler explanation is offered by H. H. Rowley who sees in the Son of Man in the Similitudes simply 'the personifying of the Danielic concept of the Son of Man in a supramundane person who stood for the representative and head of the kingdom that concept symbolized'.[2] We shall see presently that the notion of 'corporate personality' implicit in this interpretation is developed by a number of scholars to explain certain features about this figure which otherwise might be difficult to explain.[3]

On any of these interpretations, then, the Son of Man in the Similitudes can be traced back through Daniel into the tradition of the Old Testament itself. Echoes of this tradition can be heard in a number of references to the Son of Man[4] which, though they may not indicate literary dependence, show clearly how the apocalyptic figure was deeply influenced by biblical thought.

The occurrence of the Son of Man in II Esdras and the Sibylline Oracles V can be explained along similar lines. In both these sources the 'Man' is identified as the Messiah, as we have seen, but in each case there are echoes also of the Danielic Son of Man. In the

[1] Cf. *Old Testament Apocalyptic*, 1952, p. 223.
[2] *The Relevance of Apocalyptic*, 1945, p. 57. [3] See pp. 350ff.
[4] Glasson, for example, points out the connection of I Enoch 48.10 with Ps. 2.2; also 49.3 with Isa. 11.2; and 48.4 with Isa. 49.6, *op. cit.*, p. 34.

Sib. Or. V. 414–6 we read how 'there has come from the plains of heaven a blessed man with the sceptre in his hand which God has committed to his clasp: and he has won fair dominion over all.' This recalls the dominion given by God to the Son of Man in Dan. 7.14. This same connection is evident also in the case of II Esdras where the Man from the Sea, like the Danielic Son of Man, flies with the clouds of heaven (13.3, cf. Dan. 7.13), cuts out for himself a great mountain (13.6, 36, cf. Dan. 2.45) and appears as a deliverer chosen by God (13.26, cf. Dan. 7.14). Once again there would appear to be a dependence on the biblical apocalypse.

But does this line of interpretation really explain the features of the Son of Man as they appear in the extra-biblical apocalypses; and further does it explain the differences between these and the presentation in the Book of Daniel? Is it adequate to interpret this emerging figure simply in terms of Jewish presuppositions? A considerable number of scholars would argue that this approach is inadequate and that the significance of the apocalyptic Son of Man must be sought, in part at least, outside the biblical tradition altogether.

5. A MYTHOLOGICAL INTERPRETATION

The figure of the heavenly transcendent Son of Man, as it appears in the apocalyptic writings, has very little in common with the messianic figure presented in the traditional Old Testament hope. It is clear that they have different origins and, in the beginning at any rate, represent two quite distinct ideas. We have traced the roots of the Son of Man idea back through Daniel into the Old Testament Scriptures; but there are certain features about him, it can be argued, which find no precedent there either in terms of the Messiah or of Israel as a corporate unit. He is presented not only as a transcendent but apparently also as a pre-existent heavenly figure whose 'name was named before the Lord of Spirits' before the sun and the stars were created (I Enoch 48.3); he has been chosen and hidden by God from the beginning (I Enoch 48.6, cf. 46.3; 62.7); he is an object of worship to all that dwell on the earth (I Enoch 48.5); he remains hidden till the time appointed by God when at last he will be revealed in all his glory (I Enoch 62.6f.). When he appears at the end of the age he takes his seat as judge of kings and the mighty upon the earth and executes judgment upon them in the name of the Lord of Spirits (I Enoch 45.3; 61.8ff.; 62.1ff.). The 'Day of the Lord', so familiar in

Old Testament prophecy, is now described in terms of the 'Day of the Elect One' (I Enoch 61.5) when all secrets will be revealed and the righteous will be saved.

Apart from these general considerations, there are certain points of detail which find no parallel or precedent in the Old Testament and can hardly be explained simply as imaginative developments. He is quite unlike the Messiah, for example, in the role he plays as king of Paradise, in his connection with the work of creation, in his rising from the sea, and in his coming on the clouds of heaven. Such allusions as these strongly suggest that the writers were using and adapting traditional material from their apocalyptic lore and that that tradition was itself deeply influenced by ideas foreign to the biblical tradition. This is further suggested by one other factor which defies explanation along the line of purely Jewish thinking, the identification of the patriarch Enoch with the Son of Man to whose stature, apparently, he is exalted at the time of his translation to heaven (I Enoch 71.14).[1]

It has been argued by a number of influential scholars that many of the features of the apocalyptic Son of Man bear a striking resemblance to the figure of the Primal or Heavenly Man, belief in whom it is claimed was widespread throughout the oriental and Hellenistic world during the post-exilic period, and that the Son of Man idea is to be traced back to its origin in the mythology of that time. This mythology appears in different forms in different places, and many figures appearing in it have been claimed as the prototype of the apocalyptic Son of Man—Adapa, Ea-Oannes, Saoshyant, Gayomart and many more besides. Behind all these various presentations stands the figure, in some form or another, of the Primal or Heavenly Man who is revealed as a quasi-divine being, often with cosmological as well as eschatological features. He is variously presented as the supremely wise man, the ideal man, who is closely related to the act of creation and in the end will sit as judge; in him the souls of all men consist and to him they will return. It may well be that there is a historical connection between all these various forms and that they are to be traced back to their origin in those 'Chaldean' sources which reveal a syncretism of Iranian, Mesopotamian and Babylonian religious traditions.[2]

The general features of the Son of Man—as a pre-existent, heavenly figure who nevertheless represents the ideal man and who

[1] See further pp. 348f., 351f. [2] Cf. S. Mowinckel, *op. cit.*, pp. 422, 432.

will sit as judge in the last days—are reflected in this picture of the mythological Man. Even in points of detail there is a certain correspondence between the two figures. C. Kraeling, for example, has noted points of correspondence between Daniel 7 and the Babylonian myth of Marduk's conflict with Tiamat. Among the features appearing in both accounts are the description of the monster, the stirring up of the sea and the four winds that disturb the deep.[1] Mowinckel suggests that the Son of Man's rising from the sea in II Esdras and II Baruch reflects a wider reference in mythological sources;[2] he points to the fact that in Mandean sources the Primal Man is said to live in the sea and to come forth from there to effect deliverance.[3] It is said, moreover, of the Persian Saoshyant that a virgin gave birth to him after she had bathed in a lake where Zoroaster's seed had been concealed so that it could be said of him that he was 'born from the waters of the lake'. The obviously forced exegesis of the coming of the Man from the sea in the apocalyptic writings indicates that this material had been received as part of their tradition and explained without being perfectly understood. The same writer sees a covert allusion to the Primal Soul idea in I Enoch 49.3 which says of the Son of Man 'in him dwells . . . the *spirit* of those who have fallen asleep in righteousness'; the meaning of the reference has now changed, but it reflects an earlier stage of the myth in which it was taught that the souls of men will one day be liberated and restored to the Primal Soul in whom the souls of men have their pre-existence and to which they return at death.[4]

Other writers have pointed out the similarities between the Danielic Son of Man and the figure of Gayomart, the Primal Man in certain Iranian sources,[5] who frustrates the efforts of the Evil One and his demons for 3,000 years. At the close of this time he perishes; but in the end his bones are raised in resurrection, then the first human pair, then the rest of mankind. In this same form of the myth Gayomart is closely associated with the act of creation; from his seed come forth the first human pair, and from the seed of his ox come forth beasts, birds, fish and plants. In the apocalyptic literature, no

[1] Cf. *Anthropos and the Son of Man*, 1927, pp. 145ff., quoted by M. Black, *op. cit.*, p. 11.

[2] Cf. *op. cit.*, p. 392.

[3] Cf. R. Reitzenstein, *Das Iranische Erlösungsmysterium*, 1921, pp. 50f., 121f.

[4] Cf. *op. cit.*, p. 377.

[5] *E.g.* Bousset, Gressmann, Reitzenstein and Creed; cf. J. M. Creed, 'The Heavenly Man', *JTS*, vol. XXVI, pp. 113–36.

doubt under the influence of messianic ideas, stress is laid not so much on the cosmogonic features of the Son of Man as on his eschatological features; and here again we observe that in the Iranian myth Gayomart, after his resurrection, takes his place alongside Zoroaster and the Saoshyant in the final judgment of the world.

This mythological interpretation has been used by some scholars to explain the particularly difficult passage in the last two chapters of the Similitudes where the patriarch Enoch is carried up bodily into heaven to be with the Son of Man (70.1) and in the following chapter is apparently identified with that heavenly figure (71.14). Elsewhere in I Enoch it is reported that he is carried into heaven in visions and is there initiated into all the secrets of the universe (cf. 1.2ff.; 37.1ff.; 72.1ff., etc.); he is able to reveal all the secrets of wisdom (51.3), and all the treasures of what is hidden (46.3) he records for the comfort and enlightenment of God's people (82.1ff., etc.). Thus he is called 'Enoch the scribe of righteousness' (12.3f., cf. 15.1; 92.1, etc.) and has the reputation of great wisdom and understanding.

In all this, however, we have no indication of the apotheosis of Enoch such as is suggested in 71.14. But corroboration of this is to be found in two other apocalyptic books of a somewhat later date, in the second and third books of Enoch. In II Enoch 22 the patriarch again assumes the role of a heavenly scribe who both records and reveals the secrets of the universe and of the age to come. But here we observe an advance on previous descriptions of him. Having been transported into heaven, he is anointed with holy oil and clothed in glorious garments and is transformed into the likeness of God's glorious angels (22.8–10). The evidence of III Enoch is even more striking still.[1] There the heavenly scribe Enoch is introduced by the name Metatron in whom we are probably to see a variant of the Primal Man.[2] He is given a throne lower only to that of God himself and is actually described as 'the lesser Yahweh' (12.5). He is given charge of all the treasures of heaven (10.3ff.) and God reveals to him all the secrets of the universe (11.1). Despite the differences, there can be little doubt about the similarity between this figure and that of the Son of Man. Here, then, we have support for the evidence

[1] Cf. H. Odeberg, *The Hebrew Book of Enoch*, 1928. The relevant sections of the book are probably to be dated around the close of the first century AD, cf. Odeberg p. 42, n. 3.

[2] Cf. W. Bousset, *Hauptprobleme der Gnosis*, 1907, pp. 199ff., and Odeberg, *op. cit.*, pp. 4f.

in I Enoch 71.14 which identifies the translated Enoch with this heavenly figure.

But how are we to explain this identification? E. Sjöberg points out that what we have here is not the translation to heaven of one who had already been the Son of Man during his earthly life, but rather the exaltation of a man, like other men, who became the Son of Man at his translation.[1] He is at a loss, however, to explain how it is possible for an exalted man to become identified with an already existing, and indeed pre-existent, Son of Man.[2] Faced with this dilemma, Mowinckel offers a simple, if rather strained, solution. In I Enoch 71.14, instead of reading 'Thou art the Son of Man, thou who art born unto righteousness', he would read 'Thou art the son of man who is born unto righteousness.' Thus the phrase loses its technical meaning and signifies simply 'Thou art the man who'. In this case chapter 71 supports the evidence of chapter 70 where Enoch is exalted not to *become* but to *be with* the Son of Man.[3]

In the apocalyptic conception of the Son of Man Mowinckel finds 'a Jewish variant of the oriental, cosmological, eschatological myth of Anthropos',[4] but recognizes that there was no conscious borrowing of the idea or any awareness of its origin in oriental mythology. It is safe to say that the Jewish apocalyptic writers would have no idea that the Son of Man was, or in origin had been, the Primal Man. Instead they identified him with the Messiah and so altered his whole appearance that only by the most careful scrutiny can we detect the influence of the Primal Man idea on the Jewish faith itself.[5] Although there are similarities between the two conceptions, there are important differences which show that, if the apocalyptists did take over the idea, they at the same time made significant changes in line with their own religious heritage. In Daniel 7, for example, much of the mythological content has been removed, and the mythology that remains is only incidental to the symbolism which portrays the purpose of God through his saints. In the Similitudes of Enoch the presence of mythological elements is more obvious, but even here mythology has been to some considerable extent assimilated to the ideas of the Old Testament. Matthew Black goes so far as to say that the picture presented in the Similitudes is 'one which has been so completely assimilated to Biblical ideas that it emerges a new creation, a chaste and noble figure of

[1] Cf. *op. cit.*, pp. 168ff. [2] Cf. *ibid.*, p. 187. [3] Cf. *op. cit.*, 441ff.
[4] *Ibid.*, p. 425. [5] Cf. *ibid.*, p. 435.

righteousness, wisdom, and compassion, shorn of all the extravagant myths of the polytheistic East'.[1] Whatever influence this idea of the Primal Man may have had on Jewish thought it certainly was not taken over at any one period or from any one source, but came from many quarters and in different forms and was swept up, as it were, into the current of apocalyptic hope.

6. A CORPORATE INTERPRETATION

The attempt to explain the apocalyptic Son of Man by reference to oriental mythology has been challenged from many quarters. Nils Messel, for example, has argued that the Enochian Son of Man should be given a collective interpretation as in the Book of Daniel. His argument was partly vitiated by his drastic reduction of the relevant texts to only a few verses which best suited his theory.[2] Others, however, like T. W. Manson have tried to build up a case for this method of interpretation without recourse to such drastic measures. In his book, *The Teaching of Jesus*, Manson contends that in the Similitudes and II Esdras, as in Daniel, the expression 'Son of Man' is to be understood not in a literal sense but as a collective symbol. It represents what in the prophetic writings had been called 'the Remnant' or 'the Servant of Yahweh', an ideal figure which stands for 'the manifestation of the Kingdom of God on earth in a people wholly devoted to their heavenly King'.[3] In the Similitudes the Son of Man is known also as 'the Elect One', 'the Righteous One' and 'the Anointed One'. These references appear side by side with 'the elect ones' and 'the righteous ones', and it is arguable that the singular term in each case is a personification of the community indicated by the plurals. There is precedent in the Old Testament itself for a collective interpretation even for the phrase 'the Anointed One' (cf. Ps. 89.39, 52; Hab. 3.13, etc.). If these expressions can be interpreted in this way, so also presumably can the Son of Man. This same position is taken by Matthew Black who acknowledges his indebtedness to T. W. Manson in this respect.[4]

In a subsequent article Dr Manson maintains this collective interpretation of the Son of Man, but modifies his views somewhat.[5] He

[1] *Op. cit.*, p. 14. [2] Cf. *op. cit.*, pp. 18–32.
[3] *The Teaching of Jesus*, 1931, p. 227. [4] Cf. *op. cit.*, p. 14.
[5] Cf. 'The Son of Man in Daniel, Enoch and the Gospels', *BJRL*, vol. XXXII, 1950, pp. 171–93.

vigorously refutes the claim that in the Similitudes, for example, the Son of Man is a pre-existent, heavenly being. In 48.2–3 it is said of the Son of Man that 'his name was named before the Lord of Spirits' before the creation of the world. This need not signify, however, that he was called into existence before the time of creation, but simply that he was designated to some high destiny. It is said of him that he has been 'chosen' and 'hidden' before the creation of the world (cf. 48.6; 62.7). But neither do these passages imply a doctrine of pre-existence. The evidence points rather to a pre-mundane election of the Son of Man which does not necessarily involve a pre-mundane existence. It is the *name* of the Son of Man, and not the Son of Man himself, which has been known from the beginning,[1] *i.e.* he has had a place in the purpose of God from the beginning of the world. It is significant that nothing at all is said about the mode of his 'pre-existence'. When the patriarch Enoch, for example, is shown the secrets of heaven, he is escorted by an angelic guide; but no mention is made of the Son of Man. So hidden is he that 'he could more properly be described as unborn than as pre-existent' (p. 185). When at last he does appear it is on the plane of history and his function is to vindicate the righteous and to judge sinners. The pre-mundane decision of God in 'naming the name' of the Son of Man now has its fulfilment on earth and is given actuality in the community of the saints who are vindicated at the time of the End.

The relation between the community of the saints and the Son of Man as a collective symbol is particularly relevant to the problem of I Enoch 70–71. There, as we have seen, the exalted Enoch is apparently identified with the Son of Man. Sjöberg, on the assumption that the Son of Man represents a pre-existent, heavenly being, acknowledges the problem of such an identification as insoluble. T. W. Manson, however, attempts to explain it in terms of the Hebrew notion of corporate personality, seeing in the concept of the Son of Man both a collective and an individual reference. The Son of Man is not merely a symbol of Israel. There is an oscillation between, on the one side, the group idea which finds expression in 'the elect ones' and 'the righteous ones' (*i.e.* the Remnant, the saints of the Most High), and on the other side the individual idea which finds expression in two personalities—Enoch himself (cf. 71.14) who is regarded as the nucleus of the group of the elect ones, and the Messiah who will in

[1] Cf. M. Black, *op. cit.*, p. 14, but contrast J. Bowman, *op. cit.*, p. 288, who points out that 'to the Semite "name" is inextricably bound up with personality'.

the end vindicate the saints. The identification of the exalted Enoch with the Son of Man thus finds a solution. The divine purpose, which was formed before the creation of the world, finds its fulfilment and embodiment in Enoch who, after his life of righteousness upon earth, 'becomes the first actualization in history of the Son of Man idea and the nucleus of the group of the elect and righteous' (p. 189). This community of the saints awaits this fulfilment in the messianic vindication at the end of the days. Thus the Son of Man idea, purposed from the beginning, finds its realization first in Enoch, then in the company of the elect and righteous of whom he is the 'firstborn', and finally in the Messiah himself.

The view expressed by H. H. Rowley is in the main in agreement with that of T. W. Manson. He, too, bases his argument on the Hebrew conception of corporate personality[1] and sees 'a measure of fluidity in the significance of the term . . . so that it could stand as a symbol for the Kingdom or as a term for the representative of the Kingdom'.[2] He questions, however, Manson's reference to the Messiah in this connection, since such an identification goes beyond the actual evidence. Rather he sees the leader of the coming kingdom simply as 'the crystallization of the Danielic personification in a concrete person, who should come from above'.[3] If any more specific identification must be made, then it is possible that the author of the Similitudes thought of the return of Enoch himself.

This corporate interpretation has much to be said in its favour and helps to explain, perhaps more than most, the mysterious figure of the apocalyptic Son of Man. It has the merit of being founded on biblical ideas and of offering an explanation which does justice to the accepted texts.

[1] Cf. *The Relevance of Apocalyptic*, 1945, pp. 114f.
[2] *The Biblical Doctrine of Election*, 1950, p. 157, and the references in n. 2.
[3] *The Servant of the Lord*, 1952, p. 76; cf. *The Relevance of Apocalyptic*, 1945, p. 57.

XIV

LIFE AFTER DEATH

I. THE OLD TESTAMENT BACKGROUND

IT HAS BEEN shown in chapter V that, according to Hebrew thought, man is not a dichotomy of body and soul (or spirit) or a trichotomy of body, soul and spirit, but a unity of personality. 'Man is what he is by the union of certain quasi-physical properties of life with certain physical organisms, psychically conceived; separate them, and you are left not with either soul or body in our sense, but with impersonal energies on the one hand, and with *disjecta membra* on the other . . . the dissolution of this personal unity is the end of any real personal existence for Hebrew thought.'[1] A man's *nepeš* departs at death, not in the sense that his 'soul' leaves his body, but rather in the sense that his life ebbs away leaving behind a condition of utter weakness or lifelessness. This condition is experienced to a certain degree in times of illness or hunger or fear when vitality gives place to weakness. But it is experienced absolutely at the time of death so that death can be described as the weakest form of life.[2] With the breaking up of the unity of a man's essential being through the total disintegration of his *nepeš* he ceases to exist in terms of vital personality. He may indeed survive for a time in the elements of his personality such as the members of his body, but such survival is severely limited both in time and in space. A hint of this is given in Job 14.22 where it is said concerning a dead man, 'Only for himself his flesh hath pain, and for himself his soul mourneth' (R.V.m.). Pain and mourning are here shared by the whole man in the experience

[1] H. Wheeler Robinson, *The Christian Doctrine of Man*, 1934, p. 69.

[2] Cf. A. R. Johnson, *The Vitality of the Individual in the Thought of Ancient Israel*, 1949, p. 89.

of death. His *nepeš* remains in association with his body in his burial and, together with the body, is conscious of its fate. But its survival is only temporary 'like that of an image on the retina',[1] and soon ceases to be.

What continues after death is not a man's soul, but rather his 'shade' which is represented as a kind of 'double' or replica of the once living man. It bears a shadowy resemblance to the man as he was in this life, but is bereft of all qualities of personality such as characterized him upon earth. This belief lies behind the reference to necromancy in the Old Testament and explains how the witch of Endor, for example, is able to call up Samuel whose words she interprets to Saul (cf. I Sam. 28.3ff.). He appears in bodily form resembling that of the earthly body of Samuel, albeit in shadowy form. This association of the shade with the form and appearance of the once living man no doubt explains also the importance of the preservation of the corpse in Hebrew custom and the significance of proper burial rites. To burn a person's body or bones, for example, after his death, was a cause of great injury and ignominy. This is the form of punishment laid down in the Book of Leviticus for people who took part in certain forms of profanity (20.14; 21.9); it is the punishment meted out to Achan and his family because of his treachery in breaking a taboo (Josh. 7.25); it is the heinous crime of Moab which calls down the wrath of Amos (Amos 2.1). An almost equally severe punishment was that the body should be left unburied after death (cf. I Sam. 31.10ff.; Jer. 22.19). It seems likely that behind these notions of proper burial and respectful treatment of the corpse lay the conception that injury to the dead body involved injury to the shade whose double it was.

Reference has been made above to the description of the departed as 'shades'. This is the usual translation of the Hebrew word *repa'īm* whose use is relatively late with reference to the dead. Its derivation is not altogether clear, but it may signify 'the weak ones', *i.e.* those who are bereft of life. They are not 'ghosts' in the sense of spirits which are free to roam the earth; their abode is in Sheol or the Pit or Abaddon which lies beneath the surface of the earth (cf. Ps. 139.8; Isa. 7.11; Amos 8.2) or beneath the great cosmic ocean on which the earth stands (cf. Job 26.5; Jonah 2.3ff.). In this place of the dead they are cut off from the land of the living to which they are unable to

[1] H. Wheeler Robinson, 'The Old Testament Approach to the Life After Death', *Congregational Quarterly*, April 1925, p. 4.

return (cf. II Sam. 12.23; Job 7.9). Not only has it no continuity with life upon the earth (cf. Job 10.21f.), it is also a place of forgetfulness, darkness and despair where 'the dead know nothing, neither have they any more a reward . . . there is no work or thought or knowledge or wisdom in Sheol whither thou goest' (Eccles 9.5, 10). There are exceptions to this, but these are mentioned by reason of the fact that they are so abnormal. In Isa. 14.9ff., for example, the *repa'im* recognize the arrival of the king of Babylon in Sheol and marvel that he has become as weak as they are! Again, in the story of the witch of Endor, it is possible to think of an outstanding man like Samuel possessing not only memory of the past but also knowledge of the future and being able to communicate these things to men upon the earth (cf. I Sam. 28.3ff.). But for men of less renown Sheol remains a land of forgetfulness (Ps. 88.12, etc.) whose gates are locked fast against them (Job 38.17). What makes its isolation complete is that it is cut off from the fellowship of God himself, for 'the dead praise not Yahweh, neither any that go down into silence' (Ps. 115.17). None can escape from the power of Yahweh, even in Sheol itself (Ps. 139.8); but there is little comfort in this, for there the dead have no more any knowledge of the faithfulness and lovingkindness of God (Ps. 88.10ff.).

Sheol is the abode of *all* the dead, rich or poor, king or commoner. It is true that in one place Job refers to 'kings and counsellors of the earth', 'princes that had gold', 'prisoners (who) hear not the voice of the taskmaster', and 'the servant (who) is free from his master' (Job 3.14ff., cf. also Isa. 14.9, 10; Ezek. 32.21, 24). But the context shows that these social distinctions matter little in this realm of unbroken gloom and darkness. What is certain is that no moral distinctions prevail in Sheol; there is no difference there between the good and the bad. The *repa'īm* are incapable of receiving rewards or punishments (Eccles 9.5); 'all things come alike to all; there is one event to the righteous, and to the wicked' (Eccles 9.2).

This gloomy picture of the shades in Sheol is prevalent throughout the Old Testament; but already preparations were being made for the emergence in course of time of a belief in life after death quite unlike anything that had gone before. Of supreme importance was the sense of communion with God felt by certain pious people in Israel who could not rest content with such a forlorn faith. This attitude is well illustrated in a number of the Psalms where the ritualistic forms of worship are not simply an end in themselves but a means of entry into fuller fellowship with God; they lead not only to the Temple in Jerusalem but also to a spiritual altar where men can offer themselves in sacrifice to him. And so there emerged a pious hope that their fellowship with God in this life could not surely come to an end with death, but that even in Sheol men could praise him. This hope would be encouraged by a new emphasis on religious individualism associated with the name of Jeremiah, a man of prayer whose personal fellowship with God gave a new dimension to religious experience. Ezekiel in his turn linked this up with a doctrine of individual retribution which taught that there was a complete correspondence between the divine principles of moral government in the universe and their manifestations in human life; men were punished in proportion to their sin and rewarded in proportion to their righteousness during their lifetime upon earth (cf. 18.19–32). The problems raised by the obvious contradiction between this belief and the actual facts of experience are expressed in the Book of Proverbs, in certain of the Psalms and in the Book of Job. It is hardly surprising that in these last two books hopes begin to be expressed which find no parallel in the literature of former years. The most significant of these are to be found in Job 14.13–15 and 19.25–27 where the writer's faith, it would seem, reaches out for vindication beyond the bounds of human flesh, and also in Pss. 16, 49, 73 and 78 where the pressing problem of the prosperity of the wicked and the suffering of the righteous turns the psalmists' thoughts to the possibility of a continuing fellowship with God beyond the boundaries of this life. Scholars differ widely in their interpretation of these passages. Some see in them clear proof of belief in a life after death for the righteous in the presence of God; others deny that this is so or at most see in them a glimmering of hope which cannot yet be defined as conviction or belief. The latter view is accepted here. There is certainly no clearly defined doctrine of an after-life set forth in these passages; and yet the hope expressed is such that it can reach its logical conclusion only in the acceptance of such a belief. This conclusion is reached elsewhere in the Old Testament in two apocalyptic passages dating from the late post-exilic period, Isaiah 24–27 and Daniel 12. Fuller discussion of these will be reserved for treatment later on in this chapter. Here we simply observe that, in the latter reference and probably also in the former, a clear belief is expressed in life after death and that this belief is presented in the form of resurrection. At last the biblical writers had found that mould, as it were, into which they could pour their hopes and longings and which alone could give real shape to the belief that man's fellowship with God would not be broken by death.

2. THE IDEA OF SHEOL IN THE APOCALYPTIC WRITINGS

The typical Old Testament conception of Sheol as the abode of the shades remained the orthodox belief of Judaism down to the second century BC[1] and continued to be securely held long after that date particularly by the Sadducean party. The writer of I Enoch 91–104, for example, puts these words into the mouth of the Sadducees whom he identifies here with 'the sinners':

> As we die, so die the righteous,
> And what benefit do they reap for their deeds?
> Behold, even as we, so do they die in grief and darkness,
> And what have they more than we?
> From henceforth we are equal.
> And what will they receive and what will they see for ever?
> Behold, they too have died,
> And henceforth for ever shall they see no light . . .
> They perished and became as though they had not been, and their spirits descended into Sheol in tribulation (102.6–8, 11).

This same sentiment is expressed in II Bar. 10.6–12.4 which R. H. Charles ascribes to a Sadducean author.[2] As the writer reflects on the injustice of human life, he concludes that it is far better to depart to Sheol, a land of forgetfulness where men hear not what befalls the living (11.5); in the oblivion of Sheol the dead are more blessed than they who live with such sufferings here upon the earth (11.7). This, however, is quite an exceptional occurrence in the apocalyptic writings and stands in stark contrast to that conception of Sheol which was to undergo certain remarkable changes during the inter-testamental period.

(i) One change is that, in the extra-biblical apocalyptic, the dead are no longer described as 'shades' but as 'souls' or 'spirits' and survive as individual conscious beings. In the Old Testament the word 'spirit' is never used in this sense,[3] and many if not all of the uses of

[1] Cf. Ben Sira 14.16; 17.22f.; I Bar. 3.11; Tob. 3.10; 13.2.

[2] Cf. *The Apocalypse of Baruch*, 1896, pp. lxiiif., 14f.

[3] In Job 4.15 ('a spirit passed before my face') the word 'breath' rather than 'spirit' might give a better rendering, for *rūaḥ* does not occur anywhere else in the

the word 'soul' with reference to Sheol are subject to quite a different interpretation. On a number of occasions, for example, the hope is expressed that God will rescue a man's soul from Sheol (Pss. 30.3; 86.13, etc.); but generally speaking the word 'Sheol' is here used figuratively and signifies 'adversity' or 'death', and the man's prayer is that God will save his 'life' from any such calamity. Some scholars would contend that the use of 'soul' in such a context may on occasions express the hope that God will reveal his power in the after-life and deliver a man's life from Sheol;[1] but even if this is so, the departed as inmates of Sheol are still known as 'shades' and not as 'souls'. This typical Old Testament conception of the departed as shades in Sheol is represented in the two biblical apocalypses indicated above, Isaiah 24–27 and Daniel 12. In Isa. 26.19, for example, it is said that at the time of resurrection 'the earth shall produce the shades', the implication being that these shades have been cut off from God and from the possibility of reward or punishment and continue in the manner familiar to the Old Testament faith. In Daniel 12 the departed are not actually identified as 'shades' and are described simply as 'them that sleep in the dust of the earth' (12.2); but it is clear that once again the picture is that of a Sheol primitively conceived as in the rest of the Old Testament. In the extra-biblical apocalyptic writings, however, a significant departure is made. Here the departed are actually described as 'souls' or 'spirits' in a manner quite unlike anything that has gone before. Sometimes in this connection the word 'soul' alone is used (*e.g.* in the Similitudes of Enoch, Psalms of Solomon, II Enoch, Testament of Abraham, and II Baruch); sometimes the word 'spirit' is used (*e.g.* in the Noachic Fragments of Enoch, I Enoch 108, Assumption of Moses and III Baruch); at other times both 'soul' and 'spirit' are found side by side (*e.g.* in several sections of I Enoch and also II Esdras).[2] Thus, even in some of the earliest apocalyptic writings, 'soul' and 'spirit' are used as synonymous terms to describe the form of a man's survival immediately after death.

What we have here, however, is something much more significant

Old Testament in the sense of an apparition. Even if this passage is an exception, the reference would be in all probability to God himself and not to some ghostly creature from Sheol.

[1] Cf. H. H. Rowley, *The Faith of Israel*, 1956, p. 174, with reference to Ps. 16.10.

[2] There is a curious phrase in I Enoch 22.3 which refers to 'the spirits of the souls of the dead'.

than simply a change of name, from 'shade' to 'soul' or 'spirit'; it is a radical change in men's beliefs concerning the nature of survival in the life after death. In the Old Testament, as we have seen, the disintegration of the personal unity of body and *nepeš* at death signified for a man the end of real personal existence, even although a measure of consciousness might still remain. But now not only consciousness, but personal survival is implied in this change of outlook. There is seen to be a continuity between life on earth and life in Sheol in which the departed, as responsive and responsible 'souls' (or 'spirits'), can yet maintain a life of fellowship with God whose jurisdiction is acknowledged beyond the grave. Previously, in Old Testament thought, personality was wholly dependent on body for its expression; now it could be expressed—in some limited way at least[1]—in terms of discarnate soul which, though possessing form and recognizable appearance,[2] could live in separation from the body which had been left behind in death.

The souls or spirits of the departed are presented as individual conscious beings in passages throughout the apocalyptic writings far too numerous even to mention. In I Enoch 22.7, for example, 'the spirit which went forth from Abel, whom his brother Cain slew', makes suit against him till his seed be utterly destroyed from the earth. Sheol, to which Abel's spirit goes at death, is no longer a land of 'no-life' as in the Old Testament, but a land of conscious being and individual identity. Again, in the Apocalypse of Moses the death of Adam is described in terms of the departure of his soul (13.6) or the giving up of his spirit (31.4); but it can also be described in these words, 'Behold Adam . . . hath gone out of his body' (32.4), as though the essential personality were to be identified with his soul or spirit. In the Similitudes of Enoch the souls of the righteous are identifiable, the 'first fathers' being singled out for special mention (70.4, cf. Test. of Abr. 20); they rejoice in God and bless his name for ever and ever (61.12). As such these discarnate souls or spirits are capable also of emotional experiences. For example, they cry and make lamentations because they are conversant with the lawlessness of men on the earth (I Enoch 9.10); they can feel pain or pleasure, as innumerable passages make only too plain. According to their mood or their lot in the after-life they experience restlessness or repose,

[1] For certain qualifications see p. 375.

[2] In Apoc. of Moses 35.2, for example, the writer can speak of Adam's soul as 'lying on its face'!

remorse or gratitude, fear or calm assurance (II Esd. 7.80ff.). Indeed, where emotional experiences are concerned, there is apparently very little difference between their reactions in the life after death and those which they had during their lifetime upon earth.

(ii) A second distinction between the Old Testament conception of Sheol and that of the apocalyptists is that in the latter *moral* distinctions, and not simply social distinctions, now make their appearance. As in life so in death, men are separated into two distinct categories, the wicked and the righteous, on the basis of moral judgments. The full results of these judgments are seen only at the time of the final judgment; even in Sheol itself, however, the separation is perfectly clear. This distinction is made for the first time in the Book of Daniel where, at the time of the resurrection, the notably good and the notably bad are raised to receive their respective awards.[1] In subsequent apocalyptic books, however, these distinctions become clear not simply at the time of resurrection but beforehand, immediately after death, in Sheol itself. Man's destiny in Sheol is determined by the life which he has lived here upon earth. The dead, good and bad alike, go to Sheol (cf. II Bar. 21.23; 23.5; 48.16; 52.2; 83.17); but men determine their destiny in Sheol by the choice they make in this life: 'For though Adam first sinned and brought untimely death upon all, yet of those who were born from him each one of them has prepared for his own soul torment to come, and again each one of them has chosen for himself glories to come' (II Bar. 54.15, cf. 51.16). The writer of the Testament of Abraham tells us that, though 'all are gathered in by the sickle of death' (ch. 8), a separation is made between 'the just' and 'the sinners' whose souls are driven through different gates: 'This narrow gate is that of the just, which leads into life. . . . The broad gate is that of sinners, which leads to destruction and everlasting punishment' (ch. 11, cf. Matt. 7.13; Luke 13.24).

In a few of these books, belief is expressed in the possibility of moral change in the souls of the departed, chiefly through the power of intercessory prayer. In the Apocalypse of Moses, for example, it is said that the angels pray for the departed Adam (35.2), and that even the sun and moon fall down and intercede for him (36.1). Elsewhere Enoch is asked to pray for the angels (cf. I Enoch 13.4; 15.2; II Enoch 7.4), and great store is set by the prayers of men like Abraham (cf. Test. of Abr. 14) and Moses (cf. Ass. of Moses 12.6) who, though themselves among the departed, are able to intercede

[1] See pp. 368f.

on behalf of others. In one other passage which describes the purification of Adam's soul, the influence of Greek ideas is no doubt to be found: 'There came one of the seraphim with six wings, and snatched up Adam and carried him off to the Acherusian lake, and washed him thrice, in the presence of God' (Apoc. of Moses 37.3).

In the majority of the apocalyptic books, however, the conviction is expressed that no change is possible once a man has departed from this life. Man's destiny, both in Sheol and at the last judgment, is determined by the life he has lived upon the earth. Once inside the gates of Sheol no progress is possible for the departed soul either upwards or downwards (cf. I Enoch 22). Thus, in the words of R. H. Charles, Sheol becomes 'a place of petrified moralities and suspended graces'.[1] A man's destiny is determined the moment he passes from this life; there is no repentance after death (II Enoch 62.2), nor can the souls of the departed righteous pray for the living (53.1). The situation is made perfectly clear by the writer of II Baruch: 'There shall not be there again . . . a change of ways, nor place for prayer, nor sending of petitions, nor receiving of knowledge, nor giving of love, nor place of repentance for the soul, nor supplication for offences, nor intercession of the fathers, nor prayer of the prophets, nor help of the righteous' (85.12).[2]

(iii) A third difference between the Old Testament and the apocalyptic writings in this respect is that now Sheol is regarded, in most of these books at any rate, as an intermediate state where the souls of men await the resurrection and the final judgment and in which they are treated according to their deserts, *i.e.* Sheol becomes a place of preliminary rewards and punishments and gives a foretaste of the final judgment which will inevitably come. This can be illustrated from book after book, but II Esdras 7 gives perhaps the best example of it. There Ezra speaks to God in these words: 'If I have found favour in thy sight, O Lord, show this also to thy servant: whether after death, even now when every one of us must give back his soul, we shall be kept in rest until those times come in which thou shalt renew the creation, or shall we suffer torture forthwith?' (7.75). The answer given is that, when the soul departs from the body 'that it may return to him who gave it', it adores the glory of the Most High first of all (7.78). Then at once the souls of the wicked and the souls of

[1] *Eschatology*, 2nd ed., 1913, p. 218.

[2] For a discussion of moral distinctions and the possibility of moral change at the time of the final judgment, see pp. 380f.

the righteous go their separate ways, the former to suffering and the latter to blessing. The condition of the souls of the wicked is first described: 'Such souls shall not enter into habitations, but shall wander about henceforth in torture, ever grieving and sad in seven ways' (7.80). These 'seven ways' are seven degrees or kinds of torment which make only too clear the agonies of these wandering souls whose sufferings are made worse by reason of the fact that they are allowed to witness the joys of the righteous (7.81–87)! A description is then given of the state of the souls of the righteous: 'First of all they shall see with great joy the glory of him who receives them; and they shall rest in seven orders' (7.91). Just as the souls of the wicked are tormented, so the souls of the righteous enter into bliss where they remain in resting-places (7.95), guarded by angels (7.95) until the time of resurrection (7.32). The 'seven orders' in which they rest are conditions or dispositions in which their repose is undisturbed even by the plight and punishment of the ungodly, 'for they are hastening to behold the face of him whom in life they served, and from whom they are destined to receive their reward in glory' (7.92–98).

Similarly in I Enoch 5.5–7 the future lot of the wicked is described as 'eternal execration'; they will find no mercy and no salvation, but a curse shall be upon them. But the elect will enjoy light and joy and peace. Elsewhere it is said that when the righteous man dies the angel of peace leads his soul to eternal life (Test. of Asher 6.6); but of the wicked man it is said that 'when the soul departs troubled, it is tormented by the evil spirit which also it served' (Test. of Asher 6.5). II Enoch is peculiar among the apocalyptic writings, and no doubt reflects the influence of Greek thought on the book, in expressing belief in the pre-existence of the souls of men (cf. 23.4–5; 49.2; 58.5), and even of the souls of animals whose duty it will be to accuse men at the final judgment (58.6). Places have been prepared in the intermediate state of Sheol (58.4–6) for the repose of souls (49.2) until the final judgment when rewards and punishments will be made plain. But even concerning Sheol itself the writer can say, 'I saw how the prisoners are in pain, expecting the limitless judgment' (40.12). According to the writer of II Baruch, the good and the bad go alike to Sheol (cf. 21.23; 23.5; 48.6; 52.2; 83.17); but their destiny has been sealed in the after-life by the choice they have made in this life: 'Each one of them has prepared for his own soul torment to come, and again each one of them has chosen for himself glories to come' (54.15, cf. 51.16). The final judgment will not initiate but will increase the punishment already expressed in Sheol: 'And now recline in anguish and rest in torment till thy last time come, in which thou wilt come again, and be tormented still more' (36.11). Here also, as in II Esdras, the souls of the righteous are preserved in 'treasuries' (cf. 21.23; 23.4; 30.2) which presumably are situated in Sheol (cf. 23.4; II Esd. 4.41)[1] where they are guarded by angels (cf. I Enoch 100.5; II Esd. 4.41). Thus they remain in 'the place of faith and the region of hope' (59.10) until the day of final judgment.

In some apocalyptic books, however, the impression is given that Sheol is not simply an intermediate but the final state of judgment, particularly for the souls of the wicked. The Book of Jubilees is reminiscent of the Old Testament when it speaks of the righteous being gathered to their fathers (cf. 23.1; 36.1; 45.15); but its conception of Sheol is very different. No longer is it the place where all the departed assemble; it is the place of condemnation (7.29; 22.22; 24.31) and of darkness (7.29) into which the wicked descend (24.31). The lot of the righteous is very different, for their spirits proceed immediately at death to a blessed immortality: 'Their bones shall rest in the earth, and their spirits shall have much joy' (23.31). Again, in I Enoch 91–104[2] the souls of the righteous are apart from the souls of the wicked in Sheol, guarded constantly by God's holy angels. There they 'sleep a long sleep' in which they have 'nought to fear' (100.5); they have to live in hope and grieve not (102.4–5), for 'all goodness and joy and glory are prepared for them' (103.3); they 'shall live and rejoice, and their spirits shall not perish' (103.4). The lot of the wicked is very different, for 'they shall have no hope of life' (98.14); they are 'prepared for the day of destruction' (98.10). 'Their souls will be made to descend into Sheol, and they shall be wretched in great tribulation, and into darkness and chains, and a burning fire where there is grievous judgment, shall their spirits enter' (103.7–8). Sheol is the place where the wicked are slain (99.11); this does not necessarily imply annihilation, for it is described as a place from which they will never escape (103.7–8). Thus Sheol becomes for the

[1] The Latin text of II Esd. 4.41 reads, 'The chambers of souls in the underworld are like the womb.' The Syriac and Ethiopic versions read, 'The underworld and the chambers of souls.' Some scholars maintain that the verse refers not to resting-places of the righteous dead, but to places where the souls of the unborn righteous are held in readiness for earthly life. They would then correspond to the rabbinic conception of *Guph*, where the souls of the unborn are preserved. Cf. T. F. Glasson, *op. cit.*, pp. 45f.

[2] Except the Apoc. of Weeks in 93.1–14; 91.12–17.

wicked the final place of judgment. In I Enoch 108 Sheol is not mentioned by name, but no doubt it is regarded here also as the eternal place of judgment. The spirits of the righteous will be brought forth in shining light and sit each on the throne of his glory (108.12). But the spirits of sinners are cast into the 'chaotic wilderness' where they burn in the fire (108.3); there they will 'cry and make lamentations' (108.3) and finally be slain (108.3, cf. 32.13; 99.11). In the Similitudes of Enoch the righteous depart to the intermediate abode of Paradise, 'the garden where the elect and righteous dwell' (60.8). Elsewhere in the same book, however, Sheol and Hell (= Abaddon) are mentioned as the abode of souls (51.1). It may be that these are synonymous terms in this context and refer to the intermediate state of the wicked for whom it becomes the place of final judgment (cf. 56.8; 63.10). Or, as R. H. Charles suggests,[1] Paradise is to be regarded as a department of Sheol so that Sheol itself can still be described as the abode of the righteous and at the same time as the place of punishment for the wicked.

(iv) This last reference indicates a fourth distinguishing feature of Sheol in the apocalyptic writings. There it is divided up into two, three or more compartments corresponding to the moral and spiritual condition of the souls which go there, these compartments often being given specific names. The earliest description of such divisions is in I Enoch 22 where reference is made to four[2] compartments called 'hollow-places' (22.9–13) which 'have been created for this very purpose, that the spirits of the souls of the dead should assemble therein; yea, that all the souls of the children of men should assemble there. And those places have been made to receive them . . . till the great judgment comes upon them' (22.3–4). They have been made in such a way that 'the spirits of the dead might be separated' (22.9). The first division is 'for the spirits of the righteous, in which there is a bright spring of water' (22.9); the second is for sinners who have departed from this life without having received retribution for their sins—'Here their spirits shall be set apart in great pain, till the great

[1] Cf. *op. cit.*, p. 292, footnote.

[2] In 22.2 the number is given as four, in 22.9 as three. G. Beer (in Kautzsch's *Die Apokryphen und Pseudepigraphen des Alten Testaments*, vol. II, 1900, *ad loc.*) and others accept the number four; Charles (in *Apocrypha and Pseudepigrapha of the Old Testament*, vol. II, 1913, *in loc.*) accepts the number three. Beer finds the four divisions in vv. 5–7, 8–9, 10–11, 12–13. It is perhaps better to identify them in vv. 9, 10–11, 12, 13. We follow the latter divisions here, cf. T. F. Glasson, *op. cit.*, pp. 15f.

day of judgment, scourgings and torments of the accursed for ever, so that (there may be) retribution for their spirits' (22.10–11); the third is for the righteous who were martyred 'who make disclosures concerning their destruction when they were slain in the days of the sinners' (22.12, cf. also the reference to Abel in 22.5–7); the fourth is for sinners who have already received punishment in this present life for their sins (22.13).

In this passage we have the first reference in the apocalyptic writings to the idea of Hell as a place of torment, although the actual word itself is not used here. Sinners in the fourth compartment are made to suffer torments there; sinners in the second compartment are to be raised for further punishment in the 'accursed valley' (27.1). This is presumably the Valley of Hinnom, or *Ge Hinnom* in Hebrew, from which is derived the term 'Gehenna' which appears quite prominently in this literature. The name in its original Old Testament context refers to a valley west of Jerusalem notorious for its idolatrous worship and the offering of child sacrifices (cf. II Kings 16.3; II Chron. 28.3; Jer. 7.31, etc.); after the time of Josiah it was a general garbage heap which was always smouldering and on fire, a place of corruption and decay. In due course the name came to signify the place of punishment for apostate Jews where 'the worm dieth not and the fire is not quenched' (Isa. 66.24, cf. Jer. 7.32; Dan. 12.2). In the apocalyptic writings this conception is applied to the place of punishment in the after-life where the souls of the wicked suffer the burning fires of Hell. Sometimes this is identified with Sheol itself or part of Sheol (cf. I Enoch 51.1; 54.1; 56.7; 63.10; 90.26f.; Pss. of Sol. 14.6; 15.11; 16.2; II Enoch 10.1ff., etc.) or else it is in that place of endless torment which follows the final judgment (cf. I Enoch 48.9; II Bar. 85.12–13; II Esd. 7.36, etc., and also Matt. 5.22; 13.42); in certain cases, as we have seen, there is no distinction made between these two (cf. I Enoch 108, etc.). Sometimes Gehenna is thought to be situated 'in the midst of the earth' (cf. I Enoch 26.1; 90.26); it can be described as 'the burning coal of the furnace of the earth' (Apoc. of Abr. 14) where can be seen 'the lower regions . . . the Abyss and its torments' (ch. 21); it can be identified with Azazel (ch. 31) or with 'the belly of the dragon' which is found in the third heaven (III Bar. 4.4–5); or it is where no man knows its 'outgoings' (II Esd. 4.7) and belongs to neither earth nor heaven.

Over against the fires of Gehenna stands the Paradise of delight (cf. II Esd. 7.36). The word Paradise is of Persian origin and signifies a garden or park or orchard. In this sense it is found a few times in the Old Testament where the LXX translates by *paradeisos*.[1] This same word is used to refer to the Garden of Eden in Gen. 2.8, etc., and to certain other occurrences of the word 'garden' in the Hebrew Scriptures. But nowhere in the Old Testament does it refer to the future resting-place of the righteous. This development takes place in the apocalyptic writings. As we have seen,[2] it is sometimes earthly in character and sometimes heavenly; or it may partake of the nature of both together. Like Gehenna itself it may be situated on the earth or be found in the third heaven (II Enoch 42.3; Apoc. of Moses 37.5). It is the place to which the souls of the righteous go at death and where they see 'the righteous who from the beginning dwell in that place' (I Enoch 70.4). Thus, for some writers it is an intermediate state where the souls of the righteous await with hope the fearful day of God's reckoning (cf. I Enoch 60.8; Apoc. of Moses 37.5). For others, however, it is not an intermediate state at all, but the final abode of the righteous to which they go at once after death or else after the Day of Judgment. There is a separating of the ways: the wicked are cast into torment (II Enoch 10.1), but the righteous are taken to Paradise (42.3, etc.). It is a place 'where there is no toil, neither grief nor mourning; but peace and exultation and life everlasting' (Test. of Abr. 20); it is the Garden of Eden where the souls of the righteous enjoy 'foods and blessedness' for evermore (Apoc. of Abr. 21).

3. THE ORIGIN AND DEVELOPMENT OF THE RESURRECTION BELIEF

According to the teaching of the Old Testament the future hope was expressed, not in terms of individual destiny, but rather in terms of God's dealings with the nation. It was concerned not with solitary immortality, but with the establishment on earth of an everlasting kingdom in whose untold blessings righteous Israel would share. Its blessings would be experienced by those Israelites who would be living at the time and also, some thought, by the Gentiles who would come to acknowledge God's chosen people. They would be rewarded

[1] Cf. Neh. 2.8; Song of Songs 4.13; Eccles 2.5. The word occurs three times in the New Testament: Luke 23.43; II Cor. 12.4; Rev. 2.7.
[2] See p. 283.

with political and material security and enjoy the blessings of 'length of days'.

There were certain pious people in Israel, however, who could not rest content with such a belief as this. They were convinced that not only should the righteous nation share in the coming kingdom, the righteous individual should share in it also. This being so, God must raise men up so that they might take their place with the righteous nation in the kingly rule of God. A synthesis of the eschatologies of the nation and of the individual had been attempted by Ezekiel within the sphere of this present life; but it had broken down in face of the hard realities of human experience. It was only when men looked beyond this life to the next that a solution became possible. With the apocalyptists 'the separate eschatologies of the individual and of the nation issue finally in their synthesis: the righteous individual no less than the righteous nation will participate in the messianic kingdom, for the dead will rise to share therein'.[1] The full and final solution lay in the hope of resurrection from the dead.

The historical occasion marking the beginning of this resurrection belief is hidden from us, but it may well have arisen by reason of the martyrdom of certain righteous people in Israel. The justice of God's dealings with men required that those who had suffered martyrdom should be given the opportunity of sharing in the triumph of God's people when he came to establish his kingdom. Since this kingdom was to be on the earth, their bodies must be restored to them. The dead would be brought back from Sheol and united with their bodies so that they might join with the living in the triumph of God's kingdom.

This would appear to be the meaning conveyed by Isaiah 24–27, a late addition to the Book of Isaiah dating probably from the third or fourth century BC. This passage cannot properly be called an apocalyptic work, but it reveals certain apocalyptic characteristics which are of significance for the future development of apocalyptic thought. Scholars are sharply divided on the interpretation of 26.19 which might be translated thus: 'Thy dead shall live; their[2] corpses shall arise; they that dwell in the dust shall awake and sing; for the dew of lights[3] is thy dew, and the earth shall give birth to the shades'.[4]

[1] R. H. Charles, *Eschatology*, 2nd ed., 1913, p. 130.

[2] Following the Syriac and the Targum.

[3] *I.e.* the dew of heaven which revives the dead just as the morning dew revives the grass of the field. This is better than 'the dew of herbs' in the RV.

[4] So G. B. Gray, *The Book of Isaiah I–XXVII*, ICC, vol. 1, 1912, p. 447.

Some scholars would interpret this passage in the same way as Ezekiel's vision of the valley of dry bones (Ezek. 37) and take it to refer to a restoration of the *nation*, with no allusion whatever to a doctrine of individual resurrection. The view taken here is that we have in this verse the first reference in Hebrew literature to the resurrection of the dead; it is a resurrection not of all, or even of all the righteous, but only of the outstandingly righteous who are raised to participate in the messianic kingdom which is to be established upon the earth. Obscure reference is made in two ancient sources[1] to the destruction of Jerusalem and Jericho and the deportation of Jews to Hyrcania during the reign of Artaxerxes Ochus (358–338 BC). It is just possible that some such historical event as this may have marked the emergence of a resurrection belief in Israel.

A second passage of the utmost significance for the development of the resurrection belief is Dan. 12.2–3 which reads, 'And many of them that sleep in the dust of the earth shall awake, some to everlasting life and some to everlasting contempt.' Here again the principle of selection applies, but with an important difference. In the first passage the pre-eminently good are resurrected to receive the blessings of the kingdom; in the second passage the pre-eminently wicked are also raised to receive the punishment they had escaped on earth. The historical background of these verses is more certain than that of the Isaianic passage. The Book of Daniel, in its present form at any rate, is to be dated in 165 BC during the reign of Antiochus Epiphanes under whose tyrannical rule many faithful Jews were done to death. The author was convinced that the triumph of God and his people was assured and that soon his kingdom would be established on the earth. He had encouraged his compatriots to stand firm in the sure hope of final triumph. But he had seen many of them martyred for their faith; together with the living they would share in the glories of the coming kingdom.[2] On the other hand, there were Jews who had turned traitor and betrayed their fellows into the hand of the tyrant. Some of these had died without having paid the penalty of their wrong-doing. These, too, would be raised to receive their recompense.

We observe that, until the day of resurrection, the shades of all who have died remain in Sheol, shut off from fellowship with God. Even when the resurrection does take place, only a limited number of

[1] See L. E. Browne, *Early Judaism*, 1920, pp. 202f.
[2] Cf. also II Mac. 7.9, 14, 23, 36.

men are involved in it. For the rest—good and bad alike—Sheol remains their eternal resting-place. Behind both passages lies the belief that the righteous man's fellowship with God cannot be destroyed by death. In the Danielic passage, however, the factor of continued fellowship with God as the *raison d'être* of resurrection is lost sight of. The resurrection belief has ceased to be the spiritual matter which it was to the writer of Isaiah 26 and has become what R. H. Charles calls 'a mechanical conception'. 'Thus severed from the spiritual root from which it grew, the resurrection is transformed into a sort of eschatological property, a device by means of which the members of the nation are presented before God to receive their final award.'[1]

The subsequent development of the resurrection belief in the extra-biblical apocalyptic writings reveals a bewildering variation on the theme of these two biblical passages. Sometimes the righteous are to be resurrected to a kingdom established on this present earth; sometimes it is to be on a 'purified' or renewed earth; sometimes it is limited in duration and precedes the dawning of the age to come; sometimes it is a purely heavenly and 'spiritual' conception in which the idea of resurrection may or may not play a part.[2] In a few of these books the resurrection of the righteous only seems to be contemplated as it is in Isaiah 26. In the Psalms of Solomon, for example, it is said of the sinner, 'He falleth—verily grievous is his fall—and he shall not rise again; the destruction of the sinner is for ever. And the Lord shall not have him in remembrance, when he visiteth the righteous' (3.13f.); but concerning the righteous it is said, 'They that fear the Lord shall rise again into life eternal' (3.16, cf. 9.9; 13.3; 14.2, 7).[3] Likewise in I Enoch 83–90 no reference is made to the resurrection of the wicked. The resurrection of the righteous is at least implied in 90.33, where it is said that 'all that had been destroyed and dispersed' will be assembled to take their place in the kingdom.[4] Thereafter they

[1] R. H. Charles, 'Eschatology', in *EB*, vol. II, 1901, col. 1355.

[2] For an examination of the relationship of the resurrection to the messianic kingdom and the age to come, see ch. XI.

[3] R. H. Charles sees no allusion here to the resurrection of the body, presumably because the righteous are said to rise to 'eternal life' (cf. *Eschatology*, 2nd ed., 1913, p. 272). But rising into 'eternal life' does not necessarily preclude bodily participation in the future kingdom, as a number of references clearly show (*e.g.* Test. of Asher 5.2; 6.6, and II Mac. 7.9, 36).

[4] G. F. Moore doubts a reference here to resurrection. He suggests that for 'destroyed' it is possible that 'the Hebrew had '*abadh* in the sense of "be lost", which would go better with the parallel' (*op. cit.*, vol. II, p. 300).

are transformed into the likeness of the Messiah (90.38). R. H. Charles,[1] followed by E. Langton,[2] concludes from this that they rise into eternal life, which would make this passage the first expression of the idea in Jewish literature. This conclusion, however, is unnecessary since the Messiah is not here a supernatural being, but a man, however superior he may be to his fellows. Again, no reference to the resurrection of the wicked is made in II Enoch; the righteous dead alone are raised, but unlike the previous reference it is not a resurrection of the flesh; they rise rather in possession of heavenly or 'spiritual' bodies in keeping with their spiritual life in Paradise (cf. 8.5; 65.10).[3]

For the most part, however, these writers contemplate a resurrection both for the righteous and the wicked, as in Daniel 12. In I Enoch 6–36 only two references are made to resurrection, in 20.8 which is a general reference to 'those who rise' and in 22.13. In the latter passage it is said concerning the sinners in the fourth compartment of Sheol who have received punishment during their lifetime, 'nor shall they be raised from thence'. The assumption is that the sinners in the second compartment who have not received punishment during their lifetime will be raised for judgment and be cast into Gehenna (chs. 26–27), and that the righteous, in whole or in part, will also be raised to share in the blessings of the kingdom on a purified earth (cf. 10.17; 25.4ff.). Somewhat the same belief is expressed in the Noachic Fragments of I Enoch where it is at least implied that the righteous dead will share with the living righteous in the messianic kingdom (10.7, 20) and that the wicked, or at least some among them (67.8), will be raised up for judgment and will suffer in body and spirit in the fires of Gehenna (67.8–9). Likewise in the Similitudes of Enoch the righteous dead (presumably among the Jews) will be raised and 'return and stay themselves on the day of the Elect One' (61:5); they will rise from the earth and cease to be of downcast countenance (62.15), dwelling 'in the light of eternal life' (58.3) where they will find peace and increase in righteousness (58.4–5). Concerning the wicked it is said, 'And darkness shall be their dwelling, and worms shall be their bed, and they shall have no hope of rising from their beds' (46.6). Elsewhere in the same book, however, it is implied that both the wicked and the righteous in Israel shall rise, for 'in those days shall the earth also give back that

[1] Cf. *op. cit.*, p. 223. [2] Cf. *Good and Evil Spirits*, 1942, p. 214.
[3] See further pp. 377ff.

which has been entrusted to it, and Sheol also shall give back that which it has received, and hell shall give back that which it owes' (51.1). The resurrection of righteous Israelites is clearly taught in II Baruch where it is said that 'all who have fallen asleep in hope of him shall rise again' (30.1) to life in an earthly kingdom. Nothing is said in this passage about the fate of the wicked, but in another part of the book the wicked as well as the righteous apparently take part in the resurrection. The body rises from the earth and the soul from Sheol (42.8; 50.2ff.); the bodies of both wicked and righteous are transformed, the one to shame (51.2) and the other to glory (51.3).

In five apocalyptic books there is evidence for belief in a general resurrection of *all* men, to be followed by the judgment, although in practically every case this belief is confused with the contradictory evidence that there will be a resurrection of the righteous only.[1] The earliest is the Testaments of the XII Patriarchs which states that the patriarchs themselves will rise together with those 'who are put to death for the Lord's sake' (Test. of Jud. 25.1ff., cf. Test. of Benj. 10.6); 'then also *all* men shall rise, some unto glory and some unto shame' (Test. of Benj. 10.8). A physical resurrection of all the wicked as well as the righteous is indicated also in the Sibylline Oracles IV which states that 'God himself shall fashion again the bones and ashes of men and shall raise up mortals once more as they were before; and the judgment shall come' (181–3). The wicked will go to 'murky Tartarus and the black recesses of hell' (185–6), but the 'godly shall live again on earth' (187). The third book teaching a resurrection of all flesh is the Apocalypse of Moses. There it is said that God will raise up Adam (28.4, cf. 10.2) and all flesh from his day forward (41.2, 3, cf. 13.3); his holy people will enjoy the delights of Pāradise (13.3). This same teaching concerning a universal resurrection and judgment is found also in II Esdras where reference is made to 'the nations that have been raised from the dead' (7.37) signifying a resurrection of the entire human race. In the preceding verses it is said that at the resurrection the soul leaves its 'chamber' in which it had rested during the intermediate state, and enters into and revives the body which is restored from the earth (7.32). G. H. Box suggests that, in view of the fact that a general resurrection of righteous and wicked is implied by the context, a clause referring to the souls of the wicked may have dropped out at this point. Presumably the souls

[1] Cf. Tests. of XII Patr. (Jud. 25.1ff.; Sim. 6.5ff.; Zeb. 10.1ff.); Apoc. of Moses 13.3; II Esd. 7.78ff.; II Bar. 30.1–3.

of the wicked now leave their wandering (for the 'chambers' are for the souls of the righteous only) and are united with the body. Thus the righteous and the wicked are brought forward in resurrection for judgment, 'and recompense shall follow and the reward be made manifest' (7.35). The final reference is in II Baruch where it is said that 'corruption will take those that belong to it, and life those that belong to it' (42.7); at the time of resurrection the earth will restore the dead—presumably the wicked as well as the righteous—with no change in their appearance (50.2).

There are a few apocalyptic books in which no reference at all is made to a resurrection and which, indeed, point to quite a different form of survival. Of chief importance perhaps is the Book of Jubilees which teaches, not the resurrection of the body, but the immortality of the soul.[1] This is clearly expressed in 23.31 which reads, 'And their bones will rest in the earth, and their spirits will have much joy.' There is thus no place for the righteous dead in the coming earthly kingdom; their spirits rejoice in eternal bliss. Similarly in I Enoch 91–104 no earthly kingdom is visualized in which the righteous dead will receive due recompense. In 91.10 it is said that 'the righteous one (a collective) shall arise from sleep, and wisdom shall arise and be given to them', apparently referring to a resurrection of the righteous; but elsewhere, in 103.4 for example, it is made clear that it is a resurrection of the spirit only: 'And the spirits of you who have died in righteousness shall live and rejoice, and their spirits shall not perish.' From Sheol they are raised to heaven where they 'shine as the lights of heaven' (104.2) and have 'great joy as the angels of heaven' (104.4) whose companions they become (104.6). Neither is there a resurrection for the wicked; their lot is to suffer the eternal torments of Sheol (99.11; 103.7f.). A similar picture is given in the Assumption of Moses where there is no earthly kingdom and no resurrection either of the righteous or the wicked. The departed righteous enter into the bliss of heaven (10.9) and rejoice to see their Gentile foes in the fires of Gehenna (10.10). In the Apocalypse of Abraham it is said that the righteous dead go at once to Paradise (ch. 21) and the wicked dead to Azazel and the Abyss (chs. 12, 14, 21). There may be a hint here of a 'spiritual body' being given to the righteous (ch. 13), and the reference to 'dew' in the 'seventh firmament' (ch. 19) has elsewhere associations with the act of resurrection;[2]

[1] Cf. also Wisd. 2.23; 3.4; 5.15; 6.18; 8.17; 15.3.

[2] Reference to the dew is made in Isa. 26.19, where it is a sign of the revivifica-

but the general picture is apparently that of the immortality of the soul.

Such teaching concerning the immortality of the soul, though found in certain apocalyptic writings, is not typical of the apocalyptic tradition as a whole and no doubt indicates the influence of Hellenistic thought. Not the immortality of the soul, but the resurrection of the body is the key to the apocalyptic interpretation of the life beyond death.

There is evidence in the writings of the Dead Sea Scrolls that the Qumran Community believed in some form of life beyond death, although it is difficult to be sure what precise form such survival assumed. A significant passage in this connection is *Hymns of Thanksgiving* III.19–23:

I give thee thanks, Adonai!
For thou hast redeemed my soul from the Pit
and from Sheol-Abaddon thou hast brought me up again
to the top of the world.
Then I wandered on an endless plain;
and I knew that there was hope
for him whom thou hast formed from the dust (and destined)
for the eternal Assembly.
Yea, the perverse spirit hast thou purified of a great sin
so that he might mount guard with the army of the Saints
and that he might enter into communion with the congregation
of the Sons of Heaven.
Yea, thou hast caused to fall on man an eternal Destiny
amongst the intelligent Spirits,
that he should praise thy Name in communion (with them)
and that he should tell of thy wonders before all thy works.[1]

A. Dupont-Sommer[2] sees in these verses an expression of belief in the immortality of the soul which, after death, is taken up to the celestial heights, the abode of the just, where it dwells in the plain of heaven. Such an interpretation would tally with that given by Josephus concerning the beliefs of the Essenes and correspond to the Pythagorean belief in which the Elysian Fields are transported to heaven (cf. *War* II.viii.11 (155)). J. van der Ploeg suggests that, although it is possible that the resurrection belief may have been so commonly assumed at

---

tion of the dead, cf. also I Enoch 22.9; II Bar. 29.7; 73.2. See G. F. Moore, *op. cit.*, vol. III, p. 296, n. 3.

[1] Translation by A. Dupont-Sommer, *The Dead Sea Scrolls*, English trans., 1952, p. 72.

[2] Cf. *ibid.*, p. 72.

Qumran as to require no special mention, it is more likely that 'the thought of a blessed immortality appears to have pushed the notion of a bodily resurrection into the background'.[1]

The problem is complicated by the ambiguity of the texts concerning the final abode of the faithful Covenanters—in a restored and ideal Jerusalem or in a heavenly Paradise. In the passage quoted above it is stated that they are destined 'for the eternal Assembly' where they will dwell among 'the Saints' and have fellowship with 'the congregation of the Sons of Heaven'. The reference in each case is to the holy angels into whose likeness they are to be changed (cf. *Benedictions* III.25f.; IV.25f.). Such a conception does not, of course, preclude belief in resurrection as distinct from the immortality of the soul (cf. Luke 20.35f.). There is no clear-cut expression of this belief in the Scrolls, but it may well be that it was in fact accepted by the Covenanters in some form or another.[2] They must certainly have been familiar with the resurrection doctrine as the discovery of fragments of the Book of Daniel at Qumran clearly shows. J. T. Milik suggests as a possible piece of evidence for their acceptance of this belief the alignment of the graves at Qumran in which the heads, contrary to orthodox Jewish and Christian practice, lay towards the south; this would mean that, at the resurrection, the departed would rise facing the north where, according to Essene belief, Paradise was situated.[3]

A number of scholars have seen evidence for the resurrection of the Teacher of Righteousness, prior to the general resurrection of the righteous, in a reference to his 'rising' at the end of the days (cf. *Zadokite Document* VI.11). It is possible that some of his disciples may have cherished such a hope in the continuation of their Teacher's ministry until the dawning of the messianic age during which time he would solve all halakic problems as the rabbis believed Elijah would do as forerunner of the Messiah.

4. THE RESURRECTION BODY

It has been pointed out above that, whereas in Hebrew thought personality was wholly dependent on the body for its expression, in

[1] *The Excavations at Qumran*, English trans., 2nd imp., 1959, p. 109; cf. also *VT*, vol. II, 1952, pp. 171ff.

[2] Cf. M. Black, *The Scrolls and Christian Origins*, 1961, p. 141.

[3] Cf. *Ten Years of Discovery in the Wilderness of Judaea*, English ed., 1959, p. 104, and *RB*, vol. LXV, 1958, p. 77.

the apocalyptic writings it could be expressed also in terms of discarnate soul. The departed, dwelling in Sheol as souls or spirits in separation from the body, could nevertheless survive as conscious beings capable of expressing feelings and making responsible decisions. This form of survival, however, represents for the most part a temporary and transitional stage. As writers in the Hebrew tradition which regarded the body as an essential aspect of personality, the apocalyptists believed that survival after death could not be expressed *ultimately* in terms of soul or spirit apart from body. Discarnate souls might possess a conscious life of their own, but at best they were 'truncated personalities' awaiting the resurrection of the body for their ultimate expression. The soul must be united with the body because only in this way could the departed experience fullness of fellowship with God and participate in the coming kingdom.

For this reason a number of apocalyptists, as we have seen, draw the logical and consistent conclusion that resurrection and participation in the kingdom are for the righteous only. The wicked have no need of resurrection; they can neither share in the fellowship of God hereafter nor participate in the coming kingdom. And so they appear 'simply as disembodied souls—"naked"—in a spiritual environment without a body—without the capacity for communication with or means of expression in that environment'.[1] But logic and consistency are the least of the apocalyptists' virtues! Most of them teach that the wicked as well as the righteous will be raised. The writer of II Baruch states that the reason for this is that thereby the departed will be able to recognize one another (50.3–4). But a more important reason is that they may be presented before God for judgment. If a man is to be adequately punished for the sins which he committed in the body, then it is in the body that he must suffer punishment for them, *i.e.* he must be punished as a man, a fully 'integrated personality', and not as a 'truncated personality' in the form of a discarnate spirit or disembodied soul. Thus it can be said that the wicked will suffer in the fires of Gehenna in body as well as in spirit: 'Their spirit is full of lust, that they may be punished in their body. . . . And in proportion as the burning of their bodies becomes severe, a corresponding change shall take place in their spirit for ever and ever' (I Enoch 67.8–9).[2]

[1] R. H. Charles, *The Revelation of St John*, ICC, vol. II, 1920, pp. 193–4.

[2] Of interest in this connection is a parable current in rabbinic tradition and found in several versions. The following is the account given by G. F. Moore,

Generally speaking the nature of the resurrection body corresponds to the nature of the kingdom which is envisaged as the lot of the righteous—a physical body for an earthly kingdom, a 'spiritual' body for a heavenly kingdom. In the two biblical apocalyptic passages, for example, the righteous dead are to be raised from the dust of the earth to take part in the everlasting kingdom, presumably in their former physical bodies; for the kingdom, though everlasting, is to be established on this present earth. Again, in the Noachic Fragments of I Enoch the living righteous and those that have been resurrected 'shall live till they beget thousands of children, and all the days of their youth and their old age shall they complete in peace' (10.17). This idea is not confined to the earlier books, however. In the Sibylline Oracles IV, for example, we read that 'God himself shall fashion again the bones and ashes of men, and shall raise up mortals once more as they were before' (181–2) so that 'all who are godly shall live again on the earth' (187).[1] Such matters puzzled the writer of II Baruch who asks concerning those who are to be resurrected, 'Will they then resume this form of the present, and put on these entrammelling members, which are now involved in evils . . . or wilt thou perchance change these things which have been in the

Judaism, vol. I, 1927, p. 487: 'In time to come God will bring the soul and say to it, Why didst thou transgress the commandments? and it will say, The body transgressed the commandments; from the day that I departed from it, did I ever sin? Then God turns and says to the body, Why didst thou transgress the commandments? It replies, The soul sinned; from the time when the soul departed from me, did I ever sin? And what does God do? He brings both of them and judges them together. It is like a king who had a park in which were grapes and figs and pomegranates, first ripe fruits. The king said, If I station there a man who can see and walk he will eat the first ripe fruit himself. So he stationed there two keepers, one lame and the other blind, and they sat there and guarded the park. They smelled the odour of first ripe fruit. The lame man said to the blind man, Fine first fruits I see in the park. Come let me ride on your shoulders and we will fetch and eat them. So the lame man rode on the back of the blind man and they got the fruits and ate them. After a while the king came seeking for the first ripe fruits and found none. He said to the blind man, You ate them. He replied, Have I then any eyes? He said to the lame man, You ate them. He replied, Have I then any legs? So the king made the lame man mount on the back of the blind man and judged them together' (Tanhuma, ed. S. Buber, Wayyikra §12). Cf. M. R. James, *JTS*, vol. XV, 1914, pp. 236ff., and *The Lost Apocrypha of the Old Testament*, 1920, pp. 64ff.; H. H. Rowley, *The Relevance of Apocalyptic*, 1944, p. 101.

[1] Two dramatic illustrations of this belief in the resurrection of the physical body are given in II Mac. 7.11 (the martyrdom of the seven brothers) and 14.46 (the martyrdom of Razis).

world as also the world?' (49.3).[1] God replies that, when the earth restores the dead bodies on the day of resurrection, there will be no change in their form, but 'as it has received, so will it restore them' (50.2). The living are thus able to recognize them as those who had previously died but had come to life again (50.3–4).[2]

In certain apocalyptic books, however, man's future life is understood not in earthly but in supramundane terms, either because he goes direct to heaven at death or because the earthly kingdom in which he shares is only temporary and gives way to the age to come. The physical body is now no longer required; men are raised up in 'spiritual' bodies which correspond to their heavenly environment. These 'spiritual' bodies are described in several apocalyptic books under the figure of 'garments of light' (cf. II Esd. 2.39, 45, etc.) or 'garments of glory' (cf. I Enoch 62.15, etc.). The righteous are 'resplendent' and dwell in 'shining light' (I Enoch 108.11ff.). Thus in the Similitudes of Enoch when the kingdom is set up in a new heaven (45.4; 51.4) and a new earth (41.2; 45.5) the righteous dead are clothed in 'garments of glory' and dwell with the holy angels (39.4–5): 'The righteous and elect . . . shall have been clothed with garments of glory. And these shall be the garments of life from the Lord of Spirits' (62.15–16). In this way they are brought into conformity with their new 'spiritual' environment. In II Enoch the resurrection occurs at the close of the millennial kingdom when the final judgment takes place. The righteous dead are raised in 'spiritual' or 'heavenly' bodies to Paradise where 'all corruptible things shall pass away' (65.10). Their experience is like that of Enoch himself whose earthly body is replaced with a heavenly body so that he becomes like one of God's glorious angels (22.9, cf. 1.5; 20.1; 29.3).

Relatively little is said concerning the properties of this 'spiritual' body and its relation to the physical body; but such hints as are given are of considerable interest and show clearly that some connection does exist. In a number of places it is described in terms of a transformed physical body. This is probably the meaning of I Enoch 108.11ff. which says that God will 'transform those who were born in darkness'

[1] The account given in II Bar. 49–51 concerning the resurrection body finds a striking parallel in I Cor. 15.

[2] According to *Genesis Rabbah* 95.1 and *Eccles Rabbah* on 1.4, men are to be raised with their old physical marks and deformities so as to allow identification; thereupon, in the case of the righteous, the deformities are healed: cf. Matt. 5.29f. and Mark 9.43ff., which refer to physical infirmities even in the life after death.

and bring them forth 'in shining light'. The physical body will be raised up 'a glorious body' on the day of resurrection.[1] A fuller and clearer account is given by the writer of II Baruch. There, as we have noted, the resurrection body is identical in appearance with the physical body. But after the judgment, which immediately follows the resurrection (50.4), the bodies of those who have been raised will undergo a transformation: 'The aspect of those who now act wickedly will become worse than is that of such as suffer torment' (51.2). But the bodies of the righteous will pass through a series of changes during which 'their splendour will be glorified' (5.3).[2] They will be transformed into the splendour of angels (51.5, 12) and will be changed into any form they please 'from beauty into loveliness, and from light into the splendour of glory' (51.10). They will be ageless (51.9) in a world that ages not (51.16); but the wicked will 'waste away' (51.5) and depart to the place of torment (51.6).

Elsewhere, as in the Apocalypse of Moses, the 'spiritual' body in the heavenly Paradise is regarded as the counterpart of the physical body in the earthly Paradise. Adam's body, we are told, is buried in the earthly Paradise (38.5); but God says to the archangels, 'Go away to Paradise in the third heaven, and strew linen clothes and cover the body of Adam, and bring oil of the "oil of fragrance" and pour it over him' (40.2). It is apparently the heavenly body which awaits the resurrection. But not only is it a counterpart of the physical body, it is apparently also co-existent with it. This is indicated, for example, in II Enoch 22.8 where Michael is bidden, 'Go and take Enoch out of his earthly garments . . . and put him into the garments of my glory', *i.e.* Enoch's earthly body is to be replaced by a spiritual body, prepared beforehand, which is like those of the heavenly angels (22.9–10).[3] Later on in this same book a curious

[1] Cf. I Cor. 15.42ff.: 'It is sown in dishonour, it is raised in glory; it is sown in weakness, it is raised in power; it is sown a natural body, it is raised a spiritual body.'

[2] Cf. Ascension of Isa. 7.25, where Isaiah says, 'The glory of my appearance was undergoing transformation as I ascended to each heaven in turn'; and 10.9–11, where a change of the opposite nature takes place in the appearance of Christ as he descends through the several heavens to become man.

[3] With this we may compare the following passages in the Ascension of Isa.: 'But the saints will come with the Lord with their garments which are (now) stored up on high in the seventh heaven; with the Lord they will come, whose spirits are clothed . . . and he will strengthen those who have been found in the body . . . and afterwards they will turn themselves upward in their garments, and their body will be left in the world' (4.15–17); cf. also 8.14, 26; 9.9, 24, 25; 11.3, 5.

detail is given concerning the relation of the physical body to the 'spiritual' body. Enoch's 'spiritual' body, we are told, needs no food or anything earthly for its satisfaction (56.2); but when he returns to the earth for a space of thirty days, he is easily recognized by his friends (though his face had to be 'frozen' so that men could behold him, 37.2), and even allows the whole assembly to approach and kiss him (64.2–3).[1] The 'spiritual' body, then, has properties which are different from those of the physical body and yet it shares with it the same substructure. However spiritualized the concept may be, it is still 'body' and is to be clearly distinguished from the quite different concept of discarnate spirit or disembodied soul.

The apparent contradiction between the 'spiritual' body as a transformed physical body and as its heavenly counterpart, co-existent with it till the day of resurrection, is partly resolved by the belief that the spiritual body grows *pari passu* with the physical body and that a man's righteous acts performed in his earthly body condition the fashioning of his heavenly body. Such a belief is clearly stated in certain Christian apocalyptic writings[2] and is at least implied in the Jewish books. 'This spiritual body', writes R. H. Charles, 'is the joint result of God's grace and man's faithfulness. It is, on the one hand, a divine gift. . . . On the other hand, the spiritual body is in a certain sense the present possession of the faithful, and can, therefore, only be possessed through faithfulness.'[3] Man is created 'from invisible and from visible nature; of both are his death and life' (II Enoch 30.10).

5. THE LAST JUDGMENT

'When the Most High made the world . . . he first prepared the Judgment, and the things that pertain unto the Judgment' (II Esd.

[1] Cf. Luke 24.39ff.; John 20.17, 27, for the physical properties of Jesus' resurrection body.

[2] Cf. Rev. 3.4: 'But thou hast a few names in Sardis which did not defile their garments: and they shall walk with me in white, for they are worthy.' Cf. also 16.15.

That the 'spiritual' body is already one with the person for whom it is prepared is made clear in the Syriac 'Hymn of the Soul' which reads, 'I saw the garment made like unto me as it had been in a mirror. And I beheld upon it all myself, and I knew and saw myself through it, that we were divided asunder, being of one, and again were one in one shape' (cf. M. R. James, *The Apocryphal New Testament*, 1924, p. 414).

[3] *Op. cit.*, vol. I, pp. 187f.

7.70). The doctrine of the last judgment is the most characteristic doctrine of Jewish apocalyptic. It is *the* great event towards which the whole universe is moving and which will vindicate once and for all God's righteous purpose for men and all creation. On that day all wrongs will be set right; justice will not only be done, it will also be seen to be done.

Sometimes, as in the Old Testament itself, the great Day precedes and inaugurates the messianic kingdom; at other times it comes at its close and introduces the age to come. Sometimes it takes the form of a judgment of God in a great historical crisis in which the Gentiles are punished and destroyed; at other times it assumes a forensic character and takes the form of a Great Assize. Sometimes the catastrophic and forensic elements are clearly distinguished; at other times they are confused or else they are held side by side, the one representing a preliminary and the other the final judgment. Sometimes the judgment falls upon the Gentiles as distinct from the Jews; at other times it falls upon 'the wicked' who may be identified with the Gentiles, but who may also be found among *all* nations, Jewish and Gentile alike. Sometimes judgment is meted out to whole nations; at other times individual men come forward to receive their rewards and punishments. Sometimes it is reserved for the living; at other times the souls of the dead also receive their due awards. Sometimes it is confined to men and nations; at other times it falls upon angels and demons and even upon the sun and moon and stars. Sometimes God himself is judge; at other times he acts through a vice-regent, the Messiah, the Elect One, the Son of Man.

This judgment is universal in scope and ethical in character. Moral values are the criterion of judgment, be they of nations or men or angels. The contrast is between 'the righteous' and 'the wicked', between 'the elect' and 'the sinners'. One apparent exception to this is the frequent reference to the Gentiles as 'the wicked', as if these two terms were synonymous. But even here the criterion is not simply ethnic but essentially ethical in character, for this identification is possible because the Gentiles without exception are guilty of the sin of idolatry which to the Jews is the most terrible sin of all.[1] Many times over this sin is specified as the object of God's judgment (cf. Ass. of Moses 10.7; I Enoch 99.7, 9, etc.), for on that great Day 'all the idols of the heathen shall be abandoned, and the temples burned with fire, and they shall remove them from the whole earth'

[1] Cf. Ex. 20.3f.; Wisd. 13–15; Rom. 1.18–32.

(I Enoch 91.9). Elsewhere, however, this identification is not made; instead the distinction between 'the wicked' and 'the righteous' runs through all the nations of the earth, Gentiles and Jews alike. In the Testament of Benjamin, for example, it is said that God will gather together the twelve tribes of Israel with all the Gentiles and make known to them his salvation (9.2); he will judge Israel first of all 'for their unrighteousness' and then all the Gentiles (10.8–9); indeed the norm of his judgment of Israel will be the conduct of the most worthy among the Gentiles (10.10). Sometimes judgment falls upon an entire nation; at other times room is given for repentance and a place in the coming kingdom is offered to the Gentiles as well as to the Jews.[1]

Throughout these writings the picture of the nation predominates, and the salvation of the righteous is seen in terms of their share in the coming kingdom. But in some of the later books especially there is a marked tendency towards a more definite individualization. The future life is expressed not so much in terms of a restored nation in an earthly kingdom as in terms of individual and personal survival in the heavenly Paradise. As at the time of death, so also at the time of the final judgment, moral judgments prevail. Every man is judged according to what he has done of righteousness or of wickedness. This individual interest is stressed, for example, in II Enoch where it is stated that 'when all creation visible and invisible, as the Lord created it, shall end, then every man goes to the great judgment' (65.6). On that great Day all the deeds of men will be weighed and measured: 'On the day of the great judgment every weight, every measure, and every makeweight will be as in the market . . . and everyone shall learn his own measure, and according to his measure shall take his reward' (44.5). There will be different grades of punishment for the wicked and different grades of reward for the righteous. These awards will bring to their completion those already experienced in the state immediately after death. Similarly in the Testament of Abraham every man is judged according to what he has done or left undone during his life on earth. Two angels record the sins and righteous deeds of the departed (ch. 13) whose souls undergo two tests, one of fire (ch. 13) and one by the judgment of the balance in which a man's good deeds are weighed over against the bad (ch. 12, cf. I Enoch 41.1; 61.8). The seer observes an intermediate class of soul whose merits and sins equally balance each other. These

[1] For the place of the Gentiles in the messianic kingdom see pp. 297ff.

have apparently to undergo a process of purification; but their destiny depends largely on the prayers of the righteous on their behalf. Through their intercession they may at last be saved (ch. 14).[1] This same theme of prayers for the dead on the Day of Judgment occupies the mind of the writer of II Esdras, though his answer is very different from that of the Testament of Abraham. In answer to Ezra's question whether the righteous will be able to intercede then for the ungodly, 'fathers for sons, sons for fathers, brothers for brothers, kinsfolk for their nearest, friends for their dearest', God replies, 'The Day of Judgment is decisive.' It will be as impossible as it is for a man to appoint someone to take his place in illness or in sleeping or in eating or in being healed, 'for then everyone shall bear his righteousness or unrighteousness' (II Esd. 7.102–4). Repentance will be impossible and intercession for the dead will be of no avail. Each man must be judged by his own merits; each is responsible to God and is answerable for himself alone.

But the final judgment is not confined to the nations nor yet to the souls of men; the fallen angels and the demons have their share in it also. In I Enoch 6–36, for example, the punishment which the 'watchers' received beforehand will continue after the final judgment; the demons will be allowed to work their destructive powers until the day of the consummation, but on that day they will receive their rightful punishment (16.1). Several references are made to Azazel, the prince of the demons, who is judged and cast into the fire (I Enoch 10.6, cf. 41.1ff.; 55.3–56.4; II Enoch 7.1–3; 18.7). At the final judgment the fallen angels are 'led off to the abyss of fire and to the torment and the prison in which they shall be confined for ever' (10.13, cf. also 91.15; 100.4). According to the Similitudes of Enoch not only the fallen angels, but also the seventy 'shepherds' who slew of Israel more than God commanded, and the 'blinded sheep' or apostate Jews are likewise found guilty and cast into the fiery abyss of Gehenna (90.20ff., cf. also Jub. 5.10). Once again it can be seen that moral values form the criterion by which angels as well as men are to be judged on the great Day. Such moral delinquency can be credited even to the sun and moon and stars, who, like men and angels, have misused their God-given freedom; they too must submit to judgment (cf. I Enoch 18.13ff.; 20.4; 21.6; 23.4; 80.2–8).

[1] In the shorter recension of the text (Recension B) no reference is made to the salvation of this class of soul by intercession.

Together with this process of individualization in which angels and the souls of men are held morally responsible on the great Day there develops the notion of the last judgment as a Great Assize where justice is interpreted in forensic terms unlike those of the Old Testament Scriptures. The familiar Old Testament picture of judgment in the form of a great historical crisis in which the Gentiles are punished and destroyed is still to be found here (cf. I Enoch 38.1; 62.1ff.; Sib. Or. III. 742, etc.); but alongside this is the picture of the judgment seat before which, as we have seen, not only nations and rulers, but also angels and the souls of men appear for judgment.[1] God himself sits upon his throne and pronounces judgment; nations and rulers are destroyed from off the face of the earth (Dan. 7.9–14) and ungodly men are sent to 'the black recesses of hell' (Sib. Or. IV. 183–6). Sometimes, however, God acts through his vice-regent. The supernatural Son of Man, for example, appears with 'the Head of Days' and executes judgment in his name (cf. I Enoch 46.1ff.; 48.2), or wicked men are brought before the Messiah for judgment (cf. II Bar. 40.1–2; 72.2; II Esd. 12.33–34). Whatever agency he may use, this is certain—'The Judge will come and will not tarry' (II Bar. 48.39).

In some of these writings, as in the Book of Daniel, the catastrophic and forensic elements are combined in a judgment which includes not only the nations and their rulers but also the righteous and the wicked among the dead. In others, as in the Psalms of Solomon, stress is laid on the destruction of the Gentiles and, although reference is made to a resurrection of the righteous, there is no speculation at all on the fate of the individual. Elsewhere, as in the Testament of Abraham, there is a marked absence of any sense of *denouement* or crisis and the stress is laid almost entirely on the fate of the individual at the time of the Great Assize. In a few of these books, however, the writers envisage not one judgment but two, the one preliminary to the other. The first is usually catastrophic and involves a judgment on the nations; the second is forensic in which men and angels appear before the Judge on the last day. In the Apocalypse of Weeks, for example, where the history of the world is divided up into ten 'weeks', there is first of all a judgment of the sword; in the eighth week (representing the writer's own day) the righteous inflict punishment on the sinners 'that a righteous judgment may be executed on the

[1] Cf. Dan. 7.9–14; 12.2; I Enoch 51.1f.; 90.20ff.; Test. of Benj. 10.8; Test. of Abr. 13; Apoc. of Abr. 24; Sib. Or. IV. 41; II Bar. 36.11; II Esd. 7.32ff.

oppressors' (91.12) and in the ninth 'week' 'the world shall be written down for destruction' (91.14). But in the tenth 'week' 'there shall be the great eternal judgment in which he will execute vengeance amongst the angels' (91.15); then follows an eternal age of goodness and righteousness wherein 'sin shall no more be mentioned for ever' (91.17) in which, presumably, the righteous share in the blessings of God. Again, in II Baruch judgment is executed on the Gentiles who are slain in war or by convulsions of nature (40.1–2; 70.7ff.; 72.2ff.). The horizon is here limited to the present earth, and the judgment is that of the nations. But elsewhere in the book hints are given of a second and final judgment in which the wicked will 'be tormented still more' (36.11); 'the beginning of the day of judgment' (59.8) will reveal to men 'the mouth of Gehenna . . . and the likeness of future torment' (59.10–11). Somewhat the same picture is presented by the writer of II Esdras. Here again the final judgment is preceded by a judgment on the enemies of Israel. The Messiah destroys the power of Rome (12.33) and preserves his own people 'until the end come, even the Day of Judgment' (12.34). At the close of the messianic kingdom which follows there come the resurrection and the great judgment in which 'the furnace of Gehenna' and 'the Paradise of delight' will be made manifest (7.36).

In two other books also reference is made to more than one judgment, but in each case the idea is somewhat different from those described above. In the Life of Adam and Eve, for example, it is said that the Lord will bring down the anger of his judgment 'first by water, the second time by fire; by these two will the Lord judge the whole human race' (49.3). Here the reference is first to the Flood, and second to the day of the last judgment. More significant is the evidence of the Testament of Abraham. In chapter 13 the writer refers to three different judgments of the souls of the departed, and three different judges. In the first the judge is Abel; in the second the twelve tribes of Israel; in the third God himself. The second judgment introduces an element which is not altogether in keeping with the specifically individual interest of this book. It is probably an attempt on the part of the writer to combine in a single pattern the eschatology of the individual and that of the nation with their different conceptions of judgment and corresponds to the idea of a temporary messianic kingdom which we find in certain other apocalyptic books. The first and third judgments are in keeping with the individual interest characteristic of the book as a whole. The judgment of Abel serves as a preliminary judgment and prepares the way for the final judgment at the hands of God.

At the heart of all this speculation lay the conviction that God would not allow his people to perish at the hands of their enemies, that evil must be punished and good rewarded, that men and nations and the whole created universe would at last acknowledge his sovereignty over all his works. The final judgment is the final act of God in which his eternal purpose is at last made plain.

6. THE INFLUENCE OF FOREIGN THOUGHT

Attempts have been made by a number of scholars to prove that the belief in life after death among the Jews, and in particular the doctrine of resurrection, originated elsewhere than in Jewish thought and religious experience. Such a belief was to be found in Egypt, for example, at a much earlier stage than in Israel. But if this were the source of influence it is strange that it was not felt in Israel at a much earlier date; nor would the association of resurrection with the fertility cults of Egyptian religion commend such a doctrine to the Jews.[1] It should be noted, moreover, that in Egypt life after death was possible only for those who were mummified and that, down to Roman times at least, mummification was confined to the very wealthy, the poor being buried just as they were.[2] There is nothing corresponding to this in the Jewish faith.

Other scholars have traced back the origins of the Jewish doctrine of resurrection to the influence of Persian thought. Persian belief in survival in the form of resurrection antedates its rise in Israel. But the two notions are very different from each other. Among the Jews the disposal of the dead is by burial, and resurrection is explained as an awaking from sleep in the dust of the earth; among the Persians, however, it takes the form of an exposure of the dead bodies which are dissolved in the elements and are demanded from the elements again.[3] Once more it is most unlikely that the beginnings of the

[1] For an examination of the resurrection in relation to the Egyptian cult of Osiris, see H. H. Rowley, *The Faith of Israel*, 1956, pp. 161ff.

[2] Cf. *A General Introductory Guide to the Egyptian Collections in the British Museum*, 1930, p. 224.

[3] This last statement comes from the *Bundahishn* 30.6, which, though reflecting older sources, is itself not earlier than the ninth century AD. Cf. Alfred Bertholet, 'The Pre-Christian Belief in the Resurrection of the Body', *AJT*, vol. XX, 1916, p. 26.

resurrection belief among the Jews are to be traced to this particular source. J. H. Moulton claims the support of Bousset and Söderblom for the suggestion that Persian influences may have prompted the change from a selective resurrection, such as is found in the two biblical apocalypses, to a universal resurrection, such as is found in certain of the later apocalyptic books.[1] This may be so; but it is much less likely that we are to find that influence in Isaiah 24–27 and Daniel 12, so different is their conception of resurrection from that of the Persian.[2] Moreover, although the doctrine of a general resurrection is to be found in both literatures, nowhere is the Persian belief in the final and complete restitution of all men to be found in the Jewish apocalyptic writings.

Most scholars would agree with W. F. Albright that the value of Iranian influence for our understanding both of Judaism and of Christianity has been greatly overestimated.[3] Among those features where Persian influence may be detected Albright notes 'developing belief in the last judgment and in rewards and punishments after death'.[4] R. C. Zaehner likewise argues that, although the influence of Zoroastrianism on the Jewish resurrection belief cannot be proved, the same cannot be said about the doctrine of rewards and punishments after death and of an eternity of bliss or woe.[5] But even here the points of contact are mainly in matters of detail. It is true that there is a certain correspondence between the two literatures in their descriptions of the punishment of the wicked after death. But it is not at all clear to what extent this is due to Persian influence. J. H. Moulton, for example, notes with Söderblom 'how unlike anything in Judaism is the Avestan hell, a place of cold and stench and poison, not of fire—which was, of course, too sacred an element to be applied thus'[6] and agrees that there are no genuine contacts between the two faiths in this respect until a late epoch. In one point of detail concerning the final judgment we are probably to detect the effect of Persian influence. This is the tendency in some apocalyptic books to stress the part played in it by the individual, and the reference to the

[1] 'Zoroastrianism' in *HDB*, vol. IV, p. 993. For a list of Jewish books where a general resurrection is taught see above, pp. 37f.

[2] For points of similarity and dissimilarity see R. H. Charles, *Eschatology*, 2nd ed., 1913, pp. 139ff.

[3] Cf. *From the Stone Age to Christainity*, 2nd ed., 1957, p. 358. [4] *Ibid.*, p. 361.

[5] Cf. *The Dawn and Twilight of Zoroastrianism*, 1961, p. 57.

[6] *Op cit.*, p. 993, with reference to N. Söderblom, *La Vie Future d'après le Mazdeisme*, 1901, pp. 301–12.

weighing of men's deeds in a balance, the good against the evil (cf. I Enoch 41.1; Test. of Abr. 12). J. H. Moulton confirms that this is no doubt an old Iranian idea and agrees with the principle of Persian jurisprudence.[1] But of course the same idea is to be found in the Old Testament itself, which may be a sufficient source of the apocalyptic reference.[2] Indeed the whole conception of judgment, in terms of the prophetic Day of Yahweh, is so deeply embedded in Jewish tradition that the apocalyptic day of final judgment can be rightly described as a specialization of that Old Testament idea.[3] In particular the conception of the day of final judgment in the form of a future general Assize is to be found nowhere in the religious thought of that time except among the Jews and later among the Christians.[4] The idea of the destruction of the world by fire which appears in the apocalyptic writings[5] is sometimes claimed to be due to Persian influence; it is much more likely, however, to be derived from the Stoic conception of *ekpyrōsis* or conflagration which, as a feature of the cosmic cycle,[6] is a conception very different from the apocalyptic final judgment.

Other scholars have pointed to the contribution of Greek thought, and of Hellenistic culture generally, as a more significant factor than the Persian in its influence on the Jewish belief in resurrection and the life after death. The popular conception of the immortality of the soul, for example, which seeks release at death from the prison-house of the body, has left its mark on a number of the apocalyptic books.[7] But the idea of resurrection is so basic to apocalyptic thought that this could not possibly have been a decisive element in the birth of the resurrection belief in Israel. It is altogether alien to the Hebrew mentality for example to say with the Greeks that the souls of men are 'enclosed in the corporeal as though in a foreign hostile element, which survive the association with the body . . . distinct, complete and indivisible personalities . . . an independent substance that enters from beyond space and time into the material and perceptible

[1] Cf. *Early Zoroastrianism*, 1913, pp. 169f.

[2] Cf. Job 31.6; Ps. 62.9; Prov. 16.2; 21.2; 24.12; also Dan. 5.27; Pss. of Sol. 5.6.

[3] See pp. 92ff above.

[4] Cf. F. C. Burkitt, *Jewish and Christian Apocalypses*, 1914, p. 3.

[5] Cf. Dan. 7.10f.; Pss. of Sol. 15.14f.; Sib. Or. II. 253f., 296; III. 542, 689; IV. 176; II Bar. 27.10; 70.8; II Esd. 5.8; also Luke 17.28; II Peter 3.6ff.; II Thess. 1.7f.; Rev. 19.20; 20.10, 14f.; 21.8; and in the Dead Sea Scrolls, *Hymns* III.29ff.; *The War of the Sons of Light*, etc., XIV.17; *Manual of Discipline* II.8.

[6] See pp. 215f. [7] See pp. 153, 372f.

world, and into external conjunction with the body, not into organic union with it'.[1] A closer connection with Hebrew thought has been sought in the Greek doctrine of transmigration with its series of reincarnations at the end of which the soul, now rid of the body, returns to the realm of pure spiritual being whence it originally came. But here again the influence of such teaching on the origins of the resurrection belief in Israel is most unlikely. It is a complete exaggeration to say that the Jewish teaching concerning resurrection is 'exactly parallel to the reincarnation which brings the soul of the dead into the world of the living';[2] nor is it 'mainly a matter of terms' whether the word 'resurrection' is used in this connection or not.[3] It may be that the influence of Platonic thought, for example, with its teaching concerning the non-material nature of the world of eternal ideas and the immortality of the soul, can be detected in certain apocalyptic writings where there is a 'spiritualizing' of the resurrection body. But even here it is easy to overemphasize the importance or extent of such influence. The same response can be given to the claim that Greek influence is detectable in the apocalyptists' use of the word 'soul' (Hebrew *nepeš*, Greek *psychē*) to indicate the nature of a man's survival in the realm of Sheol. This cannot simply be taken for granted. It is quite possible that the explanation of the use of this word is to be found rather in the very nature of Hebrew psychology itself. The departed in Sheol, as conscious moral beings, could no longer be called *repa'īm* or 'lifeless ones'. From their stock of psychological terms the apocalyptists chose *nepeš* or *psychē* as best suited to describe that form of life in which men survive the grave, for according to Hebrew psychology consciousness is a function of *nepeš* as well as of body. This possibility is strengthened by reason of the fact that the apocalyptists often use the word *pneumata* ('spirits') as a synonym of *psychai* ('souls') to describe individual conscious beings after death even although this use of the word is not Greek at all.[4] Its use in this particular sense is probably to be explained rather as a development of the Hebrew word *rūaḥ* ('spirit').

In other respects, however, Greek influence is clearly to be

[1] E. Rohde, *Psyche*, English ed., 1925, pp. 468–9.

[2] I. Levy, *Légende de Pythagorie de Grèce en Palestine*, 1927, p. 255.

[3] Cf. T. F. Glasson, *Greek Influence in Jewish Eschatology*, 1961, p. 29, who qualifies Levy's statement given above.

[4] Cf. Edwyn Bevan, *Symbolism and Belief*, 1938, p. 185.

detected, as for example in certain topographical details of the after-life which abound in the apocalyptic books. This is particularly so in I Enoch 1–36 whose references to mountains at the end of the earth, the fragrance of trees and flowers and fruits, and the rivers and seas of the underworld are strongly reminiscent of Greek mythology.[1] T. F. Glasson finds such influence also in certain fundamental beliefs of the apocalyptic teaching, three of which may be mentioned here—the idea of divisions within Sheol, of rewards and punishments in the life beyond, and of Sheol as an intermediate abode. The belief in divisions within Hades, with their corresponding differentiations between the righteous and the wicked, is to be found for example among the Orphic sects where it arose at a much earlier stage than among the Jews. There is a similarity also between the two literatures in their description of the bliss of the righteous and the suffering of the wicked in the realm of the dead. The apocalyptists' picture of hell-fire, for example, is again strongly reminiscent of Orphic teaching. There, as in I Enoch, the burnings of fire are seen to be not only purgative but also punitive and are a means of torment and retributive justice. This whole conception, as we have seen, may well have had its origin in the fires of the Valley of Hinnom, but the history of its development no doubt owes much in its presentation to the popular notions of the Hellenistic world. Again, the idea of an intermediate abode—in Hades or 'the isles of the blessed' or heaven—from which men's souls come forth at each reincarnation was an inevitable presupposition of the Greek doctrine of transmigration. In a somewhat similar way in the apocalyptic literature men's souls descend to Sheol where they await the resurrection and the final judgment or else, as in a few books, they depart at death to heaven itself. It is hard to see these similarities as altogether fortuitous.

The argument of the preceding pages has indicated first that, in respect of origins at any rate, the resurrection belief in Israel grew naturally out of men's conviction that the fellowship they had enjoyed with God in this life could not be broken even by death; and secondly that, by reason of their particularly Hebrew conception of personality, it was inevitable that they should interpret such survival ultimately in terms of bodily resurrection. The most we can say is that the Jews may have been stimulated by what they saw in other religions; this would remind them of corresponding elements already present in their own religious faith. The rise of the

[1] Cf. T. F. Glasson, *op. cit.*, pp. 12f., 20f.

resurrection belief in Israel is so true to the Hebrew tradition both religiously and psychologically that it is quite unnecessary to look elsewhere for its source.

But whilst this judgment may be true in respect of *origins*, it requires qualification in respect of the *development* of belief in life after death as recorded in the apocalyptic writings. Here the influence of foreign thought, particularly that of the Greeks, can be clearly detected; indeed it is only to be expected that Judaism, in its belief concerning life after death as in other respects also, should not wholly have escaped the influence of that Hellenistic culture which pressed upon it from every side. But even where such influence is most marked the apocalyptic writers, here as elsewhere, not only adopt but at the same time adapt what they borrow and make it conform to the Hebrew tradition to which they themselves have fallen heir.

Appendix I

CHRISTIAN LISTS OF JEWISH APOCRYPHAL BOOKS

FROM THE FOURTH century onwards a distinction came to be made in the Christian Church not only between the 'canonical' and the 'apocryphal' books (signifying those which lay outside the Canon), but also within the apocryphal books themselves. Athanasius, for example, in his Thirty-Ninth Festal Letter (AD 365) indicates that there were certain books which, though not on the canonical list, were nevertheless appointed to be read for 'instruction in the word of true religion'. In this connection he names the Wisdom of Solomon, the Wisdom of Sirach, Esther, Judith and Tobit together with two Christian writings, the Teaching of the Apostles and the Shepherd. He thereafter refers to certain 'secret writings' (Greek *apocrypha*), bearing the names of men like Moses and Isaiah, as 'a device of heretics . . . vain and abominable voices'. Shortly afterwards Jerome (d. 420) drew a distinction between what he called *libri canonici* and *libri ecclesiastici*, the latter of which he placed '*inter apocrypha*', *i.e.* among the apocryphal books which lay outside the Canon. But even he is compelled to acknowledge an intermediate classification and designates certain books as *libri agiographi* over against the *libri apocryphi*. In this use of the word 'apocrypha' and in his general outlook Jerome had already been anticipated by Cyril of Jerusalem (d. 386) who likewise gave a more honoured place to certain among the apocryphal books.

There was no unanimity of opinion concerning the authority of these several writings, but a class of books emerged, indicated not infrequently by the title '*antilegomena*' ('debatable' or 'disputed' books), which might be permitted for reading and instruction; over against these are set a group, indefinite in number, called by the name '*apocrypha*' among which most of the Jewish apocalyptic writings appear. Valuable information concerning the nature and number of these books is given in certain lists or stichometries drawn up to define which were and which were not of canonical authority of which the following are the most significant for our purpose:

1. *The Stichometry of Nicephorus* is given as an appendix to the Chronography of Nicephorus of Constantinople[1] (806–15) to which it was probably attached about the middle of the ninth century. It is, however, considerably older than this and may date back to about the sixth century. It gives a list of canonical and apocryphal books of the Old and New

[1] Cf. C. de Boor, *Nicephori Opuscula Historica*, 1880, pp. 134f.; E. Schürer, *The Jewish People in the Time of Jesus Christ*, div. II, vol. III, pp. 125f.

Testaments together with the number of *stichoi* or lines which each book contained.

Under the heading of Old Testament 'disputed' books it gives the following titles:

i. I—III Maccabees (7,300)
ii. Wisdom of Solomon (1,100)
iii. Wisdom of Jesus (son) of Sirach (2,800)
iv. Psalms and Odes of Solomon (2,100)
v. Esther (350)
vi. Judith (1,700)
vii. Susanna (500)
viii. Tobit and Tobias (700)

This list is followed by another with the title 'apocrypha of the Old Testament':

i. Enoch (4,800)
ii. Patriarchs (5,100)
iii. Prayer of Joseph (1,100)
iv. Testament of Moses (1,100)
v. Assumption of Moses (1,400)
vi. Abraham (300)
vii. Eldad and Modad (400)
viii. Of the prophet Elias (316)
ix. Of the prophet Sophonias (*i.e.* Zephaniah) (600)
x. Of Zacharias, father of John (500)
xi. Of Baruch, Ambacum (*i.e.* Habakkuk), Ezekiel and Daniel—pseudepigrapha

The final entry, containing the names of four books, probably represents a later addition to the original list. The book ascribed to Zacharias is presumably a Christian writing.

2. *The Synopsis of Sacred Scripture* credited falsely to Athanasius[1] cannot be earlier than the sixth century. The list of books given here bears a close resemblance to that in the Nicephorus Stichometry, although no reference is made in this case to the length of each writing.

Under the heading of 'antilegomena' of the Old Testament the following names are given:

Wisdom of Solomon
Wisdom of Jesus son of Sirach
Esther
Judith
Tobit

[1] J-P. Migne, *Patrologiae Cursus Completus*, vol. XXVIII (Athanasius, Tom. IV), 1887, pp. 283ff., especially p. 431.

I–IV Maccabees[1]
Ptolemaica[1]
Psalms and Ode [*sic*] of Solomon
Susanna

The books appearing under the title 'apocrypha' are exactly the same, and in the same order, as those given in the Stichometry noted above.

3. The so-called '*List of the Sixty* (*Canonical*) *Books*' is found attached to certain manuscripts of the *Quaestiones et Responsiones of Anastasius of Sinai*[2] (*c*. 640–700) and is probably to be dated in the sixth or seventh century. Nine books are named as lying 'outside the Sixty':

i. Wisdom
ii. Jesus son of Sirach
iii–vi. I–IV Maccabees
vii. Esther
viii. Judith
ix. Tobit

Another twenty-four books, Jewish and Christian, are then listed under the heading of 'apocrypha' among which are the following:

i. Adam
ii. Enoch
iii. Lamech
iv. Patriarchs
v. Prayer of Joseph
vi. Eldam and Modam (or Eldad and Modad)
vii. Testament of Moses
viii. The Assumption of Moses[3]
ix. Psalms of Solomon
x. Apocalypse of Elias[3]
xi. Vision of Esaias[3]
xii. Apocalypse of Sophonias
xiii. Apocalypse of Zacharias (probably Christian)
xiv. Apocalypse of Esdras

[1] It has been conjectured by Credner that the word 'and' should perhaps be read instead of the letter *delta*, signifying 'four' (books of Maccabees). The list would then give 'Maccabees *and* Ptolemaica'. Since *three* books of Maccabees are mentioned in the Stichometry of Nicephorus and elsewhere, 'Ptolemaica' may refer to the third of these. Another title by which III Maccabees was known at an early date was 'On Providence' (cf. K. A. Credner, *Zur Geschichte des Kanons*, 1847, p. 144; E. Schürer, *op. cit.*, p. 218).

[2] Cf. J. B. Pitra, *Juris ecclesiastici Graecorum historia et monumenta*, 1864, p. 100, and E. Schürer, *op. cit.*, pp. 126f.

[3] In some manuscripts no. viii (Assumption of Moses) is missing, no. x (Apocalypse of Elias) is repeated in the list of those 'outside the Sixty' also as no. x, and no. xi (Vision of Esaias) is omitted, but appears with the same numbering in the former list. For a copy of the text representing these manuscripts see A. H. Charteris, *Canonicity*, 1880, pp. 28f.

There is again a close resemblance between this list and those ascribed to Nicephorus and Athanasius. Of the first nine books listed in the Stichometry of Nicephorus all but one (Abraham) appear here. The Psalms of Solomon which is counted among the 'apocrypha' in the list of the Sixty appears among the 'antilegomena' in the other two lists.

4. The so-called *Gelasian Decree* (*de libris recipiendis et non recipiendis*)[1] has been attributed to Damasus (384), Gelasius (496) and Hormisdas (523), but is probably the work of none of these and belongs to the sixth century. It sets out in two lists what books the catholic Church receives and what it ought to avoid.

Included in the list of accepted Old Testament books are:

Wisdom
Ecclesiasticus
Tobias
Judith
Maccabees (two books)

This is followed by a long list of sixty-one entries, mostly Christian, under the title 'apocryphal books' which are said to have been composed by heretics and schismatics and are to be avoided by the Church. It contains some obscure or unknown titles and omits other well-known Jewish writings which we might have expected to find here. In the list are six books of particular interest:

The Book of Leptogenesis ('Little Genesis', *i.e.* Jubilees), concerning the daughters of Adam.
The Book which is called the Penitence of Adam.
The Book concerning the giant, Ogias by name, who is considered by the heretics to have fought with a dragon after the Flood.[2]
The Book which is called the Testament of Job.
The Book which is called the Penitence of Jamnes and Mambres.
The Writing which is called the Interdiction of Solomon.[3]

5. *Three Armenian lists* noted by Theodor Zahn[4] supplement those already given.[5]

The first is provided by *Samuel of Ani* (*c.* 1179) who tells of certain Nestorian 'mountebanks' who came into Armenia and expounded their false books to the people there. Among the ten books mentioned two are of

[1] Cf. E. von Dobschütz, *Das Decretum Gelasianum*, 1912, pp. 5ff., 48ff.
[2] M. R. James suggests that this was circulated by the Manichaeans. There is reference to this giant also in rabbinic literature, cf. *The Lost Apocrypha of the Old Testament*, 1936, pp. 40ff.
[3] Another reading gives 'the Contradiction of Solomon'.
[4] Cf. *Forschungen zur Geschichte des Neutestamentlichen Kanons und der altkirchlichen Literatur*, vol. V, 1893, pp. 109–57.
[5] These are quoted by M. R. James, *op. cit.*, pp. xiiif.

particular interest. One is the Penitence of Adam; the other is called simply 'the Testament' by which is probably meant the Testament of Adam.

The second list is given by *Mechithar of Aïrivank* (*c.* 1290) under the title 'Jewish apocryphal books'. They are ten in number:

i. Book of Adam
ii. Book of Enoch
iii. Book of the Sibyl
iv. The XII Patriarchs, *i.e.* the Testaments of the XII Sons of Jacob
v. The Prayers [*sic*] of Joseph
vi. The Ascension of Moses
vii. Eldad, Modad
viii. The Psalms of Solomon
ix. The Mysteries of Elias
x. The Seventh Vision of Daniel

The third list is by the same chronicler and is dated 1085. Interspersed among the canonical Old Testament books the following titles are given:

I–IV Maccabees
The Vision of Enoch[1]
The Testaments of the Patriarchs
The Prayers of Asenath
Tobit
Judith
Esdras, Salathiel
The Paralipomena of Jeremiah, Babylon (mainly Christian)
Death of the Prophets
Jesus Sirach

[1] Presumably a late work.

Appendix II

A LIST OF PSYCHOLOGICAL TERMS IN THE APOCALYPTIC LITERATURE

I. Parts of the Body

Central Organs:

1. *Heart*

(*a*) Denoting full range of personality, inner life, or character:

Dan. 5.20, 22; 8.25; 11.12, 27, 28
I Enoch 81.7
Sib. Or. III. 548, 722, 733
Tests. of Jud. 13.2; 20.3, 4; Sim. 4.5; 5.2; Napht. 3.1; Jos. 4.6; 10.2; Benj. 8.2; Reub. 4.1; 6.10; Dan 1.3; Iss. 3.1, 8; 4.1, 6; 7.7; Gad 7.7; Zeb. 7.2
Jub. 1.11, 19, 21, 23 (*bis*); 2.29; 5.19; 12.3, 5, 21; 20.4; 22.18; 37.12, 24
I Enoch 93.8; 96.4; 99.8 (*bis*); 104.9
Pss. of Sol. 2.16; 3.2; 4.1; 6.1, 7; 14.5; 15.5; 17.15
II Enoch 44.4; 45.3 (*bis*); 46.2 (*bis*); 52.13, 14, 16; 53.3; 61.1, 5 (*bis*); 63.2
'Mart. of Isa.' 2.4; 3.11 (*bis*); 5.8
Sib. Or. IV. 169–70
II Bar. 9.1; 14.11; 32.1; 43.1; 46.5; 51.3; 67.7; 78.6; 85.4
II Esd. 3.20, 21, 22, 26; 4.4, 30; 6.26; 7.48; 8.6; 9.36
Apoc. of Moses 13.5; 26.1
Sib. Or. V. 111–12, 192
As 'conscience':[1]
Tests. of Jud. 20.5; Gad 5.3

(*b*) Denoting more emotional side of human consciousness:

Is softened: I Enoch 68.3
Is sad: Tests. of Sim. 2.4; Zeb. 2.5; Jos. 7.2; 15.3
Is merry: Test. of Napht. 9.2
Shows desire, etc.: Tests. of Reub. 3.6; Jos. 7.1; Napht. 7.4; II Enoch 63.3; Apoc. of Abr. 23; 30
Loves: Tests. of Gad 6.3; Sim. 4.7; Iss. 7.6; Dan 5.3; Jub. 19.31; 36.24

[1] The word *syneidēsis* is found in Test. of Reub. 4.3. It is probably a specialization of the Old Testament usage of heart.

Shows mercy and forgiveness: Tests. of Zeb. 5.3, 4; Gad 6.7
Hates: Test. of Gad 2.1; 5.1; 6.1
Shows reverence and fear: Tests. of Jos. 10.5; Levi 13.1
Shows guile: Test. of Iss. 7.4
Is disturbed: Test. of Dan 4.7
Rejoices and is glad: Jub. 19.21; 22.26, 28; 25.23; 35.12; Pss. of Sol. 15.5
Blesses: Jub. 22.27; 25.2; 29.20
Honours: Jub. 35.13
Worships: Jub. 36.20
Grieves: Jub. 13.18
Is troubled: Jub. 35.14; I Enoch 48.4; 95.1; II Bar. 55.4; II Esd. 6.36; 9.28
Is pained: Jub. 36.15; Sib. Or. IV. 18–19
Is afflicted: I Enoch 99.16
Is afraid: Pss. of Sol. 8.6
Shows distress: II Enoch 1.3
Is confident: II Enoch 2.3
Is lacerated: Apoc. of Abr. 27
Is in a stupor: II Bar. 70.2
Boasts: II Bar. 67.2
Is perturbed: II Esd. 3.30
Is terrified: II Esd. 10.25, 55
Is bloodthirsty: Sib. Or. V. 171

(*c*) Intellectual use:[1]

I Enoch 14.3
Dan. 2.30; 4.13 (*bis*); 5.21; 7.4, 28; 10.12
Sib. Or. III. 584–5
Tests. of Napht. 2.6, 8; Sim. 2.1; Benj. 2.8; Reub. 1.4; 5.3; Jud. 13.6, 8; Levi 6.2; 8.19
Jub. 1.5; 2.2; 12.17, 20; 15.17; 22.18; 24.4; 24.35; 35.3
I Enoch 94.5 (*bis*); 98.7; 101.5
Pss. of Sol. 1.3; 8.3; 16.6; 17.27
II Enoch 41.1; 43.2; 46.1; 47.1; 61.4; 65.2; 66.3
Test. of Abr. 3; 4; 5; 6
Apoc. of Abr. 23; 30
II Bar. 11.6; 20.3; 48.21; 50.1; 83.4
II Esd. 3.28; 4.2; 5.21; 8.4, 58; 9.38; 10.31; 12.38; 14.8, 25, 34, 40
Apoc. of Moses 3.3; 13.5
Sib. Or. V. 52

(*d*) Volitional use:

I Enoch 5.4; 16.3
Dan. 1.8; 6.15
Test. of Dan 1.4; 5.11

[1] To this list ought to be added the occurrences of *nous* which is a specialization of the Old Testament usage of 'heart'.

Jub. 1.15 (*bis*), 16, 23; 21.2, 3; 25.6; 37.21 (*bis*); 46.1, 13; 48.17
I Enoch 91.4 (*bis*); 98.11; 100.8
'Mart. of Isa.' 1.12, 13
II Bar. 46.1

(*e*) Figurative use = midst:
II Esd. 4.7; 13.3, 51

2. *Bowels*
Tests. of Jud. 26.3; Sim. 2.4; Zeb. 2.1, 4; 7.3, 4; 8.2; Jos. 15.3; Benj. 3.7
Pss. of Sol. 2.5
Test. of Abr. 3; 5 (*bis*)

3. *Liver*
Tests. of Napht. 2.8; Reub. 3.3; Sim. 2.4; 4.1; Gad 5.9, 11 (*bis*); Zeb. 2.4

4. '*Reins*' *or kidneys*
I Enoch 60.3; 68.3
Test. of Napht. 2.8
II Bar. 48.39

5. *Gall*
Tests. of Reub. 3.3; Napht. 2.8

6. *Spleen*
Test. of Napht. 2.8

7. *Womb*
Jub. 25.19

Peripheral Organs:

1. *Mouth*
I Enoch 5.4
Dan. 7.8, 20
Sib. Or. III. 500, 829
Jub. 12.25 (*tris*); 23.17; 25.14 (*bis*), 19; 31.12, 15; 43.16
I Enoch 39.7
Pss. of Sol. 17.27, 39
Ass. of Moses 7.9; 11.4
II Bar. 36.7
Apoc. of Moses 16.5; 17.4
Sib. Or. V. 280, 392, 439

2. *Lips*
Pss. of Sol. 13.4; 15.5; 16.10
II Enoch 1.5
Life of Adam and Eve 6.1
Sib. Or. V. 259, 280

3. *Tongue*

Jub. 25.19
Pss. of Sol. 12.1, 2, 3 (*bis*); 13.5; 16.10
II Enoch 46.2; 52.13, 14; 60.1
Sib. Or. V. 271

4. *Eyes*

Dan. 7.8, 20
Tests. of Benj. 4.2; Iss. 4.6
Pss. of Sol. 4.4, 5, 11, 15
II Enoch 29.1; 39.4; 42.1

5. *Hand*

Test. of Sim. 2.12
Pss. of Sol. 16.9; 18.1
II Enoch 39.5, etc.
Sib. Or. V. 401

Other parts of the body:

Belly:	Pss. of Sol. 2.15
Breasts:	Jub. 25.19
Knees:	Pss. of Sol. 8.5
Loins:	Pss. of Sol. 8.5
Joints:	Test. of Zeb. 2.5
Members:	II Bar. 54.7–8; 83.3
Bones:	I Enoch 25.6; Jub. 23.31; Pss. of Sol. 8.6; Test. of Sim. 6.2
Flesh:	I Enoch 14.21; 15.4, 8; 17.6; 84.1, 4, 6 (*bis*); 106.17
	Dan. 2.11; 4.12
	Tests. of Jud. 19.4; Gad 7.2; Benj. 10.8; Zeb. 9.7; Sim. 6.2
	Jub. 2.29; 3.29; 5.2, 3, 8
	I Enoch 108.11
	Pss. of Sol. 4.7; 16.14
	II Enoch 59.4; 60.1

II. Soul

1. Denoting the principle of life:

(*a*) Physical life:

Pss. of Sol. 17.19
II Enoch 19.5
II Bar. 51.15
Life of Adam and Eve 17.1

(*b*) Life force and its manifestations:

Jub. 7.32; 21.18
Pss. of Sol. 16.2
II Enoch 10.6; 21.4; 30.8
Apoc. of Abr. 10

2. Denoting human consciousness:

(*a*) Full range of conscious beings:

I Enoch 9.3; 16.1
Sib. Or. III. 230, 724
Tests. of Jud. 18.3, 6; Gad 5.3; 6.1; Iss. 4.6; Jos. 2.6; Benj. 6.1, 4, 6
Pss. of Sol. 4.25; 7.8; 9.9, 19
II Enoch 10.5; 49.2 (*bis*); 58.4, 5 (*bis*), 6; 59.1 (*bis*), 2, 4, 5; 60.1 (*bis*), 2 (*bis*)
Test. of Abr. 10
II Bar. 21.1; 46.5; 52.7 (*bis*); 54.19 (*bis*), 56.10; 85.9, 11
Life of Adam and Eve 27.1; 29.10
Sib. Or. V. 402

(*b*) Character:

Tests. of Levi 13.6; Reub. 4.6; Napht. 2.6; 3.1; Sim. 2.5; Asher 2.7; 4.4; Jud. 18.4
Jub. 7.20
I Enoch 63.10
Pss. of Sol. 9.12

(*c*) With emotional content:

Shows anguish: Sib. Or. III. 558, 678
Shows guile and jealousy: Test. of Gad 6.3; 7.7
Shows wrath: Test. of Dan 3.1; 4.2
Shows hatred: Test. of Gad 3.3; 6.2; Pss. of Sol. 12.6
Is savage: Test. of Sim. 4.8
Grows strong: I Enoch 45.3
Is troubled: Test. of Zeb. 8.6
Is disturbed: Tests. of Dan 4.7; Sim. 4.9; II Esd. 5.14
Afflicts: Test. of Sim. 3.4
Pines: Test. of Iss. 4.5
Loves: Jub. 19.27, 31; 21.3; 26.2; 36.24; Apoc. of Abr. 17
Blesses: Jub. 26.2, 13, 20, 27; 29.20; Pss. of Sol. 3.1
Lusts: Pss. of Sol. 2.27
Is glad: Pss. of Sol. 5.14
Exults: Pss. of Sol. 17.1
Is disquieted: Pss. of Sol. 6.4
Slumbers: Pss. of Sol. 16.1
Smells: II Enoch 30.9
Is perturbed: Apoc. of Abr. 11
Shows zeal: II Bar. 66.5
Desires: II Bar. 35.5
Is distressed: II Esd. 6.37; 10.50
Suffers agonies: II Esd. 5.34
Is embittered: II Esd. 9.41
Is wearied: II Esd. 12.5
Is grief-laden: Life of Adam and Eve 20.2

(*d*) Instrument of moral action, expressing volition:

Tests. of Reub. 1.9; 4.9; Dan 3.3; Asher 1.6
Jub. 1.15 (*bis*), 16, 23; 37.24
Pss. of Sol. 9.7
II Bar. 66.1

(*e*) Intellectual use:

Test. of Gad 5.7
II Enoch 56.2
Apoc. of Abr. 30
II Bar. 19.4; 21.3
II Esd. 5.22; 8.4; 10.36

3. Personal usage, denoting animate as distinct from inanimate:

(*a*) General term denoting any living creature, beast or man:

Jub. 49.4
II Enoch 30.7

(*b*) Denoting man alone:

i. Person:

Jub. 13.28; 15.14; 44.18, 22, 26, 32, 33 (*bis*)
II Enoch 24.4, 5; 30.1; 60.5; 61.1, 2
Test. of Abr. 2 (*bis*); 16
II Bar. 3.8
Sib. Or. V. 405

ii. Denoting 'self' or used as reflexive or personal pronoun:

Tests. of Sim. 4.6; Benj. 4.3, 5
Jub. 1.24; 10.3; 12.7; 17.18; 25.1; 36.4 (*bis*); 39.6; 42.18
I Enoch 99.14
Pss. of Sol. 3.8; 4.15; 12.1; 16.3, 12 (*bis*)
II Enoch 9.1; 61.2; 66.1
II Bar. 3.3; 38.4
II Esd. 12.8

4. In disembodied state after death:

I Enoch 9.10; 22.3; 93.12; 102.4, 5; 103.7–8
Sib. Or. III. 458
Tests. of Asher 6.5; Dan 5.11
Test. of Abr. 7 (*tris*); 11 (7 times); 12 (8 times); 14 (7 times); 16; 19; 20
II Bar. 30.2 (*bis*), 4
II Esd. 4.35, 41; 7.75, 80, 85, 93, 99, 100
Apoc. of Moses 13.6; 35.2; 43.3
II Bar. 10.5

5. In pre-existent state:

II Enoch 24.4, 5

III. Spirit

1. *Spirit of God*

(*a*) As inspirational agency:
I Enoch 68.2; 70.2; 91.1
'Mart. of Isa.' 1.7; 5.14
Test. of Abr. 4
II Bar. 6.3; 7.2
II Esd. 14.22

(*b*) Supernatural agency producing ethical results:[1]
Dan. 4.8, 9, 18; 5.11, 14
Sib. Or. III. 701
Tests. of Sim. 4.4; Benj. 8.2; 9.4
Jub. 5.8; 40.5
Pss. of Sol. 8.15

(*c*) Expressing the nature of God and his capacity to act in a positive way:[1]
Tests. of Jud. 24.2, 3; Levi 2.3; 18.7, 11
Jub. 25.14; 31.12
I Enoch 49.3 (4 times); 62.2
Pss. of Sol. 17.42; 18.8

(*d*) As operative in the world apart from man:
II Bar. 21.4
II Esd. 6.39

(*e*) As source of physical life:
II Bar. 23.5

(*f*) Referring to the realm of spiritual energies in contrast with the weakness of human flesh:
I Enoch 106.17

2. *Spirit of Man*

(*a*) Denoting the principle of life (in man or beast):

i. Life principle:
Jub. 12.3, 5; 20.8
II Enoch 30.7
II Bar. 3.2; 84.7
Sib. Or. IV. 46, 189

ii. Life energy:
I Enoch 60.4
Test. of Gad 5.9

[1] This use of spirit is at times hardly distinguishable from its use to denote the capacity of man to act in a positive way (III, 2, *c*), or the activity of supernatural beings (III, 3, *c*, iii–iv).

Test. of Abr. 17; 18
Apoc. of Abr. 16

(*b*) Denoting human consciousness:

i. The fundamental aspect of human personality:
I Enoch 10.15; 13.6; 41.8; 108.7, 9
Dan. 5.12; 6.3
Sib. Or. III. 295–6, 489–91
Tests. of Napht. 2.2; Benj. 4.5
Jub. 1.21, 23; 10.3, 6; 21.3; 25.7
In Ass. of Moses 11.16 'spirit' occurs with the sense of 'person'.

ii. With emotional content:
Is troubled: Dan. 2.1; Test. of Sim. 5.1; I Enoch 92.2
Is hardened: Dan. 5.20
Is distressed: Dan. 7.15 (*bis*)
Groans: Test. of Jos. 7.2
Is hasty: Test. of Gad 4.7
Is patient: Jub. 19.3, 4, 8
Is refreshed: Jub. 25.19
Is grieved: Jub. 27.14
Is sorrowful: Jub. 34.3
Revives: Jub. 31.6; 43.24
Is small: I Enoch 103.9
Longs: I Enoch 39.8
Is perturbed: II Bar. 70.2
Is wearied: Test. of Abr. 19
Is affrighted: Apoc. of Abr. 10
Grows faint: Apoc. of Abr. 16
Is stirred: II Esd. 3.3
Is inflamed: II Esd. 6.37
Is weak: II Esd. 12.5
Is vexed: Sib. Or. V. 260

iii. Expressing intelligence or thought:
I Enoch 98.7
II Esd. 12.3; 14.40

(*c*) Expressing the nature of man and his capacity to act in a positive way:[1]
Sib. Or. III. 738
I Enoch 56.5; 61.7; 71.11
Test. of Gad 1.9; 3.1; 4.7 (*bis*); 6.2
Pss. of Sol. 17.42
II Esd. 5.22; 6.26
Sib. Or. V. 67

[1] This use of spirit is at times hardly distinguishable from its use to denote the spirit of God (III, 1, *b*, *c*) or supernatural beings (III, 3, *c*, iii, iv) acting on men.

(*d*) In disembodied state:

i. That which leaves the body at death:
I Enoch 20.3, 6 (*bis*); 22.3, 5–14 (10 times); 36.4; 93.12; 98.3, 10; 102.11; 103.3, 4, 8; 108.3, 6, 11
Jub. 23.31
II Esd. 7.78, 80
Apoc. of Moses 31.4; 32.4; 42.8

ii. Related to the body after death:
I Enoch 67.8 (*bis*), 9

iii. That which is translated:
I Enoch 71.1, 5, 6, 11

3. *Describing supernatural beings*

(*a*) With special reference to angelic beings:
I Enoch 15.10
Jub. 1.25; 15.31–32 (3 times)
I Enoch 61.12
II Enoch 12.1
Test. of Abr. 4 (*bis*)
Apoc. of Abr. 19 (*bis*)
II Esd. 6.41

(*b*) With special reference to demons, fallen angels, and evil spirits generally:
I Enoch 15.8–12 (8 times); 16.1; 19.1; 69.12; 99.7
Tests. of Dan 1.7; 5.1; 6.1; Jud. 23.1; Levi 3.2; 4.1; 5.6; Benj. 3.3, 4; 5.2; 6.1; Iss. 7.7; Napht. 8.4; Asher 1.9; 6.5; Sim. 3.5; 4.9; Jos. 7.4
Jub. 10.3, 5 (*bis*), 8, 13; 11.4, 5; 12.20; 19.28; 22.17
II Enoch 31.4
Apoc. of Abr. 13

(*c*) With no special reference to angels or demons:

i. Supernatural beings generally:
I Enoch 37.2, plus 103 other instances in the same book;[1] reference is made in each case to 'the Lord of Spirits'.
Test. of Abr. 13

ii. Spirits of nature:
I Enoch 60.14–21 (11 times); 69.22; 75.5
Jub. 2.2 (5 times)

[1] For full list see Charles, *Apocrypha and Pseudepigrapha of the Old Testament*, vol. II, 1913, p. 209.

iii. Influencing man for good:[1]
Test. of Jud. 20.1, 2, 5

iv. Influencing man for evil:[1]
Tests. of Reub. 2.3–3.2 and 3.7 (12 times); 2.1, 2; 3.3–6 (7 times); Jud. 13.3; 14.2, 8; 16.1; 20.1 (*bis*); 25.3; Levi 3.3; 9.9; Dan 1.6, 8; 2.1, 4; 3.6; 4.5; 5.5, 6; Sim. 2.7; 3.1; 4.7; 6.6; Iss. 4.4; Zeb. 9.7, 8; Napht. 3.3; Asher 6.2

(*d*) Expressing capacity of angels:
I Enoch 61.11 (6 times)

[1] This use of spirit is at times hardly distinguishable from its use to denote the spirit of God acting on men (III, 1, *b*, *c*) or the capacity of man to act in a positive way (III, 2, *c*).

BIBLIOGRAPHY

1. *General Works on the Inter-testamental Period*

ABEL, F. M., *Histoire de la Palestine, depuis la conquête d'Alexandre jusqu'à l'invasion arabe*, Paris, 1952

ALBRIGHT, W. F., *From the Stone Age to Christianity*, Baltimore, 1940 (second ed. with a new Introduction, 1957)

BERTHOLET, A., *Die jüdische Religion von der Zeit Esras bis zum Zeitalter Christi* (vol. II of B. Stade's *Biblische Theologie des Alten Testaments*), Tübingen, 1911

BEVAN, E., *The House of Seleucus*, 2 vols., London, 1902

Jerusalem under the High Priests, London, 1904

A History of Egypt under the Ptolemaic Dynasty, London, 1927

Sibyls and Seers, London, 1928

'Syria and the Jews', in *Cambridge Ancient History*, vol. VIII, ch. 16, Cambridge, 1930

BICKERMANN, E., *Der Gott der Makkabäer*, Berlin, 1937

BONSIRVEN, J., *Le judaïsme palestinien*, 2 vols., Paris, 1934

Exégèse Rabbinique et Exégèse Paulinienne, Paris, 1939

BOUSSET, W., *Die Religion des Judentums im späthellenistischen Zeitalter*, third ed., revised by H. Gressmann, Tübingen, 1926

BOX, G. H., 'The Historical and Religious Backgrounds of the Early Christian Movement', in *The Abingdon Bible Commentary*, London, 1929, pp. 839–52

Judaism in the Greek Period, Oxford, 1932

BRIGHT, J., *A History of Israel*, Philadelphia, 1959; London, 1960

CHARLES, R. H., *Religious Development between the Old and the New Testaments*, London, 1914

DALMAN, G. H., *The Words of Jesus* (English translation by D. M. Kay), Edinburgh, 1902

DANBY, H., *The Mishnah*, Oxford, 1933

DAVIES, W. D., *Paul and Rabbinic Judaism*, London, 1948 (second ed. with additional notes, 1955)

Christian Origins and Judaism, London, 1962

'Contemporary Jewish Religion', in *Peake's Commentary on the Bible*, ed. by M. Black and H. H. Rowley, London, 1962

FAIRWEATHER, W., *The Background of the Gospels*, Edinburgh, 1908

FARMER, W. R., *Maccabees, Zealots and Josephus*, New York, 1956

FULLER, L. E., 'Religious Development of the Inter-testamental Period', in *The Abingdon Bible Commentary*, London, 1929, pp. 200–13

GRANT, F. C., *Ancient Judaism and the New Testament*, Edinburgh and London, 1960

Guignebert, C., *The Jewish World in the Time of Jesus* (English translation by S. H. Hooke), London, 1939
Herford, R. T., *The Pharisees*, London, 1924
Judaism in the New Testament Period, London, 1928
Talmud and Apocrypha, London, 1933
Hölscher, G., *Geschichte der israelitischen und jüdischen Religion*, Giessen, 1922
Juster, J., *Les Juifs dans l'Empire Romain*, 2 vols., Paris, 1914
Klausner, J., *Jesus of Nazareth*, London, 1925
Lagrange, M. J., *Le judaïsme avant Jésus-Christ*, Paris, 1931
Lods, A., *Histoire de la littérature hebraique et juive, depuis les origines jusqu'à la ruine de l'État juif*, Paris, 1950
MacGregor, G. H. C. and Purdy, A. C., *Jew and Greek: Tutors unto Christ*, London, 1937
Moore, G. F., *Judaism in the First Centuries of the Christian Era*, 3 vols., Cambridge, Mass., 1927–30
Noth, M., *The History of Israel* (English translation), London, second ed., 1960
Oesterley, W. O. E., *A History of Israel*, vol. II, Oxford, 1932
Judaism and Christianity, vol. I: The Age of Transition, New York, 1937
The Jews and Judaism during the Greek Period, London, 1941
Pfeiffer, R. H., *History of New Testament Times, with an Introduction to the Apocrypha*, New York, 1949
Robinson, H. W., *The History of Israel*, London, 1938
Inspiration and Revelation in the Old Testament, Oxford, 1946
Schürer, E., *History of the Jewish People in the Time of Jesus Christ* (English translation by J. Macpherson, S. Taylor and P. Christie), 5 vols., Edinburgh, 1890
Snaith, N. H., *The Jews from Cyrus to Herod*, Wallington, 1949
Tcherikover, V., *Hellenistic Civilization and the Jews* (English translation by S. Applebaum), Philadelphia, 1959
Thomas, J., *Le Mouvement Baptiste en Palestine et Syrie*, Gembloux, 1935
Zeitlin, S., *The History of the Second Jewish Commonwealth, Prolegomena*, New York, 1933

2. *General Works on the Apocalyptic Literature*

Translations

Charles, R. H. (ed. by), *The Apocrypha and Pseudepigrapha of the Old Testament*, 2 vols., Oxford, 1913; reissued 1963
Kautzsch, E. (ed. by), *Apokryphen und Pseudepigraphen des Alten Testaments*, 2 vols., Tübingen, 1900
Oesterley, W. O. E. and Box, G. H., *Translations of Early Documents*, London, from 1916

Andrews, H. T., 'The Message of Jewish Apocalyptic for Modern Times', in *The Expositor*, 8th series, vol. XIV, London, 1917, pp. 58–71
'Apocalyptic Literature', in *Peake's Commentary on the Bible*, London, 1920, pp. 431–5

van ANDEL, C. P., *De structuur van de Henoch-traditie en het Nieuwe Testament*, Utrecht, 1955

BEER, G., on the Pseudepigrapha in Hauck-Herzog, *Realenzyklopädie*, vol. XVI, Leipzig, 1896ff., pp. 229ff.

BLOCH, J., *On the Apocalyptic in Judaism* (*JQR* Monographs, no. 2), Philadelphia, 1952

BROCKINGTON, L. H., 'The Problem of Pseudonymity', *JTS*, N.S., vol. IV, Oxford, 1953, pp. 15–22

BURKITT, F. C., *Jewish and Christian Apocalypses*, London, 1914

CHARLES, R. H., 'Apocalyptic Literature', in *EB*, vol. I, London, 1899, cols. 213–50

DAVIES, W. D., 'The Jewish Background of the Teaching of Jesus: Apocalyptic and Pharisaism', *ET*, vol. LIX, Edinburgh, 1948, pp. 233–7 (reproduced in *Christian Origins and Judaism*, London, 1962, pp. 19–30)

DEANE, W. J., *Pseudepigrapha*, Edinburgh, 1891

de FAYE, E., *Les apocalypses juives*, Paris, 1892

FREY, J.-B., 'Apocalyptique', in Pirot's *Supplément au Dictionnaire de la Bible*, vol. I, Paris, 1928, cols. 326–54

'Apocryphes de L'Ancien Testament', *ibid.*, cols. 354–459

FROST, S. B., *Old Testament Apocalyptic*, London, 1952

FULLER, L. E., 'The Literature of the Inter-testamental Period', in *The Abingdon Bible Commentary*, Nashville and London, 1929, pp. 187–99

GINZBERG, L., 'Some Observations on the Attitude of the Synagogue towards the Apocalyptic-Eschatological Writings', *JBL*, vol. XLI, New Haven, 1922, pp. 115–36

HÖLSCHER, G., 'Problèmes de la littérature apocalyptique juive', in *Revue d'Histoire et de Philosophie Religieuses*, vol. IX, Strasbourg, 1929, pp. 101–14

HOOKE, S. H., 'The Myth and Ritual Pattern in Jewish and Christian Apocalyptic', in *The Labyrinth*, London, 1935 (reproduced in *The Siege Perilous*, London, 1956)

HUGHES, H. M., *The Ethics of Jewish Apocryphal Literature*, London, n.d.

JAMES, M. R., *The Lost Apocrypha of the Old Testament*, London, 1920

KAUFMANN, J., 'Apokalyptik', in *Encyclopaedia Judaica*, vol. II, Berlin, 1928, cols. 1142–54

KOHLER, K., 'The Essenes and the Apocalyptic Literature', *JQR*, N.S., vol. XI, Philadelphia, 1920–1, pp. 145–68

LÉVI, I., 'Apocalypses dans la Talmud', *REJ*, vol. I, Paris, 1880, pp. 108–14

McCOWN, C. C., 'Hebrew and Egyptian Apocalyptic Literature', *HTR*, vol. XVIII, Cambridge, Mass., 1925, pp. 357–411

MANGENOT, E., 'Apocalypses apocryphes', in *Dictionnaire de Théologie Catholique*, vol. I, Paris, 1903, cols. 1479–98

MANSON, T. W., 'Some Reflections on Apocalyptic', in *Aux Sources de la Tradition Chrétienne* (*Mélanges offerts à M. Maurice Goguel*), Neuchâtel and Paris, 1950, pp. 139ff.

MUNCK, J., 'Discours d'adieu dans le Nouveau Testament et dans la littérature biblique', *ibid.*, pp. 155ff.
OMAN, J., 'The Abiding Significance of Apocalyptic' in G. A. Yates, *In Spirit and in Truth*, London, 1934, pp. 276–93
PEAKE, A. S., 'The Roots of Hebrew Prophecy and Jewish Apocalyptic', *BJRL*, vol. VII, 1923, pp. 233–55 (reproduced in *The Servant of Yahweh*, Manchester, 1931, pp. 75–110)
PFEIFFER, R. H., *History of New Testament Times, with an Introduction to the Apocrypha*, New York, 1949
'The Literature and Religion of the Pseudepigrapha', in *The Interpreter's Bible*, vol. I, New York, 1952, pp. 421–36
The Apocrypha according to the Authorised Version, with an introduction by Robert H. Pfeiffer, New York, 1953
PORTER, F. C., *The Messages of the Apocalyptical Writers*, London, 1905
PRICE, E. J., 'Jewish Apocalyptic and the Mysteries', *Hibbert Journal*, vol. XVIII, London, 1919–20, pp. 95–112
RIST, M., 'Apocalypticism', in *The Interpreter's Dictionary of the Bible*, vol. I, New York, 1962, pp. 157–61
'Pseudepigrapha', *ibid.*, vol. III, pp. 960–4
ROWLEY, H. H., *The Relevance of Apocalyptic*, London, 1944 (second ed., 1947; third ed., 1963)
Jewish Apocalyptic and the Dead Sea Scrolls, London, 1957
'Apocalyptic Literature', in *Peake's Commentary on the Bible*, ed. by M. Black and H. H. Rowley, London, 1962, pp. 484–8
RUSSELL, D. S., *Between the Testaments*, London, 1960
'Apocalyptic Literature', in *Encyclopaedia Britannica*, vol. II, London, 1963, pp. 112–15
SCHÜRER, E., *History of the Jewish People in the Time of Jesus Christ* (English translation by J. Macpherson, S. Taylor and P. Christie), div. II, vol. III, Edinburgh, 1890
STAUFFER, E., *New Testament Theology* (English translation by John Marsh), London, 1955
TORREY, C. C., *The Apocryphal Literature*, New Haven, 1945
WELCH, A. C., *Visions of the End, a Study in Daniel and Revelation*, London, 1922 (new edition, 1958)
WELLHAUSEN, J., 'Zur apokalyptischen Literatur', *Skizzen und Vorarbeiten*, vol. VI, Berlin, 1899, pp. 215–49
WICKS, H. J., *The Doctrine of God in the Jewish Apocryphal and Apocalyptic Literature*, London, 1915

The apocalyptic literature is also dealt with in the following Old Testament Introductions:

BENTZEN, A., *Introduction to the Old Testament*, 2 vols., Copenhagen, 1948
CORNILL, C. H., *Einleitung in die Kanonischen Bücher des Alten Testaments* (third and fourth editions only), Tübingen, 1891
EISSFELDT, O., *Einleitung in das Alte Testament, unter Einschluss der Apokryphen und Pseudepigraphen*, Tübingen, 1934 (second ed., 1957; third ed., 1964) (English translation by P. R. Ackroyd, Oxford, 1964)

König, E., *Einleitung in das Alte Testament mit Einschluss der Apokryphen und der Pseudepigraphen Alten Testaments*, Bonn, 1893

Sellin, E., *Einleitung in das Alte Testament*, Leipzig, 1910 (seventh ed., 1935) (English translation by W. Montgomery, London, 1923)

Steuernagel, C., *Lehrbuch der Einleitung in das Alte Testament, mit einem Anhang über die Apokryphen und Pseudepigraphen*, Tübingen, 1912

Strack, H. L., *Einleitung in das Alte Testament, einschliesslich Apokryphen und Pseudepigraphen*, Munich, 1883 (sixth ed., 1906)

Weiser, A., *Einleitung in das Alte Testament* (second, third and fourth editions only), Stuttgart, 1939 (English translation from fourth edition by Dorothea M. Barton, London, 1961)

3. *Special Topics in the Apocalyptic Literature*

i. *Apocalyptic 'psychology' and inspiration* (*cf. chs. V and VI*)

Brockington, L. H., ' "The Lord showed me": the correlation of natural and spiritual in prophetic experience', in *Studies in History and Religion*, ed. by E. A. Payne, London, 1942, pp. 30–43

Burton, E. D., *Spirit, Soul and Flesh*, Chicago, 1918

Galatians, ICC, Edinburgh, 1921, pp. 486–95

Causse, A., 'Quelques remarques sur la psychologie des prophètes', *Revue d'Histoire et de Philosophie Religieuses*, Strasbourg, 1922, pp. 349–56

Du Groupe Ethnique à la Communauté Religieuse, Paris, 1938

Dürr, L., 'Hebr. *nephesh* = akk. napištu = Gurgel, Kehle', *ZAW*, vol. XLIII, Tübingen, 1925, pp. 262–9

Frey, J.-B., 'La Révélation d'après les conceptions juives au temps de Jésus-Christ', *RB* vol. XXV, Paris, 1916, pp. 472–510

Guillaume, A., *Prophecy and Divination*, London, 1938

Johnson, A. R., *The Vitality of the Individual in the Thought of Ancient Israel*, Cardiff, 1949

The One and the Many in the Israelite Conception of God, Cardiff, 1942 (second ed., 1961)

The Cultic Prophet in Ancient Israel, Cardiff, 1944 (second ed., 1962)

Lord, F. T., *The Unity of Body and Soul*, London, 1929

Porteous, N. W., 'Prophecy', in *Record and Revelation*, ed. by H. W. Robinson, Oxford, 1938, pp. 216–49

Porter, F. C., 'The Yeçer Ha-ra'', in *Biblical and Semitic Studies* (Yale Bicentennial Publications), 1901

Robinson, H. W., 'Hebrew Psychology in relation to Pauline Anthropology', in *Mansfield College Essays*, London, 1909, pp. 265–86

The Christian Doctrine of Man, Edinburgh, 1911 (third edition, 1926)

'The Psychology and Metaphysic of "Thus saith Yahweh" ', *ZAW*, vol. XLI, Giessen, 1923

'The Hebrew Conception of Corporate Personality', in *Werden und Wesen des Alten Testaments*, Beiheft 66 zur *ZAW*, Giessen, 1936

'Prophetic Symbolism', in *Old Testament Essays* (with an introduction by D. C. Simpson), London, 1927, pp. 1–17

'Hebrew Psychology', in *The People and the Book*, ed. by A. S. Peake, Oxford, 1925, pp. 353–82
Redemption and Revelation, London, 1942
Inspiration and Revelation in the Old Testament, Oxford, 1946
ROHDE, E., *Psyche* (English translation by W. B. Hillis), London, 1925

ii. *Time and history* (*cf. ch. VIII*)

BARR, J., *The Semantics of Biblical Language*, Oxford, 1961
Biblical Words for Time, London, 1962
BOMAN, T., *Hebrew Thought Compared with Greek* (English translation by J. L. Moreau), London, 1960
BOUSSET, W., 'Das Chronologische System der biblischen Geschichtsbücher', *ZAW*, vol. XX, Giessen, 1900, pp. 136ff.
CULLMANN, O., *Christ and Time* (English translation by F. V. Filson), London, 1951 (revised ed., 1962)
DRIVER, S. R., *The Book of Genesis*, Westminster Commentaries, twelfth ed., London, 1926, pp. 78f.
EICHRODT, W., 'Heilserfahrung und Zeitverständnis im Alten Testament', *TZ*, vol. XII, Basel, 1956, pp. 103–25
JENNI, E., 'Time', in *The Interpreter's Dictionary of the Bible*, vol. IV, New York, 1962, pp. 642–9
MARSH, J., *The Fulness of Time*, London, 1952
'Time', in *A Theological Word Book of the Bible*, ed. by A. Richardson, London, 1950, pp. 258–67
MURTONEN, A., 'The Chronology of the Old Testament', *Studia Theologica*, vol. VIII, Lund, 1954, pp. 133–7
NORTH, C. R., *The Old Testament Interpretation of History*, London, 1946
PEDERSEN, J., *Israel, its Life and Culture: I–IV* (English translation by A. Møller and A. I. Fausbøll), Copenhagen, 1926 and 1940
ROBINSON, H. W., *Inspiration and Revelation in the Old Testament*, Oxford, 1946
ROBINSON, J. A. T., *In the End, God . . .*, London, 1950
SKINNER, J., *A Critical and Exegetical Commentary on Genesis*, ICC, Edinburgh, 1910, pp. 134ff., 233ff.

iii. *Angels and demons* (*cf. ch. IX*)

BARTON, G. A., 'The Origin of the Names of Angels and Demons in the Extra-canonical Apocalyptic Literature to 100 A.D.', *JBL*, vol. XXXI, New Haven, 1912, pp. 156–67
'Demons and Spirits (Hebrew)', in *ERE*, vol. IV, Edinburgh, 1911, pp. 594–601
BLAU, L., 'Samael', in *JE*, vol. X, New York and London, 1905, pp. 665–6
DAVIDSON, A. B., 'Angel', in *HDB*, vol. 1, Edinburgh, 1898, pp. 93–97
DRIVER, S. R., 'Azazel', *ibid.*, vol. I, 1898, pp. 207–8
'The Host of Heaven', *ibid.*, vol. II, 1899, pp. 429–30
'The Lord of Hosts', *ibid.*, vol. III, 1900, pp. 137–8

GASTER, T. H., *The Holy and the Profane*, New York, 1955
'Demon, Demonology', in *Interpreter's Dictionary of the Bible*, vol. I, New York, 1962, pp. 815–24
HEITMÜLLER, F., *Engel and Dämonen: eine Bibelstudie*, Hamburg, 1948
JACKSON, A. V. W., 'Demons and Spirits (Persian)', in *ERE*, vol. IV, Edinburgh, 1911, pp. 619–20
KOHLER, K., 'Belial—in Rabbinical and Apocryphal Literature', in *JE*, vol. II, New York and London, 1902, pp. 658–9
LANGTON, E., *The Ministries of the Angelic Powers*, London, n.d.
Good and Evil Spirits, London, 1942
Essentials of Demonology, London, 1949
LODS, E., 'La chute des anges', *Revue d'Histoire et de Philosophie Religieuses*, vol. VII, Strasbourg, 1927, pp. 295–315
MORRISON, C. D., *The Powers That Be*, London, 1960
WHITEHOUSE, O. C., 'Demon, Devil', in *HDB*, vol. I, Edinburgh, 1898, pp. 590–4
'Satan', *ibid.*, vol. IV, 1902, pp. 407–12
ZIEGLER, M., *Engel und Dämon im Lichte der Bibel*, Zurich, 1957

iv. *Eschatology* (*cf. chs. X and XI*)

ADLER, E. N., 'Ages of the World (Jewish)', in *ERE*, vol. I, Edinburgh, 1908, pp. 203–5
BAILEY, J. W., 'The Temporary Messianic Reign in the Literature of Early Judaism', *JBL*, vol. LIII, Philadelphia, 1934, pp. 170–87
BEASLEY-MURRAY, G. R., *Jesus and the Future*, London, 1954
BLACK, M., 'The Eschatology of the Similitudes of Enoch', in *JTS*, N.S., vol. III, Oxford, 1952, pp. 1–10
BULTMANN, R., *History and Eschatology*, Edinburgh, 1957
ČERNÝ, L., *The Day of Yahweh and Some Relevant Problems*, Prague, 1948
CHARLES, R. H., 'Eschatology of the Apocryphal and Apocalyptic Literature', in *HDB*, vol. I, Edinburgh, 1898, pp. 741–9
'Eschatology', in *EB*, vol. II, London, 1901, cols. 1335–92
DAHL, N. A., 'Christ, Creation and the Church', in W. D. Davies and D. Daube (ed.), *Background of the New Testament and its Eschatology*, Cambridge, 1956
DAVIDSON, A. B., 'Eschatology', in *HDB*, vol. I, Edinburgh, 1898, pp. 734–41
DAVIES, W. D., *Torah in the Messianic Age and/or the Age to Come* (*JBL* Monograph Series, vol. VII), Philadelphia, 1952
FROST, S. B., 'Eschatology and Myth', *VT*, vol. II, Leyden, 1952, pp. 70–80
GLASSON, T. F., *The Second Advent*, London, 1945
Greek Influence in Jewish Eschatology (SPCK Biblical Monographs), London, 1961
VON GALL, A., *Basileia tou Theou, eine religionsgeschichtliche Studie zur vorkirchlichen Eschatologie*, Heidelberg, 1926

GRESSMANN, H., *Der Ursprung der israelitischen-jüdischen Eschatologie*, Göttingen, 1905
GUNKEL, H., *Schöpfung und Chaos in Urzeit und Endzeit*, Göttingen, 1895
JENNI, E., 'Eschatology of the Old Testament', in *The Interpreter's Dictionary of the Bible*, vol. II, New York, 1962, pp. 126–33
KOHLER, K., 'Eschatology', in *JE*, vol. V, New York, 1903, pp. 209–18
MACCULLOCH, J. A., 'Eschatology', in *ERE*, vol. V, Edinburgh, 1912, pp. 373–91
MANSON, T. W., *The Teaching of Jesus*, Cambridge, 1931
MESSEL, N., *Die Einheitlichkeit der jüdischen Eschatologie* (Beihefte zur *ZAW*, vol. XXX), Giessen, 1915
MOZLEY, J. K., 'Eschatology and Ethics', *JTS*, vol. XL, Oxford, 1939, pp. 337–45
OESTERLEY, W. O. E., *The Doctrine of the Last Things: Jewish and Christian*, London, 1909
RIST, M., 'Eschatology of Apocrypha and Pseudepigrapha', in *The Interpreter's Dictionary of the Bible*, vol. II, New York, 1962, pp. 133–5
SCHMIDT, N., 'The Origin of Jewish Eschatology', *JBL*, vol. XLI, New Haven, 1922, pp. 22–28
SÖDERBLOM, N., 'Ages of the World (Zoroastrian)', in *ERE*, vol. I, Edinburgh, 1908, pp. 205–10
VAGANAY, L., *Le problème eschatologique dans le IVe livre d'Esdras*, Paris, 1906
VOLZ, P., *Jüdische Eschatologie von Daniel bis Akiba*, Tübingen, 1903
Die Eschatologie der jüdischen Gemeinde im neutestamentlichen Zeitalter (second edition of above work), Tübingen, 1934
WILDER, A. N., 'The Nature of Jewish Eschatology', *JBL*, vol. L, New Haven, 1931, pp. 201–6
Eschatology and Ethics in the Teaching of Jesus, New York, 1939 (revised ed., 1950)

v. *Messiah and Son of Man (cf. chs. XII and XIII)*

BENTZEN, A., *Messias, Moses redivivus, Menschensohn*, Zurich, 1948
King and Messiah, London, 1954
BLACK, M., 'The "Son of Man" in the Old Biblical Literature', *ET*, vol. LX, Edinburgh, 1948, pp. 11–15
'The "Son of Man" in the teaching of Jesus', *ibid.*, vol. LX, 1948, pp. 32–36
'The Messiah in the Testament of Levi 18', *ibid.*, vol. LX, 1949, pp. 321–2
'The Servant of the Lord and the Son of Man', *SJT*, vol. VI, Edinburgh, 1953, pp. 1–11
BÖHMER, J., *Reich Gottes und Menschensohn im Buche Daniel*, Leipzig, 1899
BOUSSET, W., *The Antichrist Legend* (English translation by A. H. Keane), London, 1896
'Antichrist', in *EB*, vol. I, London, 1899, cols. 177–84
'Antichrist' in *ERE*, vol. I, Edinburgh, 1908, pp. 578–81

BOWMAN, J., 'The Background of the term "Son of Man" ', *ET*, vol. LIX, Edinburgh, 1948, pp. 283–8

BUZY, D., 'Antéchrist', in L. Pirot's *Supplément au Dictionnaire de la Bible*, vol. I, Paris, 1928, cols. 297–305

CAMPBELL, J. Y., 'The Origin and Meaning of the Term Son of Man', *JTS*, vol. XLVIII, Oxford, 1947, pp. 145–55

CHEVALLIER, M. A., *L'Esprit et le Messie dans le Bas-Judaïsme at le Nouveau Testament*, Paris, 1958

COPPENS, J. and DEQUEKER, L., *Le Fils de l'homme et les Saints du Très-Haut en Daniel VII, dans les Apocryphes et dans le Nouveau Testament*, Louvain, 1961

CREED, J. M., 'The Heavenly Man', in *JTS*, vol. XXVI, Oxford, 1925, pp. 113–36

DENNEFELD, L., 'Messianisme', in *Dictionnaire de Théologie Catholique*, vol. X, part 2, Paris, 1929, cols. 1404–1567

DRUMMOND, J., *The Jewish Messiah*, London, 1877

DUNCAN, G. S., *Jesus, Son of Man*, London, 1947

EMERTON, J. A., 'The Origin of the Son of Man Imagery', *JTS*, N.S., vol. VIII, Oxford, 1958, pp. 225–43

FREY, J.-B., 'Le conflit entre le messianisme de Jésus et le messianisme des juifs de son temps', in *Biblica*, vol. XIV, Rome, 1933, pp. 133–49, 269–93

GOODSPEED, G. S., *Israel's Messianic Hope to the Time of Jesus*, New York, 1900

GRESSMANN, H., *Der Messias*, Göttingen, 1929

HIGGINS, A. J. B., 'Son of Man-Forschung since the Teaching of Jesus', in *New Testament Essays in Memory of T. W. Manson*, Manchester, 1959, pp. 118–31

KLAUSNER, J., *The Messianic Idea in Israel*, London, 1956

KÖNIG, E., *Die messianischen Weissagungen des Alten Testaments*, Stuttgart, 1923

KRAELING, C. H., 'Anthropos and Son of Man', *Columbia University Oriental Studies*, vol. XXV, New York, 1927

LAGRANGE, M.-J., *Le messianisme chez les juifs*, Paris, 1909

'Notes sur le messianisme au temps de Jésus', in *RB*, vol. XXI (N.S. II), Paris, 1905, pp. 481–514

LASOR, W. S., 'The Messianic idea in Qumran', in *Studies and Essays in honor of Abraham A. Neuman*, ed. by M. Ben-Horin, B. D. Weinryb, S. Zeitlin, Philadelphia, 1962

MANSON, T. W., 'The Son of Man in Daniel, Enoch and the Gospels', *BJRL*, vol. XXXII, Manchester, 1950, pp. 171–93

The Servant-Messiah, Cambridge, 1953

MANSON, W., *Jesus the Messiah*, London, 1943

MCFADYEN, J. E., 'Israel's Messianic Hope', in *The Abingdon Bible Commentary*, Nashville and London, 1929, pp. 177–86

MOWINCKEL, S., *He that Cometh* (English translation by G. W. Anderson), Oxford, 1956

Oesterley, W. O. E., *The Evolution of the Messianic Idea*, London, 1908

Otto, R., *The Kingdom of God and the Son of Man* (English translation by F. V. Filson and B. Lee Wolf), London, 1938

Peake, A. S., 'The Messiah and the Son of Man', in *BJRL*, vol. VIII, 1924, pp. 52–81 (reproduced in *The Servant of Yahweh*, Manchester, 1931, pp. 194–237)

Riehm, E., *Messianic Prophecy*, Edinburgh, 1891

Rigaux, B., *L'Antéchrist et l'opposition au royaume messianique dans l'Ancien et le Nouveau Testament*, Gembloux, 1932

Ringgren, H., *The Messiah in the Old Testament*, London, 1956

Rowley, H. H., 'The Suffering Servant and the Davidic Messiah', in *The Servant of the Lord and Other Essays on the Old Testament*, London, 1952, pp. 59–88

Schmidt, N., 'Recent Study of the term, Son of Man', *JBL*, vol. XLV, New Haven, 1926, pp. 326–49

Scott, R. B. Y., 'Behold, He cometh with Clouds', *NTS*, vol. V, Cambridge, 1959, pp. 127–32

Sharman, H. B., *Son of Man and Kingdom of God*, New York, 1943

Sjöberg, E., '*Ben 'adam* und *Bar 'enos* im Hebräischen und Aramäischen', *Acta Orientalia*, vol. XXI, Copenhagen, 1953, pp. 57–65, 91–107

Stanton, V. H., *The Jewish and Christian Messiah*, Edinburgh, 1886

Stauffer, E., 'Messias oder Menschensohn', *NT*, vol. I, Leyden, 1956, pp. 81–102

Völter, D., *Die Menschensohn-Frage neu untersucht*, Leyden, 1916

van der Woude, A. S., *Die messianischen Vorstellungen der Gemeinde von Qumran*, Assen, 1957

vi. *Life after death* (*cf. ch. XIV*)

Bertholet, A., 'The pre-Christian Belief in the Resurrection of the Body', *American Journal of Theology*, vol. XX, Chicago, 1916, pp. 1–30

Burney, C. F., *Israel's Hope of Immortality*, Oxford, 1909

Charles, R. H., *A Critical History of the Doctrine of a Future Life*, second ed., London, 1913

Frey, J.-B., 'La vie de l'au-delà dans les conceptions juives au temps de Jésus-Christ', in *Biblica*, vol. XIII, Rome, 1932, pp. 129–68

Lods, A., *La Croyance à la Vie Future*, Paris, 1906

Johnson, A. R., *The Vitality of the Individual in the Thought of Ancient Israel*, Cardiff, 1949

Leckie, J. H., *The World to Come and Final Destiny*, Edinburgh, 1918 (second revised edition, 1922)

Martin-Achard, R., *From Death to Life. A Study of the Development of the Doctrine of the Resurrection in the Old Testament* (English translation by J. P. Smith), Edinburgh, 1960

Oesterley, W. O. E., *Immortality and the Unseen World*, London, 1921

Pilcher, C. V., *The Hereafter in Jewish and Christian Thought, with special reference to the Doctrine of Resurrection*, London, 1940

Robinson, H. W., 'The Old Testament Approach to Life after Death', *The Congregational Quarterly*, vol. III, London, 1925, pp. 138–51

ROWLEY, H. H., *The Faith of Israel*, London, 1956
RYDER SMITH, C., *The Bible Doctrine of the Hereafter*, London, 1958
SCHOFIELD, J. N., *Archaeology and the Afterlife*, London, 1951
SUTCLIFFE, E. F., *The Old Testament and the Future Life*, London, 1946

vii. *Foreign influences*

BÖKLEN, E., *Die Verwandtschaft der jüdisch-christlichen mit der parsischen Eschatologie*, Göttingen, 1902
BOUSSET, W., *Die Religion des Judentums im späthellenistischen Zeitalter*, third ed., revised by H. Gressmann, Tübingen, 1926
CARNOY, A. J., *Iranian Mythology*, Boston, 1917
'Zoroastrianism', in *ERE*, vol. XII, Edinburgh, 1921, pp. 862–8
CARTER, G. W., *Zoroastrianism and Judaism*, Boston, 1918
CUMONT, F., *The Oriental Religions in Roman Paganism*, Chicago, 1911
Astrology and religion among the Greeks and Romans, New York, 1912
L'Egypte des astrologues, Brussels, 1937
DIETERICH, A., *Nekyia*, Leipzig, 1893
DUCHESNE-GUILLEMIN, J., *Zoroastre, étude critique avec une traduction commentée des Gatha*, Paris, 1948
Ormazd et Ahriman, Paris, 1953
La Religion de l'Iran ancien, Paris, 1962
GASTER, M., 'Parsiism in Judaism', in *ERE*, vol. IX, Edinburgh, 1911, pp. 637–40
GLASSON, T. F., *Greek Influence in Jewish Eschatology*, London, 1961
JACKSON, A. V. W., *Die Iranische Religion*, in Geiger and Kuhn, *Grundriss der Iranischen Philologie*, 2 vols., Leipzig, 1896–1904
'Demons and Spirits (Persian)', in *ERE*, vol. IV, Edinburgh, 1911, pp. 619–20
KRAELING, C. H., 'Babylonian and Iranian Mythology in Daniel ch. 7', in *Oriental Studies in Honour of C. R. Pawry*, Oxford, 1933
LEVY, I., *La légende de Pythagore de Grèce en Palestine*, Paris, 1927
LIEBERMAN, S., *Greek in Jewish Palestine*, New York, 1942
Hellenism in Jewish Palestine, New York, 1950
MESSINA, G., *Der Ursprung der Magier und die Zarathustrische Religion*, Rome, 1930
MILLS, L. H., *Avesta Eschatology compared with the Books of Daniel and Revelation*, Chicago, 1908
Zarathustra, Philo, the Achaemenides and Israel, Leipzig, 1906
MOULTON, J. H., *Early Zoroastrianism*, London, 1913
'Zoroastrianism', in *HDB*, vol. IV, Edinburgh, 1902, pp. 988–94
'Fravashi', in *ERE*, vol. VI, Edinburgh, 1913, pp. 116–18
OLDENBERG, H., *Die Iranische Religion*, in *Die Kultur der Gegenwart*, part I (ed. P. Hinneberg), Berlin and Leipzig, 1906
PAVRY, J. D. C., *The Zoroastrian Doctrine of a Future Life*, second ed., New York, 1929
REITZENSTEIN, R., *Das iranische Erlösungsmysterium*, Bonn, 1921
SCHEFTELOWITZ, J., *Die altpersischen Religion und das Judentum*, Giessen, 1920

SÖDERBLOM, N., *La Vie Future d'après le Mazdeïsme*, Paris, 1901
STAVE, E., *Über den Einfluss des Parsismus auf das Judentum*, Haarlem, 1898
WATERHOUSE, J. W., *Zoroastrianism*, London, 1934
WIDENGREN, G., 'Juifs et Iraniens à l'époque des Parthes', *Supplements to Vetus Testamentum*, vol. IV, Leyden, 1957, pp. 197–240
ZAEHNER, R. C., *The Teachings of the Magi*, London, 1956
The Dawn and Twilight of Zoroastrianism, London, 1961

4. *Commentaries and other studies on individual books*

FRITZSCHE, O. F. and GRIMM, C. L. W., *Kurzgefasstes Handbuch zu den Apokryphen des Alten Testaments*, 6 vols., Leipzig, 1851–60
ZÖCKLER, O., *Die Apokryphen nebst einem Anhang über die Pseudepigraphenlitteratur* (in Strack and Zockler's Kurzgefasster Kommentar), Munich, 1891

i. *Daniel*

Commentaries

BENTZEN, A., *Daniel*, Handbuch zum Alten Testament, Tübingen, 1937 (second ed., 1952)
BEVAN, A. A., *A Short Commentary on the Book of Daniel*, Cambridge, 1892
CHARLES, R. H., *A Critical and Exegetical Commentary on the Book of Daniel*, Oxford, 1929
DENNEFELD, L., *Daniel*, La Sainte Bible, Paris, 1946
DHORME, É., *La Bible*, La Bibliothèque de la Pléiade, Paris, 1959
DRIVER, S. R., *The Book of Daniel*, The Cambridge Bible, Cambridge, 1900
HEATON, E. W., *The Book of Daniel*, Torch Bible Commentaries, London, 1956
JEFFERY, A., *The Book of Daniel*, in *The Interpreter's Bible*, vol. VI, New York, 1956, pp. 341–549
LATTEY, C., *The Book of Daniel*, Westminster Version, Dublin, 1948
MACLER, FR., *Daniel*, La Bible du Centenaire, Paris, 1940
MARTI, K., *Das Buch Daniel*, Kurzer Hand-Commentar, Tübingen, 1901
de MENASCE, P.-J., *Daniel*, La Bible de Jérusalem, Jerusalem, 1954
MONTGOMERY, J. A., *A Critical and Exegetical Commentary on the Book of Daniel*, ICC, Edinburgh, 1927
NELIS, J. T., *Daniël uit de grondtekst vertaald*, De Boeken van het Oude Testament, Ruremonde-Maaseik, 1954
NÖTSCHER, FR., *Daniel*, Echter Bibel, Würzburg, 1948
OBBINK, H. W., *Daniel*, Commentaar op de Heilige Schrift, Amsterdam, 1956
PORTEOUS, N. W., *Daniel*, Das Alte Testament Deutsch, Göttingen, 1962
RINALDI, G., *Daniele*, La Sacra Bibbia, Turin, 1947
SAYDON, P. P., *Daniel*, in *A Catholic Commentary on Holy Scripture*, London, 1953, pp. 621–43

Other studies

BAUMGARTNER, W., 'Ein Vierteljahrhundert Danielforschung', *Theologische Rundschau*, N.F., vol. XI, Tübingen, 1939, pp. 59–83, 125–44, 201–28

BICKERMANN, E., *Der Gott der Makkabäer*, Berlin, 1937

BÖHMER, J., *Reich Gottes und Menschensohn im Buche Daniel*, Leipzig, 1899

COPPENS, J. and DEQUEKER, L., *Le Fils de l'homme et les Saints du Très-Haut en Daniel VII, dans les Apocryphes et dans le Nouveau Testament*, Louvain, 1961

GINSBERG, H. L., *Studies in Daniel*, New York, 1948

'The Composition of the Book of Daniel', *VT*, vol. IV, Leyden, 1954, pp. 246ff.

NOTH, M., *Das Geschichtsverstandnis der alttestamentlichen Apokalyptik*, Cologne and Opladen, 1954 (reproduced in *Gesammelte Studien zum Alten Testament*, 1957)

ROWLEY, H. H., 'The Bilingual Problem of Daniel', *ZAW*, N.F., vol. IX, Giessen, 1932, pp. 256–68

Darius the Mede and the Four World Empires in the Book of Daniel, Cardiff, 1935 (reprinted in 1959)

'Some Problems in the Book of Daniel', *ET*, vol. XLVII, Edinburgh, 1935–6, pp. 216–20

'The Unity of the Book of Daniel', *Hebrew Union College Annual*, vol. XXIII, 1950–1, pp. 223ff. (reproduced in *The Servant of the Lord and other Essays*, London, 1952, pp. 235ff.)

'The Composition of the Book of Daniel', *VT*, vol. V, Leyden, 1955, pp. 272ff.

SCHMIDT, N., 'The Son of Man in the Book of Daniel', *JBL*, vol. XIX, Boston, 1900, pp. 22–28

YOUNG, E. J., *The Messianic Prophecies of Daniel*, Delft, 1954

ii. *The Ethiopic Book of Enoch* (*I Enoch*)

van ANDEL, C. P., *De Structuur van de Henoch-Traditie en het Nieuwe Testament*, Utrecht, 1955

BEER, G., 'Das Buch Henoch', in E. Kautzsch (ed.), *Apokryphen und Pseudepigraphen des Alten Testaments*, vol. II, Tübingen, 1900, pp. 217ff.

BLACK, M., 'The Eschatology of the Similitudes of Enoch', *JTS*, N.S., vol. III, Oxford, 1952, pp. 1–10

BONNER, C., *The Last Chapters of Enoch in Greek* (Studies and Documents 8), London, 1937

BRINKMANN, H., 'Die Lehre von der Parusie beim hl. Paulus in ihrem Verhältnis zu den Anschauungen des Buches Henoch', *Biblica*, vol. XIII, Rome, 1932, pp. 315–34, 418–34

BURKITT, F. C., 'Four Notes on the Book of Enoch', *JTS*, vol. VIII, Oxford, 1907, pp. 444–7

Jewish and Christian Apocalypses, London, 1914

CHARLES, R. H., *The Ethiopic Version of the Book of Enoch*, Oxford, 1906
The Book of Enoch, second ed., Oxford, 1912
Apocrypha and Pseudepigrapha of the Old Testament, vol. II, Oxford, 1913, pp. 163ff.
The Book of Enoch with an Introduction by W. O. E. Oesterley, London, 1917 (reprinted in 1952)
CLEMEN, C., 'Die Zusammensetzung des Buches Henoch, der Apokalypse des Baruch, und des vierten Buches Esra', *Theologische Studien und Kritiken*, vol. LXXI, Gotha, 1898, pp. 211–46
DILLMANN, A., *Das Buch Henoch*, Leipzig, 1853
DIX, G. H., 'The Enochic Pentateuch', *JTS*, vol. XXVII, Oxford, 1925, pp. 29–42
FLEMMING, J. and RADERMACHER, L. R., *Das Buch Henoch* (*Die griechischen Christlichen Schriftsteller der ersten drei Jahrhunderte*), Leipzig, 1901
GRY, L., 'Le Roi-Messie dans Hénoch (parties anciennes)', *Le Muséon*, N.S., Louvain, 1905, pp. 129–39
'Le messianisme des Paraboles d'Hénoch', *ibid.*, vol. IX, 1908, pp. 318–67
'Quand furent composées les Paraboles d'Hénoch?', *ibid.*, vol. X, 1909, pp. 103–41
'Le messianisme des Paraboles d'Hénoch et la théologie juive contemporaine', *ibid.*, 1909, pp. 143–54
Les Paraboles d'Hénoch et leur messianisme, Paris, 1910
JANSEN, H. L., *Die Henochgestalt*, Oslo, 1939
KAPLAN, C., 'Angels in the Book of Enoch', *Anglican Theological Review*, vol. XII, New York, 1930, pp. 423–37
'The Pharisaic Character and the Date of the Book of Enoch', *ibid.*, pp. 531–7
'The Flood in the Book of Enoch and Rabbinics', *Journal of the Society of Oriental Research*, vol. XV, Toronto, 1931, pp. 22–24
'Versions and Readings in the Book of Enoch', in *American Journal of Semitic Languages and Literatures*, vol. L, Chicago, 1934, pp. 171–7
KUHN, G., 'Beiträge zur Erklärung des Buches Henoch', *ZAW*, vol. XXXIX, Giessen, 1921, pp. 240–75
MANSON, T. W., 'The Son of Man in Daniel, Enoch and the Gospels', *BJRL*, vol. XXXII, Manchester, 1950, pp. 171–93
MARTIN, FR., *Le livre d'Hénoch*, Paris, 1906
MESSEL, N., *Der Menschensohn in den Bilderreden des Henoch* (Beihefte zur *ZAW*, vol. XXXV), Giessen, 1922
SCHMIDT, N., 'The original language of the Parables of Enoch', in *Old Testament and Semitic Studies in Memory of W. R. Harper*, vol. II, Chicago, 1908, pp. 329–49
'The Apocalypse of Noah and the Parables of Enoch', in *Oriental Studies dedicated to P. Haupt*, Baltimore and Leipzig, 1926, pp. 111–23
SJÖBERG, E., *Der Menschensohn im Äthiopischen Henochbuch*, Lund, 1946
STIER, FR., 'Zur Komposition und Literaturkritik der Bilderreden des äthiopischen Henoch', in R. Paret (ed.), *Orient. Studien Enno Littmann überreicht*, Leyden, 1935, pp. 70–88

TORREY, C. C., 'Notes on the Greek Texts of Enoch', *Journal of the American Oriental Society*, vol. LXII, New Haven, 1942, pp. 52–60

ZIMMERMANN, F., 'The Bilingual Character of I Enoch', *JBL*, vol. LX, New Haven, 1941, pp. 159–72

ZUNTZ, G., 'Notes on the Greek Enoch', *ibid.*, vol. LXI, 1942, pp. 193–204

'The Greek Text of Enoch 102.1–3', *ibid.*, vol. LXIII, 1944, pp. 53f.

iii. *The Book of Jubilees*

BAUMGARTEN, J. M., 'The Beginning of the Day in the Calendar of Jubilees', *JBL*, vol. LXXVIII, New Haven, 1958, pp. 355–60

BOHN, F., 'Die Bedeutung des Buches der Jubiläen', *Theologische Studien und Kritiken*, vol. LXXIII, Gotha, 1900, pp. 167–84

BÜCHLER, A., 'Studies in the Book of Jubilees', *REJ*, vol. LXXXII, Paris, 1926, pp. 253–74

'Traces des idées et des coutumes hellenistiques dans le Livre des Jubilés', *ibid.*, vol. LXXXIX, 1930, pp. 321–48

CHARLES, R. H., *The Ethiopic Version of the Hebrew Book of Jubilees*, Oxford, 1895

The Book of Jubilees, London, 1902

'The Book of Jubilees', in R. H. Charles (ed.), *Apocrypha and Pseudepigrapha of the Old Testament*, Oxford, 1913, pp. 1–82

FINKELSTEIN, L., 'The Book of Jubilees and the Rabbinic Halaka', *HTR*, vol. XVI, Cambridge, Mass., 1923, pp. 39–61

'The Date of the Book of Jubilees', *ibid.*, vol. XXXVI, 1934, pp. 19–24

'Criteria for the dating of Jubilees', *JQR*, vol. XXXVI, Philadelphia, 1945–6, pp. 183–90

HEADLAM, A. C., 'Jubilees, Book of, or Little Genesis', *HDB*, vol. II, Edinburgh, 1899, p. 791

JAUBERT, A., 'Le Calendrier des Jubilés et de la secte de Qumran: ses origines bibliques', *VT*, vol. III, Leyden, 1953, pp. 250–64

'Le Calendrier des Jubilés et les jours liturgiques de la semaine', *ibid.*, vol. VII, 1957, pp. 35–61

La Date de la Cène, Paris, 1957

KUTSCH, E., 'Der Kalendar des Jubiläenbuches und das Alte und das Neue Testament', *VT*, vol. XI, Leyden, 1961, pp. 39–47

LEACH, E. R., 'A Possible Method of Intercalation for the Calendar of the Book of Jubilees', *ibid.*, vol. VII, 1957, pp. 392–7

LITTMANN, E., 'Das Buch der Jubiläen', in E. Kautzsch (ed.), *Apokryphen und Pseudepigraphen des Alten Testaments*, vol. II, Tübingen, 1900, pp. 31–119

KLEIN, S., 'Palästinisches im Jubiläenbuch', *Zeitschrift der Deutschen Palästina Vereins*, vol. LVII, Leipzig, 1937, pp. 7–27

MARTIN, FR., 'Le livre des Jubilés', *RB*, vol. XX, Paris, 1911, pp. 321–44, 502–33

MONTGOMERY, J. A., 'An Assyrian Illustration to the Book of Jubilees', *JBL*, vol. XXXIII, New Haven, 1914, pp. 157–8

MORGENSTERN, J., 'The Calendar of the Book of Jubilees, its origin and its character', *VT*, vol. V, Leyden, 1955, pp. 34–76

ROWLEY, H. H., 'Criteria for the Dating of Jubilees', *JQR*, N.S., vol. XXXVI, Philadelphia, 1945–6, pp. 184–7

TESTUZ, M., *Les Idées Religieuses du Livre des Jubilés*, Geneva and Paris, 1960

TISSERANT, E., 'Fragments syriaques du Livre des Jubilés', *RB*, vol. XXX, Paris, 1921, pp. 55–86, 206–32

TORREY, C. C., 'A Hebrew Fragment of Jubilees', *JBL*, vol. LXXI, New Haven, 1952, pp. 39–41

UHDEN, R., 'Die Erdkreisgliederung der Hebräer nach dem Buche der Jubiläen', *Zeitschrift für Semitistik*, vol. IX, Leipzig, 1934, pp. 210–33

ZEITLIN, S., 'The Book of Jubilees, its Character and Significance', *JQR*, N.S., vol. XXX, Philadelphia, 1939–40, pp. 1–31

'The Book of Jubilees', *ibid.*, N.S., vol. XXXV, 1944–5, pp. 12–16

'Criteria for the dating of Jubilees', *ibid.*, N.S., vol. XXXVI, 1945–6, pp. 187–9

'The Beginning of the Day in the Calendar of Jubilees', *JBL*, vol. LXXVIII, New Haven, 1959, pp. 153–6 (with a reply by J. M. Baumgarten on p. 157)

iv. *Testaments of the Twelve Patriarchs*

ARGYLE, A. W., 'The influence of the Testaments of the Twelve Patriarchs upon the New Testament', *ET*, vol. LXIII, Edinburgh, 1951–2, pp. 256–8

BEASLEY-MURRAY, G. R., 'The Two Messiahs in the Testaments of the Twelve Patriarchs', *JTS*, vol. XLVIII, Oxford, 1947, pp. 1–12

BICKERMAN, E. J., 'The Date of the Testaments of the Twelve Patriarchs', *JBL*, vol. LXIX, New Haven, 1950, pp. 245–60

BLACK, M., 'The Messiah in the Testament of Levi 18', *ET*, vol. LX, Edinburgh, 1949, pp. 321–2

BOUSSET, W., 'Die Testamente der Zwölf Patriarchen', *Zeitschrift für die neutestamentliche Wissenschaft*, vol. I, Giessen, 1900, pp. 141–75, 187–209, 344–6

BRAUN, F. M., 'Les Testaments des XII Patriarches et le problème de leur origine', *RB*, vol. LXVII, Paris, 1960, pp. 516–49

CHARLES, R. H., 'Testaments of the XII Patriarchs', in *HDB*, vol. IV, Edinburgh, 1902, pp. 721–5

The Greek Versions of the Testaments of the Twelve Patriarchs, London, 1908 (reproduced in 1960)

The Testaments of the Twelve Patriarchs, London, 1908

'The Testaments of the XII Patriarchs in relation to the New Testament', *The Expositor*, 7th series, vol. VII, London, 1909, pp. 111–18

'The Testaments of the XII Patriarchs', in R. H. Charles (ed.), *Apocrypha and Pseudepigrapha of the Old Testament*, vol. II, Oxford, 1913, pp. 282–367

and COWLEY, A., 'An Early Source of the Testaments of the Patriarchs', *JQR*, vol. XIX, Philadelphia, 1906–07, pp. 566–83

CHEVALLIER, M.-A., *L'esprit et le Messie dans le Bas-Judaïsme et le Nouveau Testament*, Paris, 1958

EPPEL, R., *Le piétisme dans les Testaments des Douze Patriarches*, Paris, 1930

HUNKIN, J. W., 'The Testaments of the Twelve Patriarchs', *JTS*, vol. XVI, Oxford, 1915, pp. 80–97

de JONGE, M., *The Testaments of the Twelve Patriarchs, a study of their text, composition and origin*, Assen, 1953

'The Testaments of the Twelve Patriarchs and the New Testament', *Studia Evangelica* (*Texte und Untersuchungen zur Geschichte der altchristlichen Literatur*), vol. LXXIII, Berlin, 1959, pp. 546–56

'Christian influence in the Testaments of the Twelve Patriarchs', *NT*, vol. IV, Leyden, 1960, pp. 182–235

KAUTZSCH, E., 'Das Testament Naphtalis', in E. Kautzsch (ed.), *Apokryphen und Pseudepigraphen das Alten Testaments*, vol. II, Tübingen, 1900, pp. 489–92

MANSON, T. W., 'Miscellanea Apocalyptica III: Test. XII Patr.: Levi VIII', *JTS*, vol. XLVIII, Oxford, 1947, pp. 59–61

MUNCH, P. A., 'The Spirits in the Testaments of the Twelve Patriarchs', *Acta Orientalia*, vol. XIII, Copenhagen, 1935, pp. 257–63

OTZEN, B., 'Die neugefundenen hebräischen Sektenschriften und die Testamente der Zwölf Patriarchen', *Studia Theologica*, vol. VII, Lund, 1954, pp. 124–57

PASS, H. L. and ARENDZEN, J., 'Fragments of an Aramaic Text of the Testament of Levi', *JQR*, vol. XII, Philadelphia, 1899–1900, pp. 651–61

PHILONENKO, M., 'Les interpolations chrétiennes des Testaments des Douze Patriarches et les Manuscrits de Qumran', *Revue d'Histoire et de Philosophie Religieuses*, Paris, 1958, pp. 309–43; 1959, pp. 14–38 (reproduced as *Cahiers de la Revue d'Histoire et de Philosophie Religieuses*, no. 35, 1960)

PLUMMER, A., 'The Relation of the Testaments of the Twelve Patriarchs to the Books of the New Testament', *The Expositor*, seventh series, vol. VI, London, 1908, pp. 480–91

RABIN, C., 'The Teacher of Righteousness in the Testaments of the Twelve Patriarchs?', *Journal of Jewish Studies*, vol. III, London, 1952, pp. 127–8

SCHNAPP, F., *Die Testamente der Zwölf Patriarchen untersucht*, Halle, 1884

'Die Testamente der 12 Patriarchen', in E. Kautzsch (ed.), *Apokryphen und Pseudepigraphen des Alten Testaments*, vol. II, Tübingen, 1900, pp. 458–88, 492–506

SCHUBERT, K., 'Testamentum Juda 24 im Lichte der Texte von Chirbet Qumran', *Weiner Zeitschrift für die Kunde des Morgenlandes*, vol. LIII, Vienna, 1957, pp. 227–36

SINKER, R., *Testamenta XII Patriarcharum*, Cambridge, 1869

'Testamenta XII Patriarcharum', in *Smith and Wace's Dictionary of Christian Biography*, vol. IV, London, 1887, pp. 865–74

SMITH, M., 'The Testaments of the Twelve Patriarchs', in *The Interpreter's Dictionary of the Bible*, vol. IV, New York, 1962, pp. 575–9
van der WOUDE, A. S., *Die messianischen Vorstellungen der Gemeinde von Qumran*, Assen, 1957, pp. 190–216

v. *The Psalms of Solomon*

BEGRICH, J., 'Der Text der Psalmen Salomos', *Zeitschrift für die neutestamentliche Wissenschaft*, vol. XL, Giessen, 1939, pp. 131–64
FRANKENBERG, W., *Die Datierung der Psalmen Salomos* (Beihefte zur *ZAW*, vol. I), Giessen, 1896
FRITZSCHE, O. F., *Libri apocryphi Veteris Testamenti graece*, Leipzig, 1871, pp. 569ff.
von GEBHART, O., *Psalmoi Solomontos* (Texte und Untersuchungen, Band XIII, Heft 2), Leipzig, 1895
GRAY, G. B., 'The Psalms of Solomon', in R. H. Charles (ed.), *Apocrypha and Pseudepigrapha of the Old Testament*, vol. II, Oxford, 1913, pp. 625–52
GRY, L., 'Le Messie des Psalmes de Salomon', *Le Muséon*, Louvain, 1905, pp. 129ff.
HARRIS, RENDEL and MINGANA, A., *The Odes and Psalms of Solomon*, 2 vols., Manchester, 1916 and 1920
KITTEL, R., 'Die Psalmen Salomos', in E. Kautzsch (ed.), *Apokryphen und Pseudepigraphen des Alten Testaments*, vol. II, Tübingen, 1900, pp. 127–48
KUHN, K. G., 'Die älteste Textgestalt der Psalmen Salomos, insbesondere auf Grund der syrischen Übersetzung neu untersucht', in Beiträge zur *Wissenschaft vom Alten Testament* (ed. by R. Kittel, A. Alt and G. Kittel), Leipzig and Stuttgart, 1937
RYLE, H. E. and JAMES, M. R., *The Psalms of the Pharisees*, Cambridge, 1891
SWETE, H. B., *The Old Testament in Greek*, second ed., vol. III, Cambridge, 1899, pp. 765–87
VITEAU, J., *Les Psaumes de Salomon, introduction, texte grec et traduction, avec les principales variantes de la version syriaque par F. Martin*, Paris, 1911

vi. *The Assumption of Moses*

CHARLES, R. H., *The Assumption of Moses*, London, 1897
'The Assumption of Moses', in R. H. Charles (ed.), *Apocrypha and Pseudepigrapha of the Old Testament*, vol. II, Oxford, 1913, pp. 407–24
CLEMEN, C., *Die Himmelfahrt des Moses* (Kleine Texte 10), Leipzig, 1904
'Die himmelfahrt Moses', in E. Kautzsch (ed.), *Apokryphen und Pseudepigraphen des Alten Testaments*, Tübingen, 1900, pp. 311–31
FERRAR, W. J., *The Assumption of Moses*, London, 1918
FRITZSCHE, O. F., *Libri apocryphi Veteris Testamenti graece*, Leipzig, 1871, pp. 700ff.

Hölscher, G., 'Über die Entstehungszeit der Himmelfahrt Moses', *Zeitschrift für die neutestamentliche Wissenschaft*, vol. XVII, Giessen, 1916, pp. 108–27, 149–58

Kuhn, G., 'Zur Assumptio Mosis', *ZAW*, vol. XLIII, Giessen, 1925, pp. 124–9

Lattey, C., 'The Messianic Expectation in "The Assumption of Moses" ', *The Catholic Biblical Quarterly*, Washington, 1942, pp. 11–21

Mowinckel, S., 'The Hebrew Equivalent of Taxo in Ass. Mos. IX', in *Vetus Testamentum Supplement*, vol. I, Leyden, 1953, pp. 88–96

Rowley, H. H., 'The figure of "Taxo" in the Assumption of Moses', *JBL*, vol. LXIV, New Haven, 1945, pp. 141–3

Torrey, C. C., ' "Taxo" in the Assumption of Moses', *ibid.*, vol. LXII, 1943, pp. 1–7

Wallace, D. H., 'The Semitic Origin of the Assumption of Moses', *TZ*, vol. XI, Basel, 1955, pp. 321–8

vii. *The Sibylline Oracles*

Bate, H. N., *The Sibylline Oracles, Books III–V*, London, 1918

Blass, F., 'Die Sibyllinen', in E. Kautzsch (ed.), *Apokryphen und Pseudepigraphen des Alten Testaments*, vol. II, Tübingen, 1900, pp. 177–217

Bouché-Leclercq, A., 'Les oracles sibyllins', *Revue d'Histoire des Religions*, vol. VII, Paris, 1883, pp. 236–48; vol. VIII, 1883, pp. 619–34; IX, 1884, pp. 220–33

Causse, A., 'Le mythe de la nouvelle Jérusalem du Deutero-Esaïe à la IIIe Sibylle', *Revue d'Histoire et de Philosophie Religieuses*, vol. XVIII, Strasbourg, 1938, pp. 377–414

Ewald, H., *Abhandlung über Entstehung, Inhalt und Werth der sibyllischen Bücher*, Göttingen, 1858

Geffcken, J., *Die Oracula Sibyllina* (Die griechischen Christlichen Schriftsteller der ersten drei Jahrhunderte), Leipzig, 1902

Komposition und Entstehungszeit der Oracula Sibyllina (Texte und Untersuchungen, N.F., Band VIII, Heft 1), Leipzig, 1902

in E. Hennecke, *Neutestamentliche Apokryphen*, second ed., Tübingen, 1924, pp. 399–422

Lanchester, H. C. O., 'The Sibylline Oracles', in R. H. Charles (ed.), *Apocrypha and Pseudepigrapha of the Old Testament*, vol. II, Oxford, 1913, pp. 368–406

viii. '*The Martyrdom of Isaiah*'

Beer, G., 'Das Martyrium Jesajae', in E. Kautzsch (ed.), *Apokryphen und Pseudepigraphen des Alten Testaments*, vol. II, Tübingen, 1900, pp. 119–27

Burch, V., 'The Literary Unity of the *Ascensio Isaiae*', *JTS*, vol. XX, Oxford, 1919, pp. 17–23

'Material for the Interpretation of the *Ascensio Isaiae*', *ibid.*, vol. XXI, 1920, pp. 249–65
CHARLES, R. H., *The Ascension of Isaiah*, London, 1900
'The Martyrdom of Isaiah', in R. H. Charles (ed.), *Apocrypha and Pseudepigrapha of the Old Testament*, vol. II, Oxford, 1913, pp. 155–62
The Ascension of Isaiah, with an introduction by G. H. Box, London, 1919
FLEMMING, I. and DUENSING, H., in E. Hennecke, *Neutestamentliche Apokryphen*, second ed., Tübingen, 1924, pp. 303–14
TISSERANT, E., *Ascension d'Isaïe*, Paris, 1909

ix. *The Testament of Abraham*

BAMBERGER, B. J., 'Abraham, Testament of', in *The Interpreter's Dictionary of the Bible*, vol. I, New York, 1962, p. 21
BOX, G. H., *The Testament of Abraham*, London, 1927
GINZBERG, L., 'Abraham, Testament of', in *JE*, vol. I, New York and London, 1901, pp. 93–6
The Legends of the Jews, vol. I, Philadelphia, 1909, pp. 299–306; V, 1925, pp. 266–7
JAMES, M. R., *The Testament of Abraham* (Texts and Studies, vol. II, no. 2), Cambridge, 1892
KOHLER, K., *Heaven and Hell in Comparative Religion*, New York, 1923, pp. 77ff.

x. *The Apocalypse of Abraham*

BAMBERGER, B. J., 'Abraham, Apocalypse of', in *The Interpreter's Dictionary of the Bible*, vol. I, New York, 1962, p. 21
BOX, G. H., *The Apocalypse of Abraham*, London, 1919
GINZBERG, L., 'Abraham, Apocalypse of', in *JE*, vol. I, New York and London, 1901, pp. 91–92
The Legends of the Jews, vol. I, Philadelphia, 1909, pp. 209ff.; V, 1925, pp. 217, 229–30
KOHLER, K., 'The Apocalypse of Abraham and its Kindred', *JQR*, vol. VII, London, 1894–5, pp. 581–606
Heaven and Hell in Comparative Religion, New York, 1923, pp. 74ff.
The Origins of the Synagogue and the Church, New York, 1929, pp. 180ff.
SCHOLEM, G. G., *Major Trends in Jewish Mysticism*, Jerusalem, 1941, pp. 67–68

xi. *The Life of Adam and Eve* (*The Apocalypse of Moses*)

BAMBERGER, B. J., 'Adam, Books of', in *The Interpreter's Dictionary of the Bible*, vol. I, New York, 1962, pp. 44–45
FUCHS, C., 'Das Leben Adams und Evas', in E. Kautzsch (ed.), *Apokryphen und Pseudepigraphen des Alten Testaments*, vol. II, Tübingen, 1900, pp. 506–28

Ginzberg, L., 'Adam, Book of', in *JE*, vol. I, New York and London, 1901, pp. 179–80
The Legends of the Jews, vol. I, 1909, pp. 86–107; V, 1925, pp. 114–35
James, M. R., *The Lost Apocrypha of the Old Testament*, London, 1920, pp. 1–8
Mozley, J. H., 'The Vita Adae', *JTS*, vol. XXX, Oxford, 1929, pp. 121–49
Wells, L. S., 'The Books of Adam and Eve', in R. H. Charles (ed.), *Apocrypha and Pseudepigrapha of the Old Testament*, vol. II, Oxford, 1913, pp. 123–54

xii. *The Slavonic Book of Enoch* (*II Enoch, The Book of the Secrets of Enoch*)

Bonwetsch, G. N., *Die Bücher der Geheimnisse Henochs* (Texte und Untersuchungen, Band XLIV, Heft 2), Leipzig, 1922
Forbes, N. and Charles, R. H., '2 Enoch or the Book of the Secrets of Enoch', in R. H. Charles (ed.), *Apocrypha and Pseudepigrapha of the Old Testament*, vol. II, Oxford, 1913, pp. 425–69
Förster, 'Adams Erschaffung und Namengebung, ein lateinisches Fragment des sog. slavischen Henoch', *Archiv für Religionswissenschaft*, Leipzig and Berlin, 1908, pp. 477ff.
Fotheringham, J. K., 'The Date and Place of Writing of the Slavonic Enoch', *JTS*, vol. XX, Oxford, 1919, p. 252
'The Easter Calendar of the Slavonic Enoch', *ibid.*, vol. XXIII, 1921, pp. 49–56
Lake, K., 'The Date of the Slavonic Enoch', *HTR*, vol. XVI, Cambridge, Mass., 1923, pp. 397f.
Littmann, E., in E. Kautzsch (ed.), *Apokryphen und Pseudepigraphen des Alten Testaments*, vol. II, Tübingen, 1900, p. 218, note a
Morfill, W. R. and Charles, R. H., *The Book of the Secrets of Enoch*, Oxford, 1896
Schmidt, N., 'The Two Recensions of Slavonic Enoch', *Journal of the American Oriental Society*, New Haven, 1921, pp. 307ff.
Vaillant, A., *Le Livre des Secrets d'Hénoch*, Paris, 1952

xiii. *The Syriac Apocalypse of Baruch* (*II Baruch*)

Burkitt, F. C., 'Baruch, Apocalypse of', in *Hastings Dictionary of the Apostolic Church*, vol. I, Edinburgh, 1915, pp. 142–4
Charles, R. H., *The Apocalypse of Baruch*, London, 1896
'2 Baruch or the Syriac Apocalypse of Baruch', in R. H. Charles (ed.), *Apocrypha and Pseudepigrapha of the Old Testament*, vol. II, Oxford, 1913, pp. 470–526
The Apocalypse of Baruch, with an introduction by W. O. E. Oesterley, London, 1918
Fritzsche, O. F., *Libri apocryphi Veteris Testamenti*, Leipzig, 1871, pp. 654ff.

GINZBERG, L., 'Baruch, Apocalypse of (Syriac)', in *JE*, vol. II, New York, 1902, pp. 551–6

GRY, L., 'La date de la fin des temps selon les révélations ou les calculs du pseudo-Philon et de Baruch', *RB*, vol. XLVIII, Paris, 1939, pp. 337ff.

KABISCH, R., 'Die Quellen der Apokalypse Baruchs', *Jahrbücher für protestantische Theologie*, vol. XVIII, Braunschweig, 1892, pp. 66–107

RYSSEL, V., 'Die syrische Baruchapokalypse', in E. Kautzsch (ed.), *Apokryphen und Pseudepigraphen des Alten Testaments*, vol. II, Tübingen, 1900, pp. 406–46

SIGWALT, C., 'Die Chronologie der syrischen Baruchapokalypse', in *Biblische Zeitschrift*, Paderborn, 1911, pp. 397ff.

VIOLET, B., *Die Apokalypsen des Esra und des Baruch in deutscher Gestalt*, Leipzig, 1924

xiv. *The Greek Apocalypse of Baruch* (*III Baruch*)

GINZBERG, L., 'Baruch, Apocalypse of (Greek)', in *JE*, vol. I, New York, 1901, pp. 549–51

HUGHES, H. M., '3 Enoch or the Greek Apocalypse of Baruch', in R. H. Charles (ed.), *Apocrypha and Pseudepigrapha of the Old Testament*, vol. II, Oxford, 1913, pp. 527–41

JAMES, M. R., *Apokrypha Anecdota* (Texts and Studies, vol. V, no. 1), Cambridge, 1897

RYSSEL, V., 'Die griechische Baruchapokalypse', in E. Kautzsch (ed.), *Apocryphen und Pseudepigraphen des Alten Testaments*, vol. II, Tübingen, 1900, pp. 446–57

LÜDTKE, W., 'Beiträge zu slavischen apokryphen', *ZAW*, vol. XXXI, Giessen, 1911, pp. 219–22

xv. *II Esdras* (*IV Ezra*)

BENSLY, R. L., *The Fourth Book of Ezra, with Introduction by M. R. James* (Texts and Studies, vol. III, no. 2), Cambridge, 1895

BLAKE, R. P., 'The Georgian Version of Fourth Esdras', *HTR*, vol. XIX, Cambridge, Mass., 1926, 299–375; vol. XXII, 1929, pp. 57–105

BOX, G. H., *The Ezra-Apocalypse*, London, 1912

'4 Ezra', in R. H. Charles (ed.), *Apocrypha and Pseudepigrapha of the Old Testament*, vol. II, Oxford, 1913, pp. 542–624

ELLWEIN, E., 'Die Apocalypse des IV. Esra und das urchristliche Zeugnis von Jesus dem Christus', in *Wort und Geist. Festgabe für Karl Heim*, Berlin, 1934, pp. 29–47

FRITZSCHE, O. F., 'Das vierte Buch Esra', in *Libri apocryphi Veteris Testamenti*, Leipzig, 1871

GRY, L., *Les dires prophétiques d'Esdras*, 2 vols., Paris, 1938

'La "mort du Messie" en IV Esdras, VII, 29', in *Memorial Lagrange*, Paris, 1940, pp. 133–9

GUNKEL, H., 'Das 4. Buch Esra', in E. Kautzsch (ed.), *Apokryphen und Pseudepigraphen des Alten Testaments*, vol. II, Tubingen, 1900, pp. 331–401

JAMES, M. R., 'Ego Salathiel qui et Esdras', *JTS*, vol. XVIII, Oxford, 1917, pp. 167–9

'Salathiel qui et Esdras', *ibid.*, vol. XIX, 1918, pp. 347–9

KABISCH, R., *Das vierte Buch Esra und seine Quellen untersucht*, Göttingen, 1889

KAMINKA, A., 'Beiträge zur Erklärung der Ezra Apocalypse und zur Rekonstruktion ihres hebräischen Urtextes', in *Monatschrift für Geschichte und Wissenschaft des Judentums*, Dresden, 1932–3, pp. 76–77

KEULERS, J., *Die eschatologische Lehre des vierten Ezrabuches* (Biblische Studien, Band XX, Heft 2–3), Freiburg, 1922

MUNDLE, W., 'Das religiöse Problem des IV. Ezrabuches', in *ZAW*, N.F., vol. VI, Tübingen, 1929, pp. 222–49

OESTERLEY, W. O. E., *II Esdras*, Westminster Commentaries, London, 1933

SIGWALT, C., 'Die Chronologie des 4. Buches Esdras', *Biblische Zeitschrift*, vol. IX, Paderborn, 1911, pp. 146–8

TORREY, C. C., 'A Twice-Buried Apocalypse' (Apocalypse of Shealtiel), in *Munera Studiosa*, ed. by M. H. Shepherd and S. E. Johnson, Cambridge, Mass., 1946, pp. 23–40

VAGANAY, L., *Le problème eschatologique dans le IVe livre d'Esdras*, Paris, 1906

VIOLET, B., *Die Esra-Apokalypse:*

vol. I: *Die Überlieferung*, Leipzig, 1910

vol. II: *Die Apokalypsen des Ezra und des Baruch in Deutscher Gestalt* (with textual notes by H. Gressmann), Leipzig, 1924

VÖLTER, D., 'Die Geschichte vom Adler und vom Menschen im 4. Ezra, nebst Bemerkungen über die Menschensohnstelle in den Bilderreden Henochs', in *Nieuw Theologisch Tijdschrift*, Haarlem, 1919, pp. 241–73

5. *The Dead Sea Scrolls.* (The numbers of publications on the Dead Sea Scrolls run into many hundreds. Mention will be made below only of those books and articles to which direct reference is made in this volume.)

ALLEGRO, J. M., 'Further messianic references in Qumran literature', *JBL*, vol. LXXV, New Haven, 1956, pp. 174–87

BAILLET, M., 'Fragments Araméens de Qumran 2: Description de la Jerusalem Nouvelle', *RB*, vol. LXII, Paris, 1955, pp. 222–45

BARTHÉLEMY, D., 'Le grand rouleau d'Isaïe trouvé près de la Mer Morte', *ibid.*, vol. LVII, 1950, pp. 530–49

BARTHÉLEMY, D. and MILIK, J. T., *Discoveries in the Judaean Desert: Qumran Cave I*, Oxford, 1955

BLACK, M., *The Scrolls and Christian Origins*, London, 1961

BROWNLEE, W. H., 'The Servant of the Lord in the Qumran Scrolls',

BASOR, vol. CXXXII, 1953, pp. 8–15; vol. CXXXV, Baltimore, 1954, pp. 33–38

BRUCE, F. F., *Second Thoughts on the Dead Sea Scrolls*, London, 1956

'Qumran and Early Christianity', *NTS.*, vol. II, Cambridge, 1956, pp. 176–90

Biblical Exegesis in the Qumran Texts, Exegetica Ouden Nieuw-Testamentische Studien, The Hague, 1959 (reproduced by the Tyndale Press, London, 1960)

BURROWS, M., *The Dead Sea Scrolls*, London, 1956

More Light on the Dead Sea Scrolls, London, 1958

DAVIES, W. D., 'Paul and the Dead Sea Scrolls: Flesh and Spirit', in K. Stendahl, (ed.), *The Scrolls and the New Testament*, New York and London, 1957–8, pp. 157–82 (reproduced in *Christian Origins and Judaism*, London, 1962, pp. 145–77)

DUPONT-SOMMER, A., *The Dead Sea Scrolls: a preliminary survey* (English translation by E. Margaret Rowley), Oxford, 1952

The Jewish Sect of Qumran and the Essenes (English translation by R. D. Barnett), London, 1954

The Essene Writings from Qumran (English translation by G. Vermès), Oxford, 1961

GASTER, T. H., *The Scriptures of the Dead Sea Sect*, London, 1957

GUILLAUME, A., 'Some readings in the Dead Sea Scroll of Isaiah', *JBL*, vol. LXXVI, New Haven, 1957, pp. 40–43

KUHN, K. G., 'The Two Messiahs of Aaron and Israel', in K. Stendahl (ed.), *The Scrolls and the New Testament*, London, 1958

LEANEY, A. R. C. (ed.), *A Guide to the Scrolls*, London, 1958

MILIK, J. T., 'Le Testament de Lévi en Araméen: Fragment de la Grotte 4 de Qumran', *RB*, vol. LXII, Paris, 1955, pp. 398–406

' "Prière de Nabonide" et autres écrits d'un cycle de Daniel', *ibid.*, vol. LXIII, 1956, pp. 407–15

Ten Years of Discovery in the Wilderness of Judaea (English translation by J. Strugnell), London, 1959

PHILONENKO, M., 'Les interpolations chrétiennes des Testaments des Douze Patriarches et les Manuscrits de Qumran', *Revue d'Histoire et de Philosophie Religieuses*, Paris, 1958, pp. 309–43; 1959, pp. 14–38 (reproduced as *Cahiers de la Revue d'Histoire et de Philosophie Religieuses*, no. 35, 1960)

van der PLOEG, J., 'L'immortalité de l'homme d'après les textes de la Mer Morte', *VT*, vol. II, Leyden, 1952, pp. 171–5

The Excavations at Qumran, London, 1958

RABIN, C., *The Zadokite Documents*, second ed., Oxford, 1958

REIDER, J., 'On MŠHTY in the Qumran Scrolls', *BASOR*, vol. CXXIV, Baltimore, 1954, pp. 27–28

ROWLEY, H. H., *The Zadokite Fragments and the Dead Sea Scrolls*, Oxford, 1955

Jewish Apocalyptic and the Dead Sea Scrolls, London, 1957

RUBINSTEIN, A., 'Isaiah LII.14—*mishhath*—and the DSIa Variant', *Biblica*, vol. XXXV, Rome, 1954, pp. 475–9

SCHONFIELD, H. J., *Secrets of the Dead Sea Scrolls*, London, 1956
STENDAHL, K. (ed.), *The Scrolls and the New Testament*, London, 1958
STRUGNELL, J., 'The Angelic Liturgy at Qumran', in *Congress Volume, 1960*, *Supplements to Vetus Testamentum*, vol. VII, Leyden, 1961, pp. 318–45
VERMÉS, G., *The Dead Sea Scrolls in English*, Harmondsworth, 1962
van der WOUDE, A. S., *Die messianischen Vorstellungen der Gemeinde von Qumran*, Assen, 1957

INDEX OF SUBJECTS

INDEX OF AUTHORS

INDEX OF TEXTS

I. THE OLD TESTAMENT

II. THE APOCRYPHA AND PSEUDEPIGRAPHA OF THE OLD TESTAMENT

TESTAMENTS OF THE XII PATRIARCHS

III. THE QUMRAN LITERATURE

IV. THE NEW TESTAMENT

V. THE RABBINIC LITERATURE

VI. GREEK, LATIN AND OTHER WRITINGS (*alphabetically arranged*)